EUROPEAN LEGAL CULTURES IN TRANSITION

Are national legal cultures in Europe converging or diverging as a result of the pressures of European legal integration? Åse B. Grødeland and William L. Miller address this question by exploring the attitudes and perceptions of the general public and law professionals in five European countries: England, Norway, Bulgaria, Poland and Ukraine. Presenting new findings, they challenge the established view that ordinary citizens and people working professionally with the law have different legal cultures. Their research in fact reveals that the attitudes of citizens in Eastern and Western Europe towards 'law in principle' are remarkably similar, whereas perceptions of 'law in practice' differ by country and often correlate with GDP per capita and country ranking in rule of law indices. Grødeland and Miller's innovative methodological approach will appeal to both experts and non-experts with an interest in legal culture, European integration, or European elite and public opinion.

ÅSE B. GRØDELAND is Senior Researcher at Fafo Institute for Applied International Studies (Oslo). Her recent publications on legal culture include *The End of National Legal Culture? The Case of Norway* (with Janne H. Matlary and Morten Kinander, 2016).

WILLIAM L. MILLER is Professor Emeritus and former Edward Caird Professor of Politics at University of Glasgow. His most recent books include *Multicultural Nationalism: Islamophobia, Anglophobia and Devolution* (with Asifa Hussain, 2006) and *The Open Economy and Its Enemies: Public Attitudes in East Asia and Eastern Europe* (with Jane Duckett, Cambridge University Press, 2006).

EUROPEAN LEGAL CULTURES IN TRANSITION

ÅSE B. GRØDELAND AND *WILLIAM L. MILLER*

CAMBRIDGE
UNIVERSITY PRESS

CAMBRIDGE
UNIVERSITY PRESS

University Printing House, Cambridge CB2 8BS, United Kingdom

Cambridge University Press is part of the University of Cambridge.

It furthers the University's mission by disseminating knowledge in the pursuit of education, learning and research at the highest international levels of excellence.

www.cambridge.org
Information on this title: www.cambridge.org/9781107050358

First published 2015

A catalogue record for this publication is available from the British Library

Library of Congress Cataloguing in Publication Data
Grødeland, Åse B., author.
European legal cultures in transition / Åse B. Grødeland and William L. Miller
pages cm
Includes bibliographical references and index.
ISBN 978-1-107-05035-8 (Hardback)
1. Law–Europe. I. Miller, William Lockley, 1943– author. II. Title.
KJC147.G725 2015
340′.115094–dc23 2015008243

ISBN 978-1-107-05035-8 Hardback

CONTENTS

List of tables x
Preface xvii
List of abbreviations xx

1 **One European legal culture or several?** 1
Introduction: European legal integration 1
Legal culture 2
Legal transfers and legal culture: convergence versus divergence 5
Methodological approach 8
Western versus Eastern Europe 9
Legal outsiders versus legal insiders 15
Measuring legal culture 17
Thick descriptions of legal culture 18
Dimensions of legal culture 21
Data collection: FGs, quantitative surveys, IDIs 23
Presentation of data 26
Plan of the book 27

2 **Concept or meaning of law** 30
Introduction: law and everyday life 30
Legal outsiders' perspectives on law 31
Images of law 31
Good versus bad law: helpful? fair? complex? Moral values or state power? 34
The preferred basis of law 39
Stricter law? 44
Perceptions of change 46
Legal insiders' perspectives on law 51
The preferred basis of law 51
Perceptions of change 64
Assessment of changes 64

Causes of change 72
Conclusions 81

3 **Law in principle** 83
Introduction: the role of law 83
The role of law: the legal outsiders' perspective 84
Public ideals and attitudes towards law in principle 85
Reflect or reform? 95
Stepping outside the law? 99
The role of law: the legal insiders' perspective 101
Reflect or reform? 102
Flexibility or rigidity? 108
Stepping outside the law? 117
Conclusions 123

4 **Law in action** 125
Introduction: "exit", "voice", "loyalty" 125
Law in practice: the legal outsiders' perspective 126
General perceptions of law in action 126
Reasons for turning/not turning to court 132
"Exit", "voice", "loyalty" 135
Law in action: the legal insiders' perspective 145
"Exit", "voice", "loyalty" 145
Responding to laws that are contrary to one's religion 175
Conclusions 182

5 **Perceptions of legal outsiders** 184
Introduction: reasons for obeying or breaking the law 184
Legal outsiders' perspectives on legal outsiders (like themselves) 185
Trustworthy and law-abiding? 185
Legal insiders' perspectives on legal outsiders 201
Law-abidingness: past and present 202
Law-abidingness at present: the majority population 211
Law-abidingness at present: the ethnic and religious minorities 219
Excuses for breaking the law? 228
Conclusions 235

6 **Perceptions of legal insiders** 237
Introduction: the people making, implementing and applying the law 237
Legal outsiders' perspectives on legal insiders 238

Government officials 238
Lawyers 238
Judges, prosecutors, juries and lay judges 241
The police 246
The lawmakers: government and Parliament 251
In summary, positive public perceptions of legal insiders 255
Legal insiders' perspectives on how the public view their profession 258
The elected representatives 259
The government officials 263
The legal professionals 268
The lawyers 269
The judges 273
The prosecutors 279
The police 283
Legal insiders' perspectives on legal insiders (like themselves) 285
The legal professionals 286
The lawyers 286
The judges 291
The police 298
Conclusions 312

7 **Legal change and legal transfers** 315
Introduction: legal integration 315
Legal transfers 316
External influences on the law and legal system: the legal outsiders' perspective 319
The potential for external learning: the legal insiders' perspective 328
External influences on the law and legal system: the legal insiders' perspective 340
European legal integration? The legal insiders' perspective 355
Looking to the future 365
Conclusions 375

8 **Muslims and Euro-migrants as carriers of legal culture** 378
Introduction: carriers of legal culture 378
'Adaptive' legal cultures 379
Minorities and Euro-migrants: long-term and short-term adaptation 383
Long-term adaptation: Muslim minorities 385

Short-term adaptation: Euro-migrants 393
Conclusions – culture, context and behaviour: the legal outsiders' perspective 402

9 Balancing civil rights against a 'war on terror' 404

Introduction: the 'war on terror' 404
Perceptions of terrorism: the legal outsiders' perspective 413
FG discussions 413
Quantitative surveys: general public and Muslims 416
Paying the price: combating terrorism versus rights and freedoms 417
Staying within the law – or stepping outside 419
Reacting to international pressure 421
Risk assessment 423
The impact of risk assessment on the general public 425
The impact of risk assessment on "paying the price" to combat terrorism 425
The impact of risk assessment on respecting, changing or disregarding the law 426
Comparing the impact of risk and religion 426
The impact of risk and religion on prioritising "individual freedom" 430
The impact of risk and religion on prioritising "the rights of individuals and minorities" 431
Perceptions of the 'war on terror': the legal insiders' perspective 432
External pressure and the 'war on terror' 440
Protecting civil rights versus combating terrorism 444
Perceptions of how to fight terrorism 447
Conclusions 451

10 The role of religiosity in European popular legal cultures 454

Introduction 454
The impact of religiosity on European legal cultures 454
Religiosity 456
The impact of religiosity on attitudes towards law 458
The weaker second decile: religiosity and 'secular authoritarianism' 460
The stronger first decile: religiosity and specifically religious attitudes to law 462
Conflicting authoritarianisms: church versus state 475
Conclusions 498

11 A European legal culture? 503
Introduction: common Europe 503
Western versus Eastern Europe 503
Legal outsiders versus legal insiders 506
Legal transfers and European integration 507
Conclusions: looking to the future 509

Appendix: data collection 512
Bibliography 516
Index 541

TABLES

2.1 Notions of law: the legal outsiders' perspective 32
2.2 Perceptions of law: the legal outsiders' perspective 35
2.3 Preferred basis of law: the legal outsiders' perspective 41
2.4 Requirements for a country to be truly European: the legal outsiders' perspective 44
2.5 Attitudes, behaviour and law: the legal outsiders' perspective 45
2.6 Quality of law, implementation and enforcement of law: the legal outsiders' perspective 45
2.7 Law and change: the legal outsiders' perspective 47
2.8 Influences on law: the legal outsiders' perspective 49
2.9 EU standards, laws, regulations and minority rights: the legal outsiders' perspective 50
2.10 Preferred basis of law: the legal insiders' perspective 52
2.11 Law and change: the legal insiders' perspective 65
3.1 Law as justice: the legal outsiders' perspective 86
3.2 Individual freedom versus order: the legal outsiders' perspective 87
3.3 Penalties for lawbreakers: the legal outsiders' perspective 87
3.4 Strict versus flexible law: the legal outsiders' perspective 88
3.5 Legal controls: the legal outsiders' perspective 89
3.6 Law, court and Parliament: the legal outsiders' perspective 91
3.7 The letter of the law: the legal outsiders' perspective 92
3.8 Decision-making in court: the legal outsiders' perspective 94
3.9 Law and minorities: the legal outsiders' perspective 94
3.10 Special laws for minorities: the legal outsiders' perspective 96
3.11 Preferred basis of law revisited: the legal outsiders' perspective 97
3.12 Law and changing public opinion: the legal outsiders' perspective 98
3.13 Law and changing normal behaviour: the legal outsiders' perspective 99
3.14 When it is acceptable for government to step outside the law: the legal outsiders' perspective 100
3.15 How government and security services should respond to the threat of terrorism: the legal outsiders' perspective 102
3.16 Law, social norms and behavioural change: the legal insiders' perspective 103

3.17 Circumstances versus the letter of the law: the legal insiders' perspective 110
3.18 Whether it is acceptable for legal insiders to use discretion or step outside the law: the legal insiders' perspective 118
4.1 Law-abidingness, crime and corruption across Europe: the legal outsiders' perspective 126
4.2 Legal fairness and state power: the legal outsiders' perspective 127
4.3 Expectations of fair treatment by officials: the legal outsiders' perspective 128
4.4 Law and law enforcement: the legal outsiders' perspective 129
4.5 Law, law-abidingness, law enforcement, crime, bribery and corruption: the legal outsiders' perspective 131
4.6 Stricter law enforcement: the legal outsiders' perspective 132
4.7 Reasons that people go to court: the legal outsiders' perspective 133
4.8 Reasons that people avoid the courts: the legal outsiders' perspective 134
4.9 Alternatives to court: the legal outsiders' perspective 137
4.10 Informal methods of mediation: the legal outsiders' perspective 137
4.11 Dealing with law: the legal outsiders' perspective 140
4.12 Dealing with religious law: the legal outsiders' perspective 143
4.13 Whether people should turn to court more often: the legal outsiders' perspective 144
4.14 How people should relate to lawbreakers: the legal outsiders' perspective 145
4.15 Court and alternatives to court: the legal insiders' perspective 149
4.16 Dealing with unreasonable or unjust laws: the legal insiders' perspective 165
4.17 Dealing with law that goes against one's religion: the legal insiders' perspective 176
5.1 Personalised trust: the legal outsiders' perspective 186
5.2 Feelings about law-breaking: the legal outsiders' perspective 188
5.3 Law as the power of the state versus the people: the legal outsiders' perspective 189
5.4 Willingness to break the law: the legal outsiders' perspective 190
5.5 Reasons for obeying the law: the legal outsiders' perspective 192
5.6 Reasonable excuse for breaking the law? the legal outsiders' perspective 194
5.7 Reasons for breaking the law: the legal outsiders' perspective 196
5.8 Law-obedience amongst religious and ethnic groups: the legal outsiders' perspective 196
5.9 Reasons for breaking the law: the legal outsiders' perspective 198
5.10 Perceptions of government and corruption: the legal outsiders' perspective 199
5.11 Perceptions of law, courts, crime and bribery: the legal outsiders' perspective 200
5.12 Reasons for obeying the law revisited: the legal outsiders' perspective 201
5.13 Reasons why Euro-migrants obey the law: the legal outsiders' perspective 201
5.14 Likelihood and reasons for obeying versus breaking the law: the legal insiders' perspective 204

5.15 Law-abidingness – majority population: the legal insiders' perspective 211
5.16 Law-abidingness – religious and ethnic minorities: the legal insiders' perspective 221
5.17 Reasonable excuses for knowingly breaking the law: the legal insiders' perspective 229
6.1 Expectations of fair treatment from officials: the legal outsiders' perspective 239
6.2 Perceptions of lawyers: the legal outsiders' perspective 240
6.3 Basis of perceptions of lawyers: the legal outsiders' perspective 241
6.4 Perceptions of judges: the legal outsiders' perspective 243
6.5 Perceptions of more independent judges: the legal outsiders' perspective 245
6.6 Basis of perceptions of courts and judges: the legal outsiders' perspective 245
6.7 Perceptions of prosecutors and judges: the legal outsiders' perspective 246
6.8 Perceptions of the informedness and trustworthiness of juries and lay judges: the legal outsiders' perspective 247
6.9 Basis of perceptions of juries and lay judges: the legal outsiders' perspective 247
6.10 Perceptions of the police: the legal outsiders' perspective 249
6.11 Perceptions of law-abidingness amongst the police: the legal outsiders' perspective 250
6.12 Basis of perceptions of the police: the legal outsiders' perspective 251
6.13 External influences on law: the legal outsiders' perspective 252
6.14 Whether a country has a lot to learn from other countries, European and international organisations: the legal outsiders' perspective 254
6.15 Government's and Parliament's ability to draft clear and effective laws: the legal outsiders' perspective 254
6.16 Perceptions of government and Parliament: the legal outsiders' perspective 256
6.17 Perceptions of the manner in which political leaders relate to the rulings of supra-national courts 256
6.18 Awareness of EU standards, laws, regulations and minority rights: the legal outsiders' perspective 257
6.19 Perceptions of legal insiders: the legal outsiders' perspective 257
6.20 Perceptions of legal outsiders' perceptions of legal insiders: the legal insiders' perspective 258
6.21 Perceptions of lawyers: the legal insiders' perspective 287
6.22 Perceptions of judges and juries: the legal insiders' perspective 292
6.23 Perceptions of the police: the legal insiders' perspective 299
6.24 Perceptions of government and Parliament: the legal insiders' perspective 306
7.1 Whether (this country) has a lot to learn from other countries, European and international organisations: the legal outsiders' perspective 321
7.2 Cultural and legal convergence: the legal outsiders' perspective 323
7.3 Perceptions of the ECtHR: the legal outsiders' perspective 324
7.4 Whether the ECtHR or Parliament should have the final say: the legal outsiders' perspective 325

7.5 European and international standards, and EU pressure: the legal outsiders' perspective 326
7.6 How to handle EU/UN standards: the legal outsiders' perspective 327
7.7 EU standards and the ECtHR: the legal outsiders' perspective 327
7.8 EU standards privileging minorities: the legal outsiders' perspective 328
7.9 Learning from others about law: the legal insiders' perspective 329
7.10 European, international and universal standards: the legal insiders' perspective 343
7.11 Whether (this country) should have broadly the same laws and law-enforcement as the rest of Europe: the legal insiders' perspective 356
7.12 Whether national laws becoming much more similar across the whole of Europe: the legal insiders' perspective 366
8.1 Government regard for law across Europe: the legal outsiders' perspective 386
8.2 Law in principle versus law in practice: the legal outsiders' perspective 387
8.3 Law-abidance amongst the public: the legal outsiders' perspective 390
8.4 Reasons for obeying the law: the legal outsiders' perspective 391
8.5 A reasonable excuse for breaking the law: the legal outsiders' perspective 391
8.6 Pressure for bribes: the legal outsiders' perspective 392
8.7 Lawbreaking – whose fault? The legal outsiders' perspective 393
8.8 Whether incoming Euro-migrants obey the law more than others: the legal outsiders' perspective 395
8.9 Whether incoming Euro-migrants soon adapt to the law and become the same as others: the legal outsiders' perspective 396
8.10 Background influences on law-abidance amongst Euro-migrants: the legal outsiders' perspective 398
9.1 Respect for law and threat of terrorism by rule of law: the legal outsiders' perspective 408
9.2 Combating the threat of terrorism versus protecting individual freedom: the legal outsiders' perspective 418
9.3 Combating the threat of terrorism versus protecting the rights of citizens and minorities: the legal outsiders' perspective 420
9.4 Government response to the threat of terrorism: the legal outsiders' perspective 422
9.5 Pressure from the United States on how to deal with the 'war on terror': the legal outsiders' perspective 422
9.6 Pressure from the European Union on how to deal with the 'war on terror': the legal outsiders' perspective 424
9.7 A real threat of terrorism: the legal outsiders' perspective 424
9.8 Main priority – fighting terrorism versus protecting individual freedom – by sense of feeling threatened: the legal outsiders' perspective 427

9.9 Main priority – fighting terrorism versus protecting the rights of individuals and minorities – by sense of feeling threatened: the legal outsiders' perspective 428
9.10 Main priority – fighting terrorism versus protecting individual freedom: the majority/minority perspective 430
9.11 Main priority – fighting terrorism versus protecting the rights of individuals and minorities: the majority/minority perspective 431
9.12 Terrorism – a real threat?: the legal insiders' perspective 433
9.13 How to fight terrorism: the legal insiders' perspective 441
9.14 Combating the threat of terrorism versus protecting the rights of individual citizens and minorities: the legal insiders' perspective 445
9.15 Preferred government response to the 'war on terror': the legal insiders' perspective 448
10.1 Religiosity: the legal outsiders' perspective 457
10.2 The 'top 20' correlations with religiosity: the legal outsiders' perspective 461
10.3 Impact of religiosity on attitudes towards 'the law should be based on religion': the legal outsiders' perspective 464
10.4 Impact of religiosity on the view that to be 'truly European' a country must have a Christian tradition: the legal outsiders' perspective 466
10.5 Impact of religiosity on attitudes towards "mediation" by "a local religious leader": the legal outsiders' perspective 468
10.6 Impact of religiosity on the assertion that law should be based on the views of local religious people rather than on International Standards: the legal outsiders' perspective 472
10.7 Impact of religiosity on perceptions that "very religious people" are more obedient to the law: the legal outsiders' perspective 473
10.8 Impact of religiosity on whether respondents feel "religious and ethnic minorities" are more or less obedient to the law than others: the legal outsiders' perspective 474
10.9 Impact of religiosity on whether law should be based on customs and traditions: the legal outsiders' perspective 476
10.10 Impact of religiosity on attitudes to conflict between church and state: the legal outsiders' perspective 479
10.11 Impact of religiosity on attitude towards "church and state": the legal outsiders' perspective 480
10.12 Impact of religiosity on attitudes to how unnecessarily complicated and troublesome law should be dealt with: the legal outsiders' perspective 485
10.13 Impact of religiosity on how really unfair and unjust law should be dealt with: the legal outsiders' perspective 488
10.14 Impact of religiosity on how a large majority of people should deal with really unfair and unjust law: the legal outsiders' perspective 490
10.15 Impact of religiosity on law declared contrary to religion: the legal outsiders' perspective 493

10.16 Impact of religiosity on how to deal with religious law: the legal outsiders' perspective 496
10.17 Impact of religiosity on whether ethnic and religious minorities must always obey the law: the legal outsiders' perspective 499
10.18 Impact of religiosity on whether there should be special laws for ethnic or religious minorities: the legal outsiders' perspective 501

PREFACE

This book is about European legal cultures in transition. Our main objective is to establish whether national legal cultures in Europe are converging or diverging – or whether they are converging on some dimensions, whilst diverging on others. We seek to answer this question by exploring attitudes of 'law in principle' and perceptions of 'law in practice' amongst 'legal outsiders' (majority populations, Muslims, Euro-migrants) and 'legal insiders' (elected representatives, government officials, lawyers, prosecutors, judges, police) in five European countries that are very different from each other, yet are all exposed to the pressures of European legal integration.

In this book we challenge the established view that legal culture in Western and Eastern Europe is inherently different. In terms of attitudes towards law in principle, East and West Europeans are remarkably similar. As for perceptions of law in action, on the other hand, they are fairly different. Further, there appears to be a correlation between perceptions, GDP (PPP) per capita, and the rule of law: people living in poorer countries with less rule of law, for example, are more negative about legal insiders and the institutions they represent than people living in wealthier countries with more rule of law.

We also challenge the view that popular legal culture and professional legal culture are inherently different. Our starting point is that legal professionals are not only legal professionals, but they are also members of the general public. As such they have been socialized into the same legal culture as the non-professionals. The legal culture of the two groups is likely to differ on more technical aspects of law. However, they are remarkably similar in terms of attitudes to law in principle and perceptions of law in practice.

Although our work is essentially a book about legal culture, at a broader level the themes addressed are relevant to the quality of democracy and rule of law across Europe more generally, and to European integration in particular. We explore attitudes towards, and perceptions of, legal transfers more generally with a view to establishing whether there is scope for further legal harmonization and integration in Europe. The tension between 'liberal' and 'illiberal' legal transfers is addressed in a chapter exploring perceptions of the relationship between civil rights and the 'war on terror'.

Finally, in this book we explore the impact of religion on legal cultures across Europe. Data presented in the book suggest that the European majority populations favour a secular society and secular law. The established view that religiosity correlates strongly with authoritarianism is questioned: our data show that religiosity correlates only moderately with aspects of purely 'secular authoritarianism', and correlates much more strongly with specifically religious aspects of law, even when these conflict with 'secular authoritarianism'.

Our research was funded by the Research Council of Norway's Europe in Transition (EUROTRANS) programme (2007–17). The programme was launched in response to Parliamentary Report No. 20 (2004–5), with a view to researching changes taking place in Europe at a more general level, and Norway's role in Europe, in particular. The programme covers four main themes: law and democracy in Europe, economic development and integration, cultural change, and European foreign and security policies.

Phase 1 of the programme, (2007–12/13) provided funding for three large-scale projects. One of them – 'Legal Cultures in Transition: The Impact of European Integration' (2007–13, Award 182628/F10, NOK 16.3 million) – generated the data for this book.

The project covers five European countries: Norway, the United Kingdom (data were collected in England only), Poland, Bulgaria and Ukraine. Data were collected in four stages: we first conducted a series of focus groups with members of the public to allow for a general discussion of key issues within the seven dimensions of legal culture. Data from the focus groups then 'informed' the questionnaire we used in nationally representative surveys and for booster samples amongst Muslims in all five countries. Further, data from the focus groups and surveys 'informed' the interview guide used in our structured, open-ended, elite in-depth interviews. Finally, to gain a proper understanding of how the general public and the legal professionals interact with each other, observation of small-scale civil court cases was carried out in all countries.

We base this book on findings from the focus groups, quantitative surveys and elite in-depth interviews. Each chapter addresses one key dimension of legal culture – first by exploring the views of the legal outsiders, and then the views of the legal insiders.

We received a great deal of helpful advice, comment and encouragement from colleagues at NIBR, Fafo, Glasgow University and elsewhere. Some of their ideas have been taken on board, whereas others we have contested. Our colleagues bear no responsibility for what we have written here, but we are deeply grateful for their generosity. We would like to thank all those who have been involved in providing access to the judiciary, organizing and collecting data presented in this book – and in particular (and in alphabetical order) the following:

Sjur Egstad, Anita Lynne and Ole F. Ugland, TNS Gallup Norway
Elizabeth Bailey, Rachel Skevington Britton, Johnny Heald, Richard Hooper, Alan Hyde, Sarah Murphy and Sarah Oliver, ORB
Genoveva Petrova, Alpha Research
Barbara Badora, Jolanta Kalka, Magdalena Gwiadzda and Małgorzata Omyla, CBOS
Tetiana Diyeva and Alexander Shulga, SOCIS-Gallup

We would also like to thank Kjersti Asland and Lillian Børresen at the Research Council of Norway for their assistance.

Further, we should thank the anonymous readers who provided feedback on our book proposal and two draft chapters.

Our heartfelt thanks are due to the Commissioning Editor at Cambridge University Press, Finola O'Sullivan. We would also like to thank our editors, Richard Woodham and Helen Francis for their patience and kindness. Thanks are also due to Senior Production Editor Jonathan Ratcliffe and Assistant Editor Fleur Jones for their professionalism and assistance. We would also like to express our thanks to Bindu Vinod and Sundararajan Rengarajan at SPI Global who have been overseeing the production of our book. Our gratitude is also due to Robert and Cynthia Swanson for indexing it: we are very pleased with the result! Last but not least, we would like to express our heartfelt thanks to Alyson Platt, who has copyedited this book. We are very grateful to her for her thoroughness, helpfulness, and patience! Working with her has been a pleasure!

But most of all, we would like to thank all the anonymous respondents who took the time to contribute during all stages of data collection: without their participation and willingness to answer our questions this book could never have been written.

ABBREVIATIONS

ABA-CEELI	American Bar Association's Central and Eurasian Law Initiative
ADR	Alternative Dispute Resolution
ASA	Agency for Social Analysis
CBOS	Centrum Badania Opinii Społecznej
CEE	Central and Eastern Europe
CIA	Central Intelligence Agency
CIS	Commonwealth of Independent States
CJEU	Court of Justice of the European Union
CoE	Council of Europe
CPI	Corruption Perception Index
CPS	Crown Prosecution Service
CSD	Centre for the Study of Democracy
DIFI	Direktoratet for forvaltning og IKT [Agency for Public Management and eGovernment]
EC	European Community
ECHR	European Convention on Human Rights
ECRI	European Commission against Racism and Intolerance
ECSR	European Charter of Social Rights
ECtHR	European Court of Human Rights
EEA	European Economic Area
EFTA	European Free Trade Association
E-I Standards	European and International Standards
E-I-U Standards	European, International and Universal Standards
ENP	European Neighbourhood Policy
ESA	EFTA Surveillance Agency
EU	European Union
FG	Focus Group
FSU	Former Soviet Union
GMOs	Gene-Modified Organisms
GDP	Gross Domestic Product
HCNM	High Commissioner on National Minorities (OSCE)
HMCS	Her Majesty's Court Service

IDI	In-Depth Interview
ILO	International Labour Organisation
IMF	International Monetary Fund
IRA	Irish Republican Army
KIIS	Kyiv International Institute of Sociology
MCC	Millennium Change Corporation
MEP	Member of the European Parliament
MP	Member of Parliament
MSI	Management Systems International
NATO	North Atlantic Treaty Organisation
NHS	National Health Service
NOK	Norwegian Crowns (currency)
NOU	Norsk Offentlig Utredning [Official Norwegian Report]
OSAC	Overseas Security Advisory Council
OSCE	Organisation for Security and Cooperation in Europe
OSI	Open Society Institute
PMA	Professional Mediators' Association
PPP	Purchasing Power Parity
PR	Public Relations
RSFSR	Russian Soviet Federative Socialist Republic
UAOC	Ukrainian Autocephalous Orthodox Church
UCL	University College London
UGCC	Ukrainian Greek Catholic Church
UK	United Kingdom
UN	United Nations
UOC-KP	Ukrainian Orthodox Church under the Kiev Patriarchate
UOC-MP	Ukrainian Orthodox Church under the Moscow Patriarchate
US	United States
USAID	United States Agency for International Development
USD	US Dollars
USSR	Union of Soviet Socialist Republics
VAT	Value-Added Tax
WTO	World Trade Organisation

1

One European legal culture or several?

Introduction: European legal integration

United Europe as a concept has been pursued with considerable vigour since the collapse of Communism in 1989. Political and economic integration has been sought through European Union (EU) enlargement to the east and deeper integration within the EU, through the European Economic Area (EEA) and the European Neighbourhood Policy (ENP). Integration is being implemented primarily through the streamlining of institutional frameworks and the harmonisation of national legislation.[1] However, former British Member of the European Parliament (MEP), Glyn Ford, has argued that 'genuine partnership (in Europe) can only develop on the basis of shared common values – in particular, democracy, the rule of law and respect for human and civil rights' (Kuzio 2004) – which presupposes some harmonisation of legal culture as well as legislation and legal institutions.

More than a decade ago Lawrence Friedman (1997, p. 34) noted that 'we have, for almost every society, precious few data about legal culture, because we have never bothered to gather them'. Since then we have systematically collected such data in three EU member states (the United Kingdom – below referred to as the UK,[2] Poland and Bulgaria), one EEA member state (Norway) and one ENP[3] member (Ukraine).

These countries not only have distinct legal cultures, but they also differ on a number of dimensions of relevance to legal culture. Yet, they are all exposed to the same external factors and pressures intended to facilitate

[1] European elites are also using culture as a tool for forging a sense of cohesion and belonging among Europeans (Shore 2000; Checkel and Katzenstein 2009).

[2] As England, Wales, Scotland and Northern Ireland have different legal systems we collected data in England only.

[3] For an overview, see http://ec.europa.eu/world/enp/index_en.htm

(legal) convergence.[4] As a result, all of them are formally transitioning from *less* to *more* integration and thus possibly also from *less similar* to *more similar* legal cultures.

This book provides a comprehensive and empirically based analysis of these five national legal cultures, with a view to establishing whether – and to what extent – national legal cultures in Europe are converging.

Legal culture

Legal culture may be defined as a 'way of describing relatively stable patterns of legally oriented social behaviour and attitudes' (Nelken 2004, p. 1).[5] To some scholars this phenomenon constitutes an inherent part of the wider political culture. Others argue that legal culture, political culture and economic culture carry equal weight and are closely interconnected, even dependent on each other (Trubek 1985, p. 919; Ewing 1987, p. 487; Tamanaha 1995, p. 470). They all agree, however, that the study of legal culture facilitates a better understanding of the context into which legal transfers (i.e. the transfer of law from one geographical, cultural, political and/or economic setting into another) are introduced, and thus also some explanation as to why some such transfers succeed while others fail.

Legal culture may manifest itself at different *levels*, for instance as *supranational legal culture*, *national legal culture* or *subnational culture* – at regional or local levels within a country (De Sousa Santos and

[4] These include EU law (Regulations, Directives and Decisions), case law from the Court of Justice of the EU (CJEU), the European Convention of Human Rights (ECHR) and the case law of the European Court of Human Rights (ECtHR), the United Nations (UN) Human Rights Conventions, international trade agreements and others. Norway, for instance, is bound by the decisions of the EFTA (European Free Trade Association) Court and the EFTA Surveillance Authority (ESA), which oversees the implementation of the EEA Agreement.

[5] Some academics (Legrand 1996; Spamann 2009) prefer the terms *legal mentalities* or *legal families* over the term *legal cultures*. It could be argued that the former are more narrow concepts than the latter in that they primarily – though not only – refer to legal traditions rather than the wider, cultural setting within which law and legal institutions operate. The same may be said for the concept of *legal consciousness*. Silbey, cited in Smelser and Baltes (2001, p. 8626), describes the difference between the two terms as follows: 'if research on legal culture focuses attention on the myriad of ways in which law exists within society generally, the study of legal consciousness traces the way in which law is experienced and interpreted by specific individuals as they engage, avoid, or resist the law and legal meanings'. For an in-depth discussion of legal consciousness, see Barclay and Silbey (2008).

Rodriguez-Garavito 2005). Such legal cultures may also reflect *religious traditions*. Within Europe it makes sense to talk about the existence of a *Judeo-Christian legal culture* and an *Islamic legal culture*,[6] though there are clearly subcultures within both of these.[7] Added to this, the *different actors* operating within the wider supranational, national or religious legal culture may have different legal cultures.

Research on *supranational legal culture*, for instance, has addressed global legal culture (Menyhart 2003), the Western European legal tradition (Gessner, Hoeland and Varga 1996) and European legal culture.[8] Studies of the latter tend to focus on specific aspects of European legal integration,[9] such as compliance or non-compliance with EU directives (Falkner, Treib, Hartlapp and Leiber 2005) or with the rulings of the Court of Justice of the European Union (CJEU) (Carrubba and Murrah 2005) – with a view to establishing whether or not legal systems in Europe are converging. Hesselink (2009, p. 7) claims that 'there are still signs of a transformation from a rather formal, dogmatic and positivistic national legal culture into a more substance-oriented and pragmatic European legal culture'. Others suggest that on some levels there is convergence, whereas on others there is divergence. Kjær (2008), for instance, believes that language both hinders and facilitates European legal integration.

Research on *national legal culture* (Zirk-Sadowski 2006) usually addresses one or two key formal features of the legal culture of a country (see, e.g. Nethercott 2007), such as its economic basis (Ogus 2001) or historical context (Nenner 1977; Watson 1983; Wieacker and Bodenheimer 1990). Studies of the legal culture of one or several countries during particular historical period(s) (Lemmings 2000; Burbank 2004; Sunde 2007) or contemporary national legal culture are also common.

[6] For an overview of human rights as a concept in Islam and the West, see Sadurdin (2010). Ramadan (2005) advocates the modernisation of Islam – including its legal aspects.

[7] For discussions of the link between religion and (legal) culture, see McConnel, Cochran Jr and C. Carmella (2001); Yilmaz (2005); Mayer (1991); and Katz (2008).

[8] Although some scholars believe that a European legal culture already exists, others claim that it is being created through the Europeanisation of law (Wieacker and Bodenheimer 1990; Michaels in Basedow, Hopt and Zimmermann 2012, p. 4).

[9] Madsen, Kjær, Krunke and Petersen (2008, p. 1) claim that there is 'surprisingly little consensus on what is implied by the terminology *European legal integration*'. Referring to Gessner and Nelken (2007), they suggest that 'the term covers a plurality of processes and subject-matters, ranging from basic analysis of the European institutions and their competences to the impact of supranational law-making on national ways of producing law, even national ways of life'. We address this issue by exploring attitudes and perceptions rather than specific law or institutions.

The study of *subnational legal* culture tends to focus on the legal culture of specific ethnic minority groups (Ravna 2010) or nations within larger states (Forte 2010).

Friedman (cited in Nelken 2004, p. 1) distinguishes between *internal legal culture* (i.e. the ideas and practices of legal professionals) and *external legal culture,*[10] which refers to the opinions, interests and pressures brought to bear on law by the wider society, from political elites to the general public. Other terms used to distinguish between those working professionally with the law and those being affected by law are *professional* and *popular legal culture*, or the legal culture of *legal insiders* (i.e. those working professionally with the law) and *outsiders* (i.e. non-legal professionals who are affected by law). Subcultures exist within both sets of categories.

The rationale behind these concepts is that the views and behaviour of legal professionals are likely to differ depending on the educational establishment in which they received their training or on the type of institution or even the part of the country within which they operate.[11] The attitudes, perceptions and behaviour of the general public, on the other hand, may differ by gender, age, level of education, area of residence, ethnicity or religion, to mention but a few.[12]

The link between law and popular culture has been given considerable – and increasing – attention in recent years (see, e.g. Black 2010; Freeman 2010; Menkel-Meadow 2010): legal scholars have investigated the manner in which law, legal institutions, legal professionals and legal negotiations are depicted in religious texts as well as in world and/or national literature (Freeman 2010), and in films and television series (Machura 2010; Nead 2010).[13] Much attention has also been given to the manner in which the latter affects perceptions of right and wrong, law and legal institutions amongst legal outsiders (Harding 2010), legal insiders (Denvir 2010) as well as contemporary law.

There is a considerable literature on *legal outsiders* – either *within* or *across* national legal cultures. Such works usually explore perceptions

[10] Some scholars use the term *popular legal culture* instead of *external legal culture* (MacAuley 1989).

[11] To give an example, the style of judgement in the first instance court in Bergen (West Coast) is said to differ considerably from that of the first instance court in Oslo (Bratholm 1957).

[12] For an account of several dissimilar subcultures within popular legal culture in America, see Yngvesson (1989, p. 1694).

[13] Films and television series addressing law and legal issues in a popular manner are referred to as 'reel justice'.

amongst legal outsiders on key dimensions of legal culture, for instance, attitudes towards norms, tradition, religion and state law (Bierbrauer 1994); support for the rule of law, perceptions of law as a non-neutral, repressive force, and support for individual liberty (Gibson and Caldeira 1996) and punishment preferences (Sanders and Hamilton 1992).

The legal culture of *legal insiders within national or supranational legal cultures* has also been studied in-depth. Such studies have investigated the behaviour of a specific type of legal insider (usually lawyers or judges, but also prosecutors) within one single country (Barry and Berman 1968; LoPucki 1996; Polak and Nelken 2010), within several countries whose legal traditions are similar,[14] or within countries whose legal traditions differ (Goutal 1976; Kűhn 2004).

More recently, academics have turned their attention to legal insiders operating at a supranational level. Arold (2007), for instance, in her study of the legal culture of judges at the European Court of Human Rights (ECtHR) in Strasbourg, concludes that even though judges from 47 different countries are represented in that court, they have developed a distinct legal culture. Franklin (2010) reaches similar conclusions with regard to the CJEU in Luxembourg.

The majority of studies of legal culture have been conducted in a limited number of countries – usually one or two (Blankenburg 1994), considerably more rarely in more (Blankenburg, Tromp, Kana, Notten, Maracz and Geerts 2000; Nolan Jr 2009). Further, they tend to draw on written materials (usually formal texts or formal legislation), small-scale qualitative data or quantitative survey data collected for purposes other than the studies for which they are used. One of the largest studies of legal culture conducted by means of large-scale quantitative data to date is that of Gibson and Caldeira (1996).[15]

Legal transfers and legal culture: convergence versus divergence

The world is becoming increasingly interconnected due to globalisation and economic integration. Globalisation and European integration have

[14] For examples, see Blankenburg (1994), Blankenburg, Tromp, Kana, Notten, Maracz and Geerts (2000), and Herron and Randazzo (2003).

[15] Gibson and Caldeira's study of legal culture in Europe is based on data from the 1992 Eurobarometer Survey – for which they commissioned several questions concerning the CJEU, and on re-interviews of subsamples of the 1992 Eurobarometer respondents as part of the 1992–3 Panel Survey.

largely been law-driven. Although some analysts perceive globalisation as a process of homogenisation or convergence, others argue that globalisation also brings about heterogenisation, localisation or divergence – as local environments reject the dominant global culture. Yet others believe that the end result of globalisation is more likely to be some kind of 'hybridization'(Berger) or 'glocalization'(Roland), that is, 'difference-within-sameness', rather than sameness or differentness only (Nolan Jr 2009, p. 25).

The idea that political and/or economic reform may be achieved by legal 'borrowing' – that is, by introducing legislation from systems perceived to be more efficient or successful – is not new. As the purpose of such borrowing is typically to enhance economic performance or to promote democracy – including the rule of law – transferred law may be referred to as 'liberal' transfers. Perhaps the two most wide-ranging liberal transfers carried out to date are the democratisation of Europe's post-communist states and their adjustment to, and eventual admission to, the EU.[16] Studies of the link between legal culture and globalisation (Friedman and Pérez-Perdomo 2003) and legal culture and democratisation in developing states (Gloppen, Gargarella and Skaar, 2004) provide in-depth analyses of such legal borrowing. The 'war on terrorism', on the other hand, has produced what could be described as a set of 'illiberal' legal transfers – that is, laws curtailing basic civil and human rights in the name of national security.[17]

One group of scholars believes that legal systems are not easily altered and that for this reason they simply cannot converge. Balas, La Porta, Shleifer and Lopez-de-Silanes (2008, cited in Voeten 2008, p. 420), for instance, claim that differences among legal systems have deep historical roots that are not easily open to external influences and that have enduring effects on the performance of legal, economic and political institutions. Legrand (1996, pp. 61–2) is even more pessimistic, maintaining that 'legal systems, despite their adjacence within the European Community (EC), have not been converging, are not converging and will not be converging. It is a mistake to suggest otherwise ... such

[16] Ajani (1995, pp. 93–4) notes that 'Central and Eastern Europe, as well as Russia, has again openly become a large-scale borrower of Western models. During the Socialist era, despite declamations on the "originality of socialist law", Western models were borrowed, even if a careful legal scholarship disguised them, or judges were unaware of their origin. But the scale was slight, if compared to today's situation'.

[17] A more detailed discussion of the literature on legal transfers is provided in Chapter 7.

convergence, even if it were thought desirable (which, in my view, it is not), is impossible on account of the fact that the differences arising between the common law and the civil law *mentalités* at the epistemological level are irreducible'. Even when some of the formal legal rules are converging, they continue to have a different meaning in common law countries due to cultural and historical differences in the nature of legal reasoning.

Another group of scholars believes that legal systems may converge *given certain conditions*. The 'culturalists', for instance, hold the view that 'the success or failure of a legal transplant depends on the culture from which the law originates and the culture into which it is transplanted'. Consequently, legal transplants from 'same-type' cultures are more likely to succeed than transplants from 'other-type' legal cultures.[18] Graziadei (2009, p. 697) suggests that 'legal systems can accommodate a plurality of models, though most transplants probably still occur across legal systems that already have much in common'.[19]

By contrast, Husa (2004, p. 13) and Reimann (2002) – both referred to in Voeten (2008, p. 429) – claim that legal systems are converging *regardless of whether they are similar or different* due to regional integration and the prominence of international legal rules. As noted by the 'transferists' (Small 2005, p. 1431) 'law is autonomous from culture and, as such, good law is transplantable irrespective of culture'.

Legal transfers usually, though not always, occur at the initiative of an external party and tend to be accompanied by some pressure (Hiscock 1995; Mayhew 1998; Van Olden 2002, p. 4; Kochenov 2008). For this reason, some scholars believe that legal transfers are not likely to succeed given that they tend to be 'exported to' rather than 'imported by' its new setting. They therefore tend to be perceived as non-legitimate in their new setting and are simply unused (Seidman 1978). There is also some evidence that legal transfers frequently fail to perform as intended because they are based on legal paradigms that do not fit the recipient state's context (Miller 2003, p. 840).

As regards the question of whether legal transfers within Europe facilitate convergence or divergence, findings are not conclusive. Levitsky

18 Other scholars study legal transplants in relation to context – that is, those circumstances that specifically drive the development of a particular rule, rather than in relation to culture – that is, 'a society's entire background' (Small 2005, p. 1438).

19 Nolan Jr (2009), for instance, explores the 'export' of American-style problem-solving courts to five other common law cultures.

(1994) claims that there is such convergence in the English legal system due to influences from the EU, whereas Ajani (1995, p. 113) observes that countries in Central and Eastern Europe (CEE) and the Commonwealth of Independent States (CIS) seem to have adopted 'common law solutions, because of the insistence of proponents and commentators who are more familiar with such solutions in a body of law having continental style and structure'. Weick (1999, p. v) claims that a dualism between competition and convergence is found in 'the whole spectrum of the law of the (EU) Member States' and that such dualism is beneficial for – rather than posing an obstacle to – European (legal) integration.

Although there is some disagreement with regard to the various factors that either on their own or in combination affect and ultimately determine the outcome of legal transplants (Kahn-Freund 1974, p. 7), legal culture is perceived as a key component. Wang (2010, p. 83) notes that 'since transplantation involves the transfer of the conceptual thinking of the imported law, legal transplants often bring about a transfer of legal culture'.[20] Friedman and Scheiber (1995, p. 9) are somewhat more cautious, suggesting that 'just as we are seeing a palpable convergence in popular culture worldwide ... we may also be witnessing a convergence in legal cultures'.[21]

Methodological approach

Our starting point is that whereas there appears to be convergence of European national legal cultures as a result of globalisation and European integration, there simultaneously appears to be divergence of such cultures – due to (i) the historic divide between common law and civil law, (ii) the legacy of Communism, and most recently (iii) the pressure of international terrorism and (iv) to some extent also between broader society, on the one hand, and Muslims, on the other – all of which divides European national legal cultures. On some of these issues the divisions are historic and possibly fading, but on others they are contemporary and possibly increasing.

[20] Some academics view the translation of legal texts as a legal transfer (Mochny 2002).

[21] Wiegrand, for instance, has identified several ways in which American legal culture has shaped European legal culture, institutions, law and legal practices (ibid., p. 12). Most studies of legal convergence focus on contemporary legal integration processes. However, Watson (1997) investigates legal transfers in the historical context.

This is therefore a time and place to explore legal cultures in similarities, in traditions and in transitions. Such a study merits considerable depth rather than breadth at the expense of depth – valuable though studies with a wider but more superficial approach are. This book does not pretend to be an 'all-inclusive' or 'representative' study of national legal cultures across Europe: with finite resources (albeit with large – but limited – resources) we could not and should not 'trade breadth for depth'. In generating new knowledge on legal cultures in five European countries and the manner in which they respond to current pressures towards greater similarity this book makes an important contribution to debates over legal transfers, global governance, as well as the relation between universal norms and cultural differences.

Western versus Eastern Europe

Comparative studies usually apply a *most similar* or a *most different systems design*. In the most different systems design one selects a number of very different countries that do, however, share the phenomenon in which one is interested (Lor 2010). Our project compares the perceptions and experiences of *legal outsiders* and *legal insiders* in five countries across Europe from east (Poland, Ukraine) to west (the UK) and from north (Norway) to south (Bulgaria) on several key dimensions of legal culture. Our five countries belong to 'new' and 'old' Europe (Case 2009, p. 112), and they differ significantly as regards a number of factors 'informing' legal culture. Yet they are all exposed to the same external pressures towards greater similarity.

To start our discussion with the differences, our choice of countries first allows for an investigation of legal culture in countries that *belong to different legal families* (Legrand 1997): the common law family (the UK), the Nordic – sometimes also referred to as the Scandinavian – legal family (Norway) and civil law legal family (Bulgaria, Poland, Ukraine). The latter three countries belonged to the socialist legal family and traces from the socialist legal tradition are still present in all of them.[22]

Second, nation states never exist in complete isolation from one another and neither do their legal systems. Consequently, national legal culture reflects not only internal factors but also external factors that

[22] In the late 1990s Kőtz claimed that the Socialist legal family was dead and buried. However, some legal academics, such as Mańko (2013a; 2013b) disagree, claiming that the Socialist legal tradition is still affecting Eastern Europe.

have influenced – in some instances even shaped – the former, over time.[23] The five countries selected for our study *have different legal traditions*. Poland has historically been affected by three distinct legal cultures: the Prussian Rechtstaat culture (characterised by a strong, but law-bounded state and an uncorrupted civil service), the Austro-Hungarian multicultural society under one legal regime, and Russian legal culture, where the law was subordinated to absolutist rule (Skąpska 2003, pp. 588–9). Bulgaria was under Turkish rule for more than 500 years and has therefore been heavily influenced by Ottoman legal culture. Ukraine has been affected not only by Polish and Russian legal culture but also by Austro-Hungarian and Ottoman legal culture. England has a common law tradition, whereas legal tradition in Norway combines features from both civil law and common law (Sunde 2005). Such influences and experiences have produced a set of distinct, contemporary legal cultures, some more 'liberal' than others.

Third, these countries *have different relations with Brussels*: three countries are EU members (UK, Poland, Bulgaria), one is an EEA member (Norway) and one has signed up to the ENP (Ukraine). Norway and the UK are generally Euro-sceptic: Norwegians have rejected EU membership in two national referenda (1972; 1994). A recent poll conducted by the Chatham House (2012, p. 25) shows that 49 per cent of the Brits are in favour of pulling out of the EU.

Despite being one of the most ardent critics of legislation and regulations emanating from Brussels, England is one of the most conscientious implementers of the very same legislation and regulations (Nelken 2004, p. 1). Norway's compliance with EU law is also high (NOU 2012, p. 125). Poland and Bulgaria were very keen to join the EU[24] and did so in 2004 and 2007, respectively. Ukraine aspires to EU membership but is politically unstable and currently embroiled in civil war.

Legal reform undertaken in post-communist states has been referred to as 'voluntary harmonisation' with EU standards (Vachudova 2006). In practice, however, these states had little choice but to comply if they

[23] Ajani (1995, p. 94) notes that 'before socialism, the legal systems of Central and Eastern Europe were deeply influenced by Roman-Germanic law, by scholarly works and statutes originated in the French, German and Austrian, but also Italian and Swiss, legal systems'.

[24] Poland held a referendum on EU membership on 7–8 June 2003. Of the votes cast, 77.5 per cent were in favour of membership. Bulgaria did not organise a referendum prior to joining the EU, but opinion polls conducted before the accession showed that there was huge support amongst Bulgarians for EU membership.

wanted the anticipated benefits of EU membership.[25] Legal transfers have affected the *role* of law in Poland, Bulgaria and Ukraine, effectively redefining the formal legal sphere (Zirk-Sadowski 2010, p. 300). But the power of EU conditionality usually ends once its purpose has been attained.[26]

Whereas the present formal political, economic and legal context of post-communist states differs considerably from that of Communism, 'old thinking' and indeed 'old behaviour' to some extent still prevails (Galligan and Kurkchiyan 2003; Grødeland 2007). *Legal nihilism* is widespread in all of them. Thus, although a convergence has taken place with regard to the formal status of law – that is, from *rule by law* to *rule of law*[27] – legal cultures may be more resistant to change and, to the extent they are, may therefore limit the strength of law and consequently also the (intended) impact of legal transplants. Individual or institutional opposition to EU membership may further limit its impact.[28]

Fourth, our five countries have more and less rule of law, and they differ considerably in terms of socioeconomic development.

As regards the rule of law the World Bank produces an annual 'rule of law'-index ranking most of the countries in the world. This ranking provides a useful starting point for the research of legal culture, as the two concepts are closely interconnected.[29] In the 2010 index, Norway and the UK are located at the top end – Norway in the 99th percentile and the UK in the 94th. By contrast, Poland, which was admitted to the EU in 2004, is located in the 69th percentile, Bulgaria, which was admitted in 2007, is located in the 53rd percentile, and Ukraine, which aspires to EU membership, is located in the 25th percentile.[30] A similar pattern is observed in the World Justice Project's 2014 Rule of Law Index.[31] Our

[25] Mitsilegas (2000); Vachudova (2006).

[26] In the case of Bulgaria, however, conditionality has continued beyond formal membership (Tærum 2014).

[27] Rose (2009, p. 5) notes that in post-communist states 'democratization began backwards, for free elections were introduced before the rule of law was properly established'.

[28] Ukraine is politically divided between a Europe-leaning West and a Russia-leaning East.

[29] The World Bank ranking is a simple index providing numbers. It is based on multiple sources and largely reputation-based rather than experience-based. Besides, it is based on descriptions provided by businesspeople about somebody else's culture rather than their own culture.

[30] World Bank Rule of Law Index 2010, http://info.worldbank.org/governance/wgi/index.asp

[31] The index, which ranks countries from 1 (most rule of law) to 0 (least rule of law), ranks Norway second (score: 0.94), the UK 10th (score: 0.81), Poland 22nd (score: 0.73),

selection of countries thus allows for a comparison of states that provides a 'benchmark' with regard to the rule of law, and states at different stages of transitioning from 'less' to 'more' rule of law – that is, two 'extremes' within the European context. Further, World Bank data suggest that there is a correlation between rule of law and size of gross domestic product (GDP) Purchasing Power Parity (PPP) per capita in all countries covered by our project; that is, the more rule of law a country has, the bigger its GDP (PPP) per capita.[32]

Fifth, the legal culture in Poland, Bulgaria and Ukraine is likely to exhibit a set of common features that may be attributed to the shared communist experience. However, as each country followed different brands of Communism, the communist experience may have affected their legal cultures in rather different ways. Ukraine was a part of the former Soviet Union (FSU), whereas Poland and Bulgaria were considered the least and the most orthodox non-Soviet communist states in the Soviet Bloc, respectively. Added to this, the eastern parts of Ukraine were under communist rule for some 70 years, whereas the western parts – just like Poland and Bulgaria – were under such rule 'only' for some 40 years. Consequently, the communist legacy is likely to have left different imprints on their legal cultures.

Sixth, organised religion sometimes finds itself at odds with state law, and it may in specific circumstances cause people to violate such law. As already noted, within Europe it is possible to distinguish between two broad religious legal traditions – the *Judeo-Christian* and the *Islamic*.[33]

Bulgaria 58th (score: 0.53) and Ukraine 84th (score: 0.41). The World Justice Project (2014, pp. 14–15).

[32] The ranking of the 'rule of law' index matches World Bank figures for GDP per capita based on purchasing power parity, thus suggesting that there is more rule of law in wealthier than in poorer countries. World Bank figures for GDP PPP (2008) and Population (2008) show that Norway has the second-highest GDP (PPP) per capita in the world, at USD 58,141. The UK ranks 15th (USD 35,445), followed by Poland, ranked 39th (USD 17,625), Bulgaria, ranked 56th (USD 12,394) and Ukraine, ranked 83rd (USD 7,271). The ranking was made by dividing World Bank GDP PPP figures for 2008 with population figures for 2008. World Development Indicators Database, www.worldbank.org accessed on 15 September 2009. The ranking may be viewed in full at http://en.wikipedia.org/wiki/List_of_countries_by_GDP_(PPP)_per_capita#cite_note-1 IMF figures for 2013 show the same pattern: Norway has the fifth largest GDP (PPP) per capita (54,947), followed by the UK, which is ranked 21st (37,307), Poland, which is ranked 49th (21,214), Bulgaria, which is ranked 69th (14,499) and Ukraine, which is ranked 107th (7,423). See ranking based on estimates of projected data, World Economic Outlook Database, April 2014, cited in 'List of Countries by GDP (PPP) per Capita', http://en.wikipedia.org/wiki/List_of_countries_by_GDP_(PPP)_per_capita accessed 10 August 2014.

[33] For an introduction to Islamist legal culture, see Sykiäinen (n.d.).

Religious subcultures exist within both.[34] Our five countries are all Christian. One of them – Norway – is Protestant and until recently the Church of Norway was a fully state-funded church. England is religiously more diverse.[35] Poland is Catholic, and Catholicism largely defines 'Polishness'; Bulgaria is Orthodox but also has a significant Muslim minority (ethnic Turks, ethnic Pomaks). Western parts of Ukraine are predominantly Greek Catholic and Catholic, whereas Eastern Ukraine is predominantly Orthodox. Until the Russian Federation annexed the Crimea in 2014, Ukraine had a large Muslim minority – the Crimean Tatars – living in the Autonomous Republic of Crimea. Religious people might be more law-abiding as they have a moral imperative to obey the law. Further those who belong to a different ethnic group than the majority population might try to compensate for their ethno-religious minority status by being more law-abiding than the majority group. But it is equally plausible that religious people are less law-abiding if state law and religious law clash. Another possibility is that religion simply does not have any significant impact on law-abidingness at all.

Above we have outlined factors that might contribute to the divergence of legal cultures across Europe. The five countries covered in this book are recipients of a large body of law from supranational organisations and supranational courts. Such law includes the transfer of EU law from Brussels, CJEU case law, the ECHR and ECtHR case law, European Free Trade Association (EFTA) Court decisions, EFTA Surveillance Agency (ESA) decisions and various international conventions – such as United Nations (UN) Conventions, International Labour Organisation (ILO) Conventions and others.[36] The formal transfer of such law facilitates formal – but not necessarily actual – legal convergence across Europe. There are two other factors that are likely to contribute to convergence:

First, globalisation and the almost unlimited access to information that it has brought about through the internet, television and radio is likely to

[34] There appears to be a distinct, Catholic legal culture. See 'Mirror of Justice. A Blog dedicated to the Development of Catholic Legal Theory', www.mirrorofjustice.com/mirrorofjustice/2006/11/theocrats_in_po.html accessed on 13 February 2007.

[35] The 2011 Census fixed the Muslim population in the UK at 2,786,635, or 4.4 per cent of the total population. Most Muslims live in England, where they account for 5.02 per cent of the population (2,660,116 people).

[36] As an ENP state, the Ukraine is not bound by EU law and CJEU case law. However, it aspires to EU membership, and some effort has therefore been made to harmonise national law with European law.

affect both legal insiders and outsiders.[37] To what extent globalisation affects legal culture, however, is still not clear. Even if it affects attitudes toward the law and legal preferences at a more general level, it may still 'fail' to translate into actual behaviour. Intra-EU migrants – being more directly exposed to 'foreign' legal culture – are more likely to be affected by external influences than non-migrants. If they perceive legal culture in their (temporary) country of residence as more 'legitimate' than legal culture in their country of origin, they may – consciously or unconsciously – exert influence on the latter through the interaction with individuals and institutions there. But it is also possible that such migrants are so strongly influenced by the legal culture in their country of origin that they, rather than being influenced by it, may actually influence the legal culture in their new country of residence – especially if there are many of them. Intra-EU migrants, for their part, might simply adjust to the legal culture in whatever country they happen to be in, neither being influenced by, nor exerting any influence upon it.

Second, the war on terror is likely to have influenced legal culture in all five countries, though to different degrees. The English may be more willing to accept a reduction in their civil liberties than Norwegians, Poles, Bulgarians and Ukrainians as the UK has been directly affected by terrorist acts – previously orchestrated by the Irish Republican Army (IRA), more recently organised by 'Muslim terrorists'. By contrast, Norway had not been affected by terrorism on its own territory when data for our project were collected there. However, a few years earlier, in 2006, Osama Bin Laden had issued a threat against Norway. At the time of data collection Norway hosted (and it still hosts) an alleged terrorist (Mullah Krekar), but the country resisted efforts to have him extradited and refused to return him to his home country of Iraq, on the grounds that it would not be safe for him to return.[38] Courts have withstood political pressure in cases involving so-called terrorists. Politicians and the general public, however, may be less liberal than their legal institutions.[39] European

[37] For an analysis of globalisation in East Asia and East Europe, see Duckett and Miller (2006).

[38] In March 2012 the First Instance Court in Oslo sentenced Mullah Krekar to five years in prison for having issued death threats against the leader of the Norwegian Conservative Party, Erna Solberg.

[39] In the spring of 2006, TNS Gallup and TV2 polled 1,000 Norwegians on their attitudes toward terrorism. Some 55 per cent of non-Muslim Norwegians feared such terrorism. Only 22 per cent of the Muslim respondents expressed similar fears. TNS/TV2 survey, http://pub.tv2.no/nettavisen/innenriks/article642147.ece accessed on 19 February 2007.

post-communist states have been accused of extracting confessions from alleged terrorists under duress – and without the consent of their general publics. Although this may negatively affect legal culture, it may also trigger demands for more political accountability and more rule of law.

The aforementioned factors are likely to affect not only European legal integration but also contemporary *national legal culture.*

Legal outsiders versus legal insiders

Rather than approaching legal culture through the study of law or legal institutions this book explores legal culture through the eyes of those making, implementing and enforcing the law as well as those affected by the law. Our focus is on their attitudes and perceptions.

The academic literature on legal culture makes a clear distinction between *popular legal culture* and *professional legal culture* – or between the legal culture of ordinary people and legal professionals. We distinguish between *legal outsiders* (i.e. the general public) and *legal insiders* (i.e. those working professionally with the law).

We define *legal insiders* broadly so as to include elected representatives, government officials, judges, prosecutors, lawyers and police officials – not only the legally trained specialists responsible for applying the law but also those passing and implementing the law. We have included the elected representatives as they inform the content of and also pass the law at a national level and are engaged in decision-making at the local and regional levels. The executive implements the law and in doing so interprets the law. Besides, the executive is in a position to make certain amendments to the by-laws to ease its implementation. Lawyers interpret the law and interact with the court, whereas courts interpret and apply the law. The police enforce the law and the general public is affected by, and responds to, the law.

The *legal outsiders* refer to the general public. This category includes the majority population as well as Muslims and Euro-migrants. We include Muslims because they often have a stronger religious than ethnic identity[40] and because Islam has its own law and a distinct legal culture. A further distinction is made between 'domestic' and 'foreign' Muslims. The former includes Muslims who have lived in a given country for

[40] Predelli (2008, p. 243) observes that 'for many Muslim immigrants in Norway religion is the most important aspect of their identity'.

centuries, such as the Bulgarian Turks, the Polish Tatars and the Crimean Tatars.[41] The latter refers to Muslims who have migrated to Europe from Asia or Africa more recently – such as the Pakistani communities in Norway and the UK, and Turks and Muslims from the FSU living in Poland. The term *Euro-migrants* refers to citizens of one European country who temporarily move to another European country to work, to study or to spend an extended period of time there.

Neither professional legal culture nor popular legal culture is homogeneous: both consist of subcultures. Research on the legal culture of teachers of law in British universities show that there are some differences between law teachers based at old and new universities – even though the two groups also have much in common (Cownie 2004). Besides, although the legal professionals category previously consisted of a limited number of people primarily recruited from the elites, the number of people educated in law and/or certified to practice law has greatly increased in recent years.[42]

This book questions the established view that the legal culture of legal outsiders and insiders are inherently different. Our starting point is that legal professionals are not only legal professionals: they are also citizens. As such, they have been socialised into the same national legal culture as the non-professionals (Grødeland 2014b). Consequently, the legal culture of the legal insiders is likely to be influenced not only by profession-based or institution-based codes of conduct but also by the same factors that influence general (or popular) legal culture. The latter might influence legal professionals to a greater extent in countries where the distance between elites and ordinary citizens is small – that is, in countries where the legal professionals consider themselves to be a part of the broader 'we/us' (i.e. country nationals) rather than defining themselves as 'we/us' and ordinary citizens as 'them'.[43]

41 The Crimean Tatars were deported from the Crimea to Central Asia in 1944, but were allowed to return in the late 1980s.

42 In the UK, for instance, figures from the Law Society show that the number of solicitors qualified to work in England and Wales has increased tremendously in recent years. The number of holding certificates (i.e. excluding retired lawyers and those no longer following a legal career) has increased by 36 per cent during the last ten years. Simon Rogers, 'How many solicitors are there in England and Wales? And who are they?', *theguardian.com*, 4 April 2011, www.theguardian.com/news/datablog/2011/apr/04/solicitors-number-england-wales-ethnicity accessed on 10 September 2014.

43 For an analysis of elite perceptions of 'we/us' versus 'them', see Aasland, Grødeland and Pleines (2012).

We therefore assume that on some dimensions of legal culture the views of legal outsiders and insiders are likely to differ, whereas on others they are likely to be less pronounced. On some dimensions of legal culture the convergence–divergence dichotomy is likely to apply differently to those affected by law (the general public) and those passing, implementing and enforcing the law (legal professionals). It is also likely to apply differently to subgroups within both categories, such as Muslim minorities and Euro-migrants. On other dimensions, however, the difference between the two groups is likely to be less pronounced. The former is likely to include the more technical aspects of law, whereas the latter might include more general attitudes towards, and perceptions of, law and its role in society.

Measuring legal culture

Legal culture covers, amongst other things, the history of law, the law itself, the content of the law, the institutional settings within which the law is applied, the people applying the law and the people affected by the law. And it covers attitudes, perceptions and behaviour towards law – which relate to the more recent concept of *legal consciousness*, defined by Silbey (2008) as follows: 'the concept of legal consciousness is used to name analytically the understandings and meanings of law circulating in social relations. Legal consciousness refers to what people do as well as say about law'. Ewick and Silbey (1998) explored the manner in which American citizens *interact* with the law. Our focus is somewhat different: we are primarily interested in people's more *general attitudes and perceptions* of law.

Legal culture may be approached in several different ways. Legal anthropologists, for instance, have studied ethnic communities with a view to establishing whether – and in case what – rules they abide by. Studies have also focused on conflict management in various forms and on the manner in which institutions work.[44]

Those who have a legal background often apply what could be described as a *systems' approach* to legal culture: their focus is on legal systems, legal families or legal practice. Legal sociologists, for their part, study legal practices by looking at the manner in which individual citizens or legal professionals behave in specific settings – including in

[44] Forsyth (2009), Chapter 2. The possibilities and limitations of legal pluralism.

court. Or they address specific legal procedures in different countries to identify differences and similarities. Some legal sociologists, and also political scientists, have taken a *clusters of attitudes approach* to the study of legal culture – investigating the opinions of legal outsiders and occasionally also legal insiders in a more systematic manner by means of quantitative surveys and/or in-depth interviews (IDIs). However, survey-based studies of legal culture are fairly rare.

Though useful, legal culture as a concept is not unproblematic. One criticism that has been raised against its use is that the notion of 'culture' is too broad, almost 'all-inclusive' and thus very difficult to break down into something tangible and researchable. Another major objection is that differences observed between countries regarding legal behaviour may essentially be a result of institutional restrictions rather than legal culture as such, though it could perhaps be argued that institutional restrictions are, essentially, a reflection of the wider legal culture.

Further, it is sometimes difficult to distinguish between legal culture at the global and national levels, and between internal and external culture.[45] There is also a problem with causation: does legal culture shape the law or is the law shaping legal culture? Or is it a case of the two mutually shaping and supporting each other?[46] Nelken (2004, p. 9) argues that despite the ambiguities of causation, *thick descriptions* of legal culture are still important. Whatever its origins a distinctive legal culture is consistent with and helps to support and maintain distinctive patterns of institutional and public behaviour with regard to the law.

Thick descriptions of legal culture

Anthropologists define *thick descriptions* of a human behaviour as an approach that explains not just behaviour, but its context as well; that is, the description explains with as much detail as possible the reason behind human behaviour. Geertz, who effectively invented the term, sought to interpret the guiding symbols of cultures, which he defined as 'system(s) of inherited conceptions expressed in symbolic forms by means of which men communicate, perpetuate, and develop their knowledge and attitudes toward life' (Geertz 1973, p. 89). Common language, philosophy and literary analysis were therefore considered to have major explanatory force.

45 For a response to and theoretical discussion of these problems, see Friedman in Nelken (1997).

46 Marina Kurkchiyan, 'Placing law in the cultural context'. Unpublished teaching materials.

This book focuses on people and their opinions on several key dimensions of legal culture rather than on institutions, institutional settings and specific legislation. Opinions matter because they shed light on phenomena of importance to our understanding of legal culture, but also because they effectively 'inform' behaviour. Although it is possible to observe some behaviour (e.g. how citizens behave in court), other types of behaviour, such as the violation of specific types of law, is not easily observable. Mapping the opinions 'informing' certain types of behaviour is thus useful in that it allows one to predict the likelihood of certain types of behaviour and the reasons for such behaviour.

Within the legal insiders a *thick description* of legal culture requires attention to the variations in legal cultures within individual institutions, within different professions and within different regions, as well as to the different roles of legal experts, such as legal experts, on the one hand, and as ordinary citizens, on the other.[47] A recent study of informal practice amongst legal insiders suggests that legal professionals (judges, prosecutors) make less use of informal practice (i.e. the use of contacts and informal networks) than other elites, but that when they use them, they use them in the same manner and for the same purposes (Grødeland 2014b). Although some of these purposes are legitimate, others are clearly not. This, in turn, suggests that legal insiders sometimes comply with internal legal culture, and at other times external legal culture. Consequently, the distinction between internal and external legal culture appears to be fluid rather than fixed.

The legal culture of the legal insiders, on the other hand, is most likely influenced not only by their personal perceptions, attitudes, experiences and behaviour but also by professional legal culture and institutional legal culture – and the interplay between them.

Within the legal outsiders a *thick description* requires attention to the variations in legal cultures across different socioeconomic, regional and cultural groups. In the case of legal outsiders, the legal culture amongst the higher educated may be more convergent across Europe than

[47] Their attitudes, preferences and behaviour are therefore to some extent influenced by the general legal culture, to some extent by professional legal culture, to some extent by institutional legal culture (i.e. legal culture as manifested within their institution) and to some extent by institutional and other constraints – such as budget size, access to equipment, staff size and competence and political pressure. As concerns professional legal culture, for instance, lawyers may have more in common with other lawyers both within their own country and in other countries, than they have with other types of legal experts – such as judges or prosecutors – with whom they frequently interact in court.

amongst the lower educated. Moreover, Muslims and Euro-migrants may have a different legal culture from the majority population. Socio-economic factors may also affect the legal culture of the legal outsiders: rich and poor people may have different perceptions of law and legal professionals and they may also behave differently vis-à-vis the law. We would also expect to find variations in legal cultures amongst the 'legal outsiders' across different regional and cultural groups. Generation, education, religiosity, gender and cosmopolitan contacts are likely to be especially important.[48] Finally, people living in the centre (capital) as opposed to the periphery (regions) may also have different legal cultures.

Public perceptions of elite behaviour – from local officials to national government and indeed to the EU level – are likely to affect the structuring of the public's own attitudes and behaviour with regard to the law. Some of these influences and relationships may prove to be quite complex. Our *thick descriptions* include some description of the interconnectedness of perceptions, attitudes, experience and behaviour.

We are interested not only in people's opinions per se but also in *the manner* in which they convey their opinions – that is, what words they use and what connotations they make when talking about issues of relevance to legal culture. In this book we therefore complement statistical findings on attitudes and perceptions with an analysis of (i) the language in which attitudes and perceptions are conveyed and described, and, where relevant (ii) references to relevant events and developments that help explain the attitudes and perceptions conveyed by the legal outsiders and insiders. In doing so we provide what Nelken describes as *thick descriptions* of legal cultures based on a wide-ranging analysis of the perceptions, attitudes, experiences and practice of the people in these countries, rather than the views of external observers.

Such *thick descriptions* of legal culture are a useful tool for understanding the context into which legal transfers, or transplants, are introduced and for how they are likely to function within their new cultural, geographical and socioeconomic context.[49]

[48] For an account of several dissimilar subcultures within popular legal culture in America, see Yngvesson (1989, p. 1694).

[49] As European integration is primarily law-driven, *thick descriptions* of legal culture also serve as a useful starting point for examining to what extent soft law from Brussels facilitates convergence or divergence. For an overview of why some legal transplants succeed while others fail, see Berkowitz, Pistor and Richard (2003); Galinou (2004); Spamann (2009).

Dimensions of legal culture

One study of legal culture cannot possibly provide an all-exhaustive account of five European national cultures. For this reason we have investigated seven dimensions that we perceive to be of crucial importance for the mapping of European legal culture.

First, attitudes to, and perceptions of, law are an essential part of legal culture. The notion of *law as culture* emphasises that 'law is more than just a set of rules and concepts. It is also a social practice within a legal community' (Van Hoecke and Warrington 1998, p. 498) and also amongst those interacting with the legal community. We therefore explore the understandings legal outsiders and insiders have of law as a concept. Do they think laws should reflect social norms or be used to change people's behaviour? Should judges take account of circumstances or should they apply the law strictly? Should disputes be solved in court or would it be better to solve them in other settings? What changes have taken place in national legislation in recent years? Are such changes good or bad – and what has caused them in the first place?

Second, attitudes to the *role/status of law – including 'rule of law'* – also represent an important element of legal culture. Although democratic societies are characterised by the rule *of* law, rule *by* law is a typical feature of authoritarian societies. Added to this, some democratic societies may have more rule of law than others. Individuals' understanding of the role of law tells us something about how democratically or authoritarian-minded they are. We therefore asked legal outsiders and insiders what they think should be the basis of law – that is, whether it should be customs and traditions, religion, moral values, practical considerations of usefulness or something else. Our questions about how people should deal with unreasonable or unjust laws, or laws that are contrary to their religion, allowed us to explore their understanding of law as well as their tolerance of otherness.

Third, globalisation and European integration affect national law and legal institutions in a profound manner. These processes are primarily conducted by means of *legal transfers*, such as the transfer of legislation, institutional structures and best practices, from one cultural and/or geographical setting into another. Besides, the role of supranational courts has significantly increased as a result of globalisation and European integration. We therefore asked our respondents and focus group (FG) participants whether they think their country has a lot to learn from other countries and international organisations about law, the way law is applied, or about the way ordinary people deal with the law. And we asked them whether standards set by organisations such as the EU and the UN impose foreign ideas on ordinary people in their country, and also, whether they give too many privileges to minorities or whether they protect them from discrimination. We asked them whether their country should have broadly the same laws and law enforcement as the rest of Europe or whether they should have different laws and law enforcement that better suit their country and people. We explored their views on how political leaders and legal professionals should respond to rulings of international courts – and how they actually respond. Finally, we asked them whether they would trust the judgements of supranational courts more or less than those of national courts.

Fourth, a *thick description* of legal culture should also address images of the actors dealing with and/or being affected by law. We therefore asked both the legal outsiders and insiders (i) *how they perceive legal insiders* and the institutions in which they work and (ii) *how legal outsiders relate to the law.* We asked them whether they think government and parliament are capable of drafting clear and effective laws and whether they trust them to do so, whether they expect various types of legal insiders to be well informed about recent changes to the law, whether they are fair and/or can be trusted and whether they are capable and effective. We asked the legal insiders how they think ordinary people perceive their profession, and we asked them what they think are the most important changes that have occurred in their profession in recent years as far as the law is concerned. We asked the legal outsiders and insiders whether ordinary citizens generally obey the law, whether religious or ethnic minorities are generally more or less obedient to the law than other people, whether people are more or less likely to break the law now than they were in the past and whether people who knowingly break the law usually have a reasonable excuse for doing so.

Fifth, the war on terror has since 9/11 been fought by introducing measures that curtail the civil rights not only of terrorist suspects but also of ordinary citizens. Above we refer to such measures as *illiberal transplants.* Perceptions of such transplants are likely to differ depending on citizens' perceptions of the terrorist threat, measures introduced in their country and their democratic/authoritarian preferences. For this reason, we included some questions on the war on terror more generally, and the tension between civil and human rights and security in our questionnaire, FG and IDI guides. We asked the legal outsiders and insiders whether they think their country is faced with a real threat of terrorism;

whether they believe their country's government has been under pressure from international organisations or foreign countries to stay within the law or under pressure to step outside the law when combating terrorism; whether it is more important to combat the threat of terrorism or to protect the rights of individual citizens and minorities. And we asked how the government in their country has responded to terrorism, and how it should ideally respond – that is, whether it should pass new, tougher laws, keep the existing laws but, if necessary, step outside the law, or stay strictly within existing laws.

Finally, 'European values' and 'European culture' are concepts frequently used by the EU to describe the European project. It is not entirely clear, however, what they entail, nor what associations they evoke in European citizens. We therefore also explored these concepts by asking legal outsiders and insiders what they understand by *European culture and values* and how they differ from 'culture and values' outside Europe.[50] Further, we asked them whether they would be pleased or displeased if national cultures and values became more similar across the whole of Europe. And, more importantly, whether they would be pleased or displeased if national laws became much more similar across the whole of Europe.

Data collection: FGs, quantitative surveys, IDIs

To enable us to provide a *thick description* of European legal culture we opted for a mix of qualitative (FGs; IDIs) and quantitative (nationally representative surveys with booster samples amongst Muslims) methods.

Triangulation allows us to combine the richness of the qualitative methods with the precision of the quantitative methods. As questions asked during the FGs were repeated in the quantitative surveys and IDIs, our data allow for an unusually integrated and innovative analytical approach to the concept of legal culture. More specifically, our data allow for (i) a comparison of large-scale qualitative (IDIs) and quantitative (survey) data (frequencies, cross-tabulations), (ii) a comparison of how legal outsiders and legal insiders talk about legal culture (FG, and IDI data), (iii) an in-depth statistical analysis of quantitative data and (iv) an illustration of quantitative (survey) data with freely expressed and representative comments from the FGs.

[50] These findings have been presented elsewhere (Grødeland 2009) and are not included in this book.

Data were collected in three stages: first, we collected qualitative, then quantitative data on the legal outsiders – that is, the general public. The FGs allowed us to explore the dimensions described above, and also to conduct a comparative analysis of attitudes to the law amongst the general public, religious minorities (Muslims) and people migrating around the European common space (intra-EU migrants). They also 'informed' the content of the questionnaire used for the quantitative study, ensuring that the questionnaires were framed in easily understood and relevant terms. Second, we conducted IDIs with legal insiders. These interviews were informed by qualitative and quantitative findings on the legal outsiders.[51]

In Norway, England, Poland and Bulgaria we conducted a total of 14 FGs per country: two in the capital (one with higher educated and one with lower educated people), two in a large city (one in a wealthy and one in a poor region), two in a small town (one in a wealthy and one in a poor region), two in a village (one in a wealthy and one in a poor region), three with Muslims (different locations) and three FGs with intra-EU migrants (different locations).

To allow for an exploration of attitudes to legal culture in Western Ukraine, Eastern Ukraine and the Crimea – as well as in a wealthier and poorer region within each of them – we conducted a total of 28 FGs in Ukraine – in the capital, in a large city, small town and village in a wealthier and also a poorer part of Western Ukraine, Eastern Ukraine and the Crimea, amongst Muslims and Euro-migrants. Background information about each FG-participant, collected through mini-questionnaires, allows for a more rigorous analysis of the FGs.

Each FG lasted on average for two and a half hours. They were both audio- and video-recorded. Complete transcripts were provided both in the native language and in English.

The FGs were followed by *nationally representative surveys* and additional *booster samples with Muslims*, in each country covered by the project. The booster samples allow us to investigate whether ethnic minorities adhering to Islam relate differently to the law than the ethnic titular groups (or majority populations).

[51] Finally, court observation allowed for a thorough investigation of the interaction between legal 'insiders' and 'outsiders'. IDIs supplementing such observation were in part informed by qualitative and quantitative findings on the legal insiders and outsiders, and in part by the court cases themselves. Findings from the court observation have been published separately.

In all we interviewed 5,156 respondents drawn from the general public – 911 in Norway, 1000 in England, 1,027 in Poland, 1,018 in Bulgaria and 1,200 in Ukraine;[52] and 1,008 respondents in special Muslim samples – 201 in Norway, 200 in England, 200 in Poland, 207 in Bulgaria and 200 in Ukraine. There were, of course, a few Muslims in the samples of the general public, especially in Bulgaria. Each interview lasted approximately one hour.

Structured, open-ended IDIs were conducted with the legal insiders, including (i) elected representatives, (ii) prosecutors, (iii) lawyers, (iv) judges, (v) government officials and (vi) police (rank-and-file police officers, police investigators), at national, capital, regional and local levels. In each country except Ukraine we conducted a total of 150 IDIs – 25 interviews per category of respondents.[53] In Ukraine, we conducted 186 IDIs – 31 interviews per category of respondents – to allow us to explore attitudes towards legal culture amongst legal insiders in Western Ukraine, Eastern Ukraine and the Crimea, and in wealthier as well as poorer regions within each of them. Interviews lasted for approximately one hour. They were audio-recorded, transcribed and translated into English. Background information about each respondent, collected through mini-questionnaires, allowed for a more rigorous analysis of the IDIs.

The FGs, quantitative surveys and IDIs were commissioned from professional pollsters (see the appendix for details), but the FG guide, IDI guide and survey questionnaire were prepared by the project team. The FGs and survey interviews with the general public and IDIs with legal insiders (elected representatives, government officials, lawyers, prosecutors, judges and the police) were provided by TNS-Gallup (Oslo), ORB (London), CBOS (Warsaw), Alpha Research (Sofia) and Socis-Gallup (Kyiv). The authors attended and directly observed a sample of the FGs (some with, others without, simultaneous translation) in each

[52] In Ukraine we conducted 1,200 interviews to facilitate comparisons of East Ukraine, West Ukraine and the Crimea.

[53] For each category, we conducted eight interviews at the national level, five interviews at the capital level, eight interviews at the regional level (four in a large city in a wealthy area and four in a large city in a poor area, respectively) and four interviews at the local level (two in a small town in a wealthy area and two in a small town in a poor area, respectively). In Ukraine, in addition to the interviews at the national and capital levels, we conducted one set of interviews in West Ukraine, one in East Ukraine and one in the Autonomous Republic of Crimea, and in one wealthy and one poor region within each.

country. We analysed the data by means of QSR NUD*IST and Nvivo (FGs, IDIs) and SPSS (quantitative surveys).

Presentation of data

The first part of the chapters in this book investigates the attitudes and perceptions of the legal outsiders, drawing on survey and FG-data, and the second part of each chapter investigates the views of the legal insiders, drawing on IDI data. Survey findings are illustrated by analysis and verbatim from the FGs. IDI findings are presented in statistical form (frequencies; i.e. percentages of the total number of statements made by the legal insiders on a given issue) and complemented by a content analysis of these statements. Data presented in the book are complemented by relevant country information explaining them. To give the legal insiders their own voice, summaries of findings that precede the actual citations contain words and phrases used by the legal insiders themselves. Such words and phrases appear in double quotation marks in the text.

The book makes extensive use of citations from the FGs and IDIs.

FG participants are referred to as follows: country-FG number-FG location-FG participant number. *N* refers to Norway, *E* refers to England, *P* refers to Poland, *B* refers to Bulgaria, and *U* refers to Ukraine. Muslim FG participants are marked 'Muslim'. Thus, 'E4-Bath-4' indicates participant number four in the fourth English FG, which was held in Bath.

IDIs are referred to as follows: country-type of legal insider-respondent number. Again, *N* refers to Norway, *E* refers to England, *P* refers to Poland, *B* refers to Bulgaria and *U* refers to Ukraine. Further, *ER* refers to elected representative, *GO* refers to government official, *LA* refers to lawyer, *JU* refers to judge, *PR* refers to prosecutors and *PO* refers to the police. The number given indicates the number of the interview conducted within the given category of respondents. Thus, 'N-JU-6' refers to the sixth interview conducted with judges in Norway.

Data in Ukraine were collected before the Russian annexation of the Crimea in March 2014. As we have collected extensive data in the Crimea and as the Russian annexation of this territory has not been approved by the international community de jure, we have included these in our analysis of Ukrainian legal culture.

For reasons of space, detailed analyses of data on Muslims and Euro-migrants appear in Chapter 8 (Muslims and Euro-migrants as carriers of legal culture) and Chapter 9 (Balancing civil rights against a 'war on terror') only. Qualitative data on Muslims are included for illustrative purposes in Chapters 5 (Perceptions of legal outsiders) and 6 (Perceptions of legal insiders), but not analysed in detail. Verbatim from the Muslim FGs are included in the analysis of FG data where appropriate throughout the text.

Plan of the book

This book investigates not only differences between groups within countries but also in the convergence between countries as a whole and even more so, in the degree of pan-European convergence of legal cultures within particular groups across – both amongst the legal insiders and outsiders. The following chapters show whether patterns of pan-European convergence vary in these ways and, more generally, reveal the socioeconomic, religious and other factors that encourage or discourage the pan-European convergence of legal cultures.

First, we investigate attitudes towards law, that is, what 'law' is (Chapter 2) and what role law should have in society (Chapter 3). Such attitudes are important in that they provide an indication as to how democratically minded (how rule-of-law oriented) the general public, the legal professionals, elected representatives and government officials actually are. By comparing such perceptions in both Western and Eastern Europe we are able to establish whether citizens in these regions have a common understanding of the rule of law – and what it actually entails.

Second, we investigate attitudes towards the use of law, that is, how law should be used – but also perceptions of how it actually is used. First we look at 'law in action', investigating how citizens think legal professionals apply the law and how they themselves would solve disputes: would they turn to law or would they seek alternative solutions? (Chapter 4). We then look at law-abidingness, trying to establish in what circumstances people obey or ignore the law. Further, we try to establish whether – when they do break the law – they have any reasonable excuses for doing so (Chapter 5). Thus, we effectively investigate whether – and why – people abide by law ('Loyalty'), resist the law ('Exit'), or challenge the law ('Voice'), to borrow Hirschman's terminology.

Third, we investigate perceptions of those people and institutions who make, implement and enforce the law (Chapter 6). We look at how the public perceive these people and institutions; how these people and institutions think they are perceived by the public; and how these people and institutions perceive each other. The purpose of this exercise is to establish whether the distance between legal outsiders and insiders is narrow or broad as this, in turn, may tell us something about the legitimacy of the people and institutions administering law and thus also about the quality of democracy. Further, the perceptions the legislative, executive and judiciary have of each other are important in that they also say something about the quality of democracy. If there is mutual distrust between the three, or if one of them tries to meddle in the affairs of the other two, then this would suggest poor quality rule of law, or even its absence.

Fourth, we investigate legal transfers from two different angles. We first investigate the general attitudes of legal outsiders and insiders towards legal transfers more generally, and towards transfers protecting the weaker segments of society (various types of minorities), in particular. We then also explore their attitudes towards European legal integration (Chapter 7). However, in addition, we investigate 'carriers' of foreign legal culture (e.g. Muslims and Euro-migrants) within the context of national legal cultures (Chapter 8). Such people embody foreign legal culture. Do they shed their native legal culture in the meeting with the legal culture of the majority population? Or, on the contrary, do they try to preserve it? The answers to these questions are important as they provide a better understanding of the plurality of legal culture.

Fifth, we investigate the (potential) conflict between 'liberal' and 'illiberal' values and laws. We do this by exploring two potentially 'illiberal' influences on law: 'the war on terror' and 'religiosity'.

As concerns the former, our focus is on the tension between 'civil rights' and 'the war on terror' (Chapter 9). Although civil rights are deeply embedded in the constitutions of European democracies, security measures introduced to fight terrorism encroach on people's civil rights. The former represents a legal transfer in that some such measures are 'exported' by those countries most directly threatened by terrorism, to countries that perceive terrorism as a lesser threat. Although immediately after the collapse of Communism the West engaged in 'liberal legal transfers' to the East, in recent years legal transfers have become increasingly 'illiberal'. How do legal outsiders and insiders across Europe perceive this clash between liberal and illiberal values and laws? The answers to these questions are important as they say something about the kind of society Europeans want for themselves.

As concerns the latter, our focus is on the impact of religiosity on national legal cultures (Chapter 10). European democracies are secular in form: in most of them state law is above religion and organised religion belongs to the private sphere. The academic literature cites religiosity as correlating strongly with authoritarianism. Added to this, deeply religious people sometimes find themselves in a moral dilemma if and when their religious beliefs clash with state law. Although the role and impact of religiosity is addressed in several chapters, the link between religion and legal culture is investigated at more length in a separate chapter.

In Chapter 11 we ask whether national legal cultures in Europe are converging or diverging. We answer this question by discussing similarities and differences between Western and Eastern Europe, legal outsiders and legal insiders, majority populations, Muslims and Euro-migrants. In addition we discuss the tension between liberal and illiberal factors within national legal cultures: first by discussing the impact of the war on terror on liberal legal culture, and second by discussing the impact of religion on secular legal culture.

2

Concept or meaning of law

Introduction: law and everyday life

A key feature of modern society in the late twentieth/early twenty-first century has been the *judicialisation* of politics (Vallinder 1994; Goldstein 2004) – defined by Hirschl (2009, p. 253) as 'the reliance on courts and judicial means for addressing core moral predicaments, public policy questions, and political controversies'. Another closely related feature is what Susskind (2010, pp. 18–19) calls *hyper-regulation.* In his view 'we are all governed today by a body of rules and laws that are so complex and so large in extent that no-one can pretend to have mastery of them all . . . not that there is too much law by some objective standard, but there is too much law given our current methods of managing it'.

As law is becoming increasingly more important in people's lives it is crucial to establish what their thoughts about law are. To gain a better understanding of how the public and the legal professionals relate to law and changes in law we 'go back to the basics'. In this chapter we explore the attitudes legal outsiders and insiders across Europe have towards law: what law means to them, what it should be about and how it evolves. Our reason for doing so is twofold.

First, we seek to establish whether the public in Western and Eastern Europe have similar or different understandings of law. Attitudes towards law are a key dimension of legal culture. People's attitudes towards law can tell us much about their legal culture – including whether it is democratic or authoritarian.

Second, we seek to establish whether – and to what extent – the attitudes of legal outsiders and insiders across Europe are similar or different on these issues. In Chapter 1 we suggested that legal insiders are not only legal professionals. They are also citizens, socialised into the same national legal culture as their fellow citizens. The legal culture of legal outsiders and insiders may therefore differ on some dimensions, whilst being similar or even identical on others.

The purpose of this chapter is to establish whether there is convergence or divergence across Europe and between legal outsiders and insiders on their understandings of law.

LEGAL OUTSIDERS' PERSPECTIVES ON LAW

Images of law

Even as legal insiders make, implement, apply and enforce the law, legal outsiders are *affected* by law. Their influence on lawmaking is mostly indirect through the Members of Parliament (MPs) they elect in general elections. However, as we will see in Chapter 4, citizens may also influence draft laws directly, for instance, by communicating directly with their MPs, by presenting their views through the media or by engaging in civil society. Given their different roles with regard to law, legal insiders' understanding of what law is might differ from the understanding of legal insiders. In this part of the chapter we focus on the general public.

Right at the start of each survey interview, legal outsiders were questioned about their own general perspectives on law. Our data show that although legal insiders tend to associate the word *law* with formal law, legal outsiders in different countries have very different perceptions of law.

When Norwegians are asked what images come to mind when they think about law, 87 per cent cite 'written laws, rules and regulations' and only a mere 2 per cent cite 'people involved in making or applying the law' such as MPs or the police. By contrast, when the English think about law, only 32 per cent cite 'written laws, rules and regulations': no more than those in England who cite 'people involved in making or applying the law'. So the English focus as much on 'people involved in making or applying the law' as on 'written laws, rules and regulations'. 'Embodiment' matters in England but not in Norway.

In Poland, Bulgaria and Ukraine only approximately 11 per cent cite 'people involved in making or applying the law' and the public focus on a combination of 'written laws' and 'order and discipline'. In Ukraine especially the primary image of law is 'order and discipline', cited by 54 per cent of the public (Table 2.1).

During the Soviet period law was used to create and shape 'Soviet Man'. Enforcement of laws aimed at achieving this objective was diligently pursued. Other types of law, however, were enforced in a more lax

Table 2.1 *Notions of law: the legal outsiders' perspective*

	Norway (%)	England (%)	Poland (%)	Bulgaria (%)	Ukraine (%)
PQ1: When I say the word *law*, what images come to your mind? Do you think primarily of:					
written laws, rules and regulations?	87	32	43	44	38
order and discipline?	11	36	42	46	54
people involved in making or applying the law?	2	32	16	10	8
PQ2: And when I say the word *law*, do you primarily think of:					
justice, fairness and legal rights?	95	87	77	83	73
unfair and oppressive laws?	5	13	24	17	27

Note: without offering other replies, interviewers noted the very few who answered 'mixed'/'both', 'none'/'neither', 'don't know', 'other' or simply 'no'. These are excluded from this table. In subsequent tables the few who answered 'both agree and disagree', 'neither agree nor disagree', 'don't know' or simply 'no answers' are also excluded.

manner. Ukrainian citizens' image of law is therefore likely to have been shaped by the role of law during the Soviet past.[1]

Sajo (1990, p. 333) claims that during Communism 'politically the law became a means of repressing political opposition. The general public was sceptical of the legal system as it was unclear, offered no protection, and was considered an irrelevance or obstacle to be outmanoeuvred in order to survive'. Bodnar and Schmidt (2012, p. 291) observe that 'much of the legal culture of these countries (i.e. the post-communist ones) is a legacy of the Soviet legal tradition with its doctrine of the "unity of state

[1] Implementation of other law, however, was more lax. Soviet environmental legislation, for instance, was designed for idealistic rather than realistic purposes: their main purpose was to show the world that Soviet environmental legislation was superior to that of the West. It was commonly known and accepted that it could not be implemented in practice (Goldman 1975).

power" and an instrumental approach that "treated law as simply one of a number of instruments of rule, and not even as the dominant one"'.

Those focus group (FG) participants who associate the word *law* with *enforcement* mostly have in mind the police, prosecution or prison. Norwegian FG participants mostly associate law with the police – and the Muslims in Norway do so in a negative sense. Quite a few of them speak about the police exceeding their powers. Bulgarian FG participants are not happy with the police, whereas the Ukrainians describe a harsh police force. The English FG participants, for their part, think the police are not doing enough to help people. They also express dissatisfaction with lenient sentencing for criminal offenses. Those who associate *law* with *order* usually do so without explaining what exactly they understand by order and discipline:

> B2-Sofia-8: 'it's no good dealing with the police . . . the [police] officer tells you straight to your face to handle the situation yourself.' E4-Bristol-5: 'the punishment's not harsh enough. It's not enough of a deterrent for people'. E7-Sheffield-2: '[I associate law with] jail.' P1-Warsaw-lower education-6: 'public prosecution'. U1-Kiev-1: 'the dictatorship of the proletariat. There were laws there, too'. U4-Yasinovataya-4: 'a . . . strong hand, even a fist.' N5-Muslims-3: 'you read in the newspaper that the police break laws and regulations, they should . . . abide by them.'

Democracy is the ideal for both West and East Europeans – even though it is not yet a reality in all of Europe's post-communist states. Dryzek and Holmes (2002), Miller et al. (1998) and others have documented that citizens across Europe have similar understandings of key aspects of democracy. Rule of law is such a key feature. West and East Europeans may therefore have similar understandings of what law is and what it should be about.

Large majorities amongst legal outsiders in all five countries associate the word *law* with 'justice, fairness and legal rights' rather than with 'unfair and oppressive laws'. In Norway very few people (only 5 per cent) associate the word *law* with the latter. On an average only 15 per cent in England and Bulgaria also do so, but this percentage rises to 24 per cent in Poland and 27 per cent in Ukraine (Table 2.1).

East European FG participants in general – and Bulgarians in particular – associate the word *law* with *Themis (Θέμις)*, the ancient Greek goddess 'of good counsel', and the personification of 'divine order, law, natural law and custom'.[2] However, the Bulgarian *Themis* is not always blindfolded.

[2] 'Themis', Wikipedia, http://en.wikipedia.org/wiki/Themis accessed on 5 September 2014.

Rather, she sees everything and endorses that which should not be endorsed. The Ukrainian *Themis*, on the other hand, is blind to the injustices taking place in domestic courts:

> B2-Sofia-4: 'there is an image of the law in our Court of Justice. *Themis* who is blindfolded, pronouncing the verdict'. U15-Plotica-1: 'the scales symbolise the impartial attitude towards both parties . . . [the intention] to judge by the law.' B3-Varna-7: '*Themis*, but not the blind[folded] *Themis*. [The] *Themis*, who can see very well and whose scales bend to the money'. B8-Dolna Mitropolia-1: 'the image of *Themis*, although in Bulgaria she appears to have her eyes open.' U1-Kiev-5: 'the figure with [her] eyes shut. People with shut eyes, they are blind, they do not see what's going on'.

Other FG participants associate law with those enforcing the law (judges), premises (the court room), colours (red – i.e. the colour of the gowns of the judges in England; blue – the colour of the police uniforms; white – i.e. the colour of purity) or have their own more original spin on the term. English FG participants, for instance, mostly associate the word *law* with the judge:

> E1-London-8: 'old men in wigs'. E4-Bristol-9: 'some of the judges are way too old, they're in their seventies, aren't they? They should have retired years before.' P3-Katowice-5: 'the law is punishment and a judge.' U1-Kiev-6: 'crystal clean colours . . . white . . . the colour of purity.' E2-London-5: 'red . . . judges wore red.' N3-Muslims-5: 'I visualise the court room.'

Good versus bad law: helpful? fair? complex? Moral values or state power?

European media create the impression that in Western Europe there are too many detailed regulations, whereas in Eastern Europe there are too many contradicting laws. As law in both regions is continuously evolving, ordinary citizens have to make their way through a complicated legal landscape. It is thus useful to look into their perceptions of whether the law is helpful, fair, too complex or based on generally shared moral values.

Helpful? Perceptions that the law is 'helpful' rather than 'making problems for people' vary dramatically across the five countries from a truly remarkable 92 per cent in Norway to a mere 29 per cent in Ukraine, through 66 per cent in England and around 53 per cent in Poland and Bulgaria (Table 2.2).

Findings for Norway do not support the impression created by the Norwegian media: that ordinary citizens find law too detailed, complicated and thus unhelpful. But findings for Eastern Europe do support the

Table 2.2 *Perceptions of law: the legal outsiders' perspective*

	Norway (%)	England (%)	Poland (%)	Bulgaria (%)	Ukraine (%)
PQ9: Do you think the law in [this country] . . .					
. . . generally helps people like yourself?	92	66	50	56	29
. . . generally makes problems for people like yourself?	8	34	50	44	71
PQ14: On the whole, do you feel the law in [this country] . . .					
. . . is fair?	90	72	35	52	21
. . . is unfair?	10	28	65	48	79
PQ15: On the whole, do you feel the law in [this country] . . .					
. . . is often too complex and too frequently changed to be obeyed?	35	48	64	51	65
. . . can and should be obeyed?	65	52	36	49	35
PQ16: On the whole, do you feel the law in [this country] reflects . . .					
. . . generally recognised moral values that are shared?	83	58	50	39	26
. . . the power of the state to control people?	17	42	50	61	74

common view that law is not necessarily helpful. As we will show in the second part of this chapter East European legal professionals are often dealing with poor quality national law – including so-called designer laws (i.e. laws created for the benefit of narrow political and/or economic interest), old and new legislation (in Ukraine, for instance, some Soviet laws are still in use) that frequently contradict one another and poorly translated 'imported' law.

It is therefore not always clear to legal professionals which law they should apply – or how it should be applied. Further complicating matters, *legal dualism*, *legal nihilism* (Hendley 2011; 2012) and *informal practice* (i.e. the use of connections and informal networks) (Ledeneva 1998; Grødeland 2007) are common across Eastern Europe, effectively allowing people to get by without law. These factors help explain why citizens in Ukraine – but also to quite some extent citizens in Bulgaria and Poland – find law unhelpful. Ordinary citizens in England, for their part, are negative to the number of laws and detailed regulations that have been introduced in recent years. Many of these originate in Brussels and are considered to be foreign.

Fair? Perceptions that the law is 'fair' vary even more, from 90 per cent in Norway to 21 per cent in Ukraine, though it reaches 72 per cent in England and drops sharply to only 35 per cent in Poland. On the issue of the law being fair, Bulgarians at 52 per cent are more positive than either Poles or Ukrainians. Public attitudes are mixed in Bulgaria – but very positive in Norway and England and very negative in Poland and Ukraine (Table 2.2).

Two factors help explain why citizens in Eastern Europe – to a greater extent than citizens in Western Europe – perceive laws as unfair: notions of fairness and absence of legitimacy. First, notions of *fairness* vary across Europe. In Western Europe fairness is typically associated with "reasonable" or "equal", treatment before the law.[3] By contrast, in Eastern Europe and the West Balkans fairness tends to be understood as "what is good for me personally" (Grødeland 2013). What is good for one person, however, is often to the detriment of another. In Bulgaria and Ukraine, for instance, designer laws are good for narrow political and/or business interests but bad for society at large (Grødeland 2007). Further, in some countries in the West Balkans – particularly in Macedonia – the law itself is perceived as fair, but the size of the fines incurred when violating it is considered unfair (Grødeland 2013).

Second, historically the gap between rulers and ruled in Eastern Europe has been huge – especially in countries such as Bulgaria and Ukraine that were for centuries ruled by illegitimate outsiders. The laws of the latter were therefore, when possible, largely ignored by ordinary

[3] The *Cambridge Dictionaries Online* defines fairness as 'the quality of treating people equally or in a way that is right or reasonable', http://dictionary.cambridge.org/dictionary/british/fairness accessed on 1 September 2014.

citizens (Grødeland and Aasland 2007). Current rulers, though democratically elected, often lack legitimacy in the eyes of the general public. Politicians tend to be viewed as representing and promoting vested interests rather than the common good.

Complex? Conversely, perceptions that the law is often too complex and too frequently changed to be obeyed rises from only 35 per cent in Norway to around 49 per cent in England and Bulgaria and rises further to around 65 per cent in Poland and Ukraine (Table 2.2).

Overall, legislation in Norway is fairly stable. This might explain why Norwegians are rather positive to the law and conscious of the need to obey it. By contrast, Norwegian regulations are detailed and complex. They tend to be introduced quickly and are frequently updated.[4] Legal professionals are therefore not – as we will see below – impressed with their quality. Former prime minister for the Labour Party, Oddvar Nordli, in a newspaper interview recently stated that one of the things he regrets is that his government (1976–81) introduced a large number of such regulations.

Brits, for their part, object to what English legal insiders refer to as *knee-jerk legislation* (i.e. legislation introduced in response to individual incidents reported by the media). Such legislation is, as a rule, ill thought out and fairly complex. Besides, frequently changing laws and regulations are difficult for ordinary citizens to keep track of and make sense of:[5] even 'professional users can find [English] law complex, hard to understand and difficult to comply with' (Office of the Parliamentary Counsel, Cabinet Office 2013, p. 1).

Citizens in Eastern Europe, for their part, are faced with frequently changing law, old and new laws that often contradict each other and foreign (read: EU) legal terms that are difficult to understand even for legal

[4] As of 26 March 2011 there were 700 laws and 11,500 regulations in Norway. Although the number of new laws and regulations has dropped in recent years, existing laws and regulations are constantly updated. Direktoratet for forvaltning og IKT, DIFI [The Agency for Public Management and eGovernment, DIFI], 'Regelproduksjon' [The production of rules], 26 March 2013, www.difi.no/ledelse-og-organisering/statsforvaltningen-i-fakta-og-tall/statsforvaltningen-i-tall/regelverksproduksjon accessed on 1 September 2014.

[5] According to the BBC the number of laws passed by Parliament increases significantly during the run-up to parliamentary elections. This was the case in 2001 and also in 2010, when a total of 3,506 laws were passed – an increase of 41 per cent over the previous year. Some 51 per cent of these laws were introduced before the 6 May election. BBC News, *Politics*, 'Record number of new laws made in 2010', 27 May 2011, www.bbc.co.uk/news/uk-politics-13569604?print=true accessed on 1 September 2014.

professionals. Besides, it is more difficult for them to access law than it is for citizens elsewhere. In Western Europe. state bodies usually provide citizens with information about their entitlements and obligations on their websites. As most people have access to the internet they can easily access such information. By contrast, in East European countries such as Ukraine, this type of information is often not placed on the internet. More importantly, many people in these countries neither know how to use the internet, nor do they have access to a computer. Newspapers such as the Ukrainian *Uriadoviy Kur'er* and *Holos Ukrainy* publish new laws, but they are expensive. Besides, in Ukraine newspapers – especially those supporting the political opposition – face distribution problems in the regions (WAN/IFRA 2012).

Moral values or state power? Perceptions that the law in this country 'on the whole, reflects generally recognised moral values' rather than 'the power of the state to control people' drops from a very high 83 per cent in Norway, through around 54 per cent in England and Poland, to a low 39 per cent in Bulgaria and a mere 26 per cent in Ukraine (Table 2.2). Our findings thus correlate with the country rankings in the 2010 World Bank's Rule of Law Index: the more rule of law there is in a country, the higher the percentage of citizens stating that 'the law reflects generally recognised moral values' rather than 'the power of the state to control people'.

Our findings suggest that a sense of ownership to the law on the part of ordinary citizens, facilitates respect for it. Elected representatives in post-communist states are largely perceived as illegitimate as their primary loyalty is to themselves and their own circles rather than to the electorate that voted them into Parliament. Added to this, the ruling elites in these states frequently disregard the law. Inasmuch as the law is applied to ordinary citizens, elites know how to evade it. More importantly, elites have the necessary 'protection', should they be caught breaking the law.

As noted above, in England there is considerable unease with knee-jerk legislation – a phenomenon that has been largely attributed to the former Labour government. Further, legislation targeting terrorists has been much criticised not only abroad, but also within the UK, for being applied in a haphazard manner. The English are also wary of what they perceive as efforts (meaning 'imported' law) from Brussels to control them. These factors explain why the English, to a greater extent than the Norwegians, believe that law 'reflects the power of the state to control people'.

The preferred basis of law

What are the bases that morally and psychologically legitimise law? Given a choice of five bases for law, the general public overall puts the most weight on "general moral values" as the proper basis for law followed by "current life-styles" and "custom and tradition". "European and international standards" are rated considerably less important, and religion is rated at the bottom of the list and far behind the other bases for law (Table 2.3). The strength of support for basing law on "general moral values" and the weakness of support for basing it on religion varies little across countries: public support for the former is uniformly high and for the latter uniformly low.

Customs and traditions? First, we consider whether the law should be based on "this country's customs and traditions". There is overwhelming agreement, averaging 81 per cent across the five countries – slightly more in Norway and Bulgaria (85 per cent agreed in both) and slightly less in Ukraine (76 per cent agreed) – that it should (Table 2.3).

As noted in Chapter 1 Norwegians and Brits are fairly negative in their attitudes toward the EU. Both groups emphasise the differences between their countries and other European countries, which explains their preference for law *informed* by national customs and traditions.

In Eastern Europe, on the other hand, citizens largely abide by social norms but often ignore formal law. Although legitimacy (or rather the lack of it) obviously helps explain this phenomenon, failure on the part of the legislators to allow social norms to inform formal legislation may also have something to do with it. For instance, citizens in Eastern Europe oppose legislation granting legal rights to homosexuals, facilitating euthanasia or legalizing prostitution or the use of light drugs. Such legislation is perceived as imposed, culturally foreign and thus inappropriate. They also strongly object to EU rules barring people from preparing traditional food and drink (Grødeland 2013).

Our FGs shed some light on the reasons that citizens across Europe think customs and traditions should inform law. FG participants in all countries believe that law should preserve national identity. If law fails to do so it will produce lawbreakers rather than facilitate change:

> B1-Sofia1–3: 'the Bulgarian mentality must be considered . . . they [i.e. the EU] prohibit the production of *rakia*, which is ridiculous'. B1-Sofia-5: '[the authorities tell us], well, we have adopted this law but you [just] keep on producing *rakia*: no one is going to come and sanction you'. B1-Sofia1–4: 'it is sometimes impossible to break tradition.' U26-Poles-Kiev-1: 'if the law is not based on traditions, history, [people's] sense of

> justice, [it] will be empty. And as a result people will not observe [it]'. N7-Brits-7: 'I like the thing in Norway where you've got the right to be on free land, [there is] much more open access to land in Norway than in England. That's part of the tradition in Norway, and it is in the law.'

Current life-styles? There is slightly more support for basing the law 'not on the past, but on current life-styles, the way most people live now' in all countries. In the public's mind there seems to be no significant conflict between the country's "customs and traditions" and the country's "current life-styles". There is a "sense of ownership" about each country's customs and "current life-styles" despite the attempt apparent in the questions to separate them (Table 2.3).

FG participants stress that law must be useful – that is, bring some benefit to society, and most of all to the people living there:

> B4-Topoli-1: 'our law should correspond to the European [law] in order to make our economy competitive.' E-13-Ukrainians-London-7: 'the law [should] make sure everyone feels secure ... that's the core [significance] ... of law.' P10-Białystok-2: 'the law should be accessible, clear and understandable, so that people can understand what it is all about.' U5-Krasnogorovka-8: 'the law should work for the people.' N12-Tromsø-6: 'one should make laws that most people find appropriate.'

Religion? The issue of whether the law should, or should not, be based on religion clearly divides Norway and England where around only 17 per cent say that the law should be based on religion, from Poland and Bulgaria where around 36 per cent say the same, and still more from Ukraine where this view is held by 44 per cent of the respondents (Table 2.3).

People may have different understandings of religion: some people may understand our question as a question about faith (religion as faith), whilst others may understand it as a question about culture (religion as culture). We will return to the subjects of religion and law further in the chapter and also in Chapter 10; suffice it to say here that Catholicism has largely defined Polishness. Catholicism in general and Pope John Paul II in particular have been credited with paving the way for the collapse of Communism. As for Bulgaria and Ukraine, there was a religious upsurge in both countries in the late 1980s/early 1990s. Even though active religious worship has dropped in recent years, the Orthodox Church has consistently received high scores on surveys about trust.[6] Unlike the

[6] Survey data from December 2013 show that 64.5 per cent trusted religious institutions. Razumkov Centre, www.razumkov.org.ua/ukr/poll.php?poll_id=83 accessed on 5 September 2014.

Table 2.3 *Preferred basis of law: the legal outsiders' perspective*

	Norway (%)	England (%)	Poland (%)	Bulgaria (%)	Ukraine (%)
PQ41A: The law should be based on this country's "customs and traditions":					
Agree	85	81	80	85	76
Disagree	15	19	20	15	24
PQ41B: The law should be based, not on the past, but on "current life-styles, the way most people live now":					
Agree	86	81	86	89	82
Disagree	14	19	14	11	18
PQ41C: The law should be based on "religion":					
agree	19	15	38	33	44
disagree	81	85	62	67	56
PQ41D: The law should be based on "general moral values, what most ordinary people in this country think is right and wrong":					
agree	93	91	93	89	91
disagree	7	9	7	11	9
PQ41F: The law should be based on "European and International Standards, like those set by the EU":					
agree	73	52	79	88	77
disagree	27	48	21	12	23

Catholic Church, the Orthodox one has supported (and been supported by), rather than challenged, the political establishment.

Both the People's Church of Norway and the Church of England historically have had a more prominent formal role in society than organised religion in Eastern Europe. Yet religiosity in both countries is fairly low.[7] This might, in turn, explain why Norwegians and Brits are less favourable to religion informing the law.

FG participants in Eastern Europe to quite some extent associate religion with the Ten Commandments – which, in their view, represent universal rather than narrow Christian values. And those who are in favour of religion informing law mostly refer to the general principles of religion that resonate with people of many faiths. Some FG participants note that many laws are based on such principles. One Polish FG participant expresses his frustration with the growing number of laws by advocating a return to the Ten Commandments. English and Norwegian FG participants talk about religious values that are acceptable also to non-religious people:

> P4-Lubliniec-3: 'The Ten Commandments were enough to regulate relations between people [in the past] ... but during the next centuries they [i.e. the societies] multiplied their laws and in the end there were 613 Commandments because ten was not enough ... the number of laws grows with the progress of civilization ... but who says there must be law? ... let's go back to the Ten Commandments and live like the people did 2,000 years ago.' U6-Kharkiv-5: 'you could add some sub-paragraphs to each law in the Bible.' E12-Scandinavians-London-8: 'the laws here are all based on ... the original Christian values.' N1-Oslo-2: 'I am not personally Christian ... but there is something in the Ten Commandments [that might be useful].' N5-Muslims-6: 'whether it is the Bible or the *Quran*, it doesn't matter where it comes from, there are morals in there.'

General moral values? In sharp contrast to the relatively few who would base the law on religion, there is overwhelming agreement across Europe that the law should be based on "general moral values": "what most ordinary people in this country think is right and wrong". On an average across the five countries, 91 per cent say the law should be based on general values (Table 2.3). The lowest is 89 per cent in Bulgaria and the highest is 93 per cent in Norway and Poland.

FG participants mostly just mention moral values without elaborating on why they are important. However, some elaborate on what they themselves understand by moral values:

[7] A poll conducted throughout Europe in 2008 shows that in Norway 17.4 per cent of those polled did not believe in God (in the UK the percentage was 18). Further, 25.5 per cent said they have never believed in God, whereas 35.6 per cent said they believe in God now and always have (in the UK the percentages were 20 and 36.7 respectively) (T. Smith 2012).

> B5-Aksakovo-2: 'moral values. But they are only relevant for the lower levels of society. For the ruling circles there are no laws. That is the problem ... ordinary people abide by the law, with some small exceptions'. B10-Momchilgrad-3: 'the moral norms also matter because the moral values are very poor amongst the youth under [the age of] 25'. E1-London-3: 'values: do as you would be done by.' U6-Kharkiv-7: 'the only criterion is morality ... if we have it, then there will be no need to issue any laws.' N13-Finnsnes-4: 'laws that clash with people's moral values cause trouble'.

European and international (E-I) standards? Overall, a very large majority in every country except England agree that the law 'should be based on E-I standards, like those set by the EU'. In Poland, Bulgaria and Ukraine, around 81 per cent agree that the law should be based on such standards. In Norway 73 per cent also agree, but only 52 per cent agree in England (Table 2.3).

Our findings for Norway and England might reflect the public's greater regard for the national tradition of law there than in the former communist countries, especially Bulgaria. Findings for Eastern Europe might, to some extent, reflect a wish on the part of citizens there to attain the same living standard as citizens have in Western Europe. The EU is perceived as a facilitator of economic growth – which may, in turn, explain why East Europeans are more positive to such standards informing law than West Europeans – even though they are opposed to giving legal rights to homosexuals and are generally opposed to European and international standards providing such rights on the grounds that they clash with national traditions and national culture. It is of course also possible that E-I standards are perceived as morally superior to those standards influencing national law at present (see Chapter 7).

Surprisingly, perhaps to be "truly European" the public suggests that it is most important to "respect ethnic and religious minorities" and least important to have a "Christian tradition". The importance assigned to "respect for ethnic and religious minorities" is uniformly high. But there are sharp cross-national differences on the importance of a "Christian tradition" – which is given much more weight in Bulgaria and Ukraine, than in Norway and England (Table 2.4).

In every country except Norway a majority are flexible when asked about changing attitudes and behaviour. Interviewees were reminded that 'public attitudes on matters like smoking, drugs or personal relationships can change over time'. And then asked: 'when public attitudes and behaviour changes, should the law then be changed to reflect the

Table 2.4 *Requirements for a country to be truly European: the legal outsiders' perspective*

	Norway (%)	England (%)	Poland (%)	Bulgaria (%)	Ukraine (%)
Q122: Agree: To be truly European a country must have:					
Q122H: respect for ethnic/religious minorities (v. not)	90	83	93	81	91
Q122I: respect for sexual minorities (v. not)	85	82	66	48	54
Q122E: a secular system (v. not)	58	62	70	80	65
Q122D: a Christian tradition (v. not)	41	30	55	87	85

changes in public opinion, or remain unchanged, as a fixed standard of acceptable behaviour?'

In Norway a majority of 59 per cent opt for an 'unchanged, fixed standard'. Conversely, in England a majority of 60 per cent opt for changing the law 'to reflect the changes in public opinion' (Table 2.5). In Poland public opinion is slightly more flexible than in England, and flexible but slightly less so in Bulgaria and Ukraine. Our findings might simply reflect the fact that East European citizens are mostly in favour of moving away from the communist path and acquiring a higher living standard. They might therefore be more open to legislative change – to the extent such changes help achieve these two objectives. The English are critical of EU law – both in terms of quantity and quality. Such laws are perceived as not being in line with the English mentality. Norwegians, for their part, might think that key legislation is already in line with public attitudes and thus being in need of no change – even though they are being fairly averse to detailed regulations.

Stricter law?

When asked: 'for the country at this time, which should be more important: to have better laws or to have stricter implementation and enforcement

Table 2.5 *Attitudes, behaviour and law: the legal outsiders' perspective*

	Norway (%)	England (%)	Poland (%)	Bulgaria (%)	Ukraine (%)
PQ32: When public attitudes and behaviour change on smoking, drugs, relationships, etc. Should the law:					
be changed to reflect the changes in public opinion?	41	60	66	56	56
remain unchanged, as a fixed standard?	59	40	34	44	44

Table 2.6 *Quality of law, implementation and enforcement of law: the legal outsiders' perspective*

	Norway (%)	England (%)	Poland (%)	Bulgaria (%)	Ukraine (%)
PQ5: Which should be more important at this time? To have:					
better laws?	30	28	46	33	42
stricter implementation and enforcement of the law?	70	72	54	67	58

of the law', around 71 per cent in England and Norway opt for 'stricter implementation and enforcement' rather than 'better laws'. A majority in Poland, Bulgaria and Ukraine also opt for 'stricter enforcement', but the majority is less – around 60 per cent (Table 2.6).

At the time of interviewing, the Norwegian police trade union (*Politiets landsforbund*) was staging several actions – including strikes – in the hope that this would make the government realise that the Norwegian police force was understaffed and short of resources. The Norwegian media regularly reported incidents of the police failing to investigate burglaries as they simply lacked the capacity to investigate them. It is therefore plausible that Norwegian citizens – when answering our question – primarily have in mind stricter implementation and enforcement of the law on the part of the police. But it is of course equally plausible that they are fairly happy with the quality of national laws.

The English, for their part, might also be sceptical of the performance of the national police force. British newspapers have provided extensive coverage of the manner in which the police have gone about enforcing anti-terrorism legislation. People of colour have regularly been stopped and searched in contravention of the terrorist act. A few years ago a foreign national was mistaken for a terrorist and shot down in the London Underground. What is more, the media have suggested that British courts are too lenient with criminals, handing out (too) mild sentences. British citizens may therefore prefer stricter implementation and enforcement of the law over better laws. But it is of course also possible that the English – just like the Norwegians – are happy with existing legislation.

In Eastern Europe the law is not being applied and enforced in a consistent manner. Informal law appears to be more important than formal law and *legal nihilism* is widespread. Wealthy people and people holding important political positions in society are placed above the law in countries such as Ukraine and Bulgaria. These factors help explain why East Europeans are largely in favour of stricter implementation and enforcement of the law – even though there is much to be desired in this region in terms of quality of law.

Perceptions of change

Everywhere, a majority of the public complain that there have been too many changes to the law rather than too few – only a small majority in Norway (55 per cent) but more in England and Poland (average 62 per cent) and especially in Bulgaria and Ukraine (average 77 per cent) complain about changing laws (Table 2.7).

In Norway, but nowhere else, the public feel that recent changes have *improved* the law. Elsewhere members of the public are critical – indeed more so in England than in Poland or Bulgaria, though most critical of all in Ukraine. On balance the public feel the changes have increased citizens' rights in Norway and Bulgaria but reduced such rights in England and Ukraine.

FG participants for their part are mostly critical of changes to the law. Some Norwegian FG participants are positive to some of the new laws – for

Table 2.7 *Law and change: the legal outsiders' perspective*

	Norway (%)	England (%)	Poland (%)	Bulgaria (%)	Ukraine (%)
Q54: too many changes (v. not enough)	55	64	60	79	74
Q55: changes made law better (v. worse)	75	34	41	41	10
Q56: changes increased rights and liberties (v. restricted)	57	27	48	61	25

instance, laws about children are regarded as more humane now. Other laws – such as laws aimed at preventing forced arranged marriages – are stricter. One Muslim woman approves of such strictness. Other Muslim FG participants think it is unfair. Some FG participants are negative about the slowness of law; others believe that punishment for serious crimes is too soft, that there is too much surveillance in Norwegian society, or that the law is getting increasingly complex, which alienates ordinary people from it. The English are concerned with the sheer amount of law and number of criminal offenses but also with what they perceive as the increasing level of surveillance in the UK. They tend to blame negative legal change on *active government* and on the EU:

> N14-Bardufoss-6: 'laws that are being made [now] are more humane'. N9-Stavanger-3: 'we had a government that a few years ago promised that they would simplify the legislation, but they have done so by passing more laws and regulations . . . it has [all] become very complex.' N9-Stavanger-7: 'I personally feel more distanced from the law now than I did earlier'. E5-Bristol-7: 'in the last 10–12 years they've drafted 3,000 or 30,000 new laws.' E11-Leeds-Muslims-1: 'any offence now is an arrestable offence. Even spitting on the street'. E9-Leeds-Muslims-8: 'it's a George Orwell thing, isn't it, going on. Big Brother state . . . laws should be something that frees people, it shouldn't subdue and enslave people . . . the cameras and security and this and that'.

Poles are concerned both about the large number of new laws (especially EU law) and frequent amendments to existing laws. They find the latter particularly confusing:

> P2-Warsaw-7: 'what's astounding is the high number of badly drafted laws.' P2-Warsaw-2: 'there were amendments to amendments, and

> further amendments to those … it would be better to design those regulations again instead of making thousands of amendments that make you confused.' P4-Katowice-3: 'when Napoleon introduced his legal code in 1805 he … revolutionised [the law] but it was just one book, a new civil code for the citizens. And today we get 100,000 pages [of law from the EU].'

FG participants in Bulgaria blame the authorities for frequently changing the law and for passing poor law. Ukrainian FG participants are mostly concerned with designer laws, created specifically for the politicians themselves or for other vested interests. They are also disillusioned about new laws that have no impact as they are never implemented:

> B9-Pleven-1: 'the rulers adapt the laws to [suit] their interests.' B5-Aksakovo-1: 'when new laws are meant for personal favour they get adopted very fast, but when they are in favour of the people – a lot was said about the pension security – nothing gets done.' U16-Alushta-8: 'since the Soviet times all laws are designed for the officials and the administrative personnel. The wishes and life of ordinary people are hardly considered.' U1-Kiev-4: 'these laws can remain unwritten … nobody follows them … they don't even plan to follow them … if everything [in our country] is decided by phone, through some channels: … uncle Vanya knows uncle Petya, and uncle Petya knows aunt Masha … that's it, that's [the] law.' U8-Lypci-5: '[there is] no law here. It depends on who pays more. Those who pay more will be right'.

Members of the public do not see themselves as the most important influence on changes to the law in any of the countries. Although Norway comes closest, there is no country in which the public feel predominant 'ownership' of changes in the law. Everywhere, such changes are perceived as an imposition – sometimes welcomed, sometimes not, but always imposed. Asked "when making changes to the law in this country, do you feel our government listens more to foreign governments and international organisations, to ordinary people in this country or to minorities and special interests in this country?" an average of 48 per cent cite "foreign governments and international organisations", 30 per cent cite "minorities and special interests", and only 22 per cent cite "ordinary people in this country" (Table 2.8).

Norway comes closest to being viewed as a *popular democracy* in this respect, though with only 40 per cent viewing changes in the law as responsiveness to "ordinary people", followed by England with only a low 25 per cent citing responsiveness to ordinary English people, and with the three former communist countries averaging a mere 15 per cent

Table 2.8 *Influences on law: the legal outsiders' perspective*

	Norway (%)	England (%)	Poland (%)	Bulgaria (%)	Ukraine (%)
Q64: When changing law, government listens more to:					
foreign governments and international organisations	43	42	52	75	30
minorities and special interests in [this country]	16	33	34	14	51
ordinary people in [this country]	40	25	14	11	19

citing responsiveness to their general publics! The public, especially in Eastern Europe but also in England, do not therefore feel 'ownership' of legal changes. This, in turn, explains why they do not abide by the law. Although in Eastern Europe the authorities – and thus also the laws they pass – lack legitimacy, citizens in the West object to knee-jerk legislation passed in response to, or anticipation of, popular demand.

In public perceptions the influence of foreign governments and international organisations is perceived to be greater than anything else. It is cited by around 43 per cent in Norway and England, 52 per cent in Poland and 75 per cent in Bulgaria. Ukraine is a striking exception, however: the Ukrainian public most frequently cite "minorities and special interests" at 51 per cent, far ahead even of "foreign and international" influences at 30 per cent.

At the time of interviewing, Ukraine had joined the European Neighbourhood Policy (ENP). Although Bulgaria and Poland had to implement the *acquis communautaire* before joining the EU, as an ENP member Ukraine was not obliged to do so. However, the country had to honour its international commitments – including observing the rights of ethnic minorities such as the Crimean Tatar community and other ethnic groups. This probably explains why foreign and international influences are seen as less significant in Ukraine than in Bulgaria and Poland.

However, nationalist reactions against perceived foreign influences may be offset by general perceptions that foreign influences are generally

Table 2.9 *EU standards, laws, regulations and minority rights: the legal outsiders' perspective*

	Norway (%)	England (%)	Poland (%)	Bulgaria (%)	Ukraine (%)
Q71: Heard of EU standards, laws or regulations being applied (v. not)	76	41	50	50	32
Q77: Minorities gained more rights and privileges from EU pressure (v. political deals within [this country's] Parliament)	24	57	72	50	65

good. Significant numbers claim to have "heard news stories about particular EU standards, laws or regulations being applied in this country or others": 76 per cent in Norway, 50 per cent in Poland and Bulgaria, though only 41 per cent in England and 32 per cent in Ukraine.

In Bulgaria the public perception is that minorities have gained rights and privileges in equal measure from "EU pressure" and "political deals within our Parliament" and in Norway a large majority of the public (76 per cent) claim minorities have gained more rights and privileges from local political deals than from EU pressure. But in England, Poland and Ukraine, a majority feel that "minorities have gained more rights and privileges from EU pressure" rather than from "political deals within our Parliament" (Table 2.9).

Findings for Bulgaria are probably related to the fact that Turks had their rights reinstated after the collapse of Communism. There has also been considerable focus on the Roma community. Added to this, the predominantly ethnic Turk Movement for Rights and Freedoms has been part of most government coalitions since 1991.[8]

8 The Movement for Rights and Freedoms provided support in Parliament for the Union of Democratic Forces government (1991–2). It was part of the government in 2001–5 (the Tsar Simeon government, which was also supported by some independent representatives from the Bulgarian Socialist Party); 2005–9 (together with the Bulgarian Socialist Party and the National Movement for Stability and Progress, previously also known as the

LEGAL INSIDERS' PERSPECTIVES ON LAW

The preferred basis of law

Table 2.3 shows that members of the public (i.e. the legal outsiders) voice the highest support for values informing law – though they are also very positive to law being based on current lifestyles and customs. Their support for law based on European, international or universal standards (below referred to as E-I-U standards), is slightly lower. Fewer than 50 per cent (all countries) of their statements suggest that religion should inform law.

By contrast, legal insiders across Europe are in favour of a mix of several factors – rather than one particular factor – forming the basis of law.[9] As we will see, perceptions of which factor(s) that are more and less important in the mix differ by country.

In addition, Norwegian legal insiders are quite positive to law being informed by *values* (universal values, rather than national ones) whereas legal insiders in England voice some support for law being informed by considerations of *usefulness* (Table 2.10).

Norwegian legal insiders who express a preference for law informed by a mix of different factors predominantly have in mind most of, or all of, the elements listed in the question – except religion, which they prefer to leave out of the mix. Most references are made to practical considerations of usefulness (36 mentions), moral values (27 mentions) and tradition (26 mentions). Values that are more general (11 mentions) and human rights (4 mentions) are less popular. Only four Norwegian legal insiders prefer law to be informed by all four factors listed in our question (i.e. *tradition*, *religion*, *values* and *consideration of usefulness*):

> N-LA-25: '[law should be based on] a mix of everything'. N-JU-22: '[laws] build on our entire culture, the culture is built upon religion and morals and everything'. N-PO-16: 'moral values . . . customs and traditions . . . our opinion of what is right and wrong'.

At the time of interviewing, Norway had an official, state-funded religion – that is, the Evangelical-Lutheran faith: at the time §2 of the Norwegian Constitution stated that 'all citizens of the Norwegian state

National Movement Simeon II); and the current government that took office in 2013 (together with the Bulgarian Socialist Party).

[9] One reason for this might be that while legal insiders were asked to choose one of four different factors, legal outsiders gave their assessment of each individual factor.

Table 2.10 *Preferred basis of law: the legal insiders' perspective*

	Norway (%)	England (%)	Poland (%)	Bulgaria (%)	Ukraine (%)
What should be taken as a basis when a law is drafted? Customs and traditions, religion, moral values, practical considerations of usefulness or something else?					
Tradition	8	4	11	12	7
Religion	1	1	1	–	1
Values	23	13	7	9	10
Considerations of usefulness	8	19	7	12	9
Mix	60	63	74	68	74

Note: Entries are based on the percentages of relevant 'text units' – the total number of answers to a given question, so entries sum up to approximately 100 per cent (decimals are rounded up or down to the nearest whole number).

have freedom of religion. The Evangelical-Lutheran faith remains the official religion of the state. Those citizens who belong to it are obliged to raise their children within it'.[10] In 2008, all parties represented in Parliament signed the so-called Church Agreement, which resulted in the status of the Church of Norway being changed from that of a state church (*statskirke*) to that of a people's church (*folkekirke*).[11] As of May 2012 §2 states that 'The Church of Norway, an Evangelical-Lutheran Church, remains Norway's People's Church and as such, is supported financially by the State'.

[10] The Norwegian Constitution was passed in 1814, and at that time §2 read as follows: 'the Evangelical-Lutheran religion remains the official religion of the state. Those citizens who belong to this religion are obliged to raise their children within it'. This paragraph was amended in 1964.

[11] Several paragraphs of the Constitution (§§ 2, 4, 12, 16, 21, 22 and 27) had to be amended to facilitate this change. 'Norges grunnlov § 2' [§ 2 of the Norwegian Constitution], Wikipedia, http://no.wikipedia.org/wiki/Norges_grunnlov_%C2%A7_2 accessed on 8 January 2014.

Until 1 January 2013 the Church of Norway was 100 per cent state-funded,[12] and Norwegian citizens automatically became members of it at birth – unless their parents did not belong to the Church of Norway or made it explicitly clear that they did not want their child to become a member.[13] Church of Norway clergy were effectively civil servants. They received their salary from the state and had the same rights and obligations as any other civil servant. Yet religious law was subordinated to state law. Some elements within the Church of Norway therefore advocated severing the link to the state several years prior to the 2008 Church Agreement.[14] Since 1 January 2013 the Church itself is responsible for the employment of priests and other staff, but it still receives its funds from the Norwegian state as well as from the municipalities. The Norwegian Humanist Society, *Human-Etisk Forbund*, therefore claims that in reality there has been no division between the Church of Norway and the State.[15]

Research on religiosity suggests that highly educated people are generally less religious than lower educated people (Albrecht and Heaton 1984; Sacerdote and Glaeser 2001) and that older people are generally more religious than younger people (Hunsberger 1985). The Norwegian legal insiders we interviewed were both highly educated (71 per cent are university educated and another 21 per cent have higher non-university education)[16] and fairly young (their average age

[12] Until the 2013 parliamentary elections one of the ministers of the Norwegian government was responsible for all matters pertaining to the Church of Norway, including employer responsibilities for church staff and maintenance of church property. In 2014, responsibility for church staff and other church matters was transferred from the state to the church. See the Church of Norway's website, www.kirken.no

[13] Citizens aged 18 or above could cancel their membership in the Church of Norway by writing a letter to their local parish.

[14] In the 1980s two priests, Børre Knudsen and Ludvig Næssa, decided to perform only the religious part of their job and to boycott their administrative duties, to protest the national law on abortion. Both were eventually dismissed for failing to carry out their duties towards the state.

[15] Kristin Mile, 'Intet brudd for stat og kirke' [No division of the state and the church], *NRK*, 7 December 2014, www.nrk.no/ytring/intet-brudd-for-stat-og-kirke-1.12082078, accessed 17 December 2014.

[16] In addition to universities Norway has an educational establishment called *høyskole* – normally referred to in English as 'university college'. The university colleges do not have university status, although it is possible to obtain degrees from these institutions that roughly correspond to university degrees. In recent years some Norwegian university colleges have received university status, whilst others have been incorporated into Norway's existing universities. Britain used to have the same type of institutions – the so-called polytechnics – which obtained university status in the 1990s. Peter Scott, 'It's

was 47.5 years at the time of interviewing). A majority of them have been legally trained. These factors – together with the fact that only 41 per cent of Norwegian legal insiders consider religion to be (very) important for them personally – explain their scepticism towards religion as a source of law.

Those few Norwegian legal insiders who are positive towards religious influences of law refer to "the Christian traditional heritage", "The Ten Commandments" and "the insight of religion". They note that "religion and morals are often connected" and that law should therefore "possibly also (be informed) by religion". And they equate religion with the "the Protestant faith" rather than with religion more generally.

Most legal insiders explicitly object to religion being a source of Norwegian law (32 mentions), and they give three reasons for their position. First, religion has "nothing to do with laws" and should therefore "not be the foundation of law": it is not desirable for religion in the "narrow sense" to exert influence on the law. Some legal insiders explain why religion and law should be kept separate by referring to §142 of the 1902 Norwegian Criminal Code (*Straffeloven*) – popularly referred to as the 'Blasphemy paragraph'.[17]

Second, because there are "different religious preferences in society", law and religion should "mix to the least possible extent" as one faith should not be favoured over others. "Adjusting law to [any] specific religion" would, in the view of Norwegian legal insiders, be "dangerous" and cause "conflicts". To the extent religion should influence Norwegian legislation such influence should be "indirect" (i.e. in the form of generally accepted moral values).

Third, Norwegian legal insiders' view religion as an element of the past. In their opinion it has caused much harm throughout history and

20 years since polytechnics became universities – and there's no going back', www.theguardian.com/education/2012/sep/03/polytechnics-became-universities-1992-differentiation).

[17] The paragraph states that blasphemy – defined as 'in words or action to chide or in a hurtful manner disregard someone's faith, provided that this faith is legal in Norway, or religious teachings or worship in a religious community which lawfully exists in Norway – is punishable by fines or by up to six months in prison'. The paragraph was revised in 1934, following the court case against the Norwegian poet Arnulf Øverland, who was charged with blasphemy after giving a public lecture entitled 'Christianity – the 10th Plague' at the Norwegian Student Society in January 1933. He was later acquitted in court. The Criminal Code Commission proposed to abolish §142 in 2002. However, due to political pressure it was retained. *Store norske leksikon*, 'Blasfemi' [Blasphemy], http://snl.no/blasfemi accessed on 8 January 2014.

it is of "increasingly less significance" to modern society. Consequently, there is "no basis for religious influences" on law:

> N-ER-16: 'I have been Chairman of the Church Council in Norway, but I objected to us having a blasphemy paragraph [in the Norwegian Criminal Code].[18] This [i.e. blasphemy] . . . should not be regulated by law'. N-PR-25: 'I do not think that religion should have any great significance in the legislation . . . one thing is to . . . have legislation that protects the right [of the individual] to have religious [beliefs]. But one cannot have legislation that is based upon the religious [element] . . as there are very different religious preferences in society'. N-ER-12: 'I would like [to see] a secular society . . . I do not want religion to [influence] laws and rule'.

English legal insiders – just like the Norwegian ones – prefer law to be influenced by a mix of factors. Within this mix they make a larger number of references to *practical considerations of usefulness* (39 mentions) and *moral values* (36 mentions) – that is, the two factors that have the highest support amongst English legal outsiders (see Table 2.3). By moral values legal insiders also understand "human rights", "tolerance", "[civil] liberties", "justice", and "fairness" – that is, common, universal values rather than values underpinning "Englishness". Surprisingly, "traditions" and "customs" (20 mentions) are considered a less important part of the mix. Very few legal insiders advocate a mix of *all* four factors listed in our question:

> E-LA-14: 'perhaps a bit of everything but moral values and practical considerations would come [on] top of my list'. E-ER-3: 'you've obviously always got to consider people's religious cultural backgrounds in particular, even more so in this country, but obviously the main practical things to consider are the general civil liberties of everybody'. E-ER-11: 'it could be all of the above.'

England does not have a state church. However, the Church of England in practice enjoys many of the privileges that the Norwegian Protestant Church enjoyed prior to the 2012 amendment of the Norwegian Constitution. The Queen is the supreme governor of the Church of England. Appointments of archbishops, bishops and deans of cathedrals are made at the advice of the British prime minister. More importantly, the two archbishops and 24 senior bishops of the Church of England sit in the

[18] *Kirkerådet* (The Church Council) was established on 13 June 1969 as the preparatory and executive body of *Kirkemøtet* [the Church Meeting]. Den norske kirke, 'Kirkerådet' [the Church Council], www.kirken.no/?event=doLink&famID=237 accessed on 24 August 2014.

House of Lords – thus taking part in the British Parliament's legislative work.[19] In this sense the Church of England exerts more direct influence on state matters than the Church of Norway did prior to the 2012 constitutional amendment.

Still, English legal insiders – just like legal insiders in Norway – perceive religion to be the least important factor in the mix. They note that "religion does come into it" "through customs and tradition"; religion "complements the morals of society" and "fuses values". Further, "religion is already influencing the law" as it is "the basis for [its] moral norms".

A fairly large number of English legal insiders are actively opposed to religion influencing law (26 mentions). Their objections are in part based on their preference for a secular society, in part by the fact that England is religiously diverse, in part by their scepticism of specific religions – notably Islam – and in part on the view that religion is outdated.

First, in secular society "civil liberties are more important" than religion. The latter is a "secondary issue [that should] not be the basis of law". Rather, religion "belongs to the private sphere" and has "no [official] role in secular societies" – even though in Northern Ireland "religion is manifested in law". One English legal insider notes that although he is himself a religious person, there are "many pathways to heaven" exclusive of law.

Second, English legal insiders think there are "too many religions" in their country – each of which is "very different" and has "different roles". As religions are sometimes "contradicting" of each other, law based on religion could "easily isolate segments of society" as a country can "not have different laws for different groups". Legal insiders therefore prefer law not to "be informed by religion".

Third, some legal insiders draw attention to what they perceive as negative aspects of religion. They associate such aspects mostly with Islam, claiming that "Islamic practice is not acceptable" and that "shari'a [law] is not appropriate" for England. Further, they object to "forced marriages" and "forced sexual relationships", which they attribute to Islam. Few references are made to Christianity, though one legal insider – referring to the Tea Party Movement and Sarah Palin in the United States (US) – concludes that mixing "religion and moral values is dangerous".

[19] The Church of England, 'Bishops in the House of Lords. The Lords Spiritual', www.churchofengland.org/our-views/the-church-in-parliament/bishops-in-the-house-of-lords.aspx accessed on 24 August 2014.

Other legal insiders state that allowing religion to inform law "would imply banning homosexual practice" – which would be "unacceptable".

Fourth, some legal insiders hold the view that religion is "not [particularly] relevant" in English society. It simply does "not [have] too much precedence in the twenty-first century". For this reason it "should not be a key determinant", "not [even] be an issue" in lawmaking. But law should provide people with "protection to freely worship":

> E-GO-1: 'religion . . . is just not relevant . . . I don't think . . . it should dictate the masses'. E-GO-16: 'religion itself, it's something that's private sphere really'. E-ER-14: 'there are too many religions that you would have to take on board in constructing your laws effectively so I'm not sure that religion has such an important part to play [in lawmaking]'. E-PO-11: 'the law should be . . . less tied into religion. Because there are lots of people out there who are atheists or agnostics . . . if we were still linking our laws into religious views then we'd be banning people from having homosexual relationships. So no, is the answer'. E-GO-6: 'moral values, religious approaches . . . are dangerous things, really. One man's moral value is another one's extreme right. Sarah Palin . . . you know'. E-PR-21: 'of course [the law should provide] protection of people to freely worship'.

To recap, then, legal insiders in Norway and England mostly oppose religious influences on law – even though the Church is influential in both societies. To the extent they accept such influences they do so more for cultural than for religious reasons.

By contrast, legal insiders in Poland are fairly *accepting* of religious influences on law (36 mentions) – and not only on cultural but also on purely religious grounds. Further, they favour "tradition" (55 mentions) over "moral values" (41 mentions) and "practical considerations of usefulness" (27 mentions). As in Norway and England, very few legal insiders favour a mix of all four factors (9 mentions):

> P-GO-10: 'we should look forward, but we should also consider our customs, religious values and moral aspects, and make all these useful to the citizens'. P-GO-2: 'I would mostly follow practical criteria of usefulness . . . moral values, too'. P-LA-21: 'there is this Latin sentence – "*dura lex, sed lex*" – which can be translated as "the law is harsh, but it is the law". As far as possible, the law of the community should be based on customs, traditions, moral values, on religion. We live in Białystok,[20]

[20] Białystok hosts some of Poland's Lipka Tatars (Polish Tatars) who arrived in Poland in the fourteenth century. There were some 100,000 Tatars in Poland in 1630, but only 447 people declared themselves to be Tatars in the 2002 census. The real number of Lipka Tatars in Poland is estimated at 3,000 to 5,000 people. Wikipedia, http://en.wikipedia.org/

where there actually are many religions. They could be contradictory. The law should be for the people'.

Some 88 per cent of the Polish population define themselves as Catholics and 58 per cent are practicing Catholics.[21] Whereas in other East European countries religious worship peaked immediately after the collapse of Communism and later dropped sharply, the number of practicing Catholics in Poland has remained stable.[22] Added to this there are few ethnic and religious minorities in Poland. The Polish Tatars (also known as *Lipka Tatars*), who are Muslim, are held in high regard by ethnic Poles – much as a result of their prominent role in fighting for Polish and Lithuanian independence in several insurrections during the period of partitions of Poland.

Historically, the Catholic Church has defined 'Polishness' – distinguishing the Poles from their Orthodox neighbours in the East and their Lutheran neighbours in the West – thereby acting as the cultural guard of the Polish nation. However, in addition to *preserving* the Polish nation, the Catholic Church has played an important role in *changing* it: during Communism the Catholic Church was an important moral beacon for Poles yearning for democracy. Later, Pope John Paul II (1978–2005) became a moral symbol and a source of pride for Poles regardless of faith. The Pope has been credited with paving the way for the collapse of Communism. Even though the average age of our respondents was fairly low (43 years on an average), a large majority of the legal insiders we interviewed – 77 per cent – claim that religion is (very) important to them. These factors explain the fairly positive views of Polish legal insiders regarding religion informing law.

Polish legal insiders distinguish between religion as *history and tradition* (Judeo-Christian tradition) and religion as *faith*. They note that Polish "society's moral and legal order" and also "the current [legal] system" are

wiki/Demographics_of_Bia%C5%82ystok#Tatars accessed on 24 August 2014; Corey Jentry, Karolina Sacha and Nadiia Sokolova, 'To be or not to be: the Tatar identity ... promise or problem?', www.humanityinaction.org/knowledgebase/66-to-be-or-not-to-be-the-tatar-identity-promise-or-problem accessed on 24 August 2014.

21 These figures roughly correspond to those in our sample: 88 per cent of the legal insiders we interviewed say they are Catholics, 7 per cent are non-religious, 4 per cent are Orthodox and 1 per cent belongs to other faiths.

22 Centrum Badania Opinii Społecznei (CBOS), 'CBOS potwierdza. Zdecydowana wiĺkszoúś Polakůw uznaje siĺ za katolikůw', *wPolityce.pl*, 12 April 2012, http://wpolityce.pl/wydarzenia/26517-cbos-potwierdza-zdecydowana-wiekszosc-polakow-uznaje-sie-za-katolikow accessed on 12 January 2014.

based on the Judeo-Christian tradition. Further, "Catholicism is dominant in Poland" and national law is "mostly consistent with religion". Legal insiders refer to the Ten Commandments in this regard, but they claim that "religious [basic] standards are the same for all religions". Yet there are situations in which "religion ... clashes with societal norms" and "religious values clash with the rule of law". Besides, "religion often imposes prohibitions" on people:

> P-PR-8: 'our moral and legal order derives from the Judeo-Christian tradition, with a very strong accent on classical culture, so it is mainly about Roman law'. P-LA-25: 'the law mustn't be out of touch with reality ... Poland is not a religious country as there is no mention of this in the Constitution. But ... legal norms can't be created in isolation from the fact that the majority of Poles are Catholics .. the law somehow reflects this'. P-PR-7: 'religion comprises of something like the Ten Commandments, that is, the set of behaviour patterns desirable not only from a religious perspective but also from the general social perspective ... [but] customs absolutely cannot dictate the law'.

Not surprisingly, therefore, Poles are not only considered to be the most religious nation in Europe, they are also highly tolerant of religious minorities (Karpov 1999; Golebiowska 2004). Polish legal insiders, to a greater extent than legal insiders elsewhere, stress the need for *tolerance*: they note that Catholics "must be tolerant of other religions". In their view, "relying on one religion only" in the area of legislation would be wrong as this would "offend" people of other faiths. One legal insider claims that "life is a matter of compromise". Another insists that the extent to which religion should influence law very much "depends on (the type) of law" in question:

> P-JU-2: 'if we want to be driven by religious justifications we have to bear in mind that we have to be tolerant towards other religions'. P-PR-4: 'we cannot impose the law that would take religious values into account on the whole of society, because not every citizen shares these values'. P-GO-7: '...the majority of Poles claim that they are Catholics, but this doesn't mean that we should crucify members of the Orthodox Church or Muslims.'

However, only few Polish legal insiders are completely *opposed* to religion influencing law (13 statements). Those who do, do so for the sake of tolerance:

> P-PO-17: 'plenty of religions tend to impose prohibitions on their followers. Hence, many Poles would not want to be punished for eating [pork] meat, which is forbidden in other denominations ... there are certain

values, fundamental to all people, on the basis of which the law should be built. Religion will of course have some significance here, but it can't be seen as the imperative factor.' P-PR-18: 'the scope of legal protection of the State cannot include all religious prohibitions, because then it would be a religious State. Similarly, in many Arab countries, or even, broadly speaking, Islamic ones, in which the *Quran* generally replaces the whole legal system and all aspects of life, including penalties, divorces'.

Unlike legal insiders in Norway, England and Poland, Bulgarian legal insiders mostly prefer a mix of *all* elements listed in our question – *tradition*, *religion*, *values* and *practical considerations of usefulness* (35 mentions). But like the legal insiders in Poland they have a fairly strong preference for *tradition* (25 mentions). *Moral values* (17 mentions), *practical considerations of usefulness* (17 mentions) and *religion* (12 mentions) trail somewhat behind:

> B-LA-8: 'the law . . . should be based on everything you listed . . . [it] should regulate the protection of state interests and . . . individuals'. B-JU-14: 'the law must first of all reflect the public relationships and dress them in a legal norm . . . the way of life and culture could possibly be based on religious convictions . . . the local or national tradition should have priority . . . the practical rules of behaviour are equally a priority because, rude as it may sound, many people do not have the capacity, including intellectually, to make a proper judgement about the appropriate behaviour'.

As concerns *considerations of practical usefulness*, specific references are made to "the present situation", "the current reality", "common sense", "utility", existing "court practice" and "future conditions". Bulgarian law should respect "social relationships", "the state and citizens" and "European law". A "complex approach" is therefore called for:

> B-PR-7: 'the most important thing for a law is to be easily applicable, clear to all . . . law . . . consistent with religion . . . European law prevails over national [law]'. B-PO-12: 'most of all [it should reflect] the social and economic situation in the country'. B-JU-15: 'the law should be written in a way that allows easy compliance'.

Even though the average age of the Bulgarian legal insiders we interviewed is low – 41 years – religion is (very) important to 70 per cent of them.[23] This explains why in Bulgaria – just like in Poland – the number

[23] Of our respondents 84 per cent are Orthodox, 15 per cent are non-religious and 2 per cent are Muslims or Catholics.

of explicit statements made by legal insiders to the effect that law *should not* be based on religion is limited (5 mentions).

Ukrainian legal insiders – just like legal insiders in other parts of Europe – prefer sources of law to be *mixed.* Within this mix, *moral values* (74 mentions), as opposed to "immoral" or "selfish" interest, are considered most important. Ukrainian legal insiders understand "moral values" to include "human values", "human rights" and "justice". *Tradition* comes a close second (67 mentions), followed by a mix of *all four factors* (51 mentions) and *practical considerations of usefulness* (46 mentions).

It is possible that the stronger preference for *tradition* in Ukraine (and to some extent also in Poland and Bulgaria) than in the other countries is a response to European legal integration. Our data show that people in Bulgaria and Ukraine identify not only with European but also with Asian culture and mentality (Grødeland 2009). People in Ukraine (legal insiders and outsiders), for their part, associate Europe with Western Europe and West Europeans. They therefore refer to Europeans as 'them' rather than as 'us', and many consider West European culture to be of *higher quality* (i.e. 'better') than Ukrainian national culture. But our data suggest that the EU's efforts to integrate Bulgaria and Ukraine into Europe have triggered a desire to preserve what is perceived to be authentically 'Ukrainian' (and, in the case of Bulgaria, 'Bulgarian'):

> U-JU-3: 'the more morals there are in laws the more laws are voluntarily executed by citizens'. U-LA-11: 'moral values ... but everything [should be included] ... every nation has its own laws, own nuances, which are based on culture ... the same religious culture, the national values of society, social practice in this society, the trends that are taking place in this society'. U-PR-31: 'all that you have mentioned ... we cannot talk about usefulness for the whole nation. Just for some influential personalities.'

Some 45 per cent of the Soviet population were believers (Fletcher, referred to in Yelensky 2002, p. 456). A secret report prepared by party officials reveal that in 1985 26 per cent of new-borns were baptised, that nearly 3 per cent consecrated their marriage in a church, and over 40 per cent of the dead were buried with a church's assistance. The real figures are probably higher as baptisms and funerals conducted in underground religious institutions, by clergymen in private, or by those not registered in a special book, are not included (ibid., p. 456).

The 1,000th anniversary of Kiev Rus' baptism, which was celebrated in Ukraine in 1988, triggered changes in the religious situation in Ukraine (ibid., p. 458). The Ukrainian Greek Catholic Church (UGCC)[24] and the Ukrainian Autocephalous Orthodox Church (UAOC) that were both banned during Communism, re-emerged in 1989. What is more, some priests and parishes left the Ukrainian Orthodox Church under the Moscow Patriarchate (UOC-MP) and established a separate Orthodox Church under the Kiev Patriarchate (UOC-KP).[25] More than half of the religious communities in Ukraine are Orthodox, 20 per cent are Greek Catholic (Uniates) and 20 per cent are Protestants (ibid., p. 453).[26]

A poll conducted in December 2011 by the Ukraine Sociology Service shows that approximately 31 per cent of the population identifies with the UOC-KP, 26 per cent with the UOC-MP, 2 per cent with the UOAC (United States Department of State [USDS], Bureau of Democracy, Human Rights and Labor 2011, p. 1). Relations between these four churches have been tense.[27] They have clashed on numerous issues, including over ownership of churches and monasteries. The Moscow Patriarchate has labelled both the UAOC and the Ukrainian Orthodox Church (Kiev Patriarchate) as 'heretic splits' (Yelensky 2002, p. 473). In the seven Western regions of Ukraine, where approximately half of the religious communities in Ukraine are located, blood has even been shed as a result of such clashes.[28] Still, some 75 per cent of the Ukrainian population trusts the church more than any other social institution (ibid., p. 460).

Those Ukrainian legal insiders who are positive to *religious influences* on law (26 mentions) emphasise the link between religion, culture, tradition and mentality, using expressions such as "religious culture" and "religious values". Religion is perceived as "part of (Ukrainian) customs" but it is also linked to universal values ("Ten Commandments"):

[24] Some 93 per cent of the UGCC members live in Western Ukraine (USDS 2011, p. 1).

[25] Ukraine's first president, Leonid Kravchuk, supported the latter, viewing it as an important part of the Ukrainian state building project (Yelensky 2002, p. 478), Leonid Kuchma who succeeded him, initially supported the former. Plokhy (n.d., p. 11) claims that 'the religious conflict that independent Ukraine inherited from the former Soviet Union was inflamed by the active participation of the state apparatus at the oblast and republic levels. For an overview of church–state relations in Ukraine, see Gvosdev (2010, pp. 171–92).

[26] Approximately one million people in Western and Central Ukraine are Roman Catholics. There are some 500,000 Muslims and 103,600 Jews in Ukraine (ibid., p. 452).

[27] By mid-1999 conflicts among the Ukrainian Orthodox churches and the Ukrainian Greek-Catholic Church had been registered in 350 population points (Yelensky 2002, p. 474).

[28] Yelensky (2002, p. 459) claims that in the western parts of Ukraine, which were incorporated into the Soviet Union after World War II, 'the church preserved the functions of social communication, ethnic identification, and moral arbitration'.

> U-ER-14: 'the Ten Commandments were written a long time ago. And if we could live in accordance with [them] . . . we wouldn't have to draft so many laws and make additions to them . . . but these changes reflect somebody's interest, [they] are made for somebody to make profit'.

However, some legal insiders note that "religion is in accordance with [current] national values" and that "Ukrainians have Christian norms". Religion "may [therefore] influence lawmaking" indirectly, as "values should influence the law". The extent to which religion should be a source of law depends on "the aim of" and/or type of law. Legal insiders note that the "Law on Deported People" is of relevance to religion as the Crimean Tatars that are affected by this law happen to be Muslims. Further, "the court sometimes has to deal with religious disputes" (USDS 2011, p. 6).

Ukrainian legal insiders stress that Ukraine is "a secular state" in which there is "religious freedom". There are "many religious confessions" in the country and they "all [have] different interpretations" of matters. Those who explicitly object to religion influencing the law (18 mentions) do so for the sake of tolerance. They note that Ukraine is a "multi-national", "multi-religious", and "secular" society. Consequently, faith is "a personal matter" and society "must not favour one" religion over others by having religion "affect state law":

> U-LA-21: 'the moral values of religion should . . . also be in the foundation of the law'. U-PR-1: 'we are Christians, we have . . . Christian norms. . . U-LA-4: religious values should influence law.' U-PO-1: 'Ukraine is such a multi-religious country . . . there are more than 100 registered confessions. And each religious group has its own customs and traditions . . . the law cannot be developed according to all religious (denominations).'

Yelensky (2002, p. 466) notes that 'the Ukrainian Orthodoxy's tradition of a sufficiently tolerant attitude towards the adherents of other faiths is an important distinction between Ukrainian and Moscow Orthodoxy'. Yet most of the statements of the Ukrainian legal insiders refer to Christianity. Only two of them refer to Islam even though Islam is "the religion of the Crimean Tatars". They note that Islam has its own "legal system" and claim that "shari'a would not work in Ukraine". They view some aspects of Islam – such as "polygamy" – as undesirable. It should be noted that the Spiritual Directorate of Muslims of Ukraine has reported some difficulties in registering new religious communities in the Crimea – allegedly due to political biases on the part of some local authorities (USDS 2011, p. 5).

Perceptions of change

In the rule of law-based societies, law is predictable – and stable. Former chairman of the Norwegian Supreme Court Carsten Smith notes that 'the law in the country shall be stable. It shall be predictable for the citizens in their civilian lives and for the enterprises in the economic life. This is a profound requirement of the rule of law' (Smith 2012, p. 12). However, our findings show that across Europe legal insiders believe that the number of laws have increased a lot in recent years (Table 2.11) – though, as we will see below, for different reasons.

Ukrainian legal insiders stand out in that they to a greater extent than legal insiders elsewhere believe that there have been few or no legal changes in their country in recent years. There are probably several reasons for this. First, some Soviet laws are still in use. Second, years of stalemate between the presidential administration, government and Parliament in the aftermath of the Orange Revolution made it almost impossible for Parliament to pass new laws. Several important legislative initiatives therefore were put on hold. This stalemate was not broken until the 2010 presidential elections. What is more, many laws passed in Ukraine in recent years are essentially designer laws (i.e. laws promoting vested interests rather than the interests of society as a whole). Finally, information about new legislation is difficult to access in Ukraine – even for legal professionals (Rechberger 2009).

Legal *outsiders* in all five countries – with the exception of those in Norway – think the many legal changes in recent years have been for the worse (Table 2.7). Legal *insiders* – to an even greater extent than the outsiders – claim that there have been a lot of changes and that these have not been helpful in terms of improving the law (Table 2.3). The English legal insiders are the most negative to recent changes.

Further, while legal insiders in Norway, Poland and Bulgaria primarily attribute legal change to *European and international integration*, English legal insiders attribute them to *active government*. Ukrainian legal insiders for their part, view legal change as a combined result of *post-communism* and *European and international integration*.

Assessment of changes

Norwegian legal insiders who voice their *disapproval* of recent legal changes are negative for a number of reasons. The *judicialisation* of society and the increased power of supranational courts at the expense

Table 2.11 *Law and change: the legal insiders' perspective*

	Norway (%)	England (%)	Poland (%)	Bulgaria (%)	Ukraine (%)
What do you think has been happening to the law and the legal system in [this country] over the past few years? How would you describe the tendency of the recent changes?					
Quantitative change (in law)					
Lot	81	98	89	91	62
Little/no change	18	2	11	7	37
Mix	1	–	–	1	1
Attitude to changes					
Good	30	12	30	25	20
Bad	52	79	57	58	61
Mix	18	10	13	17	19
Cause of changes					
Post-communism	n.a.	n.a.	10	17	45
EU and international integration	84	31	79	70	45
Security	4	10	–	–	–
Active government	7	53	1	–	10
Mix	4	6	10	13	–

Note: Entries are based on the percentages of relevant 'text units' – the total number of answers to a given question, so entries sum up to approximately 100 per cent (decimals are rounded up or down to the nearest whole number).

of national ones have, in their view, negatively affected democracy. However, the majority of the legal insiders are concerned with the negative impact the sheer amount of new legislation and its level of detail is having on those administering and enforcing the law. They also object to the level of detail contained in the current legislation – and, again in their view, to the increasingly rushed legal process. The growing eagerness of Norwegian politicians to pass new laws is an issue of concern:

> N-JU-1: 'the development of the legislation [in Norway] has to some extent been marked by politicians nowadays being more concerned with legislating good aims and intentions that were earlier only expressed . . . [in] political declarations, but which are now fixed [i.e. in formal law].' N-GO-8: 'in the development of the welfare society, my impression is that laws are increasingly often used as a tool . . . more legislation on rights has the consequence that . . . jurists and courts become more important, that we have to move decision-making powers from the political elites or publicly elected bodies, from the municipal council to the local court . . . which I think is unfortunate'. N-ER-25: 'the law is one thing, another thing is that . . . the regulation [accompanying it] . . . is so detailed that one may freak out'.

Legal insiders who are *positive* to changes in Norwegian legislation highlight the, in their view, *good quality* of law: recent legislation has improved the circumstances of those affected by it. Statements to the effect that current legislation is more in tune with the development of society are also made.

English legal insiders are negative to recent legal changes mostly for reasons of *quality*. They claim that the quality of British law has deteriorated in recent years and that current legislation (anti-terrorism legislation in particular) is undermining civil rights and liberties. Added to this, frequent legal changes cause problems for those tasked with implementing and enforcing it.

Several English legal insiders believe that contemporary British law suffers from *populism*. In their view there is a tendency amongst politicians "to legislate for everything": new laws are often passed as a knee-jerk reaction to specific "unimportant issues" and events. They are therefore "ill thought out", "poorly drafted" and "rushed through" Parliament. Criminal law, for instance, is suffering from "too frequent changes" as "new criminal offences [are created] daily". Regulating these new offenses is "unnecessary" and "interfering". What is more, they promote "the nanny state".

A fairly large group of English legal insiders believe that as a result of the tendency to legislate more and more areas of society British law has become "more specialised", more "complicated" – even "too complex and fractured" – as there is "too much [focus] on detail". Problems that in the past found political solutions are now "solved by [means of] legislation". As a result, "hyper-regulation" requires "too much micromanagement" whereas unclear legislation produces inconsistent interpretations:

> E-GO-21: 'instead of tinkering, if you like, loosening a bolt off here, tightening a nut off there, we're inclined to change the whole concept.

> That is unsettling for people'. E-LA-14: 'some particularly horrific crime occurs [and] there's a knee-jerk reaction legislation-wise. Sometimes they're not very well thought out'. E-LA-3: 'ultimately there is less freedom for individuals to do things . . . the phrase "the nanny state" is often bandied about and I think that is very true'. E-GO-16: 'we make more and more law, and then the law we make is more and more complex'. E-JU-4: 'I think over the last few years there has been . . . hyper-regulation. It's a proliferation of a lot of laws that have led to all sorts of complications and obfuscation . . . it has led to conflicting statutory interpretation.'

Some English legal insiders claim that the sheer amount of new law and legal change, as well as their poor quality, put "a huge burden" on legal professionals – making it "difficult [for them] to keep track". Legal insiders believe that "[British] law is made for lawyers [not ordinary people]", given their "complex[ity]". This, in turn, makes such law difficult to "interpret and apply". New legislation therefore creates "an added workload" for the legal professionals.

Some legal insiders believe that law has become "more intrusive" and "difficult to understand" – and that it does "not have enough focus on [citizens'] rights". The 'Dangerous Dogs' Act' and the 'Hunting Act' are singled out as "laws causing concern". British anti-terrorist legislation, for its part, is perceived as "disproportionate", "difficult to apply" and "intrusive". The 1998 Human Rights' Act allegedly causes problems for "[national] security":

> E-PR-14: 'criminal law is becoming more complex and has become more fractured, and also . . . more difficult for the ordinary layman to understand and for the practicing lawyer to apply. Governments seem to micromanage the legal system . . . the judiciary and . . . all parts of the law'. E-PO-20: 'we probably have had too many new pieces of legislation being introduced so much so that it becomes increasingly difficult for those professional practitioners to interpret and apply the law appropriately, effectively and efficiently'. E-LA-2: 'people are being prosecuted . . . and fined for minor things when they are basically . . . decent or law-abiding people'. E-PR-18: 'the last government created criminal offences at about the rate of one a day for its entire tenure . . . it's become far too complicated'. E-ER-7: 'some of the new laws have . . . a damaging effect on civil liberties.'

Legal insiders in Poland – just like those in Norway and England – are rather *negative* above recent legal changes. They make an almost equal number of statements about excessive, as they do about poor-quality, law. As in England, a limited number of statements concern the difficulties legal changes cause for those tasked with implementing and enforcing the law.

As for the *quantity* of law, Polish legal insiders believe that "over-regulation" is causing "legal confusion", even "legal chaos" in their country. Further, "illegible regulations" are of "poor quality", "difficult to grasp", and cause problems in terms of "interpretation". Even worse, such regulations produce "poorly informed citizens". The sheer number of new laws and legal amendments is preventing "legal stability". What is more, they "slow [down] legal reform", do not "keep up with the needs [of society]", are "unreliable" and therefore frequently "not implemented":

> P-LA-10: 'I think that the law is heading towards absolute positivism, which means that we are moving towards the situation where even the least significant questions need to be defined by acts, decrees, or any other written forms of legal regulations.' P-LA-2: 'the last few years have been characterised by an excessive production of written law, an excessive number of amendments to this law, low quality of regulations issued and an excess of interpretations resulting in confusion concerning the application of the law . . . this trend is very dangerous since it creates chaos not only in terms of the law itself, but [also] for its execution.'

Polish legal insiders refer to the *quality* of law in highly negative language. In their view laws are generally "too detailed", "increasingly complex", and "non-transparent", often even "mutually inconsistent". One legal insider refers to them as "legal junk". As in England, legal changes in Poland are "ill thought through". As a result, laws tend to be "vague" and full of "contradictions and loopholes". Some of them are "incomprehensible" and thus "difficult for practitioners to handle". It is difficult for them "to keep track of – and understand – [current] regulations". This, in turn, causes "legal instability and public disapproval" and is ultimately "detrimental" to the development of society. Very few legal insiders blame current problems with the law on *judicialisation* and only two of them view the EU as the culprit of poor quality domestic law:

> P-JU-25: 'in many fields legal regulations are just legal junk'. P-GO-14: 'more and more regulations determine our lives, but often these regulations are bad . . . and require amendment right after their being passed'. P-LA-5: 'they [i.e. the legal changes] are not guided by the welfare of the country or its citizens, but by the welfare of a given political group, which is able to vote an Act into law.' P-ER-19: 'the Polish law and its rules to the norms of the European Union bring no good . . . this is what I personally regard as negative in recent times.' P-PR-21: 'well, as a practitioner, I can only say [that] it is a disaster . . . the mess is huge'. P-PR-18: 'practitioners have great difficulties in . . . finding out which rules are currently in force'.

Polish legal insiders who are *positive* to legal changes are appreciative of the fact that domestic law has been harmonised with EU law, for ideological reasons (i.e. because Polish law has become more democratic), or because in recent years the quality of law has, in their view, improved.

Bulgarian legal insiders – just like legal insiders elsewhere – are predominantly *negative* towards recent legal changes. However, their reasons for being negative differ from those of Polish legal insiders both in terms of *number* and *strength.*

First, Bulgarian legal insiders are concerned with the *frequent changes* to Bulgarian law. Such changes occur "too frequently". What is more, they are "turbulent", "dramatic", and even "chaotic". In the view of some legal insiders there have simply been "too many amendments" to the law in Bulgaria in recent years. Yet in areas in serious need of change, legal changes have been "piecemeal":

> B-ER-11: 'for the last 20 years laws in Bulgaria have suffered from constant changes . . . the legal framework has no actual frame, no structure, there is scaffolding on which to build things, so this dynamic creates chaos in all sectors of society.' B-GO-2: 'in recent years Bulgaria has undergone turbulent processes of amending and supplementing the laws, repealing the laws'.

Second, frequently changing laws cause problems for Bulgarians both in terms of *quality* and *implementation.* As for quality, there are "weaknesses", "loopholes" and "gaps" in Bulgarian laws. Bulgaria has "no clear policy for legal change" and new legislation and legal amendments therefore tend to be "ad hoc". As a rule they are "poorly conceived", "poorly prepared", and written in "poor language". At best new laws are "imperfect"; at worst they are "inconsistent" or "mutually contradicting". Many new laws and legal amendments are "inappropriate for (Bulgarian) reality" and "serve society badly".

As for implementation, poor quality law leaves room for "a variety of interpretations" and it makes it difficult for legal professionals to perform their duties as such laws are generally "difficult to implement". Bulgaria is therefore suffering from "poor implementation" and "poor enforcement" of national law:

> B-GO-20: '[the legal] changes are not appropriate and they are not based on the people's needs'. B-GO-12: 'the laws should change and not be to the benefit of the ruling [elites] regardless of who they are'. B-PR-11: 'the laws, both the commercial [ones] and penal [ones], not to mention the

> penal procedure, are amended way too often to allow for any stability to be established in the enforcement [of these laws]'.

Third, Bulgaria's accession to the EU has further complicated matters. EU directives, for instance, are often "directly translated" into Bulgarian, rather than being "transposed". Besides, the translation itself is often "poor". Our findings thus confirm Mattila's observation that 'the linguistic plurality of the European Union – a richness which needs to be protected – causes a major problem which endangers the results of European legal integration: imprecise, even entirely incorrect translations of legal documents in cases of an international nature' (Mattila, cited in Kjær 2008, p. 155).

Fourth, Bulgarian legislation is plagued by leftovers from the Communist period. Such "old law" is sometimes disregarded when "new law" is introduced.

Finally, new Bulgarian legislation is often "too accommodating of public opinion" or "public pressure". Laws therefore tend to be "short-lived" as they go through "frequent revisions". And they are often "improper" as they fail to take account of "new social relations" and tend to be "unjust":

> B-GO-6: 'it is still developed socialism [in Bulgaria] ... in our legal base ... bad translation [of EU law] leads to ... absurdities that trigger lots of problems ... the administration does not know what to do'. B-LA-11: 'the Parliament's willingness to harmonise legislation in Bulgaria with [that of] the EU allows [for] too many mistakes ... this is a problem we face daily in our practice: one rule annuls the other'. B-JU-14: 'there are cases where in a single article [of a law] the first paragraph was modified and no one paid attention to the second [paragraph] and a contradiction emerged, which creates enormous problems for us ... if a law is unclear or allows for a variety of interpretations you cannot explain to the citizen that the penalty [for a given violation] derives from a specific provision'.

Being no exception to the rule, the legal insiders in Ukraine are also predominantly *negative* to recent legal changes – and as in the other countries partly for reasons of *quantity*, partly for reasons of *quality*.

In terms of quantity, Ukrainian legal insiders – just like legal insiders elsewhere – object to *the vast number* of laws that has been introduced in their country in recent years. In their view there are simply "too many laws" – especially in the economic sphere. "Duplication of laws" is therefore common and there are many "contradicting legal acts". Some laws even "contradict the Constitution". Added to this, "frequently changing legislation" causes legal "instability", even "chaos": U-LA-7: "laws have become more complex ... there are far more of them'.

As regards quality, Ukrainian laws are "poorer" nowadays than they were in the past. Then "brainless lawmaking" produces "imperfect" legislation which suffers from "gaps" and "loopholes". Such laws "lack subordinate acts". In the view of Ukrainian legal insiders national legislation is unnecessarily "complex" and "the legal language is too complicated".

However, some Ukrainian legal insiders note that there is "not sufficient legislative change" in Ukraine. "Old legislation" – including legislation from the Soviet period – is still in use. Such "outdated legislation" and "slow legal change" have a "negative impact" on the country more generally and on the "social interests of the population" in particular. Ukraine is in "a permanent political crisis" and necessary "legislation is [therefore] not passed". A number of "legal amendments" (including "Constitutional reform") are therefore required to make law work:

> U-GO-17: 'there are laws in Ukraine . . . which . . . date back to the Soviet period. Of course this legislation should be updated'. U-LA-1: 'the legislation is lagging behind. The Housing Code . . . is still called the Housing Code of the Ukrainian Soviet Republic. We have private ownership for a long time and the standards in the Housing Code do not regulate this sphere. We have a lot of failures'.

Ukrainian legal insiders – to an even greater extent than legal insiders in Poland and Bulgaria – voice their dismay with so-called designer laws (see above), that is, laws designed by "unprofessional politicians" to "protect specific groups". In Ukraine the beneficiaries of such laws include "politicians", "government officials", and "the rich". As lawmaking in Ukraine "corrupts", national legislation tends to be both "anti-citizen" and anti-"civil society":

> U-JU-30: 'I would describe the changes as legal anarchy . . . a step towards nowhere.' U-LA-22: 'one legal act may be totally contradicting the other'. U-GO-20: 'laws . . . are created . . . for the sake of the interests of a small group of people . . . they are written for special political forces, for special businesses'. U-JU-22: 'I have the impression that they [i.e. the laws] serve not so much the needs of society but [more] some . . . very narrow, in some cases extremely narrow, interests.' U-PO-8: 'laws should be written extremely simply, in an extremely understandable way, clearly, and [they should] give no possibility for interpretation'.

The vast number of laws – as well as their poor quality – is causing problems in terms of implementation. Ukrainian legal insiders note that "contradicting legislation is difficult to use" for them and their colleagues. Further, "poor law enforcement" and the "chaotic application of the law" result in its "non-implementation": "judges are unable to interpret the law" in an adequate manner due to its poor quality. The Ukrainian legal system has therefore in reality become "a legal system for criminals". Still, the number of "legal disputes are increasing":

> U-JU-14: 'we don't have consistent, systematic and clear law-enforcement. For judges, lawyers and attorneys the judicial system is not well developed and clear'. U-JU-7: 'even we, the judges ... don't understand how to interpret the law.' U-PR-20: 'if, in the Former Soviet Union, we worked with Codes that were 40 years old and we had huge experience using them, now the problem is another. A law is passed and nobody knows how to use it – including us [i.e. the prosecutors]'. U-PO-1: 'the legislation has stopped working. Corrupted judges, corrupted prosecutors ... one can get five years in prison for stealing a sack of grain but for premeditated murder one can get a suspended sentence or avoid punishment altogether'.

To conclude then, the amount, complexity and poor quality of law not only in Eastern Europe but also in Western Europe clash with a core principle of the rule of law – that law should be stable, predictable and clear.

Causes of change

Norway joined the European Economic Area (EEA) in January 1994. Since then it has incorporated a large body of EU law into national law (Fredriksen 2011). Norway is formally bound by case law from the European Free Trade Association (EFTA) Court – which has roughly the same jurisdiction over the EFTA states that are party to the EEA agreement (i.e. Norway, Iceland and Lichtenstein) as the Court of Justice of the European Union (CJEU) has over the EU member states.[29] However, in a recent case the Norwegian Supreme Court set aside a decision made by the EFTA Court – causing consternation in the latter.[30] As noted above the European Convention of Human Rights (ECHR) was incorporated into Norwegian law in 1999 (Lov 1999–05–21–30) and

[29] 'Introduction to the EFTA court', www.eftacourt.int/the-court/jurisdiction-organisation/introduction accessed on 5 September 2014.

[30] The President of the EFTA court in October 2013 accused the Norwegian Supreme Court of not adjusting its rulings to EEA law. Gunnar Kagge, 'Frontalangrep på Høyesterett' [Frontal attack on the Supreme Court], *Aftenposten*, 21 October 2013, www.aftenposten.no/nyheter/Frontalangrep-pa-Hoyesterett-7344283.html accessed on 8 January 2014.

Norwegian courts are bound by European Court of Human Rights (ECtHR) case law. It is therefore not surprising that Norwegian legal insiders largely attribute the cause of recent changes in national law to *European and international influences.*

Even though Norwegians are generally positive to supranational courts the transfer of European and international law to Norway has, in the view of the legal insiders, mostly had *negative* consequences. Some legal insiders view the sheer *amount* of rules and regulations transferred from Brussels to Oslo – as well as their level of detail – as problematic:

> N-GO-6: 'we [i.e. Norway] are being more and more ruled by foreign law, by the EEA rules and by ESA[31] – which results in several situations where we have to adjust Norwegian legislation'. N-GO-2: 'we have had a huge import of rules from the EU through the EEA agreement . . . [if the rules had been made in Norway] we would have had . . . a more easily understandable set of rules . . . more based on common sense and general Norwegian culture. At present the set of rules is fairly extensive and it often contains many legal definitions which we often consider to be unnecessary in Norway'. N-LA-13: 'all EU directives . . . [are] more detail-oriented in some areas . . . less discretion is left to the implementer of the law'.

Many Norwegian legal insiders perceive EU directives, rules and regulations as irritating or confusing, but their views differ with regard to *the impact* of European legal transfers on Norwegian sovereignty. One legal insider claims that EU law "is *incorporated* into Norwegian law", whereas another believes that Norwegian law has become "*subordinated* to European law". Yet others believe that most EU directives are "adapted to Norwegian law" (i.e. "given Norwegian form"). Norwegian legal insiders also express unease about the "high level of *integration* of EU law" in(to) Norwegian legislation, which, in their view has resulted in "more control and less personal freedom":

> N-PR-8: 'there is a tendency towards the transfer of power from the popularly elected parliament to international legal bodies'. N-ER-12: 'some rules . . . have not been so well adjusted to Norwegian conditions'. N-ER-8: 'during the past 15 years . . . a substantial part of our legislation has been influenced by the EU collaboration . . . through the EEA agreement . . . as a rule laws have become stricter as far as the environment, safety, legislation on chemicals, etc. are concerned'.

[31] This body is tasked with monitoring that the EEA agreement is being implemented and adhered to in the EFTA countries. 'EFTAs overvåkningsorgan, ESA' [the EFTA surveillance body, ESA], www.regjeringen.no/nb/sub/europaportalen/eos/eos-organene/esa.html?id=685043 accessed on 17 March 2014.

Further, "the sources of [EU] law" sometimes cause problems for Norwegian legal insiders as "the emphasis during the preparation of law differs" in Oslo and Brussels. Added to this, "*double legislation* (i.e. both Norwegian and EU law)" sometimes occurs. Some Norwegian legal insiders believe that not all EU legislation is relevant for their country. As a result of the internationalisation and Europeanisation, some legal insiders claim that (Norwegian) law is increasingly suffering from a "democratic deficit":

> N-JU-23: '[we see] a more continental manner of applying the sources of law ... in Norway ... the preparatory sources of law [*lovforarbeider*] ... represent one of the absolutely most important sources of law, while in EU law they are not ... given any particular emphasis at all'. N-JU-12: 'a huge amount of rules have been introduced after we entered the EEA agreement. They change very quickly and are based on a different legal tradition than the one we are used to ... the sources of law are different ... that causes a difficult conflict as the Norwegian law enforcers apply the Norwegian sources of law and the Norwegian method of applying legal sources to interpret the rules ... while the very same rules are interpreted differently in another EU state'. N-GO-7: 'we do of course have to follow the EU rules ... [but] the EU rules are not relevant [for Norway] in all areas'.

Some legal insiders in Norway note that the globalisation of law affects Norwegian law by means of "binding treaties" – especially in the field of "human rights" – that is, through ECHR and the case law of the ECtHR.

Decisions made by the Norwegian Supreme Court are binding or at least advisory (*retningsgivende*) for lower instance courts. Decisions that are justified by reference to specific circumstances are less applicable by lower instance courts than decisions that are justified by more general considerations. In the latter case the line of reasoning applied by the Supreme Court judges is in reality binding for other courts (Smith 2012, p. 23). In the 1990s Norwegian 'lawyers challenged the Supreme Court' by making use of the ECHR and ECtHR case law – and in some instances lower-instance courts (Gulating Court of Appeal; Asker and Bærum Court of First Instance) passed rulings that interpreted the ECHR differently from what the Supreme Court had previously done (ibid., pp. 57–8).[32]

[32] Asker and Bærum First Instance Court reached its conclusion based on a ruling made by the ECtHR after the Supreme Court had made its ruling. Shortly after, the Supreme Court – based on the new ECtHR ruling – reached the same conclusion as Asker and Bærum First Instance Court in a similar case (ibid., p. 58).

The 1999 Human Rights Act 'incorporated the ... three most basic conventions on human rights into Norwegian law ... in the event of conflict with other legislation, the provisions of these three conventions are to take priority over the legislation ... national courts must apply the result of an interpretation of the Convention even if established national legislation or practice will be set aside' (ibid., pp. 135–6). The Norwegian Supreme Court "[has] provided assistance in interpreting" supranational legislation. Legal insiders perceive the ECHR as "a very important source of law" and ECtHR rulings no doubt "influence Norway". The rights of the Sámi minority, for instance, have increased because of "the ECHR, the ECtHR and its case law":[33]

> N-JU-7: '[the current situation] puts the courts in a kind of intermediate position between the government and *Stortinget* [the national parliament] on the one hand, [and] national bodies, and international systems [on the other hand] ... the Supreme Court becomes the facilitator'. N-JU-21: '[EU] directives are incorporated into Norwegian law, but also through the ECHR and some other [international] conventions ... the Supreme Court helps us quite a bit ... it makes decisions based on these rules and then we [who work in the lower courts] can read the decisions of the Supreme Court [and apply them]'.

Even though quite a few legal insiders feel that international conventions affect their own work to an ever greater extent, others (though substantially fewer) believe that European integration has not had any substantial impact on Norwegian law:

> N-PO-8: 'the ECtHR's decisions have taken on a much more specific significance in the everyday work than it had when I started working [in the police] in the early 90s'. N-PR-18: '[laws] are to an increasing extent influenced by the ECHR – i.e. the European practice. We have been seriously afraid of not being the best [country] in class [in terms of implementation] and that is somewhat irritating.' N-LA-12: 'I do not see any big changes ... the situation [at present] is the same as it was some years ago.'

Legal insiders in England stand out from legal insiders elsewhere in that they primarily attribute recent legal changes to *active government*. Statements to the effect that legal changes in England are facilitated by British

[33] The international convention that has been most helpful to the Sámi people, however, is ILO Convention 169 on the rights of indigenous peoples, which was ratified by Norway in 1990 (ibid., p. 175).

EU (and CoE) membership are significantly fewer in number. This is somewhat surprising given the British scepticism to the EU.

Legal insiders who attribute recent legal changes to *active government* stress that more and more areas of life are being legislated. Rather than responding politically to developments in society, the British government has responded by introducing new legislation. Such legislation is largely media or survey driven. It is often ill thought out, introduced quickly, paves the way for centralisation, and in some cases, restricts civil liberties. Legal professionals, in particular, feel rather daunted by the pace with which law is changing – a development that they attribute to the Labour government (1997–2010). Some legal insiders claim that increased government activity in the sphere of law is caused by politicians' wish to be re-elected rather than by a real societal need:

> E-GO-18: 'in recent years, under the Labour government, there was a lot of change, a lot of prescription about how we do things in local government. A lot of centralised direction'. E-LA-1: '[there is] a tendency to legislate more, and to be more prescriptive in terms of what you can and can't do, rather than simply limiting things to what you can't do'. E-LA-8: 'it's a result of governments feeling the need to show they're doing something'. E-PR-21: 'there seems to be a greater response now, to media issues . . . the government does something about those issues in a rather speedy way'.

Those English legal insiders who see legal changes as a result of *European integration* and *British EU membership* partly speak about "European legislation" (rather than about more specific laws), about the ECHR and the ECtHR, or about non-specified "European courts". Although some legal insiders are positive about European influences on British law, others are negative, perceiving European law as "complex" and "not popular in the UK".

By contrast, despite "eroding local legislation" the ECHR is viewed as "a most effective [piece of] legislation". Supranational courts, for their part, are seen as "influencing the UK". Even though the UK has had to "modify the terrorism act" following pressure from Europe, such pressure is "positive". The ECtHR has also exerted positive influence on the "Data Protection Act", British "criminal law", "immigration law", and "equalities law":

> E-ER-18: 'there is . . . more and more law floating across the channel from Brussels.' E-ER-2: 'our involvement with Europe . . . has created a lot more rules and laws, which don't always sit well with the general British public.' E-ER-9: 'clearly UK law does have to have more regard to what is

> happening in relation to EU law, and also the European Court of Human Rights . . . in the last couple of weeks the UK law had to be changed in relation to the way Section 44 was being implemented to allow people to be stopped and searched in relation to alleged terrorist involvement. That's had to be changed as a result of the ECHR and that's something I welcome.'

Polish legal insiders, just like the Norwegian ones, primarily view recent legal changes as a result of *European integration* and *legal harmonisation.* In Poland legal change has been "constant" and "significant" – yet "complicated" – facilitating "multiple changes" to national law.

Although some of the Norwegian legal insiders believe Europeanisation and internationalisation have caused a "democracy deficit" in their country, Polish legal insiders who express *positive* views about European legal harmonisation think it has "improved [Polish] law" by facilitating "more democracy and transparency". In their view a general "improvement of the legal system" has also taken place, due to "shorter proceedings" in court. Further, official documents that were previously not available are now "accessible". But legal diversity has been replaced by "legal uniformity". European harmonisation has facilitated not only "more legal awareness amongst citizens" but also "a new legal culture"! Legal insiders stress that Poland is "applying only what is favourable" for its citizens:

> P-LA-17: 'the law is being unified in terms of European law and more and more democratic and transparent procedures are introduced. The law is increasingly clear.' P-LA-16: 'this seems to be the right direction, given that the European Union law brings us a certain legal experience and legal culture, which is the sum of all legal cultures in the EU member states . . . by introducing European solutions we get a fresh and distant view of our problems.'

Still, a fair share of the Polish legal insiders voice their *concern* over the huge amount of European law that has been introduced in their country in recent years. Echoing the views of legal insiders in Norway and England, they note that EU law contains "too much detail". Besides it has been "adapted uncritically" by the authorities. The sheer amount of EU law has brought about "legal chaos" in Poland. The country is therefore experiencing "a loss of sovereignty", thus moving in "the wrong direction". A sense of resignation is noticeable amongst some legal insiders. Despite the many perceived negative consequences of "EU law" – including "the modification of social life" – they note that Poland is simply "obliged to adjust" to it and accept "EU control":

> P-JU-22: 'there has been a lot of chaos in the legislation over the past few years; we have been trying to change this system after … 1989 and it seems to me that we are still working on it, adapting this legislation to [the transition from Communism] … as well as to changes resulting from our accession to the European Union.' P-ER-19: 'I have the impression that the alterations resulting from the need to align the Polish law and its rules to the norms of the European Union bring no good'.

Polish legal insiders make few references to the ECHR and the ECtHR. Only two of them mention the CJEU:

> P-GO-25: 'European norms have priority in applying the law, so regulations as well as the judgement of the European Court of Justice and also directives … only afterwards, so to speak, is Polish law applied … when European and Polish law collide, then we apply European law'. P-PR-6: 'the rulings of the Court of Justice of the European Union play a vital role in criminal law … in criminal procedures … our citizens … have … the right to file their complaints to the Court of Justice of the European Union'.

Not surprisingly, legal insiders in Bulgaria predominantly attribute recent changes in laws and regulations to the EU in general and European legal harmonisation, in particular. Most of their statements are negative – primarily as a result of problems caused during the *implementation* of EU law in Bulgaria. Unlike Polish legal insiders, however, Bulgarian legal insiders do not object to legal harmonisation per se. Rather, they note that national law has *improved* as a result of legal harmonisation within the EU.

Those Bulgarian legal insiders who *explicitly object* to European legal harmonisation describe this process as "unsuccessful" – mostly due to the speed with which it has been conducted. In their view legal integration is "forced" and suffering from "many mistakes", even "absurdities". For a start EU-initiated legal reform is "not easy to implement": due to "legal discrepancies" between EU law and Bulgarian law there is a general "problem with compliance". What is more, "some EU norms are [simply] not suitable" in the Bulgarian context. Worse, there is "no overall concept for legal change" in the country. Changes therefore tend to be "piecemeal and contradictory" and they often cause "legal chaos". Even though directives from Brussels "must also [be] adjusted to local conditions" to function properly, Bulgaria "is overridden by European states":

> B-JU-21: 'some practices that are … slightly irrelevant for our country are copied … borrowed from other European countries … the[y] … are not subject to extensive public discussion'. B-LA-11: 'the legislature's

> willingness to harmonise legislation in Bulgaria with [that of] the EU allows for too many mistakes, the literal translation of laws'. B-JU-4: 'we have chaotic legislative changes that are often designed to meet the recommendations of the European Commission'.

Those Bulgarian legal insiders who are *positive* to European legal harmonisation make use of *democratic* arguments. They believe that this process enhances the quality of law in Bulgaria, thus "protecting individual interests": European legal integration has facilitated "an impressive advance", which is "positive for Bulgarian legislation". Due to EU requirements Bulgaria now even has "a better legal framework than the old EU states". Besides, legal procedures are "faster" now than they were in the past:

> B-GO-1: 'we consider the changes in legislation in relation to the introduction of European legislation and amendments to the law [to be] for the better.' B-GO-3: 'the European rules and norms which are entering our legislation and that the state has to ratify are . . . mostly focused on the protection of individual interests . . . I find this trend positive.' B-PR-14: 'in the past 15 years Bulgaria took an extraordinary step forward in the field of legislation . . . Bulgaria has made an impressive improvement and has bypassed some of the European states.'

Ukrainian legal insiders differ from those in Poland and Bulgaria in that they make an equal number of statements attributing legal changes to the *transition* from Communism to post-communism, and to the EU. Those who attribute legal change to post-communism note that the Soviet legacy still continues to exert influence on the Ukrainian legal system. The country continues to apply "a Soviet understanding of law" and use some "Soviet legislation". Such legislation is "not up to date" and "not adjusted to new purposes". Further, there have been "no substantial changes" in the legal sphere in recent years, possibly even "no development" at all. Those changes that have occurred represent "a perfection of the Soviet legislation" rather than something radically new: U-ER-20: "we inherited much of the Soviet system and then we began to go our own way and change the legislation'. U-PO-16: "in principle nothing has changed substantially".

The majority, however, hold the view that post-communism has caused "legal deterioration" in Ukraine. Those changes that have occurred have been "destructive": Ukrainian legislation is characterised by "contradictions", "imperfections", and "lack of stability". This, in turn, has facilitated frequent "disregard for the law". "Legal nihilism" is widespread, especially in business, and designer laws are commonplace.

> U-ER-23: 'up until 1989 everybody was a law-abiding citizen. People were afraid to break laws ... in case of breaking it they were punished. Unfortunately the situation is different now. This negative tendency has caused disregard for the government and [its] legislation.' U-GO-8: 'stability of laws ... does not exist today. U-ER-17: there is complete legislative *nihilism*'.

However, some Ukrainian legal insiders believe that positive changes have emerged out of post-communism. Ukraine now has a "modern" legal system, which is "connected to democratic principles". It has "a new Constitution" and "new legislation". Added to this, "legal reform is [still] ongoing":

> U-LA-14: 'practically all our legislation has changed ... before it was the legislation of the USSR [Union of Soviet Socialist Republics]'. U-LA-17: the legal system of Ukraine has become more modern'. U-PR-13: 'reforms ... have been ongoing from the moment Ukraine gained its independence'.

Legal insiders, who believe Ukraine's wish to join the EU and its subsequent adjustment to EU law is the major cause of legal change, assess this process positively. Even though Ukraine is under "some influence from Europe" and even though EU adjustment requires "frequent" and "extensive" changes, legal harmonisation is essentially "voluntary". Adjusting domestic law to EU law will "make Ukrainian legislation more progressive" and take the country in "a democratic direction", thus bringing about "more democracy". Ukraine will therefore "reach the European level over time":

> U-JU-17: 'in my opinion [European] law positively influences Ukrainian law.' U-LA-19: 'to some extent we are coming closer to the European and international standards, to the Continental system of law that we actually belong to.'

The minority, who are sceptical of European legal integration, on the other hand argue that it has come about at a "great cost". In their view Ukraine must not "uncritically" adapt to Europe. Rather, it must "lobby [its] expectations" – or at least "be selective and adapt [the European experience] to the local [Ukrainian] mentality":

> U-JU-10: 'a lot of legislation from the European countries comes to us ... our lawmakers are trying to incorporate it into our system. But we have different mentalities and that legislation [i.e. the European one] should be applied very carefully.'

A limited number of legal insiders generally believe that Ukraine should honour its "specific obligations" towards "international organisations": U-GO-2: "the constant changes that are happening ... are not very effective. From my point of view international obligations are very positive for Ukraine ... because they have strengthened our legislation and legal system and do not permit [us] to develop in those directions which, let's say, are not necessary'.

Conclusions

In this chapter we have explored public and professional attitudes towards law: what law is and what law should be about.

Dryzek and Holmes (2002) found that attitudes towards democracy are remarkably similar across Europe. Our findings show that attitudes towards law and what law is all about are also fairly similar. European publics primarily associate the word *law* with justice, fairness and legal rights – that is, with a democratic understanding of law. In all five countries the public is in favour of law informed by customs and traditions, current life-styles, and moral values And they oppose the idea of law being informed by religion. Publics in Western and Eastern Europe agree that to be "truly European" a country must have respect for ethnic/religious minorities and also have a secular political system. They agree that stricter implementation and enforcement of law is more important than better laws. And they believe that too much law has been introduced in recent years – and that such law has mostly made law worse. Only the public in Norway think law has changed for the better.

An East–West pattern emerges in terms of perceptions of realities and law: the East European publics are more negative in their assessment of the fairness of law; whether law reflects the power of the state to control people or generalised moral values that are shared; whether law can and should be obeyed; and whether it is often too complex, and too frequently changed to be obeyed. In other words publics across Europe share the same democratic ideals about law, but the actual law they deal with in their everyday lives differs and so does their expectations towards law.

In the introduction to this chapter we suggest that the attitudes of the general public and the legal professionals towards law might differ: the latter are legally trained and have been socialised into the legal profession. And they may have a different ideological understanding of law than the public at large. However, attitudes towards law and what law should be about is not so much a question about legal technicalities: rather it is a question about society at large.

Our findings show that across Europe legal outsiders and insiders have fairly similar understandings of law. Both groups have the same preferences regarding the basis of law – and both are sceptical about religion informing law. Like the legal outsiders, legal insiders also believe that laws change too often. And they – to a greater extent than the legal outsiders – believe that law is changing for the worse. Legal insiders – just like legal outsiders – across Europe have fairly similar attitudes towards law, although their perceptions of law are more varied.

Legal insiders in England, for instance, attribute frequent legal changes to *active government*, whereas legal insiders in Norway, Poland and Bulgaria attribute them to *European and international legal integration*. Legal insiders in Ukraine blame negative legal developments on the *transition from Communism* and on *European integration*.

Although the socialist past and the realities of transition affect East Europeans' *perceptions* of law, they do not affect their *attitudes* towards law. The attitudinal dimension of popular and professional legal culture in Europe is democratic and secular.

3

Law in principle

Introduction: the role of law

Rule of law is a key feature of democracy. It presupposes the supremacy of law: law is above the rulers as everybody is equal before the law. In democracies law serves as the guarantor of people's civil rights, thereby preventing excesses on the part of the rulers. Even though there are many different definitions of the rule of law, there is consensus that law must be stable, predictable and clear.

By contrast, authoritarian and totalitarian regimes are characterised by 'rule *by* law' (i.e. law serving as the extended arm of the rulers). During the communist period the Communist Party stood above the law, modifying or setting it aside at will. Law was used to achieve the objectives of the party (i.e. to build socialism) (Sajo 1990, p. 33) – not to safeguard civil rights. Socialist law thus had both a conserving and a reformist purpose.

In the previous chapter we investigated what legal outsiders and insiders understand by *law*, what the basis of law should be and how law evolves. In this chapter we will explore legal outsiders' and insiders' attitudes towards *the role of law* in society.

As we noted in Chapter 2 Dryzek and Holmes (2002) show that the various views of democracy are fairly similar across Europe. As the *rule of law* is a key component of democratic society European publics might have similar understandings of what the *role of law* in society should be (i.e. what the law should do). But it is also possible that East and West Europeans have different views on this matter. First, the socialist experience might have positively affected attitudes towards the role of law: having moved from rule *by* law to rule *of* law East Europeans may appreciate the formal limits on law that transition has brought about. They may also appreciate their newly won civil rights. Second, the socialist experience might have affected attitudes towards the role of law in Eastern Europe negatively: in many East European countries the ruling elites lack legitimacy and *legal nihilism* is widespread. Third, the current 'war on terror' has negatively affected attitudes towards civil rights in Western Europe (NatCen 2007; Staksrud et al. 2014).[1]

Legal professionals abide by strict professional codes, defining the way they should relate to law. The public is not bound by such codes, which might, in turn, affect their views. The role of law in society is not only a technical legal question but also a very political one. Even though legal outsiders and insiders might have similar ideas about what the role of law should be at a more general level, their views on the more technical aspects are likely to differ.

This chapter is very much about attitudes and less about perceptions.

The role of law: the legal outsiders' perspective

Taken together, the public's principles and perceptions of law in five countries spread across Europe from Norway and England, through Poland, to Bulgaria and Ukraine constitute the two broad elements of "popular legal cultures", and reveal the degree of variation in them across Europe from east to west.

But we need to contrast attitudes and perceptions of law and law enforcement. This chapter focuses on 'attitudes, ideals and principles of law'. Public ideals and principles include public attitudes towards such issues as the 'proper' basis for law (Chapter 2), 'proper' authority for law, and the 'proper' approach to enforcement (this chapter). The next chapter contrasts that with public perceptions of "law in action" – that is, the manner in which citizens and institutions use the law and the manner in which state bodies enforce and implement the law. It also investigates public attitudes towards alternatives to state regulation – both suprastate and substate approaches to resolving disputes and setting authoritative standards; and at both the "duty to obey" and the "duty to resist" state law.

[1] Some analysts claim that the terrorist threat is greatly exaggerated and that the authorities in some Western states use this threat as a pretext for massive surveillance of their own citizens (Greenwald 2014, pp. 219–22). Although polls show that citizens in Western Europe are increasingly willing to relinquish some of their civil rights for the sake of protection against terrorism, there is also growing awareness of the importance of civil rights and growing opposition to mass surveillance in the name of national security – suffice it to mention here Wikileaks and Julian Assange, the Manning case, the Snowden case and the CJEU's recent ruling on the Data Retention Directive (Court of Justice of the European Union, Press Release No 54/14, Luxembourg, 8 April 2014; Greenwald 2014; Harding 2014).

Across Europe from Norway to Ukraine principles and attitudes vary significantly less than perceptions. There is therefore more evidence of an emergent pan-European legal culture in terms of attitudes than in terms of perceptions, though also some evidence of a self-conscious willingness to adapt behaviour without necessarily adapting attitudes or principles.

By "popular legal culture" we mean street-level ideals, attitudes towards law and perceptions of law and law enforcement: what the public thinks law should be (i.e. "attitudes"), and what the law actually seems to be in practice (i.e. "perceptions"). Public attitudes may be perverse and public perceptions erroneous, but together they nonetheless constitute "popular legal culture". In focusing on public "legal cultures", the objective is not to investigate specific laws and legal systems but to understand public opinion – public attitudes towards law and public perceptions of law.

To varying degrees, public opinion across Europe may be affected by moves towards European unity (which exerts pressure in a generally liberal direction, protecting or extending the legal rights of individuals and minorities) but also the concurrent war on terror (which exerts pressure in a generally authoritarian direction eroding the legal rights of individuals and minorities – especially Muslims). We will briefly touch on these issues here and discuss them at greater length in Chapters 7 and 9.

Public ideals and attitudes towards law in principle

In this part of the chapter we focus on public preferences, attitudes and ideals rather than perceptions – what members of the public want, what they think law 'should' be in principle, rather than in any reality that they observe in practice. We look at these public attitudes and ideals under the following headings:

1. Law as justice or oppression?
2. Law as freedom or order?
3. An authoritarian public?
4. The 'nanny state'?
5. Parliamentary supremacy?
6. Flexibility versus rigidity?
7. Reflect or reform?
8. Stepping outside the law?

In the next chapter, we contrast the public's attitudes and ideals about law with their perceptions of the "law in action".

Table 3.1 *Law as justice: the legal outsiders' perspective*

	Norway (%)	England (%)	Poland (%)	Bulgaria (%)	Ukraine (%)
Q2: Law is justice, not oppression	95	87	76	83	73

Notes:
1. Norway, England, Poland, Bulgaria, Ukraine indicate the general publics in these five countries.
2. In each country, samples comprise approximately 1,000 interviews.
3. For simplicity, all percentages in this chapter are calculated by excluding 'mixed', 'both', 'neither', and DK/NA from the calculations.

Law as justice or oppression?

Before going into detailed questioning, the interviews began with the question: "when I say the word *law*, do you think primarily of justice, fairness and legal rights, or do you think of unfair and oppressive laws?" As noted in Chapter 2, overwhelmingly, the instinctive response of the public was justice, not oppression (Table 3.1) As might be expected the Norwegians are the group most likely to equate law with justice, but three out of four Ukrainians also cite justice, fairness and legal rights as their instinctive response. So in terms of principles, differences between countries are not nearly as great as a cynic might expect.

Law as freedom or order?

In every country public opinion prioritises "ensuring order" over "protecting individual freedom", though this encompasses only around 64 per cent in Norway and England, but around 71 per cent in Poland, Bulgaria and Ukraine (Table 3.2)

During the communist period citizens in Eastern Europe had less individual freedom than did citizens in Western Europe. Following its collapse many citizens mistakenly understood democracy as "the right to do as one pleases". There is widespread agreement that *legal nihilism* and observing informal rather than formal law pose significant obstacles to economic development and growth in Europe's post-communist states. What is more, amongst ordinary people in Ukraine and Bulgaria in

Table 3.2 *Individual freedom versus order: the legal outsiders' perspective*

	Norway (%)	England (%)	Poland (%)	Bulgaria (%)	Ukraine (%)
PQ6: Which should be more important at this time:					
to protect individual freedom?	36	37	26	30	31
to ensure order in our country?	64	63	74	70	69

Table 3.3 *Penalties for lawbreakers: the legal outsiders' perspective*

	Norway (%)	England (%)	Poland (%)	Bulgaria (%)	Ukraine (%)
PQ8: In this country would it be better generally to have:					
harsher penalties for lawbreakers?	91	93	94	96	92
more lenient penalties for lawbreakers?	9	7	6	4	8

particular, there is a sense that they are not protected as crime rates have soared, and corruption and organised crime are widespread (Centre for the Study of Democracy [CSD], 2009). This might, in turn, explain why citizens in Bulgaria, Poland and Ukraine favour order over individual freedom.

Findings for Norway and England might reflect the fact that the police are understaffed and under-resourced and thus less able to deal with crime than they were in the past (Norway). As for England, fear of terrorism – which, according to the 2007 NatCen survey has made British citizens more willing to sacrifice some of their civil rights to ensure personal protection – might also have something to do with it.

This might, in turn, explain why in every country around 93 per cent of the public opt for "harsher" rather than "more lenient penalties for lawbreakers" (Table 3.3).

Table 3.4 *Strict versus flexible law: the legal outsiders' perspective*

	Norway (%)	England (%)	Poland (%)	Bulgaria (%)	Ukraine (%)
Q8: want harsher penalties (v. more lenient)	91	94	94	96	92
Q5: stricter implementation and enforcement (v. better laws)	70	72	54	67	58
Q6: protect individual freedom (v. ensuring order)	36	37	26	30	31
Q7: protect individual freedom (v. combat threat of terrorism)	50	36	54	67	74
Q115: more important to protect rights of individuals and minorities (v. combat threat of terrorism)	37	40	44	48	67

An authoritarian public?

In both secular and religious literature *justice* has frequently been linked with *mercy*. But the general public put more weight on justice than mercy: over 90 per cent of the public in every country want "harsher" rather than "more lenient" penalties. Over 70 per cent in Norway and England thinks "stricter implementation and enforcement" is more important than having "better laws" – though attitudes are more balanced between "stricter enforcement" and "better laws" in the three former communist countries. But across all five countries around two-thirds make "ensuring order" a higher priority than "individual freedom". By that measure the public in all of the countries is authoritarian rather than libertarian (Table 3.4).

When faced with the choice between 'combating the threat of terrorism' and 'protecting individual freedom', Bulgarians and Ukrainians come down strongly in favour of "individual freedom", but Norwegians and Poles are evenly divided, and two-thirds of the English prioritise "combating the threat of terrorism". By that measure, the Ukrainian public are the most liberal, and the English are the most authoritarian!

Table 3.5 *Legal controls: the legal outsiders' perspective*

	Norway (%)	England (%)	Poland (%)	Bulgaria (%)	Ukraine (%)
PQ11: Which would you prefer:					
more legal controls on safety, quality, standards?	73	52	65	95	81
fewer legal controls leaving people to choose?	27	48	35	5	19

But, as we will see in Chapter 9, the Ukrainian public – at the time of interviewing – felt less threatened by terrorism and thus also less inclined to fight it, than the English.

In a different part of the interview respondents were faced with the choice between 'combating the threat of terrorism' and 'protecting the rights of individuals and minorities'. In every country except England, that additional focus on the "rights of minorities" evokes a more authoritarian response from the general public, though Ukrainians remain by far the most liberal.

On an average across the five countries, only 32 per cent prioritise "individual freedom" over "ensuring order". But 56 per cent prioritise "individual freedom" over "combating the threat of terrorism" and that slips only to 47 per cent who would prioritise "the rights of individuals and minorities" over "combating the threat of terrorism".

The 'nanny state'?

We asked respondents whether they would prefer "more legal controls – for example, on safety at work, the quality of goods in shops, or house-building standards" or alternatively, "fewer legal controls – leaving people to make their own choices about such things". Support for the "nanny state" – interfering in the details of everyday life – is most popular in Bulgaria (95 per cent) and Ukraine (81 per cent), somewhat less so in Poland and Norway, and by far the least popular in England, where opinion is almost evenly divided (52 per cent) (Table 3.5).

In Eastern Europe the state has traditionally played a big role in people's lives. During Communism people were 'taken care of' – for better and for worse. Transition and economic reform have come at a cost in post-communist societies, and the authorities do not have the means necessary to provide people with a proper safety net (Berend 2009). As a result there is a level of nostalgia for the past in Eastern Europe – and it encompasses both generational differences and general discontent. However, communist nostalgia is 'more closely related to dissatisfaction with the present system's ability to produce output than to genuine non-democratic values' (Ekman and Linde 2015, p. 354).

In England *knee-jerk legislation* has caused considerable irritation amongst both legal outsiders and insiders (see Chapter 2). The large number of such laws passed in recent years probably explains why support for the "nanny state" is lower amongst English legal outsiders. The average number of government bills in a typical parliamentary session is between 35 and 50, but the average number of acts has slightly declined over the past 40 years. However, the areas covered by law have significantly increased: between 1983 and 2009 more than 4,000 new criminal offences were created (Office of the Parliamentary Counsel, Cabinet Office 2013, p. 6). These factors help explain the English findings.

Weak parliamentary supremacy?

Public support for the concept of "parliamentary supremacy"[2] is remarkably weak – even in England, despite England's historic association with that concept. We asked, "if Parliament passed a law but the courts said it was illegal, who should have the final say? Parliament, because it is democratically elected by the people or the courts because they are the guardians of the law?" On an average, only 36 per cent (35 per cent in England) would choose Parliament over the courts, if the courts declared a law illegal (Table 3.6).

And there is even less support for Parliament "forcing" the courts to apply a law rather than redraft it – on an average only 18 per cent (still less, 13 per cent in England and 10 per cent in Norway). In "constitutional regimes", the Constitution and the constitutional court[3] are in theory

[2] In the UK, parliamentary supremacy 'makes Parliament the supreme legal authority ... which can create or end any law. Generally, the courts cannot overrule its legislation and no Parliament can pass laws that future Parliaments cannot change. Parliamentary sovereignty is the most important part of the UK constitution.' See 'Parliamentary sovereignty', www.parliament.uk/about/how/sovereignty accessed on 5 January 2014.

[3] In Norway, which does not have a constitutional court, this function is carried out by the Supreme Court.

Table 3.6 *Law, court and Parliament: the legal outsiders' perspective*

	Norway (%)	England (%)	Poland (%)	Bulgaria (%)	Ukraine (%)
Q20: If Parliament passed a law but the courts declared it illegal, Parliament should have the final say (v. courts)	41	35	35	35	34
Q29: If the courts refuse to apply a law, Parliament should force the courts to apply it (v. change law)	10	13	15	33	17

supreme. But in countries such as the UK, there is no written Constitution[4] and no constitutional court.[5] Moreover the contemporary public find it difficult to distinguish between the government (which cannot claim supremacy over the courts even in England) and the Parliament (which does claim such supremacy in England).

Flexibility or rigidity?

A *top-down view* of the law envisages an enormous amount of detail, fully specified at the top, leaving little or no discretion at the bottom. The model is that of the Old Testament story of the Ten Commandments 'carved on

[4] Some would argue that there is a British Constitution, but that it is found in several documents rather than in one document only. The main sources include statutes (e.g. the Magna Carta of 1215 and the Act of Settlement of 1701) laws and customs of Parliament, political conventions, case law, constitutional matters decided in a court of law, and constitutional experts who have written on the subject – e.g. Walter Bagehot and A. V. Dicey. See History Learning Site. 'The British Constitution', www.historylearningsite.co.uk/british_constitution1.htm, accessed on 20 August 2014. See also University College London (UCL), 'What is the UK Constitution?', www.ucl.ac.uk/constitution-unit/whatis/uk-constitution accessed on 2 September 2014, and Bogdanor (2009).

[5] The Supreme Court is 'the final court of appeal for all United Kingdom civil cases, and criminal cases from England, Wales and Northern Ireland; hears appeals on arguable points of law of general public importance; concentrates on cases of the greatest public and constitutional importance; maintains and develops the role of the highest court in the United Kingdom as a leader in the common world.' The Supreme Court, 'Role of the Supreme Court', http://supremecourt.uk/about/role-of-the-supreme-court.html accessed on 25 August 2014.

Table 3.7 *The letter of the law: the legal outsiders' perspective*

	Norway (%)	England (%)	Poland (%)	Bulgaria (%)	Ukraine (%)
Q27: Laws should be very detailed (v. set principles, for court to decide)	41	31	60	70	78
Q26: Courts should apply letter of law (v. decide what is fair and reasonable)	34	26	48	53	64

tablets of stone' and brought down the mountain by Moses to be applied rigidly without debate, discussion, interpretation or discretion.[6] The alternative model, the New Testament commandment simply to 'love thy neighbour as thyself',[7] leaves greater scope for interpretation and discretion, in which courts and judges 'interpret' and even 'make law' as well as 'apply law'.

Not surprisingly, given England's common law tradition, the English are the most inclined to reject the concept of 'detailed laws' and its corollary of 'applying the letter of the law' rather than deciding 'what is fair and reasonable' in the circumstances. Public support for detailed laws runs at only 31 per cent in England. It is somewhat higher in Norway, though still supported only by a minority of 41 per cent. But there is a very clear majority support for detailed laws in Poland (60 per cent), Bulgaria (70 per cent) and most of all in Ukraine (78 per cent) – even though *legal nihilism* is widespread, particularly in the latter two countries.

Support for courts to "apply the letter of the law" rather than deciding what is "fair and reasonable" follows the same cross-national pattern – though at a significantly lower level: there is only a clear majority preference for applying the "letter of the law" in Ukraine. Whether that reflects the Imperial or Soviet tradition or simply the very low opinion of the Ukrainian public about Ukrainian judges is not immediately clear (Table 3.7). However, surveys suggest that judges are the least trusted

[6] See Exodus 20:2–17 or Deuteronomy 5:6–21.

[7] See John 13:34–35 and Matthew 22:35–40.

professionals in Ukraine.[8] They are also considered to be highly corrupt (Kyiv International Institute of Sociology [KIIS] 2006). People might therefore think that the "letter of the law" is applied in all court cases, and that equal treatment before the law will automatically follow.

Verbatims from the focus groups in Bulgaria and Ukraine support this view. The large majority of the Bulgarian FG participants are in favour of strictly applying the letter of the law to ensure that all citizens are treated equally before the law. Bulgarian FG participants believe that at present this is not the case: although ordinary citizens are treated according to the law, the wealthy stand above the law:

> FG1-Sofia-7: 'we should all be equal before the law.' B5-Aksakovo-1: '[the law] must be the same for everyone. [It must] not [be] fully applied for some and [only] partly for others.' B8-Dolna Mitropolia-6: '[the law] should be the same for the rich and the poor.' FG2-Sofia-4: 'the circumstances are always in favour of the wealthy.'

FG participants in Ukraine make a point of the fact that at present the law is applied differently to different people. They believe that the situation may only be remedied by applying the law strictly. Then in Ukraine at present, who you know is more important than what you do:

> U11-Zubra-3: 'if there is law there are no circumstances.' U16-Alushta-2: 'I think the judges should follow the law strictly ... if judges would consider all circumstances then ... the law would be on the side of the stronger person, because the circumstances ... [favour] the strong and wealthy person'. U13-Zbarash-1: 'in the given situation, in our country, one should unambiguously strictly follow the law.' U15-Simferopol-1: 'the concept "it's a matter of give-and-take" is very common in our country. Brother, father of the son-in-law, any friend – these relations must be avoided, especially in the courts. Somebody gives something to someone, somebody calls somewhere ... if this mess continues then where will we end up'. U14-Plotica-4: 'we have to punish not only the poorer people but the wealthy ones as well'.

When asked to reflect on disputes amongst the "people you meet at work or in your neighbourhood" and about whether it is most important to settle these disputes "strictly according to the letter of the law", or

[8] Acknowledging this situation, the Ukrainian Parliament in April 2014 passed a law called 'On Restoring Trust in the Court System of Ukraine'. The purpose of the law is to reduce corruption in Ukrainian courts. A special commission has been established to examine judges of general jurisdiction. If judges have engaged in misconduct they may be disciplined, reprimanded or dismissed.

Table 3.8 *Decision-making in court: the legal outsiders' perspective*

	Norway (%)	England (%)	Poland (%)	Bulgaria (%)	Ukraine (%)
Q37: Most important:					
letter of the law	5	11	18	26	28
accepted ideas of right and wrong	43	41	36	25	29
preserve good human relations	52	48	46	49	43

Table 3.9 *Law and minorities: the legal outsiders' perspective*

	Norway (%)	England (%)	Poland (%)	Bulgaria (%)	Ukraine (%)
Q52: Which closest?					
minorities must obey	61	57	37	76	50
law should not offend minorities	34	30	40	19	39
not enforce, if no harm	5	13	23	4	11

"generally accepted ideas of right and wrong", or in such a way as to "preserve good human relations between those in dispute", Ukrainians are more likely than those in other countries to cite "the letter of the law" – and less likely than those in other countries to cite "good human relations". But nonetheless, "good human relations" are the top priority within each and every country (Table 3.8).

Court judgements that take account of individual circumstances can sometimes prompt the legislature to rewrite the law. But there can be a degree of flexibility built into the law itself. This is particularly relevant for minorities rather than individuals. We asked whether "ethnic and religious minorities" should be required "always to obey the law"; whether the law should be so "tolerant of individual freedoms that it does not offend these minorities"; or whether "some laws should simply not be enforced on these minorities, provided this does no harm to other people" (Table 3.9).

On an average, 56 per cent of the general public insist that minorities "must always obey the law"; 32 per cent agree that the law should be designed to avoid offence to minorities; but only 11 per cent opt for "not enforcing" some laws on minorities, "if they did no harm to other people".

The general public in Poland is by far the most flexible about simply not enforcing laws that offend minorities. According to the 2002 national census, ethnic minorities account for less than 4 per cent of the country's population. They include the Lipka Tatars (though Muslims, the Tatars are held in high regard amongst Poles, given their historical contribution to securing Polish independence), Belorussians, Ukrainians, Germans and Jews. Besides, religious tolerance is high in Poland (Golebiowska 2004; 2009).

Conversely, there is little public support in Norway, England or Bulgaria for "special laws that apply only to ethnic or religious minorities – on marriage, divorce or inheritance, for example", though considerably more in Poland (28 per cent) and Ukraine (39 per cent).

Our question is in reality a question about Muslims and about the desirability of *shari'a law* and *shari'a courts*. Although shari'a courts exist in England, they are banned in Norway. Debates on whether to allow shari'a courts in Norway suggest that opposition to such courts is considerable. There is also unease about shari'a courts amongst the majority population in the United Kingdom (Griffith-Jones 2013). As for Bulgaria, the majority population are tolerant of the fairly secular and well-integrated Turkish minority but highly sceptical of the Pomaks (Zhelyazkova, Kosseva and Hajdinjak 2010). The latter are Muslim ethnic Bulgarians who primarily identify with religion rather than with ethnicity. Besides, they are to an increasing extent turning to the Middle East for religious guidance and support (Ghodsee 2010).[9] These factors explain why there is less support for special laws in Norway, England and Bulgaria.

Obviously support might have been still less if we had presented respondents with more sensational examples of "special laws", but the examples given are very important for everyday life (Table 3.10).

Reflect or reform?

Should the law reflect the way people live? Or should it be used for social engineering, imposing change on a perhaps unwilling public? In every country a large majority say the law should reflect how most people live,

[9] The Roma community (Zhelyazkova, Kosseva and Hajdinjak 2010) has its own court – the *Meshere*.

Table 3.10 *Special laws for minorities: the legal outsiders' perspective*

	Norway (%)	England (%)	Poland (%)	Bulgaria (%)	Ukraine (%)
Q53: Should be some special laws for minorities	7	13	28	11	39

and on an average, half the public say a law should be abolished if most people ignore or evade it.

Large majorities, around 73 per cent in Norway and England, rising to around 91 per cent in Poland, Bulgaria and Ukraine back the proposition that "the law should reflect the way most people actually live". Our FGs shed some light on the reasons why.

In Poland and even more so in Bulgaria, FG participants express their unhappiness with the fact that laws do not always take into account local customs and traditions. Although Poles talk about legislation more generally, Bulgarians frequently talk about EU law. Both Poles and Bulgarians believe that some types of behaviour should be taught from an early age rather than being legislated. Poles to a greater extent than the Bulgarians stress the importance of free will:

> P3-Katowice-3: 'most of us . . . are Catholics. Catholics don't need the law because religion does it for them.' P7-Zambrow-10: 'why should I wear seatbelts if I don't like wearing them? . . . it's my personal choice.' P2-Warsaw-2: 'there was a mayor of a town who decided that dogs may not bark after 10 p.m. . . . this is absurd but there are already two towns that have these regulations.' B2-Sofia-4: 'can the law teach us to clean the space in front of and behind our apartment buildings and pick up packages thrown in the street? This cannot be done by law. These are manners that are formed in the first seven years of your life . . . the law cannot help us have a clean city.' B3-Varna-7: 'the laws that come from Europe and . . . are imposed on us in contradiction with our social norms . . . the Bulgarians simply do not abide by them.'

Smaller majorities in Poland (54 per cent), Bulgaria (51 per cent) and Ukraine (66 per cent) agree that "if the law is ignored or evaded by most people it should be abolished". In Norway only a very small majority oppose such abolition, but in England there is clear opposition to bringing the law into line with existing behaviour (Table 3.11).

At the same time, large majorities back at least the occasional use of law to change and reform the people: majorities ranging from 73 per cent

Table 3.11 *Preferred basis of law revisited: the legal outsiders' perspective*

	Norway (%)	England (%)	Poland (%)	Bulgaria (%)	Ukraine (%)
Q30A: Law should reflect how most people actually live	70	76	90	91	91
Q30C: Abolish law if disregarded	45	27	54	51	66
Q30D: Law should sometimes be used to improve the way most people behave	75	73	94	88	81

in England to 94 per cent in Poland agree that "to improve their behaviour the law should sometimes be used to change the way most people behave". In our interviews we had given a mixed set of examples: "laws about car seat-belts, smoking or restrictions on abortion".

FG participants in Eastern Europe express some support for using laws to change behaviour. People believe that if used properly, law can change society – and relations between people – for the better:

> P8-Turośń Kościelna-5: 'society needs to be educated to civilised coexistence'. P8-Turośń Kościelna-4: 'our norms should match other countries' norms, at least to some degree'. B3-Varna-3: 'the law should change things for the better, drive the entire society in a positive direction'. B3-Varna-5: 'laws . . . should change us for the better. We have to be more careful when we elect the people who are supposed to change the laws because it often happens that they act against our interests and our way of life.' U16-Alushta-8: 'the law is education.' U14-Plotica-3: 'the law should improve life'. U12-Ternopil-3: 'man should constantly improve him/herself.'

In Norway and England, on the other hand, FG participants recommend that law be used to rid society of anti-social behaviour. Several Norwegian FG participants are smokers and they were sceptical about the smoking ban when it was introduced. But they are now happy with it as they smoke less than they used to do. Still, some Norwegian FG participants caution against using law to change behaviour as, in their view, this is dangerous:

> N11-Klepp-1: 'I smoke, but I think [the smoking ban] is good, because . . . I don't really want to smoke'. N13-Finnsnes-2: 'the authorities think . . .

Table 3.12 *Law and changing public opinion: the legal outsiders' perspective*

	Norway (%)	England (%)	Poland (%)	Bulgaria (%)	Ukraine (%)
Q32: Law should reflect changing opinion (v. remain a fixed standard)	41	60	66	56	56

> our use of snow-scooters is not sufficiently controlled. The central authorities must have the right to intervene [and regulate scooter-driving]'. E5-Bristol-6: 'there's a lot of binge drinking . . . the law should do something to curb that.' E6-Sheffield-8: '[the law] should improve certain people's behaviour.' N1-Oslo-3: '[using law to change behaviour would turn Norway] into a police state . . . one must consider public opinion.'

Overall the public is ready – indeed it is all too ready – to agree with both the objectives of reflection and reform. So perhaps we should focus on one question that poses a very sharp alternative: whether the law should "remain unchanged as a fixed standard of acceptable behaviour" or "reflect the changes in public opinion and behaviour on matters like smoking, drugs or personal relationships". Except in Norway, a small majority agree that "when public attitudes and behaviour change, the law should be changed to reflect the changes in public opinion". If there is to be reform, therefore, a majority believe the law should follow public opinion rather than lead it (Table 3.12). Only amongst Norwegians is there a modest but clear majority in favour of laws 'remaining unchanged, as fixed standards of acceptable behaviour'.

Sometimes the agent for change is not a spontaneous change of public opinion or behaviour but legislation to reform the public. And then there is the question of how to change and reform their behaviour. Or more immediately, there is a question of how to engineer a change in public behaviour by imposing a new law on a perhaps reluctant public. If a new law "required many people to change what used to be regarded as normal behaviour in the past" only an average of 28 per cent agree that it should be "applied strictly as soon as it becomes law". There is more support for strict and immediate enforcement in Bulgaria and Ukraine, but that is balanced by more support for "waiting until a majority of people change their behaviour before trying to enforce a new law strictly". Conversely

Table 3.13 *Law and changing normal behaviour: the legal outsiders' perspective*

	Norway (%)	England (%)	Poland (%)	Bulgaria (%)	Ukraine (%)
Q31: Law changing normal behaviour:					
apply strictly immediately	16	18	25	50	30
apply less strictly at first and issue warnings	76	73	69	38	55
wait until a majority obeys	8	9	6	13	15

there is more support in England and Norway for "just warning people that they are now breaking the law" and only gradually moving towards enforcement (Table 3.13).

Stepping outside the law?

In every country a majority feel it is "acceptable for the government to suspend the usual rights of citizens and step outside the law in order to combat widespread corruption", to combat "widespread organised crime", or to combat "the threat of terrorism" (the latter is discussed at length in Chapter 9). On an average 54 per cent would accept their government "stepping outside the law" to combat "widespread corruption", 60 per cent to combat "organised crime", and 63 per cent to combat the "threat of terrorism".

Regarding corruption the margin of support for "stepping outside the law" is very small (though uniform across countries), but the margin is significantly larger on "organised crime" and "terrorism". Remarkably, there is very little difference between attitudes towards "stepping outside the law" in the five countries (Table 3.14).

FG participants, for their part, stress that it would only be acceptable for government to step outside the law in *extreme emergencies* to bolster national security and protect people's lives. Some Norwegians are sceptical, however. They see lawbreaking on the part of the government as being equal to dictatorship and emphasise that no one has the right to place him- or herself above the law. Several English FG participants feel it is acceptable for the government to break the law to protect them from terrorism, though some (particularly the Muslims) are sceptical:

Table 3.14 *When it is acceptable for government to step outside the law: the legal outsiders' perspective*

	Norway (%)	England (%)	Poland (%)	Bulgaria (%)	Ukraine (%)
Q45A: Acceptable for government to step outside law to combat corruption (v. not)	54	53	56	51	57
Q45B: Acceptable for government to step outside law to combat organised crime (v. not)	63	58	63	55	60
Q45D: Acceptable for government to step outside law to combat threat of terrorism (v. not)	63	64	69	56	62

> N12-Tromsø-2: 'war and disasters.' N12-Tromsø-6: 'situations might arise where you have to set some laws aside in order to be able to act swiftly and not get stuck in bureaucracy.' N1-Oslo-3: 'natural disasters.' N8-Muslims-8: 'national security.' N9-Stavanger-7: '[it would be dangerous] especially with minority governments that represent only some 10 per cent of the population.' N2-Oslo-9: 'in that case we are back to dictatorship.' E5-South-West-8: 'a national emergency'. E6-Sheffield-4: 'I think they can more or less make their own rules when it comes to terrorists these days, providing they get the right man ... because terrorists aren't bothered whom they kill or how many they kill.'

FG participants in Eastern Europe talk more about other types of emergency situations – including force majeure:

> P1-Warsaw1–2: 'it's the same thing all around the world. Governments lie to people. And the government's job is to break the law because it's the government that set the law and it has the right to break it . . . certainly, if it's about national security.' P8-Turośń Kościelna-8: 'if there is a genuine threat, law can be broken, if human lives are at stake.' P10-Białystok-Tatars-5: 'there isn't always enough time to follow all the procedures. Sometimes you need to dodge a procedure.' B3-Varna-3: '[it would be acceptable] in a situation where national security is at stake, the security of the people, extraordinary circumstances.' B4-Topoli-2: 'on the occasion of [natural] disasters or emergencies'. B6-Enchetz-1: 'the law does not

> have to change, but [it] should be broken, if need be . . . you break it, but you help [people], which is not a true violation.'

Even though the FGs in Ukraine were carried out well ahead of the Ukrainian revolution of February 2014, many of the statements made by the FG participants in West Ukraine, East Ukraine and the Crimea are highly relevant with regard to these events:

> U1-Kiev-4: 'if it is an emergency, then of course . . . let's say, force majeure . . . a revolt. Or some [kind of] counter-revolution . . . for power.' U9-Lviv-2: 'if the national dignity of the state is violated.' U11-Zubra-1: 'if there is a threat to the unity of the state'. U15-Simferopol-3: '[to prevent] civil war.' U12-Ternopil-8: 'the Crimea, if a Russian force were landed there . . . they could [i.e. the government could violate the law in such a case].' U2-Kiev-4: 'to [allow the government] to somehow govern the country.' U14-Plotica-7: 'force majeure . . . wars, state upheaval, aggression.' U13-Zbarazh-7: 'of course . . . to preserve [Ukraine's] energy security . . . the life of the nation, the health of the nation.' U7-Chuguev-7: '[for the sake of] national security . . . to preserve the state'.

Yet, although "stepping outside the law" might be "acceptable" it is not the public's first choice even for combating the threat of terrorism. When given four options and asked "what do you feel should be the government's and security services' main response to the threat of terrorism?" the top choice in every country is "new and tougher laws" (41 per cent), followed by "enforcing the law more strictly" (31 per cent). On an average only 15 per cent chose either of the more extreme options of "staying within existing laws and procedures" (the liberal extreme) or "stepping outside the law" (the authoritarian extreme) (Table 3.15). We will return to these issues in more detail in Chapter 9.

The role of law: the legal insiders' perspective

We asked the legal outsiders to give their assessment of several dimensions of law. The format of the in-depth interview (IDI) places a limit on the number of questions that may be asked. We therefore could not ask the legal insiders the same number of detailed questions that we asked the legal outsiders. However, we did ask them about whether law should reflect social norms or be used to change people; whether judges should apply the law flexibly or whether they should follow the letter of the law; and whether it is acceptable for legal insiders to use discretion or to step outside the law. Our findings are discussed below.

Table 3.15 *How government and security services should respond to the threat of terrorism: the legal outsiders' perspective*

	Norway (%)	England (%)	Poland (%)	Bulgaria (%)	Ukraine (%)
Q112: In response to the threat of terrorism government and security services should:					
stay within existing laws and procedures	15	11	21	5	21
enforce law more strictly	27	28	25	40	34
introduce new and tougher laws	36	49	34	48	36
step outside the law	21	12	19	8	9

Reflect or reform?

As we have seen, a majority of the legal outsiders in all countries except Norway prefer law to reflect changing opinion rather than remain a fixed standard (Table 3.12). Further, there is high public support for law to reflect how most people actually live, but also for sometimes using law to improve the way most people behave (Table 3.11). Table 3.16 shows that legal insiders in Norway, England and Poland prefer law to do *both*. Legal insiders in Bulgaria have a stronger preference for using law to *change* rather than preserve people's behaviour, while legal insiders in Ukraine are divided on this issue.

Bulgaria has had a harder time with transition than Poland: its socio-economic development is worse, corruption is more widespread and organised crime is flourishing (CSD 2007; OSAC 2013). More importantly, citizens in Bulgaria feel less ownership of the changes than Polish citizens do. There is also less trust in the state and in state institutions in Bulgaria than in Poland.

During the spring and early summer of 2014 Bulgarians took to the streets in large numbers to protest abnormally high electricity bills. The demonstrations turned into a mass non-partisan movement against the government and the political system, and the Borisov government was eventually forced to resign. However, the government that was appointed in its place failed to address the demands of the protesters, triggering a wave of nationwide demonstrations in support of changing

Table 3.16 *Law, social norms and behavioural change: the legal insiders' perspective*

	Norway (%)	England (%)	Poland (%)	Bulgaria (%)	Ukraine (%)
Should the law *reflect* social norms, i.e. the way *most people* actually live? Or should it sometimes be used to *change* the way most people behave, to reform people and improve their behaviour?					
Reflect social norms	14	22	31	24	37
Change behaviour	26	25	24	45	34
Mix	60	53	45	31	29

Note: Entries are based on the percentages of relevant text units – the total number of answers to a given question – so entries sum up to approximately 100% (decimals are rounded up or down to the nearest whole number).

the political model and nationalizing strategic economic sectors.[10] Our findings reflect such sentiments. Bulgarians think EU law and ECtHR case law are of higher quality than Bulgarian law and that such law should therefore be implemented in their country to facilitate change (Grødeland 2014a; see also Chapter 7).

Findings for Ukraine most likely reflect the sharp division between 'reformers' and 'conservatives' – that is, between the West-leaning portion of the legal insiders and those legal insiders who prefer closer ties with Russia, with which they feel closer cultural and linguistic affinity. The division between reformers and conservatives has been visible since 1991 and culminated with the 2014 revolution in Kyiv, the loss of Crimea to Russia, and civil war in the Eastern parts of the country.

A read-through of all statements coded as "mixed" in the Norwegian data set shows that Norwegian legal insiders think law must reflect *social norms* to be "legitimate".

[10] '2013 Bulgarian protests against the Borisov cabinet', Wikipedia, http://en.wikipedia.org/wiki/2013_Bulgarian_protests_against_the_Borisov_cabinet accessed on 30 August 2014.

In their view, norm-driven laws are "based on the collective conscience" – that is, of people's perceptions of "right and wrong" and of "what is reasonable". Such laws reflect the "common interests" and most people can therefore "identify" with them. More importantly, such laws are considered to be "just". In this sense norm-driven laws serve as a "moral compass" for people by "cementing good attitudes". Laws informed by social norms have a "stabilizing effect" on society. In the view of the legal insiders national law should therefore "mostly [reflect] social norms":

> N-LA-22: 'one should consider a combination of what is socially acceptable and what one wishes to achieve. It would often be difficult if one should introduce ... reforms that ... clash with socially accepted common norms ... it does not make much sense ... to introduce a piece of law that a large majority ... are really against'. N-GO-12: 'if the law imposes upon people something which is totally different from their own norms, then they will not abide by [it]'. N-ER-11: 'I think legislation that to a too limited extent harmonises with general perceptions of right and wrong will over time result in big problems'.

But in addition to reflecting the norms of society, law must also *educate people*, or change and improve their lives, by removing undesirable behaviour. In other words, the law should act as a "corrective" to, and even "influence" social norms, thus over time changing "opinions" and giving people "something to strive for". Several Norwegian legal insiders refer to the smoking ban in this regard. In their view, the smoking ban has facilitated a change in people's attitudes towards smoking. Some legal insiders believe that law could have a similar effect in a wide range of areas. As "norm-based punishment works best" criminal law should reflect social norms. Civil law, on the other hand, could have more of an educational role, though it should not veer too far away from the commonly accepted norms. In the view of Norwegian legal insiders implementing laws that "do not reflect society" would be difficult:

> N-ER-16: 'the challenge must be to give people that which they do not know that they would like until they get it ... the anti-smoking law ... is an example of an "attitudinal" law that has created a change in society ... if you ask people [what they think about the ban on smoking in public places] now, they think it is excellent ... sometimes one should not only aim for the [preferences] of the majority, because the majority is always conservative-minded'. N-JU-23: 'laws should both reflect [social norms] and reform [people]. The point is that the distance between what is perceived as a good norm by the population and the norm of the law must not be too big'.

English legal insiders – just like those in Norway – predominantly hold the view that law should reflect both social norms and be used to change people's behaviour.

As for *social norms* legal insiders simply state that law should "reflect", "stay within", or "respond to" social norms. But if necessary, it should also be used to "reform people to adhere to social norms" – that is, to ensure that their behaviour is "keeping within the boundaries of society", thus "protecting [it] from damage". Social norms essentially reflect "public opinion" or "the consensus view". Society drives law, and the latter should therefore "not get out of synch with society", nor "restrict behaviour". Laws should, as a rule, be driven by "consent":

> E-ER-24: 'I think the law should, in the vast majority of cases, reflect social norms . . . I think that we should be very cautious before trying to use the law as a means of nudging people into different types of behaviour. It's far more effective as a way of policing or reinforcing views about the unacceptability of existing behaviour, as opposed to some sort of social engineering tool.' E-ER-23: 'I think legislators have to be aware of what the norm is, but [that they] also have to be prepared to operate on certain principles, such as individual rights of choice, lifestyles, diversity of our population and community.'

Those English legal insiders who opt for the law to also have an *educational* role mostly express a preference for law reflecting social norms. But they add that it should occasionally be used as a "driver of change". Law promoting change should "lead public opinion" – thereby "changing [their] attitudes", "constraining" and "regulating" their behaviour. In doing so, law effectively "changes norms". Even though law may in some instances "drive social change", it should not be used for "social engineering". However, norm-driven law should not be static but should rather evolve to "reflect change in social norms" and in this way "adapt to changes in society". Just as legal insiders in Norway, English legal insiders give several examples of legislation aimed at changing behaviour:

> E-LA-14: 'if a social norm is "let's all go out and get pissed on a Saturday night" then sometimes you do have to have laws to enforce the way society should behave rather than the way society does [behave]. Just because everybody wants to drive at 200 miles per hour doesn't mean it should be legal'. E-PR-20: 'to get a perfect balance, you need the social side, but people also often need their attitudes changing'. E-JU-7: 'I think discrimination is a good example of where the law may very well have been ahead of most people's perceptions, and I think it changed the perceptions for the better.'

Close to half the statements made by legal insiders in Poland suggest that law should both reflect social norms and be used to change people's behaviour. As for *social norms*, the law should reflect the "ethical and moral order" of society – including its "norms" and "standards". It should reflect "the beliefs of most citizens" whilst "referring to values promoted by the state". Polish law should be rooted in "common sense", yet also be an "instrument to force change" – partly by reinforcing existing social norms, partly by engineering change.

First, it should reinforce existing social norms as "not all people abide by" these. In doing so, law should take on "a corrective function", putting an end to "socially reprehensive" or "undesirable" behaviour. The law should shape "awareness" and instil "social attitudes" – thus "changing life" in society "for the better".

Second, law should sometimes "be ahead of the normative development" in society. In Poland there is [still] a "need to change habits from the socialist period". Law should therefore remove "negative codes" and "pathological patterns" from society by "imposing certain behaviour" on people – thus "[facilitating] progress".

Polish legal insiders note that it is not so much a question of law either cementing social norms or promoting change, but rather a question of finding the right balance between the two:

> P-ER-16: 'I don't think that social norms constitute the way of life of the majority of the people. A social norm is not a statistical average of how people live but what they believe in, what they consider to be right or wrong.' P-LA-23: 'the law should be linked to what happens in reality. Most of all it should concern situations that we deal with every day. Undoubtedly, it should aim to change negative behaviour and strive to improve [it], first of all [the behaviour] of those … who act against social norms.' P-GO-9: 'because if [there are] some social norms that have been developed due to bad habits, or, let's say, our past socialist era, then the law should be created so that it changes such habits. However, in healthy, democratic societies, where the canon of moral values is stable, the law should reflect the norms, customs'. P-ER-10: 'there are some areas where the law practically should be a kind of creator of society's thinking, but in other cases it should specify certain limits. Let's discuss the death penalty. The question is: do we follow what society thinks … in many cases it acts under the influence of emotions'.

Roth (2007, p. 13) observes that people in the Balkans want to become Europeans – though without losing their social logic. Our findings for Bulgaria do not support this assumption. Unlike legal insiders in

Norway, England and Poland, Bulgarian legal insiders believe that law should to a greater extent *change people's behaviour* by changing the social norms that "inform" it in the first place.

They note that Bulgarian people's behaviour is in need of "correction" and "improvement". The "moral and ethical norms", "the social norms", and "the mentality [of Bulgarian citizens]" – or "the [Bulgarian] way of life" – should therefore be changed with a view to "regulating and improving social relationships" and "the Bulgarian lifestyle". Some legal insiders even claim that Balkan norms must be substituted by "North European [ones]":

> B-LA-3: 'social norms in Bulgaria are very Balkan, Oriental . . . they are more degraded . . . the West or North European norms are a better example'. B-ER-18: 'Bulgaria is not yet such a democratic state . . . the citizens are still very passive and therefore I think that the legislator and the government should provide laws that pursue strategic changes in the way of life . . . we must build a nice home where everyone will be able to enter and enjoy [themselves]'.

In Ukraine there is as much support for laws reflecting social norms as there is for law to change behaviour.

Legal insiders who express a preference for law reflecting *social norms* believe that it should reflect "tradition, customs, the way of life, and practice" of society. More specifically, it should reflect its "norms", "social standards", and "morals" – thus "reflecting the interests of the majority". Some legal insiders claim that the law "cannot change behaviour" and that it "should not" aspire do so. Then it is "difficult to change people" as it takes "a lot of time to change behaviour":

> U-PR-31: 'social norms stand above the law in some cases, this is why it is natural [for law to reflect social norms].' U-PR-26: 'certainly the law must reflect social norms and the way of life'. U-JU-14: 'the law has to reflect the social standards, the lifestyle of most people. But unfortunately, it doesn't do that. It reflects the will of those people who adopt it.' U-GO-26: 'the . . . conduct of the people will change only when they will feel that the law works for [them].' U-PO-4: 'the law cannot change an individual under any circumstances.'

Those Ukrainian legal insiders who hold the view that law should *change* the way people behave speak at length about how it should "make people more law-abiding" and improve "[social] behaviour", thus "creating a better society". They stress that law should not change people's behaviour by force. Rather, it should be used as "an educational instrument", "teaching and guiding" people and "encouraging [them] to develop" by showing them "a more pleasant option". This, in turn, will make them realise that there are benefits to be had from changing one's behaviour – which, in turn, will ensure voluntary compliance:

> U-ER-2: 'Ukrainian society . . . was deprived of independence for a long time as it was a part of the Soviet Union . . . legislation has to create modern society.' U-PR-31: '[the law should improve behaviour] because the conduct of many people is inadequate'. U-JU-25: '[the law] should influence the citizens for the better . . . because by nature a person needs to be taught and guided . . . most of the time people disobey the laws and do whatever they want.'

Flexibility or rigidity?

A core principle of the rule of law is that people should be treated equally before the law (i.e. that there should be *legal certainty*). Yet, law should also be flexible 'to allow for just decisions in individual cases' (Wolff 2011, p. 549): law cannot address all possible scenarios regarding a particular issue. Judges therefore sometimes have to venture into new territory, effectively creating law.

Some legal systems allow for more flexibility than others. Wolff (ibid.) asserts that 'flexibility is sometimes even regarded as a distinguishing feature of the common law as such.' A key principle is to do what is reasonable rather than to follow the letter of the law. England belongs to the common law tradition.

The Scandinavian legal system is of a hybrid character (Easterly 1977, p. 216; Nylund 2010; Smith 2012, p. 91). The Norwegian legal tradition combines elements of both common law and civil law – thus allowing for some flexibility in the interpretation of law. Torstein Eckhoff, one of the most prominent experts on Norwegian jurisprudence, in 1971 identified seven key elements of legal reasoning in Norwegian case law. One of these is *reelle hensyn* – deliberations of what would be equitable solutions both in the individual case under consideration and at the more general level (Eckhoff 2001, p. 23).

Bulgaria, Poland and Ukraine follow the civil law tradition – having transitioned from the socialist law tradition. A key feature of the latter is *legal positivism* – that is, a school of jurisprudence according to which 'the only legitimate sources of law are those written rules, regulations, and principles that have been expressly enacted, adopted, or recognised by a governmental entity or political institution, including administrative, executive, legislative, and judicial bodies.'[11] However, laws are not always enforceable. During Communism some flexibility was therefore applied – sometimes with the unspoken consent of the Communist Party.

Post-communist states are characterised by the co-existence of formal and informal law. Galligan (2003, p. 6) notes that 'substantial areas of social life are regulated by informal social norms rather than state law, where the norms are well developed and by and large comprehensive.' Further, formal rules have largely been informalised – much as a result of the fact that they are simply not working properly (Radaev 2000). Informal contacts and networks are widespread (Ledeneva 1998).

It could be argued that civil law jurisdictions allow for less flexible interpretation of the law than common law jurisdictions. Judges working within the former are bound by codes and statutes, which have to be strictly interpreted. They are not bound by previous interpretations of these codes and laws in cases that are factually similar. Judges working within the latter, on the other hand, interpret the law, thus effectively writing it, while hearing their cases. Cases that are factually similar to cases previously addressed by court have to be interpreted in the same manner.

Based on the this, we would expect legal insiders in England, and to some extent Norway, to be more in favour of judges interpreting law flexibly, than legal insiders in Eastern Europe. Data presented in Table 3.17 supports our assumption for England (flexible), Norway (mixed), Bulgaria and Ukraine (strict). However, Poland stands out in that more than half of the statements made by the legal insiders there favour flexible application of the law.

Former chairman of the Norwegian Supreme Court, Carsten Smith (2012, p. 14), holds the view that Norwegian judges must 'to the best of our ability abide by the Constitution, the law and recognised sources of law[12] – together with our conscience and our understanding of what is to the best for society'. Norwegian legal insiders convey similar views: they prefer law to be applied flexibly, yet strictly.

[11] 'Legal Positivism', *The Free Dictionary* by Farlex, http://legal-dictionary.thefreedictionary.com/Legal+Positivism accessed on 30 August 2014.

[12] These are '(i) statutory law (the Constitution, acts, regulations); (ii) preparatory work, other background materials, and the legislator's subsequent statements on how the law is to be understood; (iii) case law (especially that of the Supreme Court); (iv) decisions of other state institutions; (v) customs; (vi) understandings of law (especially in legal writing) and (vii) *reelle hensyn* – i.e. deliberations of what would be equitable solutions both in the individual case under consideration and at the more general level' (Eckhoff 2001, p. 23).

Table 3.17 *Circumstances versus the letter of the law: the legal insiders' perspective*

	Norway (%)	England (%)	Poland (%)	Bulgaria (%)	Ukraine (%)
Should courts and judges take account of circumstances and try to do what seems reasonable in these circumstances – or should they apply the written law strictly, whatever the circumstances? Why?					
Apply flexibly	33	66	52	31	19
Apply strictly (but flexible within the law)	23	11	17	45	60
Mix	44	23	31	24	20

Note: Entries are based on the percentages of relevant 'text units' – the total number of answers to a given question, so entries sum up to approximately 100% (decimals are rounded up or down to the nearest whole number).

As regards *the flexibility of law*, judges should "not be too stuck on the letter of the law". Rather, they should allow for some "flexibility" in their decision-making – but just enough to avoid unequal treatment. Even though Norwegian law allows for considerable discretion, legal insiders believe that the main emphasis should be on what one judge defined as the "the legal norm plus equity". Lawyers and judges, in particular, consider "equity" to be a key component of decision-making in Norwegian courts. However, they acknowledge that "equity has its limits". Judges must be guided by "the facts" of a case, "not ... by their [personal] feelings". Under no circumstances may they "side-step the law":

> N-PR-12: 'each case has to be treated individually ... having judges who read the law as a certain man reads the Bible would not in my opinion result in anything good ... equality before the law is the overriding principle.' N-ER-6: 'judges are good at finding the balance ... [they] mainly emphasise the letter of the law and this is how it should be.' N-LA-15: 'within criminal law one naturally has to relate to the fact that is sought proven in court ... it would be wrong to ... judge based on emotions. But in civil cases I actually think it happens ... sometimes a pragmatic solution can be better than a rigid [one].'

In the view of Norwegian legal insiders, more than anything democracy implies "equality before the law". To ensure that people get "the same treatment" before the law, judges should therefore combine "the letter of the law" with "flexibility" – "flexibility" meaning "interpretation" of both the law and the circumstances of the given case. But judges should not interpret the law in such a way that they would end up "going against the law". Still, one lawyer claims that judges sometimes push their interpretations of the law too far:

> N-GO-24: 'there is the principle of equal treatment. I think that is important.' N-JU-1: 'judges should not feel slave-bound by the letter of the law . . . [they] should apply considerations of what is reasonable . . . but there are limits'. N-PR-11: 'the judges must abide by the rules that have been set by *Stortinget* [the national parliament] . . . drawing on individual reasonability can often be difficult and take one in the wrong direction'. N-LA-10: 'the consideration of reasonability is also a source of law. In my view it is used to quite some extent, perhaps sometimes to too great an extent because the law is interpreted further than there is a basis for'.

Legal rules must be "predictable" but also "open to interpretation". Then Norwegian judges must often act where no law exists (Smith 2012, p. 77): no law "regulates everything" and "most laws are not crystal clear". It is sometimes "difficult to understand the letter of the law". In general terms "Norwegian laws allow for much flexibility". Whether a judge should strictly abide by the letter of the law or apply some flexibility in his or her decision-making to some extent depends on *the type of law* to be applied. Legal insiders note that when dealing with contractual law the judge must strictly follow the letter of the law. However, in other cases – especially cases regarding family law – he or she may pay more attention to circumstances. Judges have considerable discretion with regard to sentencing. Most importantly, Norwegian judges must be "reasonable" in their application of the law:

> N-ER-16: 'the letter of the law is not always equally understandable . . . human beings are different, circumstances are different, and judges are different. Law is no exact science'. N-JU-11: 'there is a margin of discretion in all laws and rules that we rule by'. N-GO-14: 'any law may be interpreted . . . if you read the Bible in the manner that the devil reads the Bible, you do not catch its meaning . . . one has to understand the intention [behind the law] and the considerations that the law is to promote'.

As already noted there are seven main sources of law in Norway (Eckhoff 2001, p. 23). Norwegian legal insiders highlight three of these: in addition to the letter of the law and equity, judges must, in their view, also consider "the intentions of the law" by consulting its "sources" [i.e. the documents from the preparatory stage of a given law]. In Norwegian these documents are referred to as *lovforarbeidene.* N-ER-4: "the preparatory work [of a given law] . . . [judges] must find . . . guidance from them . . . the letter of the law is almost never applied on its own."

Slapper and Kelly (2011, p. 95) note that 'in order to apply legislation, [English] judges must ascertain the meaning of the legislation, and in order to ascertain the meaning, they are faced with the difficulty of interpreting the legislation . . . legislation therefore involves an inescapable measure of uncertainty that can only be made certain through judicial interpretation.'

Not surprisingly, therefore, several English legal insiders claim that common law is essentially about "common sense". They believe that the English legal system is not compatible with the "strict application of the law". Rather, judges should apply *the spirit of the law* and their ultimate objective should be to make "fair" and "just" decisions. To achieve this objective, they must consider "the merits of the case", including its "history", "context" and "factual background". As each case has its "unique circumstances" the law should be applied on a "case-by-case" basis. Some English legal insiders claim that doing what is "right" and "reasonable" is "more important [for English judges] than [abiding by] the letter of the law". Several respondents refer to Lord Denning[13] and his refusal to strictly apply the law, in support of their position:

> E-LA-2: 'the strict application of the law doesn't really have much of a role to play in the English legal system'. E-ER-11: 'in my experience, judges always try to act in the interests of justice and always take into effect all the circumstances of any particular case.' E-GO-13: 'the written law can take you only so far, and the beauty of the English system is that equity is the overriding concern of judges. People like Lord Denning were clearly of the view that you simply can't treat each case just on the black-and-white letter of the law, you have to look at the circumstances of the individual, or indeed the family unit or what have you. To do anything else would be inequitable and therefore unjust.'

Compared to Norwegian legal insiders, English legal insiders prefer judges to take on a more activist role using discretion "to mitigate the

[13] Lord Denning is 'known as "the people's judge" for his willingness to override precedent to do what he saw as justice.' Clare Dyer, 'Lord Denning, controversial "people's judge", dies aged 100', *The Guardian*, 6 March 1999, www.theguardian.com/uk/1999/mar/06/claredyer1/print accessed on 9 January 2014.

ill effects" of certain laws. As "most laws allow for discretion", judges should first and foremost be driven by "purposeness". However, respondents admit that judges occasionally do make incorrect decisions:

> E-PR-14: 'strict interpretation of the law can often lead to injustice ... which is why you should always look at common sense and a reasonable approach in the interpretation of legislation.' E-JU-19: 'they [i.e. judges] should ... use any discretion in the law they apply to mitigate the ill effects of either a badly drafted law, or a law, which, if strictly applied would be unjust.' E-LA-22: 'I have found judges looking at the merits, not necessarily the letter of the law, which technically, is probably wrong.'

As for the judges themselves, some indicate that they are closer to, others that they are more distanced from, the letter of the law in their own decision-making:

> E-JU-1: 'there always have been two schools, the black letter people and the slightly more purposey ... I suppose I'm more the latter class.' E-JU-25: 'in civil law, at my level, which after all disposes of 95 per cent of all cases, I'm far more conscious of trying to do the right thing than say, "what does the letter of the law say?" Some of my colleagues are far more legalistic ... I regard a judge's function to be to apply probably 80 per cent common sense'. E-JU-23: 'I have always tried to do what is just. If you accept the written letter of the law, sometimes it produces a bad result. So I always try to produce a fair result when I've been listening to cases'.

Peczenik (2003, p. 182) notes that:

> when interpreting the 'new' law, Polish judges feel loyal to its value basis, yet they often perceive the need to resort to quite flexible interpretations, sometimes *praeter legem* (i.e. outside of the law) or even *contra legem* (i.e. in contradiction with the law), based on a judicial sense of justice, rationality and morality. Further, the 'old' law must be interpreted in the context of the new values of a democratic state of law – which justifies flexible interpretation. The 'old' law is often clearer and more coherent than the new, thus easier to interpret literally.

Transition brought about a need for legal flexibility.

Polish legal insiders caution against "black-and-white" application of the law. Even though Poland is not a common law country, they advocate the use of "common sense" and proper consideration of the "circumstances" of each individual case in court. As in England, judges should apply "the spirit of the law" rather than "the letter of the law". There is "no law for all events": "the law is open to interpretation" and "each case is different". Judges should therefore do what is "reasonable" to ensure "fairness" and "justice". As laws are sometimes "impractical", judges should "not totally obey" them:

> P-GO-7: 'sometimes we talk about something which is called "the spirit of the law" and "the letter of the law". Abiding by the "letter of the law" may lead to many absurd judgements'. P-JU-1: 'courts of law and judges should obviously take into account the circumstances of a given case. What we deal with here are two opposing concepts which have somehow reappeared throughout the centuries. They can be expressed, in simple terms, by quoting two old Roman maxims: *dura lex sed lex* [the law is harsh but it should prevail], and "the law is the art of doing what is good and just". For me, these two rules stand for two concepts of the law – one is mechanical, simplified and, in my opinion, primitive, while the other one is more humane and assumes that the judge, or the lawyer, is dealing with something which borders on art, rather than being a simple worker who stands on the assembly line, where everything is regulated in terms of seconds and minutes'. P-JU-9: 'each judge ... has the obligation to apply the law. So even if the law appears to be unfavourable or unfair, it has to be obeyed. Although there is a margin of interpretation of these provisions and the judge ... should interpret the law so that the judgement is simply fair.'

Polish legal insiders strongly advocate that judges take into consideration the "social environment", "social circumstances" and "socioeconomic conditions" in their decision-making. Prosecutors call for "social justice", recommending that the "upbringing" and "family situation" of the offenders be taken into account. In their view judges must consider whether offenders violate the law because they are "hungry" or whether they do so with a view to "improving their living standard". They should also consider whether somebody is a "first-time" or "multiple" offender, and whether serious crimes such as murders are "premeditated" or "accidents":

> P-PO-5: 'one thing is stealing bread because you're starving to death and another is stealing it to throw it in the dustbin.' P-ER-5: 'the judge has to make judgements ... of the situation on the basis not only of available documents but also ... social circumstances, the logic of certain events. Then the courts will be more just instead of being a bureaucratic machine.'

Legal insiders note that Polish judges formally have considerable "freedom": "flexibility [on the part of the judge] is provided by the law", and they are therefore free to adapt "a pragmatic approach". When making decisions they should rely on their "life experience" and "inner conviction", "applying their experience and knowledge" and striving to be "objective":

> P-GO-12: 'they should consider the circumstances and apply the rules in some reasonable way, based on specific situations . . . laws are sometimes completely impractical'. P-JU-14: 'the law cannot be dehumanised and common sense always overrides the law'. P-ER-14: 'our system is so inflexible that there is almost no margin . . . I stand for a more reasonable system, more flexibility and more trust in judges.'

By contrast, Smilov (2010, p. 120) notes that 'according to Bulgarian legal doctrines, judges do not have discretion – they cannot resort in their judicial decision-making to anything but the law, which is supposed to provide them with a single right answer in every dispute . . . the stark rejection of judicial discretion . . . has deep roots in Bulgarian legal history.' Statements made by the Bulgarian legal insiders reflect these doctrines. Nearly half of their statements suggest that judges should apply the law *strictly*. Bulgarian legal insiders make two types of statements in support of their position.

First, they argue that "the court is subordinated to the law" and that the "role of judges is to adhere to the law": Bulgarian judges "should (therefore) apply, not comment on" the law. In order to "ensure equality before the law" they should "enforce [it] strictly". However, Bulgarian legal insiders acknowledge that this is not always as straightforward as it might seem. Then judges often have to "interpret badly written and unclear laws":

> B-PO-18: 'the law is for everyone. It doesn't matter whether poor or rich, politicians or VIP or ordinary people . . . everyone should abide by the law. From this perspective the judges must implement the law the way it was written.' B-PR-16: 'we adhere to the continental system and cannot afford to discuss circumstances as is the case in the Anglo-Saxon law. Our legal doctrine is different . . . the law does not allow the judges to discuss anything beyond the presented evidence. Circumstances are something outside the evidence material'. B-PR-9: 'the law has to be applied strictly as written. Of course, the question is *what* is written because sometimes there are many different interpretations of the same legal norm'.

Second, Bulgarian "laws [do] take account of circumstances". Even though judges are strictly bound by the law they should "judge fairly on evidence" – applying "the general principles of law" and its "specific provisions", thus "complying with existing [legal] norms". This is absolutely necessary as "each case is unique":

> B-PO-22: 'well, in principle, every judge follows his internal convictions, but that internal conviction is formed on the basis of the law that requires strict implementation.' B-GO-18: 'the law must be applied . . . in the field of criminal law there are mitigating circumstances, of course, that should

be considered by the courts but only within generally provided ... principles of law and specific provisions of law'.

Those few Bulgarian legal insiders who advocate a *flexible* application of the law emphasise that no law can possibly take into account all possible circumstances, and that judges should therefore apply the spirit of the law. In doing so, they should strive for fairness and justice.

Kyselova (2013, p. 17) claims that 'the independence of judges remains the Achilles' heel of (the) Ukrainian judiciary' Popova (2012, pp. 140–1) documents how in Ukraine there is scope for influencing judges' appointments. Further, judges are dependent on the authorities for premises, equipment and personal benefits – which, in turn, renders them vulnerable to political pressure (ibid., p. 145; Rechberger 2009, pp. 73, 75). It is commonly accepted amongst judges to advise the parties to a case on the specific case outside the court room (Popova 2012, p. 129), thus leaving room for influence.

Ukrainian legal insiders are even more strongly in favour of strict application of the law than Bulgarian legal insiders – possibly as Ukrainian courts have a very poor reputation. They use rule of law arguments to justify their position. As everybody is "equal before the law" judges should strive to be "impartial" and "apply the law equally to all" by strictly applying "the letter of the law". This is simply their "obligation". Law is "reason free of passion" and judges should be "guided by the norms of the law, not [their] inner conviction". Law is "not law if interpreted": U-ER-12: "[the] judge ... must observe the letter of the law strictly".

The judges themselves advocate "flawless application of the law". Members of their profession should be guided by the "principle of legality", "the law", "norms and legal provisions", their "conscience" and their "convictions". As "servants of the law" they are obliged to be "objective". However, national laws do "not foresee all" circumstances, and many of them contain "discrepancies" and "loopholes". There are many "contradicting laws" in Ukraine, and it is therefore "difficult [for judges] to be fair and just". Sometimes they are prevented from applying the law strictly. However, they admit that members of their profession do "not always make morally correct rulings":

> U-JU-20: 'all citizens must be equal before the law ... the judge ... must follow the law blindly. But unfortunately ... there are cases when the law has some contradictions ... we have several laws which say something and other [laws that say something] different ... the judge must determine whether to use this or that law'. U-JU-14: 'it's difficult to be a fair judge. It's difficult to be just towards all people'.

Circumstances essentially represent a "subjective factor". If courts were to take them into account this would, in the view of Ukrainian legal insiders, introduce a "bias" by facilitating "inequality before the law". This, in turn, would pave the way for "advocacy" in court and "legal nihilism", possibly even "anarchy", or "tyranny". Ukrainian judges must "avoid emotions" to avoid "errors". They should be guided only by the "norms of law":

> U-ER-2: 'we must learn to stick to the legislation. For the last decade in the judicial system many decisions were made not on the basis of legislation but on the basis of political or economic expediency.' U-GO-1: 'public sector workers, judges, professionals must work within the law. If the law is not spelt out the judge may use the analogy of the law but he should not have the discretion to interpret [it], should not go beyond [it] because that is [when] legal nihilism and anarchy begin.' U-ER-3: 'the judicial system [in Ukraine] needs serious reform . . . the citizens' confidence in the judicial system . . . is very low . . . if we give additional motivation to the judges to take into account the circumstances [of a given case] . . . we will continue to promote that tyranny which is now [prevalent] in the judicial system.'

Stepping outside the law?

Legal outsiders were asked whether it would be acceptable for government to step outside the law to combat corruption, organised crime or the threat of terrorism. Table 3.14 shows that a majority are in favour of government stepping outside the law to combat terrorism, organised crime and corruption – but that they are more positive to government stepping outside the law to combat terrorism and organised crime, and less positive to do so if the purpose is to combat corruption.

Again, given the format of the IDI, we could not ask legal insiders to answer three different questions on stepping outside the law. However, we did ask them whether it would ever be acceptable for members of their profession to use discretion or step outside the law. Table 3.18 shows that legal insiders in all countries believe it is acceptable to use discretion, but that it is unacceptable to step outside the law.

For reasons of space we will not explore the reasons why legal insiders think it is acceptable or not acceptable to use discretion in their work in this chapter. Rather, we will focus on the reasons why legal insiders across Europe find it unacceptable to step outside the law. This is very much an 'attitude' question rather than a question about 'perceptions'. Essentially it is a question of the quality of democracy and the rule of law.

Table 3.18 *Whether it is acceptable for legal insiders to use discretion or step outside the law: the legal insiders' perspective*

	Norway (%)	England (%)	Poland (%)	Bulgaria (%)	Ukraine (%)
Are there situations or circumstances in which it would be acceptable for [respondent's profession] to use *discretion* or *step outside the law*?					
Discretion					
Acceptable	97	83	77	73	60
Not acceptable	3	17	23	27	40
Step outside the law					
Acceptable	0	10	6	4	16
Not acceptable	100	90	94	96	84

Note: Entries are based on the percentages of relevant 'text units' – the total number of answers to a given question; so entries sum up to approximately 100% (decimals are rounded up or down to the nearest whole number).

Norwegian legal insiders make it clear that breaking the law is neither acceptable from an ethical point of view, nor possible from a practical point of view. Lawbreaking is "never an option" – and they have "limited possibilities" to do so. Such behaviour "is not possible to defend" and several legal insiders emphasise that they themselves would never step outside the law: N-GO-10: "from a normative point of view [setting the law aside] is not acceptable." N-PO-3: "one starts moving into . . . dangerous territory, if [one is] to place [oneself] above the law'.

As laws are a "prerequisite for a functioning society" rather than setting laws aside one should "initiate legal amendments" or seek "change through politicians" if one disagrees with them. Alternatively, one may turn to court as the courts "can test the constitutionality of a law" and set them aside if they contradict the Constitution. In "extreme situations" – that is, in situations such as *nødrett* or *nødverge* (i.e. when defending oneself, one's property, or other people and their property against crime or destruction) – the law may be circumvented. However, such lawbreaking is sanctioned by law and does not therefore constitute a crime. Legal insiders note that there are limited amounts of so-called sleeping laws (i.e. laws that are outdated and no longer applied) in Norway.[14] There is no need for people to abide by such laws. One legal insider claims that "civil disobedience" is essentially a form of lawbreaking:[15]

> N-LA-18: 'one must relate to the laws as they are. And then one should rather try to change them through the politicians or some other type of work if one disagrees [with them].' N-JU-10: 'the court is tasked with controlling the constitutionality of the laws. If we do not do this, nobody will.' N-PR-11: 'civil disobedience . . . is, in my view, completely undemocratic. Then [in such cases] one . . . places oneself above laws and rules given by *Stortinget* [the national parliament]. And the [legal] frame . . . is, in a way, what makes our society work.' N-PR-14: '*nødrett* and *nødverge* are embedded in the law: when certain situations arise you are allowed to do things which would otherwise be punishable, but that is not setting aside the law'.

English legal insiders – to an even greater extent than the Norwegian ones – caution against stepping outside the law. Elected representatives take care to explain that members of their profession are not above the law. Politicians and ordinary citizens are "equal before the law" and no politician should therefore "play God". Government officials note that stepping outside the law would be unacceptable for members of their profession. The "law provides adequate remedies" for any situation and attempts to go beyond the law would therefore reflect "badly on" them and their colleagues:

> E-ER-2: 'an elected representative has not got the authority to step outside the law'. E-GO-1: '[government officials should not step outside the law]. I think it reflects badly on them and on the people they represent if they do that'.

The views of the elected representatives and government officials are echoed by the legal professionals. Lawyers stress the need to "keep within the law". Members of their profession simply "cannot do anything illegal". Judges voice their apprehension about stepping outside the law in even stronger language than the lawyers. For them, doing so would be "contrary to the judicial oath". Not only would it be "completely" unacceptable, but it would also be a "very dangerous" and "very unwise"

[14] An example in this regard is Chapter 41 ('Provisions on misdemeanors in employment relations') of the 1902 General Civil Penal Code.

[15] In Norway civil disobedience is considered by many to be a legitimate means of protest when used to protect the environment – provided that those who engage in it accept punishment for breaking the law.

thing to do so as such behaviour would "undermine the [very] purpose of being a judge". Prosecutors, for their part, claim that "no circumstances [could] justify [such behaviour]". Finally, police officers "are bound by oath" not to step outside the law:

> E-LA-14: 'we should never bend [the law], tinker with it or do anything that's outside the letter of the law'. E-JU-10: 'it would be contrary to the judicial oath . . . it is very dangerous deliberately to disregard the written law'. E-JU-25: 'stepping outside the law . . . undermines the whole purpose of being a judge'. E-PR-14: 'the legal profession by its very nature is a profession bordered by, framed by and controlled by, the law'. E-PO-1: 'we are here to uphold the law'.

Polish legal insiders objecting to law evasion do so in fairly general language. However, some give normative reasons as to why the law should be obeyed. To start with the *normative* reasons, legal insiders note that there are "no . . . circumstances" that may justify lawbreaking in Poland. "Politicians should not evade" or "break" the law. Rather, they "create and should [therefore] uphold the law". Government officials must obey even "imperfect law". Lawyers "cannot evade" the law, either because "ethical rules do not allow it" or because "it is not possible in court". Prosecutors have "no possibility" to evade the law "even if this [would be] for the best". The Polish police, for their part, have "no opportunity" to break the law:

> P-ER-4: 'a Member of Parliament . . . is a person forming the law [and thus] in my opinion [he] can't evade the law'. P-GO-1: 'the law . . . is sometimes faulty, imperfect, imprecise; however, one should never go as far as to totally evade the law'. P-GO-13: 'in our situation it is not possible. We have to abide by the law and we do.' P-LA-13: 'I don't want to take the risk.' P-PR-13: 'when they bring me a suspect who pleads guilty but doesn't have a permanent place of residence it would be best to evade the law, to let him go, but I can't do that . . . according to the Legal Code he goes behind the bars.'

Legal insiders who use more *general language* to explain why members of their profession cannot engage in lawbreaking simply state that in democratic societies one "should respect the law". For instance, "MPs shape the law [and therefore] they must not evade it". The MPs' position before the law is "the same as [for] other citizens": they have "a duty" to abide by it. For government officials law abidance is "a duty based on the rule of law". Their work is "guided by regulations" and bending the law would simply "not be tolerated".

Lawyers, for their part, "have to" obey the law. They should never "flout" it as such behaviour would be "unacceptable". For judges it would be "completely improper" to step outside the law. Rather than doing so he or she "should cease to be a judge". For judges lawbreaking "is (simply) out of the question" as they "safeguard the law". They are therefore "obliged to apply the law":

> P-LA-2: 'a person of public trust should never evade the law'. P-PR-2: '[the prosecutor] is the guardian of law and order. People place confidence in him. That is why he has to stick to the letter of the law.' P-PO-17: '[the police] protect the law on account of their profession and the Police Act so any cases of violation of the law would not only be unethical but unfounded as well.'

Legal insiders in Bulgaria are also very much opposed to members of their profession breaking the law. Some of them simply note that *laws cannot be broken*, period. Others have *normative objections* to lawbreaking. Legal insiders who state that laws cannot be broken stress that doing so is simply "not an option". Lawyers, for instance, can "use all legal opportunities", but they cannot "act beyond the law". For judges it is simply "impossible" to violate the law:

> B-LA-7: 'the lawyer . . . has the right to interpret the law in favour of his client, but interpreting the law broadly or narrowly does not mean acting beyond the law.' B-JU-24: 'that's difficult . . . it will mean numerous sleepless nights and lifelong tortures.' B-PO-13: 'I cannot infringe the law because in my work I implement the law.'

As for normative objections, Bulgarian elected representatives argue that laws "should [definitely] not" be broken. Infringements of the law would be "unacceptable". Government officials are even more strongly opposed to breaking laws – and on moral grounds. As government officials they have signed a declaration confirming that they will abide by the law. They must therefore "work strictly within legal frames" and "always comply with the law". For government officials it will "never [be] acceptable" to break the laws and even the most "stupid laws" should be observed: B-ER-21: "it is unacceptable for us to act beyond the law." B-GO-5: "however stupid you think this law is you must abide by it, especially if you're a civil servant."

Almost all the statements made by the Bulgarian lawyers suggest that breaking laws is unacceptable. In their view members of their profession "must always abide by the law" and the "law prohibits lawyers from violating it". As legal professionals they and their colleagues "must observe the Bar Law and the Code of Conduct". Bulgarian judges, for their part, "should not allow themselves to go beyond the law". In their case "even actions beyond the law must be within the law". Being "the guardian[s] of the law", prosecutors can under "no circumstances" set the law aside. The police, for their part, "cannot infringe the law as [they] implement [it]". Whether good or bad, "[it] should be respected":

> B-LA-14: 'acting beyond the law is out of question . . . [lawyers] should apply the law and strictly observe its implementation.' B-JU-3: 'even acting beyond the law has to be within the frames of the law.' B-PR-23: 'under no circumstances can a prosecutor infringe the law . . . all citizens are equal before the law and regardless of whether the accused is an acquaintance.' B-PO-19: 'if a state institution that is engaged in implementing the law decides to ignore it, it means lawlessness to me.'

Ukrainian legal insiders either dismiss the possibility of acting beyond the law outright or justify their objection to such practice from a rule-of-law point of view.

To start with the *rule of law* arguments, legal insiders note that "the law is for everybody". As "everybody is equal before the law" they themselves have "to abide by [it]". Legal insiders are "obliged to act within the limits of the law". Those who dismiss the possibility of members of their profession stepping outside the law claim that this would be "inadmissible", "very dangerous" and "not what [they would] like to see". Some legal insiders even think it would be "impossible":

> U-ER-19: 'no citizen . . . should step outside the law. The law has to be executed, no matter whether it is good or bad. And by the deputy even more. He is a person who has been entrusted with powers by hundreds or thousands of people, he must be law-abiding. He has to fulfil his obligations as a deputy.' U-GO-3: 'it is forbidden to go beyond the law . . . whether a civil servant or not a civil servant.' U-JU-19: 'I cannot go beyond the frames of the law. The law exists to be fulfilled – including by me. I am a citizen like you. And the law extends to me as well.' U-ER-1: 'I think it is inadmissible for a deputy to step outside the law . . . deputies pass laws . . . if they will step outside laws, then who will obey them?'

More specifically, elected representatives "cannot go beyond the law". Government officials, for their part, are "strictly regulated" and "obliged" to implement the law – even if "imperfect". They have "no power to step outside the law".

Ukrainian lawyers make it very clear that their profession "cannot" step outside the law. Rather, they "should act within the law" and "work within the legal framework". Law-abidingness is perceived as a "duty". This being said, lawyers should "use the laws to the advantage of their client". Judges, for their part, note that "the court must apply the rules", "act strictly within the law", or "follow the letter of the law" – in the sense that their "decisions [should be] guided by law". Prosecutors also make it clear that their profession is bound by law: as prosecutors "supervise the law" and its "implementation", they have "no right to depart from the letter of the law". Doing so would "not be acceptable"; "as jurists they must follow the [Ukrainian] Constitution".

Finally, the police note that the members of their profession "have no authority" to act beyond the law, as they are effectively "the guardian of the law". Not only would it be "a crime" for them not to observe the law – but it would also promote "lawlessness". As representatives of the country's executive, the police "must act [in accordance with] the law":

> U-GO-13: 'state officials have . . . no right to step outside the law'. U-LA-4: 'the lawyer mustn't step outside the law. But in reality he does that. Maybe it is reasonable in cases where he needs to win the lawsuit'. U-JU-29: 'the judge cannot step outside the law.' U-PR-28: 'the office of the public prosecutor is a supervising body which . . . observes the implementation of laws . . . it would be inappropriate [for them to step outside the law]'. U-PO-18: 'a policeman has no authority to go beyond the framework of the law . . . he guards the law.'

Conclusions

In the introduction to this chapter we suggested that members of the public across Europe might have similar views on what the role of law in society should be – given that their views on democracy are similar and given that the rule of law is an important component of democracy. But we also listed some factors that might differently affect the attitudes of East and West Europeans towards the role of law.

Findings presented in this chapter show that East and West Europeans have similar attitudes towards the role of law in society: both equal law with justice. Their legal culture is *democratic* in the sense that they think courts should control the legality of laws passed by Parliament and that Parliament should not have the right to force courts to comply if they refuse to apply a law.

But it is also *anti-democratic* in that the majority in all five countries think it is acceptable for government to step outside the law to combat corruption, organised crime and the threat of terrorism (even though ideally, they prefer to introduce new and tougher laws to fight terrorism rather than setting the law aside). And it is *authoritarian* in that for the average citizen the law should be strict: there should be stricter implementation and enforcement of the law, more legal controls and harsher penalties for lawbreakers.

By contrast, legal insiders in both Western and Eastern Europe think it is acceptable for members of their professions to use discretion – but a large majority are against stepping outside the law. In other words, members of the public think it is acceptable for legal insiders to step outside the law to fight those elements in society that pose a threat to it, whereas the legal insiders themselves take a more principled approach against such behaviour. However, their principled approach does not always translate into action: there is plenty of evidence that legal insiders – particularly those in Eastern Europe – do step outside the law (see, e.g. Miller et al. 2001; Rechberger 2009; Popova 2012).

Again there are almost no differences between East and West Europeans in terms of attitudes. Even though the attitudes of legal insiders and legal outsiders differ, legal outsiders across Europe share the same attitudes. By contrast, perceptions of the current role of law in society differ: East Europeans to a greater extent than West Europeans advocate more detailed laws, and they are also more favourable to courts strictly applying the letter of the law. Their perceptions are very much a reaction to *legal nihilism* – both within the judiciary and amongst members of the public who think they can buy their way to justice.

4

Law in action

Introduction: "exit", "voice", "loyalty"

In Chapters 2 and 3 we explored people's understandings of what law is, upon what elements it should be based, the manner in which it is evolving, and what its role should be. This chapter explores 'law in action' – that is, how the executive and the judiciary apply the law; how citizens themselves relate to law and how they think others should relate to it; and whether it is sometimes better to solve disputes without turning to law. Whereas Chapter 3 explored 'attitudes' (principles), in this chapter we look primarily at 'practice'.

Ewick and Silbey (1998) investigate the meaning of *legality* in the everyday lives of Americans. They explore the different ways in which ordinary people use and think about the law: sometimes they find themselves standing 'before the law'. On other occasions they move 'with the law', that is, they *play* the law to achieve the best possible outcome for themselves. But occasionally, they go 'against the law' by evading it (ibid., pp. 47–9).

Our data differ from those of Ewick and Silbey: we did not ask our respondents detailed questions about their personal experiences with the law, law enforcement or courts. Rather than applying their theoretical framework to our data on law in action, we therefore apply the phrase 'Exit, Voice and Loyalty', which is Hirschman's (1970), and which was originally applied to behaviour within firms and organisations. But in this chapter we apply it to law, and in particular to public attitudes towards finding some alternative to state law (= "Exit"); protesting against "bad" law (= "Voice"); and taking action to help enforce the law, or simply abiding by the law (= "Loyalty").

We first explore the views of the legal outsiders on "Exit, Voice, and Loyalty", before applying the phrase to the views of the legal insiders.

Law in practice: the legal outsiders' perspective

In Chapters 2 and 3 we investigated public attitudes towards law and the role of law. Such attitudes constitute the first broad aspect of popular legal culture. Public perceptions of "really existing law", "law in action" or the "law in practice" constitute its second broad aspect. In general cross-national differences in perceptions of law in action are far greater than cross-national differences in principles and abstract attitudes to law: perceptions vary much more than principles.

This part of the chapter looks at public perceptions of law in action under three main headings: general perceptions of "law in action", reasons for turning/not turning to court, and "exit", "voice" and "loyalty". We investigate public perceptions of law-abidingness in depth in Chapter 5.

General perceptions of law in action

Public perceptions that "the government and people respect the law and generally obey it more than in the rest of Europe" range down steadily from a peak of 93 per cent in Norway to around 11 per cent in Bulgaria and Ukraine. Conversely, public perceptions that "the level of crime and corruption in this country is greater than the average across Europe" range down from a peak of around 92 per cent in Bulgaria and Ukraine to just 10 per cent in Norway – though in England the public is evenly divided on whether crime and corruption are any greater or less than in the rest of Europe (Table 4.1).

Table 4.1 *Law-abidingness, crime and corruption across Europe: the legal outsiders' perspective*

	Norway (%)	England (%)	Poland (%)	Bulgaria (%)	Ukraine (%)
Q126: Government and people respect law more (v. less) than in the rest of Europe	93	58	28	12	10
Q62: Crime and corruption greater here than European average (v. less)	10	50	79	92	91

Table 4.2 *Legal fairness and state power: the legal outsiders' perspective*

	Norway (%)	England (%)	Poland (%)	Bulgaria (%)	Ukraine (%)
Q14: Law is unfair (v. fair)	10	28	65	48	79
Q16: Law = power of state v. people	17	42	50	61	74

The country pattern for Q126 and Q62 matches these countries' rankings in the 2010 World Bank's Rule of Law Index, GDP (PPP) per capita size, and their scores in Transparency International's 2013 Corruption Perception Index (CPI):[1] the more rule of law a country has and the higher its GDP (PPP) per capita, the less corruption it has, the more likely people are to think that the government and people in their country respect the law more than in the rest of Europe, and the less likely they are to think that crime and corruption in their country are greater than the European average.

Much more importantly perhaps, public perceptions that the law itself is "unfair" and that it merely reflects "the power of the state to control people" rather than reflecting "generally recognised moral values", range from a peak in Ukraine (79 per cent unfair, 74 per cent state control) down to a minimum in Norway (10 per cent unfair, 17 per cent state control). Once again, the English take a mid-position, much more critical of the law than Norwegians but less critical than any of the East Europeans (Table 4.2).

Three factors help explain the differences between Norway and England: first, Norway's population is smaller than that of England. Second, the distance between rulers and ruled has traditionally not been great in Norway. Third, and more importantly, there have been relatively few instances of misconduct involving Norwegian MPs. In such instances, the political parties have quickly forced the MPs to step down and face

[1] The CPI ranks countries by using a scale where 100 is the least corrupt and 1 is the most corrupt. In 2013 Norway was ranked 5th (score: 86), the United Kingdom was ranked 14th (score: 76), Poland was ranked 38th (score: 60), Bulgaria was ranked 77th (score: 41), and Ukraine was ranked 144th (score: 25), http://cpi.transparency.org/cpi2013/results/ accessed on 9 March 2014.

Table 4.3 *Expectations of fair treatment by officials: the legal outsiders' perspective*

	Norway (%)	England (%)	Poland (%)	Bulgaria (%)	Ukraine (%)
Q12: Expect fair treatment by officials?					
Yes	80	71	52	35	18
No	20	29	45	44	56
Only by connections or bribes	0	0	3	21	26

the legal consequences of their action. Some of them have also had to leave the political party they represent.

By contrast, British MPs have been involved in numerous scandals, more recently the parliamentary expenses scandal (2010) and the cash for influence scandal (2010). As we will see in Chapter 8, the latter have negatively affected public perceptions of British politicians. Scandals involving politicians may also have negatively affected public perceptions of the law passed by such MPs.

The numbers who would expect "fair treatment by officials" range steadily down from 80 per cent in Norway and 71 per cent in England to a mere 18 per cent in Ukraine – though another 26 per cent in Ukraine, along with 21 per cent in Bulgaria, volunteered the comment (without being asked) that they could get "fair treatment" but only by using "connections or bribes" (interviewers did not offer that answer, but were briefed to record it if the interviewee volunteered it spontaneously) (Table 4.3). Our findings thus lend support to East and West Europeans having different understandings of the term "fair".

There is a sharp gradient from Norway (92 per cent), though only 66 per cent in England, down to Ukraine (29 per cent) in the numbers who feel that on balance the law "generally helps people like myself" rather than "making problems for people like myself". A majority everywhere – though much less in Ukraine than elsewhere – feel that "stricter enforcement" of the law would "help" them rather than "cause more problems". In every country except Ukraine, close to 85 per cent of the public feel that "stricter enforcement" would help (Table 4.4). But that

Table 4.4 *Law and law enforcement: the legal outsiders' perspective*

	Norway (%)	England (%)	Poland (%)	Bulgaria (%)	Ukraine (%)
Q9: Law helps (v. causing problems)	92	66	50	56	29
Q13: Stricter enforcement would help (v. cause more problems)	87	83	84	87	59

number sinks to 59 per cent in Ukraine – a view that is consistent with the outstandingly large numbers of Ukrainians who report that they do not expect fair treatment by officials. They therefore do not find a combination of so-called stricter enforcement by "unfair officials" attractive.

The public believes the law is now much better known in Norway but not in England and Poland, and much less well known after all the changes in Bulgaria and Ukraine.

In Norway, and – though to a lesser extent – in England and Poland, the public feels that people are more willing "to go to court" now than they were in the past. In Bulgaria they are divided and in Ukraine the public perception is that people are now less willing to go to court.

Norwegians and Brits are generally better off nowadays than they were 10 to 15 years ago. They are therefore in a better position to pay court fees and lawyers' fees. Added to this, *judicialisation* has expanded the number and types of issues handled by lawyers. Judicial reforms 'have moved some way to reducing the costs, complexity, and inaccessibility of the English justice system' (Susskind 2010, p. 185). All these factors help explain why a majority of the citizens in Norway and England think people are *more willing* to go to court now than they were in the past.

By contrast, legal academics claim that people are *less willing* to turn to court now than they used to be – and that they prefer to solve their problems by means of alternative dispute resolution (ADR). Susskind (2010, p. 185), for instance, claims that 'far fewer cases are pursued through the courts (in England today) than in March 1994'. Modéer (2008, p. 297) notes that 'the conflict-solving models have turned increasingly from public to private with arbitration and later also mediation as alternative dispute resolutions. Within private law this universal change has also affected the number of cases brought to the public courts.

The number of civil cases brought to the public courts (in Scandinavia) has diminished dramatically'.

Official statistics for both countries partly confirm the latter observations for the UK, but not for Norway. During the first half of 2014 the number of civil cases brought before Norwegian courts rose by 6 per cent compared to the first half of 2013. The number of cases brought before the courts of appeal rose by 10 per cent.[2] In the UK the number of hearings and trials in the first quarter of 2014 rose by 13 per cent over the previous quarter. However, the number of family cases dropped by 6 per cent and the number of private law disputes where both parties are represented in court dropped by 50 per cent (Ministry of Justice 2014, p. 2).

In Eastern Europe the tasks addressed by courts have greatly increased following the collapse of Communism. The Polish economy has done very well since the collapse of Communism. Added to this, the country has introduced extensive – and effective – judicial reform. Poles therefore appear to be more willing "to go to court" now than they were in the past. Official statistics from Poland, for instance, show that the number of new cases at Polish ordinary courts increased by 246 per cent between 1990 and 2001 (Kühn 2010, p. 180). Kühn (ibid.) believes that 'the insufficient quality of the post-communist judiciary has kept this number (i.e. the number of court proceedings) lower than it would otherwise have been'.

Bulgarian courts are less efficient than the Polish ones and they are less trusted. In 2011, the Agency for Social Analysis (ASA Bulgaria) announced that 85 per cent of the population believes that the courts protect the rich and powerful, but that they do not protect ordinary citizens (*Novinite*, 2011, cited in Littlehale 2012, p. 40). Bulgarians also believe that the courts are corrupt (ibid., p. 40). As we will see in Chapter 6 courts in Ukraine are amongst the least trusted and most corrupted institutions in the country (KIIS 2006).

As for law enforcement, the public in all five countries believe that the law is now less respected or less strictly implemented and enforced than in the past. The editor of *The Daily Mail,* Paul Dacre, claims that whilst 'the public (in the UK) still have huge faith in the independence and integrity and incorruptibility of the British judiciary (they are becoming)

[2] Terje Helsingeng, 'Vi krangler som aldri før' [We quarrel as never before], *VG,* 28 August 2014, www.vg.no/nyheter/innenriks/vi-krangler-som-aldri-foer/a/23281916/ accessed on 28 August 2014.

Table 4.5 *Law, law-abidingness, law enforcement, crime, bribery and corruption: the legal outsiders' perspective*

	Norway (%)	England (%)	Poland (%)	Bulgaria (%)	Ukraine (%)
Q58: Now better known (v. less)	67	46	51	24	28
Q40A: People more willing to go to court now (v. less)	87	66	67	48	35
Q59: Now more respected (v. less)	21	11	35	21	11
Q57: Now more strictly implemented and enforced (v. less)	40	41	39	26	19
Q60: Crime increasing (v. decreasing)	97	83	78	91	94
Q61: Bribery and corruption increasing (v. decreasing)	87	68	76	93	96

slightly confused (because they see) political judgements being made by judges which fly in the face of what they perceive as national interests (and) an increasing lenient judiciary, handing down lesser and lesser sentences' (House of Lords 2007, p. 2). His assessment is in line with findings presented in this book: across Europe the general public advocates harsher punishment for lawbreaking.

By huge margins the public everywhere feels (rightly or wrongly) that crime, bribery and corruption are increasing rather than decreasing (Table 4.5).

Stricter Enforcement? There is a widespread public support for stricter enforcement of the laws. In every country a majority feels that stricter enforcement of the laws would 'help people like themselves'. In Norway, England, Poland and Bulgaria close to around 85 per cent say it would help them.

But there is much more scepticism in Ukraine, where only 60 per cent hold this view, whereas 40 per cent think it would 'cause more problems for people like themselves'. Even in Ukraine that is only a minority who would resent stricter enforcement of the laws – presumably as stricter law enforcement would affect ordinary citizens positively and the rich and

Table 4.6 *Stricter law enforcement: the legal outsiders' perspective*

	Norway (%)	England (%)	Poland (%)	Bulgaria (%)	Ukraine (%)
PQ13: In general, would stricter enforcement in [this country]:					
help people like yourself?	87	83	84	87	60
cause more problems for people like yourself?	13	17	16	13	40

powerful negatively. But it is a very big minority, when compared to around 15 per cent in all of the other countries (Table 4.6).

The reasons that people think stricter laws would help them are likely to vary by country. In Eastern Europe laws tend to be applied differently to different people – by government officials as well as prosecutors, judges and the police. Citizens who favour stricter law enforcement may do so on the grounds that this would facilitate more equal treatment before the law. Those opposing stricter law enforcement, on the other hand, might do so on the grounds that the law is too complex and thus not easily enforceable. Or because it is easier for people to get by when applying informal, rather than formal, law. Stricter enforcement of the law would negatively affect those seeking to evade formal law – including poor people who are compelled to break the law due to poverty. And it would negatively affect those who are unfamiliar with the law – either because access to information is difficult or because they have a preference for informal, rather than formal, law.

Reasons for turning/not turning to court

Why do ordinary people go to court? Is it 'generally to defend their personal rights, to gain some personal advantage, or just because they feel it is the best way to resolve a dispute?' Very few respondents anywhere think that ordinary people try to use the law for personal advantage (Table 4.7). A majority feel it is to defend their rights – though the English focus on 'resolving a dispute' rather than 'asserting their rights'.

Although mediation has become very popular in recent years, it is essentially focused on reaching agreements between two parties rather than on the two parties defending their rights. Yet the latter is something

Table 4.7 *Reasons that people go to court: the legal outsiders' perspective*

		Norway (%)	England (%)	Poland (%)	Bulgaria (%)	Ukraine (%)
Q34: Ordinary people go to court:						
	to defend rights	56	35	52	60	71
	as best way to resolve dispute	32	52	37	31	22
	to gain advantage	12	13	12	10	7

Note: Due to rounding of decimals, percentages do not always add up to 100%.

one can do only through the courts. This, in turn, explains why a majority in all countries except England believe that ordinary people go to court to defend their rights. They might feel compelled to turn to the courts if an injustice has been committed against them, whereas disputes of lesser importance might be better handled outside the court – for instance, through various ADR mechanisms. The advantage of turning to court is that court decisions are enforceable whereas the decisions reached through mediation require voluntary compliance.

When presented with a list of six reasons – all drawn from the FG discussions – on why people might avoid going to court and asked: "what do you feel is the most important reason why people in this country do *not* take problems or disputes to court?", by far the most frequent explanation chosen by survey respondents is that it is "slow, difficult and expensive" – cited by 90 per cent in Norway and 79 per cent in England. That explanation is the most frequent explanation in every country – though much less frequent in Poland (61 per cent), Bulgaria (56 per cent) and Ukraine (only 38 per cent)[3] than in Norway or England (Table 4.8).

That courts are far away or that legal disputes damage human relationships are seldom cited anywhere as important reasons for avoiding

[3] A poll conducted by KIIS on behalf of USAID, MSI and the Millennium Challenge Corporation in 2009 show that high costs of litigation and lawyers worry Ukrainians much less than, for instance, court inefficiency. Only 18 per cent of those polled perceived costs as one of the main problems in the judicial system (United States Agency for International Development [USAID], Management Systems International [MSI], Millennium Challenge Corporation, 2009, p. 29 – cited in Vasylyev 2013, p. 14).

Table 4.8 *Reasons that people avoid the courts: the legal outsiders' perspective*

	Norway (%)	England (%)	Poland (%)	Bulgaria (%)	Ukraine (%)
Q36A: Most important reason why people do not take problems to court					
Not insider oriented					
slow, difficult, expensive	90	79	61	56	38
damages human relationships	6	7	5	5	4
nearest court far away	1	1	4	2	4
Insider oriented					
court judgements not enforced	2	9	17	11	21
courts favour rich and powerful	1	3	11	17	20
judges and court officials seek bribes	0	1	2	10	13

Note: Due to rounding of decimals, percentages do not always add up to 100%.

courts. None of these are based on perceptions of legal insiders, however, but on the machinery of justice and its inevitable confrontational nature.

But in Ukraine, sometimes together with Poland and/or Bulgaria, significantly large numbers cite "court judgements not being enforced" (21 per cent in Ukraine, 17 per cent in Poland); "courts favouring the rich and powerful" (20 per cent in Ukraine, 17 per cent in Bulgaria); and "judges and court officials seeking bribes"(13 per cent in Ukraine, 10 per cent in Bulgaria) – as reasons why the public avoids courts.

These reasons concern the rule of law and court efficiency. The East European countries included in our study receive lower scores than Norway and the UK on the Word Bank's 2010 Rule of Law Index. Besides, their GDP (PPP) per capita are lower – which, in turn, puts greater pressure on public funds. Anderson, Bernstein and Gray (2005, p. 50) note that 'more advanced reformers tend to have higher per capita incomes and are likely to be able to provide greater capacity in the judiciary in terms of staff quality and training, buildings and other physical capital, and operating budgets'. They also note that 'although significant progress has been made in the judiciary across Eastern Europe, much remains to be done to increase the capacity of both judges and their staff, reduce case backlogs and increase court efficiency, develop the proper incentives and deterrence to address both the perception and the reality of corruption in the region's judiciaries, and promote greater access to courts' (ibid., p. 57). Judiciaries in Eastern Europe are still struggling with such problems to greater or lesser extents.

"Exit", "voice", "loyalty"

Earlier we – amongst other issues – have looked at why people turn to court. We will now turn our attention to the manner in which people deal with the law. Do they take a proactive or a passive approach to law? Do they play the law (Ewick and Silbey 1998, p. 48) by speaking up against "bad" law ("Voice")? Do they evade or ignore the law ("Exit")? Or do they abide by the law or take action to help enforce it ("Loyalty")? What are their views on what people should do if they are not happy with the law? The answers to these questions are important as they provide an indication as to how law-abiding and democratic national legal cultures are. As such they say something about the quality of democracy across Europe.

"Exit"

We sought public attitudes towards "avoiding going to court and instead asking some respected local person to act as a mediator to settle the dispute". We cited five potential mediators. In descending order of popularity, there are majorities who think it is "often or sometimes better" to approach "a local lawyer or professional mediator" (78 per cent); "family and friends" (68 per cent); "a local policeman" (61 per cent); or "a community leader, councillor or mayor"(57 per cent). But only a small minority thinks it is "often or sometimes better" to approach "a local religious leader" (31 per cent) for mediation.

Surprisingly perhaps, alternatives to courts are generally most popular in England (68 per cent) and Norway (64 per cent) – where, as we shall see in Chapter 6, perceptions of courts are relatively positive. Clearly the publics in England and Norway regard courts as a good option to dispense justice – yet not necessarily the best option to settle disputes. There may be several reasons for this – including the availability and cost of ADR. Conversely, alternatives to courts are somewhat less popular in Poland (58 per cent), Bulgaria (54 per cent) and Ukraine (51 per cent) – where public perceptions of courts are more negative.

Mediation by local lawyers, professional mediators, local police and local politicians is generally more popular in England and Norway than it is elsewhere. Conversely, mediation by family and friends – with no professional links to the law or the state – is more popular in Poland, Bulgaria and Ukraine. The latter are low-trust societies – that is, societies in which state institutions are not much trusted. Mediation by religious leaders is most popular in secular England and more religious Poland – underlining once again the distinction between personal religiosity and respect for the clergy (Table 4.9).

As regards mediation by religious leaders, findings for England probably also to some extent reflect the proactive, and sometimes also high-profile, approach. The Church of England (Patterson and McKay 2012), the Muslim shari'a courts (Griffith-Jones 2013) and the Jewish beth din (The Centre for Social Cohesion 2009) have engaged in dispute resolution. Information about the kind of mediation and arbitration they can provide is readily available through the internet.

On a general question about whether people "should rely more on these informal methods of mediation, or more on the law and courts", a large majority in England back more use of informal methods, whereas Norwegians are evenly divided on this issue, and a majority in Poland,

Table 4.9 *Alternatives to court: the legal outsiders' perspective*

	Norway (%)	England (%)	Poland (%)	Bulgaria (%)	Ukraine (%)
Q38: Often or sometimes better (v. seldom or never) to take dispute to:					
Q38C: local lawyer or professional mediator	92	86	74	69	71
Q38E: family or friends	62	66	71	71	69
Q38D: local police	73	72	54	60	45
Q38A: community leader, councillor or mayor	66	72	54	52	42
Q38B: local religious leader	28	43	35	19	28
mean	*64*	*68*	*58*	*54*	*51*

Table 4.10 *Informal methods of mediation: the legal outsiders' perspective*

	Norway (%)	England (%)	Poland (%)	Bulgaria (%)	Ukraine (%)
Q39: People should rely more on these informal methods of mediation (v. more on law and courts)	48	73	43	42	31

Bulgaria and especially in Ukraine display a lack of trust in informal methods and opt for more use of the law and courts (Table 4.10).

There are probably several reasons why support for informal methods of mediation is considerably higher in England than elsewhere. The most apparent reason seems to be that free-of-charge mediation is available to Brits for small-sum claims, whilst reasonable mediation is available for medium- and large-sum claims (Slapper and Kelly 2011, pp. 545–9). Added to this, there is a wide range of informal mediation mechanisms in England, such as professional mediators, lawyers, barristers, arbitrators, religious mediators and the like.

Flexibility and informality require a generally high degree of interpersonal trust between strangers, which is lacking in the former communist countries. Chavdarova (2007, p. 285) notes that 'the Bulgarian historical tradition is marked by a low level of impersonal trust and a higher level of trust in interpersonal and inter-organisational relations'. Although such trust extends to the friends, acquaintances and networks people are themselves involved in, there is considerable distrust towards those one does not personally know. The situation is very similar in Ukraine. The problem then is that Bulgarians and Ukrainians are too close to the people they trust (which is likely to make them biased if trying to mediate in disputes), and too distrustful of the people they do not know (which makes these less suited to act as go-betweens).

It may seem odd that the public in countries where (as we shall see) they are most critical of the courts appear, at the same time, to be the least positive of alternatives to courts. But in countries where the public is most critical of courts and judges, they are also most critical of lawyers, police and politicians (who were cited as potential mediators).

"Voice"

A culture of obedience to laws irrespective of their content is a culture of autocracy; a culture of protest, short of rebellion, is the mark of a democratic culture. In a situation where Parliament passed a law that 'some people felt was unnecessarily complicated and troublesome to obey', respondents were asked "what should these people do – (i) obey the law?; (ii) ignore or evade the law?; (iii) offer a gift or bribe to officials or the police, so that they do not enforce the law?; or (iv) protest against the law?

Second, they were asked a similar question in the situation where "some people felt the law was really unfair and unjust"; what should these people do? And then a third version of the question was asked in the situation where not just 'some people' but "a large majority of people" in the country really felt the law was unfair and unjust; what should these people do?

On "complicated or troublesome" laws, and on laws that "some people feel [are] unfair", public support for obedience to the law is highest in Bulgaria and Ukraine, and lowest in Norway and England. Conversely, support for "protest" – what Hirschman called "Voice" – is greatest in Norway and England. One likely reason is that civil society is stronger in these countries than in Eastern Europe (Howard 2003). Acts of protest are more likely to be successful in societies with strong rather than weak civil societies. The public in Western Europe has a longer tradition than people in Eastern Europe of voicing their protest with laws with which they are unhappy.

On merely 'troublesome' laws, an average of 60 per cent in Norway and England, but only 33 per cent on an average in Bulgaria and Ukraine, go further and advocate "protest" (Table 4.11). This is most likely because protesting requires effort and time – and time is a scarce commodity for people in post-communist states. It is not uncommon for people to have more than one job to make ends meet. The large majority put up with the discomforts of everyday life.

On laws that "some people feel [are] unfair", an average of 72 per cent in Norway and England, but only 51 per cent in Bulgaria and Ukraine advocate "protest" (Table 4.11).

These findings match findings from the FG discussions. Though quite a few FG participants think such laws should be obeyed – mostly to avoid the cost of breaking the law – the majority recommends some kind of protest. In most cases, the forms of protest they suggest are legal.

Norwegian FG participants mostly recommend that protesters generate publicity about their view – either through the media or the social media or by petitions, letter writing, meetings or protest letters to the head of the county (*fylkesmannen*). Other, more serious, measures include demonstrations, political participation and strikes, but also civil disobedience, which is fairly socially acceptable. FG participants think the public can:

> N5-Muslims-5: 'write in the newspaper'. N11-Klepp-4: '[start] a protest group on Facebook'. N1-Oslo-8: 'use a blog.' N11-Klepp-7: 'write to the Head of the County'. N3-Muslims-5: 'collect signatures'. N1-Oslo-3: 'demonstrate outside *Stortinget* [the Parliament]', N2-Oslo-1: '[engage in] civil disobedience. We had the Alta campaign[4] many years ago.' N2-Oslo-9: 'civil disobedience is a partially accepted reaction to make one's view clear.'

Online petitions and making contact with MPs or local councillors are popular means of protest amongst English FG participants. They

4 The FG participant refers to a campaign in the late 1970s to early 1980s concerning the decision to construct a power station by the Alta River in Finnmark (Northern Norway). Global Non-Violent Action Base, 'Saami and Norwegians protest construction of Alta Dam, Norway, 1979–81', http://nvdatabase.swarthmore.edu/content/saami-and-norwegians-protest-construction-alta-dam-norway-1979-1981 accessed on 10 September 2014.

Table 4.11 *Dealing with law: the legal outsiders' perspective*

	Norway (%)	England (%)	Poland (%)	Bulgaria (%)	Ukraine (%)
Q46: If some felt law was complicated and troublesome:					
obey	34	40	45	55	47
ignore/evade	2	3	7	14	11
offer bribe	0	1	2	3	6
protest	64	56	47	29	36
Q47: If some felt law was unfair and unjust:					
obey	29	24	30	36	33
ignore/evade	2	2	7	16	9
offer bribe	0	0	2	2	4
protest	69	74	62	47	54
Q48: If a large majority felt law was unfair and unjust:					
obey	13	16	20	17	14
ignore/evade	3	3	6	10	6
offer bribe	0	0	1	2	4
protest	84	80	73	70	76

Note: Due to rounding of decimals, percentages do not always add up to 100%.

suggest that people turn to the media, appeal to the European Court of Human Rights (ECtHR), organise demonstrations or go on strike. Examples of public protest include the demonstrations against the poll tax in the early 1990s, the protests against British intervention in Iraq and the petrol strikes (2000, 2005 and 2007). Yet some FG participants are convinced that protesting will not necessarily have an impact:

> E2-London-5: 'if you disagree with a small law you can take it to the European Court [of Human Rights]'. E3-Bristol-8: 'they have online petitions on the Downing Street website that you can go onto ... you can sign all these petitions but unless the media is pushing it out there and it's on TV 24/7, nothing really happens. I don't think petitions work.' E9-Leeds-Muslims-2: '[they can form] pressure groups.' E7-Village-Yorkshire-2: 'I should imagine, see their MP.' E4-Bath-6: 'when Margaret Thatcher brought in the Poll Tax, millions marched on Parliament in London and eventually the law got scrapped'. E9-Leeds-Muslims-4: '[during the petrol strikes] everyone ... stopped buying petrol and the government just ... did a U-turn.' E1-London-1: 'a million people took to the streets and said "don't go to Iraq!" And what did our government do? Nothing'.

FG participants in Poland mostly suggest that people could turn to court (the Constitutional Court, the ECtHR) or sign petitions. Alternatively, they could approach the ombudsman, demonstrate or turn to the media. There is some resignation amongst Polish FG participants with regard to whether such protest would be successful:

> P5-Mierzecice-4: 'they may take it to the Constitutional Court or to other institutions. Citizens do have some rights, they can take action.' P11-Warsaw-Muslims-5: 'maybe demonstrate ... go to the Supreme Court, the Constitutional Court.' P2-Warsaw-3: 'one collects an x number of signatures, say, 100,000'. P10-Białystok-Polish Tatars-3: 'they can share their views on that law with the Ombudsman'. P2-Warsaw-4: '[they should] make it known somehow. How? In writing, in the media ... to make sure that [the government] sees the light'. P9-Warsaw-Muslims-2: 'although [Poland is] a democratic state there's really not much one can do. We can protest in the streets, but ...'.

FG participants in Bulgaria suggest that people could turn to the courts, MPs or the media. Alternatively, they could organise petitions, demonstrations or go on strike. Use of the ombudsman might also be a possibility, as might be engaging in civil society. However, the latter two options are mentioned only by two FG participants. Very few FG participants recommend more radical measures:

B7-Opanetz-4: 'collecting signatures is the way.' B2-Sofia-2: '[they should] attack [the law] in every possible way . . . if they [simply] file a complaint, who will learn about it? Publicity is necessary in order to secure support . . . when this becomes the cause of many people, changes may occur.' B1-Sofia-1: 'you speak with your MP'. B5-Aksakovo-1: 'there is still no mechanism in Bulgaria for civil society to exert pressure [on the authorities] and change the law. In the worst cases people go on strike and reach some agreement [that way].' B3-Varna-6: 'if it is an absolutely unjust law that is against the interests of the whole nation, then [they could] organise rallies in the centre of Sofia and maybe it will have an effect.' B4-Topoli-5: '[they should] organise a civil mutiny'.

FG participants in Ukraine suggest that discontented citizens could organise petitions in support of a referendum, approach Parliament or government, turn to court (Constitutional Court, ECtHR), organise demonstrations, go on strike or engage in civil disobedience. The Crimean Tatars, for their part, think it might be helpful to turn to representatives of the international community for support:

U1-Kiev-4: '[they could] gather millions of signatures'. U7-Chuguev-4: 'the Supreme Court can challenge the decision of the *Verkhovna Rada* [the Ukrainian Parliament].' U7-Chuguev-2: 'the Court of Arbitration'. U7-Chuguev-4: 'there's the Court of Cassation, the Supreme Court.' U7-Chuguev-7: 'one can . . . try to get to the truth in the European Court [of Human Rights]'. U19-Bahchysaray-7: 'I addressed Yuly Borisovich Kudin, a Member of the Ukrainian Parliament, and he made an amendment in the *Verkhovna Rada* (Ukrainian Parliament) and the law was corrected.' U23-Older Male Crimean Tatars-3: '[turn to] international organisations'. U3-Donetsk-6: 'you have to strike but people here are afraid to do that'. U6-Kharkiv-4: 'civil disobedience'. U11-Zubra-8: 'hunger strikes'.

But in a situation where "a large majority feels that the law is unfair" public support for protest is much greater and the gap between attitudes in East and West is much smaller: an average of 82 per cent in Norway and England now advocate "protest", but on average so do 73 per cent in Poland, Bulgaria and Ukraine. This seems to indicate a greater element of individuality in the Norwegian and English propensity to protest. Bulgarians and Ukrainians need much more psychological reinforcement from a sense of common support before they commit to protest – but when they do, they commit in large numbers (Table 4.11): in Bulgaria large nationwide demonstrations forced the Borisov government to step down in 2013, while in Ukraine large-scale protest culminated in the president fleeing the country, Russian annexation of the Crimea and civil war in 2014.

Table 4.12 *Dealing with religious law: the legal outsiders' perspective*

	Norway (%)	England (%)	Poland (%)	Bulgaria (%)	Ukraine (%)
Q50: If religious leaders persuade Parliament to pass law, requiring everyone to obey religious law, should *non-religious* people:					
obey law	13	17	20	34	40
protest	73	48	25	40	28
obey own conscience	13	34	54	22	28
leave country	1	1	1	3	3

Note: Due to rounding of decimals, percentages do not always add up to 100%.

As noted earlier, there is considerable public support for "religious people" to obey religious leaders or their own conscience when "religious leaders oppose a law". But what should "non-religious people" do in the reverse situation, where religious leaders with the ear of government "persuade Parliament to pass a law that requires everyone to obey one of the principles of their religion"? It is easy to think of examples from banning shop-opening or sports activities on Sundays, to restricting abortion (though no particular examples were offered at this point in the interview).

On an average, only 15 per cent of the general public in Norway and England, rising steadily to an average of only 37 per cent in Bulgaria and Ukraine, advocates simple obedience to a law passed at the behest of some religious leaders. In Norway 73 per cent advocates protest, but elsewhere the weight of opposition is more divided between "protest" and "obeying your own conscience" (Table 4.12).

"Loyalty"

Hirschman's concept of "Loyalty" is close to passive conformism, but here we conceptualise it in a more active role. Should members of the public participate in the law by taking their disputes to law? Or by helping to enforce the law? Overall, only a minority – though a very large one – feels that "ordinary people should take their problems or disputes

Table 4.13 *Whether people should turn to court more often: the legal outsiders' perspective*

	Norway (%)	England (%)	Poland (%)	Bulgaria (%)	Ukraine (%)
Q35: Ordinary people should take problems to court more often (v. less)	30	41	42	47	53

to court more often". Support for more litigation is particularly low in Norway (30 per cent), where the authorities encourage state-funded alternatives to court, but rises steadily from 41 per cent in England to 53 per cent in Ukraine (Table 4.13). Even though their trust in courts and judges is limited many people in Ukraine view the courts as the only means to solving conflicts – given that courts have the power to enforce their decisions.

There is clear evidence of greater support for citizen participation in law enforcement. On an average only 31 per cent would "leave it to the police". The numbers who would "leave it to the police" are fairly uniform across all countries – with the exception of England, where very few (only 21 per cent) would do so.

Overall, 49 per cent say "ordinary people should help enforce the law by reporting lawbreakers to the authorities" – though significantly less in the former communist countries (averaging 42 per cent) compared to Norway and England (average 60 per cent), probably reflecting negative feelings about the practice of 'informing' the authorities under Communism.

On the other hand, there is greater public support in the former communist countries for "helping to enforce the law by personally 'taking action' against lawbreakers" (Table 4.14). The main reason is probably that the police are viewed as inefficient, unhelpful or even corrupt. But it is also possible that the legacy of the voluntary people's squads (*dobrovol'nie narodnie druzhiny*) has something to do with it.[5] These groups were tasked with enforcing public order in their local neighbourhoods.

[5] In the Soviet Union it was common for people to take part in maintaining public order in their local communities through such officially sanctioned watch groups as *druzhiny*. They recruited people from the *Komsomol* (the Communist Party Youth Organisation), student bodies, trade unions and work or residence groups (Friedgut 1979, p. 258). Such groups were also common in East Central and South East Europe (Makhnenko 1976, p. 254).

Table 4.14 *How people should relate to lawbreakers: the legal outsiders' perspective*

		Norway (%)	England (%)	Poland (%)	Bulgaria (%)	Ukraine (%)
Q17: Ordinary people should:						
	take action against lawbreakers	9	17	27	25	21
	report lawbreakers	57	62	42	38	46
	leave it to police	34	21	31	36	34

Note: Due to rounding of decimals, percentages do not always add up to 100%.

In recent years such informal groups have also appeared in Western Europe in response to increased crime rates – suffice it here to mention Neighbourhood Watch in England and *Natteravnene* (the Night Ravens) in Norway.

LAW IN ACTION: THE LEGAL INSIDERS' PERSPECTIVE

"Exit", "voice", "loyalty"

Throughout this chapter, we have seen how legal outsiders perceive law in action. We will now turn our attention to the legal insiders. Even though we were not able to ask as many questions about "Exit", "Voice" and "Loyalty" to the legal insiders as we did to the legal outsiders, we did ask questions that directly cover "Exit" and "Voice" – and that indirectly also address "Loyalty" – simply accepting unfair or unjust law, or taking one's problems to court. Below we will focus on "Exit" and "Voice" – though observations on "Loyalty" will be made where appropriate.

"Exit"

Randeria (2007, p. 39) claims that citizens in many countries 'are increasingly using courts at all levels rather than elections to render governments accountable'. In parallel, however, the use of alternatives to court is on the rise. By the late twentieth century there was a noticeable shift from formal towards informal modes of conflict resolution (Vasylyev 2013, p. 1).

The rationale for this strong focus on mediation is that it is cheaper, faster and that it eases, rather than reinforces, conflict. It is therefore particularly useful for resolving conflicts between people who interact on a regular basis, such as neighbours. What is more, it helps reduce the caseload of the courts as fewer cases are referred to formal court hearings (see, for instance, Sperr 2012).

Businesses and citizens preferring to solve their disputes outside the court have a wide range of ADR mechanisms at their disposal. *Mediation* and *arbitration* are by far the most common and popular forms of ADRs:

> [C]onflicting parties opting for mediation agree to allow an independent third party (the mediator) to help them reach an agreement that each party considers acceptable. The agreement is usually written down and forms a legally binding contract unless the parties state otherwise. Arbitration differs from mediation in that a third party (the arbitrator) decides how to settle the dispute. He/she may be a lawyer or an expert in the field of the dispute. Decisions made by arbitrators – awards – are made according to the law and are legally binding to the parties. If necessary, they may be enforced through the courts.
>
> (Slapper and Kelly 2011, p. 544)

Other – but less common – ADR mechanisms include *early neutral evaluation*, *expert determination*, *conciliation*, *Med-Arb* (a mixture of mediation and arbitration), *neutral fact finding*, *ombudsmen* and *utility regulators* (ibid., pp. 544–5).

Courts across Europe provide court mediation, and they may also refer disputes to mediation outside the court. In some countries various types of publicly funded ADR mechanisms also exist. Some of these are free of charge, while there is a small charge for the use of others. Solving disputes through ADR is usually cheaper than turning to court. The police occasionally engage in mediation, as do local politicians and/or other highly respected people within the local community. In the West Balkans, for instance, locally respected leaders often perform this task (Trnavei 2010). In some parts of Kosovo and Albania councils of elders solve disputes based on Albanian Customary Law – the *Kanun*. The Roma, for their part, solve their disputes in the *Meshere*.[6]

Private mediation is usually carried out by professional mediators, professional arbitrators or lawyers. Professional mediators are specially

[6] Elena Marushiakova and Veselin Popov, 'The Roma court in Central, Eastern and South-Eastern Europe', at http://romafacts.uni-graz.at/index.php/culture/culture-2/the-roma-court

trained and often have a background in psychology or social work. Lawyers, for their part, are able to advise their clients on how likely their case is to succeed in court and, more importantly, to either refer their clients to various ADR mechanisms or to mediate themselves. Sometimes it is sufficient for a lawyer to write a letter to, or meet with, the lawyer of the other party to the dispute, to settle it.

Religious communities and ethno-religious groups operate their own, alternative courts. Muslims, for instance, may turn to *shari'a councils* or *shari'a courts* to resolve family disputes, to reach divorce settlements or to resolve other types of disputes by mediation or arbitration (Edge 2013, p. 121). Jews, for their part, may turn to the rabbinic court, the beth din.[7] The beth din is 'a forum for obtaining Jewish divorces, converting to Judaism, confirming personal status and adjudicating disputes stemming from divorce, business and community issues'.[8] Although some European countries have their own beth din, others do not. Jews in the latter countries (Norway, Poland and Bulgaria being amongst them) may turn to the European beth din,[9] which is located in Switzerland.

The beth din administers Jewish law, *Halacha* (The Centre for Social Cohesion 2009), whereas the shari'a councils and shari'a courts administer Islamic law. Turning to the beth din, shari'a councils or shari'a courts is in theory strictly voluntary. David Frei, registrar of the London Beth Din, says that 'there's no compulsion, we can't drag people in off the streets'.[10] Religious people may alternatively approach their religious leaders for advice and/or assistance. In such cases, religious leaders (usually priests, rabbis or imams) or experts working for the church, synagogue or mosque mediate between the conflicting parties – provided that they belong to the same religious community.

The purpose of ADR is to achieve 'compromise, agreement and a peaceful solution' (Nosyreva, 2011, p. 11, cited in Vasylyev 2013, p. 4). However, Effron (1989, p. 481, cited in ibid., p. 9) notes that 'alternatives to litigation, when used in inappropriate cases, can deny parties the legal protection they need or frustrate beneficial public policies'. In Portugal,

[7] The beth din is typically composed of three Jewish men who know Jewish law, and it may rule on questions of divorce and approve procedures and questions pertaining to Jewish practice.

[8] 'About the Sydney beth din', http://bethdin.org.au/ accessed on 14 August 2013.

[9] 'The European beth din', http://europeanbethdin.com/index.htm accessed on 02 September 14.

[10] Nick Tarry, 'Religious courts already in use', *BBC News*, 7 February 2008, http://news.bbc.co.uk/news/7233040.stm accessed on 30 August 14.

for instance, mediation 'has experienced a fierce opposition from the bar, who labelled it as a second-class justice' (Neves 2009, p. 483, cited in ibid., p. 10).

Even though ADR is strictly voluntary and requires the consent of both parties to the dispute, it cannot be ruled out that there might be considerable peer pressure in favour of solving disputes this way. Recent research suggests that mediation tends to 'favour the stronger and more affluent' (Abel, cited in ibid., p. 3). What is more, most ADR mechanisms are not able to make decisions that are binding, and they have limited possibilities to enforce their decisions.

Below we will investigate the perceptions of legal insiders towards court and alternatives to court, with a view to establishing when and how law should be applied.

First, we asked legal insiders whether "for some kinds of disputes it would be better to ask a local religious leader, or some respected member of the local community, or relatives, to decide what should be done – rather than going to court and letting a judge decide? When? Why?"

Earlier we had asked members of the public to give their assessment of five potential mediators: "a lawyer or professional mediator", "family and friends", "a local policeman", "a community leader, councillor or mayor" and "a local religious leader". To recap, legal outsiders have a greater preference for taking their disputes to "a local lawyer or professional mediator" (78 per cent), than to "family and friends" (68 per cent), "a local policeman" (61 per cent) or "a community leader, councillor or mayor" (57 per cent). They are considerably less positive to approaching "a local religious leader" (31 per cent) for mediation (see Table 4.9).

Legal insiders were asked to choose their preferred option rather than giving their assessment of each different alternative to court. In all countries except Norway legal insiders are quite supportive of turning to court. They express a preference for combining turning to court and seeking alternatives to court. Those in England and Ukraine, for instance, prefer to solve disputes either in court only, or by combining court and alternatives to court. Legal insiders in Bulgaria have a preference for solving disputes in court. Polish legal insiders, for their part, are equally open to mediation and to addressing disputes in court. Norwegian legal insiders stand out in that they prefer either to solve disputes by mediation or to combine court and alternatives to court. Unlike legal outsiders, legal insiders are not very supportive of solving conflicts through community leaders, family, relatives or

Table 4.15 *Court and alternatives to court: the legal insiders' perspective*

	Norway (%)	England (%)	Poland (%)	Bulgaria (%)	Ukraine (%)
For some kinds of disputes would it be better to ask a local religious leader, or some other respected member of the local community, or relatives, to decide what should be done – rather than going to a court and letting a judge decide? When? Why?					
Court	13	31	31	44	36
Alternative to Court		1	4	3	1
Religious leaders	1	2	—	—	2
Community leaders	3	7	5	1	3
Family, relatives	5	—	—	—	4
Mediation	33	17	32	20	6
Mix	15	10	1	12	12
Mix – court and alternative	30	31	26	21	36

Note: Entries are based on the percentages of relevant 'text units' – the total number of answers to a given question; so entries sum up to approximately 100 per cent (decimals are rounded up or down to the nearest whole number).

religious leaders. There is almost no support in any country for engaging such people in dispute resolution (Table 4.15).

In Norway civil disputes are initially brought before *Forliksrådet* (the Conciliation Council), whereas minor crimes are addressed by *Konfliktrådet* (the conflict council). If they fail to mediate solutions between the parties, the cases are taken to court. Some more extensive civil cases may be brought before the court without first having been addressed by *Forliksrådet*.

Recently the director of the Court Administration in Norway, Sven Marius Urke, noted that 'very many disputes that would otherwise have been taken to court are being handled by the local Conciliation Councils (*forliksrådene*). This is an incredibly efficient mechanism which ensures that the number of disputes handled by the Norwegian courts is manageable'.[11]

Following the introduction of the revised Norwegian Civil Code (Lov 2005–06–17–90) in January 2008, first instance courts are obliged by law to organise court mediation (*rettsmegling*) for some types of disputes with a view to reaching a negotiated settlement. Such cases are typically mediated by a judge. If the judge's efforts are not successful then mediation is followed by formal court proceedings. Court mediation has proven highly effective, especially in divorce cases and disputes about inheritance.

Norwegian legal insiders, who refer to specific types of mediation, mostly mention *Forliksrådet* and *Konfliktrådet*. Both institutions are considered "excellent" bodies that "work really well". What is more, turning to *Konfliktrådet* is free of charge and thus accessible to all regardless of personal income. Other publicly funded mediation bodies, such as *Familievernkontoret* (the Family Protection Office),[12] unspecified *tvisteløsningsorganer* (dispute resolution bodies) and mediation by arbiters (*oppmenn*) are also mentioned – though less frequently. Legal insiders express very limited support for mediation carried out by "a [neutral] third party", "friends" or "acquaintances". Legal professionals (predominantly the judges) mostly talk about court mediation (*rettsmegling*) and mediation by lawyers (*advokatmekling*). Private court settlement (*voldgift*) is in their view also sometimes useful:

> N-PR-10: 'in Norway . . . one uses *Forliksrådet* . . . relying on the wisdom of ordinary people to try to reach an agreement regarding a conflict. And in criminal cases we use *Konfliktrådet* a lot. I absolutely think that is the way to go . . . [the court] should be the last resort.' N-LA-10: 'I absolutely think [mediation] would be a better alternative . . . perhaps especially when one is talking about personal conflicts where there . . . are just as many emotions as anything else [involved] . . . we have had *court mediation* introduced as an attempt within the courts to do something similar and my experience is that this works very well . . . one gets a dialogue across the table and it doesn't end up with who is right [and who is wrong] . . . there is also some understanding of how the other party perceives the situation.'

Norwegian legal insiders' support for mediation is primarily "informed" by its positive *impact* on the involved parties. They note that mediation

[11] Cited in Helsingeng (2014).

[12] 'Familievernkontoret' [the Family Protection Office], www.bufetat.no/familievernkontor/ accessed on 10 August 2014.

"saves money" (as "courts are too expensive"), causes "less hassle", "eases tension" and "saves time". Besides, and more importantly, in their view "a compromise is better than a court ruling" as it facilitates "win-win" rather than "win-lose" solutions. However, mediation "must be democratic" (i.e. both parties must be in favour of such mediation) and it must not be coerced. A second reason for opting for mediation is that one should "[neither] burden the courts" nor "abuse the court system" by bringing minor disputes before it. Rather, "[the] court should be the last resort" for dispute settlement:

> N-PR-11: 'for private persons the court system has become so expensive ... that in practice it is inaccessible for most [people]. There is every reason to see if the parties can reach an alternative solution'. N-ER-18: 'if both parties [to the dispute] agree that it is unnecessary to bring the dispute to court ... [mediation] will save them resources and it will save the court system's resources'. N-JU-11: 'those cases that end up in court not always but very often [do so] precisely because people have not managed to resolve them either by themselves or with the assistance of others'.

Legal insiders identify several types of disputes that are particularly well suited for mediation. These include "civil case" disputes such as "divorce", "child welfare", "inheritance", "property disputes" and "neighbourhood" disputes. Sometimes mediation is also used to resolve "labour disputes" and (smaller) "monetary disputes". Minor criminal offenses – especially those involving young first-time offenders (young "shoplifters", acts of "minor violence") – lend themselves well to mediation:

> N-LA-25: 'especially neighbour conflicts ... where one cannot agree as to whether one should have fir bushes on the lower side [of the property] or not. [This is] a typical conflict that might run over several years and cost ... a lot of money ... [as for] mediation between parents who fail to agree on [child] custody ... it is often sufficient for one [of them] to file with the court ... then they meet ... at the judge's ... they agree [and the problem] is solved.' N-JU-25: '[mediation is useful for] labour disputes ... conflicts within families, between neighbours'. N-PO-8: 'the conflict council is a good alternative for young offenders . . it is often a good alternative to meeting in court and possibly getting a sentence ... at least [one] manages to keep the [offender's] criminal record clean'.

The Church of Norway offers mediation through *Kirkens Familievern* (the Church Family Protection).[13] Religious people may turn to this body

[13] www.familievern.no/stiftelsen/vare_tjenester/mekling/ accessed on 9 September 2014.

to get the seven hours of free mediation they are entitled to by law during separations and family breakups, instead of turning to the municipal Family Protection Office *(Familievernkontoret).* The Church of Norway also mediates in other types of disputes (Sveen 2014).

As for Muslims, mosques in Norway have established conflict councils and religious leaders mediate in marital conflicts, family violence and when problems arise between children and their schools.[14] There are no shari'a courts in Norway. In recent years, however, both domestic and foreign Muslims have called for the establishment of such courts.[15]

In September 2011, the leader of *Domstoladministrasjonen* (the Norwegian Court Administration) at the time, Tor Langbach, stated that he would like to give Muslim conflict councils official status in Norway – on the grounds that in the UK such councils are officially sanctioned to engage in mediation. However, the minister of justice at the time, Knut Storberget, flatly rejected this proposition, making it clear that in Norway conflict resolution councils should follow Norwegian law and they should provide equal treatment for all. His position enjoys support across the political spectrum:[16] the prevailing view is that the establishment of such courts would create parallel legal systems in Norway and also that they would be biased against women.

Almost none of the Norwegian legal insiders are supportive of ADR conducted by religious leaders. Norwegian legal insiders who prefer *court* to settle disputes argue that this is a better solution for all parties involved as the court applies common and fixed rules, thereby ensuring equal treatment before the law. Their arguments are mostly 'informed' by rule of law considerations.

In England a small-claims mediation scheme is funded by Her Majesty's Court Service (HMCS) and is free to court users who have a small claim to defend. As of June 2008 there were 23 HMCS Court Areas in England and Wales and 'each had an in-house small claims mediator to deal with appropriate cases. In most cases such claims are settled over

[14] Ibid.

[15] Øyvind Bye Skille and Martin Herman Wiedswang Zondag, 'Omstridt muslimsk predikant ønsker shariadomstoler i Norge' [Controversial Muslim preacher wishes (to establish) *shari'a courts* in Norway], *NRK*, 20 December 2012, www.nrk.no/norge/onsker-sharia-domstol-i-norge-1.10849119 accessed on 21 August 2014.

[16] Kristian Elster, Gry Blekastad Almås and Øystein Solvang, 'Domsstolsjef åpner for å gi shariaråd plass i Norge' [Head of the court administration is open to making place for *shari'a councils* in Norway], *NRK*, 26 September 2011, www.nrk.no/norge/domsstolsjef-apner-for-sharia-1.7809190 accessed on 21 August 2014.

the telephone – though face-to-face mediation may also be arranged. If mediation is unsuccessful, the case is listed for a small claims hearing in court. Mediation for higher claims is provided by the National Mediation Helpline. A relatively modest fee is charged for such mediation' (Slapper and Kelly 2011, pp. 546–7). There is also a wide range of private ADR mechanisms in England. A large number of private, independent mediators[17] are organised in the Professional Mediators' Association (PMA). Both solicitors and lawyers provide independent mediation and arbitration.

English legal insiders to roughly the same extent express a preference for court-based dispute settlement or for a mix of court-based and out-of-court dispute settlement. Judges are particularly positive to the latter option – possibly as after retirement some of them return to chambers and engage in mediation themselves. Other legal insiders might favour court-based dispute settlements as British courts are fairly flexible in their decision-making.

As is the case in Norway, those legal insiders who prefer courts to settle disputes to some extent justify their position with rule of law arguments. They perceive courts as "independent", "[totally] impartial" and "fair". They note that the advantage of the courts is that they represent "one approach, not several" – which in turn ensures "the same treatment" before the law for everyone. What is more, courts are staffed by "reasonably objective" judges who are "better [than others] at getting it right" as they "weigh up all interests" and base their decisions on "legality principles". Court settlements also ensure "consistency" as these "decision[s] may be reviewed" by a higher-instance court. And, more importantly, they are legally binding and thus "enforceable":

> E-PR-19: one of the advantages of a centralised court system ... is that it gives the opportunity for everybody effectively to be treated the same'. E-ER-2: 'they (i.e. the courts) do try and resolve these cases in a sensible and fair manner.' E-GO-17: 'we have our legal system, we should ... fund it properly and use it'. E-LA-7: 'the trouble is that most of the other methods are not legally binding. If you want money from somebody who won't pay, for example, you have to go to law'.

Some English legal insiders caution against a "two-tier system" consisting of both "informal" and "formal" law. Courts are a feature of "civilised

[17] For an overview of procedure, see www.resolution.org.uk/mediation/resolution_first_for_family_law

Western society" and they represent something "universal" and "secular". By contrast, out-of-court dispute resolution is sometimes inconsistent, always non-binding and non-enforceable, thus opening the way for "abuse", even "corruption":

> E-GO-25: 'instead of trying to set up some parallel system it ought to be taken to the properly authorised courts.' E-LA-22: 'I think you still need the sanction . . . I think the threat of costs, the lawyers and the courts take in more than you're really arguing over, it's normally enough to bring common sense to bear. From my experience, things that go to arbitration, mediation, intellectually, it's brilliant, but I never really know anyone who comes away happy. Frequently, the disgruntled party will want to go back to court anyway'. E-GO-17: 'I think letting other . . . type people get involved is courting corruption and distortion of our society.'

In England there is 'a growing sense that reconciliation and peace-building are core gospel activities, and (within the Church of England) there is increasing familiarity with the idea of mediation' (Patterson and McKay 2012). However, mediation organised by the Church of England is less common than mediation undertaken by Jewish and Muslim religious institutions. In England there are two Jewish courts: one in London and one in Manchester.

British Muslims have established two shari'a councils – one in London and one in Birmingham – and some 80 shari'a courts (Griffith-Jones 2013, pp. 18–19). The *shari'a councils* facilitate an Islamic divorce if the couple has already begun the process that will lead to an English, civil divorce. A *Muslim arbitration tribunal* was established in 2007 to resolve commercial disputes, but in recent years it has also advised couples on Islamic divorces and protection from forced marriages. Mediation and advice is also available through Family Support Services and Counselling Clinics organised within the Mosques. Muslims may turn to these for help to solve family problems or marital issues.[18]

Opinion polls suggest that a majority of the British Muslims would prefer to live under British law (59 per cent), rather than shari'a law (28 per cent) (McGoldrick 2013, p. 52). Muslim women predominantly use the shari'a councils 'to obtain a religious divorce and state law to deal with issues of access, custody and financial settlements' (ibid., p. 67). Shari'a settlements may be endorsed by English courts, but 'enforcement of the settlement must pass under English law through the English

[18] This service is provided by the Birmingham Central Mosque, www.centralmosque.org.uk/1/services/personal accessed 2 September 2014.

courts: the decisions of religious tribunals on matters of family law are not recognised in the English courts, nor can they be enforced' (Butler-Sloss and Hill 2013, p. 109). To some, the shari'a councils represent 'an emerging parallel legal system in Europe' (Ali 2013, p. 170). However, some years ago the Lord Chancellor at the time, Jack Straw, made it clear that even though there are shari'a councils and shari'a courts in England 'there is no room for parallel legal systems. Regardless of religious belief, we are all equal before the law' (Straw, cited in Edge 2013, p. 119).

Quite a few English legal insiders spontaneously voice their objection to *religious institutions* engaging in dispute resolution. They are generally fairly "suspicious of religious or communal leaders", claiming that such people are "biased". And they mostly object to Islamic dispute resolution mechanisms such as shari'a law and shari'a courts. They view the former as "bad law" that causes nothing but "problems" – and they claim that the latter set "a dangerous precedent":

> E-LA-14: 'in the criminal side of things ... involving religion is hugely dangerous. But with civil disputes, I would defer to people who know more about that.' E-LA-5: 'some disputes between Muslims are settled by local shari'a courts rather than through the UK courts. My own view is that that sets a dangerous precedent for the Constitution of our country. We have a Constitution and a legal system and where people are in dispute, those disputes can be settled through our court system under English and Welsh law, and Scottish law in Scotland ... setting up local courts to settle disputes is not a healthy precedent'.

English legal insiders in favour of *a mixed approach* (i.e. a combination of court and out-of-court mechanisms) to dispute resolution are generally positive to mediation – be it through professional mediators or others. But they stress that if mediation fails the dispute must be resolved by court. Disputes involving lawbreaking should always be resolved in court. Judges are overwhelmingly in favour of combining mediation and dispute settlement in court. Though very positive to mediation they claim that it works only if both parties agree to it. Some judges are concerned about attempts to force one of the parties to accept mediation on the grounds that forced mediation is rarely successful.[19] Added to this, mediation may extract people from the consequences or benefits of law:

[19] Point 2.2 of the UK Register of Mediators. Code of Practice and Complaints Procedure. Mediation Services. Revision 2, July 2009 (Beeper, Derbyshire: The UK Register of Mediators Ltd) states that 'participation in mediation should be emphasized as being voluntary. Mediators shall emphasize to any referrer or any agency requesting their

> E-JU-17: 'I'm a great believer in mediation and I think every effort should be made to avoid litigation, to try to reach a compromise . . . ultimately, if they can't resolve [the conflict] then I think it should be resolved by the courts'.
> E-JU-10: 'I'm pro-mediation. What worries me is how often people would be bullied into mediation for fear of the costs that might result [if they go to court] . . . in mediation . . . the result would not be the same as if you'd gone to court. One side is getting more and the other side is getting less than they would have got in court . . . you've got to have as the last resort, the ability to go to court. If you remove that, then it's a formula for chaos, for people being strong-armed into doing things they don't want to do'.

ADR was not common in Eastern Europe before the collapse of Communism. However, officially sanctioned alternatives to court did exist. In the Soviet Union, for instance, the so-called Comrades' Courts (*Tovarishcheskie sudy*, established in 1959) – composed of three laymen – were tasked with:

> imposing non-criminal sanctions upon offenders in minor disputes between persons in factories, housing units, and other institutions. Such courts were established in enterprises, institutions, organisations, higher and specialised secondary schools, collective farms, apartment buildings, and rural villages and settlements. They also educated the public about the rules of socialist society (preventive role), and punished and re-educated violators of established laws and prescribed behaviour patterns (punitive role).
>
> (Smith 1974, p. 238)

Since the collapse of Communism mediation 'was invoked (in Eastern Europe) to serve ambitious transformational aims, in particular, to promote democracy and to find compromise' (Haynes 1999, p. 275, cited in Vasylyev 2013, p. 4). There are two competing views with regard to the usefulness of court-initiated mediation or mediation conducted by various official bodies within the post-communist context.

Some analysts claim that court mediation is particularly useful in the post-communist context as courts are short of resources and are considered to be corrupt (Buscaglia 1999; Pahis 2009; Murdock 2009); public trust in them is limited.[20] Others believe that mediation – at least if

services that parties cannot be coerced into mediation'. Even though conflicting parties cannot formally be coerced into mediation, they might give in to social pressure and take part in mediation even though they do not favour this approach.

20 An analysis of the judicial system across Europe recently conducted by the Council of Europe (CoE) shows that there is 'a strong correlation between the GDP per capita and the level of resources allocated per capita to the operation of the judicial system' (CoE 2013, p. 72). Increasing the resources of the courts would thus enhance their efficiency and, in turn, raise public trust in them.

organised by court – is less effective in post-communist societies because 'mediation . . . requires . . . public trust and respect for legal institutions for the process to function effectively as an alternative to litigation'. Sajo (1990, p. 340) notes that 'mediation and other alternatives to justice are unpopular [in Eastern Europe] because of earlier abuses of informality'. It is not only unpopular amongst the public, but also amongst legal professionals. In Bulgaria, for instance, 'the lack of legal provisions arranging the court-referred mediation resulted in . . . opposition among . . . Bulgarian judges to mediation, some of them interpreting it even as a denial of justice' (Cole and Gyaurova-Wegertseder n.d., pp. 4–5). Vasylyev (2013, p. 30) claims that 'the legacy of Soviet culture is to oppose dialogue. In Ukraine, 'the lack of culture of compromise and (the) aggressive attitude towards others' opinion . . . and collectivist tradition of burying conflicts . . . are still widely present' (Alken, Conbere and Heorhiadhi, cited in ibid.).

Polish legal insiders voice roughly as much support for settling disputes in court as they do for non-court mediation. In their view the purpose of mediation is to "look differently at a problem" from what the court would do and to reach "compromises", facilitate "reconciliation" and pave the way for "the settlement" of disputes. Mediation in Poland is "something [that is] also recommended by court". Judges therefore "often try to refer cases" to mediation with a view to reaching an "out-of-court settlement". For some types of conflict "compulsory mediation proceedings" take place through the court in the hope that the dispute may be resolved without having to go through formal court proceedings. One prosecutor advocates "more arbitration proceedings", whereas another is more pessimistic, noting that "unfortunately [such proceedings] have poor chances of success".

Those Polish legal insiders who prefer to settle disputes in court highlight the formal position of the court in their country. They note that dispute resolution is within "[the court's] jurisdiction" and also, that "[the court's] rulings are unquestionable": the courts "apply the law", make "binding decisions" and "carry out sentences". As "a professional jurist" the judge is "well prepared", "competent", and bestowed with the necessary "freedom" and "independence" to settle disputes. He or she is "a person of public trust", who is "more trusted" than other mediators. The judge "should settle [all serious] disputes" and "ambiguous matters". He or she should decide on all "legal questions" and "punishment". Court settlements represent "a manifestation of civil responsibility" and thus also "a sign of society's maturity":

> P-GO-15: 'I think that the court is the only entity entitled to administer justice.' P-PR-17: 'we should go to court . . . as the court passes final and binding sentences'. P-ER-13: 'the legal system in Poland clearly says that the judge is responsible for this . . . we have a Constitution, we live in a state of law, and not in some tribal country'. P-JU-23: 'many times I try to refer a case to mediation, however, most often it appears that some of the parties are categorically against it and demand settlement in court. This is unfortunately the kind of legal culture that we have'. P-JU-17: 'the court itself sometimes seems to move away from the trial and resort to mediation . . . this very rarely proves effective. Usually, when coming to court, people have already exhausted various possibilities of mediation'.

As we have previously noted, post-communist societies are low-trust societies. Polish legal insiders claim that one major drawback with ADR is that there are "not people of high public trust in Poland" who can conduct such mediation. Besides, it is "difficult to transfer power to local leaders". "Religious leaders and relatives" should not solve disputes as they are bound to be "subjective". Even though the Catholic Church has a strong position in Poland some legal insiders claim that "no religion has authority today":

> P-LA-15: 'there is not a single day when the [news]papers do not report on prosecutors' mistakes or on judges' mistakes or about the fact that a corruptible judge or prosecutor arranged something for somebody, especially when politicians are involved . . . there are black sheep in all professions, but . . . for the state of law where there are conflicts there is no place for shamans, witches, local sages, there the court should take action.' P-PR-3: 'I do not hold the view that spiritual leaders should influence norms established by the state, by the Sejm, by the law'. P-LA-18: 'conflicts between people are mainly family conflicts; division of property, divorces, and no . . . interference of other members of the family can help here. It can even cause damage. So it needs to be an independent arbitrator. A judge seems to be such a person'.

Polish legal insiders who favour *non-court settlements* give examples of state-funded bodies undertaking mediation as well as of more informal arrangements. As concerns the former, they claim that solving disputes outside the court is important, as Polish courts are suffering from overload. Mediation may be carried out by "different specialised institutions", "a local authority", "the head of the municipality", "court adjudication" or "a social arbitrator"[21]:

[21] Legal insiders also refer to institutions that engaged in mediation during Communism, such as "the Justice of the Peace", "the Magistrate's Office", "the Magistrate's Court", "Family Council Adjudication" and "the Barratry".

> P-JU-13: 'we have mediators available in our legal culture. This was an institution that before 1990 was also applied in various branches of law. There was mediation in economic matters and workers' matters, there were workers' councils which heard various disputes before all that was brought to the court. Then the state gave it up and now it's returning to the same concept of mediation, out-of-court settlement'. P-GO-14: 'of course, courts are overloaded with menial cases which could easily be settled by someone from outside the court. I think it would be great if there was an institution of some sort of social arbitrator ... however, unfortunately, it is Polish people's nature that they are unwilling to compromise.'.

As concerns the latter, Polish legal insiders note that mediators do not have to be state appointees. In the view of one government official, "anybody can be a mediator" provided that the "parties [to the dispute] agree" and that this person is "trusted by both parties". In Poland "psychologists" and "ex-policemen" occasionally act as mediators. Mediation may be undertaken by "a clergyman", "a Council of Elders", "the village head", "people who are respected locally", "local influential people", "people who enjoy prestige", "a third party", "a lawyer", "a familiar person" or even "the head of the family". "[Professional] mediators" – that is, "somebody with the appropriate knowledge and qualifications" – also have a role to play. It could even be "a judge":

> P-JU-22: 'it could be a person trusted by both parties, some mediator, not necessarily the court'. P-PO-6: 'if this person is really someone respected, who additionally has appropriate knowledge and qualifications and people deem him or her a genuine authority, then by all means yes. Why go to court when a dispute can be settled amicably and in a conciliatory manner?' P-ER-10: 'every kind of mediation is recommended. Whether it would be [conducted by] a clergyman, or some local authority, a commune head ... a head of a village or some person who has influence'.

Mediation can successfully be used at the "pre-court stage" with a view to "reaching a decision before [the dispute ends up in] court". Polish legal insiders also recommend mediation for a number of minor disputes, such as "minor family disputes", "divorce proceedings" and "[child] custody disputes"; but also for "smaller claims" and "minor material damage". In their view "civil law" disputes – such as "neighbour issues", "property issues" and "boundary disputes" – are particularly well suited for mediation. In criminal cases mediation should only be used for "petty" offenses such as "stealing coffee".

Polish legal insiders, just like legal insiders in Norway and England, believe that mediation is "a good solution". It is "quicker" and "easier" for citizens; it is "cheaper" as it incurs "reduced social costs", and it is better as it facilitates "amicable settlement" of disputes. Equally important, mediation is "voluntary": "the parties communicate" actively with each other rather than being "passive parties" in court. This, in turn, facilitates "a democratic process" and thus a "more respected" decision:

> P-GO-7: 'I believe that negotiations are always better than settlement by force [i.e.] a lawsuit'. P-PR-7: 'I'm very much in favour of settling disputes out of court. For a couple of years, the Polish judicial system has exercised such an option by introducing to certain cases compulsory mediation proceedings. We even have a number of properly qualified mediators . . . unfortunately, given that the parties to such proceedings are so litigious and even blinded by anger, this mediation very often has poor chances of success'. P-LA-13: 'I refer quite a lot of cases for mediation. If both parties express their consent, as this is the condition, it can end well for them'. P-JU-13: 'this [i.e. mediation] is a very, very good institution . . . it's quicker and no doubt clearer . . . encouraging the parties to make a compromise . . . makes it much easier . . . you can appoint meetings with your mediator even three days in a row . . . the costs of mediation as such are much lower [than formal court proceedings]'.

Support for settling disputes in court is higher amongst legal insiders in Bulgaria and Ukraine than elsewhere. This is a paradox given that courts in both countries are still suffering from lack of independence, lack of capacity and corruption. As we have noted a poll conducted in Bulgaria in 2011 shows that 85 per cent of those polled believe that courts protect the rich and powerful (*Novinite*, referred to in Littlehale 2012, p. 40). Ukrainian courts for their part are suffering from widespread corruption (KIIS 2006). In the following we will look into some of the reasons why legal insiders in these two countries still prefer courts to ADR.

Some Bulgarian legal insiders prefer courts to handle dispute resolution on the grounds that Bulgaria is "a modern" and "secular" state; a "state of law" composed by "three branches of power" – of which the courts represent one. In democracies the "law is for all", and it is the court that is "the structure for dealing with violations of the law". It should therefore "be exclusively responsible" for "providing justice" and "solving the issue of guilt". Even though citizens are sceptical of the courts Bulgarian legal insiders are "confident in [the state] institutions" and they endorse "the superiority of court". Further, they believe that Bulgarian judges are "competent" and "impartial" and thus well placed to "establish justice". Courts provide citizens with "equal treatment" as they are "objective and fair":

> B-ER-6: 'the court is the institution [in which] to solve arguments ... without any exceptions. There is rule of law in this country, it is an EU member'. B-PR-1: 'all disputes have to be referred to court because according to the Constitution and laws it is the only authorised body to solve disputes between citizens.' B-GO-22: 'if there is a well-functioning judicial system I do not see why there have to be double mechanisms. I do not think it is appropriate.' B-ER-20: 'our national mentality is such that we find it hard to be united and reach a final solution, especially when relatives and friends interfere'.

Some of the Bulgarian legal insiders not only give their reasons for supporting the court but also make a point of explaining why ADR should *not* be used. In their view mediation "was destroyed during Communism" and "has not yet been popularised" in Bulgaria. It would therefore be inappropriate to allow ethnically or religiously based structures, such as the Roma's *Meshere*, to address disputes.[22] Bulgarian legal insiders are sceptical of involving relatives or other close people in non-court conflict resolution. Added to this, due to "the unclear church hierarchy" in Bulgaria, turning to religious leaders is not advisable:[23]

> B-LA-16: 'in Bulgaria ... this tradition was destroyed because Communism would not allow it and it would be absurd to start creating it now.' B-LA-5: 'mediation has been introduced but this method of voluntary agreement between the parties hasn't been popularised and applied, yet.' B-GO-10: 'religion, relatives or any other type of community could bring

[22] In Bulgaria the *Meshere* – or the *Kris Romani*, as it is also called – addresses both minor and more serious disputes and crimes. In 2011 it issued a symbolic death sentence for the notorious Roma boss Kiril Rashkov, also referred to as Tsar Kiro, after he had run over and killed a 19-year-old boy in the Plovdiv district. The Meshere stated that 'if it had real power it would sentence Rashkov to death by hanging to set an example to others'. 'Bulgarian Roma "Meshere" sentences Tsar Kiro to "Death"', *Novitne.com* (Sofia News Agency), 26 September 2011, www.novitne.com/view_news.php?id=132407 accessed on 15 January 2014.

[23] A state-induced schism took place in the Bulgarian Orthodox Church in 1992 when the government of the Union of Free Democrats claimed that Maksim's 1971 election was invalid. The government therefore forcefully replaced Maksim and the Holy Synod by a Provisional Synod headed by Metropolitan Pimen of Nevrokop. In late 1992 the government of the Bulgarian Socialist Party reinstated Maksim, whom most bishops and the majority of believers supported. Since Pimen's death in 1999 the Alternative Synod has been headed by Metropolitan Innokentij. In July 2004, on orders of the Bulgarian Chief Prosecutor, police stormed 250 churches affiliated with the Alternative Synod and detained its clergy. The Bulgarian Orthodox Church under Patriarch Maxim is recognized as canonical, whereas the Alternative Synod under Metropolitan Innokentij is only recognized by the Ukrainian Orthodox Church – Kiev Patriarchate. See Broun (1997); Donev (2005); and Olteanu and Nève (2013, p. 10).

> much more subjectivism into the judgement.' B-GO-5: 'the Muslim religion ... never lead to anything good.' B-PR-1: 'we are all aware of the *Meshere* but I am strongly against this practice'.

Most of the statements the Bulgarian legal insiders make *in favour* of mediation relate to the 2007 Law on Mediation.[24] The word "mediation" is not part of the Bulgarian vocabulary. However, due to the efforts of the American Bar Association's Central European and Eurasian Law Imitative (ABA-CEELI), Bulgarians are becoming more interested in it. There are now several Centres for mediation (Dimcheva n.d.) outside the courts. Mediation also takes place within the district courts and Bulgarian judges, just as judges in other European countries may refer cases to mediation.[25] Sometimes they are even obliged by law to do so (ibid.). Professional mediators are usually competent in psychology or law, and they are listed in an official register of mediators. As in Norway and Poland, out-of-court mediation is considered to be faster and cheaper than bringing a case to court.

Ukrainian legal insiders make an equal number of statements in favour of solving disputes through court as they do in favour of combining ADR and court proceedings. Those who are in favour of letting *courts* settle disputes claim that in democratic societies it is these institutions that are tasked with dispute resolution. As in Bulgaria legal insiders use rule-of-law arguments to justify their preference for court settlements. They believe that alternatives to court are likely to cause tension rather than to solve disputes. In a "law-based and democratic state" civil law disputes should therefore be resolved in court. Some disputes simply cannot be resolved without resorting to "legal norms".

Ukrainian legal insiders believe that national courts are "the only strong institution[s]" in Ukraine. They are "independent", "democratic", "objective", "just", "fair" and "humane". Judges solve disputes in a "civilised manner", abiding by the "norms of law". Further, courts are "more efficient" than ADR and court "rulings are implemented". They provide a "guarantee of justice" since it is "possible to appeal the decision" of lower-instance courts and since courts are "more constructive". In Ukraine "people are [generally] distrustful" of each other. Courts are

[24] The Mediation Act, Code of Civil Procedure, and Ordinance No. 2 of 15 March 2007.

[25] For an overview of mediation in Bulgaria see 'Legal frame of mediation in Bulgaria', *Euro Net Mediation,* http://mediation-net.eu/index.php?option=com_content&view=article&id=24%3Aprurdedbbg&catid=6%3Abulgaria&Itemid=43&lang=en accessed on 1 February 2014.

therefore better placed than other institutions to solve disputes "given [this] mentality", and they should have "a central role" in dispute resolution and the "settling [of] all serious disputes":

> U-PO-19: 'as we are a European state, I think we must solve problems in court.' U-GO-20: 'we live in a state of law where a court of law must decide all serious disputes.' U-PO-1: 'only a judge has the necessary qualification ... the legal right to make one or the other decision and only a decision made by a judge is compulsory to enforce'. U-PO-2: 'one should go to court ... mob law must not be allowed'.

Ukrainian legal insiders – just like legal insiders elsewhere – are strongly opposed to solving disputes through *religious channels*. They note that "religion has nothing to do with [dispute resolution]". Besides, it "can confuse" people and is "not [always] reasonable". Religious leaders are neither "a great authority", nor are they "too smart". What is more, they may even have a vested interest in the outcome of the dispute to be settled. Even if their intervention is successful, the settlement may "contradict the law". Besides, it is questionable whether their decisions will actually be implemented. One should therefore "never ask ... religious leaders" to intervene in disputes:

> U-ER-12: 'what can a religious leader say? "Pray, and you will be helped"?' U-JU-16: 'religious leaders ... can simply voice their opinion, which may even contradict the law'.

Even though some legal insiders voice their concern about the objectivity of the Ukrainian courts, they see no real alternatives to court. In their view, Ukrainians – just like the Bulgarians – prefer to turn to court even if alternative means of solving their conflict might be found. Legal insiders explain this by referring to the Ukrainian mentality:

> U-ER-12: 'people are afraid of the court ... the majority ... are not able to use the law, they don't know the laws ... it is already a kind of psychological barrier ... it is easier to pay, wrest a debt or intimidate [the other party] or something else'. U-JU-5: 'since we are living in the post-Soviet space people simply want to feel protected. They therefore go to court'.

Despite the many benefits of turning to court with one's disputes, Ukrainian legal insiders note that this option is not always available to ordinary citizens. For a start, Ukraine does not have "legal aid". Second, "people do not [always] know which court to turn to", or even in which circumstances they may turn to court. What is more, courts are "not always fair" and some of them are "corrupted". The public therefore often "turn to locals and relatives" to solve their disputes. Occasionally they are even assisted by gangsters – free of charge – who take "pity" on those who are unable to get any assistance from the police:

> U-GO-16: 'it would be better to go to court. But in our life we address the local [people], relatives.' U-ER-17: 'there are cases in my practice where gangsters helped people solve their problems simply out of pity for them and without charging any money for it'. U-GO-1: 'taking into account our corrupted system, considering the legal illiteracy of most citizens . . . we have not developed a system of legal aid for the citizens . . . you have to pay big money to lawyers and these lawyers are not always acting in good faith. They take the money but don't do what they must do'.

Ukrainian legal insiders who opt for a *mixed* approach – that is, mediation followed by formal court proceedings if the former is not successful – predominantly argue in favour of court addressing criminal offenses and larger civil cases. Smaller civil case matters (in particular, family disputes), on the other hand, may be resolved with the assistance of family members, people of authority (village heads, local deputies, religious people, psychologists) or professional mediators. However, at present formal alternatives to court are not functioning well in Ukraine. Institutions that mediated conflicts in the past, such as arbitration courts, the justice of the peace, trade unions, and housing committees, either no longer exist or are too weak to exert much influence:

> U-LA-20: 'it is compulsory to bring a criminal case to court. But private, civil disputes may be settled in a peaceful manner [outside court]'. U-GO-18: 'in divorce proceedings . . . it would be better to consult a relative than to wash one's dirty linen in public . . . if there is a land dispute . . . [one] should go to court and stand up for one's rights'. U-ER-25: 'there are disputes which can be solved only by court, for example . . . divorce . . . distribution of inheritances or land disputes'. U-ER-21: 'if a conflict is [of a] moral [type], [then] of course it can be settled at the domestic level. But if [it] is of a legal character and the cost of conflict is high, I think it should be decided in court'.

"Voice"

In a democracy power is divided between the legislative, executive and judiciary. In the first part of this chapter we explored the manner in which the general public perceives the decisions of the executive – and how they relate to the judiciary (courts). We will now look at how the representatives of the legislative, executive and judiciary think members of the public should deal with unreasonable or unjust laws. This is, in

Table 4.16 *Dealing with unreasonable or unjust laws: the legal insiders' perspective*

	Norway (%)	England (%)	Poland (%)	Bulgaria (%)	Ukraine (%)
Suppose Parliament passed a law that some people felt was *unreasonable* or *unjust*. What should these people do? Can you give examples?					
Obey	13	6	14	22	12
Evade (quietly ignore, disobey)	7	9	6	1	4
Protest	4	10	2	10	1
Mild	43	41	39	47	50
Medium	4	9	2	6	4
Strong	—	1	1	1	—
Mix	31	23	36	14	29

Note: Entries are based on the percentages of relevant 'text units' – the total number of answers to a given question; so entries sum up to approximately 100 per cent (decimals are rounded up or down to the nearest whole number).

effect, also a question of how the public should relate to them personally as representatives of the establishment and of how they perceive their own institutions.

We asked the respondents the following question: 'Suppose parliament passed a law that some people felt was unreasonable or unjust. What should these people do? Can you give examples?' Table 4.16 shows that legal insiders (all countries) prefer citizens to engage in mild forms of protest against such laws (we will return to this concept and what it entails, further in the chapter).

Legal professionals in countries such as Ukraine and to some extent also Bulgaria have a reputation for flouting the law. Yet they advocate democratic protest against, rather than evading, unreasonable or unjust laws. In doing so, they exhibit a democratic mind-set. Further, perceptions of the *manner* in which such mild protest should be exercised differ across Europe. In some countries legal insiders advocate a greater variety of measures than in others. Legal insiders in countries that have a constitutional court (Poland, Bulgaria, Ukraine) are more positive to citizens turning to court about unfair legislation than legal insiders in countries that do not have such a court (Norway, England).

Norwegian legal insiders who hold the view that citizens should object to unreasonable or unjust laws through *mild protest* believe this should be done through *civic action, lobbying, formal complaints mechanisms* or through *the media.*

Norway has an active civil society,[26] which explains why respondents are mostly in favour of voicing discontent with unreasonable or unjust laws by means of *civic action.* Disgruntled citizens should "find allies", "get organised", "form a protest group"; or join an "interest organisation", "opposition group" or even "a political party". Once organised, they could engage the public by initiating "a petition". Alternatively, they could "facilitate a [public] debate", "organise hearings" or vote in "elections". Common to all these measures is that they allow citizens to take part in "the democratic process". Norwegian legal insiders view "civil disobedience" as an effective means of protest:

> N-ER-4: 'you create an opinion that puts pressure on the politicians. You contact the[m] . . . you present research materials, you put forward [your] arguments'. N-LA-15: 'they should . . . form opposition groups'. N-ER-14: 'they should join political parties and take part in changing the law . . . there are [also] many types of civil disobedience.'

In Norway *lobbying* is also considered to be a useful means of protest – though somewhat less so than civic action. Citizens can promote their cause by "lobbying Parliament", "contacting politicians and arguing [their case]" or acting "through political party representatives". Alternatively, they can "write letters to the ministries" or turn to "the central [state] administration" – including the "Ministry of Justice":

> N-LA-14: '[citizens should] engage in active lobbying and use the media'. N-GO-3: 'one has to influence those who will promote the law proposals . . . the central administration, or . . . Parliament'. N-PR-12: 'in connection with the state budget an older woman wrote an email to Kristin Halvorsen [Minister of Finance at the time of interviewing] about asset tax and she pointed out [something that was] unreasonable and that was . . . changed . . . long live democracy!'

[26] See Sivesind and Selle (2010) for an account of civil society in the Nordic countries.

Formal complaint mechanisms constitute a third means of protest. Norwegian citizens may *file a formal complaint* with the head of the county *(Fylkesmannen)*. Each county head supervises the performance of the municipal administrations within his or her county and may overturn municipal decisions if legal provisions have not been applied properly. Alternatively, citizens may file "complaints with the police" or other "official channels" against specific laws or regulations. Somewhat surprisingly, none of the legal insiders suggest that citizens turn to the civil ombudsman (*Sivilombudsmannen*) with their complaints.

Finally, citizens may address the *media*, by "writing letters to newspapers" or bringing issues to the attention of journalists, thus using "the freedom of speech" and "the freedom of the press" to "show what is unfair". Or they may turn to "*court*", which could be "the Supreme Court", the "supranational courts" (the ECtHR) or various "international organisations" for assistance:

> N-ER-17: 'you can turn to the press'. N-GO-16: 'they should . . . have it [i.e. the law] tested by . . . international courts'. N-LA-6: '[they should] go to the Supreme Court and find out whether the law contradicts the Constitution and if it does, then one has to change the law'.

Norwegian legal insiders provide several examples of unreasonable or unjust laws that have triggered protests in Norway. These include laws pertaining to family matters, education, health, labour, the environment, fishery and religion.

English legal insiders make an even larger number of statements in favour of mild protest than legal insiders in Norway. Whilst the majority of their statements pertain to various types of *civic action*, they also express a fairly strong preference for *lobbying*. Alternatively, disgruntled citizens may turn to *court*, approach *the media* or turn to *the ombudsman*. However, there is considerably less support for the latter three options.

As for *civic action*, English legal insiders – just like the Norwegian ones – suggest that citizens who are unhappy about specific legislation may either "voice their opinion" or "take direct action". In the former case they may "sign petitions" (including "e-petitions"). In the latter case they may "form political pressure groups" or work through "trade unions" to influence "public attitudes". Alternatively, they may engage in "peaceful" but "lawful" protest. More specifically, they may "sit in Parliament Square", "march", "campaign for an election", or "vote" in elections to "change [their] MPs" or "the government". In doing so, they voice their unhappiness with the law "through the democratic process", thereby ensuring that their "collective voice" is heard:

> E-GO-16: 'people got very excited about the *Ghurkhas*[27] not that long ago, didn't they? There were quite a lot of people protesting to support their case … I'm thinking about court decisions where people see a clear miscarriage of justice and come out and campaign'. E-JU-5: '[they could] ask for a general election.' E-PO-18: 'the fox hunting ban. What they should do is to use the legal system to get the law changed, either through a petition … by lawful protest, by examples of where the law works or doesn't work respectively. Not by … more direct action.'

English legal insiders – to a greater extent than legal insiders in Norway – recommend that citizens engage in political lobbying against laws that they find unreasonable or unjust. Their stronger preference for lobbying is probably a result of the simple majority election system ("first past the post"). British MPs operate political surgeries (i.e. a series of one-to-one meetings with their constituents) and thus regularly meet voters in the constituency. The English are therefore closer to their local MP than Norwegians are to theirs (Norway has a proportional election system). Citizens may lobby "[their] local councillor" or "MP", for instance, by "writing" to them or by "visiting" them. Alternatively, they may "petition" them or "ask [individual] MPs to table motions". Citizens may also "try to persuade" or "pressurise" government. On matters of local significance they may turn "to the local council". Finally, they may approach "the Crown Prosecution Service (CPS)" or "the chief constable" with some types of grievances:

> E-JU-18: 'it's got to be the democratic route … Britain has a great history of lobbying, political protest, and that sort of thing'. E-ER-15: 'they should lobby their local politicians … go to their surgeries … do a petition and present it to the local MPs … to the local councils … they could lobby the Chief Constable … the Crown Prosecution Service … there are lots of things they could do. They probably don't realise it.'

Dissatisfied English citizens may also use various *legal measures* to make their views heard, such as turning to "the courts" ("the magistrate" court, "the ECtHR"). However, the legal approach enjoys considerably less support than other means of protest. Another option available to them

[27] Hannah Vinter, 'Lost generation of elderly Ghurkhas struggle in Britain', *Reuters*, 8 November 2013, http://uk.reuters.com/article/2013/11/08/uk-britain-gurkhas-idukBRE9A70K920131108 accessed on 1 February 2014.

is to approach *the Ombudsman* with their concerns: E-LA-3: "you can go to the European Court". E-PR-11: "take [the dispute] to Europe or judicially review it or something".

Even though English legal insiders emphasise the impact of *the media* on society more generally and on public opinion regarding their respective professions, in particular, very few of them recommend that disgruntled members of the public approach the press for support in having existing legislation changed or removed. Only one lawyer, one prosecutor and one police official advocate this approach:

> E-LA-9: '[they may] make their views clear in the media, try and persuade other people.' E-PR-10: '[they may] use the press'. E-PO-2: 'you do have political pressure groups, they are very vocal, very persuasive in their argument, and will use the media as a means of really highlighting their views'.

English legal insiders mention several instances in which British citizens have engaged in mild protest against specific legislation:

> E-ER-11: '[mild protest has been used against or to facilitate] control orders, detention without charge for 28 days and above, people who've been against the Hunting Act, everything. It's always got to be a democratic process'. E-ER-13: 'look at the Poll Tax[28] ... everyone went out on the street with the placards ... I do think it's absolutely right that people take to the street and voice their protests ... don't hurt anybody or commit any crimes ... but yes, [they should] absolutely tell us how they feel and ultimately kick our arses when it comes to the election: just don't vote for us!'

During Communism people were not allowed to voice their criticisms of the Communist Party as such. Free elections, political demonstrations, political strikes and other types of civic action were therefore not available to citizens in Eastern Europe until the second half of the 1980s – with the exception of Poland, where an uprising took place in late 1970/early 1971 in protest against plans to increase prices on basic consumer goods.[29] A few years later (1980) Solidarity organised its first strikes.

[28] The Poll Tax, which was calculated based on the value of the property in which a person resided, regardless of his or her income, was a community charge introduced by the Thatcher government. Only 12 per cent favoured the tax and widespread opposition to the tax eventually facilitated her downfall. Wikipedia, 'Poll tax riots', http://en.wikipedia.org/wiki/Poll_Tax_Riots accessed on 5 September 2014.

[29] Libcom.org, '1970–71: Uprising in Poland', http://libcom.org/history/1970-71-uprising-poland accessed on 21 August 2014.

However, during Communism citizens could express their dissatisfaction with local government officials by writing letters to newspapers or by approaching their elected representatives or party officials. In the Soviet Union newspapers such as *Pravda* and *Izvestia* published letters of complaint from unhappy citizens together with the response newspaper journalists had obtained from officials on the issues addressed in these letters. The satirical magazine *Krokodil* (*The Crocodile*) exposed local officials engaging in poaching or other types of wrongdoing.

Towards the end of Communist rule (late 1980s/early 1990s) East European citizens organised strikes, engaged in demonstrations, formed informal organisations and eventually even opposition parties. East Europeans thus had some experiences with political protest at the beginning of transition, though these were very different from those of citizens in Western Europe. Although Western Europeans were able to influence both the input and output sides of government, citizens in Eastern Europe were – until the mid-1980s – only able to respond to the output side.

Legal insiders in Poland, just like legal insiders in England, predominantly recommend that citizens apply *civic measures* to protest unreasonable or unfair laws. By far the most popular measure is to collect 100,000 signatures in support of a legislative initiative to Parliament. *Lobbying* elected representatives is also viewed as useful. Polish citizens may alternatively *turn to court*. None of the Polish legal insiders suggest that approaching *the media* would be wise.

Other *civic measures* include "citizens' initiatives", establishing "associations" or organising "petitions". Citizens may initiate "interpellations" or "appeal procedures", "lodge complaints" or engage in "boycotts" of various sorts. They may organise "social actions" and "citizens' meetings" or "propose amendments" to laws. Alternatively, they may "support the political environment" by "voting" in elections or initiating a "referendum". Or, they may engage in "civil disobedience" to facilitate "changes":

> P-GO-19: 'citizens create a civil list and if there are 100,000 signatures on that list then they can petition a suitable minister, the Office of the Council of Ministers, or the President, to change a given Act'. P-ER-11: 'here, where I'm working, in ... Warsaw, there is the option of a legislative and constitutional initiative as well as ... [initiating] a referendum'. P-JU-5: '[they could] win the elections and change the regulations in Parliament. Or alternatively, meet at various social forums [or] associations; participate in the collection of signatures'.

Polish citizens may also follow various "legal paths" by *turning to court* (i.e. "the Constitutional Court", "the Supreme Court" or "the

Administrative Court") to file a "constitutional" or "legal" complaint. Alternatively, they may turn to "the ECtHR". One of the lawyers cautions that court appeals do not bring speedy results. Various formal complaints procedures are also available to the citizens. These include the "Ombudsman", "the Commission for Civil Rights" and "the Commissioner for Human Rights Protection":

> P-ER-13: 'as a last resort [they could] ... refer an Act either to the Constitutional Court or the Court in Strasbourg'. P-JU-2: 'there is the institution of the Commissioner for Civil Rights, to whom you can write'. P-PO-23: '[they may] write a letter to the Ombudsman ... appeal to the Supreme Court or the Administrative Court, or to some higher level court.'

Finally, unhappy citizens may engage in *lobbying*, by participating in "interdepartmental consultations [with MPs]". Alternatively, they may "appeal to the authorities", write "letters" or "turn to" "their own MP". Or they may approach "a Parliamentary Club"; visit "MPs", "Senators or city councillors"; or "inform Government and Parliament" about their unhappiness:

> P-ER-22: '[they could] exert influence on members of Parliament and Senators who are the direct representatives of society in the Sejm and the Senate or by the civic initiative', P-PO-5: 'they can take the citizens' initiative, they can visit a society representative, an MP, a Senator, a city councillor'.

Polish citizens have voiced their support for, or objection to, various types of legislation. Many of these pertain to moral and/or religious issues such as *in vitro* fertilisation, abortion, family matters, health, and pensions – but also a wide range of other issues. They have protested or supported restitution – including the return of property to the Catholic Church – and they have lobbied for 6 January (Epiphany) to be made a public holiday in Poland:

> P-PR-3: 'I believe life brings such examples that the law – local or national – is incompatible or even stupid, if some norms are impracticable or have grown old and do not match the modern situation but [still] exist. At times the law is dead, sometimes nobody pays attention to it, sometimes the law is not implemented but it exists ... I'm not a supporter of civil disobedience ... there are ways in a lawful state to file an application to Parliament, to Members of Parliament'.

Legal insiders in Poland who opt for *a mixed approach*, in most cases advocate obeying the law whilst working to have it changed.

Bulgarian legal insiders do not differ much from legal insiders in Norway, England and Poland with regard to the measures they recommend. The largest share of their statements recommends that citizens who object to specific laws should engage in mild protest, preferably by taking *civic action*. *Lobbying* political bodies and politicians may also be effective. As do the Polish legal insiders, Bulgarian legal insiders believe that *legal action* may be helpful. As in other countries very few legal insiders are in favour of approaching the *media*.

First, in terms of *civic measures*, Bulgarian legal insiders recommend a wider range of measures than legal insiders elsewhere. Citizens may start "a civic initiative" by setting up or joining "civic organisations" – including "NGOs", "pressure groups" or "associations" with a view to "[initiating] public debate" and "let all voices be heard". They may "listen to experts", prepare "open letters", make "proactive proposals" for "legislative initiatives", "collect signatures" and "sign petitions", or organise "meetings" and "roundtables". They may "appeal", "complain", engage in "civic protest" by organising various "protest actions", such as "demonstrations" or "strikes". Alternatively, they may "vote in elections" or demand "a referendum":

> B-GO-11: '[Bulgarians] could go on strike ... protest, sign petitions.' B-JU-16: 'lobbying in its good sense ... round-tables ... a public debate'. B-ER-11: 'civic organisations should immediately initiate a public debate'. B-ER-6: 'civic protests are also possible but in Bulgaria it is known that protests do not produce any results'. B-PO-23: 'perhaps [they could] do a referendum and collect votes.'

One lawyer, however, cautions that in Bulgaria civic measures are not likely to succeed. In his view informal approaches have a better chance of succeeding: B-LA-8: "well, if they lie on the cobblestones, organise strikes, stop the traffic – it doesn't work ... the personal relations and positions are what really work".

Second, Bulgarian citizens may engage in *lobbying*, by writing "letters to MPs", organizing "meetings with MPs and political factions", trying to "persuade politicians" (for instance, members of the Council of Ministers). They may target their lobbying efforts by "addressing a Parliamentary Committee", "negotiating with" or "pressurizing Parliament", approaching "the Council of Ministers" or trying to secure a "presidential veto". Another option available to them is to "negotiate with international representatives": B-ER-1: "[they could organise] meetings with MPs, representatives of political factions". B-ER-13: "they might get acquainted with their representatives in Parliament".

Third, Bulgarian citizens may turn to *court* (i.e. to "the Constitutional Court" or "the Supreme Court") with a view to "proving [that a given law] is unconstitutional". Formal complaints mechanisms are also available to them, including "the [Civil] Ombudsman" who may, address the Constitutional Court on their behalf. One judge is sceptical to citizens seeking redress in court as in such cases the courts rarely side with the citizens:

> B-PR-22: 'well, they can turn to the relevant institutions that are supposed to refer to the Supreme Court.' B-GO-22: '[they should] refer to the Ombudsman, through his or her political power [they should] apply to the Constitutional Court and try to change the law.' B-JU-17: 'if they seek their rights in court that would be good: in Bulgaria, however, in 95 per cent of the cases they will not get what they want because the court will say, "that is the law and you have to obey it". The question is whether in those 5 per cent [of the cases] a judge could be found who thinks differently'. B-LA-17: '[they should] inform the Ombudsman ... [who, in turn], ... may notify the European Commission'.

Finally, citizens may "engage the *media*": B-ER-14: "they could use the media to have their arguments heard".

Bulgarian legal insiders give considerably fewer examples of issues for which mild protest has been used than legal insiders elsewhere do. They simply note that Bulgarian citizens have engaged in such protest to express their objection to gene-modified organisms (GMO), tax increases, the data protection act or the management of common property: B-ER-17: "a typical example of that is the law that legitimised the GMO regime. Then the insistence of certain political forces and the civil society reaction led to its rejection and the resulting limitation on GMO".

Of the five countries studied in this book Ukraine is the one with the shortest democratic experience. However, since the collapse of Communism citizens in this country have mobilised on a great scale and successfully changed political events in their country. They did so in 2004–5 (the Orange Revolution) and again in 2013–14, but at a much greater cost, when President Yanukovych was effectively ousted from power.

Half of the statements made by the legal insiders in Ukraine suggest that *mild protest* would be the most appropriate manner in which to voice one's dissatisfaction with a piece of legislation in their country. Like legal insiders elsewhere, they have a preference for *civic measures*, though they also favour *legal measures* and *lobbying*. As in the other countries, there is next to no support for approaching the *media*.

Ukrainian legal insiders list seven different types of *civic protest.* Citizens may collect signatures or organise petitions; they may set up informal or formal groups; organise meetings; initiate referenda; vote in elections; organise lawful strikes; or engage in civil disobedience.

More specifically, they may "move away from the kitchen opposition" by actively engaging in "civil society" or "political activity". Citizens may "initiate change" by "writing something", "appealing to official institutions" or "collecting signatures". They may "gather people" at "meetings" or create "an initiative group" (to repeal a law), an "organization" or even a "political party" through which to "voice [their] discontent". They may "push for legal changes" by "demonstrating the flaw" in a given law, "proposing a new law" in its place, or by initiating "a referendum" in support of, or against, specific legislation. Finally, they may "vote in elections":

> U-ER-20: 'we have a kitchen opposition ... I will tell my wife what Yanukovych did, what President Yushchenko does ... [but] it will not become some mass protest [that way]'. U-ER-19: 'they should file a petition'. U-ER-22: '[they should] engage in political activity, create political parties, influence existing political parties'. U-PO-19: 'there must be a strong civil society with strong developed public institutions and they must exert pressure on deputies'.

Citizens wishing to turn to court to change laws may "appeal to" or "write" to "the Constitutional Court", "the Supreme Court" or "the Administrative Court". They may file a "constitutional petition" with a view to having a law "declared unconstitutional". Or they may turn to "the ECtHR". Two Ukrainian lawyers note that turning to the Constitutional Court to have bad laws repealed is effective. In the view of one prosecutor, however, ordinary citizens fail to make use of the courts due to their low level of legal culture:

> U-GO-18: 'they should turn to the Administrative Court or to the Supreme Court'. U-ER-5: 'when Parliament was passing laws that restricted some rights, especially social rights, that the citizens had, there were constitutional appeals ... not only from members of the Parliament ... but ... also ... from citizens ... the Constitutional Court ruled in favour of those citizens'. U-LA-12: 'we have a lot of laws. The norms of some were deemed unconstitutional by the Constitutional Court.' U-PR-11: 'we have examples, let's say, precedents when people go to the Constitutional Court ... there are cases concerning land disputes ... but ... there is such a concept as legal consciousness ... our level of [legal] education is low ... people don't address their complaints [to the courts]'.

Finally, citizens may engage in *lobbying* by "writing to MPs", or by "going to Parliament" and "contacting Parliamentary Committees" to present "a draft law to Parliament". Within Parliament they may also "contact political party representatives and [various] departments", "MPs", or "the Chairman of Parliament". Citizens may also approach the executive by going to "the city hall" or by "contacting governing bodies", including "the Ministry of Justice". Or they may "protest [outside] the Cabinet of Ministers". Finally, they may approach "the [Ukrainian President] to try to secure a "presidential veto":

> U-GO-21: 'you must work in Kiev, go to the Committees of the *Verkhovna Rada* [the Ukrainian Parliament] to present the law there, lobby it. Because it is practically impossible to do it at the regional level.' U-JU-22: '[they should] address the political parties that have factions in the *Verkhovna Rada*, the leaders of these factions, the deputies, [they should] write to the Ministry of Justice'. U-PR-9: 'a certain number of individuals can turn both to parliament members through a personal appointment and to the bodies of the prosecution which, in their turn, can write a constitutional appeal to the Constitutional Court'.

Civic action, legal action and lobbying may be used to promote a wide range of issues.

Responding to laws that are contrary to one's religion

There is considerable resistance both amongst publics and elites across Europe against religion "informing" law. Both groups make it clear that religion belongs to the private sphere and that in democracies religious people have to abide by state law (see Chapter 2). The two groups also believe religious leaders should not engage in dispute resolution, and that citizens should protest unreasonable and unjust legislation: they should do so by exercising their democratic rights and thus have a "voice". But does the right to a "voice" extend also to religious people who feel that state law clashes with their religion? The answer to this question is important in that it gives an indication as to how tolerant and democratic legal insiders are.

Table 4.17 shows that legal insiders predominantly think that religious people who object to laws on religious grounds should engage in mild forms of protest, just like any other citizen objecting to laws that he or she finds unreasonable or unjust. However, religious people should, to a greater extent than people who respond to troublesome, unfair or unjust laws, simply *accept* – and *obey* – laws that are not in line with their

Table 4.17 *Dealing with law that goes against one's religion: the legal insiders' perspective*

	Norway (%)	England (%)	Poland (%)	Bulgaria (%)	Ukraine (%)
Suppose *religious leaders oppose* a law passed by Parliament and declare that it is contrary to their religion. What should religious people do? Can you give examples?					
Obey	39	33	23	35	26
Evade (quietly ignore, disobey)	2	5	6	—	1
Protest	1	11	4	10	6
Mild	28	56	41	38	51
Medium	2	1	2	4	4
Strong	—	—	—	—	—
Mix	27	16	25	13	12

Note: Entries are based on the percentages of relevant 'text units' – the total number of answers to a given question; so entries sum up to approximately 100 per cent (decimals are rounded up or down to the nearest whole number).

religious faith (see Table 4.10). Obeying one's own conscience by evading state law is not considered to be an option for religious people.

Those legal insiders (all countries) who recommend that religious people engage in protest believe that they should do so by applying the same means of protest as other citizens. We will therefore not provide a detailed account of these measures, but rather highlight the reasons why legal insiders think religious people should obey laws that clash with their religious beliefs. Some attention will also be given to additional measures religious people may use to convey their concerns.

Legal insiders in Norway predominantly hold the view that religious people disagreeing with the law should nevertheless obey it as organised religion should be exercised "within the frames of the law". As "members of Norwegian society" all citizens, regardless of their faith, have "a duty to obey Norwegian laws". Put bluntly, Norway is a "democracy, not a theocracy". The law is passed "by the majority" regardless of faith and it stands "above everything". Religious people more generally (many respondents clearly have in mind Muslims rather than Christians) must either "accept democracy" or "leave the country". In the view of the Norwegian legal insiders there should be "zero tolerance for lawbreaking" on religious grounds. They believe that religious rights are well taken care of and that some domestic laws even have "the choice of conviction built into [them]":

> N-PO-22: 'those who chose to live in Norway must abide by Norwegian law regardless of what religion they belong to'. N-ER-6: 'we do not have a theocracy in Norway, we have a democracy . . . the religious leaders . . . must show societal responsibility and relate to democracy's rule and . . . laws.' N-JU-17: 'one cannot place religion above the law as long as there is a democratic society where some people have been elected to rule and give laws'. N-JU-24: 'religious people must accept the laws of the land . . . [however] when making laws one should try to do so in such a way as to not harm the most important core values of the different religions'. N-GO-15: 'one may engage in violence in the name of God . . . or in the name of Allah . . . this is a violation of Norwegian law . . . for which there should be zero tolerance'.

This being said, some Norwegian legal insiders acknowledge the difficult dilemma a conflict between state law and religious law poses for religious people. They understand that it "might be difficult" for such people to follow the law rather than their individual consciences. However, by violating the law religious people occasionally cause moral dilemmas for other people. Jehovah's Witnesses, for instance, make life difficult for doctors when declining life-saving blood transfusions. In some situations *civil disobedience* could be an acceptable solution for religious people:

> N-PR-13: 'I would think that a very religious human being places religion before the law. They would do what their God thinks they should do – but I think they should follow the law.' N-LA-12: 'one should [engage in civil disobedience] when . . . it becomes a question of conscience'.

Legal insiders in England suggest that religious people should voice their objection to laws that they feel are not compatible with their religious beliefs in the same manner as other citizens who are discontented with the law. They should do so by means of *mild protest,* such as *civic action, lobbying,* turning to the *media* or going to *court.* But, in addition, religious people may approach "the Bishops in the House of Lords". Civil disobedience ("peaceful non-compliance") is also a possibility:

> E-PO-16: 'okay, you might get a peaceful protest, the sort of thing that Ghandi did in India, marched to the sea for the salt tax, that sort of thing. So yes, there might be peaceful, civilian non-compliance, that's always one way of thinking of it. In light of the Bloody Sunday outcome recently, that's what they were trying to do in Ulster in the early '70s, late '60s, early '70s, once the troubles started unfortunately they all spiralled badly out of control'. E-GO-25: 'it's probably easier in this country for religious leaders to make their opposition known officially because of the Bishops in the House of Lords who can, you know, speak and lobby'.

English legal insiders give several examples of religious people protesting against laws that negatively affect their religion. Muslims, for instance, seek acceptance for Muslim girls wearing the *burqha* in school and for Muslim men having several wives. Some of them advocate the use of shari'a law in England. Others object to people eating pork. Sikhs, for their part, oppose any attempt to prevent them from wearing the turban. Jews and Muslims defend ritual slaughter. Religious people have objected to gay marriages. Catholic adoption agencies object to gay men adopting children. What is more, in England there has also been religiously "informed" opposition to civil partnerships, the existing time limit on abortion and equal rights legislation:

> E-ER-25: 'there are obviously those who are so fervent in their beliefs that they would like to see shari'a law coming'. E-ER-5: 'is it Sikhs who have to wear their headgear and stuff like that?' E-GO-16: 'the issue about Jewish slaughter of meat, where there has been quite a lot of campaigning to try and ban it because some animal welfare groups think it's unnecessarily cruel'. E-GO-2: 'there is quite a strong lobby around lowering the age of consent for gay men to be commensurate with heterosexual couples . . . also there was a lobby against the law to give equal access to [adoption] services for lesbian and gay people. For example the Catholic Adoption Society'.

As we have noted, Poland is one of Europe's most religious, but also most tolerant, state. Still, Polish legal insiders are slightly more tolerant towards ordinary citizens protesting law than they are towards religious people doing the same. The majority of their statements suggest that religious people who find laws unreasonable or unjust should engage in *mild* forms of *protest*. The range of activities proposed is wider than in England. Polish legal insiders distinguish between *civic protest, lobbying, turning to court, making use of formal complaint mechanisms* and approaching the *media*.

In addition, religious people may engage in advocacy through their *religious leaders* or by "voting" for "a religious party" in elections. "Spiritual leaders" may advocate religious causes "from the Pulpit" or by "making a legislative initiative". Believers may also make contact with people who share their "religious culture" and in this way "exercise [their] beliefs". One police officer referred to the Concordat between the Catholic Church (Vatican) and Poland. That agreement was signed in 1993 and entered into force in 1998:[30]

> P-JU-11: 'they should . . . support a religious party . . . which could influence a change in the law'. P-PO-25: 'there was . . . a petition to make 6 January a day off, because in the inter-war period it was a day off . . . Epiphany'. P-PO-5: 'there is such a thing as a concordat in Poland [agreement between the Vatican and the Polish state, signed in 1998] and the Church authorities can negotiate some matters with the politicians – for example the issue of abortion'. P-PR-7: 'spiritual leaders . . . have the right to criticise the law from the pulpit, in the press, in some interviews'. P-JU-22: 'spiritual leaders also have the possibility of making a legislative initiative'.

As in Norway legal insiders in Poland express some understanding for citizens who choose to abide by their own conscience rather than by national law: P-ER-16: "examples which can be provided are connected with the recent bioethical decisions, or the issues of the discussion concerning in vitro, or the issues of abortion. Here discussion is impossible".

Kanev (referred to in Ghodsee 2010, p. 233) claims that in Bulgaria 'being "religious" and believing in God had little to do with each other . . . religion is primarily about ethnic and national identity, a legacy of the state's long association with the Bulgarian Orthodox Church and the fact that "Bulgarian and Orthodoxy were synonym concepts"'. This duality is also observed amongst Muslim Turks, but to a lesser extent amongst the Pomaks (Bulgarian Muslims).

Ghodsee (ibid., p. 235) notes that 'narratives rooted in the Middle Ages . . . underpin Bulgarians' ability to have a strong religious identity

[30] The Concordat was signed in 1993. Former Polish MP, Ryszard M. Zając, has claimed that it 'restricts the sovereignty of our country, imposes on the citizens a considerable financial burden, is contrary to the constitutional principle of separation of church and state, violates the principle of equality between faiths and deviates from the principle of sovereign autonomy of the secular and (the) believers.' Concordat Watch, 'Polish Concordat (1993): text and criticism', www.concordatwatch.eu/topic-1331.834 accessed on 3 September 2014. See also Cholewinski (1998) and Delong (2012).

that can be devoid of spirituality'. Georgiev (cited in ibid., p. 236) claims that 'Bulgarians have always been independent thinkers, and that their sceptical attitude towards religious authority began in the tenth century and continues to the present day'.

The relationship between the Orthodox Church and the secular authorities are sometimes referred to as "symphonic secularism". Ghodsee (ibid., p. 241) notes that in the Bulgarian context this term 'includes a constitutionally enshrined traditional church as well as government regulation of religious activities in the country. This encompasses the government's power to dissolve churches considered a threat to public order and national security, or who violate or compromise the rights of others, as defined and adjudicated upon by the state'.[31]

Not surprisingly, therefore, legal insiders in Bulgaria are as much in favour of religious people *obeying* unreasonable or unacceptable laws as they are in favour of supporting mild protest against such laws.

Bulgarian legal insiders who advocate that law takes precedence over religious conscience do so for democratic reasons. They note that in "a secular state the law has priority" over religion – meaning that "the state [which passes law] is above religion". In Bulgaria "the law is for all citizens" and represents "the will of society". It must therefore be respected. In other words, the "religious community [must] abide by the law of the land". However, this should not really be a problem, inasmuch as Bulgaria is not "a very religious country":

> B-GO-21: 'the secular and the religious should be categorically differentiated and separated . . . I don't think it is appropriate for religious leaders to try to assume secular functions'. B-LA-25: 'the law is the will of society . . . [it] must be respected by all'.

Those who advocate *mild forms of protest* primarily support *civic*, though also to some extent *legal*, action. There is less support for lobbying, and far less support for approaching religious leaders or the media than there is in England and Poland. As in Poland, religious people in Bulgaria may turn to their spiritual leaders for assistance as "the leadership (of) religious institutions [may] object" to legislation that clashes with their faith:

[31] Bulgarian Jehovah's Witnesses, for instance, were not allowed to operate legally in Bulgaria until after they had accepted that their members would be given blood in life-threatening emergencies. Muslim teenagers have been denied the right to wear Islamic headscarves to secondary school (ibid., p. 227).

> B-LA-6: 'we are not a Caliphate, we are a Parliamentary Republic'. B-JU-4: 'I remember the disputes between the two Synods [of the Orthodox Church] ... each [Synod] has its supporters ... they brought their disputes to the European Court [of Human Rights] and obtained a decision and the state had to undertake legislative changes. I think that's the right direction.' B-GO-7: '[they could] refer to their religious leaders ... [to] determine whether this law is unconstitutional'. B-JU-21: 'the spiritual leaders of these people should hold talks with representatives of Parliament'.

As noted in Chapter 2 the early years of Ukrainian independence were characterised by religious conflict – between religious groups and between religious groups, private interest and local authorities. Many of these conflicts ended up in court. Religious disputes are still occasionally addressed by court.

Legal insiders in Ukraine acknowledge that "many laws [in their country] contradict religion" and that religious people should protest such laws. Ukrainian legal insiders recommend that religious people use the same measures as non-believers. Judges, in particular, are in favour of having courts consider religiously controversial legislation. More specifically, they should engage in *mild protest* if they feel that national legislation clashes with their religious beliefs. More specifically, they may use *civic measures*, *legal measures* or *lobbying* to voice their objections. Only one Ukrainian legal insider suggests that religious people objecting to specific legislation should turn to *the media*. In addition, however, religious people may turn to their religious leaders for assistance or initiate a "Conciliation Commission":

> U-ER-6: 'if a religious figure has influence ... [he] can take their main postulates and go with them to elections. If priests themselves would like to go into politics they should leave the church.' U-LA-19: 'they have to seek the creation of the Conciliation Commissions or the Commission to Regulate Matters'.

Ukrainian legal insiders provide several examples of situations in which religious people have objected to national legislation – notably to the introduction of "national ID cards",[32] alternative military service for conscientious objectors and the return of religious buildings to the

[32] Some 50,000 followers of the Ukrainian Orthodox Church of the Moscow Patriarchate refused to have individual identification numbers (Yelensky 2002, pp. 475–6). In Greece and Georgia Orthodox believers have made similar objections to ID cards on the grounds that in Christianity the number 666 is the symbol of the devil.

Orthodox Church. In Crimea, Muslim leaders have challenged laws that would have negatively affected their community, such as the law on Muslim holidays:

> U-ER-19: 'the identification codes were introduced [and] some religious people refused to accept them thinking they represented some kind of demonic power . . . they turned to deputies . . . the deputies made amendments that under certain conditions a person is allowed not to receive the identification code'. U-GO-18: 'an Act was passed [to the effect that] a man of faith does not have to take a weapon in his hands'.

Finally, some legal insiders note that the situation of the Orthodox Church in Ukraine is not all that bad at present as it has become fashionable to join the Church: U-GO-11: "all our officials changed their attitude towards the Church [after the collapse of Communism]. Now all of them like the Church, although they didn't want to hear anything about [it in the past] . . . it has become fashionable".

Conclusions

Going through the patterns of public attitudes and perceptions it is difficult to avoid the conclusion that "public *perceptions* of law in action" vary across our five countries very much more than "public *attitudes* towards law in principle".

Once again our data confirm that what distinguishes the popular legal culture in the different countries is not so much the legal attitudes and aspirations of the various publics but their perceptions, and in particular, as will be seen in Chapter 6, their perceptions of "legal insiders" (though not their perceptions of "legal outsiders", the general public, which are explored in Chapter 5).

As seen in this chapter the public's perceptions of 'law in action' are relatively country-specific, although their attitudes to 'law in principle' (Chapters 2 and 3) are relatively pan-European. One aspect of popular legal culture (perceptions) is very sensitive to location, whereas the other (principles) is much more detached from the environment in which people live. Popular legal culture combines both the "inner man" and the "outer environment" however, and how people act is influenced by both, and by the tension between them.

Both legal outsiders and insiders hold the view that people should protest against unfair and unjust laws (attitudes), and that they should primarily do so, using democratic means sanctioned by law ("Voice").

There is little support for protesting against such laws by evading them ("Exit"), and also little support for simply passively accepting unfair or unjust laws ("Loyalty"). But legal insiders are less tolerant of religious people who declare that a law is contrary to their religion protesting against such law. The percentage recommending that religious people should simply accept and obey the law ("Loyalty") – compared to the percentage recommending that ordinary citizens should do so if they consider the law to be unfair or unjust – is fairly high.

Although legal outsiders are in favour of several alternatives to court, legal insiders have a stronger preference for involving the courts – either by turning directly to court or by combining ADR and going to court. Though fairly positive to mediation (all countries except Ukraine), legal insiders are not very supportive of religious leaders, community leaders, family or relatives engaging in dispute resolution. Their reasoning is very much 'rule of law'-oriented: in their view ADR does not provide citizens with justice.

5

Perceptions of legal outsiders

Introduction: reasons for obeying or breaking the law

In the previous chapter we explored 'law in action' – including by investigating alternatives to court. This chapter focuses on how legal outsiders and insiders think people behave *before the law* – that is, to what extent – and why – they abide by it ("Loyalty") or break it ("Exit").

Tyler (2006, p. 3) identifies two major approaches to law-abidance: *the instrumental perspective* and *the normative perspective*. The instrumental perspective – which draws on the deterrence literature – assumes that people 'shape their behaviour to respond to changes in the tangible, immediate incentives and penalties associated with following the law – to judgements about the personal gains and losses resulting from different kinds of behaviour'. In other words, when the personal cost of breaking the law is high people are more likely to abide by it than when the cost of doing so is low. Personal costs cover a wide range of factors, such as financial cost (fines), loss of reputation, loss of employment or social exclusion. Law-abidance (or the lack of it) is influenced by social control (peer pressure) and/or the quality of law enforcement.

By contrast, the normative perspective is concerned with 'the influence of what people regard as "just" and "moral" as opposed to what is in their self-interest. It also examines the connection between normative commitment to legal authorities and law-abiding behaviour'. From this perspective, law-abidance has intrinsic value. One should follow the law regardless of personal cost as doing so represents a higher value.

Here we explore the instrumental and normative reasons why people obey – or break – the law. And we demonstrate that it is not always a question of either-or, but rather of both. We thus explore *legality* as a dimension of legal culture, but one based on attitudes and perceptions rather than personal experience. We first investigate the perceptions of the public (as potential lawbreakers) before moving on to the perceptions of the legal insiders (some of whom deal with those breaking the law) with a view to establishing whether, and in case to what extent, their perceptions differ.

The chapter is primarily 'people oriented' rather than 'principle oriented'.

Legal outsiders' perspectives on legal outsiders (like themselves)

O wad some Power the giftie gie us
Tae see oorsels as ithers see us

As Robert Burns so eloquently hinted, it is difficult if not impossible to 'see ourselves as others see us'. Public perceptions of legal outsiders are necessarily to some degree self-perceptions. If not quite self-perceptions, they are at least perceptions that include perceptions of the self or of people somewhat like the self, or at least inclusive of 'people like me' and more generous images of self, friends, neighbours and relations.

Trustworthy and law-abiding?

Public perceptions of legal outsiders – that is "ordinary people" – are clearly more positive than perceptions of legal insiders (Chapter 6) – and especially so in the former communist countries.

We did not use the same question of 'positive or negative' feelings to gauge public perceptions of legal outsiders as we did with public perceptions of legal insiders. Doing so would not be appropriate because the question lacks specificity about law when applied to anyone other than legal professionals. But on an average, 72 per cent of the public feel that 'most people they meet can be trusted'; 75 per cent feel that 'most ordinary people in this country generally obey the law'; and 88 per cent assert that people they 'regularly come into contact with personally generally obey the law'. Such personal contacts therefore rate especially highly.

Moreover the 'cross-national shape' of public perceptions of 'ordinary people' is significantly different from the 'cross-national shape' of public perceptions of legal insiders. In dramatic contrast to the progressive and precipitous drop in positive perceptions of legal insiders from 86 per cent in Norway to 38 per cent in Ukraine, the drop in positive perceptions of legal outsiders from Norway to Ukraine (Table 5.1) is neither precipitous nor always progressive.

Perceptions that 'most people you meet can be trusted and would not try to take advantage of you if they had the chance' drop only from 87 per

Table 5.1 *Personalised trust: the legal outsiders' perspective*

	NOR (%)	ENG (%)	POL (%)	BUL (%)	UKR (%)	N-MU (%)	E-MU (%)	P-MU (%)	B-MU (%)	U-MU (%)
Q99: Most 'people you meet' can be trusted (v. would try to take advantage)	94	75	62	50	77	67	47	84	54	88
Q100: Most ordinary people generally obey the law (v. disobey)	87	82	64	72	70	75	69	82	76	80
Q101: Most ordinary people you regularly come into contact with personally in everyday life obey the law (v. disobey)	94	92	84	87	83	73	86	92	91	90

Note: NOR, ENG, POL, BUL, UKR refer to the majority populations; N-MU, E-MU, P-MU, B-MU, U-MU refer to the Muslims.

cent in Norway to 70 per cent in Ukraine. (Indeed perceptions of interpersonal trust are slightly higher in Ukraine than anywhere else except Norway!) And perceptions that 'people you regularly come into contact with personally generally obey the law' drop only from 94 per cent in Norway to 83 per cent in Ukraine.

Our FG discussions show that citizens across Europe believe that people are mostly law-abiding, but they sometimes disregard "minor" law. Statements from one of the English FGs illustrate this point rather nicely. When asked "do ordinary people in England generally obey the law?" FG participants in Leeds answer as follows:

> E8-Leeds-4: 'Yes'. E6-Leeds-4: 'We are miles apart from other people in other countries'. E6-Leeds-8: 'Most people . . . obey the law'. E6-Leeds-6: 'I felt a criminal – I failed to pay a parking ticket'. E8-Leeds-4: '[Brits are] drunk and disorderly [on] weekends'. E8-Leeds-7: 'That is people who would normally be law-abiding during the week'. E8-Leeds-2: 'A lot of people break the law with motoring.'

How do the public think ordinary people "generally feel when they knowingly break the law"? The public in Norway and England most frequently cite "indifferent", but in the former communist countries they most frequently cite "nervous and afraid".

Conversely, when they are asked about three categories of legal insiders – judges, Members of Parliament and the police – when they "knowingly break the law", Norwegians most frequently answer feelings of "guilt and shame", and the English "indifferent" (though closely followed by "guilt and shame"). But in the former communist countries they cite the feelings of legal insiders who break the law as most frequently feeling "strength and self-confidence" (Table 5.2).

Members of the public do not discriminate much in their perspective on these three different sets of legal insiders: judges, MPs and police. The contrast between public perceptions of lawbreaking by legal insiders and outsiders is therefore far greater in the former communist countries than in Norway and England. In England, the public perception is that legal insiders and outsiders are much the same in their reaction to breaking the law. And in Norway, the public perception is that legal insiders who break the law are more likely to suffer greater pangs of guilt and shame than legal outsiders.

But in all three former communist countries the public perception is that legal insiders who break the law are very much more likely than legal outsiders to feel "strong and self-confident" in their lawbreaking, whereas legal outsiders who break the law are very much more likely

Table 5.2 *Feelings about law-breaking: the legal outsiders' perspective*

	NOR (%)	ENG (%)	POL (%)	BUL (%)	UKR (%)	N-MU (%)	E-MU (%)	P-MU (%)	B-MU (%)	U-MU (%)
Q103A: When *ordinary people* break the law they feel:										
nervous/afraid	24	22	36	49	45	37	21	42	37	47
guilty/ashamed	20	22	20	22	31	25	27	17	43	38
indifferent	50	51	25	14	18	28	37	25	9	9
self-confident	6	5	19	14	6	9	15	16	11	6
Q103C: When *judges* break the law they feel:										
nervous/afraid	18	13	12	11	8	25	13	16	2	7
guilty/ashamed	34	30	8	2	2	39	35	8	3	1
indifferent	26	41	28	17	32	20	28	34	27	41
self-confident	21	16	52	69	58	16	23	42	68	51
Q103E: When *MPs* break the law they feel										
nervous/afraid	21	16	9	6	3	30	10	10	4	8
guilty/ashamed	37	25	6	1	2	34	32	5	1	1
indifferent	26	40	22	14	31	19	33	32	22	26
self-confident	16	19	63	78	64	17	25	53	73	65
Q103F: When the *police* break the law they feel:										
nervous/afraid	19	17	17	14	8	27	11	21	5	4
guilty/ashamed	39	31	7	7	3	37	33	8	5	2
indifferent	24	36	26	21	34	20	28	28	29	36
self-confident	17	16	51	58	56	16	28	43	61	58

Note: NOR, ENG, POL, BUL, UKR refer to the majority populations; N-MU, E-MU, P-MU, B-MU, U-MU refer to the Muslims.

Table 5.3 *Law as the power of the state versus the people: the legal outsiders' perspective*

	NOR (%)	ENG (%)	POL (%)	BUL (%)	UKR (%)	N-MU (%)	E-MU (%)	P-MU (%)	B-MU (%)	U-MU (%)
Q16: Law = power of state v. people	17	42	50	61	74	35	53	30	49	61

Note: NOR, ENG, POL, BUL, UKR refer to the majority populations; N-MU, E-MU, P-MU, B-MU, U-MU refer to the Muslims.

than legal insiders to feel "nervous and afraid". That reflects more long-established public perceptions that in the former communist countries the law remains essentially "unfair" and continues to represent "the power of the state to control people" rather than "generally recognised moral values" – ranging from a peak in Ukraine (79 per cent unfair, 74 per cent state control) down to a minimum in Norway (10 per cent unfair, 17 per cent state control) – though now that perspective applies to human beings caught up in the process of lawmaking and law enforcement rather than the disembodied "law" in itself (Table 5.3).

Why do ordinary people disobey the law?

There is a widespread perception that 'ordinary people are more willing to break the law now than in the recent past, say ten years ago' (Table 5.4).

Our FGs show that people in England think the punishment for breaking the law is too soft. They also think that law enforcement has become too lenient. People in Norway and England make a risk assessment prior to violating minor law. Norwegian FG participants believe that if the chances of getting caught are slim and if no third party will suffer as a result of one's actions, then Norwegians will violate minor law. But they will abide by major law. English FG participants believe that if people think they can get away with it or if the punishment if caught is not so serious, they will happily break the law. The approach to (minor) lawbreaking in both countries is thus fairly instrumental:

Table 5.4 *Willingness to break the law: the legal outsiders' perspective*

	NOR (%)	ENG (%)	POL (%)	BUL (%)	UKR (%)	N-MU (%)	E-MU (%)	P-MU (%)	B-MU (%)	U-MU (%)
Q104: Ordinary people are now more willing to break the law (v. less)	79	74	50	59	72	65	64	46	52	67

Note: NOR, ENG, POL, BUL, UKR refer to the majority populations; N-MU, E-MU, P-MU, B-MU, U-MU refer to the Muslims.

> N5-Muslims-5: 'if they think they will not get caught and it is a small thing, then they break [the law].' N2-Oslo-4: 'as long as you benefit from it and it does not cause great harm to others, it is more accepted [to break the law].' E5-Village-South-West-5: 'I think we all would probably flout laws if we didn't think there was going to be [something] done to us.' E6-Sheffield-5: 'it's all purely down to the deterrent. If you're more scared of what's going to happen to you than the benefit you're personally going to get out of breaking the law then you will do it, or you might do it.'

As already noted in Eastern Europe *legal nihilism* is widespread. People feel they have a moral right to break the law because political leaders do so, thereby setting a bad example. Added to this, there are more opportunities to break laws now than there were in the past – and law enforcement is poorer than it used to be. Some people have no choice but to break the law out of poverty. They steal to feed their families.

Polish FG participants think the punishment for breaking laws is too low and that people therefore don't feel deterred from breaking it. FG participants in Bulgaria believe that some people simply cannot afford not to break the law and that, until their economic situation improves, they will keep doing so. They also think the *elites* set a bad example in terms of law-abidance. Just like the Brits, people in Bulgaria have an instrumental approach to law-abidance. They make assessments of when it will or will not pay off for them to break the law and act accordingly:

> P5-Mierzecice-6: 'the penalties are too low . . . [they don't] frighten people off.' P6-Białystok-1: 'when you feel a whip near you then you obey the law. But when you see that the whip is far away, then obeying isn't

> necessarily so strict.' B1-Sofia-1: 'internet piracy can hardly be eliminated anytime soon because we are still insolvent and cannot pay for the software products'. B1-Sofia-7: 'I was thinking that when people at the higher levels of society than us try to get round the rules we, the ordinary people, will follow suit ... my salary, for instance, is 500 leva. The employer pays social security at 220 leva, so that I can get my child allowances with the document that he issues to me. This is a violation of the law; it is cheating, but what can I do in this situation?'

Ukrainian FG participants, for their part, think people, break laws if they think there will be no repercussions. They acknowledge that some people break the law out of poverty. Others, however, are placed above the law and therefore act with impunity. If they get caught, they pay their way out of trouble:

> U16-Alushta-2: 'if they know ... there will be no punishment [they break the law].' U17-Marino-7: 'someone comes and steals a couple of your chicken and there is no law to punish [him].' U17-Marino-3: 'if you want to imprison people like him you would have to imprison all the people.' U17-Marino-5: 'someone steals pension money from an older lady. He comes, takes her money and goes. No one is chasing him. The same with potatoes'. U21-Crimean Tatars-5: 'he thinks nothing will happen to him for that. He has money and power. He can break the law.'

More revealing, however, is the question what is "the main reason why people in this country obey laws?" We listed feeling that the law is "generally fair", that it would be "morally wrong" to disobey, that it is the "duty of a citizen in a democracy to obey laws passed by the parliament they elected", and last but not least "fear of punishment". "Fair laws" are cited by an average of 22 per cent in Norway and England, but by only half as many (11 per cent) in the former communist countries. Conversely, "fear of punishment" is cited by an average of only 21 per cent in Norway and England, but by an average of 37 per cent in the former communist countries (and reaching 45 per cent in Poland). So we have a clear break between patterns of "fairness" and "fear" (Table 5.5).

Norwegian FG participants believe that Norwegians are fairly law-abiding – and that they are more law-abiding than people in many other countries. One of the British Euro-migrants thinks it is all a bit too much – meaning that people in Norway are too law-abiding:

> N12-Tromsø-7: 'ordinary people abide by the laws and regulations. It is the ones who are not ordinary who do not [obey them].' N3-Muslims-7: 'the Norwegian population obey the law to a greater extent than [people] in other countries ... there is regard for the law [here]'. N9-Stavanger-7:

Table 5.5 *Reasons for obeying the law: the legal outsiders' perspective*

	NOR (%)	ENG (%)	POL (%)	BUL (%)	UKR (%)	N-MU (%)	E-MU (%)	P-MU (%)	B-MU (%)	U-MU (%)
Q102: Why obey?										
fear punishment	18	23	45	34	32	32	39	42	34	31
morally wrong	26	31	24	23	39	24	23	20	35	44
duty as citizen in a democracy	36	22	20	29	20	28	22	26	20	18
law fair	21	23	12	13	9	17	17	12	11	8

Note: NOR, ENG, POL, BUL, UKR refer to the majority populations; N-MU, E-MU, P-MU, B-MU, U-MU refer to the Muslims.

> 'abroad we are considered to be law-abiding. Many foreigners call us naïve.' N7-Brits-2: 'I have noticed [that] they seem brainwashed by the government, like "you can't do that!" There are rules for everything . . . it's hard to explain. They seem brainwashed . . . they follow the rules.'

English FG participants mostly state that most people obey the law without providing an explanation as to why they do so. One FG participant thinks Brits are quite law-abiding compared to others. Another thinks there are some laws that everyone obeys, and other laws that they ignore:

> E5-Village-South-West-1: 'as a country, we are quite law-abiding compared to some other countries.' E6-Sheffield-8: 'most people are law-abiding.' E1-London-2: 'there is a core set of laws which . . . the majority follow and . . . there are some laws which people make their own risk assessment on, like breaking the speed limit . . . but I think broadly, most people abide by the law.'

Polish FG participants believe that people might violate some minor law, but that on the whole they are law-abiding. Some FG participants believe that ordinary people are more law-abiding than elites. The latter are considered to be above the law. One FG participant believes that people abide the law for moral reasons:

> P8-Turośń Kościelna-1: 'I guess 80 per cent of the population obeys the law.' P6-Białystok-8: 'I think they do, mostly. Some small misdemeanours, well that might happen to anyone.' P7-Zambrow-1: 'society obeys the law on the whole. It's the prominent people who don't. If I drink-drive I get caught and punished, but if it's someone prominent then the police

> turns a blind eye'. P4-Lubliniec-4: 'ordinary people are most likely to respect the law because it's simple for them ... ordinary people have nothing to hide'.

FG participants in Bulgaria partly believe that citizens obey the law out of fear, partly out of duty. Some older people have a more principled attitude towards the law – thinking that it should be obeyed regardless. Most people, however, fall into the first category. It is the fear of having the water or electricity cut, or the fear of being punished, that prevents them from breaking the law:

> B1-Sofia-2: 'the majority abide by the laws because they fear the consequences.' B8-Dolna Mitropolia-4: 'the elderly, when they receive their pensions, the first thing they do is pay their taxes and fees ... every month on the 5th or 7th when the pension arrives, they rush [off] to pay their electricity, water bills, pay debts to the state, which shows that the elderly have some trust in this state. Or feel the strength of their obligation [towards the law].' B8-Dolna Mitropolia-1: 'they [i.e. the elderly] are obliged [to pay] because otherwise ... the [electricity] cable is cut, you haven't paid your water bill and they come and stop the supply.'

Some Ukrainian FG participants think people obey the law out of duty. This is particularly the case amongst older citizens who lived through Communism and people who have been taught to abide by the law from an early age. The majority (i.e. ordinary people) obey the law because they fear the consequences of not doing so:

> U12-Ternopil-6: 'it is impossible to obey the laws 100 per cent ... [but] in most cases Ukrainians are law-abiding.' U16-Alushta-4: 'they [i.e. ordinary people] were brought up [to be] law-abiding'. U11-Zubra-1: '[ordinary people abide by the law] because they fear the law. Ordinary people are more law-abiding.' U18-Evpatoria-7: 'older people are more law-abiding.' U16-Alushta-8: 'the system is guilty ... good people make up the majority [of the population of Ukraine] but they are sometimes forced to violate the law'. U14-Plotica-4: 'if the higher officials override the law we may also override the law'. U3-Donetsk-4: 'you know, those people from our level of the population, they follow the laws.'

Some FG participants believe that people in Ukraine observe moral laws but violate state law. They do so for normative and instrumental reasons: moral laws are considered legitimate, whereas state law is largely viewed as illegitimate. If it is possible to get away with breaking the latter, most people have no moral qualms about doing so. This being said, some FG participants believe that people mostly do abide by the law – as otherwise the country would simply collapse:

Table 5.6 *Reasonable excuse for breaking the law? the legal outsiders' perspective*

	NOR (%)	ENG (%)	POL (%)	BUL (%)	UKR (%)	N-MU (%)	E-MU (%)	P-MU (%)	B-MU (%)	U-MU (%)
Q105: Ordinary people often have a reasonable excuse for breaking the law (v. no valid excuse)	31	32	42	56	72	41	42	41	42	84

Note: NOR, ENG, POL, BUL, UKR refer to the majority populations; N-MU, E-MU, P-MU, B-MU, U-MU refer to the Muslims.

> U3-Donetsk-6: 'the majority follow the law, but some kind of specific moral law. Because in a legislative sense our country does not function, and the country somehow exists only due to those moral rules'. U9-Lviv-8: 'usually, yes, [people] try to follow the laws, according to the customs and power ... that is why people who do not even know the laws are guided by their consciousness, customs, just everyday habits, the majority of them do not break the law'.

Law-abiding lawbreakers?

Lawbreaking can be as much the fault of the law as the fault of the lawbreaker. We asked, "when ordinary people knowingly break the law in this country, do you feel they often have some reasonable excuse" or do they "usually have no valid excuse for breaking the law?" Even in Norway and England around 32 per cent feel they do often have "a reasonable excuse", but that rises to 42 per cent in Poland, 56 per cent in Bulgaria and a huge 72 per cent in Ukraine (Table 5.6).

In what circumstances might "generally law-abiding people sometimes knowingly break the law?" We listed eight possible circumstances. In every such circumstance, a majority ranging from 54 per cent to 92 per cent think that "generally law-abiding people" might "sometimes knowingly break the law". More surprisingly perhaps, there is very little cross-national variation: on an average around 71 per cent in Norway, England, Bulgaria and Ukraine, together with 81 per cent in Poland think law-abiding people might break the law in these eight circumstances (Table 5.7). Unusually, it is Poland that stands apart as the least law-abiding in these circumstances.

In rising order, law-abiding people might break the law when faced with "unnecessarily troublesome laws" (54 per cent); "pressure for bribes from doctors, police or state officials" (63 per cent); "unfair and unjust laws" (67 per cent); "if they think they will do no harm to other people by breaking the law" (73 per cent); "if they think they will not get caught and punished" (73 per cent); "if they are under pressure of work, or of poverty" (73 per cent); "if they are acting in self-defence"[1] (90 per cent); and "if they are in an emergency situation"[2] (92 per cent). In most of these scenarios, perceptions of law-abiding lawbreakers do not vary greatly from country to country.

Of the eight scenarios, there is only one in which there is a large cross-national variation in perceptions of law-abiding lawbreakers: that is the public's willingness "under pressure from doctors, police or state officials to give them gifts or bribes", which averages 84 per cent in the three former communist countries but averages only 31 per cent in Norway and England. That is important in itself, but it is an exception. And it is arguably a role in which 'ordinary people' are as much or more the victims of a crime rather than the instigators.

In every country except Ukraine the general public feel, on balance, that "religious and ethnic minorities" are *less* law-abiding than the general public (Table 5.8). Muslims take a somewhat different view. On an average (and within every country except Norway) they claim that "religious and ethnic minorities" are *more* law-abiding than the general public.

The FGs shed light on what minorities the public consider to be less law-abiding. In Eastern Europe – and particularly in Bulgaria, which has a large Roma community – the Roma are singled out as the least law-abiding ethnic group.

FG participants in Bulgaria claim that the Roma do not care about law. Although they mostly blame the Roma (whom they sometimes refer to as "the Gypsies"), they also blame state representatives for being too lenient with them:

[1] If and only if the respondent asked for an example to clarify "self-defence" interviewers were instructed to say "for example, against a thief or a burglar".

[2] If and only if the respondent asked for an example to clarify "an emergency situation" interviewers were instructed to say "for example, rushing a child to hospital".

Table 5.7 *Reasons for breaking the law: the legal outsiders' perspective*

	NOR (%)	ENG (%)	POL (%)	BUL (%)	UKR (%)	N-MU (%)	E-MU (%)	P-MU (%)	B-MU (%)	U-MU (%)
Q106A: troublesome	58	55	67	47	45	58	59	35	40	35
Q106J: pressure for bribes	26	36	85	83	85	43	51	60	86	69
Q106B: unfair	74	69	74	60	58	60	65	44	56	54
Q106C: no harm	76	79	75	70	66	76	74	54	76	52
Q106D: not get caught	70	78	75	74	68	63	80	49	76	54
Q106I: pressure of work or poverty	60	69	88	69	80	64	79	57	60	69
Q106H: self-defence	95	89	92	86	88	74	89	85	81	84
Q106K: emergency	99	90	94	90	89	76	87	86	95	86

Note: NOR, ENG, POL, BUL, UKR refer to the majority populations; N-MU, E-MU, P-MU, B-MU, U-MU refer to the Muslims.

Table 5.8 *Law-obedience amongst religious and ethnic groups: the legal outsiders' perspective*

	NOR (%)	ENG (%)	POL (%)	BUL (%)	UKR (%)	N-MU (%)	E-MU (%)	P-MU (%)	B-MU (%)	U-MU (%)
Q108: Religious and ethnic minorities are:										
more obedient to law	6	8	12	15	30	17	27	19	31	44
just the same as others	62	68	69	36	57	55	68	76	50	48
less obedient	32	24	18	49	13	29	6	5	19	8
Q109: Very religious people are:										
more obedient to law	16	21	31	33	46	29	41	24	45	53
less obedient	23	23	9	19	8	22	8	5	6	17
just the same as others	61	56	60	47	45	50	51	71	49	30

Note: NOR, ENG, POL, BUL, UKR refer to the majority populations; N-MU, E-MU, P-MU, B-MU, U-MU refer to the Muslims.

> B4-Topoli-1: 'the Gypsies ... as a rule break the law' B1-Sofia-4: 'the Gypsies do not fear the authorities and therefore have no fear of laws'. B2-Sofia-6: 'they [i.e. the Roma] have more rights than obligations. They don't consider it their obligation to pay their bills, but they never forget their rights.' B3-Varna-1: 'the Gypsies, they use the electricity, water, telephone for free, they don't pay for anything while all of us here, we have to work and pay our taxes ... they [the Gypsies] ... get ... social assistance'.

Polish and Ukrainian FG participants also make negative remarks about the Roma, though most of their comments about lawbreaking minorities are about Muslims, Africans and Asians:

> P3-Katowice-3: 'I don't know if the Roma [obey the law].' P2-Warsaw-6: 'The Gypsies ... just don't respect the law at all ... they simply don't obey our laws'. P8-Turośń Kościelna-7: 'let's take the Gypsies, they are very particular ... when it comes to stealing things it's in their nature [to do so]. They do it no matter the consequences'. U9-Lviv-5: '[the minorities] are those who break the law the most ... for example, the Gypsies.' U6-Kharkiv-7: 'the Gypsies they can sell drugs everywhere but nobody notices, or doesn't want to notice.'

Only one FG participant defends the Roma population, justifying their lawbreaking by referring to their difficult social situation and the great difficulty they have in finding employment: B4-Topoli-4: "their social situation is very bad ... they are not educated. Nowadays the private sector is bigger than the state [sector]. Who will want to employ a Gypsy? Very few people ... so what can they do? When 5–6 little Gypsies are waiting at home [for something] to eat? They will steal and cheat".

By a small margin, the public in Norway and England also suggest that "*very* religious people, irrespective of which religion" are *less* law-abiding than other people. But in Poland, Bulgaria and Ukraine – again by a small margin – the public think "*very* religious people, irrespective of which religion" are *more* law-abiding than other people. Once again, however, the largest number thinks "*very* religious people" are "just the same as others" (Table 5.8).

Public perceptions of what causes "ordinary people to disobey the law" assign most blame to "the pressure of circumstances" (43 per cent) rather than "the people themselves" (27 per cent). In addition, an average of 16 per cent blames "pressure for bribes" in Poland, Bulgaria and Ukraine (though less than 2 per cent in Norway and England). Conversely, an average of 36 per cent in Norway and England, but only 21 per cent in Poland, Bulgaria and Ukraine blame "the people themselves" (Table 5.9).

Table 5.9 *Reasons for breaking the law: the legal outsiders' perspective*

	NOR (%)	ENG (%)	POL (%)	BUL (%)	UKR (%)	N-MU (%)	E-MU (%)	P-MU (%)	B-MU (%)	U-MU (%)
Q107: Fault:										
pressure of circumstances	33	51	40	44	46	28	61	42	39	50
people themselves	43	29	17	26	20	34	21	34	41	19
pressure for bribes	1	2	13	19	15	5	2	6	12	10
troublesome laws	11	7	18	6	8	12	7	16	3	9
unfair laws	12	10	10	4	11	20	9	3	5	13

Note: NOR, ENG, POL, BUL, UKR refer to the majority populations; N-MU, E-MU, P-MU, B-MU, U-MU refer to the Muslims.

Table 5.10 *Perceptions of government and corruption: the legal outsiders' perspective*

	NOR (%)	ENG (%)	POL (%)	BUL (%)	UKR (%)	N-MU (%)	E-MU (%)	P-MU (%)	B-MU (%)	U-MU (%)
Q126: Government and people respect law more (v. less) than in the rest of Europe	93	58	28	12	10	73	56	30	4	24
Q62: Crime and corruption greater than European average (v. less)	10	50	79	92	91	14	50	74	88	88

Note: NOR, ENG, POL, BUL, UKR refer to the majority populations; N-MU, E-MU, P-MU, B-MU, U-MU refer to the Muslims.

Public perceptions that "the government and people respect the law and generally obey it more than in the rest of Europe" range down steadily from a peak of 93 per cent in Norway to a mere 10 per cent in Ukraine. Conversely, public perceptions that "the level of crime and corruption in this country is greater than the average across Europe" range down steadily from a peak of 91 per cent in Ukraine to just 10 per cent in Norway (Table 5.10).

The public feel the law is now much better known in Norway but not in England and Poland, and much less well known after all the changes in Bulgaria and Ukraine. In the public's view the law is now less well respected or enforced everywhere; and by huge margins the public everywhere feel (rightly or wrongly) that crime, bribery and corruption are increasing rather than decreasing (Table 5.11).

Why do ordinary people obey the law? The Norwegian public, more than anything else, cite duty; the English and Ukrainians both cite morality; and Poles and Bulgarians cite fear (Table 5.12).

Do Euro-migrants obey the law more or less than the general public in each country? Although the most widespread view is that Euro-migrants eventually become similar to the host nation, in the meantime

Table 5.11 *Perceptions of law, courts, crime and bribery: the legal outsiders' perspective*

	NOR (%)	ENG (%)	POL (%)	BUL (%)	UKR (%)	N-MU (%)	E-MU (%)	P-MU (%)	B-MU (%)	U-MU (%)
Q58: now better known (v. less)	67	46	51	24	28	75	56	56	28	33
Q40A: people more willing to go to court now (v. less)	87	66	67	48	35	75	63	55	27	44
Q59: now more respected (v. less)	21	11	35	21	11	47	31	47	31	17
Q57: now more strictly implemented and enforced (v. less)	40	41	39	26	19	59	70	54	36	45
Q60: crime increasing (v. decreasing)	97	83	78	91	94	93	88	63	93	90
Q61: bribery and corruption increasing (v. decreasing)	87	68	76	93	96	75	72	63	97	93

Note: NOR, ENG, POL, BUL, UKR refer to the majority populations; N-MU, E-MU, P-MU, B-MU, U-MU refer to the Muslims.

Table 5.12 *Reasons for obeying the law revisited: the legal outsiders' perspective*

	NOR (%)	ENG (%)	POL (%)	BUL (%)	UKR (%)	N-MU (%)	E-MU (%)	P-MU (%)	B-MU (%)	U-MU (%)
Q102: Why obey?										
fear punishment	18	23	45	34	32	32	39	42	34	31
morally wrong	26	31	24	23	39	24	23	20	35	44
duty as citizen in a democracy	36	22	20	29	20	28	22	26	20	18
law fair	21	23	12	13	9	17	17	12	11	8

Note: NOR, ENG, POL, BUL, UKR refer to the majority populations; N-MU, E-MU, P-MU, B-MU, U-MU refer to the Muslims.

Table 5.13 *Reasons why Euro-migrants obey the law: the legal outsiders' perspective*

	NOR (%)	ENG (%)	POL (%)	BUL (%)	UKR (%)	N-MU (%)	E-MU (%)	P-MU (%)	B-MU (%)	U-MU (%)
Q110: Euro-migrants obey law:										
more	4	8	33	58	58	8	12	52	74	53
less	24	37	14	16	12	44	31	8	9	10
soon become the same	72	55	53	26	30	48	56	40	17	36

Note: NOR, ENG, POL, BUL, UKR refer to the majority populations; N-MU, E-MU, P-MU, B-MU, U-MU refer to the Muslims.

Norwegians and English feel that Euro-migrants are less law-abiding than the host public, while Poles, Bulgarians and Ukrainians feel Euro-migrants obey the law more than the host public (Table 5.13). We will return to this issue in greater depth in Chapter 8.

Legal insiders' perspectives on legal outsiders

As noted in previous chapters, research on attitude towards laws and law-abidingness in Eastern Europe indicates that *legal nihilism* is fairly widespread – particularly in the successor states to the Soviet Union, but also in some of the new EU member states. Czech and Slovenian elites, for instance, refer to lawbreaking as a "national sport", whereas elites in Bulgaria view the law as an open door in a field: there is no reason to go through the door when one may go around it (Grødeland 2007).

There appear to be two reasons for this attitude towards law: on the one hand, state institutions in Eastern Europe have historically been viewed as instruments of external, illegitimate rulers. Consequently, people have had no reason to abide by the laws of these institutions (normative perspective). On the other hand, legal nihilism also reflects an incorrect understanding of democracy: to many East Europeans democracy means unlimited freedom – including the freedom to break the law and to get away with it (instrumental perspective).

By contrast, Norwegians (just like Scandinavians more generally) seem to have a very 'correct' attitude towards law: laws exist to be kept rather than to be violated. Abiding by the law is considered a democratic duty – though there is considerable tolerance for civil disobedience in Norway in cases where one's individual conscience clashes with the law.[3]

The English, for their part, have a more flexible attitude towards law than Norwegians: while Norwegians strive to do what is strictly legal, Brits do what they consider to be reasonable. In doing so, they abide by a key principle of the English common law tradition.

Law-abidingness: past and present

Legal outsiders across Europe believe that people are less law-abiding now than they used to be. Legal insiders in Norway and England are divided on this issue: one-half believes that people are more likely to break the law now than they used to be, whereas the other half believes that there has been no change either for better or worse. Legal insiders in Bulgaria and Ukraine believe that people are more willing to break the law now than they were in the past. By contrast, Polish legal insiders mostly think people in their country are either less likely

[3] Although civil disobedience is largely accepted as a means by which to engage in environmental protection, Norwegians have been less accepting of priests making use of civil disobedience to protest the law on abortion, Rune Fredriksen and Trond Øyvind Karterud, 'Ludvig Næssa: Børre Knudsen fortjener en statsbegravelse' [Ludvig Næssa: Børre Knudsen deserves a state funeral], *NRK*, 18 August 2014, http://nrk.no/ostfold/nessa_-fortjener-statsbegravelse-1.11885898 accessed on 20 August 2014

to break the law now than earlier – or that there is no difference in terms of law-abidingness.

Those legal insiders both in Norway and England who believe that people are generally *less* law-abiding now than they were in the past, blame lawbreaking on a deterioration in public morale. Those Poles who believe that people are more law-abiding now believe that increased law-abidingness is the result of improved public morale. Bulgarians blame increased lawbreaking on deteriorating morals and poorer law enforcement, whereas Ukrainians believe that deteriorating morals and worsening socioeconomic conditions are at fault (Table 5.14).

Norwegian legal insiders predominantly believe that deteriorating moral standards in society are to blame for increased lawbreaking. In their view, Norwegians have less regard for, and less fear of, authority now than they had in the past. There is also less social control now due to increased mobility and growing secularism – the latter much as a result of better education.[4] As a result, individualism is on the rise and the community spirit is weakening. It appears that tolerance for lawbreaking has increased and that there is less stigma attached to being caught for minor offences. Besides, people are better off financially and thus better able to pay fines for minor offences than they were earlier.

> N-LA-19: 'maybe in the past one had more respect for laws and rules and authorities and judges and priests'. N-JU-13: 'the "pointing finger" was more internalised in people ... in the past than it is now. People have become more relaxed and ... more individualist .. more selfish ... less fearful of authorities'. N-JU-22: the neighbour "saw" you more ... (and) people were more religious in the past'. 'N-LA-25 'in the past it was more visible and more shameful ... (to be) investigated by the police.' N-PO-22: 'people think they can buy their way out (of trouble now), especially for traffic-related issues.'

Legal insiders also come up with a second, equally plausible, explanation: they claim that there are "more laws nowadays" than there used to be some 30 to 40 years ago. Norwegian society has become more regulated, and the large amount of detailed regulations irritates some people and exacerbates others. It is difficult for people to keep track of all the laws and consciously decide not to break them. These factors explain why people are less law-abiding now than they were in the past:

[4] Tyler (2006, p. 47) notes that education is related to legitimacy (of law). Highly educated people are less likely to evince high levels of legitimacy than less-educated people.

Table 5.14 *Likelihood and reasons for obeying versus breaking the law: the legal insiders' perspective*

Do you think people in [COUNTRY] are more or less likely to break the law now than they were in the past? Why (or why not)?	Norway (%)	England (%)	Poland (%)	Bulgaria (%)	Ukraine (%)
Frequency – lawbreaking					
More likely to break the law now	49	45	18	58	53
Less likely to break the law now	3	12	44	22	21
Mix	2	3	5	1	1
No difference	46	40	34	19	25
Reason – more frequently lawbreaking					
More laws now	19	26	4	2	2
Less caught now	4	5	0	31	15
Less educated/informed now	7	0	8	11	2
Public morale changed for the worse	50	51	38	29	38
Socioeconomic situation worse now	–	9	35	16	38
Mix	19	9	15	11	7
Reason – less frequently lawbreaking					
Better quality laws now	0	0	2	0	5
More difficult to get away with it now	75	60	12	33	42
Better educated/informed now	0	20	15	11	11
Public morale changing for the better	25	0	38	22	0
Socioeconomic situation better now	–	20	19	11	37
Mix	0	0	13	22	5

Note: Entries are based on the percentages of relevant 'text units' – the total number of answers to a given question; so entries sum up to approximately 100 per cent (decimals are rounded up or down to the nearest whole number).

N-ER-9: 'legislation has been introduced in areas where there was none earlier ... a long time ago there were many more – what should I say – local norms and local cultures that regulated behaviour, and not laws and rules'. N-PR-17: 'in some areas [people] may be more willing [to break the law] now ... because ... [they] feel that [society] is so thoroughly regulated that it is ... difficult to ... relate to all the laws and rules'.

English legal insiders – just like legal insiders in Norway – believe that people's respect for "authority" has dropped in recent years and this has negatively affected law-abidingness. British society has become less "hierarchical", and there is a stronger sense of "personal autonomy" than there used to be. "The old style community has disappeared" and been replaced by the idea that "the laws apply to others, not to me". This increased emphasis on the individual at the expense of the group has brought about a "me-me culture", which one respondent referred to as the "what can I get away with culture". This culture is driven by material interest and a certain disregard for (other) people. It has changed the very notion of socially acceptable behaviour, facilitating "more tolerance for anti-social behaviour". This alternative culture is particularly widespread amongst "younger people". As a result, there is now "more alcohol-related crime" and "more assaults":

E-PR-4: 'the way society's gone since ... Mrs Thatcher's era when she said "there's no such thing as a society", encouraged people to think of themselves as more important than society'. E-JU-8: 'people have got a greater sense of personal autonomy, which is great in one sense, but it also leads people to decide that it's up to them to choose which laws they obey and which they don't obey ... people are ... extraordinarily selfish ... now it's very much a selfish "me, me, me" culture, and, "if I want to do it, that's what I will do, and I don't really care about the consequences to anybody else"'. E-ER-18: 'there's a lack of respect for authority. . .whether it be a policeman, a vicar, MP ... the prevailing law is becoming "what can I get away with?", particularly in relation to benefit claims'. E-GO-13: 'there seems to be much more permissive, low-level kind of anti-social behaviour'.

Second, the *judicialisation* of society and *juridification* of politics have caused more areas of British society to be regulated by law. Laws and regulations are becoming increasingly complex (Office of the Parliamentary Counsel, Cabinet Office 2013) and English legal insiders note that there are more laws to break now than there were in the past. Laws and rules are therefore often broken unwittingly as people are simply not aware of them:

E-ER-3: 'there are far more laws. So the ability to not break the law is quite difficult'. E-JU-15: 'probably it is to some extent the amount of law that is being churned out . . . and a degree of confusion about what the law says . . . small print on agreements and things like that'. E-LA-4: 'that may be a product of legislating for every possibility under the sun.'

The number of statements made by English legal insiders to the effect that people "more frequently break the law nowadays" than they did in the past is almost as high as the number of statements suggesting that they are "as law-abiding now as they were in the past".

Adherents of the former position believe that human nature is fairly stable: "British community" is much the same now as it was before and there has been no significant shift either for the better or worse. Most people are simply law-abiding citizens – though there will always be criminals amongst them. The perception that people are less law-abiding nowadays is largely "media-driven" and "incorrect". There is no more crime now than in the past, but *the types of crimes* have changed. "England is [therefore still] a pretty lawful place". Some legal insiders note that people obey the law not so much because it has intrinsic value to them, but because they wish to avoid having to face the consequences if caught breaking the law:

E-ER-4: 'you will always have people who believe that the best way to live together in a good society is to observe rules which protect as well as restrict your actions. You will always have some elements in society that think "I will benefit by breaking those rules", while everybody else is keeping to the rules'. E-PR-25: 'it's probably always been the same, but because we have a lot of media exposure now I think we're more aware of it.' E-PO-21: 'I don't think there's any difference now from the nineteenth century. Just different things, they steal iPods now, and they don't get hung or they don't go to Australia, unless [they] really want to.' E-ER-19: 'there are more detection techniques than there has ever been'. E-GO-12: 'they might be more likely to be caught, because of technology that exists, CCTV, cameras, DNA'.

Dissatisfaction with Communism was particularly strong in Poland. Poles therefore embraced democracy with considerably more enthusiasm than citizens in some of the other post-communist states. During the last 20 plus years Poland has fared better financially than Bulgaria and Ukraine. The country is the largest net exporter of labour migrants within the EU. Poles are therefore more directly exposed to foreign legal culture – particularly that of West European countries – than Bulgarians and Ukrainians. Besides, given its size Poland is able to exert more influence within the European Union than Bulgaria is. Poles may therefore have a greater sense of "ownership" of the changes than Bulgarians and Ukrainians – and thus also a greater sense of duty with regard to the law.

Polish legal insiders stand out from legal insiders elsewhere in that they predominantly hold the view that people in their country are *more* rather than *less* law-abiding now than in the past – or that people's behaviour has changed neither for the better nor for the worse. They claim that Poles wholeheartedly endorse democracy. During Communism lawbreaking was for many a means of political protest against an illegitimate regime. By contrast, abiding by the laws of the democratically elected Polish Parliament is considered to be an act of patriotism. The average Pole feels a sense of ownership of current laws as he or she is able to influence the direction of Poland's legislation in parliamentary elections:

> P-JU-12: 'they [i.e. the Poles] didn't accept the previous system, including the law which was imposed and contradicted the values people believed in.' P-GO-6: 'in the past the law was identified with the communist system imposed on us, so breaking the law often had a moral justification ... nowadays ... we have democracy and we can participate in introducing changes to the law ... social awareness has changed.' P-ER-25: 'the law is ... not being imposed on us, that's why we're trying to obey it.' P-GO-16: 'there's no [longer] "us" and "them", but only "us" – our common good'.

Tyler (2006, p. 47) claims that 'the major demographic correlate of legitimacy [of law] is age. Older respondents view the law as more legitimate'. In many post-communist states older people are considered to be more law-abiding than the younger ones. However, our data suggest that old people in Eastern Europe obey the law not necessarily because they perceive it as legitimate, but because they have been socialised into abiding by the law from an early age. Besides, as pensions are low, East European pensioners are less able to pay fines for lawbreaking, should they get caught. Their law-abidance is therefore also *informed* by fear.

In Poland this generational pattern is reversed. The younger generation of Poles allegedly has a more favourable attitude towards Europe than older generations (Moes 2009, pp. 7–8). One reason might be that younger Poles travel more than older Poles. Another reason is that younger Poles are more adept at using the internet and other social media. They can thus easily obtain information about how people behave vis-à-vis the law in other democratic societies. Not only EU membership as such, but more the fact that a large number of

Poles now work in other EU member states, appears to have positively affected law-abidingness in Poland:

> P-PR-4: 'we travel a lot, have the chance to observe how it is all organised abroad . . . we . . . begin to understand: if foreigners are respectful of their laws, everything works so nicely in their countries, and living conditions are so good – why can't we have the same?'

As noted earlier, in Norway improved living standards seem to have *negatively* affected observation of minor law. People can more easily afford to pay the fine if caught breaking such law. By contrast, in Poland better living standards – as well as easier access to information – appear to have *positively* affected law-abidingness. Several legal insiders note that when people are better off and adequate social security structures are in place, there is less need for them to engage in lawbreaking. Besides, in the view of other legal insiders, many of those "elements in society" that used to break the law have left Poland to take up work elsewhere:

> P-JU-23: 'many people who used to do nothing . . . and who often broke the law for this reason, travelled to various countries of the European Union and . . . started working there . . . it started to be profitable for them to work instead of dealing with some kind of illegal activity . . . society has grown richer in recent years. The national income is increasing and so is the income of the average individual. Therefore, the temptation to commit a crime is lower.' P-PR-19: 'the quality of life has improved. So, there are unemployment benefits that constitute a . . . source of income and deter people from stealing. There are also attendance allowances, benefits from Municipal Family Support Centres, so the majority of people that used to be involved in minor thefts, now, don't have to do this anymore.'

Polish legal insiders who believe that there is *no difference* in terms of law-abidingness now and in the past in most cases simply state this as a fact – without further elaboration.

The communist period is generally perceived more favourably in Bulgaria than in Poland. The Russians liberated Bulgaria from the Turks in 1878 and relations between the two countries have historically been good. Even though the Bulgarian version of Communism was much more rigid than in, say, Hungary or the West Balkans, many Bulgarians have fond memories of that period. But nostalgia for the communist past is more driven by dissatisfaction with current polices than by normative considerations.

From a lawbreaking perspective quite a few Bulgarian legal insiders describe their country's communist past as a period during which there were "more respect for institutions", "fewer laws", "more fear of law", "more order and security", "stricter law enforcement", "more respect for law", "more disciplined citizens", "less crime" and "no corruption". However, they also acknowledge that during that period there was "more control", and "more repression". Yet only a limited number of the legal insiders refer to Communist Bulgaria as a "totalitarian state":

> B-PO-9: 'in the past . . . there was more respect for the court, the judiciary, including the police, and the people obeyed the law.' B-PO-25: '20 years ago people felt much more respect for the law'. B-JU-4: 'the rules were very strictly enforced, with very high penalties'. B-LA-2: 'the fear of punishment used to be preventive.'

Following the collapse of Communism, *absence of control* and *absence of fear* have negatively affected people's attitude towards the law and legal institutions. Bulgarians now pay less attention to the law and their own duties towards society than they did in the past. Legal insiders to some extent blame this change on the introduction of democracy. In their view, Bulgarians have "the wrong understanding of democracy". They equate freedom with "the freedom to do anything", including breaking the laws. Some even equate democracy with "free morals". As people who violate the law are less likely to get caught now than they were in the past, they do not run a big risk by disregarding the law. *Legal nihilism* and impunity are commonplace amongst those in power – which, in turn, has caused the authority of state institutions to deteriorate:

> B-PO-6: 'now everything is more democratic and there are more violations [of the law] because the fear has gone and the respect for the institutions and the law has gone.' B-JU-25: 'the public misunderstands freedom and thinks that if we are free we are allowed to do everything'. B-PO-10: 'it is the feeling of being above the law results in plenty of violations.' B-PR-14: 'people whose names are known in the community, who occupy higher positions, they [violate the law, so] why can't I do it?'. B-GO-5: 'you see how many people around you [that] violate [the law] and nothing happens to them'.

Bulgarian legal insiders believe that *the socioeconomic factor* negatively affects law-abidingness in their country.[5] Poverty is widespread and it undermines people's ability to abide by the law. Faced with the choice of

[5] Bulgaria has the highest percentage of citizens at risk of poverty in the EU. Honor Mahony, 'Risk of poverty greatest in Bulgaria', *EUObserver*, 7 October 2013, http://euobserver.com/regions/121692 accessed on 25 January 2014.

setting aside the law to feed their families or of respecting the law, people have no choice but to do the former:

> B-PO-1: 'if the social and living conditions are good, people do not steal in order to eat. When the social conditions deteriorate, the economy does not function well, unemployment exerts pressure on people and sometimes they violate the law because they have nothing to eat. I have seen such crimes lately. Robberies motivated not by the idea of enrichment, but by survival.' B-JU-24: 'the system of values is broken due to poverty and unemployment and those petty crimes are an indicator [in this regard].'

As in Bulgaria, *socioeconomic conditions* in Ukraine (Åslund 2013, pp. 6–7) sometimes make it difficult for people to abide by the law. Faced with poverty, citizens have no choice but to disregard it. Ukrainian citizens are therefore *less law-abiding now* than they were in the past:

> U-GO-17: 'the economic crisis and the social situation [in Ukraine] has its impact . . . unemployed people are more likely to break the law'. U-LA-10: 'if a person doesn't have work but needs to feed his family, he will do anything . . . of course, he breaks the law'. U-JU-26: 'now there are many problems with the banks and many people violate [the law] because . . . they cannot pay'.

Some Ukrainian legal insiders believe that the people in power have set a bad example for ordinary citizens by placing themselves above the law. Politicians and government officials "violate the law" but "go unpunished" as "the law is failing the untouchables". Consequently, ordinary citizens have no real incentive to abide by the law. Legal insiders describe Ukrainian politicians as "cynical" people and refer to the government as a group of "former criminals". Their behaviour provokes ordinary citizens who are "inspired by the injustice" they observe. By engaging in lawbreaking they try to restore a "sense of justice". Following the Orange Revolution the use of moral justifications for violating the law in Ukraine has increased:

> U-ER-19: 'all people see that the President or the Prime Minister or any government official violates certain norms but that they are not punished for that. Why shouldn't ordinary citizens think and act the same way?'. U-GO-21: 'after the Orange Revolution of disappointment [people] have a kind of moral justification when they break the law or when they give a bribe: "everybody likes it"'.

Legal insiders in Ukraine – just like those in Bulgaria – claim that citizens feel "freer" now and that the "tolerance" for law violations is higher than it used to be. Besides, there is less "discipline" now than there was in the

Table 5.15 *Law-abidingness – majority population: the legal insiders' perspective*

	Norway (%)	England (%)	Poland (%)	Bulgaria (%)	Ukraine (%)
DEP-43: Do you think most ordinary people in [COUNTRY] generally obey the law?					
Generally obey the law	49	78	65	42	55
Generally do not obey the law	4	3	9	28	22
Mix	47	19	26	30	23

Note: Entries are based on the percentages of relevant 'text units' – the total number of answers to a given question; so entries sum up to approximately 100 per cent (decimals are rounded up or down to the nearest whole number).

past and also "no fear". Ukrainian citizens are largely "profit-driven". They engage in lawbreaking knowing that it is possible to buy one's way out of trouble, should they get caught. Besides (as in Norway), fines are fairly modest and thus affordable:

> U-JU-29: 'if a person knows that there is a fine of 80 hryvnias for speeding [he] violates the law . . . as the fine is not so big'. U-PO-1: 'they are more likely to break the law only for one reason . . . there is no equality before the law'. U-ER-14: 'everybody is trying to make profits in all spheres, even the deputies – and of course illegally.' U-LA-20: 'people have changed. They are not even afraid of a criminal conviction. They know that they can be conditionally released. There are even people with a criminal background who hold positions in government.'

Law-abidingness at present: the majority population

Our in-depth interviews (IDIs) suggest that European legal insiders generally believe that citizens are fairly law-abiding – and more so in England, Poland and Ukraine, somewhat less in Norway and Bulgaria (Table 5.15).

Quite a few Norwegian legal insiders include themselves in the legal outsiders' category – referring to legal outsiders as "we", rather than "them". In doing so, they demonstrate lack of distance between legal outsiders and insiders.[6] Legal insiders primarily find ordinary citizens to be respectful of the law:

> N-ER-20: 'generally speaking, we mostly abide by laws and rules. We are a country which is . . . based on lawfulness'. N-PO-17: 'my general impression of people is that . . . 95 per cent (of them) are law-abiding'. N-JU-13: 'the ethnic Norwegian population is very law-abiding'.

In Norway, social norms dictate that one should not commit serious criminal offences such as murder, inflicting serious bodily harm on other people or committing offenses of similar magnitude. By contrast, minor infringements of the law, such as speeding, speaking on the mobile telephone while driving, downloading copyrighted material from the internet or carrying some extra bottles of wine through customs when returning from abroad, are considered fairly socially acceptable. Norwegian legal insiders to some extent blame lax attitudes towards "minor law" on their complexity and level of detail. Some of them believe that the sheer amount of law makes it difficult for citizens to keep track of new laws. They may therefore not even be aware of breaking the law. Besides, to many people breaking minor law is not such a big deal: nobody is ostracised for being fined for minor offenses such as speeding while driving. Besides, the chances of getting caught for such offenses are fairly slim:

> N-PR-11: with regard to . . . more serious types of violence . . . serious crime, Norwegians are clearly law-abiding'. N-LA-10: 'most people to a great extent abide by laws and rules, but . . . all [people] violate laws, either consciously or unconsciously . . . because there is such an enormous jungle of rules'. N-PR-18: 'violations of the law may be conscious or unconscious [i.e.] because people do not know the laws.' N-JU-18: 'everybody probably speed-drive[s]'. N-JU-8: 'the ban on using mobile telephones, hands-free in cars, is absolutely not abided by'. N-PR-1: 'smuggling alcohol, undeclared work, such things'.

Norwegians are generally supportive of the welfare state.[7] Social security in Norway is extensive, but also expensive. Legal insiders believe that

[6] The boundary between the two groups is also blurred in Eastern Europe (Grødeland 2014b).

[7] Unn Christensen, 'Stor oppslutning om velferdsstaten' [High support for the welfare state], Forskningsrådet [The Research Council], n.d., www.forskningsradet.no/servlet/Satellite?c=Nyhet&pagename=vfo%2FHovedsidemal&cid=1224698393082 accessed on 25 January 2014.

Norwegian citizens are not so willing to carry the financial burden of upholding the welfare state now as they were in the past. In some segments of the population tax evasion has become fairly socially acceptable – as have undeclared payments for cleaning services and childcare. Yet, people are more than happy to receive social security, even those who are not strictly speaking entitled to it. Claiming insurance payments to which one is not entitled is also fairly widespread:

> N-PO-4: 'it is nearly generally acceptable to have a cleaner ... a joiner whom you pay "under the table"'. N-GO-14: 'I think many people have a reasonably relaxed attitude to the tax law. *We* [our emphasis] cheat wherever we can'. N-JU-6: 'as far as paying taxes and undeclared labour are concerned, there is little understanding for the fact that these constitute criminal offences'. N-JU-9: 'there is the attitude that one pays too much tax, so therefore one may use some services without paying taxes'. N-LA-16: 'when it comes to pensions, social benefits and insurance, people's morals are put to the test'. N-LA-17: 'many people think it is OK to report something stolen or as missing to the insurance company after a trip [abroad]'.

Some of the legal insiders – just like the legal outsiders – blame such minor infringements of the law on social developments in society. Increased mobility has caused more anonymity and resulted in less social control. Ethnic Norwegians have become more secular – which, in turn, has reduced the social control exercised by the Church of Norway. Further, higher education and increased awareness amongst citizens have reduced their respect for authority, including law enforcement bodies. A general deterioration in moral standards is also blamed for this state of affairs. In the view of some legal insiders there appears to be a double standards with regard to law-abidingness: people are not accepting of other people breaking the law, yet they are perfectly happy to do so themselves:

> N-LA-15: 'you have the traditional themes where I think it is still almost a sport not to abide by them – be it traffic law, speeding ... drink-driving ... hunting and fishing ... some people find the laws too rigid'. N-GO-25: 'what frightens me a bit ... is [people's attitudes] regarding morals. Insurance claims and such things: in that field I can become a bit frightened by how cynical people can be'. N-JU-15: 'it is OK for oneself to violate the law, but it is not OK for others to do so'.

In England those legal insiders who claim that people both *obey* and *fail to obey* the law in most cases state that "serious" laws are obeyed, whereas "minor" laws are disregarded. In their view there is "lots of petty dishonesty" and "minor infractions" and "infringements" of the law in England. Even though people mostly abide by the law, everybody occasionally breaks it. As in Norway they mostly do so by engaging in speeding or speaking on their mobile telephones while driving. Other minor violations – such as exceeding the permitted alcohol quotas when returning from abroad, evading taxes, using soft drugs (cannabis), paying for undeclared work, overstating expenses following work-related travel, pirating copyrighted music, littering the streets or nicking small things from work – also occur. The seeming ease with which people engage in minor infringements of the law is blamed on lax social and cultural norms:

> E-JU-18: 'it is a sliding scale. Most people do not commit murder. [But] most people speed on the road, and I think the more significant and serious the legal provision is, the more people tend to obey it'. E-PR-1: 'it's not the mere fact that you have laws, which means that people obey them. It means that they have to make sense to people as well, and they're reinforced by social expectations and cultural norms, which are much more powerful in making the law effective than having police officers'. E-GO-20: 'most ordinary people . . . don't knick things, they don't kill people, they don't generally go around and beat people up, they generally don't abuse people . . . [but] there are a lot of little regulations and laws that people don't know about and don't realise that sometimes they're breaking'.

Legal insiders in England who hold the view that citizens either generally obey or generally disregard the law in most cases simply state this as a fact – though a very limited number of those who hold the former view claim that had they not done so, British society would have been overtaken by anarchy.

Polish legal insiders provide a greater number of explanations as to why people obey or break the law than English legal insiders do. A few of those who say that Polish citizens *obey* the law claim that people are now more willing to do so as Poland is no longer under communist rule. Besides, the quality of law in Poland has improved. But they also believe that the memory of the communist past negatively affects people's behaviour with regard to the law:

> P-GO-9: 'the law has become more just . . . democracy inspires people to obey the law. Living standards and customs have changed, and people have more trust in the courts and the police than they had in the past.

> Corruption has also declined and political influence is . . . not as strong as it used to be.' P-PR-25: '30 years ago when Communism was dominant in our country . . . the law was broken, not obeyed, evaded, this is one of the characteristics of that period. But now I think that . . . people rather begin to obey the law'.

Polish legal insiders who think that people *do not obey the law*, on the other hand, refer to tradition, which has been shaped by Poland's difficult historical experiences. Historically, illegitimate rulers passed illegitimate laws that were passively resisted by many Poles. Resisting them was considered socially acceptable. Lawbreaking is therefore blamed on Poland's historical past – that is, on the partitions of Poland (1772, 1793, 1795, 1815, 1832, 1846 and 1936), World War II and communist rule:

> P-JU-6: 'legal culture in Poland is . . . very much dependent on history. Poland was under partitions for a long time, then there was an independent state for 20 years and then, again, it suffered the yoke of Communism. Poles learnt from these times when they had no law "of their own" . . . they learnt to evade the law . . it's . . . not a matter of obeying it because it's a certain value. Such as you see in the Anglo-Saxon culture . . . where obeying the law is a value in and by itself.' P-GO-4: 'the so-called majority in Poland doesn't respect the law. This situation has its historical roots, conditions both from the times of the partition and World War II. It still lingers . . . cheating is perceived as something positive: "I'll cheat, I'll provide for my family"'. P-PR-12: 'the majority of Poles do not obey the law . . . the law is good only when it favours them, whereas if it doesn't favour them – it's bad . . . 50 years of Soviet domination caused the Poles' attitude towards law to be negative, and they think there is no necessity to obey it.' P-JU-15: 'we experienced the communist system for so many years and earlier . . . this perhaps applies more to the Eastern border, under Russian rule we learnt that in general, an annexationist was somebody enforced on society, therefore we couldn't have respected him'.

Polish legal insiders who believe that Poles regard and disregard the law in *equal measure*, just as the Norwegian and English legal insiders primarily believe that minor infringements of the law (the traffic law, troublesome law, unclear law or law that makes no sense) are considered socially acceptable. Whether people do or do not obey such laws depends on opportunity:

> P-PR-5: [they] obey the law in respect of some vital issues . . . they don't obey the law in respect of minor issues, issues which seem trivial and

> insignificant to them'. P-LA-13: '[Poles] want to circumvent troublesome laws, for example tax payments . . . the law is so ineffective'.

The reasons given for *not* abiding by the law in Bulgaria are very different from those in Poland. For Bulgarians lawbreaking is an expression of the "national psychology" and "national culture": They have "no tradition for abiding by the law"; they have "no inner conviction" of the value of abiding by the law, they are "not fond of law"; they "do not like obeying conventional rules"; and some even consider lawbreaking "a national sport". For Bulgarians informal law is more important than formal law. However, there is an element of hypocrisy involved also in Bulgaria as people "require others to observe the law, but do not do so themselves". Legal insiders are of the opinion that this Bulgarian lawbreaking culture has developed gradually, over time.

Although democracy and commitment to democracy has had a positive effect on law-abidingness in Poland, transition has negatively affected law-abidingness in Bulgaria. Paradoxically, democracy seems to be at fault: Bulgarians mistakenly equate democracy with the freedom to do as one pleases – including ignoring the law: "brazen behaviour is in fashion". Moreover, they blame lawbreaking and corruption on the Ottoman past (Grødeland 2013). In Poland legal nihilism was caused by illegitimate rule in the past and it has decreased following the collapse of Communism. In Bulgaria, however, democracy has failed to legitimatise the law and thus enhance law-abidingness. To the average Bulgarian, law is important if his or her individual rights are violated. But the average Bulgarian feels no sense of obligation or duty to the law:

> B-JU-19: 'generally, the legal culture of our society is quite low'. B-PR-24: 'it seems to be our national specific feature not to comply with the law'. B-PR-18: 'the Bulgarian national psychology is . . . [for] law not to be observed. There's this . . . contempt for the law'. B-LA-18: 'it is a national sport to avoid the law. We all do it'. B-JU-6: 'Bulgarians are fond of the law only when it . . . guarantees their personal rights. The Bulgarians will try to avoid any law that requires them to fulfil some obligation or stick to some type of behaviour'. B-JU-3: '[the law] concerns [the Bulgarian] only when his individual rights are violated'.

Still, Bulgarian legal insiders make a larger number of statements to the effect that lawbreaking is a result of *ignorance* rather than a conscious decision to break the law. They claim that people simply "do not know the law". "Messy legislation", including frequent amendments of, and contradictions in, the laws and the "lack of repercussions" for breaking the law also has something to do with it. And the elites set a bad example. When people "see those making the law not respecting it", they have no incentive to do so either:

> B-ER-13: 'many people are not well acquainted with the law'. B-GO-21: 'I believe fewer people abide by the law now due to the mess that the legislation is in at the moment.' B-JU-1: 'generally, people are honest and abide by the rules, but the legislation is so large, [it] is amended very often and is so contradictory that it frequently happens [that] the most decent man breaks the law without being aware [of it].' B-ER-7: 'we cannot hope that the people will abide by the law when they see that the people who are making the law do not abide by it.'

Bulgarian legal insiders who have mixed views on lawbreaking believe that people both abide by and break the law. In terms of law-abidingness they distinguish between (i) older and younger people, and (ii) poorer and wealthier people. Although older people (presumably because of their memory of the communist past) and poorer people (presumably because they cannot afford to pay fines) are fairly law-abiding, younger people and the well-to-do are not. In some instances poor people have no choice but to break laws to make ends meet. As laws in Bulgaria change frequently it is difficult for people to keep track of them. They therefore inadvertently break laws of which they are not aware:

> B-PR-8: 'those who actually cannot influence it [i.e. the law], I mean pensioners, juveniles, they are mostly law-abiding . . . 70 per cent are law-abiding, 30 per cent are not'. B-JU-10: 'the older generation was to a greater extent brought up to respect the law and rules. As [for] the younger generation . . . including those who are 40, 30, 30-something-years [old], perhaps because they have lived in the times of the so-called transition . . . they lack education in basic values . . . [they are] not so well behaved.' B-JU-7: 'the citizens with average social status are more diligent and law-abiding'.

Most Ukrainian legal insiders holding the view that ordinary people *mostly obey* the law, simply state this as a fact. Some, however, believe that Ukrainians have "an internal voice" that tells them to abide by the law and that they are therefore generally law-abiding. One respondent claims that law-abidingness is a genetic memory from the Soviet period. As in Bulgaria some legal insiders in Ukraine believe that older people are generally more law-abiding than younger ones. Others note that Ukraine is a "religious nation" with a "Christian history" that encourages law-abidingness. Even though they might not know the laws people abide by social norms:

> U-GO-11: 'people have a normal relation to laws in the country, especially the elderly'; U-GO-24: 'the Ukrainian people ... are a religious nation. People know God's Commandments; they read the Bible and care about the cleanness of their conscience, which helps them to be law-abiding.' U-GO-12: 'in general, of course, the Ukrainian nation is law-obedient ... [but] we need to teach our youth ... to obey the law more.'

Legal insiders who believe that Ukrainians *do not obey the law* give two major reasons for this. Some – just like the legal insiders in Poland – refer to history. They claim that lawbreaking is essentially a product of the Soviet mentality and that it has distorted the Ukrainian people's notion of acceptable behaviour. A key aspect of this mentality is no trust in the state and a general disregard for the authorities and the laws that they make:

> U-ER-2: 'we have low orderliness due to our history ... Ukraine was a colony ... the authority of the law was very low ... the most important questions were solved by bureaucrats [rather than by courts].' U-ER-5: 'the mutilated perception of law and the legal sphere in general ... we inherited [it] from the Soviet times. The vast majority of people perceive the law as kind of a small barrier which one has to jump over or get round'.

Others claim that it is the very notion of democracy that is distorted in Ukraine. Ukrainians, just like Bulgarians, mistakenly equate democracy with everything being allowed, including breaking the law. To the average Ukrainian freedom means "the right to avoid responsibility". The collapse of Communism and the introduction of democracy therefore paved the way for *legal nihilism* in Ukraine and other parts of the former Soviet Union. The notion of personal responsibility (i.e. duty to obey the law) is simply not properly understood by the citizens in Ukraine. To some extent this attitude is the result of "limited legal culture" and "low legal awareness":

> U-ER-6: Ukrainians have no legal consciousness'. U-JU-20: 'we are Ukrainians ... [we] are not law-abiding ... we don't have an understanding of personal responsibility'. U-JU-5: 'legal *nihilism* is widespread'. U-GO-6: 'the level of legal education ... is very low ... it is always easier for citizens to use the services of professional people or to give a bribe and resolve issues quickly or simply forget that you have such a need or questions.' U-LA-6: 'especially after 1991 ... people feel that it is possible to grab something somewhere ... we can only dream about the law-abiding citizen.'

Ukrainian legal insiders who believe that people obey and disregard the law in equal measure, claim that they generally try to abide by the law, but that difficult socioeconomic conditions sometimes prevent them from doing so. As in other European countries the public abide by major laws, but they break the smaller ones (e.g. traffic, administrative regulations). Those who are worse off financially make greater efforts to obey the law than those who are better off:

> U-ER-25: 'the majority of ordinary people in Ukraine are law-abiding . . . people who have money, relations and high posts don't care about the law.' U-PO-1: 'the higher echelons of power . . . the law is not written for them. They are untouchable, they are Gods. All our problems stem from this'. U-PR-3: 'the simpler and poorer a person [is], the more law-obedient [he or she] will be'.

Law-abidingness at present: the ethnic and religious minorities

The question as to how law-abiding ethnic and religious minorities are compared to the population at large is important from a legal culture point of view: if there is no perceived difference between the former and the latter one could argue that the legal culture is homogenous. If, on the other hand, ethnic and religious minorities are considered to be more or less law-abiding than the population at large, this would suggest multiple legal cultures. But it is, of course, also possible that the socio-economic factor simply affects different ethnic and religious groups differently, in turn affecting their law-abidance. Or that the majority population is prejudiced against the minority (nearly all the legal insiders in our sample belong to the majority populations).

Norway and the UK are amongst those countries in the EU/EEA that relative to population have received the largest share of immigrants from Eastern Europe (NOU 2012, p. 19). Both countries host immigrants from Asia and Africa. Some ethnic groups – notably the Pakistanis (both countries) and people from the West Indies (the UK) – have lived in these countries for several generations. Other groups have arrived more recently, such as refugees from conflict-ridden areas in the West Balkans, Iraq, Afghanistan, Somalia, Syria and elsewhere. Many of these immigrants are minorities in the double sense, that is, both in terms of ethnicity and religion.

By contrast, Poland has a very small minority population (less than 4 per cent, according to the 2001 census). What is more, the majority of the Polish immigrants are Europeans and also Christians – the exception being the Muslim Lipka Tatars and a small Jewish community. Poland hosts a modest number of refugees and labour migrants from non-European countries.

The situation in Bulgaria is rather different. During the last years of Zhivkov's rule the Communist Party undertook a forced assimilation program to "Bulgarianise" the country's Turkish minority. The effects of this program were reversed after the collapse of Communism and the Turks are now fairly well integrated. They have their own party – the Movement for Rights and Freedoms – which has been part of several coalition governments. The Pomaks (Muslim Bulgarians) and Roma, on the other hand, are viewed with hostility (Zhelyazkova, Kosseva and Hajdinjak 2010). Neither group is well integrated into Bulgarian society. Whereas the Turks are fairly secular, the Pomaks are rather conservative Muslims (Ghodsee 2010; Neuburger 2004). The Roma have been badly hit by socioeconomic problems.

Ukraine, for its part, has a large Russian-speaking population and fairly large numbers of Belarusians, Moldovans and Bulgarians. There are also smaller populations of Poles, Jews, Romanians, Armenians, Rusyns, Hungarians and other ethnic groups.[8] Until the Russian annexation of the Crimea there was a fairly large community of Crimean Tatars.[9] The latter, who were forcibly sent to Central Asia by Stalin in 1944 to prevent them from colluding with the Germans against the Soviet Army, were allowed to return to Ukraine from Central Asia and Russia in the late 1980s (Organisation for Security and Cooperation in Europe [OSCE], High Commissioner on National Minorities [HCNM] 2013, p. 2). Even though relations between the majority population and the Christian ethnic minorities are generally good (though the status of the Russian language in Ukraine has caused considerable tension), the Crimean Tatars – who are Muslims – have been regarded with scepticism and particularly so by the ethnic Russian majority in the Crimea.

Table 5.8 shows that *legal outsiders* in all countries except Bulgaria think ethnic and religious minorities are no more, no less, law-abiding than the majority population. The majority of the Muslims share this view – which also largely coincides with the view of the *legal insiders* who

[8] World Directory of Minorities and Indigenous Groups, 'Ukraine', www.minorityrights.org/5053/ukraine/ukraine-overview.html accessed on 4 September 14.

[9] OSCE estimates that there were 266,000 Crimean Tatars in Ukraine in 2013. Andrew Wilson, 'Ukraine falters in Crimean Tatar relationship', *KyivPost*, 29 August 2013, www.kyivpost.com/opinion/op-ed/ukraine-falters-in-tatar-relationship-328863.html accessed on 25 January 2014.

The Crimean Tatars made up 0.5 per cent of the population of Ukraine before the Russian annexation of the Crimea. *World Population Review, Ukraine 2013*, http://worldpopulationreview.com/countries/ukraine-population/ accessed on 25 January 2014.

Table 5.16 *Law-abidingness – religious and ethnic minorities: the legal insiders' perspective*

	Norway (%)	England (%)	Poland (%)	Bulgaria (%)	Ukraine (%)
DEP-43: Do you think religious or ethnic minorities are generally more obedient or less obedient to the law than other people in [this country]?					
More obedient than ordinary people	6	25	12	5	33
Less obedient than ordinary people	39	7	11	37	13
Mix	8	11	6	13	6
Equally obedient	48	57	71	45	48

Note: Entries are based on the percentages of relevant 'text units' – the total number of answers to a given question; so entries sum up to approximately 100 per cent (decimals are rounded up or down to the nearest whole number).

believe that ethnic and religious minorities are no more, no less law-abiding than others. Polish legal insiders hold this view to a greater extent than legal insiders elsewhere – possibly as such minorities represent a small and fairly well-integrated part of the population in their country. Norwegian and Bulgarian legal insiders – to a greater extent than legal insiders elsewhere – believe that religious and ethnic minorities are less law-abiding than the majority population (Table 5.16). We will explore the reasons here.

The majority of the Norwegian legal outsiders believe that religious and ethnic minorities are just as law-abiding as ethnic Norwegians. However, Muslims, to a greater extent than the majority population, believe that ethnic and religious minorities are more law-abiding – possibly because Muslims, to a greater extent than the majority population, fear the consequences of being caught for lawbreaking. Legal insiders share the view of the majority population.

The media create the impression that crime is more widespread amongst minorities than amongst ethnic Norwegians. Whereas ethnic minorities are overrepresented for some types of crimes, one of the judges interviewed suggests that official statistics on minority crime might be flawed. A few years ago several ethnic Pakistani taxi drivers were fined or arrested after a taxi fraud scam in Oslo.[10] Ethnic Somalis are overrepresented in the statistics for rape by assault. Other ethnic groups have been linked to drug-related crimes or social security scams.

> N-GO-4: 'I think they are just as law-abiding as others, but there are some elements that . . . become very visible. For instance these rapists who were all from Somalia . . . and the [ethnic Pakistani] taxi drivers who cheated [people]'. N-JU-6: 'I do not think they are more or less [law-abiding], but . . . many ethnic groups will be less understanding of [some] rules . . . social security fraud . . . is less frowned upon [amongst minorities than] . . . amongst Norwegian citizens.' N-PO-1: 'some of the religious or ethnic minorities live in . . . social conditions that are crime-producing- . . . if you put [ethnic] Norwegians in such a position where they do not have work . . . have poor housing, do not understand the Norwegian society, have difficulties with the language and communication . . . then [they] . . . will be just as crime-prone'.

Some Norwegian legal insiders believe that the socioeconomic conditions of these groups have something to do with their involvement in crime. For instance crime is higher amongst refugees than amongst labour migrants. Refugees are typically younger jobless males who have often been through traumatic experiences in their countries of origin (by contrast, labour migrants tend to be younger or middle-aged men who have families to support). Our respondents voice some understanding – even sympathy – for these people:

> N-JU-2: 'I do not think they are less law-abiding than others, even though much of what is written [in the media] give such an impression.' N-ER-8: 'criminal statistics . . . do not give any reason to say that there is a great difference between ethnic Norwegians and minorities [in terms of law-abidingness].' N-PR-25: 'I do not have the impression that there is any difference . . . here we have an asylum campus for minors. We see that they appear more frequently in our [crime] statistics than ethnic Norwegians, but I think that may be attributed to . . . their background, that they come alone, that they are young . . . do not have their network around them'.

[10] 'Taxi swindler finally back in Oslo', *News in English.no*, 16 January 2012, www.newsinenglish.no/2012/01/16/taxi-swindler-finally-back-in-norway/ accessed on 10 January 2014.

However, the number of statements made by Norwegian legal insiders indicates that those who believe that religious and ethnic minorities are less law-abiding than the majority population are almost as numerous as the number who believe they are equally law-abiding. In the views of the former, it is *ethnic* rather than *religious* minorities who fail to obey the law. If and when legislation clashes with life-style and attitudes, ethnic minorities opt for the latter as they place loyalty to their family members above the law. Others take the law into their own hands instead of reporting crime to the police. Only a small minority claim that religious minorities are less law-abiding than the majority population because they place religious law above state law:

> N-GO-10: some minorities . . . place family above society . . . the family's culture and values will . . . be more important than laws'. N-PO-11: 'ethnic minorities share a group affiliation which negatively affects society . . . they often take the law in their own hands'. N-ER-25: 'I perceive ethnic minorities as less law-abiding. They have a tendency to place . . . the *Tora*, the Bible or the *Quran* above Norway's laws.' N-GO-3: 'especially conservative Muslims who to a great extent set their own agenda. And sometimes . . . they challenge Norwegian law.'

Some of the legal insiders interviewed in northern Norway claim that the Sámi population there refuses to abide by Norwegian law on land use, fishing rights and scooter driving – as such legislation allegedly clashes with Sámi legal culture and Sámi customary law (see Ravna 2010; Sunde 2005; and Smith 2012 for accounts of Sámi law and legal culture):

> N-JU-24: '[the Sámi people] challenge very many Norwegian rules and hold the view that they do not apply . . . to Sámi [people] . . . the other day a lawyer argued that . . . it was against the protection of the indigenous people to put Sámi people in prison as punishment for violating the law.' N-PO-25: 'Sámi settlers claim old, traditional fishing rights. Even though this issue is later settled in Norwegian courts and not to their benefit, they do not wish to abide by [these decisions].'

In the view of Norwegian legal insiders ethnic minorities primarily engage in crime (theft) with a view to enhancing their own living standard. Their perceptions of Norwegian living standards are often unrealistic. Some claim that their views on law-abidingness amongst minorities are supported by media coverage and official statistics. Yet many seem to base their views on assumptions and impressions rather than on facts. Others believe that poor social integration explains why ethnic minorities break the law, as do lack of familiarity with Norwegian legislation and rules more generally:

> N-ER-6: 'it is a reflection of poor integration and general lack of adjustment'. N-JU-8: 'generally, in Norway . . . we have a notion of the community . . . most of us pay our tax . . . there are always some people who try to abuse the system, social security payments, but those are . . . people from different cultures who do not have the same experience with the notion of the community'. N-JU-24: 'ethnic minorities . . . are very often unfamiliar with Norwegian rules'.

Legal insiders in England are more inclined to believe that religious minorities are more law-abiding than the majority population – even though religious minorities tend to be ethnic minorities as well. It is, of course, possible that by religious minorities, they primarily have in mind members of the majority group who have strong religious beliefs, or some individuals within ethnic groups who are true believers rather than those who are religious in a cultural sense. Religious people are allegedly more law-abiding than others because of their "religious code" and "moral values". Some legal insiders claim that Muslims are more respectful of the laws of Islam than they are of national legislation:

> E-PO-9: 'genuinely religious people are more obedient . . . they're more considerate, more thoughtful and more cognisant of the effect their behaviour has on others. They also, by being religious, in a sense have signed up to a value code that is more likely to make them stay within the law.' E-JU-18: 'the Muslim community is more law-abiding, certainly of its own law. Whether it is more law-abiding of the laws of England, I would not like to say . . . that's partly because the perception of enforcement in the Muslim community is that if they don't obey their own laws then there would be consequences in a way that maybe they feel there are not consequences in terms of English law'.

Those very few English legal insiders who believe that ethnic minorities are less law-abiding than the majority population claim that this is so due to differences in legal culture. Then the "social norms", "values", "culture", "experiences" and "allegiances" of ethnic minorities differ from those of the majority. Besides, ethnic minorities tend to belong to the "lower social class". Turks, Kurds, Somalis and Caribbean youth, for instance, are particularly prone to lawbreaking, and Indians engage in "tax evasion". English legal insiders rarely cite crime statistics in support of their view:

> E-JU-10: 'I suppose [they are] marginally less [law-abiding] because . . . the allegiance is different and the culture is different'. E-PO-9: 'people's value codes are different depending on where they come from . . . the vast majority of minority ethnic people end up in lower social classes . . . the lower social classes are more likely to break the law'.

Legal insiders in England, who have *mixed views* about law-abidingness, claim that religious minorities are generally more law-abiding than the majority population, whereas ethnic minorities are less law-abiding. Legal insiders who think there is no difference between the majority and minority population in terms of law-abidingness in most cases simply state this as a fact. However, some of them note that there are good and bad people within each group, and that law-abidingness is an individual, rather than an ethnic or religious, issue.

Those Polish legal insiders who believe that ethnic and religious minorities are generally more law-abiding than the majority group mostly refer to ethnic minorities. Some mentions are also made of the Jehovah's Witnesses, who are considered to be very honest people who "must not lie". As for ethnic migrants, they risk deportation if they misbehave, and they are more closely watched than other groups. Legal insiders therefore believe that they have a strong wish to be like everybody else:

> P-ER-17: 'minorities try to obey the law as they're usually watched more closely.' P-LA-14: 'people who weren't born here ... obey the law more ... it's simply because any accusation ... or exposing themselves to risk may result in their deportation or lead to further repercussions'. P-LA-2: 'I've once met a Jehovah's Witness. It's amazing. They mustn't lie'.

In the view of Polish legal insiders, those minorities who are less law-abiding are less aware of, or knowledgeable about, the law. And some of them – such as the Roma – have different value systems from the majority populations. Socioeconomic conditions are also at play as it is more difficult for the economically destitute to abide by the law. The Roma account for one of the poorest segments of Polish society:

> P-ER-11: 'it probably results not from bad will, but from less knowledge about the law'. P-PO-24: 'people, who reside in refugee centres, rather don't obey the law. Perhaps that's because they don't know what the law is ... they are responsible for a lot of traffic violations.' P-PR-20: 'the Roma ... obey the law less than the rest of Polish society'.

However, the majority of the Polish legal insiders simply do *not* think that there is *a difference* between the majority and minority populations in terms of law-abidingness as they have not observed any such differences and have no information to this effect. There are lawbreakers in any community – including amongst the Jehovah's Witnesses – but people generally try to obey the law:

> P-ER-19: 'they obey the law to the same extent as Polish people do'. P-PR-4: 'the minorities have after all assimilated in some way . . . they feel [like] Poles, citizens of this country, and they obey the law as much as other people.' P-LA-21: 'religion, religious or ethnic views have nothing to do with law obedience . . . Jehovah's Witnesses mustn't lie; practice shows that they lie in court just like other people.'

A small number of the Bulgarian legal insiders believe that religious minorities are more law-abiding than other people as they "fear God's punishment" and therefore lead a "moral life". Religion generally promotes the view that "laws should be respected". Ethnic minorities, for their part, are considered to be less law-abiding than the majority population. The general perception is that the Turks abide by the law, whereas the Roma do not. The Roma make up some 10 per cent of the Bulgarian population.[11]

Bulgarian legal insiders – just like the legal outsiders – claim that the Roma place themselves above the law and also, that they do not fear the consequences of disregarding the law. To some extent their attitude towards law may reflect their poor socioeconomic conditions. One lawyer thinks that the Bulgarian "penal machine" is geared towards the socially and economically weakest groups in society. But it is of course also possible that lawbreaking has to do with culture. The relationship between ethnic Bulgarians and the Roma is poor (Vassilev 2004). The Roma might therefore feel that the Bulgarian political rulers are not "their" rulers, which may, in turn, explain why they disregard Bulgarian law:[12]

> B-PO-18: 'the majority of the citizens of Roma origin believe that the law is not for them and that they have no obligation to abide by it.' B-PR-25: 'the Gypsies, for instance, are less [law] abiding but there are social reasons for that. They are less educated, for them it is more difficult to earn a living, and as a consequence they are more inclined to violate the law.' B-JU-15: 'I mostly see representatives of the Roma minority in the proceedings . . . in this group the internal regulator is absent . . . I suppose they get caught more easily.' B-JU-1: 'the Turkish minority is much more

[11] Antoaneta Nenkova, 'Millions don't help Roma integration in Bulgaria', *Deutsche Welle*, 21 March 2013, www.dw.de/millions-dont-help-roma-integration-in-bulgaria/a-16691459 accessed 25 January 2014.

[12] Although ethnic Bulgarians and Turks apply various coping strategies when dealing with government officials to achieve their objectives, the Roma simply give up (Miller et al. 2001, pp. 200–3). They might also simply give up on the law rather than deliberately seeking to break it.

> disciplined and [it is] as if they respect the law more than the other minorities ... the Roma community ... has its own internal laws ... [according to] the Roma laws to steal from a non-Roma is not a crime, but if a Roma steals from another Roma, this is already a crime'.

Legal insiders who fail to see any difference in terms of how the majority population and the ethnic minorities behave, simply state that religion and ethnicity do not affect law-abidingness. To them, level of education and socioeconomic conditions are the most important determinants of behaviour before the law.

Finally, Ukrainian legal insiders – just like legal insiders elsewhere – claim that religious minorities are more law-abiding than the majority population. Almost all references to minorities are of such groups. Specific religious communities mentioned include the "church goers", "Protestants" and "sectarians" – but also "Muslims", such as the "Crimean Tatars" and "Arabs". The number of references to "Western religious groups" and "religious-sectarian groups" is limited. Legal insiders claim that the most religious regions in Ukraine are less crime prone than other regions. Christians, as a rule, obey the law due to their commitment to the "Ten Commandments" and "God's norms". Orthodox Christians believe that political authority is given by God (historically they have not challenged the authorities in the same manner as the Catholic Church has). They should abide by the laws given by those in authority:

> U-ER-2: 'they are more law-abiding ... traditional religions, as they call [upon] us to be law-abiding as the authority is from God.' U-ER-17: 'religious structures are more law-abiding than other sections of the population. Especially if we do not talk about our basic Orthodox Church ... sectarian religious confessions, Protestants and others, these religious structures are the most law-abiding.' U-LA-26: 'in most cases Crimean Tatars have to be more law-abiding simply ... because there is the stereotype that Crimean Tatars ... are ... betrayers'. U-PO-4: 'if [someone] really believes in God I think that he ... is more law-abiding. Because he doesn't limit himself to laws, he also ... takes upon himself some moral responsibility'. U-ER-15: '[they] are more law-abiding because they have moral principles and a moral basis which can't be broken – first of all ... the [Ten] Commandments.'

Ukrainian legal insiders who believe that ethnic and religious minorities are generally less law-abiding than the majority population make an almost equal number of statements about ethnic and religious minorities. The former includes the Roma, the Crimean Tatars and the Armenians.

Ethnic Russians living in Ukraine fail to observe Ukrainian legislation on the national language. They include Orthodox Christians who oppose national identity codes, whilst the Crimean Tatars seize land illegally:

> U-GO-15: 'our local Gypsies . . . Armenians . . . spit on our law'. U-PR-20: 'due to national traditions Armenians are more inclined to break the law . . . [as are] Gypsies; they are brought up to do that'. U-JU-25: 'the Russian-speaking population . . . ignores the demands of the Constitution. And nobody pays attention to that . . . they violate the law.' U-LA-31: 'they are less obedient. For example, the national leaders [of the Crimean Tatars] that seize lands . . . these people are dangerous to society.' U-LA-5: 'the [Crimean] Tatars . . . have a bomb in their bosom.'

Legal insiders who hold the view that there is *no difference* between the majority and minority populations in terms of law-abidingness claim that other factors such as socioeconomic conditions, level of education and personal qualities matter more than ethnicity and religion. In their view, some people simply abide by the law while others do not:

> U-JU-24: 'the majority . . . are law-abiding irrespective of their religious adherence and ethnic roots.' U-GO-5: 'in our state, law obedience depends on personal culture.' U-ER-6: 'the attitude toward regulations, towards morality, toward culture . . . depends more on family education.' U-LA-29: 'it depends on the level of life'.

Excuses for breaking the law?

As shown in Table 5.15 close to 50 per cent of the statements made by legal insiders in Norway, England and Poland – and the majority of the statements made by legal insiders in Bulgaria and Ukraine, suggest that people break the law *more frequently now* than they did in the past. Yet, they do not believe that people who knowingly break the law have a reasonable excuse for doing so. The percentage is highest in Norway (81 per cent) and gradually drops to 65 per cent in England, through 59 per cent in Poland, 58 per cent in Bulgaria and 52 per cent in Ukraine (Table 5.17). Our findings thus suggest that the poorer a country is and the less the rule of law, the more likely it is that people have reasonable excuses for breaking the law.[13]

[13] Norway has the highest GDP (PPP) per capita and the highest score on the World Bank's 2010 rule of law index, followed in descending order by the UK, Poland, Bulgaria and Ukraine.

Table 5.17 *Reasonable excuses for knowingly breaking the law: the legal insiders' perspective*

	Norway (%)	England (%)	Poland (%)	Bulgaria (%)	Ukraine (%)
DEP-45: Do you think people in [this country] who knowingly break the law often have some reasonable excuse for doing so?					
Have some reasonable excuse	1	7	16	26	32
Do not have any reasonable excuse	81	65	59	58	52
Mix	18	28	24	16	16

Note: Entries are based on the percentages of relevant 'text units' – the total number of answers to a given question; so entries sum up to approximately 100 per cent (decimals are rounded up or down to the nearest whole number).

Norwegian legal insiders acknowledge that citizens usually have an excuse for breaking the law. However, while this excuse may make perfect sense to the citizens themselves, it is not necessary a good excuse, and most definitely not a reasonable one.

Two major positions that are more or less identical to Tyler's two perspectives outlined above emerge from our data: the first position – *the normative position* – holds that law-abidance has intrinsic value. In democratic societies citizens have a duty to abide by democratically made law. If they do not approve of such law they should make efforts to change it. But they should not break it. For law to have intrinsic value, the authorities must be legitimate. Legal insiders note that reasons for breaking the law that they consider reasonable are, in fact, sanctioned by law. Such situations are the right to defend oneself if attacked by somebody, and the right to protect property or lives – if in danger (*nødrett* and *nødverge*):

> N-ER-18: 'I personally do not think [people] have any good reason for [breaking the law], then ... the law is democratic'. N-LA-5: 'one has to adjust to Norwegian law and use one's freedom of speech if one does not agree with the legislation, but one cannot set [the law] aside because one

> feels that it is inconvenient for oneself.' N-JU-23: 'the reasonable excuses for violating the law are usually sanctioned – [i.e.] *nødrett* and *nødverge*.' N-PR-14: 'if attacked you are [by law] allowed to hit back'.

The second position – *the instrumental position* – on the other hand, rests on the assumption that people mostly break laws for practical reasons. Laws that obstruct their personal goals and that they themselves do not approve of are set aside. Lawbreaking is therefore essentially 'selfish' and cannot be justified. An element of calculated risk seems to be involved in that utility-based lawbreaking tends to involve breaking minor laws and regulations. The punishment for violating such laws and regulations is usually a fine and chances of getting caught are not that great:

> N-LA-11: 'I do not think people have any particularly reasonable reason for [violating the law]. It is more a case of deciding that that law is not going to apply to me'. N-PR-8: 'one violates laws partly for reasons of convenience . . . I understand that it is faster to build a cottage illegally (i.e. without permission) by the sea . . . but I do not think it is a reasonable excuse.'

Norwegian legal insiders hint that in some instances they are sympathetic towards people breaking the law – even though they do not think their excuses for doing so are reasonable. They distinguish between conscious and unconscious lawbreaking. Though understandable, breaking laws because one is not aware of them does not constitute a reasonable excuse:

> N-LA-12: 'I can understand and sympathise with many [people] who violate the law, but no [they do not have a reasonable excuse for doing so].' N-JU-20: 'there is this thing called unawareness of the law [*rettsvillfarelse*] and . . . many people do not know about laws that also affect them, but in many cases they should know [them]'. N-JU-14: 'you have to distinguish between those who break the law consciously and those who break it unconsciously. If you drive at five kilometres above the speed limit because you did not pay proper attention, then you do it unconsciously. But if you consciously break the speed limit to get around faster then . . . you very rarely have a good reason for doing so.'

Only 10 statements made by the English legal insiders suggest that people have a reasonable excuse for knowingly breaking the law. Reasonable lawbreaking includes breaking poor-quality law, ignoring the law due to difficult socioeconomic conditions, bad habits (for instance drug addiction) or civil disobedience (the latter is deemed reasonable only by one legal insider): E-ER-7: "there are protests [that] are legitimate and where the police have gone over the top, and they have used the law in a way that they probably shouldn't have done, but on the whole, no".

As for the *quality* of law, some laws are apparently so "complicated" – even "stupid" or "unfair" – that people are unwilling or unable to abide by them. People "rebel" against such laws either "out of boredom" or because they "want change". According to one judge the "system is simply failing some people", which, in turn, causes them to break the law:

> E-ER-1: 'if you've got law that isn't clear, then it's not surprising if people break [it] ... we ought to try to simplify law ... we've made a lot of things too complicated ... I don't think that's an excuse, by the way, but I do think there's a responsibility on society to find a better way of doing things.' E-GO-1: 'it's just people trying to get away with [it] ... some people probably do it out of boredom ... out of ignorance ... trying to rebel against the system. I don't think there's necessarily even a good excuse for doing it.'

Some English legal insiders note that there are people who have *no choice but to break the law* due to "poverty" or "unemployment", as they suffer from "a drug habit", or because they have problems with alcohol. Karstedt and Farrall (2007, p. 2) claim that 'the mass of morally dubious behaviour is embedded in the erosion of moral standards amongst the respectable middle classes in England and Wales'. Yet, deteriorating morals and greed are mentioned by a very limited number of our respondents. One lawyer, however, believes that some people "steal for a buzz". Another – that they break the law because they "think they have a right to" do so. Judges in particular believe that everybody violates the traffic laws. Road tax and car insurance are other areas in which lawbreaking frequently occurs:

> E-ER-22: I was brought up very poor, working class, in the East End of London ... we were ... respectable working class. We wouldn't have dreamed of breaking the law so I don't think poverty is an excuse'. E-ER-14: 'one of the most common reasons why people break the law [is that] they steal to feed their drug habit'. E-PR-1: 'very often there is a social explanation ... poverty ... unemployment ... drug or alcohol problems. We could get rid of most crime in this country if we could crack our social problems'.

However, the majority do not think that lawbreaking can be justified. In their view, the law applies to everybody, and it should be respected by all. As in Norway reasonable excuses for breaking the law (protecting property or lives) does not actually qualify as violating the law in the first place:

> E-ER-10: 'there's never any justification for breaking the law, end of story.' E-GO-20: 'I don't think there's ever a reasonable excuse ... breaking the law is always a choice. I will or I won't.' E-PO-8: 'within the UK law, we do allow people to break the law if it is reasonable within certain circumstances. So if they do it within those bounds, then they haven't broken the law'.

As we have noted, in Poland lawbreaking was more accepted during Communism than it is at present. Some legal insiders are principally opposed to people breaking the law. However, they acknowledge that some violations – such as murder committed in self-defence or doctors issuing counterfeit prescriptions to the homeless – are justifiable, as they serve a higher purpose or help evade nonsensical laws. A fair share of the legal insiders views poverty as a reasonable excuse for violating the law:

> P-GO-2: 'if a father of five children who's on the lookout for a job and whose wife doesn't work ... steals because he has nothing to live on, then maybe it's a reasonable explanation although it seems to me that there's always another way out.' P-LA-2: 'if someone steals, due to hunger, a piece of bread from a shop, or a fruit from the stall, he or she has the right to do this.'

Rule of law is based on the principle that law is passed by a democratically elected Parliament and that it is clear and stable. If the legislative lacks legitimacy or if the laws themselves are not reasonable or too complicated for ordinary citizens to follow, then this does – in the view of some Polish legal insiders – constitute a reasonable reason for disregarding them:

> P-PO-1: 'there are so many absurd regulations, which are not obeyed, so why do I have to obey them? I think that from the perspective of the person it is a very rational explanation'. P-JU-1: 'some rules or restrictions are unwise, unfair, unjustified, and there is obviously an explanation that the state is not always loyal towards the citizen, so the citizen also does not feel obliged to be loyal towards society ... if public officials treat me in a bad way and if it turns out that the legislator is inconsistent in its decisions, it is difficult to expect the citizen to be 100 per cent unconditionally loyal towards the State'.

Despite difficult socioeconomic conditions and despite complicated laws most Polish legal insiders feel that laws should still be obeyed. The law must be upheld as it applies to all members of society and as those who often fail to abide by it do so for selfish reasons (greed). Rule of law is more important than people's excuses for not wanting, or claiming that they are not able to, abide by the law:

> P-JU-2: 'there is no logical explanation for breaking the law. This would require showing that the law is an absurdity, wouldn't it?' P-LA-3: 'I don't think anybody could have any logical explanation for breaking the law. People live in a society so they have to conform to certain norms . . . there is no such place on Earth where people don't have to conform to norms.' P-ER-12: 'it's for example the desire to be rich, powerful or to avoid the consequences of their own actions [that make people break the law].'

Bulgarian legal insiders, just like those in Poland, justify lawbreaking for socioeconomic reasons. However, unlike legal insiders in Poland they believe that people are sometimes justified to break laws regulating business. Besides, as law is not always applied in their country there is some rationale for disregarding it. Quite a few legal insiders note that even though people have reasonable justifications for not abiding by the law, their excuses do not necessarily hold in court:

> B-JU-1: 'each [one of them] has a reasonable excuse . . . the question is whether it is acceptable in terms of the law.' B-LA-3: 'they have completely reasonable and understandable excuses . . . they know very well that the law is not applied. It is not observed in this country . . . breaking the law does not endanger them in any way'. B-JU-16: 'a large portion of the crime that I deal with, is socially conditioned. Sometimes it's about the life and subsistence of certain people . . . [I] vindicated a person who stole a sausage from the store because he was hungry. The economic and social conditions for crimes are sometimes a reasonable justification for a violation . . . the state does nothing . . . but punish. I cannot see any educational effects'.

Most Bulgarian legal insiders, however, find it unacceptable to break the law – and for rule of law-based reasons. In their view, "the law is for all" and "norms must be followed". Consequently there is "no reasonable excuse" for breaking the law. Quite a few legal insiders simply state that lawbreaking is unacceptable without offering further explanation:

> B-PR-16: 'the justification is always reasonable in their eyes and never in ours'. B-PO-6: 'reasonable justifications, no. More likely someone is behind their back to cover them and protect them from punishment.' B-LA-13: 'they don't have any reasonable excuses, they have money.'

Ukraine is in much more dire straits economically than both Poland and Bulgaria. This is reflected in the legal insiders' statements on lawbreaking. The socioeconomic factor is the number-one reason for reasonable lawbreaking. Very strict and unreasonable business regulations comes a close second:

> U-ER-8: 'very often the legislative basis does not give ordinary people an opportunity . . . to survive'. U-JU-29: 'the economic field . . . is regulated in such a way that it is extremely difficult to obtain the necessary permits . . . sometimes people . . . work without the required . . . documents . . . part of the documents may be in the process of being registered. And it is very time-consuming. People can be understood. They cannot just be unemployed. Everybody wants to eat and [everybody] has a family to look after. This is why, in most cases, people are forced to violate the law.' U-PO-10: 'payment for public utilities is higher than the salary level [so] one will . . . manipulate the electricity counter in order to pay less.'

Other explanations for breaking the law perceived as acceptable to legal insiders – such as poor-quality legislation and inefficient legal institutions, which makes it difficult for people to resolve their problems by means of law – trail far behind the socioeconomic factor. The Ukrainian tax system and impunity on the part of Ukrainian politicians and government officials help explain why ordinary citizens violate the law. Complex legislation also has something to do with it. Some legal insiders believe that poor law enforcement explains why people do not obey the law. The socioeconomic situation also encourages lawbreaking:

> U-JU-3: 'they follow [the example] of the politicians . . . when people see that those people violate [the law] they [follow suit].' U-LA-17: 'the legal system is built in such a way that business cannot work within it'. U-ER-7: 'all the people who earn anything beside their salary . . . conceal their income, starting from the simple member of a village council and ending with the Prime Minister and the President. This happens because the existing system of taxation says you've earned 100 roubles, [now] give me 90 . . . therefore everybody conceals their income. The reason is . . . the stupid tax system'. U-GO-11: 'if [punishment would be imposed on those violating the law] then it would happen less'.

Ukrainian legal insiders who believe that people *do not have reasonable excuses* for breaking the law, claim that in most instances lawbreaking is motivated by personal interest and greed. They condemn lawbreaking by invoking the rule of law: U-JU-25: "there are no reasonable excuses. There is only gluttony and profit".

Finally, some legal insiders view lawbreaking as part of the Ukrainian legal culture: it reflects the local "mentality", people's "bad upbringing" and the fact that the distinction between "mine" (i.e. the private sphere) and "ours" (i.e. the public sphere) was messed up during Communism. A sense of "impunity" (i.e. a sense of being placed above the law) also motivates lawbreaking in Ukraine:

U-GO-18: 'no matter whether a law is good or bad . . . it is still the law'. U-LA-4: 'we are a developed country and cannot neglect laws'. U-ER-21: 'there are no reasons [for breaking the law]. It is rather our mentality and level of legal culture [that cause people to break the law].' U-GO-22: 'it is [a result of] bad upbringing.' U-LA-6: 'the concept of "mine" and "ours" are messed up. "Mine" is [placed] above "ours"'.

Conclusions

This chapter has investigated whether, and why, people obey or break the law. Tyler (2006) investigated *normative* and *instrumental* reasons why people obey or break the law. Our data suggest that across Europe people's behaviour vis-à-vis the law is informed by both instrumental and normative considerations. In doing so, and borrowing Hirschman's (1970) statement, we have investigated "Loyalty" (i.e. the reasons why people obey the law) and "Exit" (the reasons why people break the law).

As noted in previous chapters attitudes towards law are mostly pan-European, whereas perceptions are fairly country-specific. This chapter has focused on perceptions, and no clear East–West pattern emerges. However, in both Eastern and Western Europe, social norms dictate that one should abide by "major law" (e.g. that one should not commit murder, attack other people or steal from them). Breaking "minor law" (e.g. traffic law, limitations on the amount of alcohol one may bring home when returning from abroad, downloading music from the internet, etc.), on the other hand, is considered to be fairly socially acceptable. In all countries the public believe that people will break a law if it causes no harm to other people, when chances of getting caught are low, in self-defence or in an emergency.

The *normative perspective* is more prevalent in Poland. In this country many people considered lawbreaking legitimate during Communism as the Communist Party was regarded as illegitimate and people felt that the communist system was forced on them. Although transition has caused more lawbreaking in other post-communist states as people associate democracy with unlimited freedom – including breaking the law – Poles have embraced democracy. They have accepted the hardships of transition for a higher good: EU membership and thus a 'return to Europe'. Even though many are critical of the authorities, they view the law as legitimate and something one should strive to obey. Even as legal insiders across Europe believe that those people who are less lawbreaking now than they were in the past abide by the law because it has become more difficult for them to get away with such lawbreaking, legal insiders in Poland believe that increased law-abidance is a result of public morale changing for the better.

The *instrumental perspective* is most common in Bulgaria and Ukraine, but also widespread in Norway and England. However, people's reasons for disregarding the law differ. In Bulgaria and Ukraine *legal nihilism* is widespread. So is poverty. Older people (who are amongst the poorest) in the former two countries try to obey the law as they have been taught to do from an early age and because they fear the consequences of breaking the law. Ordinary citizens generally try to obey the law if they think it is likely that they will get caught if they break the law. But they happily disregard the law if they are likely to get away with it. There is an element of "Voice" in their lawbreaking: as – in their view – the ruling elites and the wealthy have placed themselves above the law. Consequently, there is no incentive for ordinary people to obey it. By contrast, people in Norway and England ignore minor law if chances of getting caught are small or if the fines for such lawbreaking are modest. Such lawbreaking is explained by deteriorating social norms, limited peer pressure, increasing individualism, higher levels of education and increased wealth.

Legal outsiders and insiders have fairly similar views about the extent of lawbreaking in their countries: a majority in both groups (all countries except Norway, where opinions are divided) believe that ordinary people mostly obey the law. They also have fairly similar views on the law-abidingness of religious and ethnic minorities: such groups are mostly as law-abiding as the majority population – though in Norway and Bulgaria both legal outsiders and insiders to a greater extent believe that they are less law-abiding than the majority.

In Chapter 1 we suggested that there appears to be a correlation between level of rule of law and size of GDP (PPP) per capita: countries with higher GDP (PPP) per capita also have more rule of law (World Bank's 2010 Rule of Law Index). Norway tops the list, followed – in descending order – by the UK, Poland, Bulgaria and Ukraine. Data presented in this chapter suggest that there is a correlation between GDP (PPP) per capita, rule of law, and reasonable excuses for lawbreaking: the poorer the country is and the less rule of law it has, the more likely both legal outsiders and insiders are to believe that people have reasonable excuses for breaking the law.[14]

[14] As shown earlier, some of our findings on law-abidingness follow the same pattern: there is a gradual slide from Norway through to Ukraine in terms of public perceptions of respect for the law, willingness to abide by the law, implementation and enforcement of the law, extent of crime and corruption and perceptions of law as the power of the state.

6

Perceptions of legal insiders

Introduction: the people making, implementing and applying the law

In Chapter 5 we explored the perceptions that legal outsiders and legal insiders have on law-abidingness amongst the general public. To get a proper picture, however, we also need to find out how both groups perceive the legal insiders and the institutions they represent.

In democracies the state is divided into three branches – the legislative, executive and judiciary – each with separate and independent powers and areas of responsibility so that the powers of one branch are not in conflict with the powers associated with the other branches.[1] The media is frequently referred to as the fourth estate (or branch) in that it influences – and sometimes even sets – the political agenda. Some also believe that there is a fifth estate consisting of digital self-publishing, bloggers, grass-root journalists and Twitter (Harding 2014, p. 60).

It is well known that in post-communist states legal outsiders perceive legal institutions with great scepticism, even distrust. By contrast, legal institutions are amongst the most respected and trusted institutions in Western Europe. Little is known about how the legal insiders think they are perceived by legal outsiders. And we have limited knowledge about how legal insiders perceive each other. This chapter explores such perceptions.

Investigating public and elite perceptions of European legal insiders enables us to explore the quality of democracy and rule of law across Europe: first, because it provides us with an idea as to how ordinary citizens perceive the people and institutions making, implementing and enforcing the law. Second, because it sheds light on how the latter

[1] Wikipedia, 'Separation of powers', http://en.wikipedia.org/wiki/Separation_of_powers accessed on 10 August 2014.

think they are perceived by the public – and thus also on perceived public perceptions of the legislative, executive and judiciary.[2] And third, because it gives us an idea as to how these three branches of power perceive, and sometimes interact with, each other.

As was Chapter 5 this chapter is more *people oriented* than *principle oriented.*

LEGAL OUTSIDERS' PERSPECTIVES ON LEGAL INSIDERS

Government officials

On an average, across the five countries, only half the public (51 per cent) say they would expect to be given fair treatment if they had some problems that they had to take to a government office; 39 per cent simply say they would not expect fair treatment and a further 10 per cent spontaneously suggest they would have to buy fair treatment by using "connections or bribes". Interviewers did not offer the bribery option, though they were briefed to record it if the interviewee volunteered it spontaneously.

The numbers who would expect "fair treatment by officials" range steadily down from 80 per cent in Norway through 71 per cent in England, 52 per cent in Poland and 35 per cent in Bulgaria to a mere 18 per cent in Ukraine. But another 26 per cent in Ukraine, along with 21 per cent in Bulgaria volunteer the comment (without being asked) that they could get "fair treatment" but only by using "connections or bribes" (Table 6.1). Very few, only 3 per cent in Poland, and none in England or Norway, mention connections and bribes.

Lawyers

Lawyers are rated highly everywhere on being "well informed" – on an average by 88 per cent. But across the range from Norway to Ukraine, their rating for "trustworthiness" drops steadily, from 88 to 53 per cent. Conversely their (adverse) rating for being "more interested in charging

[2] The elected representatives represent the legislative branch; the government officials, the prosecutors and the police represent the executive branch; and the judges represent the judiciary. The lawyers are not a part of the three branches of power, but they frequently come into contact with two of them: the executive (prosecutors) and the judiciary (courts).

Table 6.1 *Expectations of fair treatment from officials: the legal outsiders' perspective*

	NOR (%)	ENG (%)	POL (%)	BUL (%)	UKR (%)	N-MU (%)	E-MU (%)	P-MU (%)	B-MU (%)	U-MU (%)
Q12 Expect fair treatment by officials?										
Yes	80	71	52	35	18	72	72	75	47	22
No	20	29	45	44	56	28	28	23	40	56
Only by connections or bribes	0	0	3	21	26	0	0	2	13	22

Note: NOR, ENG, POL, BUL, UKR refer to the majority populations; N-MU, E-MU, P-MU, B-MU, U-MU refer to the Muslims.

money than helping their clients" rises steadily from 53 to 88 per cent. Nowhere are lawyers regarded as being more law-abiding than ordinary people, but in England and Norway lawyers are at least rated much the same as ordinary people.

By contrast, in the former communist countries a large majority rate lawyers as 'less' law-abiding than ordinary people. One reason might be that their knowledge of the law allows them to utilise the many loopholes of the law. Another – that they know how likely they are to get or not get caught and, more importantly, how to get out of trouble with law enforcement if caught breaking the law. As has been mentioned in the previous chapters, law in Eastern Europe has many flaws.

Yet despite all these criticisms, the public have, on balance, a positive attitude towards lawyers everywhere: strongly positive in Norway (80 per cent), England (75 per cent) and Poland (73 per cent), though only marginally positive in Bulgaria (54 per cent) and Ukraine (59 per cent) (Table 6.2).

To varying degrees, the public feel more positive about older lawyers than younger lawyers. Older lawyers are more experienced. Besides, and more importantly, in Eastern Europe many former judges work as lawyers. They know the courts from the inside, including the judges who used to be their colleagues. Further, the quality of education in many universities in Eastern Europe has deteriorated since the collapse of communism and corruption is rife. In some countries even faculties of law have been hit by corruption scandals – suffice it here

Table 6.2 *Perceptions of lawyers: the legal outsiders' perspective*

	NOR (%)	ENG (%)	POL (%)	BUL (%)	UKR (%)	N-MU (%)	E-MU (%)	P-MU (%)	B-MU (%)	U-MU (%)
Q78B: Lawyers well informed (v. not)	94	88	83	90	84	91	77	95	96	80
Q78C: Lawyers trustworthy (v. not)	88	82	70	61	53	83	71	84	60	58
Q78E: Lawyers more interested in money (v. helping client)	53	56	77	82	88	70	80	61	90	89
Q79: Lawyers more law-abiding than ordinary people (v. less)	44	47	23	24	23	48	36	56	37	23
Q80: Positive attitude to lawyers (v. negative)	80	75	73	54	59	82	69	87	65	63
Q81: More positive about older lawyers (v. younger)	69	71	58	57	73	64	71	72	58	81

Note: NOR, ENG, POL, BUL, UKR refer to the majority populations; N-MU, E-MU, P-MU, B-MU, U-MU refer to the Muslims.

Table 6.3 *Basis of perceptions of lawyers: the legal outsiders' perspective*

	NOR (%)	ENG (%)	POL (%)	BUL (%)	UKR (%)	N-MU (%)	E-MU (%)	P-MU (%)	B-MU (%)	U-MU (%)
Q82: Views about lawyers based on:										
personal experience	36	50	29	26	30	38	38	27	27	31
people you meet	15	19	28	32	32	28	30	40	28	31
TV and press	49	31	43	41	38	34	32	33	45	38

Note: NOR, ENG, POL, BUL, UKR refer to the majority populations; N-MU, E-MU, P-MU, B-MU, U-MU refer to the Muslims.

to mention the University of Plzeň[3] (Czech Republic) and the University of Kragujevac[4] (Serbia).

The English public claim the most direct, personal knowledge of lawyers: fully half base their views on personal experience rather than on gossip or TV and the press. In sharp contrast, Norwegians to the greatest extent base their views about lawyers on TV and the press whereas Poles, Bulgarians and Ukrainians more than others base their perceptions of lawyers on gossip with "people they meet" though they rely still more on TV and the press (Table 6.3).

Judges, prosecutors, juries and lay judges

Everywhere, large majorities feel that judges have "enough resources" (82 per cent an on average), and are "well informed" about the law (93 per cent on an average). But across the range from Norway to Ukraine their rating for "fairness" drops steadily – and precipitously so – from 92 per cent in Norway to a mere 24 per cent in Ukraine. Conversely, their adverse rating for being "willing to take bribes" rises steadily from a

3 Jan Richter, 'Plzeň law school scandal provokes nation-wide audit of over 300,000 university graduates', *Radio Praha*, 20 October 2009, www.radio.cz/en/section/curraffrs/plzen-law-school-scandal-provokes-nation-wide-audit-of-over-300000-university-graduates accessed on 18 January 2014.

4 Marina Jakovljević, 'Corruption at Serbian universities. Exam – how much?' *Wave. International Youth Web Magazine* 6 (2006), www.wavemagazine.net/arhiva/06/soc/exam.htm accessed on 18 January 2014.

mere 7 per cent in Norway to 96 per cent in Ukraine, though this is not a steady rise but a huge 'step shift' from an average of only 11 per cent in Norway and England, to an average of 86 per cent in the three former communist countries.

Perceptions that judges are too subservient to authority and "pay too much attention to whether the government will be pleased or displeased by their rulings in court" rise steadily from 31 per cent in Norway, through 42 per cent in England to 56 per cent in Poland, but then takes a sudden leap to around 83 per cent in Bulgaria and Ukraine. Conversely, perceptions that judges are more law-abiding than ordinary people declines moderately from 81 per cent in Norway to 69 per cent in England, but then drops precipitously to an average of only 25 per cent in the former communist countries. This is all too much for the public to remain positive about judges – as they do, despite criticisms, about lawyers (the independent lawyer's profession is fairly new in Eastern Europe). So, positive ratings of judges drop steadily from 97 per cent in Norway, to 82 per cent in England and 73 per cent in Poland, but then drops precipitously to 47 per cent in Bulgaria and 33 per cent in Ukraine.

In every country the public are more positive about older judges than younger judges: on an average 69 per cent feel more positive about older rather than younger judges, with no great difference between attitudes in different countries (Table 6.4).

This is a somewhat odd finding in the former communist countries where older judges might easily be associated with the 'old regime'. But it is understandable in that older judges have more experience and are sometimes better educated than younger judges. Citizens may also think that older judges are less likely to be corrupted than younger ones. Findings for England are interesting in that the judges themselves think the public perceive them as older, distanced, well-educated and wealthy men – and in a negative sense (see below).[5] Yet the public say they trust older judges more than younger ones.

If judges were given "more independence and discretion", would they then become "too lenient", "too harsh", or "more fair"; would they "favour the rich and well-educated", or "be more tempted to seek bribes"?

Except in Ukraine the public are evenly divided on whether judges would become "too lenient" (though a large majority of Ukrainians think that is unlikely). A large majority in Norway and England think judges

[5] This is confirmed in a report prepared by the House of Lords (2007, p. 1).

Table 6.4 *Perceptions of judges: the legal outsiders' perspective*

	NOR (%)	ENG (%)	POL (%)	BUL (%)	UKR (%)	N-MU (%)	E-MU (%)	P-MU (%)	B-MU (%)	U-MU (%)
Q83A: Judges have enough resources (v. not)	76	73	83	90	87	85	84	91	94	83
Q83B: Judges are well informed (v. not)	99	92	90	92	90	95	92	97	97	93
Q83D: Judges are fair (v. not)	92	73	51	43	24	89	80	74	45	30
Q83F: Judges are willing to take bribes (v. not)	7	15	72	90	96	29	28	48	81	91
Q83E: Judges are too subservient to government (v. not)	31	42	56	84	81	66	59	42	75	65
Q84: Judges are more law-abiding than ordinary people (v. less)	81	69	33	24	18	78	66	72	38	17
Q85: Positive attitude to judges (v. negative)	97	82	73	47	33	90	81	89	61	46
Q86: More positive about older judges (v. younger)	78	68	62	58	78	75	70	77	63	73

Note: NOR, ENG, POL, BUL, UKR refer to the majority populations; N-MU, E-MU, P-MU, B-MU, U-MU refer to the Muslims.

would not become "too harsh". A very large majority in Norway and England, together with a smaller majority in Poland, think that judges would make "better, more fair decisions" if they had more discretion – though Bulgarians are divided, and a large majority of Ukrainians think they would not.

In Poland, Bulgaria and Ukraine a large majority think judges would favour the rich or well educated, though a majority of Norwegians think not, and the English are evenly divided. Similarly, in Poland, Bulgaria and especially Ukraine, large majorities (83 per cent on an average) think judges would be "more tempted to seek bribes" if they had more discretion, though almost as large a majority in England and Norway think not (Table 6.5).

Even more than public perceptions of lawyers, public perceptions of courts and judges are based primarily on television or the press in every country (53 per cent on an average) and much less on personal experience (24 per cent) or gossip (23 per cent). In Norway and England perceptions are based more on personal experience than gossip, though more on gossip than experience in Bulgaria but with personal experience and gossip equally important in Ukraine (Table 6.6).

Overall the public's ratings of prosecutors are similar to their ratings of judges – though compared to positive ratings of judges, positive ratings of prosecutors are somewhat less favourable in Norway, England and Poland, though somewhat more favourable in Bulgaria and Ukraine. Of course, in theory at least, Ukrainian 'public prosecutors' claim to act on behalf of the 'public', not on behalf of the state, and indeed they claim that they frequently act against the officials of the state and on behalf of the general public (Table 6.7). It is worth noting that public prosecutors in Ukraine have seriously criticised judges for gross misconduct. However, prosecutors have also themselves been involved in scandals – most recently former Prosecutor General Viktor Pshonka, who abandoned Kiev and his grand mansion following the Ukrainian revolution in early 2014.[6]

Various countries include a role for non-professionals, without legal training, in court procedures – notably 'juries' or 'lay judges'. They are

[6] Ryan Lipman, 'A gaudy mansion of "monumental corruption": inside the staggeringly opulent home of Ukraine's prosecutor general after he flees the country to avoid retribution', 25 February 2014, www.dailymail.co.uk/news/article-2567239/Pshonkas-palace-treasure-trove-total-opulence-Journalists-protestors-enter-estate-extravaganza-luxury.html accessed on 1 August 2014.

Table 6.5 *Perceptions of more independent judges: the legal outsiders' perspective*

	NOR (%)	ENG (%)	POL (%)	BUL (%)	UKR (%)	N-MU (%)	E-MU (%)	P-MU (%)	B-MU (%)	U-MU (%)
Q28: If judges more independent (agree v. disagree):										
Q28A: become too lenient	49	48	52	47	25	61	42	29	31	18
Q28B: become too harsh	27	24	44	45	48	49	38	26	47	53
Q28C: become more fair	74	81	61	52	35	83	79	67	45	35
Q28D: favour rich/well-educated	40	49	70	78	86	48	53	49	72	80
Q28E: more tempted to seek bribes	34	29	78	82	90	44	46	52	71	87

Note: NOR, ENG, POL, BUL, UKR refer to the majority populations; N-MU, E-MU, P-MU, B-MU, U-MU refer to the Muslims.

Table 6.6 *Basis of perceptions of courts and judges: the legal outsiders' perspective*

	NOR (%)	ENG (%)	POL (%)	BUL (%)	UKR (%)	N-MU (%)	E MU (%)	P MU (%)	B-MU (%)	U-MU (%)
Q87: Views about courts and judges based on:										
personal experience	22	27	23	22	25	24	27	22	29	22
people you meet	10	18	27	29	33	20	22	38	25	34
TV and press	68	55	51	50	43	56	51	40	46	44

Note: NOR, ENG, POL, BUL, UKR refer to the majority populations; N-MU, E-MU, P-MU, B-MU, U-MU refer to the Muslims.

Table 6.7 *Perceptions of prosecutors and judges: the legal outsiders' perspective*

	NOR (%)	ENG (%)	POL (%)	BUL (%)	UKR (%)	N-MU (%)	E-MU (%)	P-MU (%)	B-MU (%)	U-MU (%)
Q88: Positive attitude to prosecutors (v. negative)	90	72	67	57	43	85	74	78	70	49
Q85: Positive attitude to judges (v. negative)	97	82	73	47	33	90	81	89	61	46
More positive to prosecutors than to judges	−7	−10	−6	+10	+10	−5	−7	−11	+9	+3

Note: NOR, ENG, POL, BUL, UKR refer to the majority populations; N-MU, E-MU, P-MU, B-MU, U-MU refer to the Muslims.

not legal insiders in the full sense, but they are temporarily legal insiders for the duration of their role in court. They are not rated highly on being "well informed about the law" (average 47 per cent); but they are rated very much higher by the public on being "trustworthy" – ranging from 84 per cent in Norway and 81 per cent in England down to 52 per cent in Bulgaria. And their overall positive ratings are also high – ranging from 82 per cent in Norway down only to 60 per cent in Bulgaria (Tables 6.8 and 6.9).

Juries are used in serious criminal court cases – though in England the civil justice system also has juries, for instance in some inquest cases (Grieve 2013, p. 2). In Norway there is growing pressure within the judiciary (especially from defence lawyers) as well as within political circles to abolish the jury and replace it with three professional judges and four lay judges – referred to as *stor meddomstol*. The main reason is that the jury does not have to explain its decision, which is viewed as a threat to justice. In England, a debate on whether jury trial is an effective guarantor of justice is ongoing (ibid. 2013, p. 1).

The police

Perhaps as an indicator of support rather than criticism, the numbers who say their police "do not have enough resources to do their job

Table 6.8 *Perceptions of the informedness and trustworthiness of juries and lay judges: the legal outsiders' perspective*

	NOR (%)	ENG (%)	POL (%)	BUL (%)	UKR (%)	N-MU (%)	E-MU (%)	P-MU (%)	B-MU (%)	U-MU (%)
Q89A: Juries and lay judges are well informed (v. not)	50	38	45	55	NA	54	43	49	46	NA
Q89B: Juries and lay judges trustworthy (v. not)	84	81	60	52	NA	69	70	69	40	NA
Q90: Positive attitude juries and lay judges (v. negative)	82	74	65	60	NA	75	72	75	54	NA

Note: NOR, ENG, POL, BUL, UKR refer to the majority populations; N-MU, E-MU, P-MU, B-MU, U-MU refer to the Muslims.

Table 6.9 *Basis of perceptions of juries and lay judges: the legal outsiders' perspective*

	NOR (%)	ENG (%)	POL (%)	BUL (%)	UKR (%)	N-MU (%)	E-MU (%)	P-MU (%)	B-MU (%)	U-MU (%)
Q91: Views about juries and lay judges based on:										
personal experience	28	31	21	20	NA	23	27	17	25	NA
people you meet	19	26	33	39	NA	30	26	60	34	NA
TV and press	52	43	46	41	NA	47	47	23	41	NA

Note: NOR, ENG, POL, BUL, UKR refer to the majority populations; N-MU, E-MU, P-MU, B-MU, U-MU refer to the Muslims.

properly" range down steadily from 80 per cent in Norway to 28 per cent in Ukraine. That pattern of public perceptions of police resources suggests that the public rating of police in Ukraine is in the "no valid excuses" category: the Ukrainian public does not accept lack of resources as an excuse for poor police performance, while the Norwegian public is more sympathetic to the needs of the police (Table 6.10).

At the time of surveying Norwegian police were involved in various types of protest for better pay and less overtime work. These protests were given broad coverage in the Norwegian media, and they were referred to by the FG participants.

Perceptions that the police are "well informed about the law" range down fairly steadily but modestly from 91 per cent in Norway to 72 per cent in Ukraine. But their "capability to enforce the law" ranges down more sharply from 89 per cent in Norway to 52 per cent in Ukraine, and whether they "can be trusted to enforce the law" ranges down even more sharply from 93 per cent in Norway to 41 per cent in Ukraine.

Around 33 per cent in England and Norway, 76 per cent in Poland, and around 64 per cent in Bulgaria and Ukraine the public say their police are "too afraid to act against armed criminals and gangsters".

The numbers who say their police "serve the government, not the public" rises steadily from 31 per cent in Norway to 88 per cent in Ukraine, and the numbers who say the police are "willing to take bribes" also rises steadily from a mere 12 per cent in Norway to an overwhelming 96 per cent in Ukraine. There thus seems to be a connection between a country's rank on the 2010 World Bank's Rule of Law Index, the size of its GDP (PPP) per capita and the willingness of the police to "serve the government, not the public": as noted in Chapter 1 Norway has the highest rank on the 2010 Rule of Law Index and the highest GDP (PPP) per capita, followed – in descending order – by the UK, Poland, Bulgaria and Ukraine.

Only 23 per cent in England say the police treat ethnic minorities worse than other people – compared to around 32 per cent in Norway, Poland and Bulgaria, and 44 per cent in Ukraine. Muslim minorities themselves disagree however: 66 per cent of Muslims in England say the police treat minorities worse – a figure that is exceeded only by the number of Muslims in Ukraine (74 per cent) who also claim that the police treat minorities worse than others.

The opinions of the English Muslims are in line with the findings of the Macpherson Inquiry, which concluded that the British police force is 'institutionally racist' (Slapper and Kelly 2011, p. 512). A report on British Muslims published by the Open Society Institute (OSI) in 2005 concluded in much the same way. Muslims in the UK, who account for some two million of the country's population, have been affected by the stop-and-search policies to a greater extent than non-Muslims.

Table 6.10 *Perceptions of the police: the legal outsiders' perspective*

	NOR (%)	ENG (%)	POL (%)	BUL (%)	UKR (%)	N-MU (%)	E-MU (%)	P-MU (%)	B-MU (%)	U-MU (%)
Q95A: Police have enough resources (v. not)	20	29	44	64	72	50	59	70	70	77
Q95B: Police well informed about law (v. not)	91	86	76	79	72	87	79	91	88	66
Q95C: Police capable of enforcing law (v. not)	89	70	62	69	52	83	78	77	70	59
Q95E: Police can be trusted to enforce law (v. not)	93	78	60	50	41	84	71	72	61	47
Q95F: Police afraid to act against armed gangsters (v. not)	34	33	76	65	63	60	51	49	62	58
Q95G: Police treat ethnic/linguistic minorities worse (v. not)	34	23	30	31	44	56	66	25	43	74
Q95H: Police serve the government, not the public (v. not)	31	45	50	73	88	56	64	37	68	89
Q95I: Police are willing to take bribes (v. not)	12	22	68	81	96	37	40	49	76	97

Note: NOR, ENG, POL, BUL, UKR refer to the majority populations; N-MU, E-MU, P-MU, B-MU, U-MU refer to the Muslims.

Table 6.11 *Perceptions of law-abidingness amongst the police: the legal outsiders' perspective*

	NOR (%)	ENG (%)	POL (%)	BUL (%)	UKR (%)	N-MU (%)	E-MU (%)	P-MU (%)	B-MU (%)	U-MU (%)
Q96: Police more law-abiding than ordinary people (v. less)	88	67	37	29	11	65	54	61	44	6
Q97: Positive attitude to police (v. negative)	91	78	76	61	27	84	66	87	69	32

Note: NOR, ENG, POL, BUL, UKR refer to the majority populations; N-MU, E-MU, P-MU, B-MU, U-MU refer to the Muslims.

In Ukraine the Crimean Tatars have been heavily discriminated against, and there is evidence of police bias against the Roma (European Commission against Racism and Intolerance [ECRI] 2012, p. 9). The Roma communities in Eastern Europe are often left without police protection or access to justice.[7]

Conversely, the numbers who say the police are "more law-abiding than ordinary people" drop very sharply from 88 per cent in Norway to 67 per cent in England and only 37 per cent in Poland. Inevitably the numbers cannot continue to drop so sharply, but they do drop further – to 29 per cent in Bulgaria and a mere 11 per cent in Ukraine. These findings are not surprising, given ample evidence of police corruption in Bulgaria and Ukraine, and also evidence of links between police and organised crime in Bulgaria (see 'legal insiders' part of this chapter).[8]

Overall, 'positive' attitudes towards the police drop steadily from 91 per cent in Norway to around 77 per cent in England and Poland, and 61 per cent in Bulgaria, but then declines most sharply to a mere 27 per cent in Ukraine (Table 6.11).

[7] Amnesty International UK, 'Roma rights', www.amnesty.org.uk/roma-rights-anti-discrimination-europe-violence-eviction-education, accessed on 16 December 2014.

[8] In late 2013 the Polish former deputy interior minister was arrested on bribery charges in the 'biggest scandal in Polish history of Polish kick-backs', IAR/PAP, 'Wide-ranging corruption scandal hits Polish ministries', *Polskie radio dla zagranicy*, 22 November 2013, www.thenews.pl/1/9/Artykul/153728,Wideranging-corruption-scandal-hits-Polish-ministries accessed 5 September 2014.

Table 6.12 *Basis of perceptions of the police: the legal outsiders' perspective*

	NOR (%)	ENG (%)	POL (%)	BUL (%)	UKR (%)	N-MU (%)	E-MU (%)	P-MU (%)	B-MU (%)	U-MU (%)
Q98: Views about police based on										
personal experience	46	59	46	32	37	45	56	37	31	30
people you meet	10	15	25	21	31	19	19	40	20	32
TV and press	44	26	28	47	33	36	25	24	48	38

Note: NOR, ENG, POL, BUL, UKR refer to the majority populations; N-MU, E-MU, P-MU, B-MU, U-MU refer to the Muslims.

Only a third of the public report that their views about the police derive primarily from "TV and the press". Two-thirds cite their own personal experience or that of their acquaintances. So, compared to public perceptions of lawyers, courts, juries and lawmakers, public perceptions of the police are self-consciously based very much more strongly on personal experience and much less on TV and the press despite the widespread coverage of police both in TV news and in TV fictional drama (Table 6.12). Gossip with acquaintances, however, has a similar impact on perceptions of all 'legal insiders' – lawyers, judges and police.

The lawmakers: government and Parliament

Remarkably, in an age of democracy, the public in every country do not see themselves as the most important influence on their government's and Parliament's changes in the law. Although Norway comes closest, there is no country in which the public feel predominant 'ownership' of changes in the law. Everywhere, changes in the law are perceived as an imposition – sometimes welcomed as a good idea, sometimes not, but always imposed.

Asked: "when making changes to the law in this country, do you feel our government listens more to foreign governments and international organisations, to ordinary people in this country, or to minorities and special interests in this country?", an average of 48 per cent cite "foreign governments and international organisations", 30 per cent cite "minorities and special interests", and only 22 per cent cite "ordinary people in

Table 6.13 *External influences on law: the legal outsiders' perspective*

	NOR (%)	ENG (%)	POL (%)	BUL (%)	UKR (%)	N-MU (%)	E-MU (%)	P-MU (%)	B-MU (%)	U-MU (%)
Q64: When changing law, government listens more to:										
foreign governments and/or international organisations	43	42	52	75	30	40	56	44	82	26
minorities and special interests in [this country]	16	33	34	14	51	9	18	17	11	58
ordinary people in [this country]	40	25	14	11	19	51	26	40	6	16

Note: NOR, ENG, POL, BUL, UKR refer to the majority populations; N-MU, E-MU, P-MU, B-MU, U-MU refer to the Muslims.

this country" (Table 6.13). Norway comes closest to being viewed as a "popular democracy" in this respect, with 40 per cent citing responsiveness to "ordinary people", followed by England at a low 25 per cent, and with the three former communist countries averaging a mere 15 per cent. But even 40 per cent indicates exclusion from lawmaking.

In public perceptions of "changing the law", the influence of foreign governments and international organisations is perceived to be greater than anything else. It is cited by around 43 per cent in Norway and England, 52 per cent in Poland and 75 per cent in Bulgaria. Ukraine is a striking exception however; the Ukrainian public most frequently cite "minorities and special interests" at 51 per cent, far ahead of "foreign and international" influences at 30 per cent.

One plausible explanation is that the Russian minority in Eastern Ukraine – and until the Crimea was annexed by the Russian Federation also the Russian majority in the Crimea – have demanded the right to use Russian as the administrative language. Another, equally plausible explanation is that the authorities in the Crimea were under a (legal) obligation to provide the Crimean Tatars with housing, land and other support. Even though ample evidence suggests that the Crimean authorities have not been very forthcoming in this regard, ordinary citizens might still feel that the Crimean Tatars have been provided with excessive privileges.

Nationalist reactions against perceived foreign influences (or minority and special interests within the country) may be offset by general perceptions that foreign influences are generally good. Around 62 per cent in Norway and England, but an overwhelming 92 per cent in Poland, Bulgaria and Ukraine feel their country "has a lot to learn from other countries and European or international organisations" about "writing good laws", "implementing and enforcing laws", and about the way "ordinary people and political leaders respect the law". Superficially, such feelings might be classed as perceptions rather than as attitudes, but in reality they are prescriptions for reform, and quite properly classed as "attitudes" (Table 6.14).

Significant numbers claim to have "heard news stories about particular EU standards, laws or regulations being applied in this country or others": 76 per cent in Norway, 50 per cent in Poland and Bulgaria, though only 41 per cent in England and 32 per cent in Ukraine – the two most peripheral countries.

Slightly less than half the public "would be pleased if national cultures and values became much more similar across the whole of Europe" but by contrast, a clear majority in every country "would be pleased if national laws became much more similar across the whole of Europe". Support for a convergence of laws averages 82 per cent in Poland, Bulgaria and Ukraine, though only 58 per cent in Norway and England. That reflects historic satisfaction with the law and lawmakers in Norway and England and historic dissatisfaction with lawmakers under Communism in Poland, Bulgaria and Ukraine – and public support for "levelling-up" to European standards.

In Norway and England a majority say the "government and Parliament can be trusted to draft clear and effective laws"; that they do not "draft laws for personal advantage or business interests"; and that they "can be trusted to ensure that the laws are implemented and enforced". But the opposite is true for Poland, Bulgaria and Ukraine (Table 6.15). Our findings for Norway are supported by Listhaug and Ringdal (2007), who suggest that high levels of public trust in state institutions in the Nordic countries should be attributed to these countries' positive economic performance, high living standards and limited distance between the public and their elected representatives.

By large majorities, the public in Poland, Bulgaria and Ukraine feel their "governments and Parliaments" are "too favourable towards the

Table 6.14 *Whether a country has a lot to learn from other countries, European and international organisations: the legal outsiders' perspective*

	NOR (%)	ENG (%)	POL (%)	BUL (%)	UKR (%)	N-MU (%)	E-MU (%)	P-MU (%)	B-MU (%)	U-MU (%)
Q65: [this country] has a lot to learn (v. not) from other countries and European or international organisations about:										
Q65A: writing good laws	66	56	93	87	92	73	63	92	92	82
Q65B: implementing and enforcing laws	69	64	93	94	95	74	72	94	93	90
Q65C: the way ordinary people respect law	61	67	92	90	92	68	73	95	88	90
Q65D: the way political leaders respect law	52	56	89	94	95	66	70	96	93	89

Note: NOR, ENG, POL, BUL, UKR refer to the majority populations; N-MU, E-MU, P-MU, B-MU, U-MU refer to the Muslims.

Table 6.15 *Government's and Parliament's ability to draft clear and effective laws: the legal outsiders' perspective*

	NOR (%)	ENG (%)	POL (%)	BUL (%)	UKR (%)	N-MU (%)	E-MU (%)	P-MU (%)	B-MU (%)	U-MU (%)
Q92C: Government and Parliament can be trusted to draft clear and effective laws (v. not)	84	63	40	37	37	91	66	55	57	37
Q92D: Government and Parliament draft laws for personal advantage or business interests (v. for good of country)	24	45	75	84	85	48	62	47	71	88
Q92F: Government and Parliament can be trusted to ensure laws are implemented and enforced (v. not)	87	71	45	29	29	83	76	59	44	35

Note: NOR, ENG, POL, BUL, UKR refer to the majority populations; N-MU, E-MU, P-MU, B-MU, U-MU refer to the Muslims.

rich and powerful", are "willing to take bribes", and are "less law-abiding than ordinary people". The opposite (of all three) is true for Norway. England falls in-between, though closer to Norway: by only small majorities the English say their government and Parliament are too favourable to the rich and powerful and that their MPs are less law-abiding than the public. In England a third, but only a third – compared to an average of 87 per cent in the former communist countries – suggest that their government and Parliament are willing to take bribes. Overall positive ratings of "government and Parliament" range steadily down from 83 per cent in Norway to a mere 14 per cent in Ukraine (Table 6.16).

Only a minority anywhere think that their political leaders always obey the rulings of international courts such as the ECtHR – though that ranges down from around 42 per cent in Norway and England to around 14 per cent in Poland and Ukraine. (At 25 per cent, Bulgarian perceptions of compliance are somewhat higher than in Poland or Ukraine) (Table 6.17).

In Norway, a large majority of the public claim minorities have gained more rights and privileges from local political deals than from EU pressure. But to varying degrees in all the other countries, a majority feel that "minorities have gained more rights and privileges from EU pressure" than from "political deals within our Parliament", though in Bulgaria the public are very close to regarding both internal local minority pressure (possibly due to the existence of a Turkish Party – the Movement for Rights and Freedoms – which has been part of several Bulgarian government coalitions and external EU pressure as equally influential (Table 6.18).

In summary, positive public perceptions of legal insiders

Public perceptions of lawyers, judges, juries, prosecutors and the police are about equally positive (close to 66 per cent, on an average). Public perceptions of juries or 'lay judges' are slightly more positive (70 per cent) than that. But public perceptions of lawmakers (i.e. Parliaments) are far less positive (at only 46 per cent).

Cross-nationally, there is a sharp trend in approval ratings for all legal insiders taken together from 86 per cent in Norway and 73 per cent in England, through 63 per cent in Poland and 50 per cent in Bulgaria, to a mere 38 per cent in Ukraine (Table 6.19).

Overall, across the five countries, Muslims feel slightly more positive about legal insiders than do the general public. The difference (5 per cent on an average) is trivial. It does not suggest much greater enthusiasm for legal insiders amongst Muslims. What is really remarkable, however, is

Table 6.16 *Perceptions of government and Parliament: the legal outsiders' perspective*

	NOR (%)	ENG (%)	POL (%)	BUL (%)	UKR (%)	N-MU (%)	E-MU (%)	P-MU (%)	B-MU (%)	U-MU (%)
Q92G: Government and Parliament are too favourable towards rich and powerful (v. not)	38	54	84	89	94	53	66	58	78	94
Q92H: Government and Parliament are willing to take bribes (v. not)	14	33	76	91	95	30	43	52	76	93
Q93A: MPs are more law-abiding than ordinary people (v. less)	75	45	15	8	4	60	42	35	23	4
Q94: Positive attitude to [this country] Parliament (v. negative)	83	61	43	30	14	79	62	48	51	20

Note: NOR, ENG, POL, BUL, UKR refer to the majority populations; N-MU, E-MU, P-MU, B-MU, U-MU refer to the Muslims.

Table 6.17 *Perceptions of the manner in which political leaders relate to the rulings of supra-national courts*

	NOR (%)	ENG (%)	POL (%)	BUL (%)	UKR (%)	N-MU (%)	E-MU (%)	P-MU (%)	B-MU (%)	U-MU (%)
Q24: Political leaders:										
obey international rulings	43	41	14	25	13	36	29	26	41	13
ignore/evade international rulings	37	31	58	57	74	34	48	47	35	61
remain unaware of international rulings	20	28	28	18	13	31	23	27	23	26

Note: NOR, ENG, POL, BUL, UKR refer to the majority populations; N-MU, E-MU, P-MU, B-MU, U-MU refer to the Muslims.

Table 6.18 *Awareness of EU standards, laws, regulations and minority rights: the legal outsiders' perspective*

	NOR (%)	ENG (%)	POL (%)	BUL (%)	UKR (%)	N-MU (%)	E-MU (%)	P-MU (%)	B-MU (%)	U-MU (%)
Q71: Heard of EU standards, laws or regulations being applied (v. not)	76	41	50	50	32	47	29	61	22	49
Q77: Minorities gained more rights and privileges from EU pressure (v. political deals within [this country] Parliament)	24	57	72	50	65	38	55	75	52	62

Note: NOR, ENG, POL, BUL, UKR refer to the majority populations; N-MU, E-MU, P-MU, B-MU, U-MU refer to the Muslims.

Table 6.19 *Perceptions of legal insiders: the legal outsiders' perspective*

	NOR (%)	ENG (%)	POL (%)	BUL (%)	UKR (%)	N-MU (%)	E-MU (%)	P-MU (%)	B-MU (%)	U-MU (%)
Q80: Positive attitude to lawyers (v. negative)	80	75	73	54	59	82	69	87	65	63
Q85: Positive attitude to judges (v. negative)	97	82	73	47	33	90	81	89	61	46
Q88: Positive attitude to prosecutors (v. negative)	90	72	67	57	43	85	74	78	70	49
Q94: Positive attitude to [this country] Parliament (v. negative)	83	61	43	30	14	79	62	48	51	20
Q97: Positive attitude to police (v. negative)	91	78	76	61	27	84	66	87	69	32

Note: NOR, ENG, POL, BUL, UKR refer to the majority populations; N-MU, E-MU, P-MU, B-MU, U-MU refer to the Muslims.

Table 6.20 *Perceptions of legal outsiders' perceptions of legal insiders: the legal insiders' perspective*

	Norway (%)	England (%)	Poland (%)	Bulgaria (%)	Ukraine (%)
DEP 41: How do you think ordinary people perceive [respondent's profession]?					
Positively	35	9	12	8	18
Negatively	24	57	52	70	51
Mix	41	35	36	22	32

Note: Entries are based on the percentages of relevant 'text units' – the total number of answers to a given question; so entries sum up to approximately 100% (decimals are rounded up or down to the nearest whole number).

that in current conditions, Muslims do not feel significantly less positive about legal insiders than do the general public. In England, Muslims do feel 12 per cent less positive than the general public towards the police, but even in England Muslims do not feel less positive than the general public towards other legal insiders.

Legal insiders' perspectives on how the public view their profession

As noted earlier, overall, the legal outsiders have *positive* views of legal insiders – though less so of lawmakers than other groups (Table 6.19). However, the legal insiders themselves – with the exception of those in Norway – think the general public perceive them *negatively*! (Table 6.20). Their perceptions seem to be largely media-driven or based on hearsay, rather than on actual feedback from legal outsiders. Those who report on their personal interactions with legal outsiders mostly describe these in positive terms.

To the extent personal experiences are referred to, most categories of legal insiders – and especially the elected representatives – distinguish between the generally negative image people have of their profession and the positive manner in which the public relate to them personally. Elected representatives make frequent references to the negative perceptions citizens generally have of MPs and the positive manner in which they relate to their own local MP and/or local councillors. This duality is common in both Western and Eastern Europe. Legal insiders in Western Europe – to a greater extent than legal insiders in Eastern Europe – report positive experiences with the public.

For reasons of space our content analysis of what the legal insiders actually say about public perceptions of their professions is focused on negative statements in England, Poland, Bulgaria and Ukraine – and on positive and negative statements in Norway.

The elected representatives

The Euro-barometer shows that across Europe elected representatives enjoy limited public trust. Only a quarter or less of those polled trust their national governments and Parliaments.[9] There may, of course, be a number of reasons for this – and they are likely to vary by country. However, it is plausible that low levels of trust are at least to some extent caused by increasing populism on the part of some elected representatives. Besides, in both Western and Eastern Europe scandals involving high-ranking politicians have in recent years tarnished the image of elected representatives as such.[10] Our IDIs suggest that the elected representatives are very much aware of such negative views of their profession – and that they are not happy with them.

Norwegian elected representatives predominantly think that people have *mixed* views of their profession. On the one hand, they believe that there is some contempt for politicians in Norway. To some extent this is due to the politicians' failure to deliver on all their promises, to some extent it is due to the privileges they have awarded themselves. The latter include a generous pension scheme for MPs, which is considerably better than that of ordinary citizens. On the other hand, public discontent is fuelled by negative media coverage of the political profession. Some elected representatives claim that politicians are perceived as "ignorant" people, as "idiots", whom the public loves to "hate", mostly apply to the national level. But local level elected representatives believe that people are generally "respectful" of them personally.

[9] Across Europe trust in national political institutions is decreasing (23 per cent, –2 percentage points since spring 2013 for national governments, 25 per cent, –1 percentage point for national Parliaments). *Standard Eurobarometer* 80 (2013).

[10] Midtbø (2007); Alex Stevenson, 'The top ten political scandals of 2013', *Politics.co.uk*, 24 December 2013; *The Spectator*, 'Top 50 political scandals. Part one', 8 July 2009 and *The Spectator*, 'Top 50 political scandals. Part two', 16 July 2009, www.spectator.co.uk accessed on 15 August 2014.

Compared to the elected representatives in Norway, English elected representatives believe that citizens have a more negative view of them: members of their profession are generally "disliked" and held in "low regard". To some, they are the "most hated people" in the country. The public allegedly generally have a "poor understanding" of what elected representatives actually do.

English elected representatives – just like the Norwegian representatives – believe that the general public distinguishes between politicians as such, and their own local MP or local councillors. Although highly critical of the former, they are mostly positive toward the latter. Public perceptions of politicians at a more general level as a group are mostly shaped by the media. Their perceptions of their local MP and local councillors, on the other hand, are usually based on their own personal experience.

Legal insiders believe that negative media coverage of their profession is to some extent justified, given the many scandals involving MPs. The Parliament expenses scandal, for instance, has caused considerable damage to their reputation, giving people the impression that politicians "abuse [their] position".[11] But English legal insiders also blame the media for projecting an unnecessarily "negative image" of politicians through "biased reporting":

> N-ER-11: 'my guess is that some [people] hate us. And there are those who have an almost unlimited trust . . . [in] the elected representatives.' N-ER-15: 'contempt for politicians . . . is really linked to central positions, to the Parliament and the government . . . I am [a politician] at the municipal level and here I do not experience that contempt . . . I have . . . almost only good, experiences'. E-ER-10: 'they perceive us generally as a bunch of incompetent oaths . . . but "my own MP is very hard working, you know, he's a good man, he's not like the rest." So, as a breed we are beneath contempt, aided and abetted by the national media'. E-ER-21: '[politicians are viewed] as a lazy bunch of money-grabbing, self-centred, egotistical, idle, useless, worthless, knuckle-dragging, scum-sucking, gutter-crawling, bottom-feelers'.

Elected representatives in *Eastern Europe* predominantly believe the general public is negative towards them. Polish and Ukrainian politicians – just

[11] In 2009 several British MPs were prosecuted and sentenced for having altered their expenses. A few years later, in December 2013, the Labour Party's former Minister for Europe, Denis MacShane, was imprisoned for bogus expenses claims. Ben Quinn, 'Ex-minister Denis MacShane jailed for bogus expenses claims', *The Guardian*, 23 December 2013, www.theguardian.com/politics/2013/dec/23/denis-macshane-jailed-bogus-expenses accessed on 18 January 2014.

like those in Norway and England – claim that public perceptions of MPs are considerably worse than those of members of local councils. The strength of negativity correlates with GDP (PPP) per capita and country score on the 2010 World Bank rule of law index: the lower the GDP (PPP) per capita and the lower score on this index a country has, the more critical the elected representatives believe the public to be of their profession.

Polish politicians believe the public perceive them as "suspicious" "caricatures". To ordinary people, politicians seek "private benefits" rather than occupying themselves with issues of importance to their electorate. The status of elected representatives is generally worse now than it was in the recent past.

The Bulgarian public's critique of their country's politicians is made with more harshness and conviction than in Poland – at least judging by the views of the Bulgarian politicians themselves. They claim that members of their profession are perceived as "arrogant", "nasty", "repulsive" and "thieving" people. Ordinary citizens perceive them as "greedy" people who promote "personal interest", whilst making "huge amounts of money". Yet the public also accuse them of being "fickle" characters who generally "do nothing". Bulgarian elected representatives are therefore "not liked" and do not command "great respect".

The most deep-seated perceived public distrust in politicians is voiced by Ukrainian elected representatives. They note that the word for elected representative – *deputat* – has very negative connotations in Ukraine. Somewhat unexpectedly, they willingly admit that citizens perceive them as "corrupt" "bribe-takers" who "bribe voters" – even as "criminals" or "thieves". Further, their profession is allegedly driven by "self-interest": many elected representatives have become "millionaires". In fact, Ukrainian politicians are so badly discredited that Ukrainian citizens do "not consider deputies to be people". Consequently, the elected representatives believe that people have "very low trust" or "no trust" at all in members of their profession.

Some of the East European elected representatives try to explain *why* citizens are so distrustful of their elected representatives.

Polish elected representatives to some extent attribute negative public perceptions of their profession to people's lack of knowledge or lack of understanding, of what politicians actually do. As in England, the media are viewed as the main culprit: the tabloids, for instance, do not have proper knowledge about the political profession. Further, the media's "thirst for sensation" and wish to "cause scandal" exceed its ability to convey accurate and correct information. Although English lawmakers express some understanding for the bad press they receive, Polish lawmakers are far less happy about it.

Bulgarian elected representatives believe that negative perceptions of their profession are predominantly the result of the "blame culture", which is so widespread in their country: when something goes wrong somebody else is always to blame. Transition has produced a large number of such wrongs – all thoroughly discussed in the Bulgarian media. Still, Bulgarian elected representatives are less concerned than Polish elected representatives with the manner in which their profession is referred to in the national press and on (national) television.

By contrast, Ukrainian elected representatives are fairly accepting of negative public perceptions of their profession. They acknowledge the public's unhappiness and unease – but without attributing it to the media. To some extent they even share the public's concerns about politicians. Local elected representatives, in particular, are critical of Ukrainian MPs. Even the MPs themselves say they are disillusioned with their fellow MPs.

To some extent negative public perceptions of Ukrainian MPs are attributed to the stalemate between the "orange" and "blue" forces that followed the 2004 Orange Revolution. Ukrainian citizens are generally unhappy with the "permanent political crisis" and national politicians have "not met [their] expectations". This, in turn, has facilitated "complete apathy and distrust" in them.

But negative perceptions of elected representatives are to an even greater extent attributed to the quality of the members of their profession. Respondents readily admit that Ukrainian MPs are "discrediting" themselves, that there are "few high-principled MPs" in their country and that most of them act in self-interest. The work of the deputies is generally "poor" and "unprofessional". Brawls in Parliament have regularly been broadcast on Ukrainian national television. Worse, elected representatives allegedly "treat criminals well". Added to this, "the executive has done much to discredit the Ukrainian Parliament":

> P-ER-13: 'the higher the level of these [politicians], the worse the perception by the people . . . I'm fortunately at the bottom, not at the top'. P-ER-16: 'ordinary people perceive councillors as idlers, as incompetent people, who take high remuneration . . . [and] require some privileges'. B-ER-18: '[politicians are perceived] as greedy, nasty, repulsive and essentially bad. No one likes the politicians [in general] and the Members of Parliament, in particular.' U-ER-19: 'this word, "deputy" has almost become a word of

abuse'. U-ER-21: 'they perceive [politicians] as thieves, bribe-takers and millionaires.' U-ER-20: 'one [politician] is a killer, the other is a paedophile – how can people behave well towards this category? . . . there were great expectations . . . in 2004 . . . [yet] we can change nothing because [now] there is complete apathy and distrust.'

The government officials

The Weberian ideal of a government official is a person who is skilled, objective and who treats all citizens equally and in accordance with the law. In a real functioning democracy government officials are responsible for the "output" side: they provide citizens with services and goods to which they are legally entitled. Reality, however, is often different. In post-communist states funds are short. Not all citizens are therefore provided with their legal rights and they are not treated equally: some are more equal than others (Miller et al. 2001). The image that government officials across Europe believe the public has of them is rather far away from Weber's ideal of the government official.

Norway and the UK have a much longer democratic tradition than Poland, Bulgaria and Ukraine. As noted in Chapter 1 they score higher on the 2010 World Bank's rule of law index and their GDPs per capita are higher. Consequently, they are in a better position to honour their obligations towards their citizens. Both countries have the funds necessary to provide citizens with benefits and services to which they are legally entitled.

Norway is a welfare state: the public sector is fairly large – in 2013 it accounted for 52 per cent of GDP.[12] High and stable oil revenues[13] have allowed the country to retain a wide range of benefits, such as free hospital treatment, extensive maternity and paternity leave, generous unemployment benefits, state pensions and a wide range of other welfare payments. Even though Norwegian political parties disagree about how extensive the welfare state should be, there is political consensus about its value as such. In recent years public services have come under

[12] 'Norway. The rich cousin', *The Economist*, 2 February 2013, www.economist.com/news/special-report/21570842-oil-makes-norway-different-rest-region-only-up-point-rich accessed on 23 August 2014.

[13] State revenues from the oil industry are transferred directly to *Statens pensjonsfond utland* (the State Pension Fund Abroad [SPU], previously referred to as the Oil Fund). No more than the annual growth of the State Pension Fund – fixed at 4 per cent by the 2001 'action rule' (*handlingsregelen*) – may be channelled into the annual state budget, and most political parties agree that this percentage should not be exceeded.

increasing pressure: extensive immigration from other European countries, increased numbers of unskilled refugees from war-torn countries in the South, an aging native population and reduced birth rates all negatively affect Norway's ability to maintain the welfare state in its current form in the future.[14]

A report on the public sector in Norway published in 2013 states that 'most citizens trust both central political and administrative institutions, and individual political and administrative actors' (Lægreid, Nordø and Rykkja 2013, p. 9). Norwegian government officials, on the other hand, claim that ordinary citizens view them as "bureaucratic", "rigid", "remote" – that is, as people very much focused on "formal rules" – thus "making issues more complex" than need be and causing "too much paperwork". Government officials are, in their own view, typically perceived as "lazy", "slow" and "servile" people who have "little work to do" and who lead "easy lives". Their jobs are considered to be "boring" and of "low status", yet secure. The common idea amongst Norwegians seems to be that government officials are "too safe in their jobs". One government official notes that the media mostly address errors made by the government administration, notably in the area of social protection. If correct, this might, in turn, 'inform' negative public perceptions of the profession as such.

As for the UK, the public sector was downsized and several state entities privatised in the 1980s. Cuts were also made in public services and social benefits. Documents recently released from Downing Street show that former Prime Minister Margaret Thatcher (1979–90) even considered introducing compulsory charges for schooling and abolishing the National Health Service (NHS).[15] In 2011–12 public spending accounted for 43.1 per cent of GNP.[16]

English government officials believe that the general public are mostly *negative* towards them. Members of their profession are, as a rule, viewed

[14] The estimated annual population growth rate for 2013 was 0.33 per cent and the estimated net migration rate was 1.68 migrants/1,000 population. See IndexMundi, 'Norway demographics profile 2013', www.indexmundi.com/norway/demographics_profile.html accessed on 23 August 2014.

[15] Alan Travis, 'Margaret Thatcher's role in plan to dismantle welfare state revealed', *The Guardian*, 28 December 2012, www.theguardian.com/politics/2012/dec/28/margaret-thatcher-role-plan-to-dismantle-welfare-state-revealed accessed on 18 January 2014.

[16] Source: HM Treasury, cited in 'UK public spending since 1963', *The Guardian*, www.theguardian.com/news/datablog/2010/apr/25/uk-public-spending-1963 accessed on 8 September 2014.

with "huge scepticism", limited or "no trust" and "no respect". Government officials in England, just as government officials in Norway, are perceived as "not sufficiently hard working", "not up to scratch", "inefficient" – and consequently of "little help". Yet, government officials claim that the public believe they receive huge salaries, thus wasting public funds. Although Norwegian government officials mostly refer to public perceptions of the *manner* in which members of their profession conduct their official duties, English government officials also talk about the perceptions they believe ordinary citizens have of them as individuals: to the average Englishman government officials are not only considered to be "dull" and "boring". They are also "vagabonds", "rogues", even "parasites" – and some of them are "corrupt".

One English government official blames the media for the poor public image of his profession. Others believe that the negative perceptions the public have of their profession are correct. However, most of them stress that citizens who have personally had dealings with members of the profession usually have a good impression of them:

> N-GO-7: '[government officials are perceived as] somewhat remote ... from ordinary people ... they give out far too many forms with a far too high level of detail'. N-GO-8: '[probably they are] a bit too inflexible'. E-GO-6: 'we're all rogues, vagabonds, parasites ... generally people say that, "except, of course, the one or two I know". Then they say "well, that's different, because I know Sue and I know David and they're not like that". But generally speaking, they are really corrupt and not to be trusted.'

In a historical perspective attitudes towards the state and state institutions have been rather negative in Eastern Europe – largely because rulers have been imposed upon people from the outside and thus been perceived as illegitimate (Grødeland and Aasland 2007). Even at present, people do not feel real ownership to the state and its institutions. The authorities are commonly referred to as "them" – whereas citizens are referred to as "us" (Aasland, Grødeland and Pleines 2012).

Our data show that East European government officials think ordinary citizens view them as the embodiment of the state: not of a state that treats its citizens equally, but rather of a state that promotes its own vested interests at the expense of the common good. This perception is particularly widespread in the successor states to the former Soviet Union (Ukraine) but also to some extent in South East Europe (Bulgaria) and the West Balkans.

Perceived public cynicism towards government officials correlates with GDP (PPP) per capita and rule of law: the lower the country's score on both indicators, the more negative the attitudes of the general public towards government officials – at least if we are to judge by the impressions of the government officials themselves.

Negative perceptions of government officials were widespread during Communism and such perceptions appear to have been "carried over" to post-communism as 'it "proved impossible to sustain" institutional discontinuity with the past, for example, most civil servants from the former regime were kept on' (Czarnota, 2009, referred to in Polak and Nelken 2010, p. 225). Even though the profession of the government official is highly discredited, it is seen as lucrative in that it provides people with a good income. The public apparently believe that government officials work for their own benefit and make life generally very difficult for ordinary citizens. They are mostly perceived as slow-working and corrupt. The government officials themselves claim that such "pre-1989 attitudes" are stereotypical rather than real:

> P-GO-23: 'I think [this negative attitude towards government officials] might be a remnant of the times before 1989, when a public official was the Master and you couldn't go to a department or [to] a specific official [just like that]. You had to knock [on doors] and ask . . . we . . . local government officials are also treated badly by people.'

Polish government officials believe that members of their profession are perceived as "silent", "malicious" and "incompetent" people who "sit behind desks" and engage in "paper-" and "pen-pushing". Further, they "hide behind rules" and "hinder people's lives". Not surprisingly, therefore, theirs is "one of the most hated professions" in Poland – some citizens even view it as "an unnecessary profession". As a general rule, Polish citizens try to avoid government officials like "the plague".

Bulgarian government officials claim that the general public are sceptical both of the title "government official" [just as the Ukrainian public is highly sceptical of the term "deputy"] and to the individuals representing the profession. Both they themselves and their colleagues are allegedly perceived as "indifferent" and "lazy" "desk-sitters" who "drink coffee" all day and fail to make "much effort". Actually some of them "do nothing" at all.

Government officials in Ukraine, for their part, note that the term "government official" –*chynovnyk* – just like the word "deputy" [*deputat*] – has negative connotations to ordinary citizens. In their view, government officials are perceived as people who do "nothing at all": they are simply "paper lifters" who do "not defend the public" and do "not want to help". Citizens are therefore generally "unsatisfied" with, or distrustful of, members of their profession, whom they perceive to be generally "unfair":

> P-GO-1: 'the general image [of government officials] is ... classical: a paper pusher sitting in an office, doing nothing for eight hours ... [just] drinking coffee and gossiping ... I often come across such opinions ... some time is still needed for this to change.' B-GO-10: 'they believe that these [officials] are people who sit all day and do nothing and then get a certain salary and want even more'. U-GO-19: 'the profession of the government official is perceived ... negatively ... it has been formed historically, when the word "official" had a more negative than positive connotation ... lately, there have been a lot of scandals connected to state officials of high rank ... [their] reputation is transferred to the government officials in general, even [to those] of middle and low ranks.'

Government officials in Poland believe that they are perceived as people "living off [people's] taxes". Most citizens view government officials as "parasites",[17] as "corrupt" people, geared towards self-interest.

Such negative views are even more pronounced in Bulgaria: Bulgarian government officials claim that ordinary citizens think their profession consists of "wealthy" people. Even though the work they do is perceived as "not prestigious", citizens believe that government officials are "privileged" people who promote their "personal interest" while "spending" "public money". They receive a good salary – which they do "not deserve" – yet want even better pay.

Ukrainian government officials believe that ordinary citizens mostly associate their profession with "corruption", "graft" and "bribes". To them, being a government official effectively means being a "dishonourable" "thief" who is "embroiled in many scandals". Government officials in Ukraine are perceived as privileged people: they have a "good salary", are "very rich", and enjoy "the good life".

[17] In the Soviet Union able-bodied citizens who refused to engage in socially useful labour or evaded work were referred to as parasites. In May 1961, the Supreme Soviet of the Russian Soviet Federative Socialist Republic (RSFSR) passed a decree entitled *On Strengthening the Struggle with Persons Avoiding Socially Useful Work and Leading an Anti-Social, Parasitic Way of Life*, which opened the way for such people to be banished 'to specially designated places for a term of from two to five years'. This decree was popularly referred to as the "Anti-Parasite Law". It is likely that legal insiders used this term as a result of the term used in the Soviet law. See Lewis Siegelbaum, '1961: Anti-parasite law', *Seventeen Moments in Soviet History*, www.soviethistory.org/index.php?page=subject&SubjectID=1961parasite&Year=1961 accessed on 18 January 2014.

Polish government officials claim that the contradicting legislation they are set to administer must take some blame for their profession's bad public image. Yet they acknowledge that the profession itself is also to blame. Very few of them claim that the manner in which they are perceived by the general public is "untrue", and some even express a dislike for other-type government officials. Our previous study of the interaction between citizens and government officials in four post-communist states show that low-level government officials receive better treatment than ordinary citizens from same-type officials, but that they are treated as any other citizen by other-type officials (Miller et al. 2001, pp. 208–9).

Bulgarian government officials attribute negative perceptions of their profession to the fact that citizens are "just ordinary people" who lack the proper knowledge of what they are (not) entitled to and who therefore have "bad experiences" with government officials.

Ukrainian government officials primarily feel that they are "not correctly perceived" by the public. In their view citizens tend not to differentiate between different *levels of officials*. Besides, they usually expect their problems to be resolved on the spot even though this is often not possible. What is more, negative perceptions of government officials mostly stem from "ignorance" or "insufficient information". It is difficult for government officials to "communicate with the public" as the latter tend to "behave in an offensive manner". Despite the public image of the wealthy government official the average official is "very poor". Ukrainian government officials do not blame the negative public image of their profession on the media:

> P-GO-16: 'generally, the profession is viewed negatively ... often public officials must be blamed for this, especially ... the "first contact-clerks" ... sometimes they're incompetent or simply unkind, which immediately discourages people'. B-GO-6: 'when I have to go to another administration, even [with]in our administration, as a citizen, I personally feel horror and fear ... the attitude [towards government officials] is very bad and it is to a large extent founded'. U-GO-17: 'there is nothing much more difficult than communicating with people every day. It can be compared to working in the coal mine ... not every citizen can understand this, because he comes with his own problem and thinks that his problem can be solved on the spot'.

The legal professionals

Legal institutions perform different functions in democratic and authoritarian societies. In the former the judiciary is independent of the legislative and executive powers. In the latter prosecutors, courts and sometimes even lawyers, function as the extended arm of the executive. In the last 20 years or so judicial reform in Eastern Europe has changed the role of such institutions in society and introduced new legislation and efforts to enhance the efficiency of legal bodies.

As noted in Chapter 1, countries in Eastern Europe receive poorer scores in the 2010 World Bank's rule of law index – and they are considerably worse off in terms of socioeconomic development than countries in Western Europe. Besides, the international donor community seems to believe that introducing new legislation will sooner or later (usually sooner) change people's behaviour. However, evidence suggests that behaviour that is "informed" by social norms is fairly resistant to change.[18] Public perceptions of lawyers, judges and public prosecutors – as perceived by these professions themselves – should therefore differ more across Europe than perceptions of elected representatives, government officials and possibly also the police.

The lawyers

From a rule of law perspective lawyers perform an important role in democratic societies: they interpret the law on behalf of private individuals, and private and public entities; they sometimes negotiate out-of-court settlements, and they assist and defend citizens in court. Lawyers thus assist citizens dealing with the state or other citizens. In order for lawyers to perform such functions it is vital that they know the law well. Yet, such knowledge does not necessarily translate into ethical and/or legally sound judgement.

Kühn (2010, p. 178) notes that 'while especially in the early communist system lawyers were pariahs, in post-communism their role was enhanced. Building a rule-of-law state to a certain extent also entails building a lawyer's state'. In the Czech Republic many former communist judges left their posts 'for much more lucrative work as private attorneys' (ibid., p. 181). It is not unlikely that many former communist judges in other post-communist states did the same. Vasylyev (2010, p. 15) claims that the 'professional standards and ethos [of the lawyers are] in reality . . . pretty vague and . . . success in litigation

[18] *Stanford Encyclopedia of Philosophy*, 'Social norms', http://plato.stanford.edu/entries/social-norms/ accessed 1 September 2014.

to a great extent depends on maintaining unlawful connections with court administration and judges'.

In Western Europe 'being a lawyer is, bluntly, not the coolest of jobs, and perhaps not as prestigious as it once was. There may even be a stigma of sorts attached to being a lawyer [hence the wealth of lawyer jokes]' (Susskind 2010, p. 5). Sunde (2005, p. 212) notes that 'just as old as the practice of using lawyers is the distrust to these judicial actors'. Former Chairman of the Norwegian Supreme Court, Carsten Smith (2012, p. 51) stresses that it is important for the lawyer's profession to change its negative public image.

The main reason for this negative image seems to be that lawyers run their own businesses and their services are fairly expensive. Susskind (2010, p. 229) claims that 'lay people have no legal resources whatsoever and, unless they are uncommonly wealthy or sufficiently impecunious to qualify for state funding, they seldom have the wherewithal to engage lawyers'. Norway and the United Kingdom both have various legal aid schemes (*fri rettshjelp* – Norway; *Legal Aid* – the UK) to ensure that citizens who cannot afford to hire their own lawyer can still access legal services.[19] Still, in Norway some legal experts claim that the middle class does not have proper access to legal services, given high lawyer fees.

Lawyers in both Norway and England acknowledge that hiring a lawyer is expensive. Presumably for this reason citizens perceive them as wealthy people, who seek to enrich themselves at their expense. Lawyers believe that the general public, therefore, have a rather negative impression of their profession.

Norwegian lawyers are of the opinion that citizens perceive members of their profession as "greedy" people who are "focused on money". To ordinary citizens lawyers apparently come across as "arrogant", "status oriented" and "cynical" people, who are "quarrel-prone" and think they "know better" than others. Such people are "rule riders" who are "not down to earth". People therefore "dislike" them, definitely do not "trust" them, and sometimes even "fear" them.

[19] Law students at Oslo University run *Jussbuss* – a service offering free legal advice to people in need of legal assistance. The Lawyer's Association (*Advokatforeningen*), for its part, offers people across the country up to half an hour of free legal advice. Advokatenhjelperdeg.no, 'Advokatvakten' [Lawyer on Duty], www.advokatenhjelperdeg.no/artikler/advokatvakten/ accessed on 1 September 2014. More importantly, however, people's home insurances provide them with sponsored legal representation should disputes arise regarding their properties.

One lawyer is sympathetic to the public perception of his profession. In his view Norwegian lawyers have moved away from serving justice and instead transformed into a profession of high earners. Corporate lawyers set the standard for other lawyers, and as a result all members of the profession have "too high incomes". This, in turn, affects the development of the profession as such. In the view of one legal insider, the Norwegian Lawyers' Association *(Advokatforeningen)* has unfortunately failed to adequately address this issue. Some of our respondents therefore voice their support for "low threshold" services such as legal aid, as they provide low-income citizens with access to justice.

English lawyers believe that citizens have negative opinions of their profession primarily as their services are rather expensive. As in Norway, lawyers in England seem to be perceived as "well-paid" people who "make lots of money" and are "very rich". Even so, they are constantly looking "for profit" and therefore come across as "greedy": they allegedly drive around in "posh cars", but "do nothing". Lawyers believe that citizens think members of their profession "overcharge" their clients. To some people, lawyers come across as "intimidating", "pompous" and generally "not trustworthy" people. Citizens therefore "lose respect for them" and view them with "suspicion".

Negative public perceptions of lawyers are, in the view of the English lawyers themselves, partly caused by a "misunderstanding", partly by "bad press". One lawyer calls for the profession to "dispel" such images. Others note that despite their general negative opinion of the lawyer's profession citizens are generally positive to lawyers when in need of their help:

> N-LA-16: '[we are perceived as being] busy catering to our own needs, concerned with income, status'. N-LA-21: 'we are perceived as a little greedy ... maybe'. E-LA-3: 'there isn't ... much respect for lawyers ... I think lawyers get a bad press because ... the headlines are all about, the big city lawyers ... and all the big legal aid barristers who make millions. So everyone thinks that we are earning lots and lots of money and that is not actually true'. E-LA-14: '(lawyers are perceived as) male, greedy, driving Porsches, getting huge amounts of money for doing absolutely nothing'.

Many of the negative images of lawyers referred to in Norway and England are echoed by Polish lawyers. In their view, Poles perceive members of their profession as "wealthy" people who have accumulated "a sack of money" [their services are therefore perceived as "expensive"]. Ordinary citizens apparently have a "general dislike" for lawyers and approach them “only when [they] have to”, and often “when it is too late”. Public perceptions of the profession are “deteriorating”. At best Polish lawyers are perceived as “unhelpful”, at worst they are branded as “criminals”. The negative image of lawyers in Poland is – in the view of the lawyers themselves – to some extent caused by negative media coverage, to some extent by Ministry of Justice criticism of their profession. They therefore believe that the image of Polish lawyers is “[very] distorted” and undeserved.

Bulgarian lawyers – just like lawyers in Norway, England and Poland – believe that they are perceived as both “wealthy” and “greedy”. Unlike the Polish lawyers, however, the Bulgarian lawyers believe that the public see them as “fixers”, capable of facilitating specific outcomes in court by bribing judges. Further, they claim that the public see them as “crooks”, who “lie and cheat”. They largely object to such an image, claiming that the public is either “badly informed” or “uninformed” about their profession as they rarely consult lawyers. Bulgarian lawyers claim that the lawyer’s profession includes many great professionals who help people and do their best to defend their clients in court. However, they acknowledge that there are some bad lawyers but that these are few in number.

By contrast, Ukrainian lawyers make more positive than negative statements about how the public perceive their profession. They claim that Ukrainian citizens have a favourable attitude towards lawyers and that they treat them with understanding and respect. As a group lawyers are generally trusted – possibly as they are non-state actors (state institutions are generally not trusted). Those who believe that lawyers are perceived negatively, on the other hand, note that members of their profession are viewed as “profit-oriented” “pettifoggers”, who “hamper cases” or are “unable to help”. Some lawyers strongly disagree with such views of their profession:

> P-LA-9: ‘the lawyer is [equalled to] a criminal . . . one could hardly find a more distorted picture.’ P-LA-10: ‘there were no such attacks on the autonomy of lawyers . . . during the times of Communism. Even Communists would not dare to carry out the attacks that today are planned by politicians, the Minister of Justice and people who work in the Ministry of Justice’. B-LA-7: ‘the lawyer lies, cons [people] or . . . is someone who carries a briefcase with a bribe for the judge . . . this is . . . an extremely uninformed opinion [but] it is widely spread.’ B-LA-8: ‘“lawyer” is a dirty word in Bulgaria . . . the Bulgarian is not accustomed to look for a lawyer, he looks for one when the things are bad, post-factum. Worldwide, [people] are looking for a lawyer before the problem occurs.’ U-LA-17: ‘they perceive the profession of the lawyer in the following way: [a lawyer]

> is a pettifogger who has learnt a number of laws, which the ordinary person could learn [himself] if he had enough time, and [who] makes a profit from it . . . a lawyer . . . hamper[s] the case and do . . . unpleasant things.'

The judges

One of the professions that has experienced the greatest changes in Eastern Europe since the collapse of Communism is that of the judge. In the past judges in post-communist states 'regarded themselves as public officials serving the respective government or ruling party – and [they] frequently still do' (Bodnar and Schmidt 2012, p. 291). The courts were politically subordinate to the Communist Party. They were managed by the executive (Ministry of Justice) and their day-to-day conduct was overseen by the Procuracy (Anderson, Bernstein and Gray 2005, p. 9): the prosecutors represented 'the main guardian of socialist legality' (Kühn 2011, cited in Komárek 2014, p. 4). In this capacity they often instructed judges on what kind of rulings to make.

In the former Soviet Union the main task of the courts was 'to aid the Communist Party and its subordinate state institutions in the implementation of policies and the creation of the "Soviet man"' (Solomon, 1996, referred to in Popova 2012, p. 139). Judges were 'trained in a tradition which made them open to extra-legal considerations' (Sajo 1990, p. 340). Compared to other professions they were poorly paid (Anderson, Bernstein and Gray 2005, p. 9) and most of them were women. In Central Europe 'the judiciary remains a predominantly female profession. In 1990, when the Polish communist regime fell, 61.6 per cent of Polish judges were women and by 2000 this percentage had increased to 63.6 per cent (66.2 per cent at first-instance courts)' (Kühn 2010, p. 191).

While under Communism East European judges were able to act fairly autonomously in smaller civil cases – their hand was forced in cases of political significance. So-called telephone justice, by which the Communist Party tried to influence outcomes of trials (Markovits, 1995, referred to in Polak and Nelken, 2010, p. 219) was common. As noted in Chapter 3, it still occurs in post-Soviet states. What is more, judiciaries in some such states 'still remain subject to political influence in the selection and disciplining of judges. Courts have little influence over the allocation of budget (funds) to the judiciary and little control over how these funds are spent' (Anderson, Bernstein and Gray, 2005, p. 28). Businesspeople rated the ability of Bulgarian and Polish courts to enforce their decisions as higher in 1999 than in 2002. The judiciary in Bulgaria was viewed as more problematic than the judiciary in Poland (ibid., p. 46). By contrast, the ability of Ukrainian courts to enforce their decisions was rated as higher in 2002 (ibid., p. 43).

West European judges, for their part, have traditionally been very independent and enjoyed high levels of public trust. Media reports suggest that Norwegian judges represent one of the most trusted professions in the country. The judges themselves, frequently referring to survey data, claim that their profession is held in high regard, possibly higher than deserved.[20] Even though citizens may disagree with specific court rulings, they still have high trust in the judges' profession (Kinander 2012). Judges note that legal professionals – notably university professors of law – are far more sceptical of judges and the decisions they make, than ordinary citizens.

Those Norwegian judges who believe that public perceptions of their profession are *mixed* claim that judges are perceived as "conscientious" "objective" people who are "doing their best". As professionals they are considered to be "fairly good": they have "much knowledge", possess "natural authority", have "no personal interest", are not "corrupt" – but rather are "very reliable", and "trusted by most people". Public regard for judges increases the higher up in the court hierarchy they are placed.

Yet, Norwegian judges are also perceived as "unapproachable", "somewhat distant", "old-fashioned" and "slow". The judges themselves claim that ordinary citizens are sometimes "scared" or "frightened" of them and their colleagues. Those who lose civil cases or who receive a sentence in criminal cases are understandably "dissatisfied with" or "negative towards" the judges' profession. Occasionally the media report miscarriages of justice *(justismord)* that have been quashed by *Kommisjonen for gjenopptakelse av straffesaker* (the Norwegian Criminal Cases Review Commission).[21] Although the total number of quashed sentences is low, several of them have occurred fairly recently and they

[20] Former chairman of the Norwegian Supreme Court, Carsten Smith (2012, p. 73), on the other hand, claims that due to misunderstandings the Supreme Court judges sometimes appear as 'distanced fools'. He would like judges to be more active in the public debate to dispel this image, but states that judges should be cautious about taking part in debates about their own decisions.

[21] During the period 2004–13, 15 per cent of the cases were reopened (197 of a total of 1,675 cases) (*Kommisjonen for gjenopptakelse av straffesaker* [*The Commission for the Review of Criminal Cases*], 2013, pp. 3, 8).

have received much publicity. Norwegian judges believe that such incidents have somewhat weakened public regard for their profession:

> N-JU-20: 'I recently saw in the newspaper . . . that judges [represent] one of the professions that enjoy the highest trust amongst the population.' N-JU-5: 'most people have relatively high regard for judges . . . the respect increases the higher up in the system one gets . . . when one gets to the court of appeal . . . there is even a little higher regard than in the first instance court and when one gets to the Supreme Court one has, in a way, reached the top of the pyramid. This is how we perceive it and I imagine that most people do so as well.'

The distance between citizens and judges is emphasised even stronger by the English judges – possibly as they are viewed as representing the upper class (Norway has no gentry and no private elite schools along the lines of Eton, Harrow and others – which may explain why the perceived distance to judges is less pronounced there).

In 1999 Professor Hazel Glenn published a report entitled *Paths to Justice* which showed a lack of general confidence in the English judiciary. Two out of three respondents claimed that judges are out of touch with ordinary people's lives and only 53 per cent thought they would get a fair hearing if they ever went to court. Glenn also found that judges could improve their image by getting rid of their wigs and gowns. In March 2006 a proposal was put forward to don the wigs. Since October 2008 they are no longer worn by judges hearing civil and family law cases. Justices of the Supreme Court also do not wear wigs when hearing cases (Slapper and Kelly 2011, pp. 479–80).

English judges acknowledge that citizens have a negative image of their profession much as a result of formal distance. In their view, the public see judges as "distanced" and "out of touch". They believe that this distance is further enhanced by the fact that judges traditionally come from privileged backgrounds (citizens perceive English judges as "well-educated" and "well off"). Judges are recruited from "a narrow stratum" and in the eyes of the public English judges are "conservative", "posh", "pompous" or even "standoffish". The typical judge is a "white", "middle aged" or "old" "male" who has received "private education" – first in "public schools", later at "Oxbridge".[22] He belongs to the "middle class", "upper middle class" or the "upper class"

[22] Slapper and Kelly (2011, pp. 478–9) cite figures issued by the Lord Chancellor's Office in May 1995 showing that 80 per cent of Lords of Appeal, Heads of Division, Lord Justices of Appeal and High Court Justices were educated at Oxford or Cambridge.

and represents "high culture". In addition he enjoys a "good standard of living" and earns "lots of money":

> E-JU-15: 'I imagine that they consider them out of touch . . . somewhat remote, toffs to some extent and well-to-do. Posh background and public schools and that sort of thing.' E-JU-20: they probably perceive them as elderly, white, middle-class, male, which most of them are . . . you're not going to become a judge until you're in your forties at the earliest'.

English judges generally *disagree* with such stereotypical images of their profession, claiming that the "public is not informed". Rather, their views of judges are based on an "unfair" "misconception" of what the judges actually do. Judges believe that the, in their view, outdated – and negative – public image of their profession is primarily caused by "bad press" – that is, incorrect or imbalanced media coverage of court cases.[23] Only one judge believes that people's perceived negative image of judges is correct. Another stresses that he himself is the antidote to the stereotypical judge as he is not rich, did not go to public school and did not study at Oxbridge:

> E-JU-12: 'if you've sat in court and listened to what I've listened to over nearly 15 years . . . you see the whole of society coming across in front of you. You're very much in touch with what's going on'. E-JU-10: 'the press are very keen to portray judges as being out of touch with ordinary society.' E-JU-16: '*The Times* said the other day, "they're the sort of people who go to the opera."' E-JU-22: 'I don't live in a giant house, and I don't drive a Rolls-Royce. I didn't go to public school and I did not to go Oxford or Cambridge, I went as a mature student to a provincial university in my 20s. [When I tell that to people] they don't believe it.'

Judges represent one of the least trusted professions in post-communist Europe. Kühn (2011, p. 31) notes that 'in Central-Eastern Europe the judiciary is one of the least popular professions among the general public; judges are distrusted, often seen as corrupt[24] (which is usually a false image) and inefficient (which is quite often a correct perception)'. Throughout the 1990s 'less than half of the respondents in any given transition country said they trusted the courts. By the end of the decade, no more than 40 per cent of respondents in any transition country said they trusted the courts. Levels of trust tended to be higher in CEE than in CIS countries' (Anderson, Bernstein and Gray 2005, pp. 19–20).

Polish judges talk at length about the factors causing *negative* opinions about their profession – but they make fewer references to what

[23] This view is held also by the House of Lords (House of Lords 2007).
[24] This view is endorsed by the findings of Anderson, Bernstein and Gray (2005, p. xiv).

this negative image actually entails. Though fairly well paid, judges in Poland do not refer to public perceptions of their salary level. [25] Instead they note that their profession is "not much trusted" by ordinary people.[26] Rather, they are perceived as "heartless", "stupid" people who engage in "politics" and "bribery". Just like the English judges, the Polish ones believe that negative perceptions of their profession are first and foremost media-driven. In their view, critical remarks about judges voiced by politicians and lack of good spokespersons in courts further compound the problem. Opinion polls largely confirm this negative public image of judges in Poland.

Bulgarian judges, just like the English ones, claim that members of their profession are considered to be wealthy, but not as a result of their privileged socioeconomic and educational background. Rather, Bulgarian judges receive good salaries that they top up with bribes! They are therefore perceived as both "privileged" and "corrupt" people and the public's perceptions of them are understandably "not favourable".[27]

Sajó (1990, p. 332) notes that during the socialist period 'judges and courts [in Eastern Europe] acted as bureaucrats and they were expected to promote the centrally determined public interest'. Further, 'the general public was sceptical of the legal system as it was unclear, offered no protection, and was considered an irrelevance or obstacle to be outmanoeuvred in order to survive' (ibid., p. 333). These factors help explain why some Bulgarian judges claim that citizens mistake them for government officials – that is, "clerks" or "bureaucrats", who happen to represent "the most despised" profession in Bulgaria. Following from this, Bulgarian citizens believe that judges must be "incompetent", "lazy", "slow" or "inaccessible" – features that they attribute to government officials.

A fairly large share of the Bulgarian judges interviewed by us – just like those in England – hold the view that negative images of judges

[25] Kühn (2010, p. 182) notes that 'the judicial salaries in Poland in the late 1990s were lower than elsewhere in Central Europe. However, there were significant improvements between 2000 and 2002, and the average salary of a district court judge reached the level of about 2.5 times the national average by 2002. Regional court judges earned 3.2 times the national average in 2002'.

[26] Poland was amongst those countries in CEE that had relatively high levels of trust in the early 1990s, but experienced declines by 1998 (Anderson, Bernstein and Gray 2005, p. 20).

[27] Anderson, Bernstein and Gray (2005, p. 20) note that 'in Bulgaria, trust in the courts was low in absolute terms throughout the period (i.e. the 1990s) and fell drastically relative to other institutions. Citizens in . . . Bulgaria . . . clearly ranked courts very poorly by the end of the decade'.

are largely *media-driven*, but that they also to some extent reflect public ignorance. Then the reality of being a judge in Bulgaria is rather different from the one attributed to them by the public: judges are often "workaholics" trying to deal with "a heavy workload". Despite their "expectations" of the judges the public have "no idea of the work of the judge". Bulgarians are generally "negative to all institutions", courts and judges included. Added to this, there will always be one losing party in every court case who will leave the courtroom with a negative perception of the judge. Some respondents believe that opening the courts to the public and providing them with information about the work that the judges do might help improve their tarnished image.

Opinion polls show that judges are the most despised and least trusted profession in Ukraine (KIIS 2006). Recent research shows that political influence on judges is exerted at all stages: from their recruitment to the decisions they make. Popova (2012, p. 134) notes that 'communication between politicians and judges about specific cases can be an efficient vehicle for influence or indirect pressure. The practice of providing judges with housing, vacations, and other perks for the duration of their tenure is an even more powerful tool for influencing judicial output. Judges who deliver rulings that anger incumbent politicians can suddenly face evictions or a transfer to another apartment'.

Power over judges is also exercised by the court chairmen: 'they control the assignment of cases and distribution of bonuses to individual judges and panels of judges. If they want to harass a judge who does not take orders well they have a variety of options at their disposal' (ibid., p. 135). Further, in 'politically sensitive cases, (Ukrainian judges) usually "receive advice" from their court chair or from procurators or lawyers they know, about how to rule' (ibid., p. 137).[28] During Kuchma's presidency there were 'strong informal links between the higher echelons of the judiciary and the Presidential Administration' (ibid., p. 140).

Vasylyev (2010, p. 11) claims that the Ukrainian judiciary 'for the whole period of the country's independence has been and still to a large extent remains a product of the Soviet bureaucratic and legal traditions'. Most of the judges 'sitting on the bench . . . in Ukraine during the 1990s and 2000s were educated and socialised within the ranks of the Soviet judiciary' (Popova 2012, p. 147). Not surprisingly, therefore, Ukrainian judges perceive the State Court Administration as more of a supervisory

[28] This was also the case in East Central Europe, including in Hungary (Sajo 1990, p. 340).

than a supporting institution, which could help or hurt judges if they wanted to (ibid., p. 144).

Ukrainian judges report very negative public perceptions of their profession. They claim that ordinary citizens view them as corrupted people who take bribes.[29] Subsequently, trust in judges is either limited or non-existent.[30] Negative public perceptions of judges are, in the view of the judges themselves, mostly "media-driven". But they are also a result of negative comments about courts made by Ukrainian politicians. The judges themselves believe that the real culprits are current "appointment procedures", "sly lawyers" engaging in "corruption schemes", "the general state of society", and "imperfect laws". One judge notes that he and his colleagues were held in higher esteem by the public in the past, while another states that he is no longer proud to be a judge:

> P-JU-14: 'the profession of the judge in Poland isn't much trusted'. P-JU-22: 'judges are perceived as bribers, as people involved in politics, not always on the right side, judges serving the [former] Communist State; these images still linger in our consciousness'. B-JU-1: 'people do not see the judge as the embodiment of law . . . but as a clerk. In their view the clerk is . . . corrupted so people perceive the judges very badly.' B-JU-5: '[we are perceived] with distrust . . . ordinary people do not differentiate between the professions of the judge, the prosecutor and the lawyer.' B-JU-24: 'we are practically workaholics, working 10–15 hours a day . . . our workload is tremendous.' U-JU-19: 'many of them think that judges . . . [are] like the official who sits all day long doing nothing'. U-JU-1: 'I am not going to say that everything is good in the courts . . . our society is ill – including the judicial system'.

The prosecutors

Prosecution is organised rather differently in the countries covered in this book, but formally it is politically independent in all of them. In Norway the National Prosecutor heads the prosecution service. He or

[29] In recent years the Ukrainian media have reported several corruption scandals involving judges; for instance, scandals involving the Lviv Appeals Court Judge Ihor Zvarych – accused of accepting a $100,000 bribe, Mykola Tyshchuk of Kyiv's Obolon District Court – accused of accepting a $3,000 bribe, and Vyacheslav Lyubashevskiy of Lviv Appeals Court – accused of accepting a $20,000 bribe. *Kiev Ukraine's News Blog*, 'Despite high-profile arrests, corruption still dogs courts', 17 May 2009, http://news.kievukraine.info/2009/05/despite-high-profile-arrests-corruption.html accessed on 18 January 2014.

[30] Polls show that only 10 per cent of the Ukrainian population trust the court system (Neutze and Karatnycky, 2007, cited in Vasylyev, 2010, p. 13).

she is not subordinated to any state ministry and is politically independent.[31] Bigger and more serious cases are prosecuted by the state prosecutors, whereas the police prosecutors handle less serious cases.[32] In England the most serious crimes are prosecuted by the Crown Prosecution Service (CPS). The CPS is accountable to Parliament[33] and the Chief Crown Prosecutors carry out prosecution according to CPS policy.[34] The Polish prosecution service used to be subordinated to the Ministry of Justice but since 2009 has operated as a formally independent unit.[35] The situation with the prosecution service in Bulgaria is similar to that in Poland.[36] Finally, in Ukraine the State Prosecutor is appointed by the president of Ukraine with the consent of Parliament.[37] In theory (but until recently not in practice), prosecution in Ukraine functions as an independent structure.

East European prosecutors have traditionally operated as the extended arm of the state. The state has lacked popular legitimacy. During Communism they had more responsibilities and more power than they have at present: not only did they investigate cases and prosecute these in court. They also supervised the performance of the judges and often instructed them on what rulings to pass in specific court cases. Whilst prosecutors previously received instructions from the Communist Party, they are now formally independent. However, in many post-communist states there are signs to the effect that the formal independence of the prosecution is greater on paper than in actual reality: in Poland, for instance, prosecutors have hinted that they are under considerable political pressure (Polak and Nelken 2010).

Given the above, citizens in Eastern Europe may be more sceptical of prosecutors than citizens in Western Europe. In Norway several high-profile miscarriages of justice have somewhat tainted the image of the prosecutors. However, the manner in which the prosecution handled the court case against the Norwegian terrorist Anders Behring Breivik

[31] www.riksadvokaten.no/no/english/ accessed on 15 September 2013.

[32] 'Welcome to the higher prosecution authorities – the director of public prosecutions and the regional public prosecution offices', www.riksadvokaten.no/no/english/ accessed on 25 January 2014.

[33] http://cps.gov.uk/about/facts.html accessed on 10 August 2014.

[34] 'Chief crown prosecutors', www.cps.gov.uk/about/ccp.html accessed on 25 January 2014.

[35] www.pg.gov.pl/en/ accessed on 25 January 2014.

[36] www.prb.bg/main/en/pages/Structure_and_Organization/ accessed on 25 January 2014. www.prb.bg/main/en/pages/History/ accessed on 25 January 2014.

[37] http://intermedia.gp.gov.ua/home accessed on 25 January 2014.

did much to restore the image of the Norwegian prosecution service. Miscarriages of justice have also occurred in the UK.[38]

Talking about public perceptions of their profession Norwegian prosecutors refer to opinion polls in which the police receive high scores for trust. The police lawyers included in our sample equal their profession's public standing with that of the police – and by referring to opinion polls on public trust in the police. Prosecutors believe that members of their profession are perceived "quite well" and that people "mostly have a positive impression" of them. In their view Norwegian prosecutors are perceived as "correct", "strict" and "just". They promote "good values" and are therefore held in "high regard".

Those prosecutors, who think public perceptions of their profession are *mixed*, believe that prosecutors generally enjoy high levels of trust amongst ordinary citizens. But there is some ignorance amongst the public as to what exactly prosecutors do. Norwegian citizens sometimes confuse the public prosecutor's profession with the lawyer's profession: there are people who believe that members of this profession are actually lawyers to whom they can turn to for help. The prosecutors themselves claim that people who have negative experiences from the court are certainly negative towards prosecutors. The public are not happy when cases are not prosecuted – and they dislike the handing out of "lenient" sentences.

English public prosecutors believe that some of the negative features attributed to lawyers are also applied to their profession, probably as prosecutors are barristers by education. The public perceive members of the prosecutor's profession as mostly "overpaid", "rich" people. Just like lawyers, prosecutors are perceived as "greedy", "arrogant", "pompous", "garrulous" and "cynical" people who are either "too clever for their own good" or simply "out of touch". Prosecutors are, in their view, perceived as "unpopular" and "unfair" people, who, if necessary, even "lie". Members of the public therefore perceive them as "parasitic", "dreadful" "bastards":

> N-PR-3: 'according to the opinion polls ... a very large share of the population have trust in us.' N-PR-16: 'many people do not know what the prosecution is, but when you ... explain ... people become very positively minded'. N-PR-2: 'we are perceived as strict, fair and that we

[38] Gwyn Topham, 'Man wrongly convicted of sexual assault is freed after 17 years in jail', *The Guardian*, 13 December 2013, www.theguardian.com/uk-news/2013/dec/13/man-wrongly-convicted-sexual-assault-freed-17-years accessed on 18 January 2014.

> work [to promote] good values . . . we stand on the barricade for the law-abiding [society] and for the interests of society.' E-PR-16: '[we are perceived as] overpaid, pompous, garrulous, cynical.' E-PR-24: 'they all think we're millionaires and greedy, grasping jurists, really. They do change their attitude when they're in trouble, but that's life, isn't it? I think we're fairly low down on the perception of being necessary to life'.

Polish public prosecutors refer to their profession as a profession that has "never been liked" by the country's public and which has traditionally been associated with "fear". The image of the prosecutor is that of an "elderly and stern man" who may be "under-educated" and who "takes bribes". His or her primary goal is "to get somebody sentenced". Citizens do not always believe that sentencing is achieved in an objective manner. In their view, prosecutors are "under political pressure", follow "bad instructions" and occasionally even "bend the law" to "suit criminals". As in England, prosecutors in Poland "earn a lot of money". Polish prosecutors object to this image, which they find "unfair", "wrong" and "hurtful". Polish citizens "do not fully understand the[ir] profession": even though prosecutors occasionally "fail", they are not as bad as the public seem to believe.

Bulgarian prosecutors believe that ordinary citizens mostly have *negative* attitudes towards them. The public prosecutor is mostly perceived as a "necessary evil" that people have "lots of reservations" against. More specifically, they are seen as "incompetent", "unscrupulous", "corrupt" and "very rich" people. The Bar Council is blamed for this negative image as it is "hopeless at PR". In the view of the prosecutors themselves negative perceptions of their profession are based on ignorance more than anything else.

Just like the Bulgarian judges, Bulgarian prosecutors also to some extent attribute the negative public image of their profession to "bad press".[39] They claim that the media is conducting an "unjustified campaign" against them. Ordinary citizens therefore have no proper understanding of the difficulties the profession is faced with and they are mostly unaware of its good qualities. Prosecutors acknowledge that the judiciary is itself partly to blame for this. Public prosecution in Bulgaria is trying to improve its image, but it "lacks PR".

Prosecutors in Ukraine note that they are mostly *negatively* perceived by the general public. Some of them simply state that people are negative

[39] 'Of politics, prosecutions, pressure, lies and umbrellas', *The Sofia Globe*, 11 February 2014, http://sofia.globe.com/2014/02/11/of-politics-prosecutions-pressure-lies-and-umbrellas/ accessed on 16 August 2014.

to prosecutors, while others claim that prosecutors – just like judges – are accused of being corrupt. Consequently, citizens do not have much trust in them:

> P-PR-1: 'public prosecutors were never liked'. 'P-PR-15: 'people don't seem to fully understand what this entire profession is about . . . we seem to close ourselves in this hermetic legal jargon, which to an ordinary man is nothing but gobbledegook . . . it is a common belief . . . that Public Prosecutors take bribes or are undereducated'. B-PR-22: 'they usually think [prosecutors] are very rich and very unscrupulous'. B-PR-23: 'most of my conversations with ordinary people disclose that they do not make much difference between the prosecutor, the judge and the investigator . . . in their minds the prosecutor and the judge somehow merge and they cannot tell exactly who decides on the sentence'. U-PR-7: '[they perceive prosecution as something] not quite positive: public scandals in the press, in the mass media [facilitate such perceptions]'. U-PR-28: 'ordinary people perceive the prosecutor's profession as if it were a punitive body [even though] it is a supervising body; [they also consider it to be] . . . the most bribeable department.'

The police

Public attitudes towards the police says something about the quality of democracy and the level of the rule of law in a society: the police maintain law and order and ensure that laws are respected by all – regardless of social status and official position. In totalitarian societies the police are used for political purposes, to identify and punish those who oppose the ruling regime. During Communism the police safeguarded the interests of the ruling party while maintaining law and order. The police were therefore referred to with some scorn, and lots of jokes about the police circulated in Eastern Europe. In the late 1980s a standard joke in Moscow was that the police would always walk around in groups of three as one of them would do the looking, one would do the listening and the third would do the talking.

Several of the Norwegian police officials we interviewed refer to opinion polls in which the police receive a very high score on trust. Some of them mention their own positive experiences with the general public. However, most of them admit that the 2009 police actions in support of higher salaries and better working conditions have eroded public trust in them. Limited police resources have also negatively affected public trust. Public satisfaction with the police appears to be generally lower than their trust in them.

Only three English police officers believe that their profession is negatively perceived in British society – and for reasons of inefficiency caused by a lack of resources rather than due to poor-quality staff. Seven police representatives believe that people view the police officer as having an "honourable profession" which has a "good reputation", and which is needed in society. The police therefore enjoy considerable public trust, which is reflected in public opinion polls. The majority believe that some people are positive whereas others are negative to them:

> N-PO-11: 'the police is one of the most trusted professions [in Norway]'. N-PO-25: 'the police have traditionally received a high score on these barometers that measure trust. The Norwegian people still trust [the police] now after a fairly hectic period of so-called police conflict ... I think the degree of satisfaction is considerably lower ... our police are good at communicating that we are short of resources and the fact that we are short of resources [may result in] a drop in the population's expectations to what we are capable of achieving ... they forgive us, are understanding and have trust'. E-PO-10: 'generally, [the attitude] is quite positive. That's from personal experience. I work in Bath, which is quite a nice, affluent area ... in general, I think [the view is] positive and I think people know that the police are there to help them.' E-PO-18: 'this country is afflicted by two things. Firstly, mass media giving a perception of what the public's opinion is and speaking on its behalf ... secondly, I believe the UK has always had, and continues to have, a massive silent majority that generally support law enforcement, that generally want to go around their day-to-day business, that are generally very good people who do know right from wrong, who want to do the right thing and want to see bad people put in prison and punished'.

Those Polish police representatives who feel that their profession is *negatively* perceived by the public claim that the latter believe the police "give tickets and fines" and "beat people with sticks". To them, the police are generally perceived as a "necessary evil" or "the enemy". Police staff "do nothing", are "incompetent" and "corrupt". People therefore have a "lack of respect" for them. This being said, quite a few police officials think the image of the Polish police is improving, or that it is even favourable.

Bulgarian police representatives hold the view that their profession is still perceived with distrust and negativity. Their fellow citizens are generally disappointed with the police: to them the police represent "dark shades" – that is, "lazy guys pretending to be important" but who are "not particularly noble". The police cite public opinion polls in support of this view. They believe that the negative public image of the police to some extent reflects its lack of resources, to some extent public ignorance. Then in their view there are good and hard-working professionals in the national police force. The police acknowledge that the profession is to some extent itself to blame for the negative public image. But they believe that it is only a matter of time before the situation will change for the better.

Ukrainian police officials mostly state that citizens are negative towards them. Their references to police corruption and the general public's lack of trust in the police force are limited. In their view, citizens try to avoid contact with the police. One police officer blames negative media coverage for this state of affairs. Another thinks the poor-quality Ukrainian legislation is at fault, while a third one blames the police itself:

> P-PO-6: 'a policeman will always be an enemy.' P-PO-7: '[the police] are [perceived as] incompetent, corrupt and generally they do not do anything.' P-PO-14: 'there is too little information concerning our profession'. B-PO-7: 'the latest polls published by the Focus Agency showed that nearly 20 per cent of the Bulgarian citizens trust the police'. B-PO-9: 'people don't trust us, they are not familiar with our work and to them we look like a bunch of lazy people who pretend to be important but are not.' U-PO-26: 'there is disregard [towards] our police force . . . because of the existing legislation, the police cannot defend [the] citizens. We cannot solve the majority of the questions that are urgent for the citizens.' U-PO-27: 'watching television you see that they show [how] the police accepts bribes . . . people don't trust the police.'

Legal insiders' perspectives on legal insiders (like themselves)

Not only the manner in which legal outsiders perceive legal insiders, but also the views legal insiders have of each other, are important from a legal culture point of view.

If, for instance, politicians or government officials were to interfere in the activities of judges this would make courts less independent. Ditto if public prosecutors were to try to "force the hand" of judges – as was the case in many East European countries during Communism. Obviously, if the police exceed their duties this undermines the rule of law. Further, if judges and courts were to interfere politically by setting aside legislation and political decisions that do not conflict with the Constitution, this would undermine the independence of the legislative.

This being said, politicians worldwide have to some extent reduced their own powers by legislating for more and more areas of society and thus transferring power to the courts. Hirschl (2006, p. 721) notes that 'over the last few decades the world has witnessed a profound transfer of power from representative institutions to judiciaries, whether domestic or supranational'. In some instances, judges – who have not been popularly elected – end up exceeding their competences and become involved in power politics. This has been the case in the German Constitutional Court (Landfried 1994, p. 113). Not all judges are happy with this development: many judges are apprehensive about the *judicialisation* of society.

Finally, if relations between public prosecution and the police are poor this might reduce the possibility for public prosecutors bringing criminal cases before the court. What is more, if police officers are not sufficiently knowledgeable of the law, they may inadvertently (or intentionally) violate people's human rights. Or cause unequal treatment of people before the law.

THE LEGAL PROFESSIONALS

The lawyers

The majority of the statements made by legal insiders in all five countries suggest that lawyers are generally well informed but that trust in them is fairly low. Even though legal insiders in all countries express greater trust than distrust in lawyers, fewer than 50 per cent of the statements made by legal insiders in Norway, Bulgaria and Ukraine suggest that members of this profession can be trusted (Table 6.21). The reasons why lawyers are viewed with some scepticism differ considerably by country.

Informedness Legal insiders in Norway believe that lawyers are fairly well informed about the law and that it is fairly easy for them to update themselves, even though frequent changes in the law make it challenging for them to stay on top of things. For lawyers being updated is "part of the job" and thus a "duty". They would provide clients with a bad deal if they did not know the law. Besides, they would encounter problems in court were they to appear unprepared before the judge. Norwegian lawyers have access to various databases and all laws are available at *Lovdata* – a database available also to the general public.

English legal insiders hold views very similar to those of legal insiders in Norway. They note that lawyers have a professional duty to keep abreast with changes in their area of specialisation. Specialised lawyers are extremely well informed: through their chambers they have access to the internet and to other sources of information. English lawyers

Table 6.21 *Perceptions of lawyers: the legal insiders' perspective*

	Norway (%)	England (%)	Poland (%)	Bulgaria (%)	Ukraine (%)
Would you expect lawyers in [this country] to be well informed about recent changes to the law? Would you trust them?					
Informedness of lawyers					
Well informed	68	78	63	68	51
Not well informed	3	1	8	17	16
Mix	29	21	29	15	34
Trust in lawyers					
Trust	46	65	50	38	41
No trust	17	12	22	36	25
Mix	38	22	28	26	34

Note: Entries are based on the percentages of relevant 'text units' – the total number of answers to a given question; so entries sum up to approximately 100% (decimals are rounded up or down to the nearest whole number).

regularly attend refreshment courses organised by the Law Society and undergo continuous professional development. Legal insiders view the Judicial Studies' Board as "efficient".[40] However, the sheer amount of law and legal amendments makes it hard for them to keep up with the changes. Lawyers should be as well informed about the laws "as a priest is informed about religion":

> N-PR-13: 'many of them are very skilled and may even discover new laws before for instance a police lawyer does'. N-PO-10: 'they must be updated in order to provide their client with the best possible assistance.' E-GO-19: 'I would expect a lawyer to be as well informed about the law as a vicar is about religion, quote the Bible.' E-JU-14: 'there's no excuse not to know with the level of information and communications technology that is at their hands.' E-PR-5: 'barristers are at the coalface of the law so often, certainly in the area that they work [in], they know more than anybody.'

[40] Since 1 April 2011 the Judicial College is responsible for the training of all judicial officeholders in England and Wales and tribunals in the UK.

In post-communist states the lawyers' profession is fairly new. A study of legal professionals in the West Balkans show that lawyers enjoy greater trust than judges and prosecutors as they do not represent the state (Grødeland 2014b). By contrast, in Norway, where state institutions enjoy fairly high levels of trust, lawyers are the least trusted type of legal professionals – and allegedly because some of them charge a lot of money for their services. Even though all of these countries have undertaken extensive legal reforms in recent years, trust in state institutions is higher in some of them than in others. Lawyers have access to various sources of law, but it might be more difficult for them to keep up-to-date than it is for lawyers in Western Europe to do the same – as the amount of law and the frequency with which it changes is greater in the former than the latter.

Polish legal insiders generally believe that lawyers in their country are "[very] well educated" and have "decent knowledge" of the law. It is in the lawyers' "own interest" to stay abreast: not only do they have "a duty to keep up-to-date" but they also essentially "live off the law". If they are not up-to-date, it will be very difficult for them to do their job properly. Polish lawyers face "no obstacles" in terms of access to current legislation. It is "easy to get information" through the internet, and lawyers also have access to legal acts, court decisions, various information bulletins, commentaries, computer programs (*Lex*), journals and newspapers such as *Gazeta Prawna* (the Legal Newspaper).

Bulgarian legal insiders – just like those in Poland – stress that lawyers have an "obligation" to stay informed. As they work in a "very competitive environment" and "earn a living from the law" they not only have a "duty", but also "self-interest", in "being well informed". Relevant information is obtained from *Darzhaven Vestnik* (the State Gazette), and from electronic databases (*Ciela*, *Apis*), but also to some extent from personal experience. Bulgarian legal insiders believe that lawyers are "generally highly qualified" people. They are "the best prepared legal professionals" – and sometimes they are "even better informed than judges and prosecutors". Lawyers "participate in the legal process" in Bulgaria both as drafters and lobbyists.

Lawyers in Ukraine tend to be "highly qualified" professionals. Even though there are "constant updates" of the law, they have "unlimited access to information": through the internet they can access the websites of the Ukrainian Parliament and the government. The database *Liha* provides them with continuous updates. They may also obtain relevant information from *Holos Ukrainy* (the Voice of Ukraine) and *Uriadovy*

Kur'er (the State Gazette) – the newspapers of the Ukrainian Parliament and government, respectively. Legal insiders note that it is in the lawyers' best interest to keep abreast with the law as they "earn a living from [it]". To "defend their client" they have to be acquainted with the law:

> P-ER-13: 'it's in their own interests to be well informed'. P-JU-19: 'lawyers are very well educated, and of course they have to constantly update their knowledge concerning significant changes in law'. B-ER-4: 'they are even better informed than the judges and prosecutors because they have incentives to be knowledgeable of all the merits, all niches and all the weaknesses of the law [in order] to be able to offer the best possible defence to their clients.' B-ER-15: 'they work in a very competitive environment and for them it is extremely important to maintain a good level.' U-GO-19: 'if, in the Soviet Union, the lawyers used to be just a formality, now they do fulfil the function of defending their clients. And to be able to do that at a proper level [they] have to be well informed.' U-JU-17: 'they work for themselves and to earn much, they must know laws.'

Trust Norwegian legal insiders who trust lawyers perceive them as "serious people" who are doing their best. Despite their slightly tainted reputation they are conscientious, serious and honest people. Norwegian legal insiders claim that the media focus on the exceptions to the rule – that is, the lawyers who engage in misconduct, rather than on those who go about their business in a conscientious and ethical manner. This, in turn, explains why the public is slightly sceptical of them. *Advokatforeningen* (the Lawyers' Association) through its disciplinary committee imposes sanctions on lawyers who fail to abide by its ethics code.

English legal insiders express a higher level of trust in lawyers than legal insiders in Norway. They emphasise the professional qualities of lawyers and claim that such people simply instil trust: English lawyers abide by "a code of conduct" and work to "a strict standard". They are "very committed" and "very professional". Most of them are "in the profession for the right reasons" and they "don't want to let their clients down". Sharp practice amongst lawyers is therefore rare. Some legal insiders base their views on lawyers on their own personal experience:

> N-ER-1: 'my experience [with lawyers suggests] that they are serious people and that the Lawyer's Association . . . is very "hands-on" to ensure that lawyers do a good job . . . [there is] also this committee which can intervene if [someone] has violated good lawyer's practice . . . they have their own . . . possibilities to sanction [such lawyers].' E-JU-23: 'on the whole I do trust lawyers. I've worked with [them] all my life, and I think they are very, very committed [people] . . . [who] do their jobs and . . . strive hard for their clients'.

Half the statements made by the Polish legal insiders indicate that they trust lawyers to quite some extent. Some of them qualify their views by stating that they trust lawyers they know personally or have had dealings with. But most legal insiders simply state that they trust lawyers, without further explanation. Legal professionals trust lawyers because they, like themselves, are jurists, or because their own job as prosecutors, judges or police representatives requires them to do so. In the opinion of one legal insider Polish lawyers are "not worse than [lawyers] in the West".

Bulgarian legal insiders both trust and distrust lawyers to roughly the same extent. They trust lawyers as they are effectively the "people's defenders" and as it is "not possible to exist without lawyers". One therefore simply "has to" trust them. There are quite a few prosecutors and judges amongst those who distrust lawyers. But they distrust lawyers because of their personal interactions with them. Judges find lawyers who appear in court to be generally "poorly prepared" and thus unable to "defend their clients".[41] Prosecutors, for their part, claim that they cannot trust lawyers as they represent the "other side" in court proceedings. For this reason they would "check laws personally" rather than rely on the interpretations and arguments presented by the lawyer.

Ukrainian legal insiders who think that lawyers may be *trusted* in most cases simply state this as a fact. Those who qualify their position emphasise that lawyers are "skilled and experienced" people. As "professionals" they "follow the laws" and should therefore be trusted. Quite a few Ukrainian legal insiders trust lawyers whom they know personally or lawyers who have been recommended to them, but not lawyers more generally.

Ukrainian legal insiders who do *not trust* lawyers claim that their level of professionalism is low and that the lawyer's profession is fairly corrupt. They note that lawyers tend to place "money above professionalism" and that they often have "a low level of education". Lawyers operate within "a dirty system" and some even "give bribes to judges". They often "confuse their clients", "spoil [their] case" and then charge "money for [their own] poor performance". Legal insiders find such behaviour "unethical":

> P-ER-14: 'many of my friends are lawyers so I trust them'. P-PR-22: 'I myself am a jurist by profession [and] because of this fact, but not only,

[41] These views contrast sharply with those of the former chairman of the Norwegian Supreme Court, Carsten Smith (2012, p. 51), who states that 'skilled lawyers are a precondition for the Supreme Court (in Norway) to do its job satisfactorily.' This is presumably also the case in Bulgaria – and not only for the higher instance courts.

I think that lawyers deserve trust.' B-ER-15: '[I trust them] because they work in a very competitive environment and for them it is extremely important to maintain a good level.' B-JU-24: 'there is no age limit for lawyers and as a result sometimes they use laws from 50 years ago in court'. U-GO-2: 'if someone had recommended the lawyer to me, then yes [I would trust him]'.

The judges

Courts in post-communist states are suffering from a number of structural and other deficiencies. For example, they often lack adequate working conditions and do not receive sufficient funds from the executive. In some countries judges even 'pay for court expenses out of their own pockets or resort to sponsorship by local authorities of various commercial entities' (Rechberger 2009, pp. 64–5). Further, they are often viewed as corrupt and unfair, and informal practice is widespread amongst them (Grødeland 2014b). Still, in all countries except Ukraine legal insiders – just like legal outsiders – have high regard for judges (Table 6.22).

Our data suggest that legal insiders in both Western and Eastern Europe believe that judges in their countries are generally well informed – though more so in Norway (91 per cent) and less so in Ukraine (72 per cent). Further, the majority of their statements (all countries except Ukraine) suggest that judges are fair and that they can be trusted. English legal insiders have more trust in, and are more confident about, the fairness of judges than legal insiders elsewhere. In sharp contrast Ukrainian legal insiders neither think that national judges are fair, nor that they can be trusted.

Informedness Norwegian legal insiders claim that judges are "obliged" to be informed and that this is indeed also the case. Judges simply cannot afford not to be well informed as, in this case, they would not be in control of court. They therefore have to be one step ahead so as to be able to assess whether the lawyers' and prosecutors' interpretation of the law is correct. Judges in high instance courts are considered to be generally better informed than judges in low-level courts. Further, legal insiders believe that younger judges, to a greater extent than the older ones, try to apply the ECHR and ECtHR case law in their rulings.

English legal insiders in most cases simply conclude that judges are well informed about law and recent legal changes. Such people are "the ultimate source of law" and they represent "the height of professional expertise". Judges have access to the law, regularly attend training courses

Table 6.22 *Perceptions of judges and juries: the legal insiders' perspective*

	Norway (%)	England (%)	Poland (%)	Bulgaria (%)	Ukraine (%)
DEP 39: What about judges and juries in [this country] – would you expect them to be fair? Would you expect them to be well informed about the law – including recent changes to the law? Would you trust them?					
Fairness of judges					
Fair	66	83	65	58	27
Unfair	0	5	19	9	47
Mix	34	12	16	34	25
Informedness of judges					
Well informed	91	89	87	86	72
Not well informed	0	5	3	4	16
Mix	9	7	10	10	12
Trust in judges					
Trust	85	91	67	68	32
No trust	0	4	20	21	43
Mix	15	6	14	11	25

Note: Entries are based on the percentages of relevant 'text units' – the total number of answers to a given question; so entries sum up to approximately 100% (decimals are rounded up or down to the nearest whole number).

to stay up-to-date, and advise the authorities on questions of law. What is more, they also have a serious job culture and they are on top of the law. English judges receive regular updates on new legislation and legal changes. They attend trainings and have access to "a team of supporters" in court. As they both advise and guide the jury it would be embarrassing for them to make mistakes:

> N-ER-1: 'it is the task of judges to be up-to-date on Norwegian legislation and to judge according to the most recent [laws].' N-PR-21: 'the court simply cannot afford not to be updated'. E-ER-19: 'I would expect judges

> to be the ultimate source of knowledge about the law ... judges should have very few misunderstandings of precedent, statutes of interpretation, and they should know the law inside out.'

Given that GDP (PPP) per capita is lower in Eastern than in Western Europe – and given that access to information is essentially a question about court resources, judges might be less informed in the former than in the latter. However, our data suggest that GPD (PPP) per capita does not seem to have much of an impact on the extent to which judges are informed and up-to-date on legal matters.

Polish legal insiders – just like those in Norway and England – believe that judges are well informed about the law and legal changes. They "know the law" and "track changes" through various "publications", "law journals", "the internet" and electronic databases such as *Lex*. Added to this, they receive "appropriate", "substantial" and "constant" training. Trainings and updates for judges are arranged by the Ministry of Justice. Judges are simply "obliged" to stay up-to-date. Polish prosecutors, in particular, think judges "know laws perfectly". In their view, being a judge is effectively "the crowning achievement in one's legal career".

Bulgarian legal insiders also consider judges to be well informed. Judges are "obliged" to know the law and they "certainly" do. They are "knowledgeable" and "very good specialists" whose competence should not be questioned. In their view no other legal profession is better prepared. Judges would simply be "fired" if they did not know the law. Still, their knowledge of the law might be a problem in that they are aware of its "loopholes" and thus able to use this knowledge for not entirely honourable purposes.

The view that judges are well informed is shared by Ukrainian legal insiders. On the positive side, judges are "obliged" to know the law and they carry a "professional responsibility" for "grounding [their] decisions" in law. Ukrainian judges have "the possibility to be well informed" through their "easy access to all materials" – including on "the internet". On the whole judges are "clever people": they are "competent" and "professional". Judges "monitor changes in the law" and "use the legislative base effectively". On the negative side, their "interpretation of the law is a problem" as "the law allows for considerable manoeuvring", and as judges are often "biased". Ukrainian judges – just like the Bulgarian ones – are therefore able to "use the pitfalls of the law", even "to violate [it]" altogether!:

> P-LA-1: 'the work of the Ministry of Justice in the field of training is visible . . . the . . . Polish National School of the Judiciary and Public Prosecution will positively influence the level of information'. P-PR-4: 'the majority of them are perfect professionals, the ones that I know, the judges of the young generation, are constantly improving their knowledge . . . they are well educated'. B-ER-8: 'the problem with our judges is not a lack of knowledge of law, but [their ability to] find the loopholes [in the law]'. B-ER-16: 'no other professionals in the legal community are better prepared than the judges'. U-LA-20: 'qualified people work in courts . . . they use the latest technologies, the internet, they update the legislative basis.' U-ER-17: 'they very often study laws well in order to interpret them on behalf of the one or the other side that will [pay] them more'.

To conclude, then, in all countries but Ukraine judges are perceived as knowledgeable and as applying the law with good intentions. By contrast, Ukrainian judges are said to know the law well, but to use it to promote vested interest rather than justice.

Fairness Even though differences between Norway, England, Poland and Bulgaria are not that great per cent-wise the reasons why they perceive judges to be fair differ significantly.

None of the Norwegian legal insiders think judges make only fair decisions. Roughly a third of their statements suggest that judges are sometimes fair, sometimes unfair. Those who endorse the former view, describe judges as "conscientious" people, who "wish" and "try to" be fair. Legal professionals – especially lawyers and prosecutors – claim that judges use their personal judgement well and make correct interpretations of the law on the basis of the case information available to them. Generally, Norwegian judges do their best and usually make good decisions. And in the event that they don't, their decisions may be appealed to a higher instance court.

Norwegian legal insiders who have *mixed* views on the fairness of judges (lawyers are overrepresented amongst these) state that there are good and bad judges. Even though judges are "mostly" fair, that the human factor sometimes comes into play: a judge may have a bad day at work. Alternatively, he or she may feel sympathetic towards one of the parties to a case. Some legal insiders believe that judges sometimes aim for the middle ground when they should make a decision clearly in favour of one of the parties to the case. Further, they believe that judges are not always well prepared. Occasionally they do make mistakes. One lawyer who has earned the right to appear before the Supreme Court states that the composition of the Supreme Court judges' panel determines the outcome of the case.

English legal insiders mostly find judges to be *fair*. However, a few (elected representatives and public prosecutors) provide an explanation as to why they think this is the case. Legal insiders who hold the view that judges are generally *unfair*, frequently claim that they are "out of touch" or "far removed from reality". As "older, privileged, white men", judges generally do "not understand ordinary citizens":

> N-ER-11: 'the Norwegian judges are particularly trustworthy.' N-PR-2: 'they have a great degree of conscience ... they try to judge according to what they feel is most correct.' N-LA-4: 'when I entered the Supreme Court the last time and I saw ... the panel of five [judges] that entered the courtroom ... I knew that the case was lost before I said "most honourable court" ... I have examples of Supreme Court judges who have not ruled in favour of the aggrieved party for 20 years'. E-LA-18: 'judges are fair and open-minded on the whole.' E-FO-17: 'most of them are so far removed from real society ... they don't live on the housing estates around here and see what people have to put up with ... they're basing decisions on their pile in Oxfordshire or somewhere, because they're pretty wealthy, judges'.

Legal insiders in Poland describe judges as "professional", "highly qualified specialists", who "do their best", to "apply the appropriate law" and make "independent decisions". But they are "poorly equipped" and there tends to be "too much pressure on the court". Negative media coverage of judges is, in the view of legal insiders, not justified: they frown at tabloid "rumours". Polish legal insiders believe that young judges are better than older ones (though Polish citizens generally place more trust in older judges – see Table 6.4). Police officials note that even though judges do not make any incorrect judgements this does not mean that they always agree with them.

Legal insiders in Bulgaria predominantly hold the view that judges are *fair*. Just like the English legal insiders most of them simply state this as a fact. Some, however, add that judges are "very well prepared", "good and competent" people who are "obliged" to be, and who indeed are, "fair-minded", "despite pressures" from the outside to favour one of the parties to a case. Bulgarian judges generally "listen to the lawyers" appearing in court.

Legal insiders in Ukraine stand out from legal insiders elsewhere. They do *not* think that judges in their country make *fair* decisions: as a matter of fact, judges often engage in corruption. Both judicial appointments and specific rulings are made following informal payments. The going rate for the position of the judge – at the time of interviewing

$100,000 – "is commonly known". In Ukraine judges are initially appointed for a five-year period, and during this period they have to recover this amount whilst accumulating sufficient funds to pay for permanent tenure. One lawyer claims that members of his profession have to pay Supreme Court judges to have their cases addressed by that court! Legal insiders therefore perceive Ukrainian judges as "cynical" people who have "vested interests" and who represent "a negative stratum of society".

The Ukrainian judges' dependence on political structures also allegedly negatively affect their rulings: judges "are dependent on local government" (see also Rechberger 2009, p. 65) and are therefore "politically and economically influenced". Courts are generally under-resourced: some do not even have envelopes. Local government provides courts with premises and equipment and is thus able to exert influence on court staff. If the judges of a court do not make the requested rulings, this affects the amount of funds allocated to that court. "Designer rulings" do occur, and as a result, the profession of the judge has become "discredited". In the view of one legal insider only those judges who practiced law during the Soviet period are "somewhat reliable". Elected representatives are particularly critical of judges:

> P-GO-4: 'judges are just [but] . . . poorly . . . equipped . . . overloaded . . . there is too much pressure . . . not only on common courts but also on the Constitutional Court'. B-PO-10: 'I cannot think of any example of a judge who. . . has done anything outside the law.' U-ER-22: 'I know from my own experience that you can buy . . . any decision in court'. U-PO-1: 'today the judge looks only at one thing: at the purse, not at the Criminal or Procedural Code.' U-LA-2: you have to pay money in the Supreme Court, too. If you don't pay money your appeal is filed as poorly grounded and is not considered . . . the judicial system in Ukraine is 90 per cent corrupt.'

Trust Table 6.22 shows that judges enjoy high levels of trust amongst legal insiders in all countries except Ukraine. The latter comes as no surprise, given that the judiciary in Ukraine is suffering from political dependence and corruption.[42]

Norwegian judges allegedly "do their best" to be "objective". They are "willing to listen" and have sufficient common sense to apply the law

[42] Maria Popova, 'Ukraine's legal problems. Why Kiev's plans to purge the judiciary will backfire', *Foreign Affairs*, 15 April 2014, www.foreignaffairs.com/articles/141187/maria-popova/ukraines-legal-problems accessed on 10 September 2014.

"correctly". Some legal insiders differentiate between judges in higher and lower courts. Their trust in the former is higher than in the latter.

English legal insiders – just like those in Norway – make fairly brief statements about trust in judges. Most of those who trust judges simply state this as a fact. Those who explain their views in greater detail believe that judges "mostly get it right" and that they can therefore "on the whole" be trusted. Overall, British judges "have integrity" and "apply the law well". Even though the prosecutors do not always agree with their decisions they understand that the hands of the judges "are tied by legislation". They therefore simply have to provide certain types of judgements:

> N-LA-11: 'I trust Norwegian judges ... the Court of Appeal or the Supreme Court ... I have much greater trust in them [than in first instance courts]'. N-LA-13: I ... trust judges, but there are some weirdos ... who have a need to get noticed, especially judges of the first instance courts ... [but] the large majority are incredibly good and know what they are doing.' E-GO-23: 'judges have got a huge amount of integrity generally, and they're very careful about what they do, and very thoughtful, I've found, about the importance of maintaining their integrity and their independence.' E-PR-11: 'I trust them.'

Polish legal insiders trust judges because they are "at a proper intellectual level", are "up-to-date" and "well-prepared" experts who "do not make mistakes because they are not informed". One prosecutor says that he has never come across judges who make "the wrong rulings". Other legal insiders note that if judges make incorrect decisions it is always possible to appeal them to a higher instance court. One government official reports with some glee that from his office window he regularly observes a female judge of the court next door dispose of her garbage in the municipal container to avoid paying for her personal waste disposal.

Most of the Bulgarian legal insiders simply state that they *trust* judges. Those who do *not* trust them claim that judges are not sufficiently independent. Structural problems within the judiciary are mentioned in this regard. Lack of trust in judges has less to do with the personal qualities of the judges.

By contrast, Ukrainian legal insiders are highly sceptical of judges, whom they refer to as "illiterate", "unprofessional", "interest-driven", "cynical" and "rotten" people. In their view judges are "corrupted" and their rulings are "not properly grounded", "unjust", "contradicting", or "ambiguous". Some of their rulings are even "illegal". Judges are "not controlled" as there are no proper "levers" in place for monitoring their decisions. As their rulings are not fair, it is simply "impossible" to trust them. Legal insiders who *trust* judges, on the other hand, argue that the judiciary should be trusted, as otherwise they themselves would not be able to do their jobs properly:

> P-ER-5: 'as a private person I trust the court. As a Member of Parliament I'd rather not speak [about this], because the Constitution professes the division of power into the legislative, executive and judiciary.' P-PR-25: 'since I started my work as a prosecutor, I haven't come across a situation where a given judge made a wrong judgement or that I regarded a judge to be incompetent or uninformed ... I can absolutely trust them.' B-PR-19: 'I should not work in this system at all if I did not have confidence in the court.' U-GO-17: 'it is a well-known fact that these are the most corrupted people in Ukraine. So I wouldn't trust them.' U-GO-24: 'I trust judges because I am often faced with the judges' decisions, which are well-grounded and fair.'

The police

Table 6.23 shows that in terms of informedness, perceptions of the police are more positive amongst legal insiders in Norway, England and Poland, than in Bulgaria and Ukraine. The level of informedness correlates to each country's GDP (PPP) per capita and their ranking on the 2010 World Bank Rule of Law Index. Our findings may, of course, have something to do with the education of the police: educational standards might be higher in countries, whose GDP (PPP) per capita and score on the 2010 World Bank's Rule of Law Index is high. But they might also reflect the fact that the resources allocated to the police – and thus their ability to update themselves on a continuing basis – are greater in Western than in Eastern Europe.

There is a noticeable difference between legal insiders in Eastern and Western Europe in terms of the perceived capacity and effectiveness of the police. The former mostly find the police incapable and ineffective, given limited resources, poor training facilities, or poorly prepared staff. But it might also indicate that police staff is poorly educated, insufficiently equipped or possibly even corrupt. The latter, on the other hand, might find the police capable but not all that effective, which might explain why a larger share of statements made by legal insiders in Western than in Eastern Europe is mixed (Table 6.23).

The police enjoy greater trust in Norway than in England and Poland, and considerably more trust than the police in Bulgaria and Ukraine (Table 6.23). Since the collapse of Communism Poland has invested considerable efforts into strengthening and modernising the national police

Table 6.23 *Perceptions of the police: the legal insiders' perspective*

	Norway (%)	England (%)	Poland (%)	Bulgaria (%)	Ukraine (%)
DEP 40: Lastly, the police in [this country]: Do you feel the police are well informed about the law? Are they capable and effective? Do you trust them?					
Informedness of the police					
Well informed	67	59	53	33	25
Not well informed	3	18	21	41	37
Mix	30	23	27	27	37
Capability and effectiveness of the police					
Capable and effective	39	48	32	20	18
Not capable and effective	20	13	43	64	49
Mix	41	40	26	16	33
Trust in the police					
Trust	82	64	68	37	25
No trust	6	11	16	49	52
Mix	11	25	15	14	23

Note: Entries are based on the percentages of relevant 'text units' – the total number of answers to a given question; so entries sum up to approximately 100% (decimals are rounded up or down to the nearest whole number).

force. This may explain why trust in the police is higher there than in Bulgaria and Ukraine. The Bulgarian police, for its part, have a poor reputation and have been linked to both corruption and organised crime.[43] The reputation of the Ukrainian police is also poor. It is short of qualified staff, as well as financial and material resources. Worse still, it is corrupt[44]

[43] 'Bulgaria arrests 17 traffic police for corruption, organized crime', *The Sofia Echo*, 27 September 2011, http://sofiaecho.com/2011/09/27/1163786_bulgaria-arrests-17-traffic-police-for-corruption-organised-crime/bulletin?ref=id accessed on 18 January 2014.

[44] The Ukrainian traffic police – *DAI* (in the Ukrainian language) – are notoriously corrupt. In the Russian language *'dai'* – means 'give me!' Russian-speaking people joke that the traffic police are stopping cars, telling the drivers to give them money (bribes).

and politicised. The Ukrainian police are ranked as the second most corrupt institution in the country.[45] What is more, it has on several occasions acted in the interests of the ruling elite. Most recently, in January 2014, Berkut – the special riot police – opened fire against the demonstrators in Kiev.

Informedness To start with Norway, roughly two-thirds of the statements made by the legal insiders there suggest that the police are *well informed*. A few of the legal insiders distinguish between police lawyers (who act as prosecutors in court) and rank-and-file police officers. Although the former are generally very well informed, the latter are well acquainted with the specific legislation they are set to enforce. Such legislation includes the traffic law, the criminal code and legislation on economic crime. The Ministry of Justice and the Police Directorate regularly update police lawyers about legal changes. Rank-and-file police also attend courses and receive information from their superiors.

Legal insiders in England in part focus on the training of the police in the area of law, in part on specific legislation they believe the police know well. In terms of training the police are regularly briefed on legal updates. Police officials are given "quite a bit of" training and they have to pass exams in law. As professional staff they have access to legal databases. They may also consult the CPS for advice. Senior police officers are especially knowledgeable about the law. Regular police officers, for their part, are "familiar with" the law in the areas in which they deal – such as "criminal law" and "anti-terrorist legislation". Legal insiders believe that the police have much better knowledge of the law now than they had in the past: their "knowledge has improved in recent years" and "is as good as can be expected". Still, they sometimes "misinterpret" the law and the "anti-terrorist legislation" is a good example in this regard:

> N-ER-18: 'they should know what to look for. If they are to detect speeding then I expect them to have a good overview ... [those] working at *Økokrim* [a special unit investigating and prosecuting economic crimes] ... must have very good competence on the economic legislation ... if you work in anti-terror you must know the [anti-] terrorist legislation'. N-ER-25: 'my wife is a police lawyer ... they gather [them] quite often ... the Ministry of Justice and ... the Police Directorate ... update them on the laws long before they are [passed].'

[45] Transparency International, 'Global corruption barometer 2013', www.transparency.org/gcb2013 accessed on 4 September 2014.

> E-ER-7: 'yes, they are well informed [about the law], but they occasionally push it a bit ... they are using anti-terrorism legislation when they shouldn't.' E-LA-1: 'they're well trained in terms of the law that they have to apply day to day, quickly and in difficult situations.'

The majority of the statements made by Polish legal insiders suggest that they consider the police to be *well informed*. However, their knowledge of the law is restricted to their "own fields". Relevant "regulations are accessible" to them through "the internet, the *Lex* database and newspapers"; through "[regular] trainings"; and through information "passed down" from their supervisors. Each police station has its own "legal unit" and the police "can also consult the prosecutor" on legal matters. The police force as such is therefore "rather well informed". Police are "better informed now than [they were] in the past" and there are "many vice policemen".

The largest share of the statements made by legal insiders in Bulgaria suggests that they do *not* think the police are adequately *informed*. However, they also make a large number of statements to the opposite effect. Those legal insiders who do not believe that the police are well informed about the law state that "the average policeman" does "not have the required legal knowledge" and is "not familiar with procedures" – partly as a result of "poor training", partly as a result of poor working conditions. In their view, Bulgarian police officials "lack funds", have "a heavy workload", work under "extraordinary conditions" and consequently have "no time for [legal] updates". This, in turn, has negative consequences in that their lack of knowledge results in the production of "poor evidence" for prosecution.

Ukrainian legal insiders feel that the police are either *not informed* about the law or that they both *are and are not informed*, to roughly the same extent. Those who express the former view in part claim that the educational level of the police is inadequate, in part that the police do not have sufficient knowledge of, or information about, the law. Respondents whose views about the police's knowledge of the law are mixed claim that police officers know the laws that they themselves apply, such as the *Law on the Police* and the *Criminal Code*. Their knowledge of other legislation, however, is limited:

> P-JU-10: 'they have training on regulations concerning their area of interest all the time.' 'P-PR-4: 'the police can always consult the prosecutor on legal matters, should any doubt arise'. B-ER-6 'the regular police officer is totally ignorant of the jurisdiction and I doubt if they have ever read the Bulgarian law.' B-JU-4: 'the police are not well informed about

> the law and this is evidenced by the poor actions to recover and preserve evidence'. U-GO-26: '[they] do not know laws well. But they know ... how to go round a law and how to benefit [from it].'

Capability and efficiency Norwegian legal insiders who feel that the police are *capable and effective* in most cases distinguish between capability and efficiency. Police officials are generally "clever" people who have "a very good education", are "competent" and "skilled". More importantly, the police "want to do a good job" and do their best with the (limited) resources that they have at their disposal. Legal insiders whose views are *mixed* on this matter suggest that the police are "professional" and "do their best", yet "could be more efficient". In their view police inefficiency is the result of poor internal organisation and lack of resources. Some legal insiders are critical of the actions that were organised by the police trade union (*Politiets Fellesforbund*) in 2009 against low pay, insufficient economic compensation for overtime, and inadequate working conditions. These included a large demonstration of uniformed police officers in front of the Parliament and massive sick leave.

English legal insiders mostly believe that the police are *capable and effective*, that they do a "decent" job, and that they are "very helpful". There are "some really good people" in the police force. They are of "higher calibre" and who work to an "extremely high standard". Police "training has increased in leaps and bounds" in recent years and the quality of police work has "improved enormously"– despite the fact that the police are "[totally] under-resourced":

> N-JU-9: 'it is difficult to get admitted to *Politihøgskolen* [the Police University College] ... the large majority [of the police] do a very good job.' N-ER-25: 'they could be more effective ... there is a little too much trade union talk within the police'. E-JU-16: 'the calibre of police officers that I see in court is higher ... they're educationally better. They speak better. They give their evidence more confidently. They appear better ... they have improved over the years.' E-PR-23: 'they are often under-resourced and they have a very difficult job. On the whole, I think they do a good job.'

Table 6.23 shows that East European legal insiders, compared to legal insiders in Western Europe, are more negative to the capability and efficiency of the police.

Most of the negative statements made by legal insiders in Poland indicate that the Polish police are "often inefficient" and that "little is done to improve [their] efficiency". The Polish police force is suffering from "bureaucracy" due to its "inefficient internal structure". "Unprofessional management" and high staff turnover are also to blame for this situation. As in Norway and England the police in Poland are under-resourced and work with "fairly poor equipment". Legal insiders criticise police staff for "not wanting to work overtime". The police are "not accessible by telephone", therefore "react too late" and have a "low detection rate for petty crime". However, legal insiders do not explicitly say that the Polish police are incapable.

Bulgarian legal insiders do *not* find the police to be either *capable* or *effective*. In their opinion police officers are "not good professionals": they are "not prepared", and they "do not do a decent job". Sometimes they even "do not do their job" (at all). When they do, they often "do not follow procedures" and "make many mistakes". Investigations are sometimes "poorly prepared" – including the "collection of evidence". This, in turn, results in "arrested people [being] released". The Bulgarian police sometimes exhibit "negativity towards prosecutors". "Much" is therefore "to be desired" in terms of police work.

Legal insiders are somewhat understanding towards the police due to their "lack of resources" and "lack of funds". Their working conditions are seen as "inadequate" and their workload is "excessive". It is therefore "very difficult" to recruit good people to the police force. Bulgarian police officers are generally "not motivated" and they have a "negative attitude towards citizens" from whom they "collect bribes" and whom they sometimes use "violence" against.

Ukrainian legal insiders predominantly believe that the police in their country are *not capable and effective.* They claim that police officers have "no proper training" and are "not sufficiently qualified". Police staff are mostly "young and inexperienced" and thus poorly acquainted with the law. Once employed, they have "no possibility to educate themselves". A "lack of decent people" is therefore typical of the Ukrainian police force: as a general rule, police staff has "poor morals", lack "motivation" and "professionalism", are "corrupted", and "defend the rich".

As in Poland and Bulgaria, a fair share of the Ukrainian legal insiders blame lack of capability and inefficiency on inadequate resources. The Ukrainian police tend to be "underfunded" and "lack a technical basis" for their work. Investigation is conducted according to "old" and "terrible" methods, and is characterised by "many omissions", even "neglect". Police officers work in "inhuman conditions"; "their salaries are low" and their living conditions are "poor". "[Staff] turnover is [therefore] high". The police force is "formal and bureaucratised" and junior staff is "capable only when pressurised from above". The police are "not properly controlled" and therefore "lack restraints". This, in turn, sometimes makes them "exceed [their] powers":

> P-LA-24: they are under-equipped, under-informed and under-financed ... activities that are commissioned by the prosecution drag on for months'. P-LA-16: 'the typewriters they use are 40 years old'. B-GO-9: 'my police [i.e. the Bulgarian police] cannot protect me'. B-PR-20: 'the facilities of the police almost everywhere around the country are in a very bad condition ... regional police stations exist in which there are 5–6 officers in one room with no computer in it, let alone [an] internet [connection]'. U-LA-28: 'they are badly qualified and not effective.' U-ER-17: 'the police are not a structure which guards public law and order ... it is a structure which [endorses] the ruling classes and defends the interests of the rich'. U-LA-2: 'if you pay money they file a criminal lawsuit or close the suit [altogether].'

Trust Despite the many problems referred to in terms of police capability and effectiveness, the police enjoy high trust in Western Europe. Legal insiders in Norway, for instance, "generally", "mostly" or "absolutely" trust them. Some legal insiders refer to the work of the police more generally, whereas others report positive, or no negative, personal experiences. Judges are mostly trusting of police representatives appearing as witnesses in court.

Many of the English legal insiders make it clear that they trust the police. Some of them feel that they simply "have to" trust the police, or that they have "no personal reason not to" do so. In their view, the performance of the police has "improved" in recent years and become "much better on race equality". Consequently, the "vast majority" of the police officers may be trusted "more now than before":

> N-ER-1: 'it would be a declaration of defeat if I ... should say that I do not trust the Norwegian police. The moment Parliament does not trust the Norwegian police ... we have a crisis in [our] law-ruled state.' N-JU-16: 'I trust ... [that the police have] a correct attitude on morals and integrity ... corruption and bribes or whatever ... that is far away'. E-LA-2: 'I find the police very trustworthy, straightforward individuals'. E-PR-10: 'the vast majority of them are hardworking and completely truthful and honest'.

Despite their misgivings about the *effectiveness* of the police, Polish legal insiders do *trust* the country's police force. They think the police – and especially younger members of staff – are "reliable people" who "protect society" and "provide safety". Despite the odd "rotten apple", the police do not engage in "gross misconduct". Even though they "receive bad press" and are short of resources, police "efficiency is increasing". Some legal insiders report that they have "received help" from, and have positive personal experiences with, the police. Thus, "despite some incidents" they therefore trust them – and more now than they did in the past.

Most of the Bulgarian legal insiders who say they do not trust the police simply state this as a fact. Those who do provide explanations suggest that the police are perceived negatively as they "turn a blind eye" to people in need of their help. Added to this, they have "poor manners", "tend to be negative" and make "people feel hopeless". The police "have no clear public priorities"; they "arrest and release people", engage in "abuse" and "violence", "do their job in a rush" and are "inefficient". Consequently, there is "no way" one can trust the police. Five legal insiders report negative personal experiences with police officers.

Ukrainian legal insiders also distrust the police, but for different reasons than the Polish and Bulgarian legal insiders. In their view the police are the "most corrupted state body in Ukraine" and they are very "dependent on politics". Besides, the personal qualities of individual police officers make it hard to trust them. Police officers frequently exhibit a "village mentality". They are "not guardians of the law" and they tend to "mess up" investigations. Even worse, they engage in "outrageous acts of violence". Public trust in the police is therefore "very low" and the profession must "improve a lot to gain public trust":

> P-ER-25: 'I trust the police quite a lot, especially the young generation'. P-LA-7: 'I certainly trust them more [now] than back then when they used to beat people with truncheons'. B-JU-22: 'if [the police] were [trustworthy] there would not be so many cases of police violence of which we learn from the media.' B-JU-9: 'I can hardly say that I trust the police. I have had many interactions with them. Sometimes they simply do their job in a rush'. U-ER-19: 'I wouldn't trust the police. I didn't have much trust in the police during the Soviet times [either], by the way.' U-GO-10: 'our police have been bought by someone'.

The law makers and the executive: government and Parliament

Table 6.24 shows that legal insiders in Norway – and to some extent also in England – have more confidence in the government's and Parliament's capability to draft clear and effective laws than legal insiders in Eastern Europe. Although most statements made by legal insiders in England suggest that the government and Parliament are *capable*

Table 6.24 *Perceptions of government and Parliament: the legal insiders' perspective*

	Norway (%)	England (%)	Poland (%)	Bulgaria (%)	Ukraine (%)
DEP 38: Do you feel the government and Parliament in [this country] are capable of drafting clear and effective laws? Do you trust them to draft good new laws?					
Capability of government					
Capable	75	57	17	45	55
Incapable	5	27	73	47	38
Mix	20	16	10	8	7
Capability of Parliament					
Capable	63	58	13	42	51
Incapable	9	27	77	47	40
Mix	28	15	10	10	8
Trust in government					
Trust	75	41	27	36	30
No trust	6	39	70	53	58
Mix	20	20	3	11	12
Trust in Parliament					
Trust	72	42	22	29	32
No trust	5	44	69	55	53
Mix	22	14	9	17	15

Note: Entries are based on the percentages of relevant 'text units' – the total number of answers to a given question; so entries sum up to approximately 100% (decimals are rounded up or down to the nearest whole number).

of drafting good new laws, their trust in government and Parliament actually doing so is much lower than in Norway for the government and somewhat lower for the Parliament.

Polish legal insiders believe that both government and Parliament are incapable of drafting clear and effective laws – and that for this reason they should not be trusted to do so. Bulgarian legal insiders have mixed views about the capability of government and Parliament to draft clear and effective laws, and a small majority of their statements suggest that they do not trust them to do so. A slight majority of the statements made by Ukrainian legal insiders suggest that government and Parliament are capable of drafting clear and effective laws, but they cannot actually be trusted to actually do so.

Capability The majority of the legal insiders in Norway hold the view that government and Parliament are capable of passing good and effective laws – and government to a slightly greater extent than Parliament.

Our finding can probably be attributed to the fact that the government draws on the capabilities and experiences of the Ministry of Justice's Law Department when preparing draft laws. This department enjoys high prestige amongst Norwegian jurists. The people who work there are considered to be "the most eminent" and "sharp jurists" in the country and job competition is stiff. Departmental staff is "dedicated" to making good laws and they do a very "thorough" job. By contrast, few MPs are legally trained. They therefore depend on the skills of the ministerial staff who prepare the draft laws. The Norwegian Parliament does not have its own drafters.

English legal insiders claim that the British government is capable of drafting good and effective laws by means of "a well-established process". The legal draftsmen are referred to as "highly trained" and "very capable" people.[46] "Some of the finest brains" in the country sit on the Parliamentary Council. They are "as capable as they could be" and they "drafts laws very well". Still, English legal insiders are concerned about political leaders' interference in the drafting process. They believe their input is negative:

> N-PR-25: 'in the law department [of the Ministry of Justice] there are very sharp jurists'. N-JU-5: 'I worked in the law department of the Ministry of Justice for several years and I have been involved in . . . preparing laws . . . I know very much about how incredibly thorough and proper the preparation of laws in Norway is'. 'E-LA-9: 'when I was at Bar School, we actually had one lecture once a week on the drafting of legislation. It was the most boring series of lectures I've ever been to! It was hard to stay awake. Everybody felt the same way, but the draftsmen do seem on the whole to get it right.' E-GO-7: 'I think the role of the House of Lords is generally important. Whatever the rights and wrongs about the way the current House of Lords is constituted and so on, you have got a lot of the right sort of people in there who are actually experts, often legal experts'.

[46] The legal drafting procedure is outlined in Office of the Parliamentary Counsel, Cabinet Office 2013, pp. 4–5.

The post-communist states covered in this book have undergone extensive change in recent years: namely, transition from Communism and preparation for/accession to the EU. Both processes have largely been law-driven and thus very demanding for those responsible for drafting and passing new laws. These factors may explain why Polish legal insiders describe the lawmaking capability of the government and Parliament in fairly negative terms.

Legal insiders in Western Europe generally have very high regard for the people drafting the laws (though not necessarily for the politicians instructing them). By contrast, Polish legal insiders claim that those drafting laws in their country are "poorly qualified", "poorly prepared" and that they "lack experience". Not all legal draftsmen are "[necessarily] aware of what they are doing". "Random" and "stupid" people are sometimes involved in such work – including "students"! Polish legal insiders would therefore like to see "more jurists" involved in legal drafting. There is some concern about drafters being "fixed on copying European law". Insufficient consultation during the drafting process is also viewed as a problem. Polish legal insiders object to draft legislation being used as a "tool for the political fight".

Bulgarian legal insiders have *mixed* feelings about the ability of politicians to make good and effective laws. They make roughly the same number of statements to the effect that they are capable as to the effect that they are not. Those legal insiders who have positive views believe that laws are drafted by "experts" who are "well trained" and who have "[sufficient] professional experience" to do a good job. These people work in the ministries and they have "a clear strategy" for what the law should look like. "Parliament" – as well as "individual MPs" – have the "capacity" to draft good laws, as "there are enough jurists" there.

On the *negative* side, the Bulgarian government is referred to as "a mess", intent on promoting "personal interest" rather than the common good. Those responsible for drafting laws tend to be "poorly educated". They "lack intellectual potential", are "not practical" and do not consider the opinions of the practitioners. Not surprisingly, therefore, they are "not the right people" for the job. For this reason there are "omissions in the law making process".

Critical remarks are also made about the lawmaking abilities of Parliament: the right of MPs to propose laws and amendments is perceived negatively, as is their level of experience. Legal insiders recommend that the personal interests of the MPs be set aside in order to facilitate good quality law. More specifically, the quality of the Legislative Commission is not considered to be good enough as few of its members are "legal professionals". Parliament does not have "enough specialists" to produce high-quality law. One judge is therefore critical of the right of individual MPs to propose new laws or amendments to existing laws – given their lack of legal qualifications.

Finally, Ukrainian legal insiders make a larger number of statements to the effect that government and Parliament *are capable* of making good and effective law, than to the effect that they are not. The difference between positive and negative statements – in per cent – is somewhat higher for the government than for the Parliament.

To start with the government: those who believe that those involved in the drafting of laws make a good job describe them as "highly qualified specialists" who are "clever and talented".

Those whose views are negative, on the other hand, refer to them as "very temporary people" who are "not specialists" and who are sometimes "incompetent". Some political leaders have even purchased "false [university] diplomas"! In the view of Ukrainian legal insiders, politics interfere too much in the drafting of laws. MPs tend to "lobby" laws for "profit" and "personal interest". In Ukraine "election campaigns" also negatively affect the drafting of good laws.

As for the Parliament, those whose views are *positive* refer to those engaged in law-drafting in Parliament as "high-class jurists". They believe that "MPs are not fools": there are "many clever people" ("good professionals") amongst them who are perfectly capable of "creating understandable law", provided that "they want to".

Ukrainian legal insiders whose views are *negative* note that those responsible for lawmaking in Parliament are neither "professionals", nor "specialists". Even worse, the "majority [of them] are not jurists". The Parliament is referred to as "a closed joint-stock company", unable "to pass high-quality laws". MPs are mostly "corrupt", "unscrupulous" and "privileged" people. Some of them are "businessmen". They do "not care about people" and excel in making "empty election promises". Laws tend to be "lobbied" and much of the lawmaking is ad hoc, rather than properly planned. The "difficult situation in Parliament" and the "political fights" that have characterised Ukrainian politics in recent years have further complicated matters: politicians simply fail to reach agreement, including on draft laws:

> P-JU-11: 'the quality of making laws is very low, it's tragic.' P-JU-6: 'Polish politicians and MPs seem to have their eyes fixed on this European law to such an extent that they mindlessly copy these patterns.' B-GO-11:

'laws are made by the experts in the ministries'. B-GO-18: 'we need to sideline political interest of a personal character . . . all [that] . . . needs to be observed is the normal functioning of state and national interests.' U-JU-5: 'in the ministries there are . . . specialist[s] who are capable of drafting laws at a high level.' U-JU-25: 'laws are drafted superficially. The deputies are not aware of what they are adopting . . . they just defend their own interests.' U-PO-29: 'the *Verkhovna Rada* [the Ukrainian Parliament] . . . is a closed joint-stock company'.

Trust Norwegian legal insiders express satisfaction with – and trust in – lawmaking procedures. These procedures are "healthy", "'long", "[very] thorough" and "democratic", and more importantly, they facilitate "good-quality [law]". Three months of hearings ensure that all relevant views are properly heard and considered before draft laws are passed onto Parliament for further consideration. Legal insiders therefore "trust the process", though they are concerned that draft laws are sometimes rushed and that they are poorly written. Some legal insiders feel awkward about the desire on the part of politicians to regulate more and more areas of society. Although good laws are prepared at the ministerial level, legal insiders indicate that there is still much to be desired in regard to detailed regulations prepared at a directorate level – that is, "delegated legislation". Norwegian MPs are generally held in high regard as they are "very clever", "competent" and "dedicated" people who do "honest work" and generally also do "a good job".

English legal insiders mostly trust the government's and Parliament's ability to pass good laws – though without shedding much light on the reasons why some note that lawmakers "come up with" "a good result". Those legal insiders who do not trust government and Parliament to draft good and effective laws are unhappy with what they perceive as politicians' "knee-jerk reaction" to developments in society. In their view the political response to public opinion is to pass an increasing number of new laws. Such laws are largely "media-driven" and intended to "appease groups". Legal insiders refer to them as "rhubarb" or "hodgepodge" laws. Typical for all of them is that they are rushed, are usually "very political", "London-centric", "vague", "full of errors" and "hideously complex". As a result, they are "unenforceable" and therefore frequently amended. The ensuing result is "over-legislation". "Rhubarb" laws are blamed on the Labour governments (1997–2010), which, given their majority in Parliament, were able to rush laws through Parliament at great speed:

N-PR-25: 'draft laws are sent out for a hearing . . . if there are things that have been forgotten, if there are contradictions in the law text, if there are

> things that have been regulated in an undesirable way, it will appear during the hearings.' N-JU-16: 'there are good people in *Stortinget* [the national Parliament]'. E-JU-22: 'although most people don't trust politicians, I think ... the majority of politicians are good men and women who are trying to do good.' E-LA-1: 'Acts of Parliament ... are poorly worded or vague and then have to be interpreted by the courts and cause problems ... the 1925 legislation is very good but the more recent legislation tends to be vague and tends to leave too much unsaid.' E-JU-16: 'they've tried to do too much too quickly ... it's been done too quickly in response to public opinion.'

Polish legal insiders are less trusting of politicians' ability to draft good laws than English legal insiders. In their view Polish laws tend to be "vague". Further, they are "of poor quality", "complicated" and sometimes even "unrealistic". They are written in a "difficult language", are "difficult to interpret" and contain several "loopholes". For this reason they are often "not enforceable" and have to be amended. Legal insiders also talk at length about the general lack of respect for politicians, which is widespread in Poland and which causes distrust.

The majority of the statements made by Bulgarian legal insiders suggest that they trust neither the government nor the Parliament to prepare and pass *quality law*. Two main criticisms are raised in this regard: on the one hand, the sheer *quantity* of law is viewed as a problem, as are the frequent amendments of existing legislation. On the other hand, *poor-quality* legislation gives reason for concern. Bulgarian laws are generally "unclear", "difficult to interpret" and therefore "confuse" people. New laws are often "poorly linked" to already existing laws. Examples of such poor-quality laws include the *Civil Procedure Code* (described as "very poor") and the recently changed *Penal Code* and *Criminal Procedure Code*. Legal insiders note that Bulgarian citizens generally do not "respect laws" given their poor quality. Therefore, the "old laws are better". Bulgarian judges are most critical of the quality of laws recently introduced in Bulgaria.

A majority of the statements made by the Ukrainian legal insiders indicate that they trust neither the government nor the Parliament. Negative comments are made with regard to the *quality of law*, on the one hand, and the *personal qualities of politicians*, on the other. Ukrainian laws are referred to as "designer laws" – that is, "lobbied" laws that "lack an economic basis" and that are "not good".

More specifically, the government's performance in lawmaking is deemed "unsatisfactory", and 'informed' by "private interest". The government is not composed of "professionals" and has "no expertise" whatsoever in lawmaking. Parliament is said to "prevent the country's progress". As per today, Ukrainian laws primarily represent "private interest" and come about as a result of "lobbying". Some laws are prepared "for elections", others "for [somebody's] profit". Yet none of them are properly planned. MPs are generally "unfamiliar with law". For these reasons neither the government nor the Parliament can be trusted to make good-quality law:

> P-LA-12: 'the law isn't clear. It's very complicated. Sometimes 3–4 persons are needed to read one article or one chapter ... no one can understand the sense of this regulation'. P-LA-16: 'haste, haste, haste – this is the greatest enemy of effective law.' B-JU-14: 'very often the laws do not introduce clarity, but just the opposite – they confuse the citizens and they confuse us ... the laws which were created in the period 1950–80 were of much better quality than the laws created during the last ten years.' B-JU-20: 'new laws are absolutely unclear to me and they absolutely make possible multiple interpretations, which I think is not right'. B-JU-18: 'I do not respect our laws'. U-GO-23: 'we can't trust our laws as they are created to the benefit of their creators.' U-PR-17: 'we have plenty of laws that have actually been passed without an economic basis and [thus do not work]. Therefore ... I do not trust our system [of lawmaking]'.

Conclusions

In previous chapters we have shown that legal outsiders across Europe have fairly similar ideas about what law is and what its role in society should be. They share the same ideals. Their perceptions of the institutions and the people who make, implement and enforce the law, however, differ considerably. Overall, the public are positive to legal insiders. By contrast, the legal insiders (Norway being the exception) believe the public are negative to members of their profession. The views of legal insiders towards other types of legal insiders vary.

Of the five countries included in our study Norway has the highest GDP (PPP) per capita, followed – in descending order – by the UK, Poland, Bulgaria and Ukraine. The same country ranking is observed in the World Bank's 2010 rule of law index. Data presented in this chapter show that the legal outsiders' perceptions of the legal insiders to quite some extent correlates with GDP (PPP) per capita and rule of law.

The poorer the country and the less rule of law there is, the

- *less likely* the public is to believe that it will receive fair treatment by government officials.

- *less likely* they are to trust the government and Parliament to draft clear and effective laws.
- *more likely* they are to think that government and Parliament draft laws for personal gain and specific business interests.
- *more likely* they are to believe that judges are unfair, willing to take bribes, subservient to government, and that they are less law-abiding than ordinary citizens.
- *more likely* they are to perceive the police as serving the government rather than the public, as willing bribe-takers, and as less law-abiding than ordinary people.
- *more likely* they are to think that government and Parliament are too favourable towards the rich and powerful, are willing to take bribes and are less law-abiding than ordinary people.

This, in turn, has a negative effect on trust in legal insiders in Eastern Europe: the lower a country's GDP (PPP) per capita and the less rule of law the country has, the less trusting the public is of judges, prosecutors, judges, lay-judges, the police, government and Parliament.

On a more optimistic note, however, legal outsiders in all countries except Ukraine generally have *positive* attitudes to legal insiders: attitudes are most positive in Norway, somewhat less positive in the UK and Poland, less positive in Bulgaria, and the least positive in Ukraine: more than 50 per cent of the respondents in all countries except Ukraine have positive attitudes to judges, prosecutors and the police.

As noted above, by contrast, the legal insiders (Norway being the exception) themselves believe that members of the public perceive them *negatively* – and there are small country differences: even in the UK, which received a high score on the World Bank's 2010 Rule of Law Index and whose GDP (PPP) per capita is high, such perceptions are common.

Our previous study of low-level government officials in Eastern Europe show that such officials generally receive better treatment than members of the public by the same type of officials[47], but that other-type officials treat them in the same manner as any other member of the public (Miller et al. 2001, pp. 208–9). Trust in own-type officials is therefore higher than trust in other-type officials.

[47] Legal insiders were – due to time constraints – not asked to give their assessment of public prosecutors.

Although legal insiders across Europe believe that different-type legal insiders are generally well informed, their trust in them varies. Trust in

- *judges* is high in all countries except Ukraine.
- *the police* is high in Norway, the UK and Poland, but fairly low in Bulgaria and Ukraine.
- *the lawmaking efforts of Parliament and government* is high in Norway, mixed in the UK, and low in Eastern Europe.
- *lawyers* is fairly low across the board, though higher in England than elsewhere.

It thus appears that trust in legal insiders – also on the part of the elites – is conditioned by socioeconomic factors and the quality of the rule of law. Although Bulgaria and Ukraine are still strongly affected by the legal *nihilism* of 'transitional' legal culture, Poland seems to be moving from 'transitional' to 'democratic' legal culture – partly due to their commitment to democracy (Chapter 5), and partly due to improved socioeconomic conditions. Thus transition appears to have had a positive impact on the behaviour of the legal insiders in Poland.

7

Legal change and legal transfers

Introduction: legal integration

Globalisation and European integration have predominantly occurred as legal transfers – that is, the transfer of law, best practices and institutional structures from 'more developed' to 'less developed' states.

Within the European area law (in the form of various EU regulations, directives and decisions) have been transferred from Brussels to EU member states, EEA states, EU candidate states, EU applicant states and members of the ENP (Kochenov 2008). Human rights conventions (UN – 1966; ECHR – 1950) have been incorporated into national law in most countries in Europe. Added to this the case law of supranational courts such as the ECtHR and the CJEU has become binding on CoE and EU member states, respectively. Decisions made by the EFTA court are binding on those EFTA states that are members of the EEA (i.e. Norway, Iceland and Lichtenstein). EEA member states are in addition bound by the decisions of the EFTA Surveillance Authority, which monitors their compliance with the EEA rules.

As noted in Chapter 1 academic studies of legal transfers/transplants[1] usually focus on the setting into which the transfer is introduced, on the transfers themselves or on the interaction between the formal institutional setting and the transfer. To date none of them have investigated public perceptions of legal transfers at a more general level. However, such perceptions are important as they tell us something about how open national legal cultures are to the reception of foreign law. This, in turn, is useful for predicting how legal transfers will be received, and thus how they are likely to 'behave' within different national legal cultures.

[1] The two terms *transfers/transplants* are used more or less interchangeably in the academic literature. In the following we will for practical purposes refer to legal transfers. In citations, however, the original wording will be retained.

How do citizens across Europe feel about the transfer of legislation from supranational structures such as the EU – or from other countries – to their own country? How do they feel about their countries effectively being under the jurisdiction of supranational courts? How do they view national courts and political institutions compared to supranational ones? Do they think external influences are (potentially) positive or negative? And do they believe that their countries have something to learn from other countries?

The answers to these questions are not only important for understanding European integration and the globalisation processes as such – but even more so for understanding national legal cultures, the interplay between different national legal cultures, and between national and supranational legal cultures.

This chapter is as much about *attitudes* as it is about *perceptions*.

Legal transfers

'Legal transplants – the movement of laws and legal institutions between states – have become central to the study of comparative and international law' (Miller 2003, p. 839).

Wise (1990, p. 6) notes that 'legal transplants can take different forms. Reception of foreign law may be partial, gradual, or indirect (as when a legal writer draws on knowledge of another system)'. Further, legal transfers may be 'imposed or voluntary, encompass entire legal systems or single legal principles and integrate similar or different cultures. Within host countries, legal transfers may permeate state and non-state social institutions, or . . . reside in state law superimposed on indigenous legal structures' (Gillespie 2006, p. 3). Legal transfers usually, though not always, occur at the initiative of an external party and tend to be accompanied by some pressure (Hiscock 1995; Mayhew 1998; Van Olden 2002, p. 4; Kochenov 2008).

Three main positions have emerged as to how likely legal transfers are to succeed. Adherents of the first position believe that legal transfers are unlikely to succeed as they tend to be 'exported to', rather than 'imported by', their new setting. For this reason they tend to be perceived as non-legitimate in their new setting and are simply unused (Seidman 1978). The more entrenched established rules, practices and institutions are, the higher the resistance to the rules imported by the EU (Sadurski 2010, p. 30).

Adherents of the second position are more optimistic, arguing that legal transfers may succeed, provided that the laws to be transferred are perceived as legitimate in their new setting. Legal transfers are therefore more likely to take hold if initiated locally – that is, if 'imported' rather than 'exported' (Goodpaster 1999, pp. 21–4).[2] Sadurski (2010, p. 30) claims that EU conditionality 'was most efficient when it resonated with domestic preferences and political aims, where there existed significant domestic factors in the "importing" states that favoured the importation, adoption and the maintenance of these mechanisms'.

The most commonly held position, however, is that it is inconceivable that a legal transfer introduced into a context very different from the one within which it was generated, will 'remain identical with itself playing its old role in a new organism' (Teubner, cited in Kingsley 2004, p. 514), even if it is supported locally (i.e. 'imported') (Watson 1974, p. 1). In other words the transfer of legislation may succeed, but the outcome may be very different from that intended.[3] For this reason, some analysts prefer to use the term *legal irritant* rather than *legal transfer* or *legal transplant* (Teubner 1998, p. 24).

Legal reception 'includes the adoption of legal institutions and institutional practices, legal rules as well as legal principles, systems of law, legal methods and fundamental legal values' (Sunde 2010, p. 29).

Not only the EU, but also various international organisations such as the International Monetary Fund (IMF) and the World Bank 'condition loans on legal reforms' (Miller 2003, p. 847). De Groot (1992, p. 54) believes that 'it is likely that the legal systems of the European States will form one great legal family with uniform or strongly similar rules'.[4]

[2] Berkowitz, Pistor and Richard (2003, pp. 164–5) claim that transplanted law – even that which has been 'imported' – tends not to be enforced in an efficient manner. Their findings suggest that 'receptive transplants, that is, those that adapted the imported law, or had a population that was familiar with it show legality ratings that are statistically no different from those of origin countries' (ibid., pp. 189–90).

[3] According to Ajani (1995, p. 112) 'experience shows . . . that bad communication between the foreign and the local experts, cultural misunderstandings on the fields that must be covered by the new legislation and, last but not least, a weak translation can heavily influence both the choice and the drafting of the new rules'.

[4] Helleringer and Purnhagen (2014, p. 8) are critical of the term *legal family*. In their view 'many legal families are far from being as homogenous as the categories of legal families would lead us to believe'. Őrűcű (2008, pp. 1, 5) is critical of the distinction between the 'common law tradition' and the 'civil law tradition' – preferring instead to 'regard all legal systems as mixed and overlapping, overtly or covertly, and group them according to the proportionate mixture of the ingredients'. Then, as noted by Monateri (1998, cited in Őrűcű 2008, p. 5) 'the actual legal world is more to be seen as a world of "contaminations" than a world split up into different families'.

It could be argued that European legal integration is a natural phenomenon that allows Europe's less developed states in the East to 'catch up with', and evolve towards, the more developed countries in the West.[5] Gedeon (1997, p. 104) claims that for Eastern Europe 'joining the European Union is now considered to be an indispensable means of catching up with the developed world and staying out of the European integration process is synonymous with the danger of preserving backwardness'. Rose (2009, p. 181) notes that 'in principle, the Copenhagen criteria were goals that CEE regimes wanted to meet as part of the process of expunging the anti-modern legacy of their predecessors'.

Moes (2009, p. 12) claims that in Poland '"European ideals" are seen as a way to "get rid of . . . (a) problematic past, as they are seen to have the potential to "move" Central Europe . . . westwards, where they can finally be a "normal" country again'.[6] Verdery and Schopflin (cited in Tanasoiu and Colonescu 2008, p. 365) note that 'for Central and East Europeans, European integration is seen as a recognition of their "Europeanness" and, as such, it carries a certainty of "belonging"'. Bulgaria rates as one of the most pro-European EU member states (Tanasoiu 2008, p. 364) and 'dissatisfaction with the national political elite is an important factor inducing (such) a pro-accession attitude' (ibid., p. 371).

By contrast, 'for average West Europeans concerns of the loss of national identity may lead to Euro-scepticism' (Cary, McLaren, Dulpy and Manigand, cited in Tanasoiu and Colonescu 2008, p. 365). In both the UK and Norway there is concern about loss of national sovereignty and the ensuing 'democracy deficit' resulting from their EU and EEA membership, respectively.

As noted in Chapter 1 quite a lot is known about various types of legal transfers, technical problems encountered during the actual transfer of law, and the impact, or lack thereof, of such transfers. We know less about public perceptions of legal transfers as such. However, opinions matter as they inform behaviour – including towards transferred law.

Investigating attitudes towards legal transfers is useful in that it allows us to investigate all the different dimensions referred to earlier – such as

[5] Trubek (2011, p. 1) claims that 'a nation's legal system affects its economic and social prospects' and that this idea 'can be traced back as far as the eighteenth century'. 'Law can either be an instrument to be used by developmental states to foster change' – or 'it may be a barrier to economic development'.

[6] Poland is also 'a new-found Eurosceptic nation because of political debates over various European issues' (ibid., p. 1).

- whether such laws and standards represent something *familiar* or *foreign* to European publics.
- whether foreign laws and legal standards are perceived as *legitimate* or *illegitimate.*
- whether such laws and standards can be implemented in the *short term*, or whether *a longer time perspective* is required.
- whether they are *likely* or *unlikely* to succeed.

Asking citizens across Europe about their attitudes towards European, international and universal (later referred to as E-I-U) standards that apply to their respective countries allows us to say something meaningful about the prospects for (further) European integration.

External influences on the law and legal system: the legal outsiders' perspective

On an average only 60 per cent in England and 68 per cent in Norway, but around 92 per cent in Poland, Bulgaria and Ukraine feel that their country "has a lot to learn from other countries and from European or international organisations" about "writing good laws" or "implementing and enforcing" the law.

Norwegian FG participants are keen to learn from countries that have stricter punishment for lawbreaking, but also from countries that have better laws than Norway in specific areas. Muslims, for their part, believe Norway has something to learn from multicultural societies including England about how to deal with ethnic minorities:

> N10-Sandnes-3: 'they can learn . . . to be a bit tougher [on lawbreakers].' N12-Tromsø-7: 'some countries handle drugs violations very strictly . . . we have to apply stricter measures [in this area].' N11-Klepp-4: 'Switzerland is more directly democratic than Norway. [They have] more referenda on important issues.' N5-Muslims-2: 'we can learn from England . . . at least as far as immigrants are concerned . . . they have better laws on racism'.

English FG participants are particularly keen to learn from countries that have stricter law and stricter implementation of the law: E8-Leeds-4: "in the US, a sentence means what it means". E6-Sheffield-1: "[we can learn from] America . . . is the length of sentencing". E7-Village-Yorkshire-2: what "we can learn from some of the punishments [the countries in the Middle East] dish out".

Polish FG participants are positive about copying specific legislation, for instance in the spheres of health care, social security, environmental protection and citizenship. Some of them think it is important to learn from countries that actually implement the law:

> P6-Białystok-1: 'simplicity of law . . . in some countries the law is simple. . .tax regulations fit into a single page.' P5-Mierzecice-2: '[we could learn] efficiency . . . in Poland court cases drag on and on, until the citizen dies, but the case will continue nevertheless.' P5-Mierzecice-1: 'in this country, you will always buy your way out, if only you've got enough money.' P8-Turośń Kościelna-8: 'Poles could certainly learn a lot from the English . . . the police are really respected there, unlike here.'

FG participants in Bulgaria are also keen to learn from other countries – particularly from Europe. They want to learn mostly about good laws and respect for the law:

> B2-Sofia-6: 'when they make laws they must think about how they will be enforced and respected. It doesn't happen in Bulgaria, so we have to draw some experience from other countries.' B5-Aksakovo-3: 'if we want to catch up with them [i.e. Europe], we have to enforce the laws like they do and have similar laws to theirs.' B3-Varna-7: 'from China we can learn how to abide by the law because the corrupt there are simply sentenced to death and the sentences are effective.'

Ukrainian FG participants mostly talk about learning from others in fairly general terms. Some of them make it clear that Ukraine could learn about specific types of law [especially in the area of social protection and health], and – more importantly – about effective law enforcement:

> U2-Kiev-7: 'from Sweden we can adopt laws on social welfare.' U6-Kharkiv-5: 'we could change the law on protection of people's [human] rights . . . we should refer to the Western countries because our laws are nothing in comparison with theirs.' U1-Kiev-4: 'from China [we could learn about] punishment for theft'. U1-Kiev-5: 'In the United States . . . Texas . . . they abolished the death penalty and then re-introduced it . . . and the quantity of murders diminished at once.'

Similarly, an average of only 62 per cent in England and 57 per cent in Norway, but around 92 per cent in Poland, Bulgaria and Ukraine feel that their country "has a lot to learn from other countries and from European or international organisations" about "the way *ordinary people and political leaders* respect the law".

Even though they talk mostly about ordinary people some FG participants in Bulgaria and Ukraine take note of how politicians who disregard the law are treated in other countries – and they state that it would be good to copy such practices:

> B1-Sofia-1: 'we have a lot to learn … especially from Germany, which is famous for their respect for the law'. B2-Sofia-1: '[we have a lot to learn in terms of] how to enforce the law and implement it … in Great Britain a minister went to work in his official car and picked up his wife on the way to take her to the hairdresser's. A scandal immediately followed … [as] he used his official vehicle for personal needs … it shows where they are and where we are.' U2-Kiev-4: 'in Italy … their Prime Minister went somewhere on the state's expense … the budget lost three million … he was immediately dismissed … unfortunately, here it will never be like that.'

Writing, implementing and enforcing law is a creative 'top-down' perspective on law. Respecting the law is a more 'bottom-up' perspective. But it seems to make little difference in terms of openness to Europe and the wider world: good ideas from abroad are welcome – especially in Eastern Europe – though without great enthusiasm in Norway or England where a degree of self-satisfaction constitutes a barrier to welcome ideas from abroad.

Superficially, such feelings might be classed as perceptions rather than as attitudes, but in reality they are prescriptions from abroad for change and reform, and therefore quite properly classed as supranational "attitudes and principles" (Table 7.1).

Table 7.1 *Whether [this country] has a lot to learn from other countries, European and international organisations: the legal outsiders' perspective*

	Norway (%)	England (%)	Poland (%)	Bulgaria (%)	Ukraine (%)
Q65: [this country] has a lot to learn (v. not) from other countries and European or international organisations about:					
Q65A: writing good laws	66	56	93	87	92
Q65B: implementing and enforcing laws	69	64	93	94	95
Q65C: the way ordinary people respect law	61	67	92	90	92
Q65D: the way political leaders respect law	52	56	89	94	95

Slightly less than half the public would be pleased if "national cultures and values" became much more similar across the whole of Europe – though attitudes vary sharply across our five countries. In Poland and Bulgaria a majority of the public would be pleased by a convergence of cultures, whereas in more peripheral Ukraine, England and especially Norway, a majority are opposed to a convergence of cultures. It is a centre/periphery pattern rather than an East/West or post-communist pattern.

Roth (2007, p. 13) claims that 'the people in the Balkans want to become "Europeans" without really becoming "Europeans", that is they want to become members of the EU without giving up their social logic and – purportedly – losing their cultural identity'. However, our findings suggest that they would be happy to change their attitudes towards law-abidingness and the manner in which law is implemented. Their wish for change is to some extent driven by a feeling of inferiority: since joining the EU Bulgaria has been branded "the bad pupil in class" and the EU has withheld funds as the country has failed to reduce corruption and effectively fight organised crime. To the average Bulgarian, lack of law-abidingness and poor implementation of law is a result of the negative imprint Ottoman culture left on their society, rather than an inherent feature of Bulgarian culture (Grødeland 2013, p. 556, note 81). Ridding themselves of this imprint on their cultural identity does not infringe on their Bulgarian identity.

A clear majority in every country "would be pleased if national laws became much more similar across the whole of Europe". Support for a convergence of laws averages a very high 82 per cent in former communist Poland, Bulgaria and Ukraine, though only 58 per cent in Norway and England. To some degree that reflects historic satisfaction with the law in Norway and England and historic dissatisfaction with Soviet or communist law (but also transition) in Poland, Bulgaria and Ukraine – and therefore public support for "levelling-up" but not "levelling-down". But it also reflects widespread Euro-scepticism in Norway and England. East Europeans would like to move on from the legal chaos of transition – and more importantly, they would like to catch up with the West. EU law provides them with a means with which to do so.

Case (2009, p. 125) notes that '"Euro-enthusiasm" and nationalism are not necessarily, or even commonly, manifest as polar opposites'. To give an example, Poles are in some ways very positive towards the EU, but also some of the most fervent Euro-sceptics and nationalist politicians are located in this country (Hesselink 2014, p. 20). Our findings show that

Table 7.2 *Cultural and legal convergence: the legal outsiders' perspective*

	Norway (%)	England (%)	Poland (%)	Bulgaria (%)	Ukraine (%)
Q125A: Pleased by convergence of cultures and values	25	40	60	63	45
Q125B: Pleased by convergence of national laws	59	56	76	90	79
Q66: Prefer to be in EU (v. not)	45	50	88	90	59
Q72: Want same laws as rest of Europe (v. more suitable)	39	29	55	67	34

European publics would like to preserve their cultural differences, whilst – for practical reasons – moving closer to each other in the legal sphere.

Although there is a small majority in both Norway and England for a convergence of laws, even that may reflect some hope or expectation that the convergence may comprise greater changes in other countries and only minor changes in Norway or England (Table 7.2). FG participants in England, for instance, suggest that other countries could learn from their country rather than the other way round: E3-Bristol-8: "there's other countries that could learn from us".

EU membership is very popular in Poland and Bulgaria (average 89 per cent); considerably less so in Ukraine (59 per cent); and least of all in Norway and England (average 48 per cent). That reflects a combination of post-communist wishes to "join Europe" (in Poland, Bulgaria and parts of Ukraine) mixed with "peripheral" reservations about "becoming European" or being ruled by Europe (in Ukraine, England and Norway).

An even clearer "centre-v.-periphery" pattern emerges in answer to a deliberately "loaded" question about an extreme convergence of laws. Asked whether "our country should have broadly the same laws and law enforcement as the rest of Europe" or "different laws and law enforcement that better suit our country and people", there is a majority for that extreme convergence of laws in Poland and Bulgaria (average 61 per cent) but only a minority in Norway, England or Ukraine (average 34 per cent).

Table 7.3 *Perceptions of the ECtHR: the legal outsiders' perspective*

	Norway (%)	England (%)	Poland (%)	Bulgaria (%)	Ukraine (%)
Q22: People can appeal to ECtHR (v. their government)					
Good	96	74	95	77	73
Too difficult	0	2	2	18	21
Bad	4	24	4	5	6

Note: Due to rounding of decimals, percentages do not always add up to 100%.

There are numerous international courts and tribunals, but in the minds of the general public throughout Europe, if not in the minds of international businesspersons or national politicians, the popular focus is on Strasbourg or Brussels rather than the Hague, and their concept of "supranational law" primarily means decisions of "the ECtHR", the adoption of the "EU standards" and, to a lesser degree, "UN standards".

The ECHR and the ECtHR are far more popular than the EU. When asked, "There is a European Court of Human Rights which meets in Strasbourg. People can appeal to that European Court if they feel their own government has treated them badly. Do you feel this is a good thing or a bad thing?" fully 24 per cent in England say it is "a bad thing", but there are negligible numbers anywhere else. Interviewers were briefed to record any spontaneous declarations, such as that it would be "*too difficult* for most ordinary people to appeal to the ECtHR" and in Bulgaria and Ukraine an average of 20 per cent do declare it to be "too difficult". But despite that, the overwhelming majority in every country think the ECtHR is "a good thing" and support the concept of "supranational" law (Table 7.3).

Although there is some normative support for the ECtHR in Norway, East Europeans are mostly in favour of the ECtHR and its case law for instrumental reasons: the ECtHR is viewed as a very effective mechanism for controlling national politicians and government officials. And the ECtHR itself is perceived as better and fairer than national courts (Grødeland 2014a).

"Suppose someone objects to a law passed in Parliament and takes the case to the ECtHR in Strasbourg", the legal outsiders were asked, "Who should have the final say?" On this question the balance is not between

Table 7.4 *Whether the ECtHR or Parliament should have the final say: the legal outsiders' perspective*

	Norway (%)	England (%)	Poland (%)	Bulgaria (%)	Ukraine (%)
Q23: ECtHR should have final say (v. their Parliament)	72	48	81	82	85

public support for the ECtHR versus "the government", but between public support for the ECtHR versus Parliament. Clearly, in the eyes of the English and Norwegian public, their Parliament has more legitimacy than their government on matters of law, and support for the ECtHR drops sharply – from 96 to 72 per cent in Norway and from 74 to 48 per cent in England. In Poland public support for the ECtHR drops much less – from 95 to 81 per cent. But in sharp contrast, in Bulgaria and Ukraine public support for the ECtHR against Parliament is greater than public support for the ECtHR against the government.

On matters of law, therefore, and measured against the ECtHR, Parliament has far more legitimacy than the government in Norway and England, and somewhat more legitimacy than the government in Poland; but in matters of law, Parliament seems to have even less legitimacy than the government in Bulgaria and Ukraine (Table 7.4).

European and International Standards Large majorities everywhere feel that European and international (E-I) standards, like those set by the EU are "generally good ideas that we should welcome" rather than "foreign ideas that do not suit our country". Added to this, large majorities everywhere would "welcome" rather than "feel insulted and resent EU pressure to reduce the level of crime and corruption" in their country.

But with the exception of Bulgarians, however, a majority do not think E-I standards should be a more important basis for law than "what ordinary people in this country think is right and wrong". And the English are by far the most unwilling to prioritise E-I standards over "what ordinary people in this country think is right and wrong". Across all three questions, Bulgarians are by far the most enthusiastic about E-I standards, and the English the least enthusiastic (Table 7.5).

Large majorities in Norway, England and, to a somewhat lesser extent, in Poland, all feel that their country should "try by argument and negotiations to get international organisations such as the EU or UN to

Table 7.5 *European and international standards, and EU pressure: the legal outsiders' perspective*

	Norway (%)	England (%)	Poland (%)	Bulgaria (%)	Ukraine (%)
Q68: European and international standards are generally good ideas (v. do not suit)	73	61	73	83	59
Q63: Welcome EU pressure to cut crime and corruption (v. resent)	78	69	75	92	79
Q42: European and international standards should be more important basis for law (v. what ordinary people think)	34	20	43	61	38

change particular international standards if we do not like them". Compared to Norway and England, the public in Bulgaria and Ukraine are 24 per cent more resigned to simply "accepting and applying" unwelcome E-I standards – and, at the same time, also 9 per cent more inclined to simply "reject" them; but Bulgarians and Ukrainians recognise their weakness and are 36 per cent less inclined than Norwegians and English to try to negotiate a change in unwelcome E-I standards (Table 7.6).

Yet their perceived weak negotiating position is almost an irrelevance to the public in the former communist countries because they are so notably positive about E-I standards. Do "EU standards, laws or regulations help to protect ordinary people from bad laws that might be made by their own governments" or "cause extra problems for ordinary people?" The English are ambivalent and only 61 per cent of Norwegians are on balance positive, but an average of 76 per cent in Poland, Bulgaria and Ukraine are positive and feel that EU standards 'protect people from bad state laws'.[7]

Support for the ECtHR is much higher than for E-I standards, but it follows the same cross-national pattern: only 67 per cent in England feel

[7] The same can be said for ECtHR case law (Grødeland 2014a).

Table 7.6 *How to handle EU/UN standards: the legal outsiders' perspective*

	Norway (%)	England (%)	Poland (%)	Bulgaria (%)	Ukraine (%)
Q69: If we do not like particular EU/UN standards we should:					
argue for changes	80	76	65	36	49
accept and apply them	7	6	19	37	25
reject them	11	16	12	22	23
pretend to accept but not apply them	2	3	5	4	4

Note: Due to rounding of decimals, percentages do not always add up to 100%.

Table 7.7 *EU standards and the ECtHR: the legal outsiders' perspective*

	Norway (%)	England (%)	Poland (%)	Bulgaria (%)	Ukraine (%)
Q70: EU standards protect people from bad laws (v. cause extra problems)	61	47	73	80	76
Q73: ECtHR protects (v. problems)	96	67	92	92	86
Q74: Trust ECtHR more (v. this country's court)	65	32	81	86	87

the ECtHR "helps to protect ordinary people from bad decisions by their own country's courts or governments", but an average of 92 per cent elsewhere. And while only 32 per cent in England "trust the ECtHR more than their own country's courts", 65 per cent in Norway and an average of 85 per cent in Poland, Bulgaria and Ukraine do the same (Table 7.7).

Criticism of EU standards for "giving too many privileges to minorities" (we cited Roma, religious, ethnic, linguistic and sexual minorities) rather than "just protecting minorities from unfair discrimination" is low in Norway, Poland and Ukraine (average 26 per cent) but higher in England (41 per cent) and Bulgaria (52 per cent) (Table 7.8). Averaged across the five countries, there is very little difference between allegations of EU privileges for different minorities.

Table 7.8 *EU standards privileging minorities: the legal outsiders' perspective*

	Norway (%)	England (%)	Poland (%)	Bulgaria (%)	Ukraine (%)
Q76A: EU standards privilege Roma (v. protect)	19	42	30	65	30
Q76D: EU standards privilege sexual minorities (v. protect)	21	29	45	46	33
Q76B: EU standards privilege religious minorities (v. protect)	33	47	22	45	21
Q76C: EU standards privilege ethnic/ linguistic minorities (v. protect)	28	46	16	50	19

But the targets of criticism vary from country to country. Norwegians are most critical of EU privileges for religious minorities; the English are most critical of EU privileges for religious and ethnic minorities; Poles are most critical of EU privileges for sexual minorities; Bulgarians are most critical of EU privileges for Roma; and Ukrainians, like Poles, are most critical of EU privileges for sexual minorities. (Ukrainians do complain about privileges for Crimean Tatars, but they do not associate that with the EU pressure.)

In sum, then, European citizens are surprisingly positive to legal transfers – and citizens in Eastern Europe more so than citizens in Western Europe. But Norwegians and the English are more sceptical about the EU and EU law than Poles, Bulgarians and Ukrainians. And the English are much more sceptical towards the ECtHR than other Europeans.

The potential for external learning: the legal insiders' perspective

As noted earlier, legal transfers are more likely to take hold if they are "imported by", rather than "exported to", a country. Asking legal insiders whether their country has something to learn from other countries and international organisations gives an indication as to how willing they are

Table 7.9 *Learning from others about law: the legal insiders' perspective*

	Norway (%)	England (%)	Poland (%)	Bulgaria (%)	Ukraine (%)
(DEP 32): In general does [this country] have a lot to learn from other countries and international organisations about law, about the way law is applied, or about the way ordinary people deal with the law?					
Learn a lot	30	33	62	52	61
Learn something	45	29	25	32	24
Not learn anything	5	22	3	8	4
Mix	5	5	5	6	9
Learn both ways	15	12	3	2	1

Note: Entries are based on the percentages of relevant 'text units' – the total number of answers to a given question; so entries sum up to approximately 100 per cent (decimals are rounded up or down to the nearest whole number).

to receive law from abroad – which, in turn, provides a measure for how open their legal culture is to legal transfers.

Table 7.9 shows that legal insiders (all countries) believe that their countries have something to learn from other countries and international organisations about law, the way law is applied, or the way ordinary people deal with the law. Although Norwegian legal insiders mostly think that their country can learn *something* from others, legal insiders in Poland, Ukraine and – to a slightly lesser extent – Bulgaria, believe that they can learn *a lot*. English legal insiders make a greater number of statements suggesting that their country *cannot learn anything* from other countries and international organisations than legal insiders elsewhere.

Due to its long coastline Norway has always had "an open culture", which has been receptive to foreign influences.[8] Historically, foreign ideas and material law were easily incorporated into Norwegian law

[8] For a historical overview of the reception of foreign law in Norway, see Sunde (2005, 2010).

(Sunde 2005, p. 169). Most of these originated in Western Europe (ibid., p. 183). During the Middle Ages Norwegian law was influenced by Irish, English and Mosaic, Canonical and Roman law (ibid., p. 326). Influences from German law also left an imprint on Norwegian law (ibid., p. 322) – both directly, and indirectly, via Danish law (ibid., p. 325). Norwegian legal theory was predominantly oriented towards the Continent until just after World War II, but has since then mostly been oriented towards the Anglo-Saxon legal culture (ibid., pp. 294, 325).

Former chairman of the Norwegian Supreme Court, Carsten Smith, refers to Norwegian law as mongrel law: 'today one cannot characterise Norwegian law by referring merely to civil law or the common law systems. By keeping an eye on the European Continent as well as to the west across the sea, we have tried to import the best from both systems' (Smith 2012, p. 89). The ability to learn from other cultures comes handy in these days of Europeanisation and globalisation. One legal insider notes that Norway may "benefit from the international legal order".

Norwegian legal insiders note that even though Norway does not have *much* to learn from others, it can still "expand [its] horizons". In their view Norway has the most to learn from other Nordic countries[9] (especially from Sweden, Denmark and Finland) and the ECtHR but also from the UK. Since the end of the nineteenth century the Nordic countries have 'harmonised their legislation in several fields of law, for example, in commercial law, contracts, maritime law, family law, security law and intellectual property law' (Modéer 2008, p. 292),[10] effectively developing a common Nordic legal culture.[11] That Norway may learn from the UK is no surprise given that the Norwegian legal system is a mixed legal system that contains elements of both civil and common law:

> N-GO-11: 'one can always learn from others . . . Norway has always been an open culture . . . with enormous trade . . . at least coastal Norway'. N-LA-14 'we have something to learn . . . [with regard to] the ECHR . . . [we]

[9] The Nordic countries (Denmark, Finland, Iceland, Norway and Sweden) have collaborated extensively since 1950s – through the Nordic Council (established in 1952), and the Nordic Council of Ministers. The Nordic Council's web page, www.norden.org/en/nordic-council/the-nordic-council Smith (2012, p. 91) claims that 'the Nordic states constitute a legal family, with fairly similar legal systems . . . one can speak of a traditional Nordic mode of legal reasoning'.

[10] Since 1972, however, the convergence of Nordic legal cultures has given way to divergent national identities and legal cultures. To some extent this trend coincided with Denmark joining the EU in 1973 (Modéer 2008, p. 295).

[11] For an analysis of Nordic legal culture see Nylund (2010, pp. 167–81).

> must to a greater extent accept that it is a set of rules to be applied also in Norway'. N-JU-13: 'all countries have something to learn from other countries ... Norway is fairly receptive to influences from the EU'. N-LA-17: 'we often compare ourselves to Sweden, Denmark ... which in a way are the closest countries and cultures that we can compare ourselves to. Maybe we should do this more with regard to the UK'.

Norway could primarily learn something from other countries in practical terms: it could learn about human rights, immigration and minority integration, international police collaboration, criminal law, and a wide range of other issues. It could learn about the EU directives – for instance about the storage of electronic data (Data Storage Directive) – and how best to implement these directives, and it could learn from the Treaty of Rome. The European legal order, the ECtHR and the UN conventions also have something to teach Norwegians:

> N-LA-19: 'Norway has not been the best [country] in class in terms of implementing human rights'. N-ER-25: 'we probably have something to learn with regard to some EU directives and how to practice [them]'. N-PR-21: '[we have something to learn regarding] our use of [pre-trial] detention'.

Quite a few legal insiders spontaneously state that in terms of law Norway is a well-functioning society: it has a "well-developed legal culture" and the legal standard is "very high". Put simply, Norway is a "well-developed country" in which "the police and the courts function well" and where people are "generally law-abiding":

> N-JU-21: '[Norway is] a well-organised society ... we are more law-abiding [than many other countries]'. N-PR-16: 'the police and the courts function very well in Norway ... [there is] no corruption and people can trust the courts and the police'.

English legal insiders hold the view that England may either learn *a lot* or *something* from other countries and international organisations.

Most of the EU's 28 member states belong to the civil law tradition. Only four of them – the UK, Cyprus, Ireland and Malta – are common law countries. Although some European legal insiders believe that the UK has something to learn from the EU, the majority believe that there is more to learn from other common law countries. More specifically, the UK may learn from the US, Canada, New Zealand and South Africa – that is, countries firmly rooted within the "Commonwealth tradition". However, Germany, Scandinavia and the ECtHR also have something to teach the Brits:

> E-LA-1: 'we're fundamentally a common law country and I think we can learn from common law countries, perhaps more than we can from Europe'. E-ER-20: 'we can learn from Scandinavian law ... we are now learning all the time through the European Union. Whether we like it or not, we are being sucked into understanding these legal systems, and the different codes that exist on the Continent.'

English legal insiders point out that there are deficiencies in the British legal system and also that the common law system is not as unique as Brits like to think.[12] Common law is essentially "mongrel law": "a hybrid" system that has adopted features of law "from other countries". In the view of one legal insider, "all [British] laws are imported". Besides, "the British system is not always best and right":

> E-ER-20: 'the English law, of course, is an amalgamation of laws that existed in Anglo-Saxon times and Norman times, and then the Latin times, so it's already not English, it's a total mongrel law. The common law is distinctive from the statutory law, but there is no doubt that we have lots to learn from other countries'. E-GO-13: 'we need to learn a degree of humility ... people are holding on to the vestiges of the Empire, but the simple fact of the matter is ... the reason common law works is because it [has] cannibalised the best bits from other legal systems. It originally was French law many centuries ago ... we've got some slightly lunatic people in this country, particularly in the judiciary, and I'd also say ossified policy officials who have a very blinkered view of the world and just don't like change on principle.' E-ER-13: 'I could be very arrogant and say, "we started it all", "we're the best we know" ... many countries take English law as the basis of their own law but then they improve it ... we're often not as forward thinking as other countries ... we can learn from others'.

English legal insiders who hold the view that England may *learn something* from other countries and international organisations are vaguer in terms of *what* exactly it may learn. Rather than referring to specific areas or types of law, they typically talk about "other countries' experience" and give non-specific "examples of good practice". More specific examples from which England may learn include "the operation [and "application"] of law abroad", giving "directions to the jury" and regulations on "jury access to the internet". Precedents from other countries are also considered useful for closing gaps and shortcomings in one's own legislation – as are "monitoring the situation of law" and "US boot camps".

[12] A similar proposition has been set forth by Őrűcü (2008, p. 5): 'English law ... is becoming more and more an overlap of common law, various civilian systems and European law'.

Those English legal insiders who specifically refer to European or Commonwealth law are mostly positive. In their view the UK may learn from "the European Community–oriented thinking" and from "incorporating European human rights instruments" into national legislation. Such knowledge may be obtained from "other legal systems", "other countries" (the Commonwealth in general, and Australia, Canada and New Zealand in particular), and "supranational courts". However, also the US, Scandinavia, the EU and the ECtHR have something to teach the Brits. Scandinavia, for instance, has "quite advanced law" and "some laws may be slightly better" there:

> E-GO-22: 'in Equalities, our laws tend to be quite advanced compared to a lot of other countries, even . . . in Europe . . . I'm not saying we couldn't learn from Canada, or South Africa. . . or, you know, some other countries. Scandinavian countries, for example.' E-PR-20: 'any nation always has something to learn from another nation . . . we incorporate within our jurisprudence a great deal from the Commonwealth countries of Canada and Australia, in particular'.

The specific areas of law or specific legislation from which England could learn include civil liberties and human rights, EU law, and international legal frameworks and conventions. It could also learn from "other's failings" and "experiences".

Some English legal insiders emphasise the practical aspects of law, claiming that by considering "opinions from elsewhere", one "makes life easier for people". They acknowledge that "other countries do things better than the UK" and that "some laws are working fantastically well" there. Consequently, there is "always stuff to learn" and it is "right to be open" – for instance by "adopting the benefits of overseas" and thus "picking up good ideas". Then "the English legal system is not perfect":

> E-ER-22: 'we should always be listening to examples of good practices and looking at what other countries are doing, but . . . this country has an extremely proud record of its legal system.' E-PR-17: 'our [legal] system is one of the best in the world . . . you can always look at laws that other countries have that seem to make sense or seem to work slightly better than ours, or are drafted a little better . . . but . . . the Crown Court system of the jury is a marvellous system.'

Quite a few legal insiders – judges (but also some of the prosecutors) in particular – find the English legal system "very" good. English law is "not inferior"; as a matter of fact "[it] is amongst the world's best", possibly even "the best". Consequently, "many" countries, including "Australia and

New Zealand", "look to the UK". Even though "any nation has something to learn" from others, it is, in the opinion of English legal insiders, "difficult to learn from other legal systems". This is particularly true for England, given its "common law system": E-JU-18: "the English law takes a lot of beating. I'm not sure that we have a huge amount to learn".

English legal insiders who believe that the UK has *nothing* to learn from other countries or international organisations in the field of law in part emphasise that England is a common law country; they also focus on the advantages and strengths of the English legal system, and in part express their negative opinions of Europe and EU law.

First, they stress that "common law is different" from civil law (one-fifth of the countries of the world belong to the common law system). As "law is culture bound" it is not automatically transferable across legal systems. As a rule the law should therefore "suit the country and [the] people" who live there:

> E-JU-19: 'law is so closely bound up with a country's culture that it grows in ways that are natural to that culture'. E-LA-1: 'we should have laws that suit our own country . . . because we have a fundamentally different legal philosophy underpinning how our legal system works . . . we're a common law system . . . and you can't bolt one onto the other successfully'.

Second, they claim that "English laws are pretty good": English criminal law, for instance, is "amongst the best in the world". "A lot of countries" could or "should" learn from England as its legal system is "the best and fairest". English legal insiders claim that even "Continental law has learnt from the UK". For instance, "the Germans think the legal process is quicker in England" than in their own country:

> E-PO-10: 'our legal system is very good. It's very adequate . . . probably one of the best in criminal law and certainly one of the best in the world. I would not be surprised if a lot of other countries use our law as a benchmark'. E-JU-11: 'Continental law has itself learnt a lot from the English method, and indeed has a high regard for the decisions of the English judges'.

By contrast, EU law is perceived as "useless" since it is "not adjusted to culture". The UK "should not be governed by Europe" and it "should not go to the ECtHR" with its disputes, but rather solve them itself:

> E-GO-19: 'we don't need the European Union to change our laws'. E-JU-17: 'I'm not anti-European but I'm not necessarily a believer in going to Strasbourg for our decisions . . . in some cases they could do well to learn from us rather than the other way round.'

Legal insiders in Poland primarily hold the view that their country may *learn a lot* from various international and regional organisations such as the EU (and especially the "old EU" member states), CoE and the ILO, but also from supranational courts such as the ECtHR and the CJEU. Poland may learn from the "democratic world" and from "more developed countries" – including Western Europe in general, and specific countries such as the UK, Germany, France, Austria, Italy and the Scandinavian countries, in particular. The US also has something to teach the Poles.

More specifically, Poland may learn a lot from these countries and organisations as "the West has a longer tradition of democracy" and as EU member states exhibit "good democracy" and "apply good solutions" to problems with which Poland is trying to come to grips. It should therefore "use European solutions" and thus "benefit from Europe":

> P-GO-10: 'Poland can learn a lot . . . what I have in mind here is the "old" European Union.' P-LA-16: 'it is great that this country has the possibility to embed in its own legal system the experience of other countries, which have been democratic for 50 or 100 years with no political breakdowns, for which the passage of time has not acted as a demoralising factor'. P-JU-15: 'Poland is a so-called young democracy . . . we take patterns from the "old" European democracies'. P-PO-2: 'a lot of things are incomprehensible to us, as well as a number of legal standards which function in the so-called democratic world . . . we associate freedom with . . . "let's party"'.

Poland may also learn a lot from the EU in terms of "EU law" – by one judge described as being "superior" to domestic law – and from the EU "regulations", "directives" and "standards". Besides, Poles could learn a thing or two about "applying EU regulations". From the ECtHR Poland could learn about "legal principles". The Helsinki Convention, the ILO Convention, international law and the British application of precedents are also useful:

> P-LA-2: 'the influence of international law is positive . . . especially the one exerted by the European Conventions . . . [for example], the European Convention on Human Rights, the Helsinki Convention on Civic, Political and Economic Rights. They have . . . great and positive influence. They fill a void in Polish law'.

Further, Poland may learn a thing or two about democracy and the rule of law, such as "good democratic traditions", "equality before the law" and "respect for the law". The latter includes "elementary respect for the executive and the judiciary" and "law-abidance". Acquiring such knowledge will "change people" and their "mentality" for the better. Legal insiders may learn from other "legal systems", "legal traditions" and "legal practice [s]" about the "application" and "everyday functioning of the law".

Poland should not only learn from the positive experiences of other countries. It should pay equal attention to – and learn just as much from – their mistakes. In other words, Poles should not simply "blindly adapt" or "adjust" to foreign law. Rather they should "choose the good and reject the bad":

> P-PR-17: 'I'm sure we may learn a lot and in fact we are learning . . . we may learn the most from the regulations of civil law, because European civil law is the most stable, and in fact it has its roots in the Napoleonic Codes adopted in the area of partitioned Poland. As far as criminal law is concerned . . . there are certain institutions, or certain European trends, which were adopted too hastily into the criminal procedure or to Polish criminal law and in practice, they don't fit into the Polish reality.'

Legal insiders in Bulgaria are less enthusiastic than Polish legal insiders about the prospect of learning a lot from other countries and international organisations – though a majority are in favour of such learning.

In terms of whom they may learn from, Bulgarian legal insiders mainly mention "experienced" and "more advanced" societies in the "West" and "worldwide". Bulgaria may learn a lot from their "experience", "practices" and "legislation". The ECtHR and "foreign country courts" also have a lot to teach Bulgarians:

> B-LA-3: 'we can learn from the practice worldwide'. B-PO-8: 'we should borrow the positive from the European states.' B-LA-21: 'first of all, the respect that the people have for the law, the respect for the institutions like the court, the prosecution, the investigation . . . their reality is so organised . . . we here in Bulgaria have a lot to learn.'

Like Poland, Bulgaria should primarily learn about democracy and the rule of law. More specifically, it should learn something about "public attitudes towards law"; the "balancing . . . [of] personal freedom"; "law abidance"; and "respect for institutions". Bulgaria may benefit from the expectations of other countries in terms of the "attitude of youth towards law" and "legal education". Educating people about the law would be useful for "changing the mentality" of Bulgarians towards law and thus also towards the institutions passing, applying, implementing and enforcing it:

> B-JU-17: 'yes of course . . . we are one hundred years behind them [i.e. the US] and perhaps 40–50 years behind Western Europe in our mentality'.

> B-PR-22: 'there is much to learn . . . ordinary people in Bulgaria usually do not distinguish [between] the attitude towards the law [and] their attitude towards politicians and a particular political party. So far I do not think there is respect for the law'. B-LA-3: 'what our society lacks is the principal respect for the institutions . . . we have no rule of law . . . we could learn . . . equality before the law'.

In the view of the legal insiders Bulgaria has a lot to learn in terms of "writing", "passing", "applying" and "implementing" laws. More specifically, Bulgaria may learn a lot from "observing the classical principles of law" with a view to making "long lasting laws". And it may learn about "access to [legal] information", "administrative legal culture", "faster proceedings", "good practice", "better implementation" of law, "compliance with law", "stricter control", and "criminal matters". Bulgaria also has something to learn about "dispute resolution":

> B-ER-10: 'naturally, Bulgaria has a lot to learn . . . in England there are laws that haven't been changed for 300 years . . . ours are changed five times a year and they are again irrelevant.' B-PR-21 'we could borrow from the experience of other countries that have much faster proceedings, much better control of the implementation and a much more adequate attitude of the citizens towards the exercise of their rights.' B-JU-13: 'our society should learn from other, more advanced and modern societies than ours [about] how to apply the law, how to apply it to law enforcement bodies . . . Bulgarian legislators should learn from foreign legislative bodies how to produce law . . . [and] from foreign judicial systems how to apply the law'.

As regards the EU, Bulgaria may learn about European "law" and "practice" more generally, and about "best European practices", in particular. It may "copy foreign law"; "borrow ideas" and learn from the "experience of other countries" – thus "adapting [Bulgarian] law to the European requirements" and ensuring "unification of law" across Europe. B-JU-10: "since Bulgaria joined the European Union, there has been a very positive impact on the legislative process".

Bulgaria may also learn a lot about quality of law and law enforcement – including "cleaning up the law", "controlling law enforcement" and dealing with "corruption": B-JU-22: "certainly there is ultimately a lot to learn, but the greatest problem is that the ordinary people have no clear idea about their rights. The average Bulgarian should learn about his or her rights and about the ways in which to defend them'.

Finally, Bulgaria – like Poland – may learn to "avoid the errors of others". It should therefore not engage in the "mechanical reception of law". Rather, reception should be "adapted to the Bulgarian reality". The country should therefore not "adopt so much US law". Legal insiders acknowledge that some weaknesses and problems have to be overcome before Bulgaria can apply what it is now learning from other countries:

> B-JU-25: 'reception of foreign law should not be mechanical, precisely because the social life in the other countries and the one in Bulgaria are not the same'. B-PR-18: 'it is not proper for foreign law to be copied . . . it has to be consistent with national traditions, psychology and so on'. B-PR-4: 'we exercise more US law than our Continental law, which for me is not proper.'

Legal insiders in Ukraine – just like those in Poland and Bulgaria – hold the view that their country has a lot to learn from other countries and international organisations. Ukraine may learn from "everybody, really", but most of all from "the West" – including "Europe". Further, it may learn from "international organisations" such as "the UN", "the World Trade Organisation (WTO)", "the EU", "CoE" and its "Venice Commission", and "international courts". Ukraine's "[closest] neighbours" – that is, "Russia", "the Baltic states", and "Poland" – all have something to teach Ukraine. Ukraine may also learn from countries located further away, such as "Germany", "France", "Belgium", "Holland", "Italy", "the US" and "Canada":

> U-ER-25: 'Ukraine must learn . . . people there . . . respect the law, since everybody is equal before the law, starting with the President and ending with the simple worker . . . in our country it is opposite: everybody breaks the law and only certain people [have to] answer for this. In Ukraine there is no equality for everybody before the law and that's why ordinary people don't respect it and officials don't obey it.'

Ukrainian legal insiders make a larger number of references to what their country may learn in terms of democracy and the rule of law than legal insiders in Bulgaria and Poland: Ukraine may learn about "equality before the law", and the "protection of rights and freedoms" – including the "freedom of speech", "the right of assembly" and "civil rights" more generally. In the view of Ukrainian legal insiders, learning also includes the "planning", "creation" and "writing" of law. Ukraine has a lot to learn in terms of "mentality" – that is, people's "attitude" and "behaviour" towards law:

> U-LA-17: 'the more receptive we are to the European legislation, the better . . . in the field of protecting the freedom of speech or . . . protecting the right to peaceful meetings, civil rights, economic law and tax

> regulations'. U-PO-18: 'a lot of people in our country know nothing about their rights, do not know laws ... in Europe even the ordinary worker knows his or her rights, he or she knows the laws'.

Ukraine could learn about "law" more generally, for instance about "case law" from the UK and about "precedent" from the US. And it could learn about more practical matters such as "electronic citizens' appeals" and "the creation of administrative courts". Ukraine should "replicate the best experiences" of other countries – applying "all that is positive":

> U-JU-20: '[we could learn] everything regarding the adoption, application [of law] and the attitude of people [towards law]. We have complete *legal nihilism* [in Ukraine]. From the President [down to] the ordinary citizen. All the problems stem from [this]'. U-JU-11: 'we should learn [from the] positive experience ... there is a proverb [saying] that the smart learns from others' mistakes ... we are not very mature in the field of law-making'.

To the extent Ukrainian legal insiders speak about the EU, they address European integration more generally, and European legal integration, in particular. As regards the latter, Ukraine could – and should – learn from "EU law", "EU directives", "European norms", "European standards of law" and "legal harmonisation":

> U-ER-23: 'we can borrow lots of things from Europe. The European legislation is much simpler and more comprehensive than ours. People in Europe respect the law ... they have been through all the stages of state building that we are going through at the moment.' U-GO-1: 'we intend to join the European Union ... [in] 1994 we signed the so-called ... agreement for partnership and collaboration with the EU ... we [therefore] adapt our legislation to the European system of law and to the world system of law'.

Legal insiders emphasise that Ukraine should learn from the experience – and mistakes – of others and especially from their "positive experiences": U-ER-1: "of course, there are a lot of good laws in the world, perfect laws, which have passed the test of time ... [Ukraine] is developing its democracy [and] should look for something better in other countries' laws, learn from them".

Even though legal insiders in Ukraine express great willingness to learn from others, they also call for caution: whilst Ukraine should learn, it should "not [engage in] plagiarism". While learning, "the Ukrainian mentality" and the country's "specificity" should be considered. Ukraine must preserve its national "foundations" and "traditions", "keeping in mind local traditions". Put bluntly, transferred law must "not contradict the Ukrainian reality" as this would be counterproductive. One legal insider labels the WTO "anti-Ukrainian" as, in his view, this organisation fails to take local realities into account:

> U-ER-24: 'we shouldn't ... adopt everything because the Ukrainian society is developing in a way that is different from that of Europe.' U-LA-6: 'in principle, it would be very nice ... [but] sometimes our society is not ready to commit to certain laws ... [from] England or Germany ... economic base is not ready for this'.

External influences on the law and legal system: the legal insiders' perspective

Some countries are generally more positive to the transfer of laws and best practices from other countries than others. Added to this, some countries are more, other less, favourably disposed towards the EU.

Norway is generally very sceptical of the EU, yet highly favourable to international collaboration. Since July 2011 more than 70 per cent of the population have been negative to EU membership.[13] There is considerable dissatisfaction with the cost of the EEA Agreement: Norway's participation in various EU programs and bureaus costs some 1.7 billion Norwegian crowns (NOK) per year.[14]

The UK is also highly EU-sceptic. Since 2010 opinion polls have consistently indicated that a majority supports a British withdrawal from the EU. A poll conducted in November 2012, for instance, shows that 56 per cent of Brits are in favour of withdrawing. Only 30 per cent prefer to remain in the EU.[15] A government study conducted in 2013, however, concluded that the economic benefits of the country's EU membership outweigh the loss of independence on policy.[16] Still, the current

[13] NTB, 'Sju av ti er imot norsk EU-medlemskap' [Seven of ten are against Norwegian EU membership], *Dagbladet*, 25 January 2013, www.dagbladet.no/2013/01/25/nyheter/politikk/eu/innenriks/euro/25429064 accessed on 15 January 2014.

[14] Nei til EU, 'EØS-kontigenten' [The EEA fee'], 5 March 2012, www.neitileu.no/om_nei_til_eu/konferanser/umulige_eoes_mulige_loesninger/hva_er_galt_med_eoes/eoes_kontingenten accessed on 18 January 2014.

[15] Daniel Boffey and Toby Helm, '56% of Britons would vote to quit EU in referendum, poll finds', *The Observer*, 17 November 2012, www.theguardian.com/politics/2012/nov/17/eu-referendum-poll accessed on 10 January 2014.

[16] Peter Griffiths, 'Britain's economy better off inside EU – government study', *Reuters*, 22 July 2013, http://uk.reuters.com/article/2013/07/22/uk-britain-europe-idUKBRE96L0H720130722 accessed on 10 January 2014.

government intends to organise a referendum on the UK's future EU membership in 2017.[17] Added to this, British Prime Minister David Cameron recently announced that the government is considering introducing various restrictions to discourage Bulgarian and Romanian unskilled workers from travelling to the UK, by limiting their access to welfare benefits and by charging them for some health benefits.[18] Citizens from both countries were given free access to the Schengen area on 1 January 2014.

By contrast, the countries in Eastern Europe see economic advantages in their EU membership: 'joining the EU significantly reduces the risk premium on investments in the East – with resulting huge benefits to new entrants ... (EU) enlargement is (therefore) a very good deal for both the EU incumbents and the new members' (Baldwin et al. 1997, p. 125).

From an economic point of view, Poland has done fairly well since joining the EU. Its share of the EU's Cohesion Policy Grants stipulated for the period 2007–13 was the highest of all the EU member states. Added to this, Poland's weight in Europe and the world has increased. According to a report issued by the Polish Ministry of Foreign Affairs in 2013, Polish GDP increased by 18.2 per cent from 2007 to 2013.[19] Passport-free travel within the Schengen area has allowed Poles to move freely across Europe in search of jobs.[20]

Bulgaria, for its part, received around 10 billion euro from the EU between 1990 and 2006, during its run-up to EU membership. From 2007 to 2009 it received a further 4.6 billion euro.[21] Even though Brussels

[17] Jason Douglas and Friedrich Geiger, 'David Cameron's referendum on UK's EU membership still set for 2017', *The Wall Street Journal*, 1 June 2014, http://online.wsj.com/articles/u-k-referendum-on-eu-membership-remains-scheduled-for-2017-1401626844 accessed on 24 August 2014.

[18] *Economic Times*, 'EU official accuses UK of immigration distortions', 10 January 2014, http://economictimes.indiatimes.com/news/international/world-news/eu-official-accuses-uk-of-immigration-distortions/articleshow/28639304.cms accessed on 10 January 2014.

[19] Ministry of Foreign Affairs, Republic of Poland, 'Social and economic impact of Poland's membership of the European Union (1 May 2004–1 May 2013). Key conclusions on the ninth anniversary of Poland's EU membership', wresour/resource/1f6677c7-cc34–45ab-9587–446ca4f33428:JCR accessed on 16 January 2014.

[20] European Commission – IP/09/5953, 29 April 2009, http://europa.eu/rapid/press-release_IP_09_595_en.htm accessed on 16 January 2014.

[21] Veselin Tsachevsky, 'Bulgaria's EU membership: the adaptation to the new status is not over', *Electronic Publications of the Pan-European Institute* 16/2010, www.tse.fi/pci accessed on 16 January 2014.

has withheld funds to Bulgaria as a result of Bulgarian governments' inability to reduce corruption and organised crime, in net economic terms the country has still benefited from its EU membership.

In November 2013, the Ukrainian president at the time, Viktor Yanukovych, changed course following Russian pressure. Ukraine is a member of the ENP and an association agreement with the EU was completed and initialled in 2012. The Ukrainian citizens were largely in favour of EU membership. By 2013, however, Yanukovych was under heavy pressure from the Russian authorities to distance himself from the EU and instead strengthen economic relations with Russia. His sudden decision not to sign the association agreement with the EU triggered huge demonstrations in Kiev and other parts of Ukraine. The demonstrations culminated in the killing of several demonstrators in Kiev, the president's sudden departure from Ukraine, Russia annexing the Crimea, and the outbreak of civil war in eastern Ukraine in early 2014. The association agreement with the EU was eventually signed on 27 June 2014.[22]

Based on the above we would expect legal insiders in Western Europe to be more negative to E-I-U standards than East European legal insiders. However, Table 7.10 shows that across Europe legal insiders do not believe that such standards are imposed on people in their country – even though a larger share of legal insiders in England than elsewhere claim that they are indeed imposed.

In 1999 the Norwegian Parliament passed the Human Rights Act, which incorporated the ECHR (1950), ECtHR case law and the two 1966 UN covenants into national law. A priority clause states that in the event of conflict with other legislation, the provisions of these three conventions are to take priority over national legislation (Smith 2012, p. 135). These conventions have since exerted 'a strong influence on (the Norwegian) application of the law' (ibid., p. 106).

Norwegian courts often refer to EU law beyond that to which Norway is bound as a relevant moment when interpreting Norwegian law. Norwegian courts are formally bound to consider the case law of the CJEU, the development of the EU Commission's decisions, the case law of the EFTA court and the decisions of ESA – EFTA's surveillance body – and the development in national case law and administrative decisions (NOU 2012, p. 39).

[22] Steven Pifer, 'Poroshenko signs EU-Ukraine association agreement', *UpFront,* 27 June 2014, www.brookings.edu/blogs/up-front/posts/2014/06/27-poroshenko-signs-eu-ukraine-association-agreement-pifer accessed on 23 August 2014.

Table 7.10 *European, international and universal standards: the legal insiders' perspective*

	Norway (%)	England (%)	Poland (%)	Bulgaria (%)	Ukraine (%)
Do you feel that 'European', 'international' or 'universal' standards, set by organisations such as the European Union or United Nations, impose foreign ideas on ordinary people in [this country]?					
Impose	23	39	18	25	26
Impose – but welcome	5	n.a.	n.a.	n.a.	16
Do not impose	57	52	66	69	52
Mix	15	9	16	6	6

Note: Entries are based on the percentages of relevant 'text units' – the total number of answers to a given question; so entries sum up to approximately 100 percent (decimals are rounded up or down to the nearest whole number).

Since the EEA Agreement came into force, Norway has incorporated numerous EU directives and regulations into national law. As of January 2012 some 170 of Norway's approximately 600 laws contained EU law (i.e. some 30 per cent in total) to a greater or lesser extent, as did some 1,000 Norwegian regulations (NOU 2012, p. 18). Through its agreements with the EU, Norway has incorporated about three-quarters of the EU legislation (ibid., p. 18). In addition, some national laws have had to be amended so they did not conflict with EU law (ibid., p. 128). The reception of EU law is Norway's largest reception of foreign law ever (ibid., p. 119). The NOU notes that 'even most jurists are not aware of what share of Norwegian law that is EU/EEA based'.[23] Still, ordinary Norwegian rules are to be interpreted based on the domestic sources of law, whereas EU-based rules are to be interpreted based on the sources of EU law – including the case law of the CJEU and the EFTA court (ibid., p. 122).

[23] The government or a ministry may appoint a committee and working groups to report on different aspects of society. A report can either be published as an Official Norwegian Report – NOU – or as a regular report, www.regjeringen.no/en/doc/norwegian-official-reports.html?id=1767 accessed on 3 September 2014.

So far Norway has not made use of its right to reserve itself against legal acts from Brussels (ibid., p. 20) though the government has considered opting out of 17 of the more than 6,000 EU legal acts that since 1992 have been incorporated into the EEA Agreement (the Schengen Agreement has since 1999 been supplemented by some 158 new legal acts) (ibid., p. 39). The Norwegian Parliament has on several occasions made it clear that it will introduce rules similar to those of the EU even though no formal agreement between Norway and the EU has been made to this effect (ibid., p. 39).

Further, Norway ratified ILO Convention 169, Concerning Indigenous and Tribal Peoples in Independent Countries in 1990. The convention states that 'the indigenous people's customs and customary law should be taken into account in national legislation' (Ravna 2010, p. 150) and its incorporation into Norwegian law through the Finnmark Act (ibid.) has positively affected the rights of the Sáami minority in northern Norway (Smith 2012, pp. 173–80).

Norwegian legal insiders predominantly claim that E-I-U standards are not imposed – partly because the ideas they reflect are not foreign, partly because Norway has formally committed itself to implementing these standards through various international treaties and agreements.

Legal insiders emphasise that Norway is "a part of [the international community]". E-I-U standards are based on "universal ideas" and "basic human rights". In this sense they are "in line with the Norwegian legal tradition", "mostly reflect Norwegian views", and therefore "mostly [enjoy] broad public support". They also note that most international organisations make decisions by consensus:

> N-GO-1: 'I never felt that [they represented] an attempt at foreign influence, but [rather] an attempt to achieve something together . . . [i.e. a] tool with which to achieve a greater goal.' N-PR-6: 'the human rights conventions, for instance . . . harmonise well with the [Norwegian] citizens' own opinions of how things should be.'

Legal insiders concede that E-I-U standards no doubt "influence Norway". Particularly the legal professionals (i.e. lawyers, prosecutors and judges) appreciate the inherent value in learning from others. In their view "it is good to look to foreign experiences". To Norwegian legal insiders foreign standards generally represent a means by which to generate "fruitful discussions"; "a tool [by which to achieve] a greater goal". Such standards are "in line with the European tradition" – that is, the tradition of countries with "a fairly common cultural heritage" – and as such they "reflect general principles". Therefore, taking them into account is "a question of solidarity" and Norway "has much to gain" from doing so. Some legal insiders note that Norway has "international obligations":

> N-JU-16: 'the point is that we should take part and that we have much to gain [from such standards] . . . we should together bring those who are a bit on the edge, the Baltics and such [areas], with us and lift them to a more reasonable level compared to what so-called wealthy [countries] have. It has to do with solidarity, in Europe, at least'. N-LA-2: 'much of what is passed in the EU is in line with the European legal tradition.' N-PR-21: 'you have the ECHR . . . and especially the rights of the accused, which I think is positive . . . [these are] not foreign ideas for us.' N-ER-20: 'if one is a part of an alliance then one has to adjust accordingly . . . when we [i.e. Norway] have ratified [a law or a rule] then we have accepted it and then we must abide by it.'

When giving examples of European and international standards that Norway is formally obliged to implement, legal insiders mention "human rights" more generally, as well as "the rights of the indigenous people". Various standards on the environment, standards concerning foreign policy and the EU are also mentioned. Legal insiders make more specific references to the Four Freedoms, EU law, EU directives, the EEA Agreement, the ECtHR and its case law, the UN, UN Conventions and various rights: N-ER-5: "every week some law comes from the EU . . . [regarding] crime, illegal border crossings . . . it is very important that the European countries stand united".

Norwegian legal insiders who hold the view that E-I-U standards are *imposed*, on the other hand, believe that these standards are not appropriate for Norway. They are particularly negative to what they perceive to be silly or meaningless standards imposed upon Norway by the EU. Such standards concern the shape of cucumbers and bananas (EU Directive 1677/88), which are referred to with some scorn. An EU directive from the 1990s about a particular type of sand to be used in playgrounds and kindergartens is considered inappropriate for northern Norway, as such sand effectively turns into concrete when temperatures drop below zero – which is often the case there.[24] Legal insiders opposed to E-I-U standards frown at the 2006 EU Data Retention Directive (this directive was scrapped

[24] Gunnar Kagge, 'Agurkenes krumning og barnehagesandens grovhet' [The curving of the cucumbers and the coarseness of the sand in the kindergartens], *Aftenposten*, 18 May 2013, www.aftenposten.no/nyheter/Agurkens-krumning-og-barnehagesandens-grovhet-7205797.html accessed on 24 August 2014.

by the CJEU on 8 April 2014 on the grounds that it amounted to a grave intrusion into the private lives of EU citizens)[25] and several other EU directives. Some legal insiders dislike the fact that such standards are imposed upon Norway by what they perceive as "illegitimate foreign bodies".

In 1974 Lord Denning likened EC law with 'an incoming tide. It flows into the estuaries and up the rivers. It cannot be held back' (NOU 2012, p. 126). As an EU member, the UK has incorporated a large body of supranational law (the ECHR, various UN Conventions, etc.) into national law. Somewhat surprisingly, a majority of the English legal insiders do not feel that such law is imposed upon their country.

Those who do *not* feel that E-I-U standards are imposed upon the UK emphasise that their country is a member of the very organisations that make these standards – that is, the EU and the UN. The UK "influences" these bodies: it sits at the same negotiation table as other member states and "thrashes things out" together with them. Several English legal insiders note that some of the E-I-U standards that the UK has ratified have either been prepared by British jurists or are heavily influenced by British thinking. The ECHR, for instance, was written by British lawyers. The UK "has [not only] chosen to be part of Europe", but it also "has a strong voice in Europe". It "drives these [international and European] standards upwards" and they are therefore "as much British as [they are] foreign" or "universal":

> E-ER-18: 'of course we mustn't see the European Union as an entirely external organisation. British Ministers help to make laws, British officials sit in the Commission and British Members of Parliament help them shape all these laws . . . [At] the United Nations . . . we are on the Security Council. We do have a sort of seat at the table. We're able to veto anything'. E-PO-20: 'we have a strong voice in Europe . . . we can decide whether we accept certain laws or not.' E-ER-4: 'the reason why there's European law being produced by the European Parliament is because I, as a European citizen, have mandated it to do so.' E-GO-13: 'take the European Convention on Human Rights, that was drafted by English lawyers . . . it more than anything else represents . . . long-standing British values'.

Further, in the view of English legal insiders E-I-U standards are based on "very good ideas" that one "can agree with" and "learn from". Still,

[25] DW, 'Top EU court overturns data retention directive', www.dw.de/top-eu-court-overturns-data-retention-directive/a-17550163 accessed on 23 August 2014.

legal insiders in England, just like legal insiders in Norway, are critical of the (in their view) ridiculous instructions such as the EU requirements regarding the metric system, the curve of bananas and the flavour of crisps:

> E-LA-8: 'if you look at major treaties, such as the European Convention on Human Rights, you've got to be a pretty warped politician . . . to spin that as imposing foreign ideas on the British people. What instruments like that actually do is distil into some pretty simple propositions things [that] are fundamental to a liberal civil society. They are a good guide, particularly in a country which doesn't have a written Constitution. If you're talking about most petty Brussels output in relation to bananas and markets, then it's easier to make a case for that, being rather unnecessary.'

One prosecutor claims that to the extent such conventions are imposed upon British society, they are imposed by the British Parliament – which ratifies them – rather than by the supranational bodies as such. Having voluntarily signed up to various international and European conventions, the UK must, of course, comply with them. However, as international conventions are usually fairly broad, they leave considerable scope for manoeuvring. Still, English legal insiders – just like some of the Norwegian ones – believe that their country is too conscientious in implementing directives, rules, regulations and standards emanating from supranational bodies. As a matter of fact, the UK "is very compliant", "applying [standards when] other European countries ignore" them:

> E-GO-9: 'maybe it's sort of like an obsession, that some European bureaucrat makes a regulation and the English follow it slavishly, and the rest of Europe ignores it'. E-PO-4: 'the issue that probably worries/irritates many of us in the UK is that . . . we work our socks off to be very compliant and ensure that we don't transgress, to see other countries who actually pay lip service to it . . . that's where our sense of unfair play comes in.'

As shown in Table 7.10, the percentage of statements made by English legal insiders to the effect that E-I-U standards *are imposed* upon their country, is larger than elsewhere. A read through of these statements show that such standards are perceived as imposed partly as the UK differs from the rest of Europe [the metric system is given as an example in this regard], and partly as it adheres to the common law rather than the civil law tradition:

> E-ER-2: 'we have developed differently [than] mainland Europe because we're an island. We have different ideas of what's right and wrong'. E-JU-

17: 'I don't think we should be governed by Europe.' E-LA-5: 'some of the legislation that comes in from Europe . . . is a bit nannyish, it's a bit bossy, and we don't really like it'.

A common British complaint against EU law is that it is too long and too complex. However, the EU is not always to blame. A review of the causes of legal complexity in England conducted in 2013 shows that 'gold-plating' – that is, government departments adding burdens to EU laws, which then impose extra costs and restrictions on business – is very much a 'British problem' (most EU member states have historically adopted a 'copy out' approach). The UK on an average provides 2.6 implementing documents per EU directive. In the case of Directive 2002/42/EC, however, the original English text consisted of 1,167 words but resulted in 27,000 words of implementing regulation in the UK! (Office of the Parliamentary Counsel, Cabinet Office 2013, p. 8): E-LA-6: "European law . . . is to do with principles. It is, however, some of the most confusing law I've ever come across. I do a lot of environmental law and the European Directives that come out, I consider myself to be a relatively intelligent person, and I can hardly understand them".

Europe's post-communist states also have a legacy of legal transfers: during the interwar period most post-communist states in Eastern Europe belonged to the civil law tradition and much of their legislation had been transposed from countries in Western Europe. During the communist period they initially received law from the Soviet Union but later mostly borrowed law from each other.[26] After the collapse of Communism they started borrowing extensively from Western Europe and the US[27] – both from civil law and common countries (Ajani 1996). Post-communist states have also been under pressure to accept legislation from various international organisations such as the IMF, the World Bank and the WTO (Anderson, Bernstein and Gray 2005, p. xv). Although some transfers have been voluntary (i.e. legal 'imports'), many have in reality been forced upon them (i.e. legal 'exports').

For post-communist states the largest source of legal transfers at present is the EU. Some analysts are critical of the manner in which

[26] For analyses of reception of Soviet law, see Péteri (1986–87) and Ajani (2005).

[27] International donor assistance in Eastern Europe at the earlier stages of transition was 'often targeted . . . toward the development of specific commercial laws and regulations' (Anderson, Bernstein and Gray 2005, p. 13). Donors have also been heavily involved in judicial reform in Eastern Europe (Krygier and Czarnota 1999; Přibáň 2010; Kühn 2004, referred to in Piana 2010, p. 202).

the EU has expanded eastwards. Olgiati (2010, p. 56), for instance, claims that 'only a veritable financial and legal colonisation of Eastern European countries made their entry into the EU possible and acceptable'. Rose (2009, p. 181) notes that 'on occasion, there was conflict between the EU's criteria and the particular practices of national governments, leading to complaints from applicants that the EU was seeking to impose conditions that infringed their national independence'.

Case (2009, p. 126), on the other hand, claims that 'joining the European Union ... was and is often celebrated by East-Central European politicians and commentators as a return to an important *national* project begun in the interwar and/or wartime periods that was aborted by the communist takeover'. For Poland the harmonisation of domestic and European law is not so problematic as 'both cultures are based on a minimum of legal positivism, namely on a similar conception of creating the law, legitimising the law, the sources of law, the structure of the legal profession and the model of legal education' (Zirk-Sadowski, cited in Peczenik 2003, p. 177). Statements made by the legal insiders largely support this view.

Polish legal insiders mostly talk about EU and UN standards (conventions). They claim that the EU and other supranational organisations represent a "Euro-Atlantic culture" or "a European culture" to which Poland has belonged "for ages". In their view, Poland is "a European society" – a "Judeo-Christian European society" – located "in the European cultural circle". When entering the EU, Poland thus joined "a group of civilised countries", promoting "the concept of the civil state" and the "rule of law". To most Polish legal insiders international standards (regulations) reflect "generally accepted norms" or "universal values" such as "equality" and "justice". In this sense they promote "ideas that are not foreign", that are in line with the Polish (legal) tradition, and that are "positive" for Poland and Polish citizens:

> P-GO-4: 'they don't impose any foreign ideas ... these are very universal regulations, very general, democratic'. P-PR-2: 'I don't think [they impose] ... the European Union puts an emphasis on equality and justice.' P-PR-12: 'we've been part of European culture for ages'. P-LA-8: '[they do not impose] ... we feel like citizens of Europe'. P-ER-18: 'I don't think that they impose. They make it possible to take advantage of foreign ideas.'

Poland joined the EU in May 2004, following a national referendum in June 2003. Legal insiders claim that EU directives and regulations can therefore "hardly [be viewed as] a matter of imposing". On the contrary, the EU has done "lots of good things for Poland", providing citizens with "more freedom and privileges". Poland has succeeded in preserving its independence within the EU and it takes part in creating EU law. Polish legal insiders view such law more as "recommendations" than as compulsory rules. EU members have some discretion in terms of what standards (or laws) to accept or reject. Poland, for its part, has retained its separate legal order:

> P-PO-16: 'I wouldn't use the word "impose", no. Our accession to the European Union was voluntary'. P-LA-15: 'we have moved from the so-called real socialism to an entirely different system so we have to absorb many things from the Western system and I am convinced that this is not detrimental to us but . . . helpful'. P-LA-3: 'the EU has brought a lot of good things to Poland'.

To the extent legal insiders in Poland speak about specific standards, they refer to "EU law", "basic human rights", matters pertaining to abortion, gay marriages and UN military missions (sending Polish soldiers to war zones). Several references are also made to the ECtHR's rulings on crucifixes in Italian schools and the case of Alicja Tysiąc, who requested an abortion for health reasons, had her request turned down, and subsequently suffered serious damage to her eyesight after giving birth.

By contrast, Polish legal insiders who believe that European, international and universal standards *are imposed* upon their country think such standards are at odds with Polish customs and Polish culture. Examples include EU regulations on the curving of the banana, EU restrictions on the preparation of traditional Polish dishes such as the *oscypek* (cheese), the EU approach to the Polish-German issue, and gay rights.

During the communist period Bulgaria was more closed-off than Poland. Added to this, the first years of its EU membership were not easy. Still, quite a few legal insiders voice their support for the "European idea". In their view, the aim of European standards is to create a "United Europe" – that is, a "uniform system across Europe" – thus ensuring that "European values" are observed by everyone. As Bulgaria "is part of Europe" and "the Bulgarian mentality is similar to the European one", this development should be applauded. Further, Bulgarian legal insiders believe that the Bulgarian people are positive to control extended by the EU as national politicians enjoy limited public trust.[28] Most Bulgarians

[28] Kaelbe (2009, p. 209) asserts that 'at least in recent years trust in and expectations of specific policies of the EU have been stronger than overall identification with the EU.

perceive them as individuals representing and promoting vested interest rather than the common good:

> B-GO-4: 'they do not impose foreign ideas . . . that is why we have agreed to become part of the European Union.' B-JU-18: 'we, as a society, are actually part of Europe. We observe European values of human life, the equality of women'. B-LA-3: 'ordinary people . . . rely on various international, external institutions, forces and institutions to control their own politicians that they have elected. . . values that are imposed by international treaties and the European Union legislation . . . are very close to Bulgarians and its old, I would call it, Renaissance, Enlightenment morality. It is a bourgeois morality'.

Bulgarian legal insiders speak favourably of the good ideas that underpin E-I-U standards. In their view, "progressive development sets [such] standards". These standards are based on "universal principles" and "common European values" that are "correct ideas" for Bulgaria. As such, they represent "compromises for the common good". As European norms are "sufficiently general" they are "beneficial for Bulgaria", "consistent" with the Bulgarian reality and "not contrary to the development" of the country:

> B-PR-7: 'I would not say [that they are] foreign. Rather they are universal ideas.' B-GO-1: 'it could not be perceived as intrusive. There are so-called "European values", which we approve [of, and] we should observe them.' B-JU-22: 'the idea of being a part of this Union is to have common values on a European scale. I am certainly not a Euro-sceptic.' B-LA-17: 'in the end we are Europeans and the norms of the European Union cannot be alien to us.' B-JU-16: 'I certainly don't think the Bulgarian mentality differs substantially from the European [one]'. B-LA-17: 'the European Union is the best thing that could happen in Europe . . . now we are really one state that can set a very serious policy anywhere in the world.'

Legal insiders believe the EU is "progressive" and good for their country as Bulgaria "must adapt to a new life-style". However, they demonstrate that joining the EU has not been easy for Bulgaria: European norms are "reasonable", but "hard". Other EU members are "more experienced"

These specific policies are above all foreign policy, defence policy, environmental policy, and the fight against organised crime and terrorism; they have been much weaker on questions of education, health, housing and pensions. According to Eurobarometer polls, and with unavoidable variations among states, in these policy fields Europeans trust the EU more than they do their national governments'. Our findings lend some support to this assertion.

and "ahead of Bulgaria" and EU law is mostly "written for [more developed] societies". Adjusting to Europe "is [therefore a] difficult, but [still a] true road" for Bulgaria. The country "could learn" from more experienced EU member states by "extracting what is relevant" and thus "taking the best" from them:

> B-GO-13: 'the ideas are correct and a good understanding and awareness will be beneficial for Bulgaria.' B-ER-6: 'I don't think foreign ideas are being imposed. It's another question that some of the standards are not readily applicable in our society because of the specific features of our nation and the place we inhabit ... the problem is rather that we do not understand what they are telling us.' B-LA-4: 'they don't impose them. They try to present them to us ... we should ... get converged with what is good for us'.

As an EU member state Bulgaria is able to influence all decisions made by the Union – and it is not prevented from having its own, unique laws. In the view of legal insiders European acts are "minimum standards". One judge, however, cautions that Bulgaria's ability to influence European decision-making is limited. The country is simply "too small" to significantly influence decision-making in the EU:

> B-ER-12: 'the European idea ... shared values, the common law, it must really be for everyone, but it does not prevent each EU member state from having its own, unique laws'. B-PO-23: 'no matter how difficult it could be for us, we are Europeans and must behave as such. It could be difficult, it could be hard, but that is the only true road for Bulgaria.' B-JU-6: 'Bulgaria, as one of the smaller countries [in the EU] cannot actively influence the decision-making since it cannot achieve a majority of the votes and impose its own decision'.

Finally, Bulgarian legal insiders speak about specific standards that Bulgaria receives from the outside – and primarily from the EU (including the *acquis communautaire*) and the UN, but also to some extent from the ECtHR.

Those Bulgarian legal insiders who believe that European, international and universal standards are *imposed* upon their country claim that this is nothing new. Then historically Bulgaria has been imposed upon by others. They note that foreign standards are not always compatible with local moral values and/or culture – and thus not with the Bulgarian way of life. In their view, foreign pressure on Bulgaria is on the increase, but efforts should be made to reduce it.

Ukraine is the country included in our study that is located furthest away from, and has the "loosest" ties with, Brussels (i.e. the periphery).

Culturally, it is divided between the Russia-leaning East, South, and the Crimea, and the Europe-leaning West and Kiev. Opinion polls have for several years consistently shown that Ukrainians favour EU membership (see, for instance, White, Korosteleva and McAllister 2008, p. 219) but that they do not wish to join the North Atlantic Treaty Organisation (NATO).[29]

EU membership would allow Ukraine to "catch up" with the affluent West (Åslund 2013). The late 2013 and early 2014 demonstrations in Kiev and other parts of Ukraine in support of signing the Association Agreement with the EU were supported not only by the democratic-minded population in Kiev and Western Ukraine, but also by young people from the Eastern parts of the country. The latter's support for the association agreement is explained by their wish for a better future – that is, the possibility to travel to Europe for studies or work. Åslund (ibid.) believes that the benefits of an association agreement between the EU and Ukraine outweigh those of membership in the Russian Customs Union.

Just like legal insiders elsewhere in Europe, Ukrainian legal insiders mostly hold the view that E-I-U standards are *not imposed* upon their country. Rather, they are "universal", "human" values that are "close to the local mentality" and thus "valuable". Legal insiders in Ukraine – just like those in Poland and Bulgaria – therefore view foreign legal transfers as "positive influence", which is particularly useful for "developing civil society" in their country:

> U-ER-20: 'they do not impose . . . human values are identical everywhere.' U-GO-5: 'as a rule, the standards are universal and very useful.' U-JU-26: 'international standards are not foreign to the ordinary people of Ukraine because . . . Ukraine is [located] in the centre of Europe.'

More specifically, Ukrainian legal insiders refer to E-I-U standards as "common European ideas". As Ukraine is "close to the EU mentality-wise" it should be able to "adapt to European norms". The country must "adjust" to the EU by "meeting [its] demands". The EU member states

[29] Interfax-Ukraine, 'Poll: Ukrainians supporting NATO membership in minority', *Kyiv-Post,* 14 May 2014, www.kyivpost.com/content/ukraine/ukrainians-supporting-nato-membership-in-minority-poll-347807.html accessed on 24 August 2014. Even after the Russian annexation of the Crimea and armed clashes in eastern Ukraine, 36.7 per cent would vote yes and 41.6 per cent would vote no if a referendum were held on NATO membership in the very near future.

are "ahead of Ukraine" and adjusting to European standards is "necessary to reach the EU level" (of development):

> U-GO-17: 'every normal person will accept the ideas that date back thousands of years in Europe'. U-GO-21: 'Ukraine is not too [different] ... in its mentality, compared to the countries of the European Union'. U-GO-19: 'Ukraine chose the path of Ukrainian integration ... we have to meet the demands that are made [by] ... the EU. We cannot talk ... about imposing foreign ideas'. U-LA-29: 'I don't think they impose anything foreign upon us ... let's say that we are at the [bottom] end of civilisation and they [i.e. the EU member states] are far ahead'. U-GO-25: 'nobody imposes anything upon us. We were closed to the whole world for a very long time and such organisations as the UN and the EU, help Ukraine feel like a European state'.

As for the UN, a Ukrainian lawyer notes that Ukraine is "one of [its] constituent states". Consequently, "nobody forces Ukraine to ratify [its] conventions". Rather these are voluntarily "accepted". UN standards, for their part, are "flexible" and generally "intergovernmental agreements" tend to be "general" and "delegative". As such they do not contradict Ukrainian legislation. In the view of Ukrainian legal insiders, international cooperation gives "positive results":

> U-LA-17: 'Ukraine is a member of the UN and one of its constituents ... we've undertaken obligations to comply with certain standards regarding some rights and freedoms ... this is our decision'. U-LA-22: 'these are general standards such as freedom of religion ... freedom of opinion ... I don't think they are foreign to any state.' U-PR-20: 'I wouldn't say that they impose ideas which are foreign to us. If we talk about ratification of different agreements, contracts and international legislation, Ukraine is far ahead of all republics of the Former Soviet Union. It is a problem that nothing changes after they have been signed. We ratify them and don't apply them here in Ukraine.'

Ukrainian legal insiders mostly refer to the EU and the UN in their statements. But some mentions are also made of the ECtHR and NATO. One judge states that he is "not always satisfied" with ECtHR rulings: U-JU-20: "the principles of the European Court of Human Rights ... are compulsory for us, [but] I couldn't find any essential contradictions with our legislation".

Ukrainian legal insiders who believe that European, international and universal standards are *imposed* upon their country claim that there is an element of coercion involved in efforts to have Ukraine join various supranational bodies. In their view, many of the standards of the supranational organisations are foreign or inappropriate for Ukraine.

European legal integration? The legal insiders' perspective

European integration primarily takes place by means of legal harmonisation: directives and rules passed in Brussels are compulsory for EU member states, EEA states and in reality also for countries holding best partner status within the ENP.[30]

A number of studies have investigated formal compliance with specific EU directives (Falkner and Treib 2008; Falkner et al. 2004; Falkner et al. 2005a; Falkner et al. 2005b; Thomson et al. 2007). Less is known about the manner in which judges across Europe apply EU law in their everyday work. Yet, the 'process of legal integration within the Union and further development of its legal order very much depends on judges' willingness to cooperate and contribute to this supranational order' (Jaremba 2013, p. 197).[31]

Little is also known about the attitudes of the legal insiders (effectively those responsible for implementing, applying and enforcing such directives) and the legal outsiders (those affected by the directives) with regard to legal harmonization at a more general level. Yet their attitudes matter as it is very much up to them whether European (legal) integration is likely to succeed.

If European citizens prefer to have different rather than similar legislation they may be less keen to implement and/or abide by legal transfers. Even though – as is the case in Norway – it is not always clear what does, and what does not, constitute legal transfers as it is not always indicated in the legislation (NOU 2012, p. 122). Attitudes towards law and the role of law are also likely to affect compliance with EU directives and thus also the eventual outcome of European legal integration. If legal insiders have a strong sense that laws should be abided by no matter what, their sense of duty may override their

[30] The ENP was launched by the EU in 2003 for North African countries, Middle Eastern countries, and the Western CIS countries and the intention was to 'standardize the EU approach to friendly neighbours, offering them more market access and interaction'. Negotiations between Ukraine and the EU on a deep and comprehensive free trade area commenced in 2008 and were concluded in 2011. The agreement was initialled but not signed in July 2012 (Åslund 2013, pp. 3–4). For details, see also http://eeas.europa.eu/enp/index_en.htm

[31] National judges of lower courts in Poland, Germany and the Netherlands, for instance, lack proper knowledge of institutional, procedural or material EU law (ibid., p. 199) and such law has no real bearing on their daily practice (ibid., p. 198). These factors 'put into question the operationalization of the most basic principles of EU law such as direct effect, harmonious interpretation or *ex officio* application of EU law' (ibid., p. 202).

Table 7.11 *Whether [this country] should have broadly the same laws and law-enforcement as the rest of Europe: the legal insiders' perspective*

	Norway (%)	England (%)	Poland (%)	Bulgaria (%)	Ukraine (%)
Should [this country] have broadly the same laws and law enforcement as the rest of Europe or should it have different laws and law enforcement that better suit our country and people?					
Same	29	27	53	27	19
Different	21	73	19	30	36
Mix	50	1	28	44	44

Note: Entries are based on the percentages of relevant 'text units' – the total number of answers to a given question; so entries sum up to approximately 100 per cent (decimals are rounded up or down to the nearest whole number).

personal dislike of European legal integration. The UK, for instance, is highly Euro-sceptic, yet it is one of the most conscientious implementers of EU directives.[32]

Conversely, in post-communist states citizens' attitudes towards laws and legal institutions are often referred to as *nihilist.* Yet as these countries have vested interests in improving their economic and political performance, EU membership is viewed as a means to this end. Practical considerations of usefulness might therefore override general disregard for law and legal institutions and facilitate compliance.

Table 7.11 shows that one-half of the legal insiders in Norway and close to half of the respondents in Bulgaria and Ukraine prefer a combination of national and supranational law. By contrast, English legal insiders have a strong preference for retaining national law. A majority of the Poles would like to have broadly the same laws and law enforcement as the rest of Europe.

[32] The UK and especially Denmark have implemented EU directives most conscientiously (Lampinen and Uusikylä 1998, p. 236).

As seen earlier, resistance to EU membership is more pronounced in Norway than in the UK. Yet Norway is less sceptical of legal receptions from the EU and other supranational bodies than the UK. Former Chairman of the Norwegian Supreme Court, Carsten Smith (2012, p. 96), is of the opinion that national courts 'should use their power to the fullest to implement the obligations deriving from international law ... one of the functions of the national courts is to bring new legal ideas from foreign soil into national case law'. He notes that 'Norway may paradoxically be the Nordic country that most easily adapts to the new European law requirements' (ibid., p. 91). However, national courts also have an obligation to 'weigh the advantages of legal unification against the need to protect the legal basis for national and local culture' (ibid., p. 96).

As for England, it is a common law country, whereas the majority of the EU member states belong to the civil law tradition. Implementing EU directives and EU regulations therefore poses specific challenges for this country.[33] First, in common law states *parliamentary sovereignty* is considered to be sacred. Such sovereignty 'makes Parliament the supreme legal authority in the UK, which can create or end any law. Generally, the courts cannot overrule its legislation and no Parliament can pass laws that future Parliaments cannot change. Parliamentary sovereignty is the most important part of the UK constitution'.[34]

Second, the UK is located on the edge of Western Europe. Brits (in this context: the English) define themselves as different from people in Continental Europe and they are proud of their differences. The fact that the EU is located in Brussels and that it may pass directives that require amendments to legislation passed by the British Parliament is therefore presumably more difficult to stomach for Brits than for people in other parts of Europe.

These two factors help explain the English legal insiders' reluctance to having the same laws and law enforcement as the rest of Europe.

Polish legal insiders endorse European integration for both normative and practical reasons. First, they see Poland as a country belonging to the Western rather than the Eastern cultural sphere. Second, and equally important, Poles are keen to improve their country's socioeconomic conditions. Third, Poland is one of the largest net-exporters of labour

[33] European Commission 2004.

[34] 'Parliamentary sovereignty', www.parliament.uk/about/how/sovereignty/ accessed on 2 April 2014.

within the EU.[35] Same-type laws and law enforcement across Europe would thus make life a lot easier for Poles living abroad.

Norwegian legal insiders note that their country is "not an island" existing in splendid isolation from other countries. It is "a Western society" and as such, part of "international society". Norway should therefore not "isolate" itself. The ever increasingly "globalised world" requires "common legislation" and Norwegian law should therefore be "internationalised": Norway "depends on Europe and the world" and it is "not so special" that it requires its own type of laws and law enforcement.

Europe should have a "common notion of law", "common [legal] norms and basic principles [of law]", and a "common legal framework". In the view of some [legal insiders] this would "not be dangerous" but rather be "an advantage". Norway should "harmonise [its] national legislation" with that of other European countries:

> N-ER-20: 'when we live in an international world, or a global world . . . our laws and rules should to a great extent be aligned with those of other countries'. N-JU-19: 'it is good to have . . . similar rules, then . . . one is more mobile nowadays than . . . one used to be 100 ago'.

Most Norwegian legal insiders think it will be useful to have common European legislation in areas where countries "depend on international collaboration". The European Charter of Social Rights (ECSR), for instance, is considered positive in that it sets minimum standards for all of Europe. "Universal models", "common foundations", "minimum thresholds" and "standardisation" are viewed as helpful tools in this regard.

Rather unexpectedly, many Norwegian legal insiders view "Federal Europe" as desirable. However, one prosecutor cautions against "uncritically applying European law" whereas another believes that "European countries are too different" for legal integration to be 100 per cent effective. The implementation of European law should therefore have a "national application" – that is, "be adjusted to Norwegian law, Norwegian priorities and understanding of law".

Norwegian legal insiders have different views as to how extensive European legal integration should be. Some prefer common legislation in "most areas". Others believe that identical legislation should pertain to

[35] According to the Polish Central Statistics Office some 2.1 million Poles are living abroad, mostly in Europe. 'Poland's emigration headache', *The Economist*, 5 November 2013, www.economist.com/blogs/easternapproaches/2013/11/poland-and-eu accessed on 25 January 2014.

"some areas" of law only. In the view of the latter "some nuances between different countries should be allowed" and Norway should retain its most prominent national features by means of *subsidiarity*:

> N-ER-7: 'it is an advantage if we handle different issues more or less in the same manner – for instance the drugs trade, terrorism, everything that has to do with cross-country crime'. N-JU-21: 'in most areas of law I believe that we to a great extent could have rules at the basis that are fairly common to Europe. But there is the democratic side to it; after all we are located on the outskirts of Europe and we probably have some views about a couple of things which are "off" and I think we should still be allowed to have these'. N-ER-13: 'we should become a member of the EU and have the same ... legislation as the rest of Europe, but only [in the areas] where it is necessary ... the principle of subsidiarity should still apply, in areas where harmonisation is not necessary each country should still be able to make its own laws and rules.'

As a general principle laws and rules must "fit local conditions" and be "adjusted ... to the people" living there. Being located at "the edge of Europe", Norway should retain some "norm-based rules" and some country-specific legislation. Then each country has its own "legal cultures", "national traditions and legislation". Legal insiders note that Norway has a "different philosophy" than other countries in Europe when it comes to caring for criminals. It also has generally "milder sentencing" and higher "fines" for criminal offenses:

> N-JU-10: 'it is obviously a great advantage that the rules, both for trade and human behaviour do not fundamentally differ ... this being said ... it is not necessarily certain that what is correct and sensible for the Netherlands suits Volda or Kautokeino [small urban areas in the North West and North of Norway, respectively] well'.

In the view of some legal insiders, Norwegian law is in some areas "more advanced" than EU law. The "Norwegian standards" should therefore be retained as should national legal peculiarities such as the "Norwegian welfare model",[36] the law-based right of the oldest child in the family to take over the family farm (*odelsloven*), and others. Norway should also retain specific national features of "criminal law".[37] Added to this, it

[36] Laws that should be preserved included "drugs legislation", "environmental law", "immigration law", laws on "pensions" and "children". "family law", legislation providing Norwegians with the right to ramble, "inheritance law", legislation on "predators", legislation on the "internet" legislation, the sex (industry) ban.

[37] These include "environmental crime" and "organised crime"; "legislation on "care for criminals".

should administer its own "natural and environmental resources" ("agriculture", "fishery", the High North, and the Antarctic). In other words, "local adjustments" should be made during the implementation of common European law in Norway so as to allow the country to "preserve [its] geographical and cultural traditions":

> N-LA-7: 'the legislation should reflect the common notion of law ... it should be in line with your and my perception of what is right and wrong ... I think it is important that national legislation be retained.' N-JU-5: 'as long as Norway is not a member of the EU and only has a kind of associated membership [with the EU] through the EEA Agreement, I do not feel that ... it would be appropriate for Norway to opt for complete unification with the rest of Europe'. N-ER-19: 'we have [hydro] power and water, fish and oil, and of course we have a big responsibility for [them] ... we may need separate legislation'. N-PO-23: 'rules for the fish industry are not exactly relevant for a country like Andorra'. N-GO-14: 'in some areas ... it is sensible to have Norwegian laws that are similar to the laws in other countries ... for instance, regulations regarding discrimination ... but as far as our welfare system ... and our health system [are concerned] ... legislation [should] ... reflect our society ... it would be totally wrong ... to create a ... universal European law system in this area'.

Legal insiders in England are overwhelmingly in favour of England having different legislation from the rest of Europe. They note that its legal system "reflects [British] values". It is an "old [legal] system" representing "centuries of law" as well as a "different legal philosophy" from that of Continental Europe. The UK and Europe have "a fundamentally different approach to law" and they have "different legal systems". For these reasons "uniformity is not the answer" and there is "no advantage in a pan-European legal system". One should therefore "preserve the difference" between countries:

> E-JU-21: 'we're not based on Roman law, we're based on English common law, and so inevitably we have a very different legal system to the ones that apply on the Continent and Scotland'. E-LA-1: 'we should have laws that suit our own country ... because we have a fundamentally different legal philosophy underpinning how our legal system works for historical reasons. We're a common law system'. E-LA-5: 'we are totally different to European culture. We have our Rule of Law, our Constitution's developed over many centuries and I think our enforcement of law must be based on our custom and tradition.'

Added to this, the UK is an "island" with its own "peculiarities", "history", "culture", "traditions", and "customs". "The concept of the national state" should be respected and "some laws [should be] specific to the nation".

Consequently, the UK should have its "own laws", "mirroring [its] social structures and values". Laws should be "based on how people do things" as the English "know [their own] tradition and culture better than the EU and the ECtHR". Some English legal insiders perceive Europe as "totally different" from the UK. They even claim that "England is not a European country" and that the English "want to be different". It is therefore impossible to "avoid different laws". Civil disputes, for instance, "simply can't be harmonised":

> E-ER-13: 'we're an island . . . so we have a lot about the water that surrounds us that a landlocked country like France wouldn't have. It's right that we have different rules that apply to our differences and that apply to the views of the majority of the people.' E-ER-2: 'we probably know our country and our conditions and our views better than people who are a long way away in Strasbourg or Brussels. Therefore we should be making our own laws'. E-PR-22: 'our law has a very long history, it has been adapted over the years to the customs, tradition, history and the national character . . . there are features of Anglo-Saxon culture that are best dealt with by the laws that this country has developed.' E-JU-18: 'our laws should be framed to suit our own people and to mirror our own social structures and our own social values and I don't think that we should be crammed into a European box.'

Other legal insiders believe that the English legal system is not only the "best for England" but also "better than many others". Law-abidingness is a key feature of the English legal culture. One government official claims that although "England is law-abiding, other [European states] are not". And this is detrimental for England. Some legal insiders object to what they perceive as the "uniformity" imposed by Europe. In their view the EU is "an economic, not a culturally driven union":

> E-GO-18: '[the English legal system] is probably better than a lot of legal systems in the rest of Europe.' E-GO-21: 'I'm English, and I live here, and I abide by the rules of England. Not of Europe . . . we [i.e. the English] stick to the rules, and we don't break them, or very seldom do . . . whereas other nations, quite frankly, they will bend them slightly. Then we get very upset when we stick to them, and they don't, but that's our way of life.' E-GO-19: 'the cultural things have got to be tailor made for the various countries because we all have a different culture.' E-JU-9: 'I don't see any reason why we need a universal European law'.

Those legal insiders who are *in favour* common European legislation, on the other hand, are either positive to the European project as such or they believe that having similar laws and law enforcement across Europe would be an advantage for business and travel.

Legal insiders in Poland mostly favour *more* European legal integration. They stress that Poland "is not a solitary island" within Europe. It shares the "same Latin culture" as other European countries and favours "unified legal systems" and "regulation[s]" within the EU. For practical purposes the EU should have a "single legal system" and "identical application of law". A common European legislation would be "more convenient" for all. Being a "part of the EU", Poland shares "the same objectives" as other member states. As "EU citizens" Poles should have the "same rights and obligations" as other Europeans. Poland stands to gain from further legal harmonisation (unification) as its own law is "faulty and bureaucratised":

> P-ER-6: 'we belong to a united Europe'. P-ER-7: 'we've always been a part of the European community, even if it didn't cross our minds that we were such a part in the Middle Ages.' P-LA-17: 'Poland should have exactly the same laws as any other European state, because there is no difference between France, Poland, Greece and Belarus'. P-GO-2: 'we are citizens of the European Union and should have the same rights, as well as obligations, as other EU citizens, regardless of obvious cultural differences.' P-JU-15: 'yes . . . because it [i.e. EU law] is good and reliable while ours is faulty and too bureaucratised'.

Polish legal insiders who *object* to laws and law enforcement becoming more similar across Europe primarily do so for nationalistic reasons. Euro-sceptic Polish legal insiders stress that the EU "is a commonwealth of independent states, not a union". As a sovereign country Poland has the right to pass its own laws. What is more, its culture, traditions and values must be preserved. Law should therefore reflect Polish history, local customs and norms as this would enhance people's respect for Polish law.

Bulgarian legal insiders are slightly more inclined to prefer a *mix* of national and European law rather than opting for the one or the other. They hold the view that the EU should provide the legal framework and key legislation, and Bulgaria should provide the rest.

Legal insiders acknowledge that the EU is moving in the direction of legal unification – through the Accession Treaty, the EU framework and common legislation. In their view, "the common European family" currently in the making should have "synchronised law". However, they note that total – 100 per cent – reception of EU law is unrealistic. National laws across Europe can "never be the same", even though it is possible to ensure that they do not directly "contradict" each other.

As for domestic law it must take account of – and also protect – Bulgarian society, including its "history", "national traditions", "morals and beliefs", "language, culture and national values", and other issues of "local significance". One government official equals "preserving national legislation" with "preserving [Bulgarian] identity":

> B-GO-2: 'a balance should be found ... we must apply the laws of the [European] Community because we wanted to be a member of that community and we are a member state now ... national, local legislation should remain autonomous and in no way should it be absolutely and completely ... carbon copies of the Community law.' B-PO-24: 'not all the laws can be introduced literally as they exist in other European states because they will not be adequate to our reality.'

Legal insiders in Bulgaria do not perceive combining compliance with EU law and preservation of Bulgarian national legislation as a problem, given that EU regulations and directives are "flexible". Although there are "common standards" and "some uniformity" in the EU, there are also "many issues that are not regulated by common specifics". Consequently, all EU member states have "autonomous national legislation":

> B-LA-18: 'the things put on paper are just 30 per cent of the entire picture, the remaining 70 per cent are a series of things such as institutional arrangements, knowledge, public attitudes ... it is simply impossible to take the German legislation and introduce it in Bulgaria ... 100 per cent reception of foreign experience is impossible; it is practical nonsense'. B-PR-20: 'I don't think there are two states with the same system of justice – it is always a reflection of the society, the history of the people, its value system, its way of life, culture and all those circumstances that differentiate it from the other ethnic communities. Therefore it is virtually impossible, but it will be good to borrow the best practices.' B-JU-18: 'Europe is not a homogenous country, it is not a state ... the right approach here is to interpret the main European laws and legislation [that] will serve our common life, but to apply [them] in a manner that is consistent with our mentality, our geography, our understanding of fast and slow.'

Some Bulgarian judges stress that their country has a legal commitment towards international organizations to implement international treaties and such treaties are "part of international law". Globalization facilitates "a uniform legal practice". However, even Bulgarian international legal obligations must be consistent with the country's "stage of development"; they must take "national specifics into consideration" and be applied "consistently with the national mentality": B-JU-1: "international treaties signed by our country become part of our national law and they rank with the Constitution". B-PO-5: "more than 90 per cent of our legislation is harmonised with the European legislation".

The EU is seeking cultural and legal convergence through its third pillar (the Lisbon Treaty). Consequently, EU member states should have the same law and the same standards. Some Bulgarian legal insiders are positive to the European project as such – and thus also to a set of common European values. The EU is developing its own, common norms and a unified normative basis. As EU legislation is "more efficient", it is "good" for Bulgaria to borrow "best practices" from other EU member states.

Bulgarian legal insiders who *object* to Bulgaria having the *same* laws as other EU member states predominantly state that Bulgarian law must reflect national culture, tradition, mentality, habits and way of life. Some of them emphasise the need to preserve national peculiarities. Others simply do not believe that different countries can have identical legislation given that law essentially reflects society.

Legal insiders in Ukraine predominantly believe that their country should have either *different* laws or a mix of its own and common European law.

Those who prefer a mix of common European legislation and Ukrainian national legislation give several reasons for their view. First, as Ukraine wishes to join the EU it will simply have to "adopt EU standards". Second, adopting some European legislation would be beneficial for Ukraine. Ukrainians should take the "best" from Europe; they should "adopt" and "apply" European experiences since these are "positive" and "better" than national law. Ukrainian legal insiders believe that it would be better for Ukraine to have "the same general platform as [the rest of] Europe" and "maybe [also] the same law enforcement" in areas such as taxation, property, trade, customs and air traffic:

> U-GO-12: 'if we aspire to the European Union . . . we need to be closer to Europe. At the same time, we don't need to [lose sight of] our national interests'. U-PR-21: 'we must take all positive features from Europe but we shouldn't copy everything . . . every country should have its priorities and views.' U-JU-19: 'we must have some common laws, because it is more suitable . . . on some questions of taxation . . . private property, it is better to have unified legislation for Europe. On some issues of criminal law it is better to have [one's] own [law]. It is also better to have [separate] labour law.'

Several legal insiders believe that Ukrainian society is "not [yet] ready" for a mix of Ukrainian and European legislation in "all areas". It is particularly important for Ukraine to retain some of its legislation in order to preserve national "history", "culture", "traditions", "mentality", "social norms", and "peculiarities". One should "proceed from national interests" when dealing with legal transfers. Ukraine's "geopolitical situation", current "economic situation", and "economic possibilities" should be the starting point for the reception of foreign law. Ukraine should first and foremost follow "its own way of development", properly addressing its "own needs and specifics". Some Ukrainian legal insiders therefore emphasise the value of national legislation which has developed from Ukraine's "historical traditions" and which "reflects [national] mentality and traditions":

> U-ER-24: 'we must be oriented towards European standards, but the majority of the laws must be Ukrainian . . . based on our mentality.' U-LA-20: 'adopting European standards and laws is good. But . . . Ukraine will not adopt a permissive attitude towards sexual minorities'. U-GO-11: 'in principle, it is necessary to use the world experience . . . but . . . it is necessary to proceed from national interests and look at the economic situation in our country'.

Those legal insiders who are in favour of Ukraine having *separate* legislation from that of the rest of Europe, on the other hand, justify this by highlighting the differences between Ukraine and Europe. The history of Ukraine – including its Soviet past – works against its legal integration with the EU. Besides, as an independent country, Ukraine should have its own national laws. EU and US law are considered inappropriate for Ukraine, given differences in "life-style", "economic development" and "socioeconomic conditions". Legal insiders conclude that Ukraine is simply not "mature enough" for European laws:

> U-LA-26: 'it is probably impossible to put a cart in front of a horse . . . it is necessary to take into account the mentality of our people and our notion of laws'. U-JU-25: 'we cannot be unified [law-wise] . . . the knowledge of laws [in Ukraine] is much lower than in other European countries. We don't have respect for law[s] . . . one law is drafted, another one is changed . . . [in Ukraine] statesmen don't obey laws. What can [then] be said about the poor people? When writing laws the mentality of people, their traditions, customs and history have to be taken into account.'

Looking to the future

Table 7.11 shows that legal insiders in Norway, Bulgaria and Ukraine prefer *combining* national and European legislation rather than selecting one at the expense of the other. However, when asked whether they would be pleased or displeased if national laws became much more similar across the whole of Europe, a majority of the statements made by the Bulgarian, Polish, Ukrainian legal insiders, and close to half of the statements made by the Norwegians show that they are in favour of

Table 7.12 *Whether national laws becoming much more similar across the whole of Europe: the legal insiders' perspective*

	Norway (%)	England (%)	Poland (%)	Bulgaria (%)	Ukraine (%)
Would you be pleased or displeased if national laws became much more similar across the whole of Europe?					
Pleased	45	32	57	76	68
Displeased	22	41	20	13	14
Mix	33	27	22	11	17

Note: Entries are based on the percentages of relevant 'text units' – the total number of answers to a given question; so entries sum up to approximately 100 per cent (decimals are rounded up or down to the nearest whole number).

integration. By contrast, legal insiders in England would be more displeased than pleased about European legal integration (Table 7.12).

Findings from Tables 7.11 and 7.12 do not necessarily suggest that legal insiders have contradictory views on the issue of European legal integration. Rather, they would ideally prefer legislation to be much more similar across Europe (Table 7.12). But for various reasons they do not think this is possible at present.

Norwegian legal insiders who favour European legal convergence primarily do so for pragmatic, rather than ideological reasons.

Those few insiders who favour legal integration for ideological reasons view the EU as "a peace project". In their opinion European integration is "good for Europe" and thus "very important" in its own right. European legal convergence is "a natural process". Even though Norway is not formally an EU member, the "common European Constitution" and European "collaboration [based] on common values" is viewed as positive also for Norwegians.

Other legal insiders note that European countries are becoming "more and more similar". Thus they are faced with "common challenges", for which "collaboration is required". As European countries are "more extroverted now" than they were in the past, legal integration will be "inevitable". European countries should therefore "cultivate what they have in common".

There would be several practical *advantages* of European legal integration: common legislation would not only make it "easier" for European citizens to "interact" and "collaborate", but it would also make life "easier for courts". This, in turn, would "enhance efficiency" and be "mostly beneficial" for Norwegian citizens. European legal convergence would also be beneficial for EU migrants and tourists: Europe has a "more mobile population" at present than it had in the past. Free movement of "people" and "labour" has "brought Europe closer". Having the same laws across Europe would be "more practical" and, more importantly, it would facilitate trade. However, achieving legal convergence in Europe would be "a slow" process:

> N-GO-17: 'there is a gradual adjustment to a [common] European legislation . . . that is also part of the internationalisation, for instance in regard to culture. And in regard to . . . the EU as a peace project'. N-PR-17: 'as long as [the laws] would be based on the same values . . . it would be a great advantage.' N-ER-2: 'it would be easier with a common set of rules'. N-PO-25: 'it is a natural process, in a way it is inevitable'. N-GO-1: 'it is . . . positive for the individual [citizen].' N-LA-6: 'the world is becoming more international, we travel around, we have more trade and interaction with each other . . . the more similar rules we get, the easier it will be to understand . . . do trade with each other'.

Those Norwegian legal insiders who *oppose* European legal convergence give several reasons for this: some voice their dissatisfaction with the European project as such; some believe that legal integration is simply not possible, whereas yet others stress the cultural, traditional, historical and geographical differences between Norway and the EU. A fairly large number of legal insiders express a preference for Norwegian law – which they find to be of high quality – rather than for European law.

English legal insiders are not positive to national legislation becoming more similar across Europe. Some of them object to the UK having the same laws as other European countries on the grounds that their country is a sovereign state that should have its own laws. In the opinion of one prosecutor, "it is the right of the nation to determine law". Another believes that "it is important to stay independent". British law is "historical law" and it must reflect national culture, traditions and local circumstances. The British legal system is right for the Brits. Besides, and more importantly, it is reasonably well-functioning – that is, fast and effective:

> E-GO-20: 'I'm not convinced they should or need to be [similar]. I think we have developed and built our legal system because it suits us and . . .

> because it is right for our country'. E-PR-7: 'the important thing is that each and every nation has the right to determine the laws under which its citizens will live'.

Some legal insiders object to legislation in Europe being passed "from the centre" (i.e. from Brussels). Laws common to several European countries are perceived as too bland, alien or foreign. The unification of the metric systems in Europe, for instance, angered many in England. In the view of some legal insiders European legal harmonisation would only be important for international trade. But one legal insider claims that if laws become more similar, citizens from other countries may be tempted to take advantage of the British system – notably by signing up for general social benefits:

> E-LA-14: 'I'd be displeased. Let's put it this way: if they have ours that is great. If we have to have theirs, I'm not so sure.' E-PR-13: 'they're more ... socialist on the Continent'. E-ER-13: 'I'd be displeased ... the law that said that people in the European Union can have access to each other's benefits after three months ... that's unfair.'

English legal insiders who are in favour of *similar laws across Europe* in part argue that this would be desirable given that European countries are fairly similar already. Moreover, Europe is populated with "the same sort of people" and the "same [types of] enterprise[s]" that have "the same problems". Europeans also have the "same concerns, regarding crime". Identical legislation would create a more level playing field for all. Although some respondents would like to see British law accepted by others, other respondents believe that the UK could benefit from the law of other countries: identical application and enforcement of the law would make life easier for everybody. Still, some English legal insiders caution that aligning the legislation of Europe's countries will either take a very long time or simply not occur. In the view a common European legislation is a "utopia":

> E-JU-16: 'our system is very insular and it's not ... very efficient ... we can learn things from Continental countries'. E-PO-1: 'I'd prefer if there was a more level playing field with regard to the law'. E-PO-16: 'from the point of view of enforcement, it would make life easier.' E-PO-23: 'it would be a good idea. I think ironing out the kinks would take hundreds of years ... I don't think it would happen.'

Most statements made by Polish legal insiders in favour of more similar laws across Europe either refer to *the type of laws* that ought to be similar and the benefits to be gained in this regard – or on *the manner* in which similar legislation would make life easier for individual citizens and businesses. Several respondents justify their position by referring to the large number of Poles living abroad or visiting other European countries as tourists.

European legal integration would have several advantages: it would promote "universal principles" as there would be "one legal system for all". Legal systems would thus become "standardised", effectively facilitating "[greater] European integration". EU member states would have "similar regulations" or identical laws for drunk-driving, speeding and environmental protection, which, in turn, would make people "more law-abiding":

> P-JU-1: 'after World War I our law was modelled on the legislation systems of other countries, even after the Second World War the Napoleonic Code was in force; most of the laws in between the two wars were based either on German law or its concept, construct, or the Austrian legal system, Russian law was unlikely to be an option . . . no one was outraged by this transfer, or should I say adoption of patterns, as it wasn't a mechanical transcription of those countries' regulations . . . the adoption of the patterns was rather welcomed'. P-PR-13: 'we, [i.e. the European Union] are heading towards a unified legal system, which will reflect one model. If we want to be a European community, both the law and the currency need to be common.'

Legal insiders argue that in the field of criminal law European countries would have "the same definitions of crime", the consequences would be the same for the same types of crime and interpretation of law would be clearer as there would be one common interpretation of laws. Court rulings would be similar across Europe and citizens would receive the same punishment for wrongdoing. Legal integration would thus facilitate "the work of the police", "the combating of crime" and consequently "protect society". Due to "greater simplicity" it would become easier "to prosecute criminals" and to "pass judgements in court". Finally, court cases would be "faster" and facilitate "more effective settlement of disputes". It would become easier "to use foreign institutions", to "interpret the law" and "apply the law and regulations" both in Poland and in other countries:

> P-GO-2: if . . . such crimes as theft, murder, robbery were defined and perceived in the same way in all European countries, it would be really good . . . I would be totally in favour.' P-JU-13: 'probably I would be satisfied . . . mainly because it would be easier for me to adjudicate in cases'.

Following from this, European common legislation would make "life" and "work" "easier" for citizens, businesses and others within Europe. People would be "more aware" of the law and "know how to behave". It would become "easier to learn" and "easier to understand law". All these factors would be "beneficial" and "more convenient" for people as everything would be "faster" and as economic growth and various other beneficial developments would be facilitated:

> P-PR-24: 'the less legal complexities, the better for the ordinary Mr Smith or, I don't know, anyone in Europe.' P-PO-24: 'this would definitely help us ... even when we travel we would know that the regulations in our country would be the same as those in another'. P-PR-25: 'now we have ... a situation [where] a lot of Poles live, work abroad ... it would be good for all of us.'

Making laws across Europe more similar would, in the view of Polish legal insiders, be "a harmonious process" by which "to [reach] common goals" and "acquire better things" –eliminating "irregularities" and "misunderstandings". This process should be "convenient for all": P-PR-4: "as an entrepreneur, as a citizen ... of Europe, a tourist ... a person who is a professional in a given field, I'd like the law to be made for me and to always know what to expect from the law, regardless of the country I go to. I'm talking about predictability; the knowledge on how to act, what is allowed and what is not, the legislation related with taxes, insurances, and the job market ... the traffic regulations'.

Despite the many perceived advantages of European legal integration many Polish legal insiders suggest that it would take a long time for legislation in European countries to become more similar, if at all possible. One particularly pessimistic respondent thinks it would be "impossible [to achieve] in 100 years". Legal integration should therefore rather be something to "aim for in the future". Other legal insiders are somewhat more optimistic: even though it would be "really difficult" to achieve, "in 100 years' time [European legal integration] will be unavoidable":

> P-JU-7: 'now we have three basic legal systems in Europe, [we have] the law stemming from Roman law, we have German law, which is different to a great extent, but ... also similar to a great extent ... and the English system, which is different to a great extent from the two systems mentioned ... in the field of civil law and criminal law. Any attempt to unify the law is at the same time an attempt to introduce disagreements ... any attempt to make one, unified law is not feasible ... look at our law ... there is still a huge difference in the legal culture in a broad sense between Western and Eastern Poland ... these

> regions were under different rules during the period of partitions. Under Prussian partition people were instilled with the obligation to obey the law, no matter if it were a German, Prussian or Pole, but in Eastern areas there was the rule "do what you want", "no holds barred" . . . it is visible even today'.

Those Polish legal insiders who *object* to the idea of European legal integration primarily refer to factors that in their view make Poland unique – such as its "history", "culture" and "traditions" – the "roots" of the Polish people; their national "mentality"; "beliefs"; "social norms"; "temper"; "habits"; "peculiarities"; "experiences" and "achievements".

Legal insiders in Bulgaria who are in favour of more similar legislation across Europe mostly highlight the benefits that EU membership bestows upon their country: European laws are "better" and "more stable" than domestic laws and Bulgarians therefore have "a lot to learn from Western Europe" in terms of law and law enforcement.

By having laws based on the "same general principles" and "same values", EU member states will be able to find "common solutions to their problems". For a start, similar laws would make it easier for citizens to familiarise themselves with the law. It would "ease foreign travel" and "ensure free movement" as the Bulgarians would know their rights and obligations. Equal rights would "protect [them]", and facilitate "predictability". But in addition same-type laws would "encourage communication", "simplify relationships", and enhance "efficiency". Legal convergence across Europe would thus "make life easier" and "better" for them:

> B-JU-17: 'this makes it easier for the people, makes them more mobile – both business and ordinary people . . . in Bulgaria . . . there is one group of people . . . who live in the nineteenth century, other groups that live in the twentieth, and a third, smaller group . . . that lives in the twenty-first . . . for those who live in the nineteenth century it will be difficult to adapt and for those who live in the twenty-first it is a necessity.'

European legal convergence would also ease *the implementation of law* in Bulgaria, which would ease the work of the "law enforcement" agencies. Some prosecutors note that same-type law would help them in the "fight against crime" – thus giving citizens "some sense of security". Police representatives believe that legal convergence would be good for Bulgaria as the Bulgarian people have "lost faith in the [national] legislative bodies":

> B-JU-2: 'the so-called convergence of both systems and the upgrading of these systems will achieve more perfect legislation and a more

> sophisticated enforcement system. It is inevitable ... it would be much more useful.' B-PR-2: 'it would definitely contribute to a more efficient, better fight against crime'.

Same-type laws would remove trade barriers. This would be "good for the Bulgarian economy" as the country "must catch up" with the rest of Europe. Everybody would "benefit" from such a process as it would facilitate "better economic development":

> B-LA-2: 'we are striving towards a practice regarding the law that was stalled in Bulgaria ... for 45 years we lived in a closed world ... we had no commercial law ... there were hardly any obligation[s] because there were no contracts ... now we must catch up, which means that we really have to copy very much.' B-ER-3: 'I believe more in European laws, European regulations and European judges'.

Bulgarian legal insiders (elected representatives only) also talk about the *desirability of the European project and legal integration* as such – though the number of such statements is considerably less than those focusing on the benefits to be had for Bulgaria having the same laws as other European countries. Legal insiders note that the EU is "one community" with "a common European identity" and EU member states should therefore have "uniform law". Creating a "pan-European space" and a "Europe of no borders" should be the ultimate goal.

Though mostly in favour of European legal convergence, Bulgarian legal insiders believe that it would be "hard to attain": it would "take a lot of effort" and be a "long road" to walk. One judge claims that it would simply not be possible for all laws to be "absolutely identical", whereas a prosecutor believes that there are differences between EU member states that "are non-negotiable". Further, "national specifics should be retained" and the manner in which convergence is facilitated must be "appropriate for Bulgaria":

> B-JU-10: 'the goal is to build a pan-European legal space ... it is a long road we should walk, but it is necessary'. B-JU-24: 'it would make life easier. The unification of the laws in a union is always desirable.' B-ER-15: 'it will be a very long process ... the United States have existed for more than 200 years and there are still huge differences in the legislation of the various states'.

Bulgarian legal insiders who are *not in favour* of European legal integration primarily emphasise the need to protect their country's national heritage: the "national identity" must be "preserved" and "respected". Further, the Bulgarian Constitution must be "of a national character".

The "national legislation" must be preserved as "laws must meet the requirements of society". Only two legal insiders object to European legal convergence for ideological reasons.

The majority of the statements made by the Ukrainian legal insiders on future European legal integration favour European legal convergence – and primarily due to the benefits Ukraine stands to gain from joining the EU. Support for the European idea as such is voiced considerably less frequently.

Ukrainian legal insiders have an instrumental approach to legal convergence. They believe it would be beneficial for their country as it would generate "more positive law", "simplify procedures" and make life (far) easier and simpler for people in terms of "orienting themselves" about the law; and "defending their rights". People would "feel more comfortable" living "by common rules". Having "the same rights" and "same obligations" would "facilitate mutual relations". The Ukrainian people "wish to live in better conditions". Legal convergence would help them achieve this goal by "raising [their] social standards":

> U-LA-4: 'I would be pleased . . . laws are a mixture of the best traditions and cultures. We have to come closer to the ideal.' U-PR-9: 'of course I would be pleased. Because it would simplify communication with Europeans'.

By facilitating better-quality legislation legal convergence would also be beneficial for Ukraine in terms of *law enforcement*. Same-type laws across Europe would make it easier for people to orient themselves about the law, understand it, observe it and thus solve their problems. In addition, it would be "difficult to hide" violations of such law and consequently there would be "more fear" of breaking it in the first place. However, citizens would have "better legal protection"; it would be easier for the judiciary to implement the law, and thereby combat crime and regulate society. In other words, legal convergence would facilitate "order" in Ukraine:

> U-PO-6: 'sooner or later it will come to the unification of European law . . . [it] will make work easier . . . because we will work with one legislative bloc, code'. U-PO-16: 'it would be better for everybody, including me, as a [police] investigator.'

Unlike legal insiders in Poland and Bulgaria, Ukrainian legal insiders also underline what their country stands to gain from legal convergence in the areas of *democracy* and *human rights*. First, citizens would gain "freedom of movement". Second, they would gain "personal" and "civil liberty".

Legal integration would also strengthen “freedom or religion”, “freedom of speech” and “freedom of the press”:

> U-LA-7: ‘it would be more convenient . . . it would be good for people’. U-JU-16: ‘I would be pleased . . . the borders would become more transparent, [that is], the possibilities and rights of a person would increase . . . the countries of the Schengen agreement . . . have similar laws: take your passport and go to any place you like.’

European laws are generally considered to be of *better quality* than Ukrainian laws, and some respondents point out that legal convergence would be “very convenient”. It would give Ukraine “the same platform” as other European countries, thus improving relations and “triggering development”; by copying high-quality legislation from other countries, Ukraine would “solve many problems”. Equally important, fewer differences between countries in terms of law would result in “less conflicts” and a more “peaceful” and “pleasant” living:

> U-ER-12: ‘when laws are similar it is easier to orientate oneself, easier to defend one’s rights, which means easier to live.’ U-GO-27: ‘we would have an opportunity to talk with other states in the same legal language.’ U-ER-3: ‘it would be very good, and countries that have lower levels of development would benefit from this.’

Legal insiders in Ukraine – just like legal insiders elsewhere – find common European legislation convenient. Such legislation would result in “fewer violations” (of foreign law). It would make travel in Europe easier as there would be more transparent borders and as European citizens would be free to travel within the Schengen area. People would be “protected” and there would be “no need to study the law while abroad” as one would already be familiar with it. Conducting business would be simpler as “states would be talking the same language” and as there would be common “European standards” that would be “fully observed” – thus “easing communication at work”, making “work easier” and “facilitating economic development”:

> U-ER-22: ‘unifying them would be beneficial . . . we have become more mobile – we go to other countries, socialise with other people. Law is rules of conduct, if they will be more compatible it will . . . simplify a dialogue with the representatives of other cultures.’ U-GO-13: ‘it would be far easier even to go to European countries . . . if cultural values were approximately the same. Probably it would influence the attitude of those citizens who live in European countries toward the citizens who live in Ukraine.’

Ukrainian legal insiders who voice their support for legal convergence as part of the wider, European project, favour Europe as "one large formation" – even a "confederation" – which should have "a single European standard" and "an equal legal system" promoting "core human values". Ukraine "should be integrated" into such a Europe and it should have "more similar laws" that "suit Europeans". "Some unification" is both "possible and necessary":

> U-GO-17: 'this is normal and ... quite a positive tendency.' U-GO-19: '[for people] to be able to live in this unified space the law should become similar. The same concerns our country if we aim to integrate into the European Union.'

Though in favour of European legal convergence some of the legal insiders caution that "Ukraine is not [entirely] ready" for EU law and that it is (unfortunately) "not possible" to apply such law in all spheres of society. "State interests", "the interests of the Ukrainian people" and "national peculiarities" would have to be considered and "nationally specific laws" should, to some extent, be retained. Ukrainian "customs and traditions" would remain in the future. At present "Europe encourages difference" rather than similarity and it would therefore simply be "impossible" to achieve legal convergence within Europe:

> U-GO-7: 'it would be very convenient ... but perhaps, in some respects, our people are not ready for European legislation.' U-JU-24: 'however hard we try to join the European community, our customs and traditions ... will remain with us. The similarity of laws is necessary to make life easier'. U-PO-15: 'it would certainly be nice, but it is impossible'.

Just like legal insiders elsewhere, Ukrainian legal insiders who object to legal convergence mostly advocate preserving the Ukrainian historical heritage, its customs, traditions, national culture and values, the national heritage, national peculiarities, and the Ukrainian mentality and way of life. As all of these are largely reflected in national law, such law should be preserved. A more limited number of legal insiders argue against legal convergence on the grounds that they either find such a project impossible to achieve or because they believe there is no need for countries to have similar laws.

Conclusions

Even though European integration and globalization to a great extent take place by means of legal transfers, to date little has been known about how ordinary citizens and elites perceive such transfers at a more general level. Our data show that Euro-identity correlates with support for European and international standards amongst legal outsiders in England and Norway but not in Ukraine and Bulgaria. But that is because European and international standards are popular in Ukraine and Bulgaria irrespective of whether they do or do not feel European. That, in turn, reflects public suspicion of local law in Ukraine and Bulgaria, but pride in local law in England and Norway.

From the legal 'import' versus 'export' perspective our data suggest that there is considerable support across Europe for 'importing' foreign law – but only law that does not clash with local mentality and local culture. Foreign legislation that does not take into account these two factors is perceived as undesirable legal 'exports'. In the case of Eastern Europe our FG data show that legal outsiders in Bulgaria, in particular, think people should feel free to ignore 'cultural exports' such as the ban on producing *rakia* at home. Such law is therefore largely ignored – and with the blessing of the Bulgarian authorities. In the case of England, there is some resistance to legal 'exports'; that is, laws that are considered to be of poorer quality than domestic law or that do not fit well with England's common law tradition.

Legal outsiders across Europe are remarkably positive to learning from others and to the reception of foreign law. In all countries (but more so in Eastern Europe and less so in Western Europe) a majority believe that their countries can learn a lot from other countries, European and international organisations about writing good laws, implementing and enforcing laws, and the way ordinary people and political leaders respect law. They are – though slightly less so in England – very receptive to the ECtHR. And they would be pleased to see national laws converge.

Further, legal outsiders think European and international standards are generally good. All but the English believe that these standards protect people from bad laws. But a fair share think such standards privilege the Roma (Bulgaria), religious minorities and ethno/linguistic minorities (Bulgaria, England), and sexual minorities (Bulgaria, Poland) – something they are less happy about. Our FG data show that across Europe there is considerable resistance to giving sexual minorities rights as doing so clashes with the long-held beliefs of the majority.

Legal insiders share the legal outsiders' view that their countries have something to learn from other countries, European and international organisations about law, about the way law is applied, and about the way ordinary people deal with the law. They are rather positive to E-I-U standards, which they do not perceive as being imposed upon their countries.

However, they are more sceptical than legal outsiders to the idea that European countries should have broadly the same laws and law enforcement. But that is mostly because they are aware of practical problems that would make this difficult, not because they think having the same laws is a bad idea as such. The English legal insiders stand out in that they do not want to give up their national legislation: many of them consider English law to be superior to European law. Others do not think it is possible for common law and civil law countries to have the same laws.

East Europeans are generally more positive to European legal convergence than West Europeans. But that is mostly because they would like to learn from the West in order to catch up with Western Europe in the economic sphere and not because they are supporters of a united Europe. In other words, their support for European legal integration is primarily instrumental, not normative.

8

Muslims and Euro-migrants as carriers of legal culture

Introduction: carriers of legal culture

Legal influences take place not only by means of legal transfers – that is, laws and legal structures being transferred from one cultural context into another – but also through travel and migration. Immigrants, for instance, are carriers of one legal culture who are exposed to the legal culture of the country in which they settle. Immigrants who permanently settle in a foreign country are likely to become more influenced by the foreign legal culture to which they are exposed than people who are exposed to such legal culture for a shorter period. However, both groups are likely to become affected in one way or the other.

In the past 30 years or so there has been a huge influx of immigrants from Asia and Africa to Europe. Added to this, free movement across Europe is a key component of the European project. The Schengen Agreement has made it possible for citizens of the EU, EEA and EFTA states to travel freely within Europe – though until 1 January 2014 some restrictions applied to citizens from Bulgaria and Romania. As a result, large numbers of East Europeans (Poles in particular) have migrated to Western Europe in search of work. West Europeans, for their part, have travelled to Eastern Europe for business, work or study.

In parallel with migration to, and within, Europe there has been pressure towards a more convergent European legal culture. But from country to country within this wider Europe there remain sharp differences in popular legal cultures. Public perceptions of law and attitudes towards law, towards observance of the law and towards law enforcement vary, sometimes sharply, from country to country.

There is no automatic guarantee that long-established minorities and/or recent *Euro-migrants* (defined as people born in one European country but now living in another European country) will necessarily adapt to the general legal culture of the majority in their current country of residence, but the natural tendency is for the larger numbers to at least influence the smaller – except in very special circumstances.

Within Europe, long-established Muslim minorities have adapted to the popular legal culture in their country over the long term. So even though they have their own particular concerns the legal cultures of Muslim minorities tend to vary from one European country to another in much the same way as the legal cultures of the majorities in these countries. To that extent, their legal cultures are as much country-specific as Muslim.

More dynamically, Euro-migrants (who are generally not Muslims) tend to adapt to the local legal culture in their new country of residence. But their adaptation is both asymmetric and benign: Euro-migrants seem more willing to adapt when they move to a more law-abiding part of Europe, and less willing – or sometimes just less able – to adapt when they move to a less law-abiding and more 'informal' society.

This chapter investigates the perceptions of both the majority populations and the Muslims and Euro-migrants on these issues.[1] Do Euro-migrants remain loyal to their native legal culture, or do they adapt to the legal culture of the country in which they settle? The extent to which such people either adapt to or reject the legal culture of their (temporary) host country says something about the stability or instability of popular legal culture at personal level as well as the responsiveness (or the lack of it!) of national legal cultures to external influences.

As noted in Chapter 1 by *legal cultures* we mean conceptions and perceptions of, and attitudes towards, law and law enforcement.[2] This chapter is about attitudes as well as perceptions.

'Adaptive' legal cultures

In principle, we can compare and contrast the legal cultures of legal insiders (legislators, lawyers, judges, prosecutors, civil servants and police) with the legal cultures of legal outsiders (the general public). We can also compare and contrast legal cultures in different countries, whether

[1] As few of the legal insiders we interviewed were migrants and as we did not ask legal insiders any questions about migrant legal culture, findings on the legal insiders are not included in this chapter.

[2] To recap from Chapter 1, the concept of popular *legal culture* was defined by Friedman (1990, p. 213) as 'ideas, attitudes, expectations and opinions about law, held by people in some given society'. This legal culture, he (Friedman 1975, p. 15) argues, determines their 'way of doing and thinking'. See also Nelken (2004, pp. 1–28).

amongst legal insiders, legal outsiders or both. And we can compare and contrast the legal cultures of different sections of the general public – different generations, the rich and the poor, the well-educated and the less well-educated, the religious and the irreligious.

With more difficulty, however, we can even compare and contrast the legal cultures of small but important sections of the public with the legal cultures of the general public as a whole. Our focus here is on 'adaptive' legal cultures – and, in particular, on how Muslim minorities (mostly well established for decades or even centuries) and Euro-migrants have adapted, or are in the process of adapting to the legal cultures of the local majority.

There are two kinds of adaptive legal culture: institutional and personal. First there is a concern that any attempt to "import" some legal institution from another country – and still more so any attempt to "export" a legal institution to another country – may trigger an adaptive response that will distort its performance. Nelken (Nelken and Feest 2001, p. 15) argues that 'legal transplants' are 'both common and reasonably successful', especially when good ideas from abroad are voluntarily 'borrowed'. But more recently, Kurkchiyan (2009, p. 337) argues that 'any [legal] institution transplanted from one social environment to another will be reinterpreted and reshaped, so that it can be accepted into the receiving society'. Thus transferred laws or legal institutions may transform and 'adapt' when applied in other cultures. Similarly, Zaborowski (2005, p. 16) contrasts the 'coercive impact of the EU and NATO' in 'Westernizing the East', with the 'more voluntary dimensions of policy diffusion' and suggests that 'the first and foremost condition of effective external influence is that it must be compatible with the norms and domestic conditions already in existence' or it will be adapted, distorted or ignored (ibid., p. 29).

But we focus here on the second kind of adaptation. Whatever moves becomes the target for pressures to adapt. If it is not legal institutions but the people who do the moving, then it is the people – not the institutions – who are under pressure to adapt. Thus Euro-migrants are under immediate 'short-term' pressure to adapt to the local legal culture.

In the case of a long-established minority, however, there is a continuous 'long-term' pressure to 'adapt' to the local majority's legal culture. That adaptation is historic rather than dynamic. But at the other extreme, highly mobile people who cross state boundaries may adapt their legal culture very quickly. Perceptions of, and attitudes towards, the law depend on the country as well as on the individual, and the same person may therefore obey the law in one country but not in another. Berry (1997, p. 18) suggests that migrants' 'behavioural adjustments' – in contrast to their 'psychological adaptation' are 'typically made with minimal difficulty'. In terms of action, if not always in terms of preference, that implies legal culture does not reside exclusively within the individual but applies rather to the amalgam of an 'individual-in-context'.

Business economists have also used the term *adaptive behaviour* or simply *adaptation*. Kay (2004, p. 204) suggests that 'the traits of behaviour we observe are those which are most likely to be replicated in the environment in which we find them . . . both corrupt and honest behaviour are self-reinforcing . . . a member of a corrupt organisation will find it difficult to be honest' – and most significantly: 'the same people might be corrupt in a corrupt environment and honest in an honest environment'.

Kay, whose main focus is on business organisations rather than states, goes on to argue that there might also be reverse causation through self-selection: 'we seek environments appropriate to us'. But while that is plausible in the context of business organisations, it is likely to be far less important in the context of states. Certainly, honest people may switch employers to get out of a corrupt business and into a more honest one, thereby reinforcing the corrupt nature of the first business and the honest nature of the second. But it is not so likely that large numbers of Ukrainians will move to England or Norway simply to avoid paying tips and bribes to officials, and even less likely that large numbers of English and Norwegian people will move to Ukraine simply to give bribes to officials. Even if they wanted to this would not be possible: Ukraine is neither a member of the EU, nor part of the Schengen Agreement.[3] Within Europe, the peculiarities of countries' legal cultures are largely home grown, not the product of selective migration; and it is the migrants who are under pressure to adapt to local circumstances.

Some migrants may already have a legal culture more compatible with their destination than with their country of origin: they are already adapted to their country of destination. Inglehart and Norris (2009) use World Values Survey data to argue that 'the basic values of Muslims living in Western societies fall roughly halfway between the dominant culture prevailing within their countries of destination and origin'. That

[3] For an overview of EU visa policy, see European Commission, Home Affairs, 'Visa policy', http://ec.europa.eu/dgs/home-affairs/what-we-do/policies/borders-and-visas/visa-policy/index_en.htm accessed on 23 August 2014.

could be interpreted as a halfway stage on the road to adaptation, but Inglehart and Norris suspect that 'self-selection' contributes, arguing that 'people already sympathetic to Western cultures' may be more likely to relocate to the West. The migrants in Inglehart and Norris's study differ most from their countries of origin on sexual liberalisation and gender equality, and differ least on religion and democratic values. Inglehart and Norris were studying migration on a worldwide scale and with serious oppression as a driving force. Such 'self-selection' is not likely to be such a significant driving force for the acclimatisation of Euro-migrants with regard to legal cultures.

When comparing the legal cultures of minorities and migrants with the legal cultures of the general public we need to take note of Schuck's (2000, Chapter 7) threefold distinction between (1) the 'law on the book' – that is the law as formally enacted, (2) 'the law in action' – that is the law as implemented, and (3) 'the law in the minds' – the law as perceived by different groups in society including the general public, migrants and their employers. It is this 'law in the minds' that comes closest to our concept of popular legal culture.

In Schuck's view, this distinction is particularly relevant to immigration inasmuch as illegal immigration is a 'victimless offence, which confers significant benefits on almost all concerned' (at least in the American context). Technically, some immigrants may work without a permit, or work for more hours than permitted (by their student visa, for example) but Schuck suggests that legalistic arguments based on the 'law in the book' ring hollow when applied to a courageous, reliable, hard-working, generally law-abiding and not at all overpaid, immigrant. Schuck claims that 'Americans like immigrants more than they like immigration' and that they might reasonably regard illegal immigration positively as a 'socially efficient offence'.

For an assessment of 'legal culture', it is important to distinguish between illegal immigration and non-law-abiding immigrants. In the British context, Ruhs and Anderson (2010, p. 207) considered the potentially positive 'functions of different types of illegality for migrants, employers and the state'. They found that a majority of their sample were 'semi-compliant', which they defined as 'legally resident but working in violation of the employment restrictions attached to their immigration status' – typically working more hours than permitted by their immigration status. There is no reason to believe that they were not law-abiding residents in other respects. Two-thirds of the sample of migrants that they studied were nationals of the so-called A8 countries that joined the EU in 2004 and 'for those A8 workers residing in the UK illegally (or working more than the legally permitted number of hours per week), EU enlargement meant a change in their legal status in the UK . . . [which was] effectively a regularisation' (ibid., p. 196). But that did not greatly alter their 'legal culture' or affect whether they were 'generally law-abiding' in terms of 'law in the minds'.

In the United States, Butcher and Piehl's (1998) analysis of official statistics shows what they describe as 'unexpected implications for crime and incarceration' linked to recent immigrants. Immigrant men were less likely than the native-born to be sent to prisons, mental hospitals or other institutions – and 'much less' likely than native-born men with similar demographic characteristics. More recently, Georgios Papadopoulos's (2010) analysis of British Home Office–sponsored data on 'Offending, Crime and Justice' in England and Wales suggests that 'the likelihood for an immigrant to commit a property crime' or indeed a 'crime against the person' is 'slightly lower than for natives'.

Whether or not immigrants have bent or broken the law on immigration itself may be an inadequate guide to whether they have a 'generally law-abiding' legal culture.

Minorities and Euro-migrants: long-term and short-term adaptation

After reviewing our 84 FG discussions with groups drawn from the general public (48 FGs), from Muslim minorities (18 FGs) and from 'Euro-migrants' (18 FGs), we interviewed a cross-section of around 1,000 members of the general public plus 200 Muslims in each of Norway, England, Poland, Bulgaria and Ukraine in 2009–10.[4] (For purely practical reasons, we did not conduct such large-scale interviews with Euro-migrants.)

Our aim was to discover how the legal cultures of Muslim minorities and incoming Euro-migrants compare with the legal cultures of the general public in these five countries using whatever analytical approach best fits the situation and, not least, the data available. We have enough

[4] As noted in Chapter 1 in all we interviewed 5,156 drawn from the general public: 911 in Norway, 1,000 in England, 1,027 in Poland, 1,018 in Bulgaria and 1,200 in Ukraine; and 1,008 in special Muslim samples – 201 in Norway, 200 in England, 200 in Poland, 207 in Bulgaria and 200 in Ukraine. There were, of course, a few Muslims in the samples of the general public, especially in Bulgaria.

interviews with Muslims to compare directly their legal attitudes and perceptions with those of the general public. In particular we can gauge the extent to which Muslims in different countries have "acclimatised" or "adapted" to local legal cultures.

Many Muslims in our chosen countries are long-established citizens, with a long family background in their current country of residence. Their legal cultures may reflect the legal culture of the general public in their country of residence. Or at the very least the legal cultures of Muslims may vary from country to country in a way similar to the varying legal cultures of the general public. Indeed the pattern of cross-national variation in legal cultures amongst Muslims may then echo the pattern of cross-national variation in legal cultures amongst the general public even if Muslim legal culture differs from the legal culture of the general public. Evidence of such long-term Muslim adaptability to the local legal cultures in different countries does not require complete assimilation. But it does require evidence of some incorporation of country-specific legal culture.

Evidence of such long-term adaptability requires two things. First, there must be a considerable difference between the legal cultures in the different countries – as evidenced by large cross-national 'standard deviation' in some aspect of the general public's legal cultures. Otherwise there are no significantly 'local' or 'country-specific' legal cultures to exert any pressure to adapt.

Second, there must be a high cross-national correlation between the variation in the legal cultures of Muslims and the variation in the legal cultures of the general public. Otherwise, there is no evidence of their general adaptation to the varied local country-specific legal cultures.

In contrast to Muslim minorities, Euro-migrants are, by definition, not a long-established minority but relatively new arrivals, still very much caught between the legal culture of their country of origin and the legal culture of their new country of residence. We do not have large-scale surveys of incoming Euro-migrants. Moreover, large-scale surveys of recent incoming Euro-migrants might not be appropriate anyway because the legal cultures of Euro-migrants are likely to be in a state of flux: the process of convergence, even if it is underway, is likely to be incomplete. We need a more dynamic approach that is sensitive to short-term adaptation-in-progress.

We rely on two different kinds of data. First, the general public's perceptions of incoming Euro-migrants and in particular the public's perceptions of how these incoming Euro-migrants adapt to the various local legal cultures. Of course, the general public might be ill-informed. In particular they might be prejudiced against immigrants of any kind, including Euro-migrants. Judging by Schuck's claims that 'Americans like immigrants more than they like immigration' the less contact they have with immigrants the more negative their perceptions. So we should regard public perceptions as biased against immigrants and treat the amount of positive perceptions as an underestimate.

Second, we can draw on some of our FG discussions with Euro-migrants themselves. We can note not only their own perceptions of, and attitudes towards, their new local legal culture, but also their direct and sometimes nuanced perceptions of being caught between, and influenced by, two different legal cultures – self-conscious awareness of the pressures, and the opportunities, to adapt.

Long-term adaptation: Muslim minorities

There is no automatic guarantee that established minorities will necessarily adapt to the general legal culture of the majority in their country of residence but, except in special circumstances, the natural tendency is for the larger numbers to at least influence the smaller. In that sense long-term adaptation is likely to be asymmetric. Within Europe, long-established minorities have adapted to the popular legal culture in their country. So even though they have their own particular concerns, the legal cultures of Muslim minorities also tend to reflect the legal cultures of the majorities in these countries. Consequently there may be a cross-national correlation between the general public's legal culture and the legal culture of these Muslim minorities.

Perceptions of general respect for the law In our survey, very general images of the government and people's "respect for the law" vary hugely across our five countries, echoing the pattern of the World Bank's 'Rule of Law' rankings. There is considerable cross-national variation in the perceptions of both Muslims and the general public.

Amongst the public as a whole, perceptions that the "government and people in [this country] respect the law more than in other countries" peak at a remarkable 93 per cent in Norway, and a moderately smug 58 per cent in England, but decline through 28 per cent in Poland to 12 per cent in Bulgaria and a mere 10 per cent in Ukraine. Amongst Muslims in our surveys, perceptions of the general public's respect for the law follows a broadly similar pattern, with a peak of 73 per cent in Norway and a moderate 56 per cent in England, followed by a

Table 8.1 *Government regard for law across Europe: the legal outsiders' perspective*

	NOR (%)	ENG (%)	POL (%)	BUL (%)	UKR (%)	N-MU (%)	E-MU (%)	P-MU (%)	B-MU (%)	U-MU (%)
PQ126: Government and people in this country respect the law, and generally obey it more (v. less) than in the rest of Europe	93	58	28	12	10	73	56	30	4	24

Notes:
1. For simplicity, all percentages in this chapter are calculated by excluding from the calculations uninvited and unprompted responses classified by interviewers as 'mixed', 'both', 'neither', 'other' and 'DK/NA'.
2. NOR, ENG, POL, BUL, UKR refer to the majority populations; N-MU, E-MU, P-MU, B-MU, U-MU refer to the Muslims.
3. Within each country, samples are based on approximately 1,000 interviews with the general public plus 200 with Muslims.

decline to 30 per cent in Poland, 24 per cent in Ukraine and 4 per cent in Bulgaria (Table 8.1).

On these perceptions, there is plenty of cross-national variation amongst both the general public and Muslims; and the cross-national correlation between the views of Muslims and the general public reaches a remarkable 0.95. That fits our criteria for a minority's long-term adaptability: large-scale cross-national variations in the perceptions of both Muslims and the general public, coupled with a high cross-national correlation between these variations in Muslims' and the general public's perceptions.

Perceptions of law in principle and practice When asked at the start of our interviews whether the word *law* conjures up an image of "justice, fairness and legal rights" or, alternatively, an image of "unfair and oppressive laws" a very large percentage, both amongst the general public (83 per cent) and Muslim minorities (85 per cent), respond with an immediate image of "justice" rather than "oppression". (In FGs, a remarkable number of majority population participants spontaneously

Table 8.2 *Law in principle versus law in practice: the legal outsiders' perspective*

	NOR (%)	ENG (%)	POL (%)	BUL (%)	UKR (%)	N-MU (%)	E-MU (%)	P-MU (%)	B-MU (%)	U-MU (%)
PQ2: Law is justice, not oppression	95	87	76	83	73	89	84	89	90	73
PQ16: Law = power of state v. people	17	42	50	61	74	35	53	30	49	61
PQ9: Law helps, not problems	92	66	50	56	29	83	68	71	66	37

Note: NOR, ENG, POL, BUL, UKR refer to the majority populations; N-MU, E-MU, P-MU, B-MU, U-MU refer to the Muslims.

cited "Themis" the Greek goddess of law, depicted in statues as blindfolded and holding a set of scales, as their own "image" of law – see Chapter 2).

Of course, there is some country-to-country variation in perceptions of law as "justice", though not much. So although there is some variation, it is not enough to indicate a fundamental difference of public attitudes towards the abstract concept of "law" or "law-in-principle" in different countries. In the abstract, in principle, this aspect of legal culture – the concept of "law as justice" – is simply not local but, at least within the scope of our five countries, fairly universal, though both the general public and Muslims are least likely, in principle, to equate law with justice in Ukraine (Table 8.2).

Perceptions of reality (or "law-in-action" rather than "law-in-principle") are strikingly different, however – much more critical and, importantly, much more variable cross-nationally.

On an average, half the public (49 per cent) view the actual, "really existing" law in their own country as "reflecting the power of the state to control people" rather than "generally recognised moral values shared by most people in this country". Only a minority of 17 per cent in Norway and 42 per cent in England envision the law in this way, as primarily state control. But Polish opinion is evenly balanced at 50 per cent, and a majority in Bulgaria (61 per cent) and Ukraine (74 per cent) see actually existing law as primarily state control.

On an average, Muslims once again do not differ much from the general public, but they differentiate somewhat less between the countries.

So although Muslims are less critical than non-Muslims of the law as state oppression in Poland, Bulgaria and Ukraine, they are more critical than non-Muslims of the law as state oppression in Norway and England.

As noted earlier, the Muslims we interviewed in Norway and England are "migrant-Muslims", whereas the Muslims interviewed in Eastern Europe are mostly "native-Muslims". Added to this, recent acts of terrorism in England have been perpetrated primarily by Muslims; and new laws against terrorism, coupled with stricter enforcement, have inevitably been used in England primarily against Muslim suspects. Consequently there is Muslim resistance to adapting to majority views on this aspect of popular legal culture. Nonetheless, perceptions of law as representing 'the power of the state' are highest in Ukraine amongst both Muslims and the general public and lowest or close to lowest in Norway.

On the more personal issue of whether 'the law in [this country] generally helps people like yourself, or generally makes problems for people like yourself' only 59 per cent of the general public – but 65 per cent of Muslims (a small difference, but a positive one) – say that the law "helps" rather than "caus[es] problems" for them personally. Though the difference between Muslims and the general public is not large, Muslims are at least as much, or slightly more inclined, than the general public to feel that the law "helps" rather than "makes problems" for them – despite all the pressures of the so-called war on terror, which certainly did cause new problems for European Muslims, and especially so in England.

Within the general public, the number reporting that the law "helps people like me" goes down from a remarkable 92 per cent in Norway, through 66 per cent in England, to an evenly balanced 50 per cent in Poland and 56 per cent in Bulgaria and an unambiguous low in Ukraine (29 per cent) – a huge difference of 63 per cent between the perceived realities of law-made problems in Norway and Ukraine. Amongst Muslims the number reporting that the law "helps people like me" goes down from 83 per cent in Norway, through 68 per cent in England, 71 per cent in Poland and 66 per cent in Bulgaria, to a low of 37 per cent in Ukraine. On this issue, the cross-national pattern of Muslim opinion closely reflects the cross-national pattern of the general public, and the cross-national correlation between the views of Muslims and the general public on whether the law helps or causes problems reaches a high of 0.89. Muslim perceptions of law being personally helpful vary greatly between countries but largely reflect the typical views of the general public in these countries.

Perceptions of 'ordinary people' We have already found that public perceptions that the "government and people in [this country] respect the law more than in other countries" ranged down dramatically from a peak of 93 per cent in Norway to a mere 10 per cent in Ukraine. But that is a comparative assessment, and it groups together government and people. A different and much less variable picture emerges when respondents are asked, non-comparatively, only about obedience to the law within their own country. And, in addition, a different and more positive picture emerges when the question's focus is exclusively on people and the reference to their government is excluded.

We asked whether "most ordinary people in this country generally obey the law", as contrasted with "frequently disobey the law". Qualified as it is by *most* but not *all* the public, and by *generally* but not *always* obeying the law, that is not a very high standard of compliance, but it is nonetheless a realistic description of actually existing "law-abiding citizens".

When asked whether "most ordinary people" in the country "generally obey the law", an average of 75 per cent of the general public (and 76 per cent of Muslims) feel that "most ordinary people" generally do obey the law. This perceived rate of compliance runs at around 85 per cent in Norway (87 per cent) and England (82 per cent), and drops – but only to around 69 per cent – in the three post-communist countries (Table 8.3).

When focusing on people whom the respondent meets regularly and knows well, perceptions of compliance increase significantly: on an average 88 per cent of the general public (and 87 per cent of Muslims) feel that most people with whom they regularly come into contact generally obey the law. The general public's perceived rate of compliance now rises to 94 per cent in Norway and 92 per cent in England. But much more significantly, it never drops beneath 83 per cent in any country.

Intriguingly, the cross-national correlation between Muslim perceptions and the general public's perceptions are negative not positive. In this respect there is no evidence of Muslims' legal culture adapting to that of the general public: quite the reverse. But the cross-national variations are very small and insignificant.

Why obey? What is the main reason why people in the country obey laws: Is it because the law is generally fair? Because it is morally wrong to break the law? Because it is the duty of a citizen in a democracy to obey laws passed by the Parliament that they themselves have elected? Or is it simply fear of punishment? On an average 30 per cent of the public cite fear of punishment; the rest cite various, more positive

Table 8.3 *Law-abidance amongst the public: the legal outsiders' perspective*

	NOR (%)	ENG (%)	POL (%)	BUL (%)	UKR (%)	N-MU (%)	E-MU (%)	P-MU (%)	B-MU (%)	U-MU (%)
PQ100: Most ordinary people generally obey the law.	87	82	64	72	70	75	69	82	76	80
PQ101: People I regularly come into contact with personally, in everyday life generally obey the law.	94	92	84	87	83	73	86	92	91	91

Note: NOR, ENG, POL, BUL, UKR refer to the majority populations; N-MU, E-MU, P-MU, B-MU, U-MU refer to the Muslims.

reasons – the moral imperative (29 per cent), democratic duty (25 per cent) or fair laws (16 per cent).

Cross-nationally there are positive correlations between the Muslims' and the general public's perceptions of why people obey the law: Poles in general, and Polish Muslims in particular, are the most inclined to cite "fear of punishment"; Ukrainians in general, and Ukrainian Muslims in particular, are the most inclined to cite a "moral" imperative; Norwegians in general, and Norwegian Muslims in particular, are the most inclined to cite "citizen duty"; and Norwegians and the English in general, and Norwegian and English Muslims in particular, are the most inclined to cite "fair law" (Table 8.4).

A reasonable excuse? To get a fully rounded picture we need to ask not just 'why obey?' but its obvious inverse, 'why not?' We posed a question about the balance between state and people in responsibility for lawbreaking: "When ordinary people knowingly break the law in this country, do you feel they often have some reasonable excuse for breaking the law, or do they usually have no valid excuse for breaking the law?"

The answers everywhere are remarkably sympathetic to lawbreakers and thus to lawbreaking. But they differ sharply across countries. Around 32 per cent of the general public in Norway or England think lawbreakers

Table 8.4 *Reasons for obeying the law: the legal outsiders' perspective*

	NOR (%)	ENG (%)	POL (%)	BUL (%)	UKR (%)	N-MU (%)	E-MU (%)	P-MU (%)	B-MU (%)	U-MU (%)
PQ102: Why obey?										
Fear of punishment	18	23	45	34	32	32	39	42	34	31
Morally wrong to disobey	26	31	24	23	39	24	23	20	35	44
Duty as citizen	36	22	20	29	20	28	22	26	20	18
The law is fair	21	23	12	13	9	17	17	12	11	8

Note: NOR, ENG, POL, BUL, UKR refer to the majority populations; N-MU, E-MU, P-MU, B-MU, U-MU refer to the Muslims.

Table 8.5 *A reasonable excuse for breaking the law: the legal outsiders' perspective*

	NOR (%)	ENG (%)	POL (%)	BUL (%)	UKR (%)	N-MU (%)	E-MU (%)	P-MU (%)	B-MU (%)	U-MU (%)
PQ105: Reasonable excuse	31	32	42	56	72	41	42	41	42	84

Note: NOR, ENG, POL, BUL, UKR refer to the majority populations; N-MU, E-MU, P-MU, B-MU, U-MU refer to the Muslims.

often have "a reasonable excuse"; but that rises to 42 per cent in Poland, 56 per cent in Bulgaria and 72 per cent in Ukraine. On an average, there is scant difference between Muslims and the general public, though about 42 per cent of Muslims in Norway, England, Poland and Bulgaria all say lawbreakers often have a reasonable excuse, whereas Muslims in Ukraine are twice as likely (84 per cent) to excuse lawbreakers. There is thus a strong cross-national correlation of 0.82 between the opinions of the general public and Muslims, though that depends largely on the huge support for "reasonable excuses" amongst both public and Muslims in Ukraine (Table 8.5).

Pursuing this concept of the "reasonable excuse", we noted that "even generally law-abiding people sometimes break the law". We specified eight such situations and asked whether "most ordinary people in this country would be generally willing to break the law, or generally unwilling to break the law" in each set of circumstances. In every one of these scenarios over half the public thought "most ordinary people in this country would be generally willing to break the law". At one extreme only just over half thought "most ordinary people in this country would be generally willing to break the law" if it was "unnecessarily troublesome", and at the other extreme over 90 per cent thought "most ordinary people in this country would be generally willing to break the law" if it was in "self-defence" or in "an emergency".

There is remarkably little cross-national variation in most of these responses. But there is one scenario in which there are huge differences between opinions across the five countries. Amongst the general public an average of 84 per cent in Poland, Bulgaria and Ukraine, compared to an average of only 31 per cent in England and Norway, think even "generally law-abiding people would break the law" if they "were under pressure from doctors, police or state officials to give gifts or bribes". It marks a very sharp difference between the Western and Eastern countries though it perhaps indicates public submissiveness rather than willing lawbreaking. Amongst Muslims an average of 72 per cent in Poland, Bulgaria and Ukraine, compared to an average of only 47 per cent in England and Norway think even "generally law-abiding people would break the law" if they "were under pressure from doctors, police or state officials to give gifts or bribes". So on that scenario there is a correlation of 0.81 between the cross-national pattern of the general public's attitudes and those of the Muslims (Table 8.6).

Whose fault? As a further check, we asked: "Overall, when ordinary people in this country disobey the law, is that mainly the fault of (1) the people themselves, (2) pressure from doctors, police or state officials

Table 8.6 *Pressure for bribes: the legal outsiders' perspective*

	NOR (%)	ENG (%)	POL (%)	BUL (%)	UKR (%)	N-MU (%)	E-MU (%)	P-MU (%)	B-MU (%)	U-MU (%)
PQ106J: Pressure for bribes	26	36	85	83	85	43	51	60	86	69

Note: NOR, ENG, POL, BUL, UKR refer to the majority populations; N-MU, E-MU, P-MU, B-MU, U-MU refer to the Muslims.

Table 8.7 *Lawbreaking – whose fault? the legal outsiders' perspective*

	NOR (%)	ENG (%)	POL (%)	BUL (%)	UKR (%)	N-MU (%)	E-MU (%)	P-MU (%)	B-MU (%)	U-MU (%)
PQ107: Fault:										
Pressure of circumstances	33	51	40	44	46	28	61	42	39	50
People themselves	43	29	17	26	20	34	21	34	41	19
Troublesome	11	7	18	6	8	12	7	16	3	9
Pressure for bribes	1	2	13	19	15	5	2	6	12	10
Unfair and unjust laws	12	10	10	4	11	20	9	3	5	13

Note: NOR, ENG, POL, BUL, UKR refer to the majority populations; N-MU, E-MU, P-MU, B-MU, U-MU refer to the Muslims.

who expect gifts or bribes, (3) the pressure of circumstances, (4) unnecessarily complicated and troublesome laws or (5) unfair and unjust laws?" (Table 8.7).

There are strong correlations between cross-country patterns of the attitudes of Muslims and the general public on blaming "pressure of circumstances" (r = 0.94) and "troublesome laws" (r = 0.93) as well as "pressure for bribes" (r = 0.89). "Pressure for bribes" is most frequently cited by the Bulgarian public and Bulgarian Muslims, "troublesome laws" by the Polish public and Polish Muslims, the "pressure of circumstances" by the English public and English Muslims and "unfair and unjust laws" by the Norwegian public and Norwegian Muslims. So although the cross-national variations are only moderate in scale (partly because this is a question that splits answers across five possible answers) there is some clearly visible evidence that Muslims' cross-national pattern of blame tends to echo the general public's.

Short-term adaptation: Euro-migrants

By definition, Euro-migrants are relatively new arrivals still very much caught between the legal culture of their country of origin and the legal culture of their new country of residence. They are caught very much at different stages in a process of adaptation depending on the timing of their arrival.

We do not have large-scale surveys of incoming Euro-migrants. For insight into Euro-migrants' "legal cultures in transition," we draw on some of our FG discussions with Euro-migrants, and note their own comparative perceptions and attitudes towards the law of both their country of origin and their country of residence.

In addition we take note of the general public's perceptions of incoming Euro-migrants and in particular the general public's perceptions of how the legal cultures of incoming Euro-migrants compare with the local legal culture, and how Euro-migrants have adapted or are likely to adapt to local legal cultures. Of course, these are only the general public's perceptions, which might be ill-informed. In particular they might be prejudiced against immigrants of any kind, including Euro-migrants. Judging by Schuck's claims that 'Americans like immigrants more than they like immigration' the less contact they have with immigrants the more negative their perceptions. So we should perhaps regard public perceptions as potentially biased against immigrants and treat the amount of positive perceptions as an underestimate.

Public perceptions that Euro-migrants have a different legal culture Amongst the general public, the numbers who think incoming Euro-migrants are more rather than less obedient to the law compared to other people in their country, peak at 83 per cent in Ukraine and 78 per cent in Bulgaria, but drop to 42 per cent in Poland, and then to a mere 17 per cent in England and 13 per cent in Norway (Table 8.8). The public's images of incoming Euro-migrants therefore correlate, inversely of course, with the World Bank's ratings and indeed with the public's own self-images of general respect for the law within their own country. Where the public are most inclined to feel that people in their country do show respect for the law (Norway and England), they are also most inclined to suspect that incoming Euro-migrants do not show such respect.

By a margin of 14 per cent, Muslims have a more favourable perspective than the general public on Euro-migrants; but cross-nationally their favourable images of Euro-migrants follow the same steep pattern from 84 per cent in Ukraine to 16 per cent in Norway, and the cross-national correlation between the views of Muslims and the general public on whether Euro-migrants obey the law more or less than others reaches 0.87.

In addition, there is a fairly general perception – in every country and amongst both Muslims and the general public – that incoming Euro-migrants from European countries outside the former communist bloc are more law-abiding than Euro-migrants from countries within the former communist bloc.

Table 8.8 *Whether incoming Euro-migrants obey the law more than others: the legal outsiders' perspective*

	NOR (%)	ENG (%)	POL (%)	BUL (%)	UKR (%)	N-MU (%)	E-MU (%)	P-MU (%)	B-MU (%)	U-MU (%)
PQ110: Euro-migrants obey law more (v. less)	13	17	42	78	83	16	28	87	89	84
PQ111: Who are the more law-abiding? Euro-migrants from outside the former communist bloc (v. Euro-migrants from inside the former communist bloc)	87	61	69	93	80	66	64	68	90	67

Notes:

1. NOR, ENG, POL, BUL, UKR refer to the majority populations; N-MU, E-MU, P-MU, B-MU, U-MU refer to the Muslims.
2. In this table the percentages obeying the law are calculated after excluding those who opted for "Euro-migrants soon become the same as other people in this country". We discuss this 'adaptive' or 'acclimatisation' option later in this chapter.

Of course this pattern of public perceptions of Euro-migrants may simply reflect public perceptions – or public fears – of the countries from which they originate. These perceptions hint at feelings, perhaps subconscious, that incoming Euro-migrants will bring their legal cultures with them: If they were likely to break or evade the law in their country of origin then they will be likely to break or evade the law in their country of destination; that they carry their legal culture with them in their baggage; and that they will not adapt to their new environment.

Public perceptions or expectations that Euro-migrants soon adapt But our question about public perceptions of Euro-migrants' obedience to the law went beyond merely asking whether they were "more or less" law-abiding than others in their country of destination. It also offered the

Table 8.9 *Whether incoming Euro-migrants soon adapt to the law and become the same as others: the legal outsiders' perspective*

PQ110: Euro-migrants obey the law:	NOR (%)	ENG (%)	POL (%)	BUL (%)	UKR (%)	N-MU (%)	E-MU (%)	P-MU (%)	B-MU (%)	U-MU (%)
more than others	4	8	33	58	58	8	12	52	74	53
soon become just the same as others	72	55	53	26	30	48	56	40	17	36
less than others	24	37	14	16	12	44	31	8	9	10
more minus less	−20	−29	+19	+42	+46	−36	−19	+44	+65	+43

Note: NOR, ENG, POL, BUL, UKR refer to the majority populations; N-MU, E-MU, P-MU, B-MU, U-MU refer to the Muslims.

option that incoming Euro-migrants "soon become just the same as others". That reveals a more important and a more dynamic pattern in public perceptions of incoming Euro-migrants. Overall, the most frequent perception is not that Euro-migrants are more or less law-abiding but that incoming Euro-migrants "soon become just the same as other people in this country" in terms of their obedience to the law. The general public are most inclined to feel that incoming Euro-migrants soon "acclimatise" or "adapt" to the local legal culture (average 47 per cent) rather than obey the law more than locals (32 per cent) or less than locals (21 per cent) (Table 8.9).

Muslims have a somewhat more favourable perspective of Euro-migrants, but 39 per cent of Muslims also feel that Euro-migrants 'soon become the same' as locals. And just as there were sharp differences between countries and a strong cross-national correlation between the general public's and Muslim perceptions of whether incoming Euro-migrants were more or less law-abiding than others in their country, there is also a strong cross-national correlation of 0.78 between the general public's and Muslims' perceptions that incoming Euro-migrants adapt to the local legal culture.

But adaptation is asymmetric Insofar as they do not appear to "adapt" or "acclimatise" and thus become "just the same as others", public perceptions of incoming Euro-migrants in the more law-abiding countries (Norway and England) are on balance negative: by an average margin of 25 per cent the public rate incoming Euro-migrants as less rather than more law-abiding than other people in Norway and England.

Conversely, however, insofar as they do not appear to "adapt" or "acclimatise" and thus become "just the same as others", public perceptions of incoming Euro-migrants in the less law-abiding, post-communist countries (Poland, Bulgaria and Ukraine) are on balance positive: by a margin of 19 per cent in Poland and by an average margin of over twice that much, 44 per cent, in Bulgaria and Ukraine, the public rate incoming Euro-migrants as more rather than less law-abiding than other people in these countries.

At the same time, public perceptions that Euro-migrants are indeed adapting to local norms (and becoming "just the same" as others in the country) rise from around 28 per cent in Bulgaria and Ukraine, to around 54 per cent in Poland and England, and to 72 per cent in Norway.

Public perceptions at least suggest that Euro-migrants are therefore more willing to adapt to more law-abiding local legal cultures than the legal cultures in their countries of origin; however, they are less willing to adapt to less law-abiding local legal cultures than the legal cultures of their countries of origin. So in the general public's perceptions at least, Euro-migrants display not only "adaptive" legal cultures, but also "asymmetric adaptive" legal cultures, and therefore what might be called 'benign adaptive' legal cultures. In the public view, Euro-migrants find it easier to become more law-abiding than to become less law-abiding.

Background influences on public perceptions of Euro-migrants' respect for the law Within each country are some 'background influences' – other than religion – that may affect the general public's perceptions of Euro-migrants' respect for the law. We looked at a wide range including age, gender, urbanisation and income, but the key factors that affect their perceptions of Euro-migrants are location, education, identity and cross-national contacts. Positive public perceptions of incoming Euro-migrants' respect for the law are greater amongst the better-educated, amongst those who identify themselves with Europe, amongst those with international contacts and, above all, amongst those who live in post-communist countries (Table 8.10).

But these factors interact with the basic division between Norway and England on the one hand, and the post-communist countries on the other. For those who live in the post-communist countries that alone seems sufficient for them to have, on balance by a majority of 36 per cent, positive perceptions of incoming Euro-migrants. Only having relatives or close friends abroad has much impact at all and then only by 9 per cent. But for those who live in Norway or England perceptions of incoming Euro-migrants are far more complex and variable. For them,

Table 8.10 *Background influences on law-abidance amongst Euro-migrants: the legal outsiders' perspective*

	Norway (%)	England (%)	Poland (%)	Bulgaria (%)	Ukraine (%)
PQ110: Euro-migrants obey the law: 'more minus less' than others here					
Overall: All respondents	−20	−29	+19	+42	+46
If feel more primarily European, or equally [Country] and European	−10	−4	+17	+46	+50
If feel more [Country]	−23	−30	+18	+39	+48
If feel only [Country]	−36	−43	+22	+48	+41
Impact of Euro-identity	*+26*	*+39*	*−5*	*−2*	*+9*
Education: university	−12	−17	+16	+48	+46
Education: other higher	−20	−30	+12	+36	+48
Education: basic	−28	−41	+19	+43	+51
Impact of university education	*+16*	*+24*	*+3*	*+5*	*−5*
Relatives or close friends: live abroad: Yes	−19	−29	+21	+47	+51
Relatives or close friends: live abroad: No	−26	−32	+14	+36	+43
Impact of having relatives or close friends abroad	*+7*	*+3*	*+7*	*+11*	*+8*

it is necessary to identify with Europe, to have a higher education, to have lived abroad or to have friends or relatives living abroad, in order to even come near to having a positive perception of Euro-migrants' respect for the law. For Norwegians and the English having relatives or close friends abroad reduces their net balance of negative perceptions of Euro-migrants by a scarcely impressive 5 per cent; but having lived abroad reduces it by 12 per cent; whereas a university education reduces it by 20 per cent. Identifying with Europe rather than exclusively with Norway or England has the greatest impact on reducing their net balance of negative perceptions of Euro-migrants by 33 per cent – but that still leaves their perceptions of incoming Euro-migrants slightly negative.

Euro-migrants speak for themselves The general public's perceptions of Euro-migrants are clear: in their perceptions, Euro-migrants display not only "adaptive" legal cultures, but also "asymmetric adaptive" legal cultures – more ready to adapt to a more law-abiding legal culture than to a less law-abiding legal culture. As a whole, therefore, the general public holds a remarkably benign view of Euro-migrants' long-term legal cultures.

By itself that is not conclusive proof of 'asymmetric adaptation', though it is the clear view of the general public. But there is some more direct corroboration in our FG discussions with Euro-migrants themselves. These FG discussions do suggest that Euro-migrants are consciously willing to adapt, and to adapt more readily, to a more law-abiding culture than to a less-abiding culture. This does not necessarily reflect high moral standards or high legal culture alone. There are practical reasons and positive advantages for Euro-migrants to adapt, and to adapt more readily to a more law-abiding culture than to a less law-abiding culture.

In FGs, Euro-migrants who are familiar with the need to give officials a tip or a bribe in their country of origin express warmth towards officials in the country in which they now live who provide the same – or better – service without extorting tips and bribes. Conversely Euro-migrants, who are unfamiliar with the possibility of resolving a problem by giving a tip or a bribe, report that they are restrained not only by their own legal culture but by their lack of knowledge and familiarity with the etiquette of bribery. In their own eyes, they are quite consciously aware that their legal culture is not only adaptive but also asymmetrically adaptive.

Our Euro-migrant FGs provide some direct evidence of a self-conscious "adaptive" or "acclimatisation" effect. As participants in a Euro-migrant FG with Poles living in Lviv (western Ukraine) explain: U27–4: "when nobody does it here and everybody there, one does not want to be different".[5] U27–3: "so the society influences the person". U27–4: "forms us". U27-ALL: "yes, yes". U27–4: "the legal system itself forces people to violate the laws because it is too complicated". U27–1: "one cannot expect people to observe laws which are unobservable".

[5] In this chapter U27–4: indicates participant number 4 in FG No. 27 that took place in Ukraine.

Participants in a Euro-migrant FG with "North-Europeans [Scandinavians, Germans etc.]" living in Kyiv expressed sympathy for badly paid Ukrainian police and officials. Indeed they made excuses for these officials:

> U28–1: 'I felt sometimes with a bad experience with police, that policemen, as persons, must do that to feed their children, for example . . . and I will not say that such policemen are pigs because I do not know what I would do if I were him in this country and I do not know whether I would not do the same . . . and I do not want to cast the first stone'. U28–1: 'I suppose that they earn less than they need'. U28–6: 'and nobody gives them a high salary because they are expected to earn in an unofficial way'. U28–1: 'the same thing with Ukrainian teachers'. U28–6: 'they get their money by private tutoring'.

Moreover the tone of comments by some North Europeans suggests that they preferred the "informal system" to the state law. There was flexibility – even warmth – amongst these North Europeans towards the predictability of the Ukrainian "system" of direct (albeit informal or illegal) payments: U28–6: "this system is supposed actually to work on other rules. The cases with traffic police – everybody actually knows what the fine is, and the police stop and say that you have to pay [an amount which is] lower than the fine. So it is a system, but it is not written and formal, not based on salaries and so on". In short, this is a vision of two competing providers in the marketplace for traffic law: first, the state; and second, quite separately, the police themselves act on their own account – and with some advantages for the customers.

No doubt some North Europeans are simply unwilling on moral grounds to adapt to a more corrupt system, but others are simply unable to adapt: They do not know the appropriate behaviour or the appropriate price in an "informal" system:

> U28-MODERATOR: 'so you do not trust the police but you have sympathy for them?' U28–1: 'in a certain way, yes.' U28–6: 'I think foreigners [like us] are very frustrated because of the police, because we are used to formal rules and formal systems. But my impression is that locals understand these informal rules much better. They are not so frustrated because they know the system somehow, though it is not written. We [foreigners] just come from different systems and this is much more frustrating for us.' U28–5: 'if the police [are] corrupted it can really take terrible forms but also there are these everyday forms, which are predictable . . . it's another story if the police are cruel and brutal . . . if the police force is physically dangerous, oppresses people.' U28–4: 'yes, [but] they are not dictatorship police, they try to tolerate people, they just have to make some money, it is everyday business. And the same is in the University,

> you have to pay for the special courses, for special exams ... this gives a person great security ... and now the government tries to change this system and there will be external exams ... and this gives great insecurity to people ... even pure people borrowed some money [to get] just the right paper ... And the police in Ukraine, in a way, give you big security too. In Germany if you go 80 kilometres fast you lose your driving license for three months, in France even worse, they are quite strict there, [but] here you can arrange everything, if you do not harm anybody, of course everything in a way can be arranged.'

– A clear invocation of the 'J. S. Mill principle'!

The complaints of the North Europeans were about the problem of access to this "informal system": U28–4: "[unfortunately] for us it is totally insecure, because we do not know the prices, we do not know the language well enough, [and] we cannot deal with them".

North European Euro-migrants try hard to depict Ukrainians as law-abiding people in overwhelmingly difficult circumstances: U28–5: "from what I see, I cannot say that there is a low level of obeying the law ... people obey the law as well as they can ... But they can reach the limits and then you really have to ask the question what is the relationship between demands made on them and their behaviour". U28–1: "I have the impression that everybody looks to live without law and without hurting anybody too much".

Despite all this sympathy for the Ukrainian condition, however, the statistical evidence of "asymmetric acclimatisation" which emerge in our survey data suggests that legal culture does not reside exclusively within the state. In particular our statistical data suggest that Euro-migrants might be more willing to adapt to a more law-abiding state culture than the one with which they are familiar, but at the same time they might be more reluctant to adapt to a less law-abiding state culture than the one with which they are familiar – though adapt to some degree they clearly do, in both these circumstances.

In the Euro-migrant FGs within Ukraine there are also some reservations about the "U28–4: informal system" even if they are not personal complaints: "but for those who have no money and cannot solve problems like this ... nobody will help ... there is no Ombudsman ... and this makes me upset".

There is certainly evidence in our Euro-migrant FGs of more unqualified enthusiasm for adapting to a more law-abiding state culture rather than to a less law-abiding state culture, however. Indeed, one of the Polish Euro-migrants in Lviv argued: U27–1: "I must tell you about the Ukrainians who came to Poland, and it turned out that observing the law did turn out to be possible for them. They are able to do this, looking for traffic lights, they know how to park, and they can behave according to traffic rules. This is not a question of nationality".

Another FG with Polish Euro-migrants, this time in England, displayed similar enthusiasm for a more law-abiding state culture – though this time Poland was depicted as the less law-abiding country. Every participant in the group felt that English law and officials, unlike Polish law and officials, helped them: E14–8: "I had a meeting with a person from the tax office [in England] . . . [she] wrote three forms for me; sent it to a tax office in another city; I was a little shocked, because in Poland that's impossible. In Poland I cannot expect any help. Here I have it". E14–2: "in our country [Poland] they are going to catch you". E14–5: "fine you and". E14–5: "not help you". 'E14–6: "law in England works a little bit . . . faster and more straight".

Conclusions – culture, context and behaviour: the legal outsiders' perspective

Do the public across Europe (or at least across the five European countries in our study) have fundamentally similar legal cultures? And do the legal cultures of Muslims and/or Euro-migrants reflect the legal culture of the country in which they live? Have they "adapted", or are they at least in the process of adapting, to the country-specific legal culture of the country where they now live?

In many respects our data suggest that public perspectives on law are similar across the five countries and similar also between the general public and Muslim minorities. The public in different countries have similar attitudes towards basing law on religion, general moral values, current life-styles, or local customs and traditions though sharp disagreement on the importance of applying E-I standards. On an average, Muslims have similar attitudes to the general public except that they would put less emphasis on local customs and traditions and more on E-I standards.

The public in different countries have similar expectations about whether "law-abiding" people would "knowingly break the law" in an emergency, in self-defence, if they thought "they would not get caught", or if they would cause "no harm to others" – even perhaps if the law was "unfair", or if they were driven by "pressures of work or poverty".

But on some aspects of legal culture the public differ sharply between countries. When they do, so do the Muslim minorities within those countries. On overall perceptions of their government and people's respect for the law, on whether the law helps them or causes problems, on whether religious or ethnic minorities obey the law more or less than others, on whether people obey the law primarily because it is fair rather than for fear of punishment, on whether "when ordinary people knowingly break the law they often have some reasonable excuse", or whether they succumb to "the pressure of circumstances", or whether "generally law-abiding people would break the law if they were under pressure from doctors, police or state officials to give gifts or bribes", or whether they think incoming Euro-migrants are more or less law-abiding than locals – on all of these there are large differences between countries but a high cross-national correlation between the pattern of general public opinion and the pattern of Muslim opinion. So we have clear evidence that suggests more or less long-established minorities have adapted to the popular legal culture in their country.

More dynamically, we have found evidence of incoming Euro-migrants' willingness to adapt – and evidence that their adaptation is both asymmetric and benign. Our survey of the general public's perceptions show that they are strongly convinced that incoming Euro-migrants are more willing to adapt when they move to a more law-abiding society; and that they are less willing – or perhaps just less able – to adapt when they move to a less law-abiding and more "informal" society.

These public perceptions are corroborated by the comments made by incoming Euro-migrants themselves in our FGs. Their own comments suggest that they adjust to the changing context when they cross state borders – and that, for Euro-migrants, it is easier to adapt to a more law-abiding context than to a less law-abiding context. It is easier to adjust to a more law-abiding context where government officials do not seek tips or bribes to perform their duties, and more difficult to adjust to a less law-abiding context where contacts and networks may take too much time and effort to establish and where "informal" rules are less explicit and more difficult for incomers to negotiate.

9

Balancing civil rights against a 'war on terror'

Introduction: the 'war on terror'

Since the collapse of Communism in 1989 the concept of a United Europe has been pursued with vigour. Political and economic integration has been sought through EU enlargement to the east, deeper integration within the EU and beyond the EU through the EEA and ENP.

At the same time, however, CoE with its strong commitment to human rights has also extended even further to the east, and it is argued that genuine partnership across the whole of Europe can develop only on the basis of shared common values – not only democracy and the rule of law but, more fundamentally, full respect for human and civil rights (Kuzio 2004).

The pressure of European Unity on legal cultures, with its emphasis on respect for human and civil rights, has been in a liberal direction. But there are other influences and pressures on popular legal cultures in Europe: historic legal traditions, religious traditions, experiences of Communism, the impact of globalisation and migration and, especially over the last decade, the adverse pressure exerted by terrorism and the so-called war on terror. Although European integration has exerted pressure on national legal cultures in a liberal and convergent direction, terrorism, the continuing threat of terrorism and the war on terror have exerted pressure on legal cultures in illiberal, authoritarian and divergent directions.

Terrorism has been divisive, targeting some European countries but not others. And its impact has been to provoke an authoritarian but variable reaction. Commenting on findings from the 2007 British Social Attitudes report, Conor Gearty concluded that:

> our survey shows a general public that remains on the whole committed to civil liberties [but] with less enthusiasm than in the past and with a greater susceptibility to be persuaded to dispense with them . . . the very mention of something being a counter-terrorism measure makes people

> more willing to contemplate the giving up of their freedoms. It is as though society is in the process of forgetting why past generations thought these freedoms to be so very important.
>
> (NatCen Press Release 2007; see also Johnson and Gearty 2007).

Increasing attention has been given to two allegedly dangerous concepts: 'the morality of the lesser evil' (Gearty 2007b, p. 351; Ignatieff 2004) and a 'war' against terrorism (Campbell and Connolly 2003; see also Zedner 2005).

The phrase *war on terrorism* has a lengthy history. In the late nineteenth century it was used by the press in connection with attempts by European and American governments to stop anarchist attacks on politicians and officials. In the 1940s it was used to describe British efforts to end attacks by Zionist Jews in British-administered Palestine – attacks that are still remembered and, perhaps more surprisingly, still cited spontaneously in at least one of our English FGs (see information to follow).

In the press and in the public mind, terrorism has often been associated with religion, indeed with many religions: in the last few decades alone it has been associated with Catholics, Protestants, Jews, Muslims, Buddhists, Hindus and Sikhs. Nonetheless, in recent times within Europe and the US, the phrase *war on terror* has been used almost exclusively in regard to Islamic terrorism, and law-abiding Muslims may therefore be particularly alienated by it. The phrase is now most closely associated with President Bush's reaction to the 9/11 (11 September 2001) destruction of the Twin Towers in New York City, and the loss of almost three thousand lives, along with a simultaneous attack on the Pentagon and a fourth plane brought down in rural Pennsylvania as passengers fought the hijackers. Five days after 9/11, Bush was widely reported as saying 'this crusade, this war on terrorism is going to take a while'. He was advised to avoid using the word *crusade* but continued to speak of *the war* on terrorism.[1]

Some critics have suggested that the use of the word *war* was an attempt to 'externalise' the threat though it had some legal significance within the complex US presidential system. The term itself was not used in the UK, but it is argued that 'the British government's response to the London bombings sought to make the terror of that day foreign, even though it appeared largely domestic' (Bulley 2008, p. 379). Others, however,

[1] Wikipedia.org/Tenth_Crusade accessed on 1 January 2011.

have emphasised the importance of links between second- and even third-generation immigrants and their ancestral lands (see Githens-Mazer 2008, p. 565), so that recent terrorism, in this view, really does have foreign overtones. Nonetheless, many of the terrorist actions in UK over the last half century have involved terrorists who were entitled to a British passport (though some were entitled to Irish passports as well as, or instead of, British passports).

In Northern Ireland where various groups of terrorists caused more deaths than in 9/11 (admittedly over a 30-year period from 1969–98, but out of a population much less than 1 per cent of that in the US) the British government did not declare a war on terror (though British troops were stationed in Northern Ireland).

From a Northern Irish perspective, Campbell and Connolly (2003, p. 341) cite 'the dangers of a "war" model in complex and violent disorders'. And even after the al-Qaeda–inspired 7 July 2005 bombings of the London Underground, which killed 56 and injured many more (followed quickly by another attempt on 21 July when further casualties were avoided only when the bombs failed to explode), the term *war on terror* was officially criticised in the UK. Writing in *The Times* (24 January 2007), Ken McDonald, British Director of Public Prosecutions, argued that the July 2005 bombers were not 'soldiers' in a war and should be dealt with by the criminal justice system. In his view a war on terrorism simply legitimised terrorists. He further argued for a 'culture of legislative restraint' in passing new anti-terrorism laws because the 'primary purpose' of these attacks was to tempt the UK to 'abandon our values': the response, he argued, should be 'proportionate, and grounded in due process and the rule of law'.

English (2009), in his major study of the IRA, 'Terrorism: How to Respond', argues that the most effective response to terrorism is to avoid over-militarisation, address the underlying causes, respect the existing legal framework and adhere to the established rule of law.

Gearty (2007a, pp. 42–9) warns at length of 'the subversive power of the counter terrorism narrative'. Indeed he argues that whereas the half century following the 1948 Declaration of Human Rights might be described as an 'age of human rights', the half century after 9/11 in 2001 may come to merit the title of an 'age of counter terrorism' if not an 'age of war on terror' (a phrase he particularly dislikes), citing the 'plethora of anti-terrorism laws' and 'the harnessing of the human rights ideal itself to legitimize action that in any other context would be condemned as being in violation of basic rights' (Gearty 2007b, p. 340)

In her study of 'the cost of counter terrorism', Donohue (2008, p. 25) warns of the 'security or freedom dichotomy' and sets out 'to recalculate the price the US and UK have paid for their counter terrorist regimes' (ibid., p. 31), citing a British law lord's claim that 'the safety of the state has always been used as a justification for undermining civil liberties' (ibid., p. 32). In her conclusion she asserts that 'the accretion of dangerous executive power is indeed the hallmark of counter terrorist law ... blinded to the broader and more profound costs of our counter terrorist regime' (ibid, pp. 359–60).

But our focus here is not on what distinguished academics or lawyers believe is the 'price worth paying' to combat terrorism; instead, our focus is on how the general publics – and Muslim minorities – across Europe feel about the 'price worth paying' to combat terrorism.

Using data from our 5,000 approximately hour-long survey interviews with the general public and 1,000 with Muslim minorities we look at the public response to the pressure of terrorism on popular legal cultures in our five countries: Norway, UK (as data was collected in England only, we refer to England rather than to the UK in this chapter), Poland, Bulgaria and Ukraine. The English sample does not include those residing in Northern Ireland, Scotland and Wales, whose opinions merit separate investigation. But, of course, terrorist actions anywhere within the UK have an impact on strictly English public opinion. We also draw insights from the 84 FGs that preceded our surveys. And using data from the 786 structured and open-ended interviews with legal insiders (i.e. legislators, prosecutors, lawyers, judges, government officials, police) that followed our surveys, we explore the manner in which the war on terror has affected professional legal culture in these four countries.

As noted in Chapter 1, our spectrum of five European countries range from Norway which regularly scores at or near the top on World Bank 2010 Rule of Law Index to Ukraine which scores nearer the bottom – a ranking that is echoed by their publics in our own survey (Table 9.1).

These five countries also range from those that have suffered major terrorist attacks (UK) to those where the people feel they are almost invisible to international terrorists (Ukraine, see Q121 later in this chapter). So the English especially might be more willing to accept a reduction in their civil liberties than Norwegians, Poles, Bulgarians and Ukrainians because the UK has been directly affected by IRA terrorism from 1969 to 1998 and by al-Qaeda terrorism since 2001. (The interviews in Norway, as with the other countries, all took place in 2008–9,

Table 9.1 *Respect for law and threat of terrorism by rule of law: the legal outsiders' perspective*

	Percentile on World Bank 2010 Rule of Law Index (Percentile)	Q126 Our government and people respect and obey the law more (v. less) than in rest of Europe (%)	Q121 There is a real threat of terrorism (v. no threat or threat exaggerated) (%)
Norway	99	93	49
England	94	58	70
Poland	69	29	44
Bulgaria	53	11	26
Ukraine	25	10	13

Note: The World Bank Rule of Law percentile for England strictly applies to Britain (though the population of England comprises 84% of the British population). The other data comes from questions Q126 and Q121 in our survey.

well before the Oslo massacre in 2011 – though that had no direct connection with organised global terrorism).[2]

In our FGs and IDIs, we avoided the emotive and much criticised phrase *war on terror* and asked instead about public perceptions of 'terrorism' or the 'threat of terrorism', about whether the supposed 'threat of terrorism' is real or exaggerated, about whether to prioritise a respect for civil rights or for combating terrorism, and about whether the government and security services should respond to the 'threat of terrorism' by 'staying within existing laws and procedures', 'enforcing existing laws more strictly', 'introducing new and tougher laws' or 'stepping outside the law whenever they think it useful'.

Terrorism or the war on terrorism is likely to have influenced both popular and professional legal culture in all five countries – though to

[2] Anders Behring Breivik, the organiser and sole executor of the car bomb attack on the Norwegian government headquarters and the massacre at the Labour Party Youth Camp at Utøya, which resulted in 77 deaths, is a fierce opponent of the 'Islamification of Europe'. Behring Breivik opposed what he perceived as the Norwegian government's promotion of multiculturalism in Norway. The coalition government at the time was headed by the Norwegian Labour Party. Breivik therefore targeted the government and the Labour Party's youth camp to draw attention to his ideas and his manifesto. His case was heard by Oslo tingrett (Oslo First Instance Court) between 16 April and 22 June 2012. Breivik was sentenced to 21 years' internment.

different degrees because previous and current experience with terrorism varies across Europe. The UK has been exposed to both 'homebred' and 'foreign' terrorism for decades. In the first half of the 1970s it experienced a very high level of IRA-inspired subversive violence (Gearty 1999, p. 369). In London, bomb scares were frequent throughout the 1980s and sporadically occurred also in the early 1990s. More recently, British-born Islamist suicide bombers from Leeds attacked the London Underground and a London bus (2005).[3] An NHS doctor from Iraq and an Indian engineering student were jailed in 2008 for detonating a car bomb at Glasgow airport in 2007.

Prior to the massacre of 22 July 2011 (by a right-wing Norwegian), two years after our surveys, Norway had little experience with terrorism within its own territory.[4] However, the country hosts an internationally recognised terrorist – Mullah Krekar – who came to Norway from Iraq as a refugee.[5] The US exerted pressure to extradite him to Iraq, but the Norwegian government resisted on the grounds that Norway is bound by international agreements not to extradite citizens of foreign origin to another country if this is likely to put their life at risk. In response, the American Central Intelligence Agency (CIA) allegedly made an unsuccessful attempt to abduct Krekar from Norway in 2009.[6]

Osama bin Laden issued a threat against Norway when the Norwegian *Magasinet* reprinted 12 cartoons he considered blasphemous of the Prophet Mohammad, which were originally published by the Danish daily *Jyllandsposten* in 2005. Shortly after, in February 2006, the Norwegian

[3] Two weeks after the blasts, six men went on trial for plotting to murder people in attempted bombings in London. See 'Six on trial over failed London bombings', *The Guardian*, 15 January 2007, www.guardian.co.uk/uk/2007/jan/15/july7.uksecurity accessed on 8 March 2012.

[4] The closest one gets to international terrorism in Norway is the assassination of a Palestinian activist by Israeli Mossad agents in the late 1970s and the attempted murder of Norwegian publisher William Nygaard in the 1980s, following his decision to do the Norwegian translation of Salman Rushdie's *Satanic Verses*. www.sa.no/innenriks/article 5322505.ece accessed on 8 March 2012.

[5] Mullah Krekar has on several occasions been taken to court – including for issuing death threats against former Minister of Municipal and Regional Affairs and current leader of the Conservative Party of Norway, Erna Solberg, during a meeting with the international press in Oslo on 10 June 2010. The Oslo First Instance Court sentenced him to five years in prison for the death threats. Krekar has hinted that terrorist acts against Norway are likely in the event that he is extradited to Iraq.

[6] 'Agenter skulle kidnappe Mulla Krekar' [Agents were to kidnap Mullah Krekar], *TV2*, 6 November 2009, www.tv2.no/nyheter/innenriks/agenter-skulle-kidnappe-mulla-krekar-2994247.html accessed on 22 February 2002.

embassy in Damascus was set ablaze in response to the publishing of these cartoons in Norway.[7] In 2012 the Oslo first instance court jailed two men for planning to bomb *Jyllandsposten* and to murder the cartoonist, Kurt Westergaard.[8] A Norwegian of foreign origin, Arfan Bhatti was charged with terrorism in 2006 after having fired shots at the Jewish synagogue in Oslo. He was acquitted of the terrorist charges by the Norwegian Supreme Court in 2009.

Norway[9] has allowed US aircraft bound for Guantanamo Bay to land on Norwegian soil and, as has the UK, it has been actively involved in US-led operations in Iraq and Afghanistan where there have been casualties – though not in the range of those suffered by the UK.

Altogether, with the exception of internal right-wing extremism, the timing of which means its horror had no impact on our survey interviews, within Norway itself, it has been a mixed bag of pressure from the US and Osama bin Laden, neither of whom resorted to terrorism against the general Norwegian public.

Poland, Bulgaria and Ukraine have not experienced domestic Islamist-motivated terrorism since 9/11, nor have they been specifically targeted by terrorists abroad. Poles, however, were amongst the casualties both in the 2004 Madrid train bombing and the London bombings the following year.

The domestic threat of terrorism is probably rather small in Poland and Bulgaria though somewhat higher in Ukraine. Poland's native Muslim Tatar community is not at odds with the ethnic titular group. Polish Tatars have played an important role in the country's historical past and

[7] Irene Elisabeth Rossland, 'Norges ambassade i Syria nedbrent' [Norway's embassy in Syria burnt down], *NRK*, 4 February 2006, http://nrk.no/nyheter/utenriks/5458523.html accessed on 22 February 2012.

[8] More recently, in July 2010, three men of Uighur/Uzbek nationality were arrested by the Police Security Service (PST) – and charged with the planning of a terrorist act. The men have been accused of having planned the largest terrorist attack against a Western country since 9/11. Two of them – Mikel Davud (an Uighur from China with Norwegian citizenship) and Shawan Sadek Saeed Bujak (an Iraqi Kurd residing in Norway) were in the beginning of 2012 sentenced to 7 and 3.5 years in prison. David Jakobsen – an ethnic Uzbek residing in Norway – was sentenced to 4 months in prison for helping the other two to procure bomb-making material. These men were the first people to be jailed for planning a terrorist act in Norway. AP. 'Men jailed for planning attack on Danish newspaper', *The Guardian*, 30 January 2012, www.guardian.co.uk/world/2012/jan/30/men-guilty-planning-attack-danish-newspaper accessed on 9 March 2012.

[9] Kjell Persen. 'Guantanamo-fly i norsk luftrom' [Guantanamo aircraft in Norwegian air space], *TV2*, 14 March 2008, www.tv2.no/nyheter/guantanamofly-i-norsk-luftrom-1686257.html accessed on 22 February 2012.

are well respected as a result. Muslim immigrants, for their part, represent a very small minority, and most of them have migrated from secular states such as the successor states to the former Soviet Union and from Turkey. Bulgaria has a sizeable Muslim minority (ethnic Turks, Bulgarian Turks – referred to as Pomaks) that has lived in Bulgaria for centuries. Though heavily discriminated against during the Zhivkov regime, the political opinions of the Bulgarian Turks do not appear to differ significantly from those of ethnic Bulgarians though some religious radicalisation has been observed in recent years.[10]

At the time of interviewing Ukraine also had a native Muslim community: Crimean Tatars. The Tatars were expelled from the Crimea to Central Asia in 1944, as Stalin feared that they would collude with the Germans against Soviet rule. In 1989 the Tatar Community was rehabilitated and allowed to return to the Crimea. By 2000 an estimated 260,000 Tatars had returned to Ukraine.[11] Since their return, however, tension between the Crimean Tatars and the ethnic Russian community in the Crimea has been considerable – though mostly pertaining to the ownership of land and political representation. Whether this in itself should cause reason for concern about the possibility of terrorism, however, is questionable.

NATO member states Poland and Bulgaria have sent troops to Iraq and Afghanistan. Ukraine has done the same through the NATO Partnership for Peace programme, though on a very modest scale. Polish soldiers have been killed in Afghanistan (34) and Iraq (23). Bulgaria and Ukraine suffered casualties in Iraq (13 and 18 soldiers respectively), but have so far not lost any soldiers in Afghanistan.

US aircraft transporting terrorist suspects to Guantanamo Bay have landed for refuelling in most of these countries. And Poland has admitted to having hosted two US-run facilities near the Szymany airfield in northern Poland (Traynor 2010), at which CIA detainees were interrogated and allegedly tortured. Bulgaria, for its part, however, has denied any involvement with US extraordinary rendition.[12]

[10] For an account of the Muslim community in Bulgaria, see Ghodsee (2010) and Neuburger (2004).

[11] For an introduction to the Crimean Tatars, see Williams (2001) and Fisher (1978). By 2000 some 260,000 of the 400–550,000 strong Tatar community had returned to the Crimea. CoE (2000).

[12] Officially, Bulgaria has denied media reports suggesting that CIA aircraft landed at the Sarafovo airport in 2005. See 'Countries involved in extraordinary renditions 18–12–05', www.statewatch.org/cia/documents/countries-in-extraordinary-rendition.pdf accessed on 22 February 2012.

Reflecting their recent experience, the English in our survey were the most concerned about the 'threat of terrorism' within their country. Nonetheless, the English were second only to Norwegians in claiming that their "government and people respect and obey the law more than in the rest of Europe". It is an odd combination, this perception of a relatively law-abiding but terrorism-prone society. Despite Bulley's (2008) logical arguments, the English public really does seem to have, in some peculiar sense, 'externalised' their perceptions of terrorism: so that their fear of terrorism does not contradict their perception of a generally law-abiding public – and indeed a law-abiding government. Their image is of a law-abiding society under attack from atypical outsiders – including, in a peculiar sense 'outsiders' that live amongst generally law-abiding citizens, hold British passports, and may well be English by birth. And their image of their government is that of a law-abiding government forced by terrorist outsiders to take harsh measures.

Al-Qaeda has targeted two of our five countries – most notably England (and to a very much lesser degree, Norway) – more than the others, partly because England is seen as an old colonial power and now as a close ally of America. Moreover al-Qaeda seeks what it describes as 'spectacular targets', and targets in London or New York City are likely to grab more international attention than targets in Kyiv or Sofia. So we might expect sharp country variations across our five countries in terms of their significance as terror targets and consequently in terms of public attitudes towards a defensive or retaliatory 'war against terror'.

Because al-Qaeda sympathisers are predominantly Muslims, Muslims in general – who may not themselves sympathise with al-Qaeda at all – may nonetheless feel, with some justice, that they are the principal targets of the security forces. Consequently we might expect sharp differences between Muslims and others in their attitudes towards a retaliatory, or even a defensive, 'war against terror'. But, on the other hand, the most direct and immediate influence on attitudes towards prioritising a war on terror over the rights and liberties of individual citizens and minorities may simply be perceptions of 'risk' or 'threat'.

The legal insiders, for their part, are responsible for providing both security and for protecting civil rights. Norway and England have been "rule-of-law"-based countries for much longer than Poland, Bulgaria and Ukraine. However, the terrorist threat appears to be greater in the former than in the latter countries. We might therefore expect to find some differences between legal insiders in Western and Eastern Europe both in terms of the terrorist threat and in terms of what measures to apply in response to it.

PERCEPTIONS OF TERRORISM: THE LEGAL OUTSIDERS' PERSPECTIVE

FG discussions

As might be expected, participants in English FGs have much more to say about terrorism than participants in any of the other countries. Their comments can be grouped into two broad categories: 'visibility' and 'fault' – comments displaying an awareness of terrorism past and present (which might be classified as 'visibility'), and comments assigning blame (which might be classified as 'fault').

Terrorism anywhere in the UK is highly visible to the English. English participants suggest terrorism is endemic. E4-Bath-1: "there has always been terrorism". E5-Bristol-3: "we have lived under the threat of IRA for I don't know how long". E4-Bath-8: "before the IRA, well, you've got the Jewish terrorists before Israel was a country".

They cite recent examples, notably the attacks on the London Underground (7 July 2005) and Glasgow Airport (30 June 2007) – though not much earlier than the Lockerbie bombing in Scotland (21 December 1988), which killed 11 people in Lockerbie in addition to the passengers and crew of the Pan Am flight that crashed on the town en route from London to New York.

Police activity also raises awareness of terrorism: E7-Village-Yorkshire-2: "you can see it's a threat because you go to an airport, there's police with guns and that never used to be". [An important perspective, though not quite historically accurate is the view that police with submachine guns have patrolled British airports since IRA terrorism erupted.] And there is more direct local awareness, sometimes very local:

> E8-Leeds-7: "I've actually met a terrorist [cites the terrorist's name] . . . he was very nice." E9-Leeds-Muslims-4: "but who'd have thought that three young Asian men from Leeds would go to London and blow themselves up – and other people." E7-village-Yorkshire-7: "it's our kids that are born and bred over here to some extent, that are going over there to train in camps . . . It's a genuine threat, there's no doubt."

Some English participants suggest that the UK is at fault – that the country itself is the real cause of terrorism:

> E2-London-5: 'I think the Government has created a terrorist situation . . . because they've invaded two countries [i.e. Afghanistan and Iraq].' E2-London-7: 'we've upset the whole world.'

Others blame America or the UK's association with America:

> E7-village-Yorkshire-1: "we joined forces with America". E4-Bath-9: "this Iraq thing . . . it wasn't too bad before that." E7-Village-Yorkshire-2: "the war in Iraq was like a recruiting ground for terrorists in this country."

The majority of the Norwegian legal outsiders feel that the terrorist threat is low in their country and that, compared to other countries, Norway is at relatively low risk. Those who believe that Norway is at risk of terrorism think the risk is primarily due to external factors and its high international profile, such as the country's support for, and participation in, US-initiated operations abroad, notably involvement in Afghanistan. Further, they express their concern with al-Qaeda's threats against Norway and the subsequent torching of the Norwegian embassy in Damascus (2006). Some FG participants believe that Norway is at risk because it is a wealthy country with a large oil industry.

Most Norwegian Muslims, however, stress that they believe the risk of terrorism in Norway is low. Very few legal outsiders believe that the presence of alleged terrorists such as Mullah Krekar or Arfan Bhatti within Norway poses a threat to their country. Only one person expressed fear of terrorism:

> N12-Tromsø-7: 'our participation abroad makes us more vulnerable than we would otherwise have been . . . Norway may be targeted.' N14-Bardufoss-1: 'the Norwegian embassy [in Damascus] was attacked . . . we have rich resources and we are involved in Afghanistan.' N-Oslo-Muslims-6: 'Norway . . . sell[s] ammunition to Israel. In addition [Norway] is a wealthy country. Al-Qaeda knows about Norway . . . [but] I feel that the probability [of an attack] is small'. N-Oslo-Muslims-3: 'there is a continuous threat against all countries. No country can say that they have no problem with this. But I don't think Norway is particularly vulnerable . . . in Norway, radicals from outside the country are a greater problem.'

Those legal outsiders who thought Norway is not at risk of a terrorist attack in most cases simply stated this as a fact. Norwegian Muslims believed that Norway is faced with only a small terrorist risk. In the view of one of them the Norwegian government's policy of dialogue rather than confrontation with Norwegian Muslims has done much to defuse tension over the Mohammad cartoons:

> N11-Klepp-4: 'I don't think the danger is as great as the media is suggesting.' N-Oslo-Muslims-9: 'Norway does not have so much power in the great matter of things and then there is no point in blowing up [something] in Norway.' N4-Oslo-Muslims-3: 'there is of course no guarantee that nothing will happen. But . . . the government has tried to establish contact with various groups, to talk and to try to [establish] a common front, and that is very good'.

Polish comments also fall into the broad categories of "visibility" and "fault". But by contrast there is no suggestion that terrorism is endemic in Poland, no recent Polish examples and no local awareness. "Visibility" comprises only police activity within Poland – together with an awareness of actual terrorism in other countries, notably the US, UK and Spain (the Madrid bombings, 11 March 2004) – all of which are cited in some detail. Participants in Bulgarian FGs have little to say about a real threat of terrorism.

Terrorism lacks any "visibility" in Bulgaria, however, and only a few comments assign "blame" – mainly to NATO, the UK or America: B8-Dolna Mitropolia-1: "terrorist acts happen in countries which have interfered with the policy of another country".

Participants in some Ukrainian FGs have a lot to say about the threat of terrorism. But in striking contrast to participants in English FGs, Ukrainian citizens express generalised impressions, or fears for the future, rather than citing specific examples of actual terrorist actions. Unlike the English, who cite a sequence of different terrorist threats from Zionists in the 1940s, through northern Irish Republicans and Loyalists in the last three decades of the twentieth century, to the contemporary international terrorism of al-Qaeda sympathisers, Ukrainians cite only a variety of contemporary terrorist threats. These include threats from Muslims reacting against the invasion of Iraq, and also threats from Russia, and most especially threats from what they call "local" terrorism, whether these are from unspecified "local gangsters" or from "local Tatars".

A few Ukrainians blame local gangsters: U12-Ternopil-3: "showdowns between all sorts of clans . . . gangsterism". Many more, especially in Crimea, blame Tatars. Participants in Ukrainian FGs nearly always refer to them as "Tatars" rather than "Muslims" – stressing the ethnic and the territorial, rather than the religious dimension:

> U16-Alushta-1: "if land lots that the Tatars want to grab are not allocated to them, there can be a terrorism threat". UKR16-Alushta-6: "we live as on a volcano". U16-Alushta-7: "the situation in Ukraine is explosive."

> U19-Bahchysaray-5: "we sleep on a volcano, frankly speaking." U20-Lobanovo-4: "Crimea is the only centre of real terrorism, in my mind." U20-Lobanovo-6: "the Tatars think that this is their Motherland, their land. They even say so; that everything will be theirs. They will take this from us."

So, in complete contrast to English references to "actually existing" and "international" terrorism participants in Ukrainian FGs talk only of "potential" and "local" terrorism. And in further contrast to the English, Ukrainians express no feelings of remorse or responsibility for triggering that "local" terrorism: they see themselves purely as victims – albeit only potential victims as yet.

Quantitative surveys: general public and Muslims

Within each of our five countries, we interviewed approximately 1,000 respondents drawn to represent the general public, together with an additional "Muslim sample" of approximately 200 Muslims using questions drawn largely from the ideas that emerged from the FG discussions.

The self-chosen "family background" of Muslims interviewed varies systematically from country to country: in Norway they are predominantly Pakistani (54 per cent); in England even more predominantly Pakistani (67 per cent); in Bulgaria overwhelmingly 'Bulgarian Turk' (92 per cent); in Ukraine overwhelmingly Crimean Tatar (99 per cent); and in Poland our sample was designed to include 50 per cent long-established 'Polish Tatars', with the other 50 per cent incomers – from Russia or Turkey. The sheer diversity of Muslims' self-declared 'family backgrounds' cautions against any assumption of monolithic uniformity. But we might expect that under the pressure of the war on terror, differences between Muslims and non-Muslims within a single country are more likely to reflect the peculiar circumstances of Muslims (any Muslims!) within that country at the present time, rather than their specific family background. It should be noted that for many Muslims, religious identity is more important than ethnic identity.

To avoid an overemphasis on differences between small samples, we focus primarily on the difference between the cross-country averages for Muslim opinion and the opinion of the general public – effectively basing our analysis on comparisons between approximately 5,000 respondents drawn from the general public and 1,000 Muslims. That provides a more general cross-European perspective on Muslim/non-Muslim reactions to the threat of terrorism and their support for counterterrorist measures.

Occasionally, however, we take the statistical risk of citing Muslim/non-Muslim comparisons within a single country – notably within England where the perceived threat of terrorism is greatest and where Muslims might reasonably feel particularly exposed to the pressures of counterterrorism.

Paying the price: combating terrorism versus rights and freedoms

As we noted earlier, the British Director of Public Prosecutions argued that the 'primary purpose' of terrorist attacks was to tempt England to 'abandon our values'. To measure the extent to which terrorism has succeeded in getting the public to abandon the value of 'individual freedom' respondents were asked to prioritise 'individual freedom' versus 'combating terrorism': Q7: "Which do you feel should be more important at this time: to protect individual freedom or to combat the threat of terrorism?"

This is not a simple question about public support for a war on terrorism. Such a question might be worded: 'How important is it to take action to combat the threat of terrorism? Very important? Somewhat important? Not very important? Not at all important?' That wording would focus on a single concept: combating terrorism. But the question asked is not so much about the importance of combating terrorism as about the 'price' – in terms of popular legal culture that the public are willing to pay for combating terrorism. Combating terror is not cost free, and the 'price' that the public is willing to pay for combating terror can be measured in terms of its impact on popular legal culture as well as in money.

On an average across the five countries, both the general public and Muslims ranked "individual freedom" above "combating terrorism" – the general public by only a very narrow margin of 9 per cent and the Muslims by a much larger margin of 32 per cent. (Reflecting their more direct experience of terrorism, however, the English public prioritises "combating terrorism" even over "individual freedom") (Table 9.2).

In Norway and Poland, the general public's opinion is fairly evenly divided. But in Bulgaria and Ukraine the priority is "individual freedom" (by a margin of around 30 per cent) – whereas in sharp contrast, the English public's priority is combating terrorism (by a margin of 25 per cent). So faced with global terrorism, Bulgarians and Ukrainians opt strongly for the 'liberal' side, whereas the English opt strongly for the authoritarian side, and Norwegians along with the Poles are split down

Table 9.2 *Combating the threat of terrorism versus protecting individual freedom: the legal outsiders' perspective*

	General Publics						Muslims (N = 1,000)
Q7: Which do you feel should be more important at this time?	Norway (%)	England (%)	Poland (%)	Bulgaria (%)	Ukraine (%)	*Mean*	*Mean*
To combat the threat of terrorism	47	58	43	25	18	*38*	*28*
To protect individual freedom	48	33	49	53	50	*47*	*60*
Net majority for combating the threat of terrorism						*−9*	*−32*

Note: For brevity, the percentages who spontaneously replied with uninvited answers such as "both", "neither", "don't know", "cannot decide", etc., are not shown in this or subsequent tables even though they can be large. They can easily be calculated, however, by subtracting the percentages shown from 100%.

the middle. That cross-national pattern of prioritising the need to combat terrorism closely reflects the cross-national pattern of perceptions of risk or threat (Table 9.2).

This question of combating terrorism at the price of "individual freedom" was asked near the start of our interview. But towards the end of the almost hour-long interview, another question posed the price to be paid for combating terrorism in slightly, but significantly, different terms: Q115: "Which do you feel should be more important – combating the threat of terrorism, or protecting the rights of individual citizens and minorities?"

When the price of combating terrorism affects not only the rights of "individual citizens" but also the rights of "minorities", the balance of opinion amongst Muslims shows remarkably little change, and a majority of Muslims remain committed to prioritising "protecting rights". But the general public switches to prioritising "combating terrorism". The general public therefore differentiates between the "rights of individuals" and the "rights of minorities" in a way that Muslims do not. So the average gap between the opinions of Muslims and the general public widens from 23 per cent to 36 per cent (Table 9.3).

Only the Ukrainian public prioritises the rights of "individuals and minorities" over combating terrorism. Poles and Bulgarians marginally prioritise combating terrorism; and Norwegians join the English in strongly prioritising the need to combat terrorism over the "rights of individuals and minorities". So once again the Ukrainians by a large margin choose the liberal option; whereas the English and now the Norwegians also, by a large margin, back the authoritarian option.

Staying within the law – or stepping outside

Moving from principle to practice, respondents were asked in more concrete, operational terms: Q112: "What do you feel should be the [COUNTRY'S][13] government and security services' main response to the threat of terrorism? What do you feel is the right thing to do? In your opinion, should they: (1) just stay within existing laws and procedures, (2) stay within existing laws, but enforce them more strictly, (3) introduce new and tougher laws, or (4) step outside the law whenever they think it is useful?'

[13] '[COUNTRY]' was replaced by the actual name of the country in which the interview took place.

Table 9.3 *Combating the threat of terrorism versus protecting the rights of citizens and minorities: the legal outsiders' perspective*

	General Publics						Muslims (N = 1,000)
Q115: Which do you feel should be more important?	Norway (%)	England (%)	Poland (%)	Bulgaria (%)	Ukraine (%)	*Mean*	*Mean*
Combating the threat of terrorism	60	55	50	37	21	45	27
Protecting the rights of individual citizens and minorities	36	37	39	34	42	38	56
Net majority for combating the threat of terrorism						+7	−29

Overall, the general public opts primarily for "new and tougher laws" whereas Muslims opt for "stricter enforcement of existing laws". By a margin of 9 per cent, the general public opts for tougher laws or even stepping outside the law; but by a larger margin of 18 per cent, Muslims opt for enforcing existing laws more strictly or even staying within existing procedures (Table 9.4).

Significantly, however, amongst both the general public and Muslims, the two most popular choices are the relatively moderate options of "stricter enforcement" of existing laws (the top choice of Muslims) or "new and tougher laws" (the top choice of the general public). There is less support for the more extreme options of just staying within "existing procedures", or "stepping outside" the law.

Reacting to international pressure

American pressure Overall, on average across the five countries, just over half the public feel their country has been under pressure from the US. And though by a very small margin, both the general public and Muslims feel US pressure has been to "step outside the law" (Table 9.5).

There is a remarkably sharp difference between public perceptions of US pressure in Norway and England on the one hand, and the three post-communist countries on the other. In Norway and England a large majority, amongst both the general public and Muslims, feel the US has encouraged their government to "step outside" the law. By contrast, in Poland, and to a greater extent in Bulgaria and Ukraine, many confess that they simply do not know whether or not the US has exerted pressure on their country; but amongst those who do claim to know, a majority feel the US has encouraged their government to act 'within the law'.

It is possible – but extremely unlikely – that public perceptions of American pressure are everywhere accurate. This would mean that the US really did put differential pressure on British and Norwegian governments to step outside the law (where that is less usual), while urging strict legality in former communist countries (where strict legality had been less usual) – what could be called a universal 'middle-way' approach to combating terrorism.

The other, more likely explanation, is that the public in former communist Europe are so used to American lectures about the need to develop the 'rule of law' in post-communist Europe that they could not believe the US would consciously undermine the 'rule of law': could the familiar preacher really be such a sinner? East Europeans had perhaps

Table 9.4 *Government response to the threat of terrorism: the legal outsiders' perspective*

	General Publics						Muslims (N = 1,000)
Q112: What do you feel should be the [COUNTRY] government and security services' main response to the threat of terrorism? I mean what do you feel is the right thing to do? In your opinion, should they:	Norway (%)	England (%)	Poland (%)	Bulgaria (%)	Ukraine (%)	*Mean*	*Mean*
stay within existing laws and procedures?	15	11	20	4	17	*13*	*20*
stay within existing laws, but enforce them more strictly?	27	27	24	32	28	*28*	*33*
introduce new and tougher laws?	36	47	33	39	29	*37*	*24*
step outside the law whenever they think it is useful?	21	11	18	6	7	*13*	*11*

Table 9.5 *Pressure from the United States on how to deal with the 'war on terror': the legal outsiders' perspective*

	General Publics (N = 1,000 / country)						Muslims (N = 1,000)
Q117: When combating terrorism or the threat of terrorism, do you feel the [COUNTRY] government and security services have been under any pressure from the US:	Norway (%)	England (%)	Poland (%)	Bulgaria (%)	Ukraine (%)	*Mean*	*Mean*
to stay within the law?	20	19	31	32	20	*24*	*24*
to step outside the law?	46	51	17	10	14	*28*	*30*
There has been no pressure from the US	27	19	27	29	18	*24*	*20*

been indoctrinated by the long years of American sermons on the 'rule of law', but the Norwegians and English, like other west Europeans, have long had more doubts about American law (so much so that the US could not meet the basic conditions for entry into the EU).

In every country, however, the net reaction to American pressure is negative – both amongst the general public (on balance by a margin of 29 per cent) and rather more amongst Muslims (on balance by a margin of 39 per cent). The reaction is especially negative in Norway and England – both amongst the general public (on balance by 47 per cent) and still more amongst Norwegian and English Muslims (on balance by 65 per cent).

EU Pressure Just under half of the general public and of Muslims feel that their country has been under pressure from the EU. But in sharp contrast to perceptions of US pressure, both the general public and Muslims (in every country and on average by a margin of around 24 per cent) feel that EU pressure has been to "stay within the law". And although reactions to perceived US pressure are on balance negative in every country, both amongst the general publics and Muslims, reactions to perceived EU pressure are on average marginally positive – though rather more positive amongst Muslims than amongst the general public (Table 9.6).

The net reaction to EU pressure is positive in England, Poland and Bulgaria, though negative in Norway and Ukraine – the two countries that are not members of the EU, and which might therefore be particularly sensitive to EU pressure of any sort. Amongst the three EU members, however, both the general publics and Muslims feel positive about EU pressure – on average by a margin of 13 per cent amongst their general publics and by a greater margin of 28 per cent amongst their Muslims.

Risk assessment

As a measure of "risk assessment" respondents were asked: "Which comes closest to your view about the threat of terrorism in [COUNTRY]? There is a real threat of terrorism in [COUNTRY]; the threat of terrorism in [COUNTRY] has been exaggerated; or there is no real threat of terrorism in [COUNTRY]". Amongst the general publics, the public in England stands out sharply with 68 per cent saying there is a "real threat" to their country; in Norway and Poland public perceptions are mixed with an average of 45 per cent who believe there is a "real threat"; but in Bulgaria and Ukraine, only an average of 17 per cent believe (Table 9.7).

Table 9.6 *Pressure from the European Union on how to deal with the 'war on terror': the legal outsiders' perspective*

	General Publics						Muslims (N = 1,000)
Q119 When combating terrorism or the threat of terrorism, do you feel the [this country] government and security services have been under any pressure from the European Union:	Norway (%)	England (%)	Poland (%)	Bulgaria (%)	Ukraine (%)	*Mean*	*Mean*
to stay within the law?	30	39	26	48	25	*34*	*33*
to step outside the law?	20	8	10	6	8	*10*	*10*
There has been no pressure from the EU.	41	40	38	21	22	*32*	*34*

Table 9.7 *A real threat of terrorism: the legal outsiders' perspective*

	General Publics						Muslims (N = 1,000)
Q121: Which comes closest to your view about the threat of terrorism in [this country]?	NOR (%)	ENG (%)	POL (%)	BUL (%)	UKR (%)	*Mean*	*Mean*
There is a real threat of terrorism in [this country].	49	68	41	22	11	*38*	*17 (−21)*
The threat of terrorism in [this country] has been exaggerated.	41	26	36	35	41	*36*	*48 (+12)*
There is no real threat of terrorism in [this country].	9	3	16	28	31	*18*	*24 (+6)*

Overall, across the five countries 38 per cent of the general public, but only 17 per cent of Muslims, acknowledge a "real threat". Muslims do not deny that there is some degree of threat: on average, across the five countries, 48 per cent of Muslims recognise some threat of terrorism but feel that the threat in their country has "been exaggerated". In England, only 12 per cent of Muslims go so far as to claim there is "no real threat" of terrorism, but 64 per cent feel the threat is real but has "been exaggerated". (There is of course no simple way of determining whether Muslims underestimate the threat or the general public exaggerate that threat. What is clear, however, is the difference between the risk-perceptions of Muslims and the general public.)

The impact of risk assessment on the general public

When the question of prioritising citizens' rights and freedoms over combating terrorism is put – in an open-ended IDI format – to legal insiders (i.e. legislators, prosecutors, lawyers, judges, government officials, police) in eastern Europe, where the threat of terrorism seems less acute, a recurrent response is to opt for prioritising "rights and freedoms", but then to add that their view might well change if the threat of terrorism increases and they have to reconsider their priorities. These legal insiders take advantage of the open-ended interview format to give – without any prompting – a flexible, conditional answer. They self-consciously link their priorities to their (potentially variable) risk assessment.

Interviews with the general public did not have such a flexible format. But we can correlate public attitudes towards rights and freedoms with their risk assessments, and thereby measure the impact of perceived risk on the public's priorities.

The impact of risk assessment on "paying the price" to combat terrorism

Overall, across the five countries, threat perceptions have an average impact of 43 per cent on the balance to be struck between protecting individual freedom and combating terrorism: those in the general public who feel there is a "real threat" of terrorism prioritise "combating terrorism" over "individual freedom" by a margin of 14 per cent; and conversely, those who feel the threat "is not real" or "has been exaggerated" prioritise "individual freedom" over "combating terrorism" by a margin of 29 per cent – a difference of 43 per cent.

Amongst the general public in Norway risk assessment has a greater than average impact, 66 per cent, on prioritising action against terrorism over protecting "individual freedom"; and in England risk assessment has a similar 65 per cent impact. Elsewhere, risk assessments have smaller, though still significant, impacts on the need to prioritise combating terrorism: an impact of 28 per cent in Poland, and only 10 per cent in Bulgaria, but an impact of 42 per cent in Ukraine (Table 9.8).

As we saw previously, citing the rights of 'minorities' along with the rights of 'individuals' elicits a much more authoritarian response amongst the general public. Nonetheless, across the five countries, threat perceptions have on average exactly the same overall impact, 43 per cent, on prioritising the need to combat terrorism over "protecting the rights of individuals and minorities". And the country profile is similar: risk assessment once again has its greatest impact in Norway and England, and its least impact in Bulgaria (Table 9.9).

The impact of risk assessment on respecting, changing, or disregarding the law

Overall, the impact of a perceived "real threat" on support for "new and tougher laws" to combat terrorism or even to 'step outside the law' is 18 per cent, though support rises to 25 per cent in Norway and 28 per cent in England.

On balance, even those who think there is a "real threat" resent American pressure on their governments – and especially so if that pressure is to step outside the law. On average across all five countries, even amongst those who feel there is a "real threat" of terrorism in their country, a majority of 20 per cent feel negative towards American pressure, rising to a majority of 48 per cent who feel negative if they think American pressure has been to step outside the law.

By contrast, amongst those who believe there is "not a real threat", or that the threat has been "exaggerated", a larger majority of 41 per cent feel negative towards American pressure, rising to a massive majority of 74 per cent if they think American pressure was to step outside the law.

Comparing the impact of risk and religion

Within the general public, risk assessment clearly has a very powerful impact on attitudes towards "paying the price" in terms of rights and freedoms to combat terrorism. Muslims are much less willing than the

Table 9.8 *Main priority – fighting terrorism versus protecting individual freedom – by sense of feeling threatened: the legal outsiders' perspective*

Q7: Which should be more important at this time?	Amongst those in the general public who feel there is areal threat of terrorism						Amongst those in the general public who feel the threat is exaggerated or not real					
	NOR (%)	ENG (%)	POL (%)	BUL (%)	UKR (%)	*Mean*	NOR (%)	ENG (%)	POL (%)	BUL (%)	UKR (%)	*Mean*
To combat the threat of terrorism	64	68	51	31	42	*51*	31	37	37	26	16	*29*
To protect individual freedom	31	23	42	52	38	*37*	64	57	56	57	54	*58*
Net majority to prioritise combating terror	+33	+45	+9	−21	+4	*+14*	−33	−20	−19	−31	−38	*−29*
Impact of a perceived 'real threat'	+66	+65	+28	+10	+42	*+43*						

Table 9.9 *Main priority – fighting terrorism versus protecting the rights of individuals and minorities – by sense of feeling threatened: the legal outsiders' perspective*

	Amongst those in the general public who feel there is a real threat of terrorism						Amongst those in the general public who feel the threat is exaggerated or not real					
Q115: Which do you feel should be more important?	NOR (%)	ENG (%)	POL (%)	BUL (%)	UKR (%)	*Mean*	NOR (%)	ENG (%)	POL (%)	BUL (%)	UKR (%)	*Mean*
Combating the threat of terrorism	76	64	60	46	50	*59*	45	38	44	38	18	*37*
Protecting the rights of individuals and minorities	20	27	29	34	30	*28*	51	59	48	39	47	*49*
Net majority to prioritise combating terror	+56	+37	+31	+12	+20	*+31*	−6	−21	−4	−1	−29	*−12*
Impact of a perceived "real threat"	+62	+58	+35	+13	+49	*+43*						

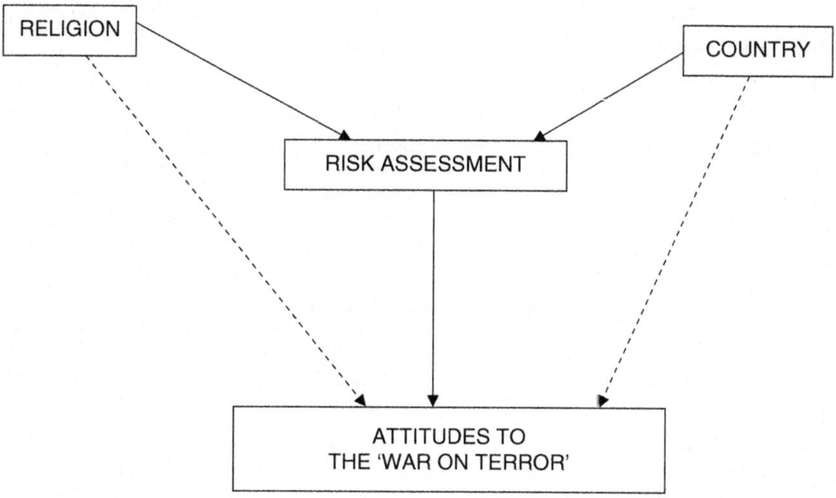

Figure 9.1 Attitudes to the 'war on terror'

general public to pay that price. But is that because they assess the risk differently, or simply because they are Muslims?

Risk assessment itself is influenced by both country and religion: risk assessment is greater in some countries than in others, and greater amongst the general public than amongst Muslims. Figure 9.1 shows a chain of influence from "country" and "religion", through "risk assessment", to attitudes towards "paying the price" for combating terrorism (the solid lines). But it also raises the possibility of a direct impact from religion (and also from country) to attitudes towards combating terrorism (the broken lines).

This analysis suggests that religion, by itself, indeed has some direct impact on attitudes towards the war on terror, not least because Muslims might be the ones most affected by counterterrorism measures in present circumstances. But it also shows that the impact of risk assessment is greater than the impact of religion. When both threat perceptions and religion are taken into account simultaneously, threat perceptions have far more impact than religion on attitudes towards the war on terror. Muslims take a different view about paying the price of the war on terror primarily (though not entirely) because they have a different level of "risk assessment".

There are, of course, some country-to-country variations, but these general conclusions from the five-country analysis are confirmed (and indeed strengthened) by analyses in England – which has been

Table 9.10 *Main priority – fighting terrorism versus protecting individual freedom: the majority/minority perspective*

Q7: Which do you feel should be more important at this time: to combat the threat of terrorism *or* to protect individual freedom

	Averaging over all five countries		
	Net majority for combating terrorism rather than protecting individual freedom		Impact of risk assessment ("a real threat")
	If feel threat of terrorism is exaggerated or not real	If feel threat of terrorismis real	
Amongst general publics	−29	+14	+43
Amongst Muslims	−43	0	+43
Impact of Muslim religion	−14	−14	

most exposed to al-Qaeda terrorism, and where in consequence "risk assessment" is greatest.

The impact of risk and religion on prioritising "individual freedom"

On the principle of giving priority to "combating terrorism" over "protecting individual freedom" the impact of "risk assessment" across all five countries is on average (43 per cent) three times as great as the direct impact of religion (14 per cent) when both risk assessment and religion are taken into account simultaneously. (In Table 9.10, the difference between the rows measures the direct impact of religion, whereas the difference between the columns measures the impact of risk assessment.)

England has been exposed to terrorism more than any of the other countries studied. Although our analysis is based on contrasting only 200 Muslims with 1,000 members of the general public, a similar calculation suggests that the impact of "risk assessment" (55 per cent) is five times as great as the direct impact of religion (11 per cent) on the principle of giving priority to combating terrorism rather than protecting individual freedom.

The impact of risk and religion on prioritising "the rights of individuals and minorities"

As we have noted, Muslims do not distinguish greatly between "the rights of individuals" and "the rights of minorities". But the general public certainly does not empathise with the "rights of individuals and minorities" as strongly as they do with the "rights of individuals". So, on the principle of giving priority to "combating terrorism" over "protecting the rights of individuals and minorities" the impact of religion (at 29 per cent) more nearly approaches the impact of "risk assessment" (almost unchanged at 44 per cent). Nonetheless, the impact of "risk assessment" remains significantly greater than the direct impact of religion. (As before, the difference between the rows measures the direct impact of religion, whereas the difference between the columns measures the impact of risk assessment.)

Closer inspection shows that this increased impact of religion is due almost entirely to the general public's lesser commitment to the rights of "individuals and minorities" rather than their commitment to "individual freedom". Muslims by contrast make no great distinction between the two questions (Table 9.11).

Table 9.11 *Main priority – fighting terrorism versus protecting the rights of individuals and minorities: the majority/minority perspective*

Q115: Which do you feel should be more important: to combat the threat of terrorism *or* protect the rights of individuals and minorities

	Averaging over all five countries:		
	Net majority for combating terrorism rather thanprotecting the rights of individuals and minorities		Impact of risk assessment ("a real threat")
	If feel threat of terrorism is exaggerated or not real	If feel threat of terrorismis real	
Amongst general publics	−12	+31	+43
Amongst Muslims	−41	+3	+44
Impact of Muslim religion	−29	−28	

Again, within England alone, the impact of "risk assessment" remains almost unchanged at 53 per cent, and still reaches well over twice as much as the increased direct impact of religion (23 per cent) on the principle of giving priority to combating terrorism rather than protecting "individuals and minorities".

Taken together, an emphasis on combating terrorism rather than the rights of individuals, or even the rights of minorities, is directly driven more by "risk assessment" than by religion, and especially so in the country (England) where risk assessment is greatest.

Perceptions of the 'war on terror': the legal insiders' perspective

Belonging to the elite, legal insiders may have more knowledge about terrorism than legal outsiders – and possibly even be involved in anti-terrorist efforts as part of their work. The elected representatives pass anti-terrorist legislation. Government officials are involved in efforts to prevent terrorism and they also implement current legislation. Prosecutors prosecute terrorist suspects, judges judge them and lawyers defend them. The police, for their part, are partly engaged in preventing terrorism, and partly in catching terrorists after an attack has taken place.

This part of the chapter is based on a systematic content analysis of 786 IDIs with legal insiders by country (see Appendix for details). Statistical findings (frequencies) are presented in the tables, which are followed and illustrated by an analysis of what the legal insiders actually said.

Our content analysis of the IDIs suggest there is a correlation between (i) the extent to which a country has (previously) been affected by terrorism, (ii) the extent of its involvement in the war on terror, and (iii) elite perceptions of whether there is a terrorist threat. Table 9.12 shows that legal insiders in Norway, England and Poland predominantly believe that their countries are faced with a real threat of terrorism. By contrast, legal insiders in Bulgaria and Ukraine do not think there is such a threat.

The majority of the Norwegian legal insiders feel that the terrorist threat is low in their country. They suggest that although it does exist, the threat is "fairly small", "small", at a "low level", "limited" or "exaggerated". Very few of them believe that Norway is a "real target".

To the extent Norway is at risk of terrorism, legal insiders believe that this is primarily due to external factors such as the country's support for, and participation in, US-initiated operations abroad, notably the involvement in Afghanistan and Iraq, its NATO membership and international

Table 9.12 *Terrorism – a real threat?: the legal insiders' perspective*

Do you think that [this country] is faced with a real threat of terrorism? Why or why not?	Norway (%)	England (%)	Poland (%)	Bulgaria (%)	Ukraine (%)
Real threat	54	95	58	38	30
No real threat	46	5	42	62	70

Note: Entries are based on the percentages of relevant 'text units' – the total number of answers to a given question; so entries sum up to approximately 100% (decimals are rounded up or down to the nearest whole number).

engagement. There is some concern with al-Qaeda's threats against Norway. As regards internal (or domestic) factors, very few legal insiders believed that the presence of alleged terrorists such as Mullah Krekar or Arfan Bhatti poses a threat to Norway:

> N-JU-6: 'Norway may be at risk of terrorism to the extent we take part in operations abroad that provoke those who apply terrorism against their adversaries'. N-PR-14: 'we are a target and some of our embassies have experienced that'.

Legal insiders who do not think that Norway is at risk refer to Norway primarily as a "small" and "insignificant" country located on the "periphery" of Europe. In their view, Norwegians tend to perceive their country as a peace-loving nation that has not taken any controversial stands abroad. The cartoon controversy that culminated in the 2006 torching of the Norwegian embassy in Damascus was amicably resolved through the intervention of the Norwegian government and in dialogue with "native" Muslim groups (both in Norway and the Middle East). Added to this, Arfan Bhatti, who was tried on terrorist charges, was eventually acquitted.[14] Consequently, terrorists have "no motive" for attacking Norway, and there are no indications that such an attack is underway. The Norwegian security services seem to be in control of the situation:

[14] Bhatti has since reinvented himself as a supporter of al-Qaeda he has grown a long beard and turned from crime to religion. Some years ago, he organised a demonstration in support of al-Qaeda in Oslo. For the last year or so he has been based in Pakistan, where he has served a prison sentence.

> N-ER-17: '[Norway] is a relatively small country even though we have a lot of money and thus have a certain influence . . . in international bodies. I [therefore] do not think that we are so interesting'. N-GO-22: 'what could they target here in Norway?' N-PR-8: 'there is no reason to assume that we are facing a real . . . threat of terrorism'.

The majority of the statements made by the English legal insiders show that they predominantly believe that the UK is at real risk of terrorist attacks. Whereas in Norway the terrorist threat is viewed almost exclusively as an external threat, in England it is perceived partly as an external, partly as an internal (domestic) threat. A distinction is made between "home-grown" terrorism (IRA) and "foreign" terrorism (Islamists):

> E-LA-2: 'England has always been faced with a threat of terrorism of one sort or another . . . [it] was a much more dangerous place when the IRA was active when I was young. There were bombs going off all over the place all the time, murders . . . day in, day out. It isn't like that now'. E-PO-10: 'back to 2007, certainly what happened in London on the Tubes and the bus as well . . . up until then it was the IRA in the seventies and eighties and then we went through a decade of calm'. E-PO-4: 'we get into a nice lull of complacency then all of a sudden with something like the Glasgow bomb or whatever, something else will come back'

Despite the numerous terrorist attacks previously carried out by the IRA, some English legal insiders feel that IRA-based terrorism was more "benign" and "moderate" than Islamist terrorism – though one of the prosecutors argues that the IRA was more dangerous as it directed its activities against the British state. By contrast, Islamist terrorism is directed against ordinary citizens:

> E-PR-12: '[Islamist terrorism] differs very much from the IRA troubles because you didn't have suicide bombers with the IRA'. E-PR-1: 'I'm sure there is a real threat, but I would make a distinction that one of our very senior judges made in the Belmarsh case,[15] which is that there's a difference between people's lives being at risk and the life of the country being at risk. I think it's an exaggeration to say that the life of the country is at risk because of al-Qaeda terrorism. It's probably less of a threat to the

[15] Nine foreigners were held for almost three years without charge or trial at the Belmarsh prison. In December 2004, the law lords in the House of Lords ruled that detaining foreign terrorist suspects without trial breaks human rights laws. 'Terror detainees win Lords appeal', *BBC News*, 16 December 2004, http://news.bbc.co.uk/2/hi/uk_news/4100481.stm, accessed on 9 March 2012.

country than IRA terrorism was 30 years ago, because they were trying to bomb their way out of the British Constitution ... they were less interested in killing people than killing the state ... we now have ... much looser networks which are interested in just killing people because they seem to hate some people for the sake of it.'

Some English legal insiders express concern that younger native British Muslims – particularly those residing in Northern England – are becoming increasingly radicalised and anti-state: much as a result of the manner in which they have been treated in the aftermath of 9/11. Police representatives, in particular, claim that there is clear evidence to this effect – a view that is, to some extent, also voiced by public prosecutors. The Islamist terrorist threat should therefore no longer be considered only as an 'external' threat:

> E-LA-5: 'we have a substantial Muslim community in this country, many of whose young ones are malignly influenced by firebrand preachers, Imams, who some feel are feeding their minds with some of this fundamentalist stuff the al-Qaeda believe in ... we're like a breeding ground ... for a lot of the potential terrorists. A lot of them go to Pakistan to the training camps'. E-PR-24: 'It's people's perception of a few people. Everybody assumes that the Muslim population are all excitable, that they're all waiting to blow us up and things like this, which isn't true. Of course, that then breeds bad feeling between the two groups, and you get things like the riots of Bradford arising out of nothing. You get the bombings that we talked about already. You get the influence.' E-JU-5: '[the UK] has a huge Asian immigrant community. It's only the Asian immigrant community which is prone to be, or liable to be, infected by ideas of terrorism and the promotion of terrorism.' E-PR-12: 'we have of course got a lot of Muslims who have come over here who will get brainwashed and the trouble is ... it differs from all other religions, as far as I know.' E-PR-20: 'our criminal courts have prosecuted a very large number of terrorists, and they are predominantly from a certain community, the Muslim community, born and bred here ... I'm looking at increased militancy amongst young people, young Muslims.'

English legal insiders argue that the terrorist threat is primarily caused by England's previous status as a colonial power, which has created numerous enemies. The British involvement in Iraq and Afghanistan is viewed as a less significant threat to national security. Being one of the US's most loyal allies also poses a security risk for the UK:

> E-JU-8: [the UK is faced with a terrorist threat] because we have behaved so extraordinarily badly across the world. I'm not surprised that a lot of people across the world would quite like to get back at us.' E-LA-4: 'we've

> managed, as a nation, to wind people up massively over the years and put people's backs up. I think the Americans have done the same by flexing their muscles in an overly aggressive way. I think we've probably allied ourselves to America in such a way that we've got ourselves in the spotlight. I think we're a prime target.' E-PO-9: 'we've gone and upset everybody. Well, they upset us first I suppose, but we've got into this tit-for-tat . . . we had this terrible event of 9/11. We have then responded to that, and I think we've probably got ourselves in a terrible pickle with it all . . . we've now got a lot of people that really, really don't like us and want to get at us'. E-PR-13: 'we are in the line of fire. We're clearly identified with the West, with particular values.' E-PR-4: 'England will go into other countries on the coat tails of America courting hatred across the world, that's why.'

Although opinions voiced in the IDIs in England are primarily based on hearsay, some legal insiders are either involved in anti-terrorist work or have, in one way or another, been affected by the war on terror. A few police representatives interviewed have taken part in anti-terrorist operations themselves, and some of the prosecutors have prosecuted cases under the Act of Terrorism. One retired judge has conducted relevant work for the war on terror in the UK; another has a son who is working for the police on anti-terror assignments. Finally, one of the elected representatives points out that three of the prisoners currently in Guantanamo belong to her constituency!:

> E-PR-17: 'if you're talking in terms of Islamic fundamentalism . . . we radicalised a lot of people in the way that people have been treated. I think that there has been a lot of knee-jerk reaction and a lot of superstition in the communities in Leeds. Some of the 7/7 bombers came from Leeds . . . some of the people that I work with, one of the probation officers, knows one of the lads because he was a supply teacher at one of the schools'. E-GO-3: 'the bombers of the 7 July [2007] in London were from Leeds; we kind of had to deal with the aftermath of all of that'.

Only two of the English legal insiders – both prosecutors – think the UK is "at no risk" of terrorism.

The majority of the statements by the legal insiders in Poland indicate that they believe that Poland is facing a real threat of terrorism. However, they are more cautious in their language than the English legal insiders. They believe that Poland is "a potential target" of terrorism, but that it is faced with a "low risk", a "small risk", or a "lower risk" than other countries. As do legal insiders in Norway, Polish legal insiders almost exclusively refer to external factors when explaining why they believe Poland to be at risk. These include the country's involvement in the international anti-terrorism block – including the wars in Iraq and Afghanistan, Poland's EU/NATO memberships, and the fact that it is a US ally:

> P-ER-18: 'our participation in wars outside our country makes us a party in conflict and we are somehow endangered because of that.' P-GO-1: 'Poland is a country which, in recent years, has become visible on the international stage; it is exposed. We were in Iraq, we are in Afghanistan, we are a member of NATO and the European Union'. P-JU-25: 'Poland is under a real threat of terrorism, because in the world of Islam . . . we are seen as an ally of the biggest Satan, the United States'.

Geography is also perceived as a risk factor. Though not wealthy, Poland is located "in the centre of Europe", "in the Northern Hemisphere". This is thought to increase the risk of terrorist attacks – though Poles living abroad are obviously more exposed to such risk:

> P-LA-2: 'Poland is not some "cottage on the outskirts of a village" but a Central European and high-population country which engages in world conflicts and sends its troops away with live cartridges'. P-LA-3: 'we travel all over the world and terrorism can reach Poles everywhere . . . something happened in Spain . . . in the train there were also Poles. In the [London] underground there were Poles as well . . . we are under threat of terrorism, but not necessarily on our territory.'

Legal insiders who believe that Poland is not faced with a terrorist threat explain their position by referring to both external and internal factors. As regards the external factors, Poland is seen as being too poor, insignificant and unimportant to warrant an attack. Any retaliation directed at their country as a result of its involvement in Afghanistan or Iraq would therefore most likely occur in these countries. As regards domestic factors, Poland is perceived as a homogeneous society, hosting very few ethnic or religious minorities – and none from the Middle East. Poland's native Muslims – the Polish Tatars – are referred to in positive terms only. Finally, no terrorist group has so far been identified in Poland:

> P-ER-7: 'our global importance is still too low to make us the target of some terrorist manipulation. What can they demolish here? The Palace of Culture and Science [a remnant of Soviet style grandiose buildings]? It won't be a tragedy [if they do].' P-GO-2: 'though we have our troops both in Iraq and Afghanistan, we grant refugees from Iraq and Afghanistan political asylum . . . [this] somehow harmonises the situation.' P-LA-5: 'they [i.e. the Muslims] know that . . . America forces us to participate [in Iraq and Afghanistan]'. P-GO-5: 'we are not under any threat coming

from domestic fundamentalists or ... religious minorities with fundamentalist tendencies – Muslims. I'm not talking about the Tatars: we've got two Tatar villages in the Podlasie region, plus there are many people of Tatar descent in the army – but they're all citizens who rendered great service to our country, being part of this culture'. P-PR-5: 'Poland is rarely visited by people from Islamic countries, there are few immigrants from Islamic countries. Islamic terrorism constitutes a tangible threat in countries which used to benefit from colonies in the past'. [And rather oddly] P-GO-14: 'there are no Muslims in our country. I haven't seen a single one in Katowice.'

The majority of the statements made by legal insiders in Bulgaria suggest that their country is not faced with terrorism. For a start, Bulgaria is too small and insignificant. Added to this, its economy is fairly weak and the country is peripheral to the international political scene. Besides, some legal insiders argued that the Bulgarian mentality is fairly similar to that of the Middle East (as a result of Ottoman rule) and that the country therefore does not pose a threat to Muslims:

B-JU-1: 'I personally do not think that there is a real threat. We are too small and insignificant'. B-LA-2: 'first, because Bulgaria is a very small country ... second, there is no such sharp dispute among the ethnic ... groups'. B-LA-4: 'we are closer to the Middle East conflict areas ... Iran, Afghanistan, and we are much closer to them as a nation'.

The statements made by legal insiders who believe that Bulgaria *is* at risk of terrorism are few in number. They view terrorism predominantly as an external threat. They point out that the war on terror is a global war, which targets European society as such and that Bulgaria is a member of the anti-terrorist coalition: B-JU-3: "in each European country there is an actual threat of terrorism". B-LA-1: "yes, we are at risk because we went into the anti-terrorist coalition".

Ukrainian, just like Bulgarian, legal insiders mostly do not believe their country to be at risk of terrorism. They justify their position by referring to Ukraine's many positive features as well as its global insignificance, which in their view render it less useful as a terrorist target: Ukraine is "no empire", it is "not strong", "not rich", "not well developed", has "no oil", does not border on the Islamic world, and has "no enemies". Besides, its role in the global war on terror is limited. Rather, Ukraine is a "peaceful country" and Ukrainians – just like other Slavs – are essentially "decent" and "kind-hearted" people:

U-GO-24: 'Terrorists want power and the Ukrainian government cannot give that as our country is young ... and ... has no means of influence,

> like the USA'. U-LA-24: 'terrorism is aimed at huge, well-developed countries.'. U-ER-31: 'not only Ukraine, but the Slav nations are very kind-hearted, ready to give the last to somebody who suffered'. U-GO-14: 'we are a quiet nation, we are not an aggressive nation ... we are not an Empire, we are ... a country that doesn't wage wars'.

Terrorism is perceived to be a much greater problem for the US – and a direct consequence of its foreign policies. Some of the Ukrainian legal insiders even imply that the Americans created terrorism as a means by which to gain global influence. In their view the US will end up having the same problems in Afghanistan as the Soviet Union had:

> U-ER-7: 'in America, it is the consequence of their globalisation policy: we are the chief on the planet, everybody should be sitting under us, do everything like [we] do. And in Afghanistan one needs to establish democracy where they always had a Tsar, a chieftain. We tried to establish Soviet rule there and the Americans are trying to establish democracy. The same as they did to Iraq and Hussein ... it is the American policy to rule over the globe. In response, they get a corresponding reaction'. U-PO-1: 'let's start with New York 2001. As they say the Americans got a dose of their own medicine. It is clear even to a fool today that terrorism was conducted with the tacit consent of the American special services, or by the American special services themselves. The aim is clear: to take control over financial flows under the cover of combating terrorism, to take control over politicians, to take control over every citizen ... of the Earth. Muslim leaders understood this very fast'.

Only a very limited number of statements by Ukrainian legal insiders suggest that they feel that their country is faced with a real threat of terrorism. To the extent it is, this is partly to do with domestic and partly to do with external reasons, such as Ukraine's political and economic weakness and the tension between Crimean Tatars, Russians and Ukrainians in the Crimea. Some view the significant number of illegal immigrants in Ukraine as a potential source of terrorism:

> U-ER-25: 'terrorism has no borders or nationality ... [it] is a political, economic threat, it is coming from everywhere, from neighbouring countries, from Russia, which can't accept Ukraine's independence'. U-JU-6: 'terrorism has no boundaries'. U-LA-2: 'the weakening of central power in Ukraine creates chaos ... creates situations when the oligarchs ... divide [Ukraine] into pieces ... the weakening of central government creates instability in Ukraine, especially in the Crimea and the East'. U-LA-1: 'the problem with the Crimean Tatars really exists ... the Tatars are humiliated'.

External pressure and the 'war on terror'

It could be argued that the war on terror is essentially a question of foreign policy and the willingness of states to join forces with the US and fight terrorism in the manner that the US sees fit. European countries can either join forces with the US but not blindly accept the means with which the war on terror is fought. Or they can oppose the war on terror altogether on the grounds that it is unnecessary or unjustified. Whether a country chooses to join or not join the war on terror not only depends on the perceived threat, but also on its relative political strength and the costs versus benefits of joining or opposing the US-led war on terror. Further, a country may accept or reject the means with which international terrorism is fought depending on its political orientation, political strength and also its legal culture.

We asked the legal insiders whether they thought their country had experienced any pressure to stay within, or to step outside, existing laws in their endeavour to fight terrorism. Table 9.13 shows that they believe that pressure to stay within existing laws primarily comes from the EU and that pressure to step outside existing laws primarily is US driven. English legal insiders primarily feel that the UK has been under pressure from the US to step outside the law. Norwegian legal insiders think their country has first and foremost been pressured into passing new laws to combat terrorism. By contrast, Polish, Bulgarian and Ukrainian legal insiders feel that their respective countries have not been put under any pressure at all. As fairly new EU and/or NATO member states, Poland and Bulgaria have probably had no wish to rock the boat by refusing to take part in EU- and NATO-led anti-terrorist activities. Poland, in particular, may have concerns as NATO and EU membership represents a safeguard against Russia. Ukraine is a member of NATO's Partnership for Peace Program only and thus is less vulnerable to such pressure.

The supremacy of the law, that is, the rule of law, is a key feature of Western democracy and also an important part of Western legal culture. In Eastern Europe, which was under communist rule for more than 50 years, such rights were until fairly recently non-existent. Law and legal institutions were subordinated to the Communist Party. Although opposition to communist rule was significant in Poland and in parts of Western Ukraine, it was largely absent in Bulgaria and Eastern Ukraine.

Lawbreaking is an important feature of post-communist legal culture: even though people are expected to comply with moral norms, ignoring formal law is considered fairly acceptable. In some countries, such as the

Table 9.13 *How to fight terrorism: the legal insiders' perspective*

Do you feel the [COUNTRY] government has been under pressure from international organisations or from foreign countries to stay within the law, or under pressure to step outside the law, when combating terrorism?	Norway (%)	England (%)	Poland (%)	Bulgaria (%)	Ukraine (%)
Pressure – keep existing laws			1		
EU	1	9	6	1	
US	1		2	1	
Pressure – step outside existing laws					
EU				4	
US	13	63	6		1
Pressure – pass new laws	34	9	7	12	1
Pressure – act	14	1	8	4	12
No pressure	18	8	51	70	56
Pressure (undefined)	18	9	20	7	30

Note: Entries are based on the percentages of relevant 'text units' – the total number of answers to a given question; so entries sum up to approximately 100% (decimals are rounded up or down to the nearest whole number).

Czech Republic and Slovenia, lawbreaking is even referred to as a national sport. What is more, in some post-communist states democracy as a concept is perceived as synonymous with freedom, including the freedom to break laws – that is, *legal nihilism* (Grødeland 2010). Following from this, one may assume that pressure exerted on the part of other states or international organisations to violate existing laws would receive a more negative response amongst legal insiders in Norway and England than in Poland, Bulgaria and Ukraine.

Statements made by legal insiders suggest that efforts on the part of the US to make their countries step outside the law are perceived negatively in all five countries. They believe that such efforts clash with the key democratic principle of the supremacy of the law. Further, many legal insiders do not approve of the US-initiated war on terror in the first place. Some of the Norwegian legal insiders point out that the US has tried to make Norway step outside the law by allowing aircraft bound for Guantanamo Bay to land in Norwegian airports for refuelling. They also believe that pressure had been exerted on the Norwegian government to extradite Mullah Krekar to the US to return him to his home country of Iraq, and they claim that the US tried to persuade Norway to bypass existing rules on surveillance, data storage and treatment of terrorist suspects. Such pressure is perceived negatively; upholding democratic principles is considered more important:

> N-ER-12: 'we have been exposed to pressure especially from the United States ... to introduce stricter terrorist legislation and also to violate our legislation on surveillance ... treatment of prisoners and such things.' N-JU-15: 'my impression is that ... the United States has gone very far in ... weakening human rights in its hunt for terrorists and that it has exerted pressure on Norway to do the same and to set aside some principles of human rights in order to achieve this'. N-PR-9: 'it is a paradox that our most important ally – until they got a new president almost a year ago – had big problems accepting a legal ban on torture ... but held the view that it was a tool that could be used ... it is a paradox that ... our closest ally ... commits the greatest violations of human rights that have probably been committed in this century. And [that these violations are taking place] on Cuba, an island that they have boycotted for 50 years exactly because of human rights [violations]'.

English legal insiders feel that the US had forced their country to go to war against Iraq and to comply with their wishes regarding Guantanamo Bay. They accuse the Americans of having initiated gross violations of human rights and international law. As in Norway, most respondents are highly negative to such pressure:

> E-GO-1: 'I certainly think with the Iraq war there is a definite sense that England was put under pressure by the United States to step outside the law ... I don't think we would stand for it again'. E-JU-2: 'there is some evidence to suppose that we have gone along with American pressures to act, underneath the law in relation to extraordinary rendition. Also emulation to go to war at all. There is some evidence to suggest the British government has been under some pressure to bypass international law'. E-PO-9: 'we've come under immense pressure to break all sorts of rules, and I think to some extent we have contributed to selling our soul with it ... we built our entire Western democracy on the fact that you've got freedoms, you're innocent until you're proven guilty, we've got war conventions, we've got legislation ... I think if ever there's going to be a war crime that'll come out it'll be Guantanamo Bay. It will live with us for decades ... and there'll be some point when people will be brought to

> justice over that. . . we didn't live up to what we set out own lifestyle to be, when it came to it. It's a shame, really.'

By contrast to legal insiders in Norway and England, Polish legal insiders feel their country has been under more pressure from the EU to abide by the law than from the US to set it aside. Just like the English legal insiders, however, they think Poland has been "forced" to collude with the Americans with regard to CIA prisoners. And just like Norwegian and English legal insiders, they are negative to American pressure to step outside the law – though one respondent suggests that violating international law may be justified in some situations:

> P-PO-7: '[Poland] is pressured by the United States [to set aside the law], just like the rest of the world'. P-GO-6: '[Poland is pressured] to disobey the law, after all America winds up all these situations: it started from the [destruction of] the World Trade Center: we have a war in Afghanistan, we have a war in Iraq, maybe we will have a war in Iran and everything under the slogan of combating terrorism'.

The majority of the statements made by legal insiders in Bulgaria suggest that the country has not been under any pressure to either comply with, or abide by, the law. Most legal insiders simply state that there is no evidence suggesting such pressure. A smaller number of legal insiders believe that fighting terrorism is synonymous with fighting a 'terrible, great evil' and 'protecting state interests'. Bulgaria is therefore 'willingly' taking part in the 'war on terror':

> B-GO-1: we are sufficiently aware of what terrorism constitutes . . . generally, this is a . . . manifestation of the great evil, so I do not think that pressure is necessary [in order to] take . . . adequate measures to combat terrorism.' B-PR-9: 'each Bulgarian government has worked to protect the interests of the state. [It is in the] interests of the state [to] fight . . . terrorism . . . it seems to me that none of the Bulgarian governments have been under pressure from abroad'.

Legal insiders in Ukraine – just like in Poland and Bulgaria – predominantly believe that the country's authorities have not been under any pressure to fight terrorism, as terrorism poses no real threat to their country. Some of them think there has been no need to pressure Ukraine as it had been a willing participant in the war on terror and as other countries are satisfied with its performance. None of the Ukrainian legal insiders believe the US has put pressure on Ukraine to step outside the law. Rather, the Americans have made efforts to persuade the Ukrainian government to take measures to prevent terrorism. Such measures do not necessitate violations of international or domestic law – though they facilitated Ukraine's participation in the wars in Iraq and Afghanistan. These wars are referred to in negative terms:

> U-ER-24: 'of course there are certain conditions from international organisations. I [think] Ukraine is a respectable country and I think other countries are satisfied with us.' UKR-PO-4: '[as regards terrorism] Ukraine voluntarily signs [the] necessary papers without any coercion.' U-PR-28: 'no international organisation can force a state to break a law or operate [with] in the framework of laws.' U-PR-23: 'there is no pressure, but there is collaboration.' 'U-PO-18: 'our government felt the pressure on the part of the international organisations . . . because they issued loans to our country'. U-PO-17: 'they forced Ukraine to dispatch forces for carrying out counterterrorist operations in Iraq. It seems to me that all other countries were forced to [do] this, too.'

To sum up, legal insiders in Norway and England feel the US has put pressure on their countries to step outside the law. They express themselves in negative terms about this, referring to international human rights and international conventions that have to be observed. By contrast, legal insiders in Europe's post-communist states are keen to emphasise that their countries have not been under any pressure either to act within, or to step outside, the law. Poland and Bulgaria are aligned with the US through NATO. However, the sense of being pressured is less felt and talked about in Eastern Europe, where the terrorist threat is perceived as less serious than in Western Europe.

Protecting civil rights versus combating terrorism

Measures taken by a country in response to the terrorist threat to some extent depend on how strongly the threat is felt in the particular country. Given the global dimension of the war on terror it also depends on the position of international organisations and foreign national states. And it is likely to reflect the local legal culture: old democracies may be keener to protect the rights of their citizens than to provide security. By contrast, states with an authoritarian past may be more willing to set aside civil and basic human rights in the name of national security. However, it is also possible that Europe's old democracies are keener to protect the democratic order – especially if the terrorist threat is perceived as small. Europe's post-communist states, for their part, may be more intent on protecting democratic and civil rights to preserve their fairly new democratic status. Or they may find it easier to set such rights aside, given their authoritarian past.

Table 9.14 *Combating the threat of terrorism versus protecting the rights of individual citizens and minorities: the legal insiders' perspective*

What would you say is most important: combating the threat of terrorism or protecting the rights of individual citizens and minorities? Why?	Norway (%)	England (%)	Poland (%)	Bulgaria (%)	Ukraine (%)
Combat terrorism	29	26	20	19	15
Protect rights	25	27	43	23	67
Mix	46	47	38	58	18

Note: Entries are based on the percentages of relevant 'text units' – the total number of answers to a given question; so entries sum up to approximately 100% (decimals are rounded up or down to the nearest whole number).

Legal insiders are reluctant to choose one option over the other: in Norway, England and Bulgaria a mixed approach of balancing security and rights receives the most support, whereas Polish and Ukrainian legal insiders are mostly in favour of protecting rights (Table 9.14).

As shown in Table 9.12, legal insiders in Norway, England and Poland perceive the threat of terrorism as real, whereas those in Bulgaria and Ukraine do not. Legal insiders generally have a more nuanced view of how to go about this threat than the legal outsiders. In Norway and particularly in England there appears to be real tension between the need for security and the need to uphold basic human and civil rights. Several legal insiders make it clear that they find it very difficult (or feel very uncomfortable) when they have to choose one over the other. Those who opt for security over rights stress that one should not necessarily sacrifice civil rights as a result. To them it is more a question of emphasis than of choosing one over the other. Ultimately, however, they believe that people's right to life is a precondition for exercising their civil rights and that it must therefore be given adequate protection:

> E-JU-13: 'they're both, obviously, highly important. It's slightly invidious to prioritise, but I think combating terrorism probably should be number one . . . we have a special procedure to deal with [terrorism] which leaves all of us, I think, feeling slightly uncomfortable because it's not open justice, but that's an example of having to tread on the rights of an individual sometimes, for the greater good to combat terrorism.' E-JU-9:

> 'how do you balance trying to give such a person [a terrorist] a fair trial or a fair opportunity to say, "I shouldn't be under this form of order", and at the same time protect the nation against the possibility of terrorism? . . . we have tried to . . . have a process under which you give the detainee what they call a special advocate who is allowed to know what this secret information is, but on the other hand, he's not allowed to communicate with his client . . . this is the duty of a country, a government, a law to protect the people who may be subject to terrorist attack.' E-PR-13: 'I don't think they're mutually exclusive. I think it's combating terrorism [which is most important]. Everybody has rights up to a point, but everybody foregoes absolute freedom where it's in the interests of the majority and a free, safe, fair society.'

Those English legal insiders who opt for maximum civil rights argue in defence of democratic society. In their view, such rights are difficult to reinstate once they have been removed. Besides, in the view of some, abiding by fundamental democratic principles is in itself an effective means by which to fight terrorism:

> E-JU-1: 'the latter [i.e. to protect civil rights]. The terrorists have won anyway.' E-PR-10: 'if you sacrifice the rights of individuals and minorities to pursue a targeted group . . . you lose out in a huge way because you may succeed in reducing terrorism . . . but you will have materially damaged your own society in order to do that'. E-PR-15: 'once you start eroding liberties it's very difficult to reinstate them.' E-PR-21: 'it should be a fundamental principle, that respect for the individual and minorities within the society should not be trampled upon'. E-PR-8: 'the best means of resisting any threat of terrorism is to protect minorities and individuals, because that is what it's for.'

However, the majority of the legal insiders argue in favour of striking a balance between civil rights and the war on terror. Some of them, notably the judges, indicate that sometimes that balance will tip in favour of civil rights, and at other times in favour of national security: the level of threat will be decisive in this regard. To some, the war on terror is essentially a balancing act between protecting the rights of the individual (civil and human rights) and those of the masses (right to life). Legal insiders think it is very difficult to get the balance right:

> E-JU-10: 'they're both important. You've got to strike a balance, really'. E-JU-11: 'it also depends on the level of the terrorist threat.' E-JU-14: 'sometimes the balance will come down in favour of taking, what some people would consider unacceptable, temporary steps to combat the threat of terrorism. By and large, they're not so ever present that they have to result in the abridgment of ordinary liberties'. E-JU-15: 'the

> balance will change from time to time. It's inevitable'. E-PR-14: 'it's a balance because I can see situations where the rights of the individual have to be subordinate to the rights of the masses . . . I think everybody, politicians and the judiciary, must agonise over the balance of those rights and I'm very glad I don't have to make that decision.'

One public prosecutor states that it a paradox that the IRA – which effectively waged a self-declared war on the UK – was treated as a criminal organisation rather than a military one, whereas Islamist fundamentalists are perceived as militants and for that reason fought with military means. Others are critical of the way in which Muslims are all branded as potential terrorists. They also express dissatisfaction with the manner in which the civil and human rights of those charged with terrorism have been grossly violated. In their view, neither has done much to reduce the terrorist threat – or to uphold democratic values:

> E-PR-1: 'for 30 years we faced IRA terrorism . . . we never took the view that the IRA was engaged in a war. We didn't use the language of war, they did. They wanted to be recognised as prisoners of war, and we never gave them that status because we said that they were criminals, and so we used the ordinary criminal justice system to put them on trial for offences . . . there's a lesson which we can learn from, which is that our way of life and our cultures, traditions, law, and so on, are strengthened if we don't step outside the law and we don't change our standards just because other people resort to violence.' E-PR-24: 'well, you've got to deal with the threat, not the perceived threat, and once you start painting a broad brush, for example, that all Muslims are trouble-makers and want to blow us up then that's when trouble starts, I think.' E-PR-4: 'there's a balance to be struck. If you can't protect the rights of individuals by tackling terrorism then you're not combating terrorism, because you're not protecting the freedoms that we have.'

In Poland and Ukraine the perceived absence of the terrorist threat also appears to have a lot to do with it. Legal insiders are not so much in favour of protecting rights because they perceive this as a means by which to protect democratic values. Rather, their position is primarily conditioned by the fact that there is no real need to combat terrorism in their country. Consequently, protecting rights makes more sense.

Perceptions of how to fight terrorism

Table 9.15 shows that legal insiders in all five countries covered by our project believe that the best way to fight terrorism is to strictly abide by

Table 9.15 *Preferred government response to the 'war on terror': the legal insiders' perspective*

What do you feel should be the [COUNTRY] government's main response to terrorism and the threat of terrorism? To pass new, tougher laws? To keep the existing laws but step outside the law when necessary? Or to stay strictly within existing laws?	Norway (%)	England (%)	Poland (%)	Bulgaria (%)	Ukraine (%)
Introduce new, tougher laws	23	18	29	19	37
Keep existing laws but step outside if necessary	16	11	8	4	5
Strictly abide by existing laws	61	72	63	77	58

Note: Entries are based on the percentages of relevant 'text units' – the total number of answers to a given question; so entries sum up to approximately 100% (decimals are rounded up or down to the nearest whole number).

existing law – regardless of whether they consider the terrorist threat to be real or not. Introducing new, tougher laws or keeping existing laws but stepping outside them if necessary, are viewed as less appropriate alternatives.

Norwegian legal insiders primarily feel that current legislation is sufficient to effectively fight terrorism. They also point out that abiding by the law is a legal norm, which should be adhered to regardless. Norwegian anti-terrorist legislation is considered to be fairly wide, leaving room for interpretation. Consequently, current legislation could be interpreted more strictly than is the case today. The need to implement existing laws properly is mentioned by fewer people:

> N-ER-12: 'the Norwegian government should observe existing laws and regulations and change its foreign policy. That will alleviate the terrorist threat.' N-GO-21: 'my experience is that ... we could practice law in a stricter manner ... I think we practice law in too liberal a manner'. N-JU-14: 'laws and regulations must be at the core of the war against terror just like they must be at the core of society as such'. N-PO-25: 'I think it is very important than when our society is put under pressure; we should demonstrate that this will not alter the values we have developed and that function so well [in our society].'

English legal insiders primarily hold the view that the war on terror 'has failed' and has gone too far in terms of violating laws and regulations. In the opinion of the majority of those interviewed, there is no need to step outside existing laws, nor is there a need for more law. Rather, existing legislation should be strictly observed, competently implemented and enforced:

> E-LA-1: 'we've got more than enough law already. Just stay within the law, but act competently when implementing laws . . . more law is not necessarily the answer when something isn't working.' E-LA-4: 'there's a great danger in chipping away at people's human rights by trying to approach terror as though it's a different sort of offence . . . I think you can deal with terrorism in the same way that you can deal with a complicated murder or a complicated fraud'. E-PR-14: 'we have at the moment extremely tough . . . and effective laws to combat terrorism. The extension of detention, even to what I think is 28 days presently, is far greater than that which is necessary for normal suspects, so we've already extended that but that is within the law and it happens within parliamentary debate, and it happened by democratic process.' E-PR-22: 'the proper approach is not to keep passing ever more extreme laws. That has the effect of penalising the law-abiding citizen and undermining trust in government and accepting that the law of the land should be obeyed.'

The war on terror could go two ways: it could bring about more or less democracy. Although one might assume that legal insiders in Eastern Europe – given their countries' communist past – would be more willing to introduce illiberal measures to fight terrorism, the opposite seems to be the case: legal insiders in the East remember the authoritarian past of their own countries and they are not willing to move in that direction again.

Legal insiders in Poland predominantly feel that existing legislation is sufficient for fighting terrorism and that much could be achieved in terms of better implementation of existing legislation. They also express their disapproval of setting aside laws more generally. These findings contrast with the prevailing attitude towards laws in post-communist states – that is, that laws are there to be broken. Several statements reveal a commitment to democratic values and to the rule of law and a fear of returning to the communist past. Some of the Polish legal insiders emphasise that allowing state institutions to break the law would be dangerous as the law could then be used against troublesome citizens (as was the case during Communism). Others stress the need to observe human and civil rights. Rather than introducing new laws and regulations to fight terrorism, they recommend better implementation of already existing ones:

> P-GO-7: 'we can't allow evasion of the law, because this is the simplest way to adopt methods and ways of functioning, which we want to eliminate. If we start to act like terrorists, breaking the law, then counter-acting terrorism will become pointless, since at some point we ourselves become terrorists'. P-GO-14: 'passing strict regulations . . . is very dangerous because it provides the authorities with a weapon which they can use against inconvenient citizens. For instance, they would pass a regulation that people suspected of terrorism could be locked [up] in prison without trial because they are suspected of terrorism. And then it would turn out that Mr Kowalski is suspected of terrorism because he frowned at some minister'. P-JU-6: 'the State should always act lawfully. State authorities . . . should never allow evading the law in order to fight anything. Because then the State . . . would be setting itself above the law. It would be difficult to retain any trust for the State authorities then'. P-LA-10: 'the problem in Poland is not that we do not have laws [that are] strict enough. Our law is quite strict. The problem is that we cannot apply the law quickly and effectively.'

Bulgarian legal insiders almost exclusively state that existing laws should be strictly observed – though some hint that law enforcement in Bulgaria is not currently good enough and that there is scope for improvement:

> B-LA-3: 'existing laws have to be strictly observed. [There is] no need to change the law. There is a need to respect the law.' B-PR-10: 'the laws adopted in Bulgaria are sufficiently stringent . . . [There is] no need of new law. Those which have been introduced must be respected'. B-PR-8: 'the laws should be respected . . . the [problem] is that the practical arrangements, I believe, of government and all law enforcement authorities, I mean prosecutors, to combat and prevent terrorism . . . are not at a sufficiently high level.'

Most of the Bulgarian legal insiders are in favour of strictly abiding by the law.

Ukrainian legal insiders think Ukraine has a sufficient number of good-quality laws to fight terrorism – though there is still much to be desired in terms of law enforcement. They stress that for democratic reasons the state should not step outside the law. A few of the respondents indicate that as Ukraine is not faced with a real threat of terrorism, there is no need for new and stricter laws:

> U-ER-19: 'if the existing legislation that we have were consecutively carried out to the full . . . we would have enough means and legal acts to avoid terrorism in Ukraine.' U-JU-18: 'our laws are good, we should only observe them.' U-JU-4: 'neither the state nor a particular person should go beyond the law. You should act within the law. The law is the law.' U-LA-2: 'we should stick to the laws that we have . . . America is not

a model to follow ... America is a police state.' U-LA-20: 'under no circumstances can the state step outside the law'.

Conclusions

This chapter has looked at the perceptions of legal outsiders and insiders of the terrorist threat and how to combat terrorism.

As regards the legal outsiders, it has explored the impacts of two significant influences on attitudes towards "paying the price" by prioritising "combating terrorism" over the rights of "individuals" or over the rights of "individuals and minorities": (i) religion (i.e. Muslim or not); and (ii) risk assessment. Muslims "as Muslims" might regard measures to combat terrorism as just another excuse for prejudice against Muslims. But they might also oppose measures to combat terrorism because they feel that the threat of terrorism is exaggerated – a panic overreaction by the authorities.

These two factors are correlated, though risk assessment does not correlate perfectly with religion. Muslims are more inclined to discount the threat of terrorism, many regarding the threat as exaggerated, though few denying its existence. Averaging across the five countries in the analysis, only a few more Muslims than non-Muslims deny there is any real threat of terrorism in their country. Even in England, where the threat of terrorism is most widely acknowledged, fewer than 10 per cent more Muslims than non-Muslims deny there is a real threat of terrorism in their country. But Muslims tend more than others to feel that the threat of terrorism is exaggerated – and especially so in England, where the threat of terrorism is most widely acknowledged.

There is, of course, no absolute standard by which to determine whether Muslims underestimate – or that the general public overestimate – the threat of terrorism. We can only note the difference between the perceptions of Muslims and non-Muslims.

Both religion and risk assessment have measurable impacts on popular legal culture, influencing the priority assigned to 'combating terrorism' over the need to defend the rights of individuals and minorities. But the more powerful influence, by a large margin, is risk assessment, not religion.

The greater the perception that terrorism poses a real threat, the greater the willingness to prioritise "combating terrorism" over the rights of individuals and minorities and this impact of risk assessment is strongest in England, where risk assessment itself is strongest. Religion also has a direct impact on attitudes towards prioritising "combating terrorism" over the rights of individuals and minorities in addition to its indirect impact through "risk assessment". The direct impact of religion is highly sensitive to the specific inclusion or exclusion of references to "minorities", which alienate the general public. But even with their inclusion the impact of "risk assessment" remains unchanged and risk assessment remains clearly greater than the impact of religion.

As for the legal insiders, there appears to be a correlation between the extent to which a country has (previously) been affected by terrorism, the extent of its involvement in the war on terror, and elite perceptions of whether there is a terrorist threat. Legal insiders (just like the legal outsiders) in Western Europe – unlike the legal insiders (and outsiders) in Eastern Europe – believe that their country is faced with a real threat of terrorism.

Legal insiders in Western Europe think the US has put pressure on their countries to step outside the law and that the EU has exerted pressure on them to stay within the law when combating terrorism. They are highly critical of American pressure. Legal insiders in Eastern Europe, for their part, do not believe their countries have been under pressure neither to stay within, nor to step outside, the law.

Legal insiders primarily advocate fighting terrorism by preservation civil rights while providing security – though some give priority to preserving civil rights. In England, which has introduced the strictest security measures against terrorism, respondents believe domestic efforts to combat terrorism have gone too far and increased, rather than decreased, the terrorist threat. Stepping outside the law in order to combat terrorism finds limited support amongst European legal insiders.

Our findings suggest that both legal insiders and outsiders believe the war on terror should be fought by means of law. However, whereas legal outsiders predominantly favour the introduction of new, tougher laws, legal insiders argue in favour of staying strictly within existing laws.

Our data thus seem to suggest that legal outsiders have a more authoritarian legal culture with regard to combating terrorism than legal insiders. Then some of the legislation that has so far been introduced to combat terrorism – notably legal procedures for how to deal with terrorist suspects and measures to prevent terrorism (notably the "stop and search" policy) in the UK – have limited the civil rights of terrorist suspects as well as ordinary citizens. Legal insiders – notably in England – warn against the introduction of new, tougher laws.

Our findings give reason for (cautious) optimism with regard to the preservation of civil rights in Europe. Then the legal insiders who are tasked with providing security and/or protecting civil rights are acutely aware of the need to preserve such rights while fighting terrorism, rather than (temporarily) suppressing them.

10

The role of religiosity in European popular legal cultures

Introduction

An extensive literature cites religiosity as correlating strongly with nationalism and authoritarianism.

This chapter is based on 168 questions about law, law enforcement, and public perceptions and attitudes towards legal insiders such as the police, lawyers, judges and lawmakers in our wide-ranging hour-long interviews in five European countries that focus on many aspects of the general publics' legal cultures. Some of these 168 questions might reasonably be classed as indicators of authoritarianism, or more clearly as 'secular authoritarianism'; but some might reasonably be classed as simply indicators of religious commitment that might conflict with secular authoritarianism; and others might not fit into either category.

Legal cultures vary across the five European countries. But they also vary across different groups within these countries. Here the focus is on the different legal cultures of the more or less religious – that is a focus on the impact of religiosity on legal culture, within each of the countries.

Religion is often associated with an authoritarian attitude towards enforcement of the law. Yet paradoxically, religion is also associated with extreme disregard for the law. Both of these aspects of the impact of religiosity on legal cultures need investigation. Religiosity is two-faced with respect to secular state law.

The impact of religiosity on European legal cultures

Do the more religious have a different conception of law from the less religious and non-religious or irreligious? It can be argued that it is in the nature of religion to 'proclaim its truth' irrespective of whether that is popular or not. So religion always has a potentially uneasy relationship with the state and with the fickle trends of the wider public opinion. In the longer term there may be a compromise between religion and broad public opinion, but there is often conflict in the shorter term.

At the state and society level there is tension between church and state, between state law and religion, and also between current public opinion and religion. But there is also tension at the level of the individual, who may simultaneously owe conflicting loyalties to political leaders (i.e. secular authority), to religious leaders (i.e. religious authority), to friends and neighbours and not least to their own conscience.

It has long been argued that 'because religious true-believers have embraced a body of received doctrines or dogmas, they have difficulty processing (in Max Weber's phrase) inconvenient facts', which makes them relatively intolerant and authoritarian (McClosky and Brill 1983, p. 411; see also Lord Percy of Newcastle 1954, p. 28.)

In a wide review of the literature, Eckhardt (1991, p. 113) cites religiosity as correlating strongly with nationalism, with opposition to civil disobedience (though in Western nations only) and generally with 'authoritarianism'. Wisneski, Lytle and Skitka (2009, p. 1060) cite a literature that 'suggests that religiosity reflects a generalised willingness to trust authority, regardless of whether the authority is secular or religious'. But how can they trust two authorities, if and when those authorities conflict?

Altemeyer and Hunsberger (1992, p. 113) claim that 'religious fundamentalism is linked with authoritarianism and prejudice toward a wide variety of minority groups'. But authoritarianism is not merely linked to religious fundamentalism: more widely it is claimed that 'religiosity induces susceptibility to authoritarian ideas and resistance to democratic ones' (Geddes and Zaller, 1989, p. 339). In more detail, Canetti-Nisim (2004, pp. 377, 388–9) claims that 'the negative effect of religiosity on endorsement of democratic values results from the mediation of authoritarianism': there is, she argues, a 'closeness found between religiosity and authoritarianism' which is the consequence of 'religiosity leading to authoritarianism' but 'not the model showing the opposite'. In her view, religiosity leads to authoritarianism, but authoritarianism does not lead to religiosity. Lakatos (2010) criticises any notion that religiosity and authoritarianism are different aspects of the same phenomenon, arguing that 'the impact of non-authoritarian religiosity is too important for religiosity to be treated as a simple correlate of authoritarianism'.

As befits a study of legal cultures, we focus on attitudes towards law rather than the psychological mindsets of individuals. Our measures of legal culture are conceptually closer to Canetti-Nisim's measure of democratic values, but far more extensive and detailed and in no way intended to form the basis of a single scale such as 'democratic values'. Even though we can classify certain laws or legal attitudes as authoritarian, we do not classify individuals as authoritarian. And as for religiosity, we rely on respondents placing themselves on a four-point scale that runs from religion being 'very important', 'somewhat important', 'not very important' or 'not at all important' to them, rather than assigning levels of religiosity on the basis of detailed questions about their religious beliefs or their participation in religious organisations. Ours is a public opinion approach, and not primarily an analysis of the interconnectedness of various psychological concepts.

Religiosity

When asked, "How important is religion to you personally – very important, somewhat important, not very important, or not at all important", almost every respondent in the surveys felt able to place themselves in one of these four categories. It is obviously not a difficult question for them.

Self-declared religiosity is strongest in Poland and weakest in Norway and England. Those who say they regard religion as "important" or "very important" are most numerous in Poland (86 per cent); somewhat less – though not very much less – in Ukraine (73 per cent); still less in Bulgaria (64 per cent); and by a large margin least numerous in England (45 per cent) and Norway (42 per cent). This cross-national pattern is broadly the same on the much tighter measure of self-declared religiosity as religion being "very important": as declared by 35 per cent of the public in Poland and 27 per cent in Ukraine, though only 19 per cent in Bulgaria, 17 per cent in England and 15 per cent in Norway (Table 10.1). On both measures, religiosity is strongest in Poland and Ukraine, and weakest in England and Norway.

At the other end of the scale, the numbers for whom religion is "not at all important" are so low in all three former communist countries – despite decades of Communism – that we need to exercise some caution when interpreting the legal cultures of the very few "most irreligious" rather than the larger numbers of the wider "less religious" (i.e. those who say religion is "not very" important to them, in addition to those who say religion is "not at all" important to them).

Within all these countries, religiosity varies across personal and social backgrounds – though to different degrees in different countries – and very occasionally in different directions in different countries.

Table 10.1 *Religiosity: the legal outsiders' perspective*

PB11: By how important is religion to you personally?	Norway (%)	England (%)	Poland (%)	Bulgaria (%)	Ukraine (%)
Very important	15	17	35	19	27
Somewhat important	27	28	51	46	46
Very +somewhat important	*42*	*45*	*86*	*65*	*73*
Not very important	25	26	11	25	19
Not at all important	34	29	3	10	8

Note: For simplicity all percentages in this chapter have been calculated after excluding those who gave mixed or non-committal answers, or who refused to answer the question.

Across the five countries, religiosity correlates most with gender and age, less with rurality and income, and even less with education. In every country – though especially in Poland and Ukraine – women are more likely than men to regard religion as "very important" (by a margin of 16 per cent in both Poland and Ukraine, though only 5 per cent elsewhere); and those aged 55 and over are more likely than those aged under 35 to regard religion as 'very important' (by margins of 29 per cent in Poland and 20 per cent in Ukraine, though much less elsewhere).

Rurality has a strong impact on religiosity in Ukraine and Poland though less elsewhere. In Ukraine, the numbers who regard religion as "very important" rise steadily from only 12 per cent in the capital, Kyiv, to 33 per cent in villages or rural areas. In Poland there is not much difference between the numbers in Warsaw (27 per cent) and even those in small towns (31 per cent) who regard religion as "very important"; but the numbers rise sharply to 45 per cent in Polish villages or rural areas. In Bulgaria there is not much difference between urban and rural areas (average 23 per cent who regard religion as "very important") except for an exceptionally low number (just a mere 7 per cent) in the capital, Sofia.

In every country, by a margin of 13 per cent on an average (though by a margin of 21 per cent in Poland) – those who feel their income and "standard of living" is "below average" are more likely to regard religion as "very important".

Education has little impact on religiosity in Norway and England but, if anything, religiosity in Norway and England appears very slightly greater amongst the well-educated. That is in very sharp contrast to Poland and Ukraine where low, not high, levels of education correlate with religiosity. Compared to those with minimal education, those with university education in Poland are 25 per cent less likely to feel religion as "very important" for them, and in Ukraine 17 per cent less – very different from the pattern in Norway and England.

In Poland especially, though much less elsewhere, those who identify exclusively with their country and not at all with Europe are on an average 21 per cent more likely than 'Euro-identifiers' (i.e. those who combine a national and European identity), to regard religion as "very important" to them "personally". In Poland a strong and exclusively national identity combines to a significant degree with strong religiosity.

Sectarian divisions also have an impact on religiosity, especially in Eastern Europe. By small margins of only 7 per cent in England, and 10 per cent in Norway, Catholics are more likely than Protestants to say religion is "very important" to them "personally". But Catholics are much more likely than the Orthodox to say religion is "very important" to them "personally", and by much larger margins, of 14 per cent in Bulgaria, 22 per cent in Poland and 33 per cent in Ukraine.

Clearly religiosity is widespread, and in some degree it is endorsed by a majority in all of the five countries. Indeed, religion is not merely "important" but regarded as "very important" by a large majority in the three East European countries and by a very large minority in the two West European countries. And religiosity tends to be particularly strong – though not necessarily in every country – amongst women, the poor, the old, the low-educated, those who live in rural areas, Euro-sceptics and Catholics (in contrast to Protestants or Orthodox).

But the primary focus here is not on the factors that encourage and sustain religiosity, nor even on the social or personal nature of religiosity, but on the role and impact of religiosity on legal cultures – a primary focus on the 'consequences' of religiosity rather than the 'causes' of religiosity.

The impact of religiosity on attitudes towards law

Given the findings of Geddes and Zaller (1989) that religiosity induces susceptibility to authoritarian ideas, or the findings of Canetti-Nisim (2004) that religiosity leads 'directly' to authoritarianism, we might expect that the impact of religiosity would encourage a generally more authoritarian legal culture that would support strict adherence to the law.

But which law? Religiosity may encourage more specific attitudes towards the defence of religion, religious institutions, religious leaders and their pronouncements, ordinary religious people and religious practices – any of which may conflict with the wider legal culture of the general public – and potentially lead to conflict with state law itself.

Although the more religious may be more inclined to bow to authority, the concept of authoritarianism depends critically on the issue of 'who has recognised authority'. Amongst those who are willing to take instruction from a recognised 'authority', some religious people may regard the state as the ultimate authority, but others may regard their religious leaders as the ultimate authority; or they may regard the state as the ultimate authority in one context, but their religious leaders as the ultimate authority in another. In a broad sense, authoritarianism is a willingness to bow before recognised authority, coupled with a willingness to challenge other self-proclaimed, but unrecognised, authorities. For the deeply religious, deference to religion and religious leaders ('religious authoritarianism') may therefore take priority over the purely 'secular authoritarianism' of the state whenever there is a conflict between these two 'authorities'. And then the religious authoritarians may morph into 'secular troublemakers' – or into something much worse.

The impact of religiosity within legal culture can be assessed by correlating indicators of legal culture – that is, indicators of public perceptions of law, and of public attitudes towards law – with varying degrees of religiosity. Most of these perceptions or attitudes were measured by offering either two alternatives or a four-point scale; and only those unprompted answers in the categories of "both/depends", "neither", "other/don't know/no answer" are, as usual, excluded from the calculation of correlations. (The very few questions where more meaningful answers were also excluded from the calculation of correlations because these answers did not fit into a one-dimensional scale are discussed in detail later.)

Across 168 indicators of legal culture, the correlation with religiosity (measured on a four-point scale) equals or exceeds 0.10 on only 36 of these 168 indicators of legal culture in Poland, on 29 indicators in Norway, 25 in England, 19 in Ukraine and 14 in Bulgaria. More narrowly, the correlation with religiosity equals or exceeds 0.15 on just 14 of these indicators of legal culture in Poland and Norway, just eight in England and Ukraine, and only four in Bulgaria. (All of these correlations – and more – exceed statistical significance at conventional levels, but here we are more concerned with substantial significance, which requires a higher standard.)

On these calculations, religiosity therefore does *not* have a strong impact "across the board" on most, or even on very many, aspects of legal culture. But religiosity does have a strong impact on some limited but substantial aspects of legal culture in every country, though this impact is most widespread in Poland, and least in Bulgaria.

Each of these 168 indicators fall naturally into one of three categories: (1) "religious authoritarian" or "strictly religious"; (2) "secular authoritarian" and (3) "other". This classification suggests that where religiosity has its strongest (and most complex) impact is in the explicit defence of religion, or explicit support for religious authority in relation to law. Where religiosity has a detectable, but clearly lesser, impact is on more general, "secular authoritarian" issues.

On the top 10 issues where legal attitudes correlate most strongly with religiosity, all but one has a clear and direct connection, specifically with religion, and none are linked to secular authoritarianism. (The one remaining issue is linked to the EU.) Of the next 10 issues where legal attitudes correlate most strongly with religiosity, eight are linked to secular authoritarianism and none are explicitly linked to religion. (The two remaining issues are linked to attitudes towards the EU; see Table 10.2.) And beyond this top 20, there are very few legal issues where attitudes correlate with religiosity at 0.15 or more in any country except Poland. Altogether this reveals a very sharp division between the impact of religiosity on "religious authoritarianism" and purely "secular authoritarianism".

So across the very wide-ranging investigation of the public attitudes and perceptions that together constitute popular legal culture, the evidence suggests that religiosity has: (i) a very strong impact on issues of law that are specifically and explicitly religious, (ii) a clear but lesser impact on some essentially "secular authoritarian" issues of law, and (iii) little or no impact on any of the remaining large majority of legal issues included in the survey.

The weaker second decile: religiosity and 'secular authoritarianism'

In descending order, the strongest correlation in the second decile is between religiosity and positive attitudes towards the police: the more religious are more inclined than others to regard the police as "more law-abiding than ordinary people" and, in general, they tend to feel "overall

Table 10.2 *The 'top 20' correlations with religiosity: the legal outsiders' perspective*

PQ			*Mean*	Norway	England	Poland	Bulgaria	Ukraine
Q41c:	Authoritarian Religious or Other	Topic						
Q122d:	**R**	Base law on religion	*0.35*	**0.36**	**0.42**	**0.37**	**0.30**	**0.32**
Q38b:	**R**	Christian tradition	*0.25*	**0.27**	**0.27**	**0.39**	0.11	**0.23**
Q43:	**R**	Go to religious mediator	*0.24*	**0.30**	**0.27**	**0.27**	**0.17**	**0.21**
Q109:	**R**	E&IS v. religious people	*0.22*	**0.25**	**0.21**	**0.32**	**0.17**	**0.16**
Q108:	**R**	Very religious more obedient	*0.18*	**0.27**	**0.37**		0.13	
Q41a:	**R**	Relig and ethnic minorities more obedient	*0.17*	**0.23**	**0.20**		**0.21**	**0.13**
Q49:	**R**	Base law on customs and traditions	*0.13*	**0.16**		**0.15**		**0.24**
Q122e:	**R**	Follow advice of religious leaders	*0.12*	0.12	**0.19**	0.10	0.11	0.10
Q66:	**R**	NOT Secular system	*0.07*	**0.15**	0.14	**0.18**		−0.14
	Oth	Prefer being in EU	*−0.02*		−0.11	−0.12		**0.19**
Q97:	**A**	Positive to police		0.14	**0.15**	0.10		
Q96:	**A**	Police more law-abiding		0.14	0.11		0.12	
Q7:	**A**	Combat terror v. protect freedom			**0.16**	**0.15**		
Q41b:	**A**	(Not) base law on current life-styles		0.13	**0.19**			0.11
Q121:	**A**	Real threat of terror			**0.20**		0.10	
Q32:	**A**	Fixed standard		0.12	**0.17**			
Q76d:	**A**	Privilege sexual minorities			0.11	**0.18**		
Q68:	**Oth**	E&IS do not suit			0.14	0.13		
Q60:	**A**	Crime increasing			0.10	**0.15**		
Q123:	**Oth**	Country truly European				0.14		0.11

Note: For simplicity, correlations less than 0.10 are not shown. All correlations shown are statistically significant at the 1% level or better, but it is their size that makes them substantively significant. Correlations of 0.15 or more are in bold. All entries are listed in order from the greatest correlation with religiosity (averaged across the five countries) to the least.

more positive" than others towards the police. The more religious are also more inclined than others to feel there is a "real threat of terrorism", and more inclined to prioritise "combating terrorism" over "individual freedom". They are less likely than others to support basing laws on "current lifestyles", and more inclined than others to say that "when public attitudes and behaviour changes" the law should "remain unchanged as a fixed standard of acceptable behaviour" rather than "be changed to reflect changes in public opinion". They are also more inclined than others to feel that "European and International Standards" privilege sexual minorities. And the more religious are more inclined to feel that crime is increasing.

All of these correlates with religiosity could be categorised as issues of 'secular authoritarianism' with no essentially religious content. So there is evidence in the survey of some degree of correlation between religiosity and these indicators of secular authoritarianism. But the range of issues is limited, and the correlation between religiosity and secular authoritarianism is much weaker than the correlation between religiosity and more specifically religious issues.

The stronger first decile: religiosity and specifically religious attitudes to law

Within the wide range of our 168 indicators of popular legal culture, only a few questions raise specifically religious issues, but religiosity correlates much more strongly with these issues than with secular authoritarian issues – and most strongly with the simple issue of whether "the law should be based on religion".

Basing law on religion? Not entirely surprisingly, religiosity has its greatest impact on public support for "basing law on religion". Across the five countries the correlation between religiosity and support for basing the law on religion averages 0.35 with only a small variation between countries: 0.36 in England, 0.42 in Norway, 0.37 in Poland, 0.30 in Bulgaria and 0.32 in Ukraine.

However, in every country the pattern depends not so much on the positive impact of strong religiosity as on the much greater negative impact of "strong irreligiosity" on "strong opposition" to basing law on religion. Amongst those who feel religion is "not at all important" to themselves, 79

On an average across the five countries only 20 per cent of those for whom religion is "very important" strongly agree that the law should be based on religion, but 68 per cent of those for whom religion is "not at all important" strongly disagree. On the issue of basing the law on religion therefore, the most secular are very strongly opposed, while the most religious are only moderately favourable if at all (Table 10.3).

Do "truly European" countries have a "Christian history and tradition"? The correlation between religiosity and the assertion that "to be truly European" a country must have "a Christian history and tradition" averages 0.25 across the five countries (though it is particularly high in Poland at 0.39, and particularly low in Bulgaria at only 0.11). "History and tradition" incorporates law even though it is not explicit about details of the law, and that correlation with religiosity suggests that the more religious are more inclined than others to want Christian traditions to be preserved even though they do not go so far as to demand that the law be openly and explicitly based on religion (Table 10.4).

Local religious leaders as mediators Support for avoiding courts and using a "local religious leader" as a mediator correlates with religiosity at 0.24 on an average across the five countries – somewhat less in Bulgaria and Ukraine but more everywhere else. There is no evidence of great enthusiasm for religious leaders as mediators: outside England, where only 25 per cent even amongst the most religious, say a religious leader is often better, on an average across the other countries, a mere 12 per cent even amongst the most religious, say that a religious leader is often better. But in every country, the irreligious are far more sceptical than the religious of any mediation by local religious leaders. The irreligious are on an average 33 per cent more inclined than the most religious to say that such mediation is "never better" than going to court.

There is of course nothing authoritarian in the concept of mediation – quite the opposite. It is very much an example of "soft law" rather than "hard law" – depending as it does on voluntary agreement between the two contending sides in the dispute. So here it is the irreligious, not the religious, who recommend taking the more "authoritarian" option of "going to court" and letting the court impose its law (Table 10.5).

European and International Standards versus the views of local religious people For the general public, both "European and International Standards" and "religious people in this country" might seem somewhat outside the mainstream – the one with an increasingly liberal agenda, the other with perhaps more conservative views. Agreement that law should be based on the views of "religious people in this country" rather than on "European and International Standards" correlates strongly with religiosity – at a high of 0.32 in Poland though at 0.22 on an average across all the five countries. Even amongst the most religious,

Table 10.3 *Impact of religiosity on attitudes towards 'the law should be based on religion': the legal outsiders' perspective*

			By how important religion is to you personally			
PQ41C: The law should be based on religion . . .		Impact of religiosity (%)	If very important (%)	If somewhat important (%)	If not very important (%)	If not at all important (%)
In England:						
	Agree strongly	***+17***	18	3	1	1
	Tend to agree	***+17***	21	13	7	4
	Tend to disagree	***+9***	25	32	33	16
	Disagree strongly	−***43***	36	52	59	79
	Correlation	r = 0.36				
In Norway:						
	Agree strongly	***+8***	11	3	1	3
	Tend to agree	***+42***	45	19	10	3
	Tend to disagree	***+12***	27	31	27	15
	Disagree strongly	−***61***	17	47	62	78
	Correlation	r = 0.42				
In Poland:						
	Agree strongly	***+20***	20	6	1	0
	Tend to agree	***+38***	38	26	11	0
	Tend to disagree	***+3***	27	34	45	24
	Disagree strongly	−***61***	15	34	43	76
	Correlation	r = 0.37				

In Bulgaria:						
	Agree strongly	***+23***	24	8	6	1
	Tend to agree	***+13***	31	24	15	18
	Tend to disagree	***+9***	31	40	46	22
	Disagree strongly	−***45***	14	28	33	59
	Correlation	r = 0.30				
In Ukraine:						
	Agree strongly	***+22***	29	10	7	7
	Tend to agree	***+30***	36	34	23	8
	Tend to disagree	−***16***	23	31	39	39
	Disagree strongly	−***35***	12	26	30	47
	Correlation	r = 0.32				

Note: The 'impact of religiosity' is the difference between the views of those who regard religion as 'very important', and those who regard religion as 'not at all important'.

Table 10.4 *Impact of religiosity on the view that to be 'truly European' a country must have a Christian tradition: the legal outsiders' perspective*

			By how important religion is to you personally			
PQ122D: To be truly European a country must have a Christian history and tradition . . .		*Impact of religiosity* (%)	If very important (%)	If somewhat important (%)	If not very important (%)	If not at all important (%)
In England:						
	Agree strongly	***+19***	26	14	8	7
	Tend to agree	***+13***	23	16	24	10
	Tend to disagree	***0***	33	43	39	33
	Disagree strongly	−***33***	17	27	30	50
	Correlation	r = 0.27				
In Norway:						
	Agree strongly	***+18***	27	19	13	9
	Tend to agree	***+16***	35	27	24	19
	Tend to disagree	−***5***	22	34	36	27
	Disagree strongly	−***29***	17	21	27	46
	Correlation	r = 0.27				
In Poland:						
	Agree strongly	***+28***	32	11	4	4
	Tend to agree	***+42***	42	41	21	0
	Tend to disagree	−***30***	20	34	49	50
	Disagree strongly	−***40***	6	15	27	46
	Correlation	r = 0.39				

In Bulgaria:						
	Agree strongly	***+20***	61	55	42	41
	Tend to agree	−***14***	25	34	47	39
	Tend to disagree	−***4***	11	9	6	15
	Disagree strongly	−***3***	2	3	5	5
	Correlation	r = 0.11				
In Ukraine:						
	Agree strongly	***+32***	57	43	31	25
	Tend to agree	−***5***	36	41	52	41
	Tend to disagree	−***13***	5	13	12	18
	Disagree strongly	−***13***	2	4	6	15
	Correlation	r = 0.23				

Note: The "impact of religiosity" is the difference between the views of those who regard religion as "very important", and those who regard religion as "not at all important".

Table 10.5 *Impact of religiosity on attitudes towards "mediation" by "a local religious leader": the legal outsiders' perspective*

PQ38b: Sometimes people avoid going to court and instead they ask some respected local person to act as a mediator and help settle the dispute. Please tell me if you feel that asking a local religious leader to settle a dispute or solve a problem is often, sometimes, seldom, or never better than going to court.		*Impact of religiosity* (%)	By how important religion is to you personally If very important (%)	If somewhat important (%)	If not very important (%)	If not at all important (%)
In England:						
	Often better	**+22**	25	11	7	3
	Sometimes better	***+13***	35	40	35	22
	Seldom better	***−6***	22	27	29	28
	Never better	***−29***	18	22	29	47
	Correlation	r = 0.30				
In Norway:						
	Often better	**+8**	12	3	3	4
	Sometimes better	**+32**	45	27	23	13

	Seldom better	***−10***	28	43	38	38
	Never better	***−30***	15	27	37	45
	Correlation	r = 0.27				
In Poland:						
	Often better	***+7***	12	6	5	5
	Sometimes better	***+33***	38	25	11	5
	Seldom better	***+12***	30	35	41	18
	Never better	***−53***	20	35	43	73
	Correlation	r = 0.27				
In Bulgaria:						
	Often better	***+8***	9	3	1	1
	Sometimes better	***+6***	22	15	12	16
	Seldom better	***+11***	39	36	37	28
	Never better	***−24***	31	47	51	55
	Correlation	r = 0.17				

Table 10.5 (*cont.*)

			By how important religion is to you personally			
PQ38b: Sometimes people avoid going to court and instead they ask some respected local person to act as a mediator and help settle the dispute. Please tell me if you feel that asking a local religious leader to settle a dispute or solve a problem is often, sometimes, seldom, or never better than going to court.		*Impact of religiosity* (%)	If very important (%)	If somewhat important (%)	If not very important (%)	If not at all important (%)
In Ukraine:						
	Often better	***+14***	15	4	4	1
	Sometimes better	***+8***	24	23	14	16
	Seldom better	***+5***	28	29	28	23
	Never better	***−28***	33	44	54	61
	Correlation	r = 0.21				

Note: The 'impact of religiosity' is the difference between the views of those who regard religion as 'very important', and those who regard religion as 'not at all important'.

however, a narrow majority in England and Poland – and a large majority elsewhere – would defer to "European and International Standards" rather than defer to the views of "religious people in this country" (Table 10.6).

Perceptions that the very religious are more law-abiding When articulated by religious people themselves, the claim that "very religious people, irrespective of [which] religion, are more obedient to the law than others", it is a claim – and possibly a proud claim – to be observant of the law. But it is not a demand to impose a tougher legal regime on others. It is about religion and religious people, not an authoritarian demand by religious people that others should be forced to become more law-abiding.

In England and Norway the correlation between religiosity and perceptions that "very religious people" are more obedient to the law averages at a very strong 0.32. But in Poland, Bulgaria and Ukraine the correlation is weak – not, however, because the religious fail to claim that they are law-abiding, but because a majority of even the irreligious in these countries are so generously willing to concede that very religious people tend to be more law-abiding (Table 10.7).

Perceptions that "religious and ethnic minorities are more law-abiding than others" On an average, the most religious are 21 per cent more inclined than the irreligious to say that "religious and ethnic minorities" are more law-abiding than others. The correlation between religiosity and perceptions that "religious and ethnic minorities" are more law-abiding than others correlates on average at 0.17. On this issue, the more religious are clearly more tolerant rather than more authoritarian: they are more than averagely tolerant of "minorities" – albeit in the context of a specific reference to "religious" minorities along with "ethnic" minorities (Table 10.8).

Basing law on "customs and traditions" Finally, the more or less religious are not so sensitive to basing the law on "customs and traditions" as they were with basing the law explicitly on "religion", or recognising as "truly European" only those countries that had an explicitly Christian history and tradition.

Nonetheless, on the issue of whether the law should be based on a country's "customs and traditions" – which in the European public imagination probably includes their Christian heritage along with other traditions – the correlation between personal religiosity and support for basing the law on heritage and traditions averages at 0.13 across the five countries. It is particularly weak in Norway and Bulgaria, but rises to

Table 10.6 *Impact of religiosity on the assertion that law should be based on the views of local religious people rather than on International Standards: the legal outsiders' perspective*

		By how important religion is to you personally			
PQ43: Which should be more important as a basis for law in our country today?	*Impact of religiosity* (%)	If very important (%)	If somewhat important (%)	If not very important (%)	If not at all important (%)
In England:					
What religious people in our country think is right and wrong, not European and International Standards	**+32**	46	32	22	14
Correlation	r = 0.25				
In Norway:					
What religious people in our country think is right and wrong, not European and International Standards	**+22**	28	12	6	6
Correlation	r = 0.21				
In Poland:					
What religious people in our country think is right and wrong, not European and International Standards	***+45***	49	23	8	4
Correlation	r = 0.32				
In Bulgaria:					
What religious people in our country think is right and wrong, not European and International Standards	***+15***	24	8	4	9
Correlation	r = 0.17				
In Ukraine:					
What religious people in our country think is right and wrong, not European and International Standards	***+17***	36	20	14	19
Correlation	r = 0.16				

Note: The 'impact of religiosity' is the difference between the views of those who regard religion as 'very important', and those who regard religion as 'not at all important'.

Table 10.7 *Impact of religiosity on perceptions that "very religious people" are more obedient to the law: the legal outsiders' perspective*

			By how important religion is to you personally			
PQ109: Are very religious people, irrespective of which religion . . .		*Impact of religiosity* (%)	If very important (%)	If somewhat important (%)	If not very important (%)	If not at all important (%)
In England:						
	More obedient than others to the law?	**+33**	65	58	39	32
	Correlation	r = 0.27				
In Norway:						
	More obedient than others to the law?	**+58**	82	43	33	24
	Correlation	r = 0.37				
In Poland:						
	More obedient than others to the law?	***+18***	81	78	73	63
	Correlation	r = 0.08				
In Bulgaria:						
	More obedient than others to the law?	***+13***	71	65	51	58
	Correlation	r = 0.13				
In Ukraine:						
	More obedient than others to the law?	***+4***	90	85	80	86
	Correlation	r = 0.07				

Note: The 'impact of religiosity' is the difference between the views of those who regard religion as 'very important', and those who regard religion as 'not at all important'.

Table 10.8 *Impact of religiosity on whether respondents feel "religious and ethnic minorities" are more or less obedient to the law than others: the legal outsiders' perspective*

			By how important religion is to you personally			
PQ108: Religious and ethnic minorities are . . .		*Impact of religiosity* (%)	If very important (%)	If somewhat important (%)	If not very important (%)	If not at all important (%)
In England:						
	More obedient	**+29**	44	27	20	15
	Correlation	r = 0.23				
In Norway:						
	More obedient	**+27**	40	12	8	13
	Correlation	r = 0.20				
In Poland:						
	More obedient	**+18**	43	40	38	25
	Correlation	r = 0.06				
In Bulgaria:						
	More obedient	**+20**	41	24	10	21
	Correlation	r = 0.21				
In Ukraine:						
	More obedient	**+9**	78	72	56	69
	Correlation	r = 0.13				

Note: The 'impact of religiosity' is the difference between the views of those who regard religion as 'very important', and those who regard religion as 'not at all important'.

around 0.16 in Poland and England, and to an even stronger 0.24 in Ukraine (Table 10.9).

Conflict between church and state Across the five countries the correlation between religiosity and feeling that religious people should obey their religious leaders, rather than the law, in circumstances of conflict correlates on an average at only 0.12. Though the correlation may not be very strong, it shows that in a conflict between church and state the most religious are the least willing to simply obey the law. This is also one of the questions where correlations are a somewhat inadequate measure of the complexity of the potential alternatives to simply obeying the law; it merits further discussion (see Table 10.10).

On the issue of whether 'to be truly European there must be a secular system with complete separation of church and state', in England, Norway and especially in Poland, the most religious are the least willing to agree. But in Bulgaria, personal religiosity has little or no impact. And perhaps surprisingly, in Ukraine, where the "very religious" were so favourable towards merging law with "national customs and traditions" (see PQ41a) the most religious are nonetheless the most favourable towards a "complete separation of church and state".

At first that is surprising, but it is unlikely to be a statistical blip. A much more plausible and substantive explanation is that in West European countries a close relationship of church and state has been seen for a long time as giving the church access to some influence over the state; on the other hand, in the history of the USSR, as in its predecessor, a close relationship of church and state was seen as continuing to give the state excessive influence and power over the church. So rightly or wrongly, a separation of church and state could be seen as giving more freedom to the state in the West, but more freedom to the church in the East, and consequently the separation is most popular with the irreligious in the West, but with the most religious in the East (Table 10.11).

Conflicting authoritarianisms: church versus state

So on a range of legal issues in the "second decile", including public attitudes towards legal-insiders such as the police and judges, the most religious are somewhat more authoritarian than the irreligious – but what the most religious display is a somewhat greater degree of "secular authoritarianism", confined as it is to issues that do not focus explicitly on religion.

Table 10.9 *Impact of religiosity on whether law should be based on customs and traditions: the legal outsiders' perspective*

PQ41A: Law should be based on customs and traditions . . .		*Impact of religiosity* (%)	By how important religion is to you personally: If very important (%)	If somewhat important (%)	If not very important (%)	If not at all important (%)
In England:						
	Agree strongly	***+20***	59	52	42	39
	Tend to agree	*−7*	29	34	36	36
	Tend to disagree	***−9***	8	12	17	17
	Disagree strongly	***−3***	5	3	4	8
	Correlation	r = 0.16				
In Norway:						
	Agree strongly	***+13***	39	34	35	26
	Tend to agree	*−7*	52	48	52	59
	Tend to disagree	***−4***	7	13	11	11

	Disagree strongly	***–1***	3	5	3	4
	Correlation	r = 0.07				
In Poland:						
	Agree strongly	***+15***	34	27	21	19
	Tend to agree	***+13***	52	53	45	39
	Tend to disagree	***–24***	11	16	30	35
	Disagree strongly	***–5***	3	3	5	8
	Correlation	r = 0.15				
In Bulgaria:						
	Agree strongly	***+10***	46	44	42	36
	Tend to agree	***–14***	36	39	46	50
	Tend to disagree	***+5***	14	11	8	9
	Disagree strongly	***–3***	3	6	3	6
	Correlation	r = 0.01				

Table 10.9 (*cont.*)

PQ41A: Law should be based on customs and traditions . . .		*Impact of religiosity* (%)	By how important religion is to you personally If very important (%)	If somewhat important (%)	If not very important (%)	If not at all important (%)
In Ukraine:						
	Agree strongly	***+27***	48	33	22	21
	Tend to agree	***+3***	40	42	49	37
	Tend to disagree	***−17***	8	18	16	25
	Disagree strongly	***−13***	4	7	13	17
	Correlation	r = 0.24				

Note: The 'impact of religiosity' is the difference between the views of those who regard religion as 'very important', and those who regard religion as 'not at all important'.

Table 10.10 *Impact of religiosity on attitudes to conflict between church and state: the legal outsiders' perspective*

PQ49: If religious leaders oppose a law, religious people should . . .		*Impact of religiosity* (%)	By how important religion is to you personally: If very important (%)	If somewhat important (%)	If not very important (%)	If not at all important (%)
In England:						
	Obey the law, not their religious leaders	***−18***	66	79	76	84
	Correlation	r =−0.12				
In Norway:						
	Obey the law, not their religious leaders	***−12***	88	96	98	100
	Correlation	r = 0.19				
In Poland:						
	Obey the law, not their religious leaders	***−13***	79	88	87	92
	Correlation	r = 0.10				
In Bulgaria:						
	Obey the law, not their religious leaders	***−8***	86	93	96	94
	Correlation	r = 0.11				
In Ukraine:						
	Obey the law, not their religious leaders	***−8***	84	90	93	92
	Correlation	r = 0.10				

Note: The 'impact of religiosity' is the difference between the views of those who regard religion as 'very important', and those who regard religion as 'not at all important'.

Table 10.11 *Impact of religiosity on attitude towards "church and state": the legal outsiders' perspective*

			By how important religion is to you personally			
PQ122E: To be truly European there must be a secular system with complete separation of church and state . . .		*Impact of religiosity* (%)	If very important (%)	If somewhat important (%)	If not very important (%)	If not at all important (%)
In England:						
	Agree strongly	***−14***	24	24	22	38
	Tend to agree	***−4***	28	35	42	32
	Tend to disagree	***+7***	26	27	26	19
	Disagree strongly	***+12***	23	13	10	11
	Correlation	r = − 0.15				
In Norway:						
	Agree strongly	***−16***	24	19	22	40
	Tend to agree	***+2***	30	33	31	28
	Tend to disagree	***+10***	28	31	34	18

	Disagree strongly	***+5***	19	17	14	14
	Correlation	r = − 0.14				
In Poland:						
	Agree strongly	−***54***	26	34	44	80
	Tend to agree	***+27***	35	40	32	8
	Tend to disagree	***+19***	31	21	18	12
	Disagree strongly	***+7***	7	5	6	0
	Correlation	r = − 0.18				
In Bulgaria:						
	Agree strongly	***+11***	49	52	53	38
	Tend to agree	−***22***	21	28	33	43
	Tend to disagree	***+8***	22	15	10	14
	Disagree strongly	***+3***	8	5	4	5
	Correlation	r =−0.04				

Table 10.11 (*cont.*)

PQ122E: To be truly European there must be a secular system with complete separation of church and state . . .		*Impact of religiosity* (%)	By how important religion is to you personally If very important (%)	If somewhat important (%)	If not very important (%)	If not at all important (%)
In Ukraine:						
	Agree strongly	***+22***	41	22	21	19
	Tend to agree	***−11***	34	41	37	45
	Tend to disagree	***−6***	15	24	27	21
	Disagree strongly	***−5***	10	13	16	15
	Correlation	r = + 0.14				

Note: The 'impact of religiosity' is the difference between the views of those who regard religion as 'very important', and those who regard religion as 'not at all important'.

But in the "first decile", where the correlations with religiosity are much stronger, the more religious are not necessarily more willing to obey the laws of the state. For religious people in particular, authority does not always mean the state: for them there are two, potentially conflicting, authoritarianisms. It is an age-old problem. As the King James Version of the Gospel of St. Luke puts it (in chapter 20, verse 25) 'render unto Caesar the things that are Caesar's and unto God the things that are God's'. Provided there is no conflict between state and church, the deeply religious appear to be a little, but only a little, more authoritarian than others – as commanded by the first part of this text. But if there is a conflict between state and church, the deeply religious may be the least law-abiding – as also commanded by the second part of the text. At the extreme, it is worth recalling that terrorist campaigns have often been linked to religion.

Obedience to the law depends on the law as well as on the citizen. In many cases the citizen has a clear duty to obey the law. But in some cases the citizen may feel a duty to protest against an unjust law, evade it, or simply reject it. The survey investigated public support for obedience – and for justified disobedience – towards various kinds of unpalatable laws. It is worth looking at public attitudes towards these laws in more detail than one-dimensional correlations permit. In particular there are a variety of possible responses to an offensive law: so the options include more than simply 'obey' or 'disobey'. The correlation analysis has been based only on those who advocated obedience or disobedience to the laws of the state – those who opted for answers such as 'both/depends', 'neither', 'other/don't know/no answer' were, as usual, excluded from the calculation of correlations.

On one important sequence of questions about obedience to the law, however, it was necessary to exclude those who opted for all but two of the answers in order to calculate correlations with religiosity because the excluded answers did not fit into a meaningful one-dimensional scale; they were multidimensional alternatives. One set of these alternatives were (1) "obey the law"; (ii) "ignore or evade the law"; (iii) "offer a gift or bribe to officials or the police, so that they do not enforce the law" and (iv) "protest against the law".

Troublesome laws If Parliament passed a law that "some people felt was unnecessarily complicated and troublesome" a clear majority in England and Norway say that people should "protest" against that law rather than meekly "obey it" – but very few say people should "evade" the law, or offer a "bribe" to officials or the police to avoid enforcing it. But, most important, there is little difference between the very religious and the irreligious on this issue: in both countries, the very religious are a mere 5 per cent more in favour of simple obedience than the irreligious – that is the limited extent of their (secular) "authoritarianism" on this issue.

In Poland, and more especially Bulgaria, there is less support for "protest" but the impact of religiosity is greater: the most religious are on an average 12 per cent more inclined than the irreligious to advocate simple obedience to troublesome laws. But in Ukraine the most religious are 9 per cent more inclined than the irreligious to advocate protest rather than simple obedience.

Overall, however, the impact of religiosity on attitudes towards merely "troublesome" laws is weak. The more religious people do take a slightly more "authoritarian" attitude on this issue, but it is only very slightly: on an average across the five countries, the impact of religiosity increases support for simple obedience by 5 per cent and reduces support for protest by 4 per cent. In short the impact of religiosity is weak on this issue (Table 10.12).

Unfair and unjust laws If "some people" felt the law was "really unfair and unjust" – rather than merely "troublesome", however, general public support for them to protest is considerably greater. But on an average across the five countries, the impact of religiosity only increases support for simple obedience by 3 per cent and reduces support for protest by 2 per cent. Again, the most religious are only slightly more authoritarian than the irreligious (Table 10.13).

If a "large majority" of people – rather than just "some" people – felt the law was "really unfair and unjust" public support for protest is greater still, especially in Eastern Europe. A reference to a "large majority" in the question gives a degree of democratic credibility to the argument that the law is unjust, and ultimately a greater threat that the weight of opposition may force a change in the law.

But once again the very religious are, on an average, a mere 2 per cent more than the irreligious in favour of simple obedience, and 3 per cent less inclined than the irreligious to advocate or support protest. (On an average, the most religious are also under 3 per cent less inclined than the irreligious to advocate "ignoring or evading" the law; and under 2 per cent less inclined than the irreligious to advocate "offering a gift or bribe"). So once again, the very religious are scarcely any more authoritarian than the irreligious on this issue – contrary to the claims that religious people are generally more authoritarian and more willing than others to simply obey the law. In these situations, the most religious simply hold "mainstream" attitudes (Table 10.14).

Table 10.12 *Impact of religiosity on attitudes to how unnecessarily complicated and troublesome law should be dealt with: the legal outsiders' perspective*

		By how important religion is to you personally			
PQ46: If Parliament passed a law that *some people* felt was unnecessarily *complicated and troublesome* to obey should they …	*Impact of religiosity* (%)	If very important (%)	If somewhat important (%)	If not very important (%)	If not at all important (%)
In England:					
Obey the law	***+5***	39	43	43	34
Ignore or evade the law	***−2***	2	2	2	4
Offer a gift or bribe so that officials or police do not enforce the law	***0***	1	1	1	1
Protest against the law	***−3***	58	54	54	61
In Norway:					
Obey the law	***+5***	36	36	36	31
Ignore or evade the law	***0***	2	3	2	2
Offer a gift or bribe so that officials or police do not enforce the law	***0***	0	0	1	0

Table 10.12 (*cont.*)

			By how important religion is to you personally			
PQ46: If Parliament passed a law that *some people* felt was unnecessarily *complicated and troublesome* to obey should they . . .		*Impact of religiosity* (%)	If very important (%)	If somewhat important (%)	If not very important (%)	If not at all important (%)
	Protest against the law	**−4**	63	61	62	67
In Poland:						
	Obey the law	**+13**	49	44	36	36
	Ignore or evade the law	**−1**	7	6	9	8
	Offer a gift or bribe so that officials or police do not enforce the law	**+2**	2	2	2	0
	Protest against the law	**−14**	42	49	52	56
In Bulgaria:						
	Obey the law	**+11**	58	57	51	47
	Ignore or evade the law	**−3**	11	14	17	14
	Offer a gift or bribe so that officials or police do not enforce the law	**−2**	5	2	2	7
	Protest against the law	**−7**	26	28	31	33

In Ukraine:

Obey the law	***−9***	51	42	46	60
Ignore or evade the law	***−4***	8	14	8	12
Offer a gift or bribe so that officials or police do not enforce the law	***+4***	5	6	10	1
Protest against the law	**+9**	36	38	35	27

Note: The 'impact of religiosity' is the difference between the views of those who regard religion as 'very important', and those who regard religion as 'not at all important'.

Table 10.13 *Impact of religiosity on how really unfair and unjust law should be dealt with: the legal outsiders' perspective*

			By how important religion is to you personally			
PQ47: If Parliament passed a law that *some people* felt was really *unfair and unjust* should they . . .		*Impact of religiosity* (%)	If very important (%)	If somewhat important (%)	If not very important (%)	If not at all important (%)
In England:						
	Obey the law	**+5**	25	27	23	20
	Ignore or evade the law	***+1***	2	2	1	1
	Offer a gift or bribe so that officials or police do not enforce the law	***+1***	1	0	0	0
	Protest against the law	*−7*	72	71	76	79
In Norway:						
	Obey the law	***0***	25	33	32	25
	Ignore or evade the law	**−2**	0	3	2	2
	Offer a gift or bribe so that officials or police do not enforce the law	***0***	0	0	0	0
	Protest against the law	**+2**	75	64	67	73
In Poland:						
	Obey the law	***+16***	32	28	30	16
	Ignore or evade the law	**−2**	6	7	9	8

	Offer a gift or bribe so that officials or police do not enforce the law	***+4***	4	1	3	0
	Protest against the law	***−18***	58	65	58	76
In Bulgaria:						
	Obey the law	***+3***	34	37	37	31
	Ignore or evade the law	***−12***	12	14	17	24
	Offer a gift or bribe so that officials or police do not enforce the law	***+2***	4	1	1	2
	Protest against the law	***+8***	50	48	45	42
In Ukraine:						
	Obey the law	***−12***	31	31	33	43
	Ignore or evade the law	***+2***	8	10	11	6
	Offer a gift or bribe so that officials or police do not enforce the law	***+1***	5	3	4	4
	Protest against the law	***+9***	56	55	53	47

Note: The 'impact of religiosity' is the difference between the views of those who regard religion as 'very important', and those who regard religion as 'not at all important'.

Table 10.14 *Impact of religiosity on how a large majority of people should deal with really unfair and unjust law: the legal outsiders' perspective*

		By how important religion is to you personally			
PQ48: If Parliament passed a law that *a large majority of people* felt was really *unfair and unjust* should they. . .	*Impact of religiosity* (%)	If very important (%)	If somewhat important (%)	If not very important (%)	If not at all important (%)
In England:					
Obey the law	***+5***	18	17	17	13
Ignore or evade the law	***+1***	5	2	3	4
Offer a gift or bribe so that officials or police do not enforce the law	***+1***	1	0	0	0
Protest against the law	*−7*	77	81	80	84
In Norway:					
Obey the law	*−1*	12	15	13	13
Ignore or evade the law	***+1***	4	3	3	3
Offer a gift or bribe so that officials or police do not enforce the law	***0***	0	0	0	0
Protest against the law	***0***	84	83	85	84

In Poland:						
	Obey the law	***+12***	24	20	11	12
	Ignore or evade the law	***+2***	6	5	13	4
	Offer a gift or bribe so that officials or police do not enforce the law	***−4***	0	1	2	4
	Protest against the law	***−10***	70	74	74	80
In Bulgaria:						
	Obey the law	***−4***	17	16	18	21
	Ignore or evade the law	***+1***	9	11	12	8
	Offer a gift or bribe so that officials or police do not enforce the law	***+3***	6	1	1	3
	Protest against the law	***0***	68	72	70	68
In Ukraine:						
	Obey the law	***−3***	17	12	13	20
	Ignore or evade the law	***0***	4	6	11	4
	Offer a gift or bribe so that officials or police do not enforce the law	***+4***	5	3	5	1
	Protest against the law	***0***	74	80	71	74

Note: The 'impact of religiosity' is the difference between the views of those who regard religion as 'very important', and those who regard religion as 'not at all important'.

Laws that conflict with religion But if "religious leaders oppose a law passed by Parliament and declare it is contrary to their religion', the impact of religiosity is no longer negligibly small and positive. Now it is large and negative.

Across the five countries, those for whom religion is "very important" are 19 per cent less likely than the irreligious to agree that religious people should simply obey the law; they are only 6 per cent more likely to say they should "follow the advice of their religious leaders", but 13 per cent more likely to say they should "follow their own conscience" (and no more or less likely to say religious people should emigrate).

The consequence is that amongst the most religious, only in Bulgaria is there a clear majority who advocate obedience to a law that has been declared to be contrary to religion. But amongst the most religious, only half in Ukraine, slightly less than half in Norway, and only one-third in England or Poland advocate simple obedience to such a law. In these circumstances, the religious are the very opposite of secular authoritarians. Authoritarians they may be, but their "authority" is their religious leadership, not the state (Table 10.15).

Attitudes towards secular protest If some religious leaders persuade Parliament to pass laws that require everyone to obey the principles of their religion, what should non-religious people (or those belonging to other religions) do? No examples were given in the interview, though one classic example might be the ban on Sunday shopping which remained in force until 1994 in England, though other examples might include laws on abortion or euthanasia. On an average the most religious are no more likely than others to say the non-religious should obey such laws, but they are 10 per cent less likely than the irreligious to say the non-religious should "protest" against such laws, and 10 per cent more likely than the irreligious to say the non-religious should "follow their own conscience" (Table 10.16).

Adjusting the law Religiosity has very little impact on public support for adjusting the law to suit the needs of ethnic and religious minorities – either by ensuring the law is "sufficiently tolerant of individual freedoms that it does not offend minorities", or by "not enforcing some laws on minorities provided that does no harm to other people". Only in Bulgaria is there a large majority in favour of requiring strict obedience to the law by minorities, and very few support non-enforcement. But religiosity has little or no impact on these attitudes in Bulgaria. In England and Norway there is a narrower majority in favour of requiring strict obedience to the law by minorities – with Norwegians relying on tolerance of individual

Table 10.15 *Impact of religiosity on law declared contrary to religion: the legal outsiders' perspective*

PQ49: Suppose religious leaders oppose a law passed by Parliament and declare it is contrary to their religion, what should religious people do?	*Impact of religiosity* (%)	By how important religion is to you personally: If very important (%)	If somewhat important (%)	If not very important (%)	If not at all important (%)
In England:					
Obey the law	***−21***	36	48	47	57
Follow the advice of their religious leaders	***+8***	19	13	15	11
Follow their own conscience	***+12***	39	33	31	27
Go and live somewhere else	***0***	6	5	6	6
In Norway:					
Obey the law	***−40***	47	76	83	87
Follow the advice of their religious leaders	***+6***	6	3	1	0
Follow their own conscience	***+32***	43	16	11	11
Go and live somewhere else	***0***	3	5	5	3

Table 10.15 (*cont.*)

PQ49: Suppose religious leaders oppose a law passed by Parliament and declare it is contrary to their religion, what should religious people do?		*Impact of religiosity* (%)	By how important religion is to you personally If very important (%)	If somewhat important (%)	If not very important (%)	If not at all important (%)
In Poland:						
	Obey the law	***−11***	31	33	37	42
	Follow the advice of their religious leaders	***+4***	8	5	6	4
	Follow their own conscience	***+7***	61	62	57	54
	Go and live somewhere else	***0***	0	1	1	0
In Bulgaria:						
	Obey the law	***−6***	68	72	77	74
	Follow the advice of their religious leaders	***+6***	11	6	3	5
	Follow their own conscience	***−1***	18	19	15	19
	Go and live somewhere else	***+1***	3	4	5	2

In Ukraine:						
	Obey the law	*−16*	50	56	59	66
	Follow the advice of their religious leaders	*+4*	10	6	5	6
	Follow their own conscience	*+14*	35	31	30	21
	Go and live somewhere else	*−3*	5	6	7	8

Note: The 'impact of religiosity' is the difference between the views of those who regard religion as 'very important', and those who regard religion as 'not at all important'.

Table 10.16 *Impact of religiosity on how to deal with religious law: the legal outsiders' perspective*

			By how important religion is to you personally			
PQ50: Suppose some religious leaders persuade Parliament to pass a law that requires everyone to obey one of the principles of their religion. What should non-religious people, or those who belong to other religions, do?		*Impact of religiosity* (%)	If very important (%)	If somewhat important (%)	If not very important (%)	If not at all important (%)
In England:						
	Obey the law	***+5***	19	20	16	14
	Protest against this law	***−16***	41	41	50	57
	Follow their own conscience	***+11***	38	38	33	27
	Go and live somewhere else	***+1***	2	2	1	1
In Norway:						
	Obey the law	***−5***	9	16	10	14
	Protest against this law	***−1***	70	73	78	71
	Follow their own conscience	***+7***	21	11	11	14
	Go and live somewhere else	***−1***	0	0	1	1

In Poland:						
	Obey the law	***+9***	24	20	15	15
	Protest against this law	***−24***	18	26	36	42
	Follow their own conscience	***+15***	57	54	49	42
	Go and live somewhere else	***+1***	1	1	0	0
In Bulgaria:						
	Obey the law	***−4***	40	31	32	44
	Protest against this law	**+2**	38	39	46	36
	Follow their own conscience	***0***	20	26	18	20
	Go and live somewhere else	**+2**	2	4	4	0
In Ukraine:						
	Obey the law	***−4***	*42*	39	41	46
	Protest against this law	***−9***	24	30	27	33
	Follow their own conscience	***+15***	31	29	29	16
	Go and live somewhere else	***−1***	4	3	4	5

Note: The ‘impact of religiosity’ is the difference between the views of those who regard religion as ‘very important’, and those who regard religion as ‘not at all important’.

freedoms and the English on a mixture of tolerant laws coupled with non-enforcement. To an even greater degree, Poles would rely on a mixture of tolerant laws coupled with non-enforcement, and only a minority would insist on strict obedience to the law.

In four of the countries, however, degrees of religiosity have little impact. But in Ukraine the irreligious differ sharply from other Ukrainians: they are 17 per cent more insistent than others that the law must be obeyed by ethnic and religious minorities, 10 per cent less willing to have tolerant laws and 8 per cent less willing to avoid enforcing laws which offend minorities. What is very significant, however, is that it is the irreligious, and not the most religious, who take the most authoritarian position.

In fact this same pattern – of relatively tolerant religious people and relatively authoritarian irreligious people – is visible in all the other countries, though the differences between the religious and irreligious are very small. Overall those differences do not suggest a strong liberal tendency amongst the most religious, but they refute any expectation that the most religious would be more strongly authoritarian (Table 10.17).

Special laws for minorities Going beyond tolerance or non-enforcement, there is the issue of special laws for minorities however. Should there be "some special laws that apply only to ethnic or religious minorities – on marriage, divorce, or inheritance, for example?" On this issue, the differences between the attitudes of the most religious and the irreligious are small and not entirely consistent. But on an average the most religious are 4 per cent more favourable than the irreligious towards such "special laws" (and more than twice that in Bulgaria and Ukraine). Of course these numbers do not suggest great support for such special laws. But they clearly refute the proposition that the most religious might have a particularly authoritarian, one-size-fits-all attitude, on this issue of law (Table 10.18).

Conclusions

This chapter has focused on the impact of mainstream religiosity, based not on small numbers of zealots, but on the broad numbers of the general public who declare that religion is at least as "important" or even "very important" to them. Across the five countries – Norway, England, Poland, Bulgaria and Ukraine – almost two-thirds regard religion as at least as "important" and a quarter regard it as "very important" – somewhat less than average in Norway and England, but more than

Table 10.17 *Impact of religiosity on whether ethnic and religious minorities must always obey the law: the legal outsiders' perspective*

		By how important religion is to you personally			
PQ52: Some people say that the government should make a special effort to adjust the laws of a country to the needs of ethnic and religious minorities. Others disagree. Which of the following statements comes closest to your view?	*Impact of religiosity* (%)	If very important (%)	If somewhat important (%)	If not very important (%)	If not at all important (%)
In England:					
Ethnic and religious minorities must always obey the law of a country	***−1***	58	55	57	59
The law should be sufficiently tolerant of individual freedoms that it does not offend such minorities	**−3**	28	30	31	31
Some laws should not be enforced on minorities, if no harm to other people	**+4**	14	15	12	10
In Norway:					
Ethnic and religious minorities must always obey the law of a country	**−8**	53	63	63	61
The law should be sufficiently tolerant of individual freedoms that it does not offend such minorities	**+5**	40	32	31	35
Some laws should not be enforced on minorities, if no harm to other people	**+4**	7	5	6	3
In Poland:					
Ethnic and religious minorities must always obey the law of a country	**−3**	39	38	34	42
The law should be sufficiently tolerant of individual freedoms that it does not offend such minorities	***0***	39	38	51	39

Table 10.17 (*cont.*)

		By how important religion is to you personally			
PQ52: Some people say that the government should make a special effort to adjust the laws of a country to the needs of ethnic and religious minorities. Others disagree. Which of the following statements comes closest to your view?	*Impact of religiosity* (%)	If very important (%)	If somewhat important (%)	If not very important (%)	If not at all important (%)
Some laws should not be enforced on minorities, if no harm to other people	***+4***	23	24	15	19
In Bulgaria:					
Ethnic and religious minorities must always obey the law of a country	***−4***	71	79	75	75
The law should be sufficiently tolerant of individual freedoms that it does not offend such minorities	***+1***	24	16	20	23
Some laws should not be enforced on minorities, if no harm to other people	***+3***	5	5	5	2
In Ukraine:					
Ethnic and religious minorities must always obey the law of a country	***−17***	49	49	46	66
The law should be sufficiently tolerant of individual freedoms that it does not offend such minorities	***+10***	39	40	42	29
Some laws should not be enforced on minorities, if no harm to other people	***+8***	12	12	12	4

Note: The 'impact of religiosity' is the difference between the views of those who regard religion as 'very important', and those who regard religion as 'not at all important'.

Table 10.18 *Impact of religiosity on whether there should be special laws for ethnic or religious minorities: the legal outsiders' perspective*

			By how important religion is to you personally			
PQ53: Should there be some special laws that apply only to ethnic or religious minorities – on marriage, divorce or inheritance for example?		*Impact of religiosity* (%)	If very important (%)	If somewhat important (%)	If not very important (%)	If not at all important (%)
In England:						
	Yes	***+1***	11	15	16	10
In Norway:						
	Yes	**+5**	12	7	6	7
In Poland:						
	Yes	**−3**	29	28	28	32
In Bulgaria:						
	Yes	**+9**	21	8	8	12
In Ukraine:						
	Yes	**+8**	41	36	46	33

Note: The 'impact of religiosity' is the difference between the views of those who regard religion as 'very important', and those who regard religion as 'not at all important'.

average in Poland and Ukraine. With only a slight exception in Bulgaria, the religious are overwhelmingly Christian, though they vary from primarily Protestant to Catholic to Orthodox.

An extensive literature cites religiosity as correlating strongly with authoritarianism, but the analysis here shows that religiosity correlates only moderately with aspects of purely "secular authoritarianism", and correlates much more strongly with specifically religious aspects of law, even when these conflict with "secular authoritarianism". To describe religiosity as exerting an influence towards "authoritarianism" in legal cultures is therefore only a misleading half-truth.

For deeply religious people, authority cannot and does not always mean the state. Provided there is no conflict between church and state, the deeply religious appear to be a little – though it is only a little – more authoritarian than others. But if there is a conflict between church and state the deeply religious suddenly become the least law-abiding. In these circumstances, the very religious are much *less* likely than the irreligious to automatically advocate obedience to the law, and much *more* likely to advocate following the advice of religious leaders or more especially their "own conscience", even if that breaks "state law".

11

A European legal culture?

Introduction: common Europe

In Chapter 1 we cited British former MEP Glyn Ford, who has argued that 'genuine partnership (in Europe) can only develop on the basis of shared common values – in particular, democracy, the rule of law and respect for human and civil rights' (Kuzio 2004). This presupposes some harmonisation of legal culture as well as legislation and legal institutions. In the following chapters we provided in-depth analyses of the attitudes and perceptions of legal outsiders and insiders on several key dimensions of legal culture.

The World Bank's 2010 Rule of Law Index – and more recently, the World Justice Project's 2014 Rule of Law Index – ranks Norway at the top end, followed in descending order by the UK, Poland, Bulgaria and Ukraine. World Bank (2008) and IMF (2013) GDP (PPP) per capita figures follow the same pattern, descending from higher (Norway) to lower (Ukraine). In addition, the five countries investigated in this book differ on several other parameters, outlined in Chapter 1. Yet, all of them are recipients of law transferred from European and international supranational bodies.

This chapter seeks to establish whether – and to what extent – legal cultures across Europe are actually converging or diverging, or whether they are converging on some dimensions, whilst diverging on others. The chapter first summarises findings presented in previous chapters – organised around three themes: Western versus Eastern Europe, legal outsiders versus legal insiders, and legal transfers. In the second part these findings are used to discuss where legal culture in Europe is headed in terms of attitude and perceptions.

Western versus Eastern Europe

The most important finding from our country comparisons is that legal outsiders and insiders across Europe have fairly similar attitudes to "law in principle" – that is, what law is and what its role in society should be.

Their attitudes are largely *democratic*: everybody should be equal before the law; nobody should place him- or herself above it. Law should provide justice. It should be strict, yet fair, and it should protect the weaker groups in society. There should not be too many laws; laws should be clear and easily understandable to people; and they should not change often. People should make use of their democratic rights to protest cumbersome or unfair law ("voice") – but whilst working to change such law, they should abide by it ("loyalty").

Their attitudes are also *secular*: both East and West Europeans are in favour of secular states, having secular law. There is little support for religion *informing* law. A majority think that religious people should protest secular law clashing with religious law ("voice"). However, the percentage that thinks religious people should simply accept and abide by the law ("loyalty") is greater than for citizens who are unhappy with cumbersome or unfair law. There is minimal support for religious leaders engaging in dispute resolution. But it is not intolerance that informs reluctance to mix religion and law: both East and West Europeans stress that there are many religions, and it is therefore important that they be treated equally. Besides, many people have no religion. Allowing religion to inform law would thus discriminate them.

Finally, their views on law highlights what could be coined *the 'democratic' crisis*. A core principle of the rule of law is that law should be stable, clear and predictable. Legal outsiders and insiders believe that law is not stable (but that it should be): that it is changing rapidly (but that it should not), and not for the better (which it should). And even the legal professionals find it difficult to keep up with, and understand, the large amount of often poor-quality law that is churned out as a result of European integration, or active government. European countries are thus faced with a potential 'democratic' crisis as regards the legitimacy of law and equal treatment before the law.

Perceptions of "law in practice", on the other hand, are more *country-specific*. Such perceptions often correlate with GDP (PPP) per capita and ranking on the World Bank's (2010) and the World Justice Project's (2014) Rule of Law Index: in countries that do well in both areas, perceptions of legal insiders and the institutions they represent are generally more positive than in countries that do not do so well.

There is also *a centre-periphery dimension* to the perceptions' part of legal culture: on some parameters perceptions in Europe's 'fringe' states – the UK and Ukraine – are very similar. These differences seem to be informed primarily by a sense of distance to 'core Europe': English FG participants talk about the UK being an island and as such, being naturally closed off from the rest of Europe. Ukraine is culturally diverse: while western Ukraine and Kiev are predominantly West-leaning (EU), eastern and southern Ukraine have stronger affinity with the East (Russia).

The perceptions of Muslims within Europe are not specific to Muslims as such: rather they vary by country, just as the perceptions of the majority populations do. It is therefore not possible to speak about one homogeneous Muslim legal culture. Rather, there are several legal cultures just as there are several types of European Muslims. Some have lived in Europe for centuries, whereas others have migrated from Asia and Africa to Europe fairly recently. The former are carriers of *native* Muslim legal culture, which is fairly similar to the legal culture of the majority population. The latter are carriers of *migrant* Muslim legal culture or elements of such migrant Muslim legal culture – and in the process of adapting to the legal culture of the majority population.

In their study of US immigrants Algan and Cahuc (2010, p. 1) claim that 'the inherited trust of descendants of US-immigrants is significantly influenced by the country of origin and the timing of arrival of their forbears'. They find that immigrants from Scandinavia and the Netherlands and their descendants have a high degree of trust, whereas immigrants from Africa, Portugal and the former Yugoslavia are the least trustful. A majority of the Muslims in Norway and England have either migrated from, or are descendants of people who have migrated from, low-trust societies in Asia and Africa. To the extent Muslims have different perceptions from the majority populations these appear in part to be informed by a sense of being excluded – that is, 'not belonging' or feeling discriminated against, more so than by 'inherited perceptions'.

As for *Euro-migrants,* our data suggest that Europeans who settle in other European countries are fairly adaptable – but that their level of adaptation is greater amongst those who settle in countries with 'same-type' legal cultures than amongst those who settle in countries whose legal culture is very different from that of their country of origin. What is more, Euro-migrants find it easier to adapt to more than to less law-abiding legal cultures: Euro-migrants from Western Europe are reluctant to adjust to informal law and corruption, which characterises many East European legal cultures. By contrast, East European Euro-migrants find it fairly easy to adapt to the more law-abiding legal cultures of Western Europe. Polish FG participants in Norway made this explicitly clear in their statements.

Legal outsiders versus legal insiders

We have used our own definition of 'legal insiders' by including not only the legal professionals (lawyers, prosecutors, judges) in this category, but also those making the law (the elected representatives), those implementing the law (government officials), and law enforcement (the police). It could, of course, be argued that elected representatives, government officials and the police are not legal professionals in the traditional sense. Yet they all work professionally with the law: the laws they pass and the manner in which they implement and enforce the law affects ordinary citizens (legal outsiders).

The academic literature on legal culture makes a clear distinction between popular and professional legal culture, or the legal culture of the legal outsiders and the legal insiders. In this book we have argued that both legal outsiders and insiders are effectively socialised into the same national legal culture. What is more, the term *legal professional* is no longer as exclusive as it used to be in the past: in recent years not only the number of legal professionals but also the social strata from which the legal professionals are recruited have expanded significantly. Even though they have been socialised into the same professional legal culture, the 'baggage' the legal insiders bring with them is diverse.

In this book we have shown that the legal culture of the legal outsiders and insiders is fairly similar as far as attitudes to law in principle are concerned. There is also some similarity in terms of law in practice or law in action. However, legal outsiders and insiders have fundamentally different views on three issues of key importance to democracy and the rule of law: on whether governments may occasionally step outside the law, whether national security should take precedence over civil rights in the 'war on terror', and on the flexibility of law.

First, legal outsiders across Europe are open to governments stepping outside the law to combat corruption, organised crime and terrorism. By contrast, legal insiders (also across Europe) are massively opposed to members of their professions stepping outside the law. In this sense the legal insiders exhibit a greater 'in-principle' commitment to the rule of law than the general public does.

Second, legal outsiders believe national security should be prioritised at the expense of civil rights. Further, support for civil rights is higher in those countries where the threat of terrorism is weaker. And it is stronger amongst Muslims – who in Western Europe have been targeted by those fighting the war on terror. Legal insiders, for their part, believe that governments should fight terrorism by strictly abiding by existing laws. The alternatives – introducing new, tougher laws, or if necessary, stepping outside existing laws – have less support. In this sense it is the legal insiders, rather than the legal outsiders, who stand up in defence of civil rights. Again, the legal insiders have a stronger in-principle attitude.

Third, the legal culture of the legal outsiders is authoritarian in that the public believe the law should be harsh. In their view there should be stricter implementation and enforcement of the law, more legal controls on safety, quality and standards and harsher penalties for lawbreakers. Even though legal insiders stress that there are no reasonable excuses for knowingly breaking the law, some make allowances for civil disobedience (Western Europe), whilst others excuse lawbreaking caused by poverty or ignorance (Eastern Europe). They are more open to judges in court applying the law flexibly – that is, by considering the circumstances of a given case.

Sceptics might argue that some of our questions are essentially political questions. Yet it is difficult to deny that issues such as the meaning of law, the role of law and legal transfers are not also core components of legal culture. Whilst we do not deny that legal outsiders and insiders might have different views on more technical aspects of law, their views are fairly similar as far as law in principle and law in practice are concerned. As few comparative studies of legal outsiders and insiders have so far been carried out, it would be useful to conduct further studies of legal outsiders and insiders with a view to establishing how similar or different their views are on other aspects, or dimensions, of legal culture.

Legal transfers and European integration

The literature on legal transfers suggests that they are more likely to be embraced locally and to take proper hold if initiated or endorsed by the recipient state ('legal imports') than if initiated or enforced upon the recipient state from the outside ('legal exports'). It is also often claimed that legal transfers will never behave in exactly the same manner in the legal culture into which they are transferred as they do in the legal culture within which they originate.

The general views of legal outsiders and insiders on legal transfers are important in that they tell us something about countries' readiness to accept such transfers and thus also about whether transferred law is perceived as *imports* or *exports*. This, in turn, allows for some predictions as to whether, in the future, law in Europe is likely to converge or diverge.

Our data show that citizens across Europe are not in favour of cultural integration (Grødeland 2009). However, there is considerable support for legal borrowing, even for legal integration. Across Europe both legal outsiders and insiders believe their countries can learn from other countries and from supranational organisations about writing, implementing or obeying the law. Across Europe legal insiders agree that their countries can learn from other countries or from international organisations about laws, the way law is applied or about the way ordinary people deal with the law. And they do not consider E-I-U standards to be imposed. However, they are more cautious about the value of having much more similar law across Europe. Where legal outsiders see opportunities and benefits, legal insiders see practical obstacles and difficulties that would have to be overcome for legal convergence to become a reality.

Support for learning from Europe is fairly high in Eastern Europe: copying good law is seen as a prerequisite for catching up with the more affluent countries in Western Europe. East Europeans are generally positive to legal convergence, EU standards and the ECtHR. Whereas the Poles favour legal integration for both *normative* and *instrumental* reasons, Bulgarians and Ukrainians primarily do so for *instrumental* reasons.

By contrast, the English rate their country's legal system – and the common law – very highly. Many legal outsiders and insiders in England believe that other countries could learn from the UK rather than the other way round. Further, they claim that the UK has more to learn from other common law countries than from continental Europe. They would therefore be displeased if national laws were to become much more similar across Europe – unless European law is adjusted to British law. Still, English legal outsiders and insiders do not believe that E-I-U standards are imposed upon their country: in their view the UK was instrumental in writing up the ECHR. What is more, the UK does have a strong voice in the very international fora that make these standards.

Sceptics claim that it is impossible to transfer law from civil law to common law systems and vice versa. Our data does lend some support to this position: a fair share of the English legal insiders believes European legal integration neither possible, nor desirable, given the differences between common law and civil law. On the other hand, research shows that law is transferred not only between civil law systems, or between common law systems – but also between civil law and common law systems. Post-communist states in Eastern Europe, for instance, have copied laws from both systems. It is also worth noting that some English legal insiders believe the UK have something to learn about law from the Scandinavian countries whose legal systems are hybrid mixtures of civil and common law. Norwegian legal insiders, for their part, believe Norway has something to learn from the UK.

Conclusions: looking to the future

Hesselink (2009, p. 7) claims that 'there are still signs of a transformation from a rather formal, dogmatic and positivistic national legal culture into a more substance-oriented and pragmatic European legal culture'. But do Europeans really want a common European legal culture?

Findings presented in this book show that there is convergence across Europe in terms of attitudes to 'law in principle'. There is a declared wish both in Eastern and Western Europe to learn from other countries in terms of making, implementing or enforcing the law. But there is divergence in terms of law in practice: perceptions of law in practice frequently correlate with GDP (PPP) per capita and level of rule of law in that perceptions of legal insiders and the institutions they represent are generally more positive in Western than in Eastern Europe. A convergence in perceptions of law in practice is unlikely to occur in the short term – and for two major reasons.

First, our data suggest that there is a correlation between perceptions of law in practice, GDP (PPP) per capita and rule of law. Academic research suggests that there appears to be a link between economic growth and corruption (Mo 2001, p. 66), and also between GDP per capita, corruption and the rule of law (see, for instance, De Mendonça and Da Fonseca 2012) – though the manner in which these three factors affect each other is disputed.

We will not enter into a discussion on the causal relationships between GDP per capita, rule of law and corruption. But it seems reasonable to assume that wealthier countries are able to make more resources available to the judiciary and the police than poorer countries to enhancing their efficiency – which, in turn, is likely to affect people's perceptions of them. Bulgaria is one of the poorest countries in the EU,[1] and Ukraine is suffering the effects of civil war. Corruption is widespread in both of

[1] Wikipedia, 'Economy of the European Union', 'Economies of member states', http://en.wikipedia.org/wiki/Economy_of_the_European_Union#Economies_of_member_states accessed on 30 August 2014.

them. Neither country is therefore likely to catch up with the countries in Western Europe, or for that matter other countries in Eastern Europe, in the short term.

Second, as Algan and Cahuc (2010) suggest, trust is passed on from one generation to another. One reason might be that trust is partly rooted in social norms. And social norms do not easily lend themselves to change. Data presented in the previous chapters suggest that in Eastern Europe perceptions of legal insiders and the institutions they represent are to some extent informed by social norms: centuries of foreign rule have fostered lack of trust in the state and state law. In Poland such attitudes are gradually being replaced by a normative commitment to democratic society and its laws. But in Bulgaria and Ukraine, the historically informed scepticism prevails. And it is reinforced by the actions of the ruling elites. In Ukraine, even the ruling elites themselves are sceptical not only of other ruling elites but of their own profession. Their views are not likely to change overnight.

Across Eastern Europe, foreign rule has historically been imposed upon reluctant populations that considered not only the rulers but also their laws illegitimate. Ethical dualism is therefore common in many post-communist states. In such states people in the past applied a strict moral code in their interaction with people belonging to their own group, but the manner in which they treated other people in general, and state institutions in particular, was very different (Suhara 2004, pp. 393–4). This ethical dualism is still prevalent in Eastern Europe through the widespread continued use of informal law and informal practices.

After the collapse of Communism *normative* deliberations – that is, support for the democratic project and for European integration – appears to have positively affected people's behaviour vis-à-vis the law in Poland. By contrast, Bulgarians and Ukrainians appear to have less regard for the law now than they had in the past – partly due to a distorted understanding of what democracy entails, partly as they perceive the ruling elites and their laws as illegitimate, and partly due to poverty.

The academic literature suggests that identities and mindsets change slowly. Cownie (2004, p. 206) found 'considerable evidence of the enduring nature of certain core aspects of the culture of academic law, which suggests that the professional identities of legal academics may be more resistant to pressure than some commentators have acknowledged'. Dahrendorf (quoted in Pedersen and Johannsen 2005, p. 19) has predicted that 'it will take six months to reform the political systems (in post-communist states), six years to change the economic systems and sixty years to effect a revolution in the people's hearts and minds'. The latter are of particular importance to legal culture.

The Poles held on to a strong 'alternative' (democratic) mindset during the Communist period and therefore easily adapted to democracy – and for normative reasons. Bulgarians and Ukrainians, for their part, have embraced democratic attitudes towards law in principle. But they have largely done so for instrumental, rather than for normative, reasons. This helps explain why the gap between attitudes and perceptions is bigger in these two countries than in Poland.

In conclusion we can say that there is convergence across Europe in terms of law in principle, but divergence in terms of law in practice. It remains to be seen whether legal cultures in Europe will also converge in terms of law in practice. In any event, such convergence is not likely to occur in the near future.

Appendix

Data collection was commissioned from professional pollsters working to ESOMAR standards: TNS Gallup (Norway), ORB (UK), CBOS (Poland), Alpha Research (Bulgaria) and SOCIS-Gallup (Ukraine).

	Focus groups (84)				
	Norway	England	Poland	Bulgaria	Ukraine
Capital (2)	Oslo (high/low)	London (high/low)	Warsaw (high/low)	Sofia (high/low)	Kiev (high/low)
Wealthy region (3/9)	West (Stavanger-Sandnes-Klepp)	South-West (Bristol-Bath-mixed large village)	South-West (Katowice-Lubliniec-Mierzęcice)	North-East (Varna-Aksakovo-Topoli)	West (Lviv-Horodok-Zubra) East (Donetsk-Yasinovata-Krasnogorovka) Crimea (Simferopol-Alushta-Marino)
Poorer region (3/9)	North (Tromsø-Finnsnes-Bardufoss)	North-East (Leeds-Sheffield-mixed large village)	North-East (Białystok Zambrów-Turośń Kościelna)	North (Pleven-Dolna Mitropolia-Opanets)	West (Ternopil-Zbarash-Plotyca) East (Kharkiv-Chuguev-Liptsy) Crimea (Evpatoria-Bakhchisaray-Lobanovo)

(*cont.*)

	Focus groups (84)				
	Norway	England	Poland	Bulgaria	Ukraine
Muslims (3/4)	Oslo Ethnic Pakistanis	London Ethnic Pakistanis	Warsaw (FSU Muslims, Turks) Białystok (Polish Tatars)	Kardjali, Momchilgrad, Enchets Bulgarian Turks	Simferopol (2) Bakhchisaray (2) Crimean Tatars
Euro-migrants (3/4)	Oslo (Brits-Poles-Ukrainians)	London (Scandinavians-Poles-Ukrainians)	Warsaw (Scandinavians-Brits-Ukrainians)	Sofia (Scandinavians) Varna (Ukrainians) Elhovo (Brits)	Kiev (Russians, Poles) Lviv (Poles, Northern Europeans)

	Nationally representative surveys (5)				
	Norway	England	Poland	Bulgaria	Ukraine
Sample size	**Main sample** (911) **Muslim booster** (201) – mixed Muslims	**Main sample** (1,000) **Muslim booster** (200) – mixed Muslims	**Main sample** (1,027) **Muslim booster** (200) –Polish Tatars (100) –FSU/Turks (100)	**Main sample** (1,018) **Muslim booster** (207) –Bulgarian Turks	**Main sample** (1,200) **Muslim booster** (200) –Crimean Tatars

	Structured, open-ended in-depth interviews (786)				
	Norway	England	Poland	Bulgaria	Ukraine
Judges	25	25	25	25	31
Prosecutors	25	25	25	25	31
Lawyers	25	25	25	25	31
Police officials	25	25	25	25	31
Elected representatives	25	25	25	25	31
Government officials	25	25	25	25	31
Total	(150)	(150)	(150)	(150)	(186)

Note: Interviews were carried out at national level, capital level, in a wealthy region (big city and small town) and a poorer region (big city and small town) in Norway, England, Poland and Bulgaria. In Ukraine, interviews were carried out at national level, capital level, in the West (one big city in a wealthy region, one big city in a poorer region), East (one big city in a wealthy region, one big city in a poorer region), and the Crimea (one big city in a wealthy region, one big city in a poorer region). The regional interview locations were as follows:

Norway: Stavanger and Sandnes (wealthy region), Tromsø and Finnsnes (poorer region);

England: Bristol and Bath (wealthy region), Leeds and Sheffield (poorer region);

Poland: Katowice and Lubliniec (wealthy region), Bialystok and Zambrow (poorer region);

Bulgaria: Varna and Aksakovo/Devnia (wealthy region), Pleven and Dolna Mitropolia/ Cherven Briag (poorer region) – please note that interviews with judges and prosecutors in the regions (small towns) had to be conducted in Devnia and Cherven Briag as there are no courts and prosecutor's office in Aksakovo and Dolna Mitropolia;

Ukraine: (1) Western Ukraine: Lviv (wealthy region), Ternopil (poorer region); (2) Eastern Ukraine: Donetsk (wealthy region), Kharkiv (poorer region) and (3) Crimea: Simferopol (wealthy region), Evpatoria (poorer region).

BIBLIOGRAPHY

Aasland, Aadne, Åse Berit Grødeland, and Heiko Pleines, 2012. 'Trust and informal practice among elites in East-Central and South East Europe', *Europe-Asia Studies* 64(1): 115–43.

AFP, 15 October 2013. 'Polish Muslims drop Eid sacrifice amid protests, Halal Ban', http:/tribune.com.pk/story/618920/polish-muslims-drop-eid-sacrifice-amid-protests-halal-ban/

'Agenter skulle kidnappe Mulla Krekar' [Agents were to kidnap Mullah Krekar], 6 November 2009. *TV2*, www.tv2.no/nyheter/innenriks/agenter-skulle-kid nappe-3mulla-krekar-2994247.html

Ajani, Gianmaria, 1995. 'By chance and prestige: Legal transplants in Russia and Eastern Europe', *The American Journal of Comparative Law* 43(1): 93–117.

13–16 June 1996. 'Transformations of systems in Middle and Eastern Europe and its consequences for banks, stock exchanges and security risks', Paper prepared for the Max-Planck Institut Symposium, Hamburg, www.jus.unitn.it/cardozo/review/Business/Ajani-1997/ajani.htm

2005. *Das Recht der Länder Osteuropas*. Berlin: Berliner Wissenschafts-Verlag.

Albrecht, Stan L., and Tim B. Heaton, 1984. 'Secularization, higher education, and religiosity', *Review of Religious Research* 26(1): 43–58.

Algan, Yann, and Pierre Cahuc, 2010. 'Inherited trust and growth', *American Economic Review* 100(5): 2060–92. http://econ.sciences-po.fr/sites/default/files/file/yann%20algan/Inherited%20Trust%20and%20Growth_AER.pdf

Ali, Shaheen Sardar, 2013. 'From Muslim migrants to Muslim citizens', in Griffith-Jones (ed.), 157–75.

Altemeyer, Bob, and Bruce Hunsberger, 1992. 'Authoritarianism, religious fundamentalism, quest, and prejudice', *International Journal for the Psychology of Religion* 2(2): 113–33.

Anderson, James H., David S. Bernstein, and Cheryl W. Gray, 2005. *Judicial Systems in Transition Economies – Assessing the Past, Looking to the Future.* Washington DC: World Bank.

AP, 30 January 2012. 'Men jailed for planning attack on Danish newspaper', *The Guardian*, www.guardian.co.uk/world/2012/jan/30/men-guilty-planning-attack-danish-newspaper

Arold, Nina-Louisa, 2007. *The Legal Culture of the European Court of Human Rights.* Leiden: Martinus Nijhoff Publishers.

Åslund, Anders, September 2013. 'Ukraine's choice: European association agreement or Eurasian union?' *Peterson Institute for International Economics*, policy brief 13–22.

Aziz, Miriam, 2004. *The Impact of European Rights on National Legal Cultures.* Portland, OR: Hart Publishing.

2010. 'Constitutional tolerance and EU enlargement: The politics of dissent?', in Sadurski et al. (eds.), 237–61.

Baldwin, Richard E., Joseph F. Francois, and Richard Portes, 1997. 'The costs and benefits of Eastern enlargement: The impact on the EU and Central Europe', *Economic Policy* 12(24): 125–76. http://faculty.london.edu/rportes/Bfp.pdf

Barclay, Scott, and Susan S. Silbey, 2008. 'Understanding regime change: public opinion, legitimacy, and legal consciousness', in Keith E. Whittington (ed.), *Oxford Handbook of Law and Politics.* Oxford University Press, 663–78.

Barry, Donald D., and Harold J. Berman, 1968. 'The Soviet legal profession', *Harvard Law Review* 82(1): 1–41.

Basedow, Jurgen, Klaus J. Hopt, and Reinhard Zimmermann, 2012. *Max Planck Encyclopedia of European Private Law.* Oxford University Press.

BBC News. 2004 December 16 . 'Terror detainees win Lords appeal', http://news.bbc.co.uk/2/hi/uk_news/4100481.stm

Berend, Ivan T., 2009. *From the Soviet Bloc to the European Union. The Economic and Social Transformation of Central and Eastern Europe since 1973.* Cambridge University Press.

Berkowitz, Daniel, Katharina Pistor, and Jean-Francois Richard, 2003. 'The transplant effect', *European Economic Review* 47(1): 163–203.

Berry, John W., 1997. 'Immigration, acculturation, and adaptation', *Applied Psychology: An International Review* 46(1): 5–68.

Bierbrauer, Gűnter, 1994. 'Toward an understanding of legal culture: variations in individualism and collectivism between Kurds, Lebanese, and Germans', *Law & Society Review* 28(2): 243–64.

Black, David A., 2010. 'Narrative determination and the figure of the judge', in Freeman (ed.), 677–85.

Blankenburg, Erhard, 1994. 'The infrastructure for avoiding civil litigation: comparing cultures of legal behaviour in the Netherlands and West Germany', *Law & Society Review* 28(4): 789–808.

Blankenburg, Erhard, Nena Tromp, Airi Kana, Michiel Notten, Laszlo Maracz, and Hank Geerts, 2000. *Legal Culture in Five Central European Countries.* The Hague: WRR Scientific Council for Government Policy W111.

Blichner, Lars Chr., and Anders Molander, 2005. 'What is juridification?', Arena working paper no. 14, Oslo: Arena.

Bodnar, Adam, and Eva Katinka Schmidt, 2012. 'Rule of law and judicial independence in Eastern Europe, the South Caucasus, and Central Asia', in *OSCE Yearbook 2011. Yearbook of the Organization for Security and Co-operation in Europe*. Baden-Baden, Nomos Verlag, 289–301.

Bogdanor, Vernon, 2009. *The New British Constitution*. Oxford and Portland, OR: Hart Publishing.

Bonner, David, 2000. 'The United Kingdom's response to terrorism: The impact of decisions of European judicial institutions and of the Northern Ireland "peace process"', in Fernando Reinares (ed.), *European Democracies Against Terrorism. Governmental Policies and Intergovernmental Cooperation*, Aldershot: Ashgate, pp. 31–71.

Broun, Janice, 1993. 'The schism in the Bulgarian Orthodox Church', *Religion, State and Society* 21(2): 207–20.

Bőrzel, Tania, 2001. 'Non-compliance in the European Union: Pathology or statistical artefact?' Robert Schuman Center, RSC no. 2001/28, San Domenico: EUI Working Papers.

2002. 'Pace-setting, foot-dragging, and fence-sitting: Member state responses to Europeanization', *Journal of Common Market Studies* 40(2): 193–214.

Bratholm, Anders, 1957. *Pågripelse or vareteksfengsel [Arrest and Custody]*. Oslo: Universitetsforlaget.

'Britain slips to 20th in global probity index', 2010, October 27. *The Guardian*.

Broun, Janice, 1997, Spring. 'Divisions in Eastern orthodoxy today', *East–West Church Ministry Report* 5(2): 1–3.

Bulley, D., 2008. 'Foreign terror? London bombings, resistance and the failing state', *British Journal of Politics and International Relations* 10(3): 379–94.

Burbank, Jane, 2004. *Russian Peasants Go to Court: Legal Culture in the Countryside, 1905–1917*. Bloomington, IN: Indiana University Press.

Buscaglia, Edgardo, 1999, March 1. 'Judicial corruption in developing countries: Its causes and economic consequences', *Berkeley Program in Law and Economics, Working Paper Series, Berkeley Program in Law and Economics, UC Berkeley*.

Butcher, Kristin F, and Anne Morrison Piehl, 1998. 'Recent immigrants: Unexpected implications for crime and incarceration', *Industrial and Labour Relations Review* 51(4): 654–79.

Butler-Sloss, Elizabeth, and Mark Hill, 2013. 'Family law: Current conflicts and their resolution', in Griffith-Jones (ed.), 108–15.

Campbell, C., and I. Connolly, 2003. 'A model for the "war against terrorism"? Military intervention in Northern Ireland and the 1970 falls curfew', *Journal of Law and Society* 30(3): 341–75.

Cane, Peter, and Joanne Conaghan (eds.), 2008. *The New Oxford Companion to Law*. Oxford University Press.

Canetti-Nisim, Daphna, 2004. 'The effect of religiosity on endorsement of democratic values: The mediating influence of authoritarianism', *Political Behaviour* 26(4): 377–98.

Carrubba, Clifford J., and Lacey Murrah, 2005. 'Legal Integration and the use of preliminary ruling process in the European Union', *International Organization* 59(2): 399–418.

Case, Holly, 2009. 'Being European: East and West', in Checkel and Katzenstein (eds.), 111–31.

Centre for Social Cohesion, 2009. *The Beth Din. Jewish Law in the UK*. London: The Centre for Social Cohesion.

Centre for the Study of Democracy (CSD), 2007. *Organized Crime in Bulgaria: Markets and Trends*. Sofia: CSD.

2009. *Crime without Punishment: Countering Corruption and Organised Crime in Bulgaria*. Sofia: CSD.

Chatham House – YouGov Survey, 2012. *British Attitudes towards the UK's International Priorities. Survey Results*. London: Chatham House.

Chavdarova, Tanya, 2007. 'Business relations as trusting relations: The case of the Bulgarian small business', in Roth (ed.), 277–302.

Checkel, Jeffrey, and Peter J. Katzenstein, 2009. *European Identity*. Cambridge University Press.

Cholewinski, Ryszard, 1998. 'The protection of human rights in the new Polish Constitution', *Fordham International Law Journal* 22(2): 236–91.

Christensen, Unn, n.d. 'Stor oppslutning om velferdsstaten' [High support for the welfare state], Forskningsrådet [The Research Council], www.forskningsradet.no/prognett-vfo/Nyheter/Stor_oppslutning_om_velferdsstaten/1224698393082?lang=no

Cole, Lynn H., and Bilyana Gyaurova-Wegertseder, n.d. 'A journey in mediation: The Bulgarian path', *Annual Meeting and Convention. Special Section*, www.baadr.com/en/archive.php? . . . Journey-in-Mediation.doc

Comparato, Guido, 2014. 'Europe vs the nation-state in private law? Legal cultures and their community-building function', in Helleringer and Purnhagen (eds.), 329–49.

Council of Europe, 2000. Parliamentary assembly, 'recommendation 1455, repatriation and integration of the Tatars of Crimea', www.assembly.coe.int/Documents/AdoptedText/ta00/EREC1455.htm

Council of Europe. Directorate General of Human Rights and Rule of Law, 2013. 'Eastern partnership. Enhancing judicial reform in Eastern partnership countries. Working group on "efficient judicial systems". Project report', Strasbourg: Council of Europe.

'Countries involved in extraordinary renditions 18–12–05', www.statewatch.org/cia/documents/countries-in-extraordinary-rendition.pdf

Cownie, Fiona, 2004. *Legal Academics: Culture and Identities*. Oxford and Portand, OR: Hart Publishing.

Darian-Smith, Eve, 2013. *Laws and Societies in Global Contexts: Contemporary Approaches*. Cambridge University Press.

De Groot, Rene, 1992. 'European education in the 21st century', in Bruno de Witte and Caroline Forder (eds.), *The Common Law of Europe and the Future of Legal Education*. Maastricht: Kluwer Law and Taxation Publishers.

De Mendonça, Helder Ferreira, and André Oliveira Da Fonseca, 2012. 'Corruption, income, and rule of law: Empirical evidence from developing and developed countries', *Revista de Economia Politica* 32(2): 305–14.

De Sousa Santos, Boaventura, and César Rodriguez-Garavito, 2005. *Law and Globalization from Below: Towards a Cosmopolitan Legality*. Cambridge University Press.

Dedek, Helge, 2014. 'When law became cultivated: "European legal culture" between *Kultur* and civilization', in Helleringer and Purnhagen (eds.), 351–74.

Delong, Marek, 2012. 'The Polish episcopate and Poland's signing and ratifying of the Concordat with the Holy See (28 July 1993)', *Polityka i Społeczeństwo (Studies in Politics and Society)* 9: 89–98.

Denvir, John, 2010. 'What movies can teach law students', in Freeman (ed.), 183–93.

Dimcheva, Ekaterina, n.d. 'Mediation country report Bulgaria', *JAMS International ADR Center*, www.adrcenter.com/jamsinternational/civil-justice/Mediation_Country_Report_Bulgaria.pdf

Doe, Norman, 2011. *Law and Religion in Europe: A Comparative Introduction* Oxford University Press.

Donev, Dony K., 2005. 'Church and state in Bulgaria today', *East-West Church & Ministry Report* 13(3): 11–12, www.eastwestreport.org/articles/ew/3306.htm

Donohue, Laura K., 2008. *The Cost of Counterterrorism*. Cambridge University Press.

Dryzek, John S., and Leslie T. Holmes, 2002. *Post-Communist Democratization: Political Discourses Across Thirteen Countries*. Cambridge University Press.

Duckett, Jane, and William L. Miller, 2006. *The Open Economy and Its Enemies*. Cambridge University Press.

Dyson, Matthew, 2014. 'Ligations divide and conquer: Using legal domains in comparative legal studies', in Helleringer and Purnhagen (eds.), 115–37.

Easterly, Ernest A., 1977. 'Global patterns of legal systems: Notes toward a new geojurisprudence', *Geographial Review* 67(2): 209–20.

Eckhardt, William, 1991. 'Authoritarianism', *Political Psychology* 12(1): 97–124.

Eckhoff, Torstein, 2001. *Rettskildelære [Sources of Law]*, 5th ed. Jan E. Helgesen (ed.) Oslo: Universitetsforlaget.

Edge, Ian, 2013. 'Islamic finance, alternative dispute resolution and family law: Developments towards legal pluralism?', in Griffith-Jones (ed.), 116–43.

Ekman, Joakim, and Jonas Linde, 2005. 'Communist nostalgia and the consolidation of democracy in central and Eastern Europe', *Journal of Communist Studies and Transition Politics* 21(3): 354–74.

English, R., 2009. *Terrorism: How to Respond.* Oxford University Press.

European Commission, 2013, November 21. 'Building trust in justice systems in Europe: "Assises de la Justice" forum to shape the future of EU justice policy', press release, Brussels.

2013. *Standard Eurobarometer 80. Autumn 2013. Public Opinion in the European Union. First Results*, Brussels: European Commission, http://ec.europa.eu/public_opinion/archives/eb/eb80/eb80_first_en.pdf

2014. *Report from the Commission to the Council and the European Parliament. EU Anti-Corruption Report*, Brussels: European Commission.

European Commission against Racism and Intolerance, 2012. *ECRI Report on Ukraine, Fourth Monitoring Cycle*, Strasbourg: ECRI Secretariat, Council of Europe.

European Commission, Legal Service, Legal Revisers Group, 2004, September 22. 'Seminars on quality of legislation. Challenges facing a common-law system,' Brussels, 2 July 2004.

European Neighbourhood Policy website, http://ec.europa.eu/world/enp/index_en.htm

Ewick, Patricia, and Susan Silbey, 1998. *The Common Place of Law: Stories from Everyday Life.* University of Chicago Press.

Ewing, Sally, 1987. 'Formal justice and the spirit of capitalism: Max Weber's sociology of law', *Law and Society Review,* 21(3): 487–512.

Fatková, Gabriela, 2012. 'Revisiting the conceptualization of "Turks" in Bulgaria', *Antrocom Online Journal of Anthropology* 8(2): 315–26.

Falkner, Gerda, Miriam Hartlapp, Simone Leiber, and Oliver Treib, 2004. 'Non-compliance with EU directives in the member states: Opposition through the backdoor?', http://www2000.wzb.eu/alt/ab/pdf/Hartlapp%202004WestEuropeanPolitics.pdf

Falkner, Gerda, Miriam Hartlapp, and Oliver Treib, 2005a. 'Worlds of compliance: Why leading approaches to EU implementation are only "sometimes-true theories"', www.mpi-fg-koeln.mpg.de/socialeurope/downloads/2005WorldsOfCompliance.pdf

Falkner, Gerda, Oliver Treib, Miriam Hartlapp and Simone Leiber, 2005b. *Complying with Europe: EU Harmonization and Soft Law in the Member States.* Cambridge University Press.

Falkner, Gerda, and Oliver Treib, 2008. 'Three worlds of compliance or four? The EU-15 compared to new member states', *Journal of Common Market Studies* 46(2): 293–313.

Febbrajo, Alberto, 2010. 'Legal cultures in transition: A system-theory approach', in Febbrajo and Sadurski, 35–71.

Febbrajo, Alberto, and Wojciech Sadurski (eds.), 2010. *Central and Eastern Europe After Transition: Towards a New Socio-legal Semantics*. Farnham: Ashgate.

Fisher, Alan W., 1978. *The Crimean Tatars*. Stanford, CA: Hoover Institution Press.

Fogelklou, Anders, 2003. 'Introduction: From transition to integration', in Fogelklou and Sterzel, 11–28.

Fogelklou, Anders, and Fredrik Sterzel (eds.), 2003. *Consolidating Legal Reform in Central and Eastern Europe – an Anthology*. Uppsala: Iustus Förlag.

Forsyth, Miranda. 2009. *A Bird That Flies with Two Wings: Kastom and State Justice Systems in Vanuatu*. Canberra: Australian National University E-Press, http://epress.anu.edu.au/titles/kastom_citation

Forte, Angelo, 2010. 'Mixing and remixing Scots law – an historical perspective of Scots law 1100–1707', in Sunde and Skodvin, 133–48.

Franklin, Christian, 2010. 'The melting pot or the salad bowl revisited (again)', in Knut Einar Skodvin and Jørn Øyrehagen Sunde (eds.), *Rendezvous of European Legal Cultures*. Bergen: Fagbokforlaget, 77–96.

Fredriksen, Haavard Haukeland, 2011. *EU/EØS rett i norske domstoler [EU/EEA Law in Norwegian Courts]*. Oslo: Europautredningen, www.europautredningen.no/eksterne-utredninger/

Freeman, Michael (ed.), 2010. *Law and Popular Culture*. Oxford University Press.

Friedgut, Theodore H., 1979. *Political Participation in the USSR*. Princeton University Press.

Friedman, Lawrence M., 1975. *The Legal System: A Social Science Perspective*. New York: Russell Sage Foundation.

1990. *The Republic of Choice: Law, Authority and Culture*. Cambridge MA: Harvard University Press.

1997. 'The concept of legal culture: a reply', in Nelken (ed.), 33–40.

Friedman, Lawrence M., and Harry N. Scheiber, 1995. 'Legal cultures and the legal profession', *Bulletin of the American Academy of Arts and Sciences* 48 (5): 6–13.

Friedman, Lawrence M., and Rogelio Pérez-Perdomo (eds.), 2003. *Legal Culture in the Age of Globalization*. Redwood City, CA: Stanford University Press.

Føllesdal, Andreas, 2013. 'Much ado about nothing? Claims about political appointment to the Norwegian Supreme Court – and what to do – and not to do – about it', *Tidsskrift for rettsvitenskap* 126(3): 364–71.

Galinou, Eirini Elefthenia, 2004. 'Legal borrowing: why some legal transplants take root and others fail', *Comp. Labour Law & Policy Journal* 25(3): 391–422.

Galligan, Denis, 2003. 'Legal failure: law and social norms in post-communist Europe', in Galligan, Denis, and Marina Kurkchiyan (eds.), *Law and Informal Practices: The Post-Communist Experience*. Oxford University Press: 1–24.

Gargarella, Roberto, Siri Gloppen, and Elin Skaar (eds.), 2003. *Democratization and the Judiciary: The Accountability Function of Courts in New Democracies*. Abingdon, Oxon: Routledge.

Gearty, Conor, 1999. 'Terrorism and human rights: As case study in impeding legal realities', *Legal Studies* 19(3): 367–79.

(2007a). *Civil Liberties*. Oxford University Press.

(2007b). 'Terrorism and human rights', *Government and Opposition* 42(3): 340–62.

Geddes, Barbara, and John Zaller, 1989. 'Sources of popular support for authoritarian regimes', *American Journal of Political Science* 33(2): 319–47.

Gedeon, Peter, 1997. 'Hungary: German and European influences on the post-socialist transition', in Peter J. Katzenstein (ed.), *Mitteleuropa. Between Europe and Germany*. Providence: Berghahn Books, 101–48.

Geertz, Clifford. 1973. *The Interpretation of Cultures*. New York: Basic.

Gessner, Volkmar, Armin Hoeland, and Csaba Varga (eds.), 1996. *European Legal Cultures*. Aldershot: Dartmouth.

Gessner, Volkmar, and David Nelken (eds.), 2007. *European Ways of Law: Towards a European Sociology of Law. Onati International Series in Law and Society*. Oxford: Hart Publishing.

Ghodsee, Kristen, 2010. *Muslim Lives in Eastern Europe: Gender, Ethnicity and the Transformation of Islam in Postsocialist Bulgaria*. Princeton University Press.

Gibson, James, and Gregory A. Caldeira, 1996. 'The legal cultures of Europe', *Law & Society Review* 30(1): 55–86.

Gillespie, John, 2006. *Transplanting Commercial Law Reform: Developing a Rule of Law in Vietnam*. Farnham: Ashgate.

Githens-Mazer, J., 2008. 'Islamic radicalisation among North Africans in Britain', *British Journal of Politics and International Relations* 10(4): 550–70.

Gloppen, Siri, Roberto Gargarella and Elin Skaar (eds.), 2004. *Democratization and the Judiciary. The Accountability Function of Courts in New Democracies*. London: Frank Cass Publishers.

Goldman, Marshall, 1975. *The Spoils of Progress. Environmental Pollution in the Soviet Union*, Cambridge, MA: MIT Press.

Goldstein, Leslie Friedman, 2004. 'From democracy to juristocracy', *Law and Society Review* 38(3): 611–29.

Golebiowska, Ewa A., 2004. 'Religious tolerance in Poland', *International Journal of Public Opinion Research* 16(4): 391–416.

2009.'Ethnic and religious tolerance in Poland', *East European Politics and Societies* 23(3): 371–91.

Goodpaster, Gary, 1999. 'The rule of law, economic development and Indonesia', in Tim Lindsey (ed.), *Indonesia: Law and Society*. Sydney: Federation Press, 21–32.

Goutal, Jean Louis, 1976. 'Characteristics of judicial style in France, Britain and the U.S.', *The American Journal of Comparative Law* 24(1): 43–72.

Graziadei, Michele, 2009. 'Legal transplants and the frontiers of legal knowledge', *Theoretical Inquiries in Law* 10: 693–713.

Greenwald, Glenn, 2014. *Overvåket. Edward Snowden, NSA og overvåkningsstaten [No Place to Hide: Edward Snowden, the NSA and the U.S. Surveillance State]*. Oslo: Cappelen Damm.

Grendstad, Gunnar, William R. Shaffer, and Eric N. Waltenburg, 2014. 'Høyesterettsdommerne er politisk farget – Svar til Morten Nadim' [The Supreme Court Justices Are Politically Biased – a Reply to Morten Nadim], *Lov og rett* 53(2): 109–24.

2011. 'When justices disagree: the influence of ideology and geography on economic voting on the Norwegian Supreme Court', *Retfærd* 34: 2–25.

2012, March 22–24. 'Social-political experiences of Norwegian supreme court justices', Paper prepared for delivery at the Annual Meeting of the Western Political Science Association, Marriott Waterfront, Portland, OR.

Grieve, Dominic, 2013. 'Speech in defence of the jury trial – speech at the Politeia Forum', *GOV.UK*, www.gov.uk/government/speeches/in-defence-of-the-jury-trial

Griffith-Jones, Robin (ed.), 2013. *Islam and English Law*. Cambridge University Press.

Grødeland, Åse B., 2005. 'Informal networks and corruption in the judiciary: elite interview findings from the Czech Republic, Slovenia, Bulgaria and Romania', paper presented at the World Bank Conference "New Frontiers of Social Policy", Arusha, 12–15 December 2005. http://siteresources.worldbank.org/INTRANETSOCIALDEVELOPMENT/Resources/informalnetworks.pdf

2007. 'Informality, legal institutions and social norms', in *Transparency International: Global Anti-Corruption Report 2007*. Cambridge University Press, 306–9.

2009. 'Culture, context, and values: public perceptions of law', paper prepared for The Santiago – 21st World Congress of Political Science, SS01: Special Session General Pool, 465: European Legal Cultures in Transition.

2010. 'Elite perceptions of anti-corruption efforts in Ukraine' (special issue) Anti-Corruption for Eastern Europe, Diana Schmidt-Pfister and Holger Moroff (eds.), *Global Crime* 11(2): 237–60.

2013. 'Public perceptions of corruption and anti-corruption reform in the West Balkans', *The Slavonic and East European Review* 91(3); 535–98.

2014a. 'Public and elite perceptions of supranational courts: The European perspective', *Review of Central and East European Law* 39 (1): 41–94.

2014b. 'Informal practice in the judiciary: A comparison of East Central Europe, South East Europe and the West Balkans', in William Simons (ed.), *East*

European Faces of Law and Society: Values and Practices Leiden/Boston: Brill, 95–150.

Grødeland, Åse B., and Aadne Aasland. 2007. 'Informality and informal practices in east central and south east Europe. Contemporary Europe Research Centre (CERC), University of Melbourne, working papers series, no. 3.

2013. 'Elite perceptions of the judiciary in East Central and South East Europe', *European Review* 21(1): 70–102.

Guarnieri, Carlo, and Patrizia Pederzoli, 2002. C. A. Thomas (ed.),*The Power of Judges: A Comparative Study of Court and Democracy*. New York: Oxford University Press.

Gvosdev, Nikolas K., 2010. 'The new emperors? Post-Soviet presidents and church-state relations in Ukraine and Russia', *Sophia Institute Studies in Orthodox Theology*, part no. 3, 171–92. http://academiccommons.columbia.edu/download/fedora_content/download/ac:156387/CONTENT/Sophia Vol3_-_Gvosdev.pdf

Harding, Luke, 2014. *Snowdenfilene: Historien om verdens mest ettersøkte mann [The Snowden Files]*. Oslo: Forlaget Press.

Harding, Roberta M., 2010. 'Reel violence: Popular culture and concerns about capital punishment in contemporary American society', in Michael Freeman (ed.), *Law and Popular Culture*. Oxford University Press, 358–74.

Haynes, Emily Stewart, 1999. 'Mediation as an alternative to emerging postsocialist legal institutions in central and eastern Europe', *Ohio State Journal on Dispute Resolution* 15(1): 257–83.

Helleringer, Geneviève, and Kai Purnhagen, 2014a. 'On the terms, relevance and impact of a European legal culture', in Helleringer and Purnhagen (eds.), 3–14.

(eds.), 2014b. *Towards a European Legal Culture*. Baden-Baden: Nomos Verlag.

Helsingeng, Terje, 2014 August. 'Vi krangler som aldri før' [We are quarrelling as never before'], *VG* 28.

Hendley, Kathryn, 2009. '"Telephone law" and the "rule of law": The Russian case', *Hague Journal on the Rule of Law* 1(2): 241–62.

2011. 'Varieties of legal dualism: Making sense of the role of law in contemporary Russia', *Wisconsin International Law Journal* 29(2): 233–363.

2012. 'Who are the legal nihilists in Russia?', *Post-Soviet Affairs* 28(2): 149–86.

Herron, Erik S., and Kirk A. Randazzo, 2003. 'The relationship between independence and judicial review in post-communist courts', *The Journal of Politics* 65(2): 422–38.

Hesselink, Martijn W., 2009, December 7. *The New European Legal Culture – Ten Years On*. Amsterdam: Centre for the Study of European Contract Law. http://ssrn.com/abstract=1519939 or http://dx.doi.org/10.2139/ssrn.1519939

2014. 'The new European legal culture – ten years on', in Helleringer and Purnhagen (eds.), 17–24.

Hirschl, Ran, 2006. 'The new constitutionalism and judicialization of pure politics worldwide', *Fordham Law Review* 75(2): 721–54.

2008. 'The judicialization of mega-politics and the rise of political courts', *Annual Review of Polital Science* 11: 93–118.

2009. 'The Judicialization of Politics', in Robert E. Goodin (ed.), *The Oxford Handbook of Political Science*. Oxford University Press, 253–74.

Hirschman, Albert O., 1970. *Exit, Voice and Loyalty: Responses to Decline in Firms, Organizations and States*, New Haven: Harvard University Press.

Hiscock, Mary, 1995. 'Changing patterns of regional law making in Asia', *Australian Journal of Corporate Law* 5, 367.

Holmøyvik, Eirik, 2010. 'A little bit of this and a little bit of that – the complexity of legal reception', in Sunde and Skodvin (eds.), 45–59.

House of Lords, 2007, July 11. *Constitution: Sixth Report. Session 2006–07*, Publications on the Internet, Constitution Committee Publications. www.publications.parliament.uk/pa/Id200607/Idselect/Idconst/151/15106.htm

Howard, Marc Morjé, 2003. *The Weakness of Civil Society in Post-Communist Europe*, Cambridge University Press.

Hunsberger, Bruce, 1985. 'Religion, age, life satisfaction, and perceived sources of religiousness: A study of older persons', *Journal of Gerontology* 40, 615–20.

Husa, Jaakko, 2004. 'Classification of legal families today – is it time for memorial hymn?', *Revue Internationale de Droit Comparé* 56(1): 11–38.

Ignatieff, Michael, 2004. *The Lesser Evil: Political Ethics in an Age of Terror*. Edinburgh University Press/Princeton University Press.

Inglehart, Ronald, and Pippa Norris, 2009. 'Muslim integration into western cultures: Between origins and destinations', Harvard Kennedy School working paper.

Jaremba, Urszula, 2013. 'At the crossroads of national and European Union law: Experiences of national judges in a multi-level legal order', *ELR*, 3/4, 191–203.

Johnson, Mark, and Gearty, Conor, 2007. 'Civil liberties and the challenge of terrorism', in Alison Park, John Curtice, Katharina Thomson, Miranda Phillips, and Mark Johnson (eds.), *British Social Attitudes: The 23rd Report: Perspectives on a Changing Society*. British social attitudes survey series, no. 23. London: Sage Publications, 143–82.

Kaelbe, Hartmut, 2009. 'Identification with Europe and Politicization of the EU since the 1980s', in Checkel and Katzenstein (eds.).

Kagge, Gunnar, 2013, October 21. 'Frontalangrep på Høyesterett' [Frontal Attack on the Supreme Court], *Aftenposten*. www.aftenposten.no/nyheter/Frontalangrep-pa-Hoyesterett-7344283.html

Kahn-Freund, Otto, 1974. 'On uses and misuses of comparative law', *Modern Law Review* 37(1): 1–27.

Karpov, Vyacheslav, 1999. 'Religiosity and political tolerance in Poland', *Sociology of Religion* 60(4): 387–402.

Karstedt, Susanne, and Stephen Farrall, 2007, June. 'Law-abiding majority? The everyday crimes of the middle classes'. London: Centre for Crime and Justice Studies, King's College, briefing 3.

Kate, Jan Ten, and Peter J. Van Koppen, 1994. 'Judicialization of politics in the Netherlands: Towards a form of judicial review', *International Political Science Review* 15(2): 143–51.

Katz, Paul R. 2008. *Divine Justice: Religion and the Development of Chinese Legal Culture*. Oxford: Routledge.

Kay, John, 2004. *The Truth About Markets*. London: Penguin.

Keller, Helen, and Alec Stone Sweet (eds.), 2008. *A Europe of Rights: The Impact of the ECtHR on National Legal Systems*. Oxford University Press.

KIIS, 2006. *Analitichniy zvit za rezultatami doslidzhennia "Koruptsia ta nadannia poslug u sudoviy sistemi Ukraini" [Analytical Report on the Results of the Research "Corruption and the provision of Services in the Court System of Ukraine]*. Kiev: KIIS.

Kinander, Morten, 2012. *Cases observed in the Oslo City Court 13 March – 20 November 2012* (unpublished research report). Oslo.

Kingsley, Jeremy, 2004. 'Legal transplantation: Is this what the doctor ordered and are the blood types compatible? The application of interdisciplinary research to law reform in the developing world – a case study of corporate governance in Indonesia', *Arizona Journal of International and Comparative Law* 21(2): 493–534.

Kjær, Anne Lise, 2008. 'Introduction: Language as barrier and carrier of European legal integration', in Petersen, Kjær, Krunke and Madsen (eds.), 149–56.

Kochenov, Dimitry, 2008. *EU Enlargement and the Failure of Conditionality*. Alphen aan den Rijn: Kluwer Law International.

Komárek, Jan, 2014. 'The struggle for legal reform after Communism: A review of Zdeněk Kűhn, *The Judiciary in Central and Eastern Europe: Mechanical Jurisprudence in Transformation?*, LSE Law, Society and Economy working papers, no. 10.

Kommisjonen for gjenopptakelse av straffesaker, 2014. *Årsrapport 2013 [Annual Report 2013]*. Oslo: Kommisjonen for gjenopptakelse av straffesaker.

Korosteleva, Jelena, and S. White, 2006. '"Feeling European": The view from Belarus, Russia and Ukraine', *Contemporary Politics* 12(2): 193–205. http://eprints.gla.ac.uk/5266/

Krindatch, Alexei D. 2003. 'Religion in postsoviet Ukraine as a factor in regional, ethno-cultural and political diversity', *Religion, State and Society* 31(1): 37–73.

Krygier, Martin, and Adam Czarnota (eds.), 1999. *The Rule of Law after Communism*. Dartmouth: Aldershot.

Kühn, Zdeněk, 2004. 'Worlds apart: Western and central European judicial culture at the onset of the European enlargement', *The American Journal of Comparative Law* 52(3): 531–67.

2010. 'The democratization and modernization of post-communist judiciaries', in Febbrajo and Sadurski (eds.), 177–200.

2011. 'Judicial independence in central-eastern Europe: The experience of the 1990s and 2000s', *The Lawyer Quarterly* 1(1): 31–42.

Küpper, Herbert, 2003. 'Romania's legal system: Transition halfway on its road to modernity', in Fogelklou and Sterzel (eds.), 197–232.

Kurkchiyan, Marina, 'Placing law in the cultural context', unpublished teaching materials.

2009. 'Russian legal culture: an analysis of adaptive response to an institutional transplant', *Law and Social Inquiry* 34(2): 337–64.

Kuzio, Taras, 2004, March 25. 'Ten ways Ukraine is a neo-Soviet country', *Ukrayinska Pravda*. www.artukraine.com/old/buildukraine/kuzio13.htm

Kyselova, Tatiana, 2013, December. 'Judiciary reform under the pressure of EU: One step forward, two steps back', National University Kyiv-Mohyla Academy, Ukraine. http://dx.doi.org/10.2139/ssrn/2391082

Lakatos, Zoltan. 2010. Paper to first international conference of the society of sociologists from Romania, Cluj-Napoca.

Lampinen, Risto, and Petri Uusikylä, 1998. 'Implementation deficit – why member states do not comply with EU directives', *Scandinavian Political Studies* 21 (3): 231–50.

Landfried, Christine, 1994. 'The judicialization of politics in Germany', *International Political Science Review* 15(2): 113–24.

Laurence, Jonathan, 2012. *The Emancipation of Europe's Muslims: The State's Role in Minority Integration*. Princeton and Oxford: Princeton University Press.

Ledeneva, Alena, 1998. *Russia's Economy of Favours*. Cambridge University Press.

2011. 'Telephone justice in Russia: an update', *The EU-Russia Centre Review* 18.

Legrand, Pierre, 1997. 'European legal systems are not converging', *The International and Comparative Law Quarterly* 45(1): 52–81.

Lemmings, David, 2000. *Professors of Law: Barristers and English Legal Culture in the Eighteenth Century*. New York: Oxford University Press.

Levitsky, Jonathan E., 1994. 'The Europeanization of the British legal style', *The American Journal of Comparative Law* 42(2): 347–80.

Listhaug, Ola, and Kristen Ringdal, 2007, January 3–5. 'Trust in political institutions: The Nordic countries compared to Europe', paper presented at the Norwegian Political Science Meeting, NTNU Trondheim.

Littlehale, Stephanie A., 2012. 'A study of corruption in the Bulgarian legal system', Honors College, Paper 66. http://digitalcommons.library.umaine.edu/honors/66

LoPucki, Lynn M., 1996. 'Legal culture, legal strategy, and the law in lawyers' heads', *Northwestern University Law Review*, 90, 1498–1556.

Lor, Peter. 2010. 'Methodologies in comparative research', *International and Comparative Librarianship*. http://pjlor.files.wordpress.com/2010/06/chapter-4-draft-2011-04-20.pdf

Lord Percy of Newcastle, 1954. *The Heresy of Democracy*. London: Eyre and Spottiswood.

Lorenz, Nina-Louisa Arold, Xavier Groussot, and Gunnar Thor Petursson, 2013. *The European Human Rights Culture – A Paradox of Human Rights Protection in Europe?* Leiden: Martinus Nijhoff Publishers.

Lægreid, Per, Åsta Dyrnes Nordø, and Lise H. Rykkja, 2013, May. 'Public sector reform in Norway: views and experiences from senior executives. Country report as part of the COCOPS research project'. www.cocops.eu/wp-content/uploads/2013/06/Norway_WP3-Country-Report.pdf

MacAuley, Stewart, 1989. 'Popular legal culture: An introduction', *The Yale Law Journal*, Symposium: Popular Legal Culture 98(8): 1545–58.

Machura, Stefan, 2010. 'Procedural unfairness in real and film trials: Why do audiences understand stories placed in foreign legal systems?', in Michael Freeman (ed.), *Law and Popular Culture*. Oxford University Press, 148–59.

Madsen, Mikael R., Anne Lise Kjær, Helle Krunke, and Hanne Petersen, 2008. 'General introduction: Paradoxes of European legal integration', in Petersen, Kjær, Krunke and Madsen (eds.), 1–6.

Mahoney, Honor, 2013, October 7. 'Risk of poverty greatest in Bulgaria', *EUObserver*.

Mak, Chantal, 2014. 'Judges in utopia: Fundamental rights as constitutive elements of a European private legal culture', in Helleringer and Purnhagen (eds.), 375–95.

Makhnenko, Aleksandr Kharitonovich, 1976. *The State Law of the Socialist Countries*. Moscow: Progres.

Mańko, Rafał, 2013a. 'Proprietary right to a cooperative apartment: A survival of the socialist legal tradition in Polish private law', in Bronisław Sitek, Jakub J. Szczerbowski, Aleksander W. Bauknecht (eds.), *Public Interest and Private Interest in the European Legal Tradition*. http://ssrn.com/abstract=2170845

2013b. 'Survival of the socialist legal tradition? A Polish perspective', *Comparative Law Review* 4(2): 1–28.

Marushiakova, Elena, and Veselin Popov, 'The Roma court in central, eastern and south-eastern Europe'. http://romafacts.uni-graz.at/index.php/culture/culture-2/the-roma-court

Mattila, Heikki, 2008. 'European integration and legal communication', in Petersen, Kjær, Krunke and Madsen (eds.), 253–76.

Mayer, Ann Elizabeth. 1991. *Islam and Human Rights: Tradition and Politics.* Boulder, CO and London: Westview Press.

Mayhew, Alan, 1998. 'The European Union's policy towards Central Europe: design or drift', in Carollyn Rhodes (ed.), *The European Union in the World Community.* Boulder, CO: Lynne Rienner Publishers, 105–26.

McClosky, Herbert, and Alida Brill, 1983. *Dimensions of Tolerance.* New York: Russell Sage Foundation.

McConnel, Michael W., Robert F. Cochran Jr and Angela C. Caramella (eds.), 2001. *Christian Perspectives on Legal Thought.* New Haven and London: Yale University Press.

McGoldrick, Dominic, 2013. 'The comparability of an Islamic/shari'a law system or shari'a rules with the European convention on human rights', in Griffith-Jones (ed.), 42–70.

Menkel-Meadow, Carrie, 2010, January. 'Can they do that? Legal ethnics in popular culture: of characters and acts', *Georgetown Law Faculty Publications.*

Menyhart, Russell, 2003. 'Changing identities and changing laws: possibilities for a global legal culture', *Indiana Journal of Global Legal Studies* 10(2): 157–99.

Metodiev, Momchil, 2009. 'Bulgaria', in Stan (ed.), 152–75.

Michaels, Ralf, 2012. 'Legal Culture', in Jűrgen Basedow, Klaus J. Hopt, Reinhard Zimmermann, and Andreas Stier (eds.), *Max Planck Encyclopedia of European Private Law.* Oxford University Press. http://scholarship.law.duke.edu/faculty-scholarship/2390

Micklitz, Hans-W., 2014. 'The (un)-systematics of (private) law as an element of European culture', in Helleringer and Purnhagen (eds.), 81–113.

Midtbø, Tor, 2007. *Skandaler i norsk politikk*: [Scandals in Norwegian Politics]. Oslo: Universitetsforlaget.

Miller, Jonathan, 2003. 'A typology of legal transplants: using sociology, legal history and Argentine examples to explain the transplant process', *The American Journal of Comparative Law* 51(4): 839–85.

Miller, Russel A., 2004. 'Lords of democracy: The judicialization of "pure politics" in the United States and Germany', *Washington and Lee Law Review* 61(2): 587–662.

Miller, William L., Annis May Timpson, and Michael Lessnoff, 1996. *Political Culture in Contemporary Britain.* Oxford University Press.

Miller, William L., Stephen L. White, and Paul M. Heywood, 1998. *Values and Political Change in Postcommunist Europe.* Basingstoke: Palgrave Macmillan.

Miller, William L., Åse B. Grødeland, and Tatyana Y. Koshechkina, 2001. *A Culture of Corruption? Coping with Government in Post-communist Europe.* Budapest: Central European University Press.

Ministry of Justice, 2014. *Court Statistics Quarterly January to March 2014.* London: Ministry of Justice.

Mirror of Justice. A blog dedicated to the development of Catholic legal theory. www.mirrorofjustice/2006/11/theocrats_in_po.html

Mitsilegas, Valsamis, 2000. 'New forms of transnational policing: The emergence of financial intelligence units in the European Union and the challenges for human rights', *Journal of Money Laundering Control*, 3(3): 250–9.

2003. 'The new EU–US co-operation of extradition. mutual legal assistance and the exchange of police data', *European Foreign Affairs Review* 8, 515–36.

Mo, Pak Hung, 2001. 'Corruption and economic growth', *Journal of Comparative Economics* 29, 66–79.

Mochny, Daniela, 2002. 'Translating law texts in translating culture', *Ccaps Translation and Localization, Ccaps Newsletter*. www.ccaps.net/newsletter/06-05/art_1en.htm

Modéer, Kjell Å., 2008. 'Adjustment or reluctance? Scandinavian exceptionalism in legal cultures', in Petersen, Kjær, Krunke and Madsen (eds.), 287–98.

Moes, Jeroen, 2009. 'CosmoPolesA A mixed methods study of the European identity of higher educated Polish youth', *Studies in Ethnicity and Nationalism* 9(3): 429–51.

Monateri, Pier Giuseppe, 2003. 'The "weak law": contaminations and legal cultures (borrowing of legal and political forms)', published in *Transnational Law & Contemporary Problems* 13, 575, and reprinted by Alan Watson Foundation, University of Belgrade, School of Law, Belgrade, 2008. www.alanwatson.org/PGMonateri.pdf

Munger, Michael C., 2002. 'Comment on Ferejohn's "judicializing politics, politicizing law"', *Law and Contemporary Problems* 65(3): 87–93.

Murdock, Charles W., 2009. 'Corporate corruption and the complicity of Congress and the Supreme Court – the tortuous path from "central bank" to "Stoneridge Investment Partners, LLC v. Scientific-Atlanta Inc.', *Loyola University Chicago, School of Law, LAW eCommons*, 1(1).

NatCen 2007. 'New British social attitudes report'. http://discover.ukdataservice.ac.uk/catalogue/?sn=6240

Nead, Lynda, 2010. 'Courtroom sketching: Reflections on history, law and the image', in Michael Freeman (ed.), *Law and Popular Culture*. Oxford University Press, 173–82.

Nelken, David (ed.), 1997. *Comparing Legal Cultures*. Aldershot: Dartmouth Publishing.

2001. 'Towards a sociology of legal adaptation', in Nelken and Feest (eds.), 7–54.

2004. 'Using the concept of legal culture', *Australian Journal of Legal Philosophy* 29(1): 1–28.

2008. 'Normalizing time: European integration and court delays in Italy', in Petersen, Kjær, Krunke and Madsen (eds.), 299–324.

Nelken, David, and Johannes Feest (eds.), 2001. *Adapting Legal Cultures*. Oxford: Hart Publishing.

Nenner, Howard, 1977. *By Colour of Law: Legal Culture and Constitutional Politics in England, 1660–1689*. University of Chicago Press.

Nethercott, Frances, 2007. *Russian Legal Culture before and after Communism: Criminal Justice, Politics, and the Public Sphere. BASEES/Routledge Series on Russian and East European Studies*, no. 39, London: Routledge.

Neuburger, Mary C., 2004. *The Orient Within: Muslim Minorities and the Negotiation of Nationhood in Modern Bulgaria*. Ithaca/London: Cornell University Press.

Neuman, Iver B., 2006. 'European identity and its changing others', NUPI [710] Paper.

Nolan Jr, James L., 2009. *Legal Accents, Legal Borrowing: The International Problem-Solving Court Movement*. Princeton University Press.

Norges offentlige utredninger (NOU), 2012. *Utenfor og innenfor: Norges avtaler med EU [Outside and Inside. Norway's Agreements with the EU]*. Oslo: NOU, 2.

Nylund, Anna, 2010. 'Mixing past and future – the making of a Nordic legal culture 1850–2050', in Sunde and Skodvin (eds.), 167–81.

Office of the Parliamentary Counsel, Cabinet Office, 2013, March. 'When laws become too complex. a review into the causes of complex legislation'. London.

Ogus, Anthony, 2001. 'The contribution of law and economics analysis to legal transplants', in Jan Smiths (ed.), *The Contribution of Mixed Legal Systems to European Private Law*. Antwerp: Intersentia, 27–37.

Olgiati, Vittorio, 2010. 'The eastern EU enlargement and the Janus-headed nature of the constitutional treaty', in Sadurski et al. (eds.), 51–71.

Olteanu, Tina, and Dorothée de Nève, 2013. *Religious Pluralism in Europe – Orthodox Churches and their Members in the Process of European Integration*, IPW working paper no. 2.

Open Society Institute, 2005. *Muslims in the UK: Policies for Engaged Citizens*. Budapest/New York: Open Society Institute.

Őrűcű, Esin, 2008. 'What is a mixed legal system: Exclusion or expansion?' *Electronic Journal of Comparative Law* 12(1): 1–18.

OSCE High Commissioner on National Minorities, 2013, August. 'The integration of formerly deported people in Crimea, Ukraine', *Needs Assessment*, The Hague.

Overseas Security Advisory Council (OSAC), 2013. *Bulgaria 2013. Crime and Safety Report*. Washington, DC: OSAC. www.osac.gov/pages/ContentReport Details.aspx?cid=13951

Pahis, Stratos, 2009. 'Corruption in our courts: What it looks like and where it is hidden', *The Yale Journal* 118(8): 1900–43.

Papadopoulos, Georgios, 2010, January 20–22. 'Property crime and immigration in England and Wales: Evidence from the offending, crime and justice survey', paper for the conference on Economics of Culture, Institutions, and Crime, University of Padua and Centre for Economic Policy Research, Milan.

Patterson, Colin, and Alastair McKay, 2012. *Making Mediation Work – in the Church of England*. London: Bridge Builders Ministries.

Peczenik, Aleksander, 2003. 'The rule of law in Poland', in Fogelklou and Sterzel (eds.), 171–95.

Pedersen, Karen H., and Lars Johannsen, 2005, May 19–21. '*Corruption: Commonality, causes and consequences: Comparing 15 ex-communist countries*', paper for the 13th NISPAcee Annual Conference, Moscow.

Persen, Kjell, 2008, March 14. 'Guantanamo-fly i norsk luftrom' [Guantanamo aircraft in Norwegian air space], TV2. www.tv2.no/nyheter/guantanamofly-i-norsk-luftrom-1686257

Péteri, Zoltán, 1986–87. 'The reception of Soviet law in Eastern Europe: Similarities and differences between Soviet and Eastern European law', *Tulane Law Review* 61, 1397–1412.

Petersen, Hanne, 2008. 'Introduction: Exceptionalism and normalization: Ambiguity and honour in European integration processes', in Petersen, Kjær, Krunke and Madsen (eds.), 279–85.

Petersen, Hanne, Anne Lise Kjær, Helle Krunke, and Mikael Rask Madsen (eds.), 2008. *Paradoxes of European Legal Integration*, Aldershot: Ashgate.

Piana, Daniela, 2010. 'Bureaucratic and managerial cultures in central eastern European courts', in Febbrajo and Sadurski (eds.), 201–18.

Plokhy, Serhii, n.d. 'Church, state and nation in Ukraine'. www.georgefox.edu/ree/Plokhy_Church_Oct%201999.pdf

Polak, Paulina, and David Nelken, 2010. 'Polish prosecutors, political corruption and legal culture', in Febbrajo and Sadurski (eds.), 219–54.

Ponterotto, Joseph G., 2006. 'Brief note on the origins, evolution, and the meaning of the qualitative research concept "thick description"', *The Qualitative Report* 11(3): 538–49.

Popova, Maria, 2012. *Politicized Justice in Emerging Democracies: A Study of Courts in Russia*, Cambridge University Press.

Predelli, Line Nyhagen, 2008. 'Religion, citizenship and participation: A case study of immigrant Muslim women in Norwegian mosques', *European Journal of Women's Studies* 15(3): 241–60.

Přibáň, Jiří, 2010. 'Constituting the heterarchy of European constitutionalism in the EU's new member states', in Febbrajo and Sadurski (eds.), 13–33.

Radaev, Vadim, 2000. 'Return of the crowds and rationality of action: a history of Russian "financial bubbles" in the mid-1990s', *European Societies* 2(3): 271–94.

Ramadan, Tariq, 2005. *Western Muslims and the Future of Islam*, Oxford University Press.

2013. 'Following Shari'a in the West', in Griffith-Jones (ed.), 245–55.

Randeria, Shalini, 2007. 'De-politicization of democracy and judicialization of politics', *Theory, Culture, Society* 24(4): 38–44.

Ravna, Øyvind, 2010. 'Sámi legal culture – and its place in Norwegian law', in Sunde and Skodvin (eds.), 149–65.

Rechberger, Walter, 2009. 'Judicial independence in Ukraine', in Juliane Besters-Dilger (ed.), *Ukraine on its way to Europe: Interim results of the Orange Revolution*, Frankfurt am Main: Peter Lang, 61–78.

Reid, Sue, 2011, July 29. 'As Islamic extremists declare Britain's first sharia law zone, the worrying social and moral implications', *Mail Online*, www.dailymail.co.uk/news/article-2020382/You-entering-Sharia-law-Britain-As-Islamic-extremists-declare-Sharia-law-zone-London-suburb-worrying-social-moral-implications.html

Robertson, Roland, 1995. 'Glocalization: Time-space and homogeneity-heterogeneity', in Mike Featherstone, Scott Lash and Roland Robertson (eds.), *Global Modernities*, London: Sage

Rose, Richard, 2009. *Understanding Post-Communist Transformation: A Bottom Up Approach*, Abingdon, Oxon: Routledge.

Rossland, Irene Elisabeth, 2006, February 4. 'Norges ambassade i Syria nedbrent' [Norway's embassy in Syria burnt down], *NRK*. http://nrk.no/nyheter/utenriks/5458523.html

Roth, Klaus (Hg.), 2007. *Soziale Netzwerke und soziales Vertrauen in den Transformationsländern: Social Networks and Social Trust in the Transformation Countries*, Zűrich/Berlin: Lit Verlag.

Ruhs, Martin, and Bridget Anderson, 2010. 'Semi-compliance and illegality in migrant labour markets: An analysis of migrants, employers and the state in the UK', *Population, Space and Place* 16, 195–211.

Sacerdote, Bruce, and Edward L. Glaeser, 2001. 'Education and religion', NBER working paper series, working paper 8080. www.nber.org/papers/w8080

Sadurdin, Soomro, 2010. *Concept of Human Rights in Islam and West*, Saarbrücken: VDM Verlag.

Sadurski, Wojciech, 2010. 'Constitutional courts and constitutional culture in Central and Eastern European countries', in Febbrajo and Sadurski (eds.), 99–118.

2010. 'EU enlargement and democracy in new member states', in Sadurski et al. (eds.), 27–49.

Sadurski, Wojciech, Adam Czarnota, and Martin Krygier (eds.), 2010. *Spreading Democracy and the Rule of Law? The Impact of EU Enlargement on the Rule of Law, Democracy and Constitutionalism in Post-Communist Legal Orders*, Dordrecht: Springer.

Sajo, Andras, 1990. 'New legalism in East Central Europe: law as an instrument of social transformation', *Journal of Law and Society* 17(3): 329–44.

Sanders, Joseph, and V. Lee Hamilton, 1992. 'Legal cultures and punishment repertoires in Japan, Russia, and the United States', *Law & Society Review* 26(1): 117–38.

Sarat, Austin, 1977. 'Studying American legal culture: An assessment of survey evidence', *Law & Society Review* 11(3): 427–88.

Sasse, Gwendolyn, James Hughes, and Claire Gordon, 2010. 'Sub-national governance in Central and Eastern Europe: Between transition and Europeanization', in Sadurski et al. (ed.), 121–47.

Schuck, Peter H., 2000. *The Limits of Law: Essays in Democratic Governance*, Boulder, CO: Westview Press.

2007. 'Law and the study of migration', in Caroline B. Brettell and Games F. Hollifield (eds.), *Migration Theory: Talking Across the Disciplines*, 2nd edn, London and New York: Routledge, 239–57.

Seidman, Robert B., 1978. *The State, Law, and Development*, Kent: Croon Helm.

Semmelmann, Constanze, 2014. 'Legal principles in EU law as an expression of a European legal culture between unity and diversity', in Helleringer and Purnhagen (eds.), 303–27.

Shore, Cris, 2000. *Building Europe: The Cultural Politics of European Interation*, London and New York: Routledge.

Silbey, Susan, 2005. 'After legal consciousness', *Annual Review of Law and Social Science* 1, 323–68.

2008. 'Legal consciousness', in *New Oxford Companion to Law*, Oxford University Press. http://web.mit.edu/anthropology/pdf/articles/silbey/silbey_Legal_consciousness.pdf

Simantiras, Nicos, 2014. 'A common culture in European legal education? A constitutional approach on applied pluralism', in Helleringer and Purnhagen (eds.), 223–41.

Sivesind, Karl Henrik, and Per Selle, 2010. 'Civil society in the Nordic countries: Between displacement and vitality', in I. R. Alapuco and H. Stenius (eds.), *Nordic Associations in a European Perspective*, Baden-Baden: Nomos Verlag, 90–120.

'Six on trial over failed London bombings', 2007, January 15. *The Guardian*. www.guardian.co.uk/uk/2007/jan/15/july7.uksecurity

Skąpska, Grażyna, 2002. 'Law and society in a natural laboratory: The case of Poland in the broader context of East Central Europe', in Max Kaase, Vera Spatschuh, and Agnieszka Wenninger (eds.), *Three Social Science Disciplines in Central and Eastern Europe: Handbook on Economics, Political Science and Sociology (1989–2001)*, Berlin: Informationszentrum sozialwissenschaften, 588–603.

Slapper, Gary, and David Kelly, 2011. *The English Legal System, 12th edn*, Abingdon, Oxon: Routledge.

Small, Richard G., 2005. 'Towards a theory of contextual transplants', *Emory International Law Review* 19, 1431–56.

Smilov, Daniel, 2010. 'Constitutional culture and the theory of adjudication: Ulysses as a constitutional justice', in Febbrajo and Sadurski (eds.), 119–46.

Spamann, Holger, 2009. 'Contemporary legal transplants – legal families and the diffusion of (corporate) law', *Brigham Young University Law Review*, 1813–77.

Smelser, N. J., and Paul B. Baltes (eds.), 2001. *International Encyclopedia of the Social and Behavioural Sciences*. Oxford: Pergamon.

Smith, Gordon, 1974. 'Popular participation in the administration of justice in the Soviet Union: Comrades' courts and the Brezhnev regime', *Indiana Law Journal* 49(2): 238–52.

Smith, Karsten, 2012. *Dommersyn utenform dommen*. Oslo: Universitetsforlaget.

Smith, Tom W., 2012, April 18. 'Beliefs about God across time and countries', report for ISSP and Gesis, NORC at the University of Chicago.

Sperr, Anneken Karl, 2012. 'Mediation in Norway. "Faster, cheaper and more friendly"', in Klaus J. Hopt and Felix Steffek (eds.), *Mediation: Principles, Regulation and Reform in Comparative Perspective*. Oxford: Oxford Scholarship Online, 1137–64.

Staksrud, Elisabeth, Kari Steen-Johnsen, Bernard Enjolras, Maria Helena Gustafsson, Karoline Andrea Ihlebæk, Arnfinn H. Midtbøen, Synne Sætrang, Sissel C. Trygstad, and Maria Utheim, 2014. *Ytringsfrihet i Norge: Holdninger og erfaringer i befolkningen [Freedom of Speech in Norway: The Attitudes and Experiences of the Public]*. Oslo: Institutt for samfunnsforskning.

Stan, Lavinia, 2009. 'The former Soviet Union', in Stan (ed.), 222–46.

(ed.), 2009. *Transitional Justice in Eastern Europe and the Former Soviet Union. Reckoning with the Communist Past*. London and New York: Routledge.

2009. 'Poland', in Stan (ed.), 76–101.

Suhara, Manabu, 2004. 'Corruption in Russia: A historical perspective', in Tadayuki Hayashi (ed.), *Democracy and Market Economics in Central and Eastern Europe. Are New Institutions Being Consolidated?* Hokkaido: University of Hokkaido, The Slavic Research Centre, 383–403.

Sunde, Jørn Øyrehagen, 2005. *Speculum Legale – Rettsspegelen*. Bergen: Fagbokforlaget.

2007. *Den juridiske komedien. Ein antologi over tanke og praksis i den norske rettskulturen si historie* [*The Juridical Comedy: An Anthology on Thought and Practice in the History of Norwegian Legal Culture*]. Bergen: Fagbokforlaget.

2010. 'The art of being artful – the complex reception of law', in Sunde and Skodvin (eds.), 29–43.

Sunde, Jørn Øyrehagen, and Knut Einar Skodvin (eds.), 2010. *Rendezvous of European Legal Cultures*. Bergen: Fagbokforlaget.

Sunkin, Maurice, 1994. 'Judicialization of politics in the United Kingdom', *International Political Science Review* 15(2): 125–33.

Susskind, Richard, 2010. *The End of Lawyers? Rethinking the Nature of Legal Services*. Oxford University Press.

Sveen, Anne Kjersti Landsverk, 2014, Spring. *Meklerrollen ved konflikthåndtering i Den norske kirke* [*The Role of Mediation in Handling Conflicts within the Church of Norway*], Master dissertation, Faculty of Theology, University of Oslo. http://brage.bibsys.no/xmlui/bitstream/handle/11250/218561/AVH501-kand-nr-5066-masteravh-Sveen-navn.pdf?sequence=1&isAllowed=y

Sykiäinen, Leonid, n.d. 'Shari'ah and Muslim-law culture', Sweden: CA&CC Press AB. www.ca-c.org/dataeng/08.syki.shtml

Tamanaha, Brian Z., 1995. 'The lessons of law-and-development studies', *American Journal of International Law* 89, 470–86.

2008. 'Understanding legal pluralism: Past to present, local to global', *Sydney Law Review*. 30(3): 375–411.

Tanasoiu, Cosmina, and Constantin Colonescu, 2008. 'Determinants of support for European integration: The case of Bulgaria', *European Union Politics* 9 (3): 363–77.

Teubner, Gunther, 1998. 'Legal irritants: Good faith in British law or how unifying law ends up in new divergences', *The Modern Law Review* 61(1): 11–32.

Thomson, Robert, Rene Torenvlied, and Javier Arregui, 2007. 'The paradox of compliance: Infringements and delays in transposing European Union directives', *British Journal of Political Science* 37(4): 685–709.

TNS Gallup (Norway). Findings from survey on terrorism. http://pub.tv2.no/nettavisen/innenriks/article642147.ece

Traynor, Ian. 2010, February 22. 'Poland admits role in CIA rendition programme', *The Guardian*. www.theguardian.com/world/2010/feb/22/poland-cia-rendition-flights

Trnavei, Gene, 2010. 'The intervention of customary law with the modern rule of law in Albania and Kosova', *The Rule of Law in Comparative Perspective: Ius Gentium: Comparative Perspectives on Law and Justice* 3, 201–15.

Trubek, David M., 1985. 'Kronman, Max Weber', *Stanford Law Review* 37, 919–36.

2011. 'Law and development in the twenty-first century', in McAlinn and Pejovic (eds.), *Law and Development in Asia*. London: Routledge. https://media.law.wisc.edu/s/c_638/myzm5/21st_century_law-brasilia_2009.pdf

Tyler, Tom R., 2006. *Why People Obey the Law*. Princeton University Press.

Tærum, Johanne Lie, 2014, May. *EU conditionality and anti-corruption: The case of Bulgaria and its incentive game*, Masters thesis, Department of Political Science, University of Oslo.

United States Department of State (USDS), Bureau of Democracy, Human Rights and Labor, 'International religious freedom report for 2011. Ukraine'. www.state.gov/documents/organization/193085.pdf

Vachudova, Milada A., 2006. 'Democratization in postcommunist Europe: Illiberal regimes and the leverage of international actors,' Centre for European Studies working papers series no. 139, Harvard University,

2009. 'Corruption and compliance in the EU's post-communist members and candidates', *JCMS* 47 Annual Review, 43–62.

Vallinder, Torbjörn, 1994. 'The judicialization of politics: a world-wide phenomenon: introduction', *International Political Science Review/Revue international de science politique* 15(2): 91–9.

Van Hoecke, Mark, and Mark Warrington, 1998. 'Legal cultures, legal paradigms and legal doctrine: Towards a new model for comparative law', *The International and Comparative Law Quarterly* 47(3): 495–536.

Van Olden, Jan, 2002. 'Legal development cooperation: Transplanting or transforming legal systems?' In *Legal Development and Corruption. CILC Seminar in Tribute to Jan van Olden*. The Hague: Center for International Legal Cooperation, 4–8.

Vassilev, Rossen, 2004. 'The Roma of Bulgaria: A pariah minority', *The Global Review of Ethnopolitics* 3(2): 40–51.

Vasylyev, Yegor, 2013, June 5. 'Alternative dispute resolution in a global perspective: legal, political and cultural factors in introducing mediation in post-Soviet Ukraine'. http://papers.ssrn.com/sol3/papers.cfm?abstract_id=2274627

Voeten, Erik, 2008. 'The impartiality of international judges: Evidence from the European court of human rights', *The American Political Science Review* 102 (4): 417–33.

WAN/IFRA, 2012. *Sustainable Businesses in News Media: The Need for a Free Market for a Truly Independent Ukrainian Press to Flourish*. Paris: WAN.

Wang, Ling, 2010. 'Legal transplant and cultural transfer: The legal translation in Hong Kong', *Across Languages and Cultures* 11(1): 83–91.

Watson, Alan, 1974. *Legal Transplants: An Approach to Comparative Law*. Edinburgh: Scottish Academic Press.

1977. *Society and Legal Change*. Edinburgh: Scottish Academic Press.

1983. 'Legal change: Sources of law and legal culture', *University of Pennsylvania Law Review* 131(5): 1121–57.

1993. *Legal Transplants: An Approach to Comparative Law*. Athens, GA: University of Georgia Press.

1995. 'From legal transplants to legal formants', *The American Journal of Comparative Law* 43(3): 469–76.

Weick, Günter (ed.), 1999. *Competition or Convergence. The Future of European Legal Culture*. Frankfurt am Main, Berlin, Bern Bruxelles, New York, Wien: Peter Lang.

White, Stephen, Jelena Korosteleva, and Ian McAllister, 2008. 'A wider Europe? The view from Russia, Belarus and Ukraine', *Journal of Common Market Studies* 46(2): 219–42.

Wieacker, Franz, and Edgar Bodenheimer, 1990. 'Foundations of European legal culture', *The American Journal of Comparative Law* 38(1): 1–29.

Williams, Brian G., 2001. *The Crimean Tatars: The Diaspora Experience and the Forging of a Nation*. Leiden: Brill.

Wise, Edward M., 1990. 'The transplant of legal patterns', *The American Journal of Comparative Law* 38, Supplement U.S. Law in an Era of Democratization, 1–22.

Wisneski, Daniel C., Brad L. Lytle, and Linda J. Skitka, 2009. 'Gut reactions: Moral conviction, religiosity, and trust in authority', *Psychological Science* 20(9): 1059–63.

WND Faith, 2012, May 25. 'Norway separates church, state after 198 years'. www.wnd.com/2012/05/norway-separates-church-state-after-198-years/#AvzotLU4W5PXvmOR.99

Wolff, Lutz-Christian, 2011. 'Law and flexibility – rule of law limits of a rhetorical bullet', *The Journal of Jurisprudence* 11, 549–67.

World Bank's 2010 Rule of Law Index. http://info.worldbank.org/governance/wgi/index.asp

World Bank. World Development Indicators Base. www.worldbank.org

World Justice Project, 2014. *Rule of Law Index 2014*. Washington: The World Justice Project.

Yelensky, Victor, 2002, June 6. 'Religion, church, and state in the post-communist era: the case of Ukraine (with special references to orthodoxy and human rights issues), YEL-FIN.DOC, 453–88. http://digitalcommons.law.byu.edu/cgi/viewcontent.cgi?article=2120&context=lawreview

Yilmaz, Ihsan. 2005. *Muslim Law, Politics and Society in Modern Nation States: Dynamic Legal Pluralisms in England, Turkey and Pakistan*. Aldershot: Ashgate.

Yngvesson, Barbara, 1989.'Inventing law in local settings: Rethinking popular legal culture', Symposium: Popular Legal Culture, *The Yale Law Journal* 98(8): 1689–1709.

Zaborowski, Marcin, 2005. 'Westernizing the East: external influences in the post-communist transformation of Eastern and Central Europe', *Journal of Communist Studies and Transition Politics* 21(1): 16–32.

Zedner, Lucia, 1995. 'In pursuit of the vernacular: comparing law and order discourse in Britain and Germany', *Social & Legal Studies* 4(4): 517–34.

2005. 'Securing liberty in the face of terror: Reflections from criminal justice', *Journal of Law and Society* 32(4): 507–33.

Zhelyazkova, Antonina, Maya Kosseva, and Marko Hajdinjak, 2010. 'Tolerance and cultural diversity discourses in Bulgaria: The Bulgarian ethnic model –

parallel cohabitation or multicultural recognition?' Accept Pluralism working paper 15.

Zirk-Sadowski, Marek, 2010. 'Transformation and integration of legal cultures and discourses – Poland', in Sadurski et al. (eds.), 299–311.

Legislation

LOV-1999–05–21–30: Lov om styrking av menneskerettighetenes stilling i norsk lov (menneskerettighetsloven) [The Law on the Strengthening of the Position of Human Rights in Norwegian Law (The Human Rights' Law)], *Lovdata*, www.lovdata.no/all/hl-19990521-030.html

LOV-2005–06–17–90: Lov om mekling og rettergang i sivile tvister – tvisteloven [The Law on Mediation and Court Procedure in Civil Disputes – the Disputes Law], *Lovdata*, http://lovdata.no/dokument/NL/lov/2005-06-17-90

INDEX

acquis communautaire, 49, 352
active government, 47, 64, 75–6
actors, in legal cultures, 3
'adaptive' legal cultures, 379–83
ADR. *See* alternative dispute resolution
Alpha Research, 25
alternative dispute resolution (ADR) mechanism, 146–7
anthropologists, legal, 17
Arold's study on ECtHR, 5
asymmetric adaptation, 396–7. *See also* Muslims and Euro-migrants
attitudes, behaviour & law (legal outsiders' perspective), 43–4
Austro-Hungarian multicultural society, 10
authoritarian republic (legal outsiders' perspective), 88

bad v good law (legal outsiders' perspectives), 32–5
behaviour, attitudes & law (legal outsiders' perspective), 43–4
behaviour and law, changing (legal outsiders' perspective), 98–9
Bhatti, Arfan, 410, 414, 433
Bin Laden, Osama, 14, 409–10
"Blasphemy paragraph," 54–5
bombings. *See* terrorism
booster samples, 24
borrowing, legal, 6
Breivik, Anders Behring, 280–1, 408
bribery
  crime, bribery & corruption (legal outsiders' perspective), 129–31
  law, courts, crime & bribery (legal outsiders' perspective), 199–200
  pressure for bribes (legal outsiders' perspective), 392
Brussels, 10–11
Bujak, Shawan Sadek Saeed, 410
Bulgaria. *See also* religiosity; war on terror
  acquis communautaire, 49, 352
  attitudes, behaviour & law, 43–4
  authoritarian republic (legal outsiders' perspective), 88
  behaviour and law, changing (legal outsiders' perspective), 98–9
  bribes, pressure for (legal outsiders' perspective), 392
  Brussels' relations with, 10–11
  circumstances v letter of law (legal insiders' perspective), 109
  'complex' law, 35, 37–8
  court alternatives (legal insiders' perspective), 148–9, 160–2
  court alternatives (legal outsiders' perspective), 136
  courts, avoidance of, 133–5
  courts, reasons for turning to, 132–3
  crime, bribery & corruption (legal outsiders' perspective), 129–31
  cultural and legal convergence (legal outsiders' perspective), 322–4
  'customs and traditions' (preferred basis of law), 39–41
  designer laws, 36, 70–1
  ECtHR, perceptions of (legal outsiders' perspective), 324
  ECtHR or parliament, who should have final say (legal outsiders' perspective), 324–5

Bulgaria. (cont.)
E-I-U standards (legal insiders' perspective), 342, 350–2
elected representatives (legal insiders' perspectives on how public view their profession), 259–63
EU standards, laws, regulations & minority rights, 49–50
Euro-migrants adapting to law (legal outsiders' perspective), 395–6
Euro-migrants' law-abidance, background influences on (legal outsiders' perspective), 397–9
Euro-migrants obeying the law (legal outsiders' perspective), 394–5
Euro-migrants' reasons for obeying the law, 199–201
'fair' law, 35–7
government and corruption (legal outsiders' perspective), 199
government and parliament (legal outsiders' perspective on legal insiders), 251–5
government and parliament, capability of, 305–9
government and parliament, trust in, 305–7, 311
government officials (legal insiders' perspectives on how public view their profession), 263–8
government officials (legal outsiders' perspectives on legal insiders), 238
government officials, fair treatment by (legal outsiders' perspective), 128
government regard for law across Europe (legal outsiders' perspective), 385–6
Greek Goddess of Law *(Themis)*, 33–4, 386–7
'helpful' law, 34–6
instrumental perspective, 236
judges, 115–16
judges (legal insiders' perspectives on how public view their profession), 273–9
judges, fairness of, 291, 295
judges, informedness of, 291, 293
judges, prosecutors, juries (legal outsiders' perspectives on legal insiders), 241–6
judges, trust in, 291, 297
law, courts, crime & bribery (legal outsiders' perspective), 199–200
law, dealing with (legal outsiders' perspective), 142–3
law, flexibility or rigidity (legal insiders' perspective), 108–17
law, flexibility or rigidity (legal outsiders' perspective), 91–5
law, good v bad, 32–5
law, images of, 32–64
law, influences on (legal outsiders' perspective), 48–9
law, preferred basis of (legal insiders' perspectives), 51, 60–1
law, preferred basis of (legal outsiders' perspectives), 35–41
law, preferred basis of (revisited) (legal outsiders' perspective), 97–8
law, reflect or reform (legal insiders' perspective), 102–8
law, reflect or reform (legal outsiders' perspective), 95–9
law, stepping outside (legal insiders' perspective), 117–23
law, stepping outside (legal outsiders' perspective), 99–101
law, stricter, 44–6
law, stricter enforcement (legal outsiders' perspective), 131–2
law, unreasonable or unjust (legal insiders' perspective), 165–6, 172–3
law, willingness to break (legal outsiders' perspective), 189–90
law and change (legal insiders' perspectives), 64, 69–70, 78
law and change (legal outsiders' perspectives), 46–8
law as freedom or order (legal outsiders' perspective), 86–8
law as justice or oppression (legal outsiders' perspective), 86

law as power of the state v the people (legal outsiders' perspective), 187–9
law enforcement and law (legal outsiders' perspective), 128–9
law in principle v law in practice (legal outsiders' perspective), 386–8
law-abidance amongst public (legal outsiders' perspective), 389
law-abidingness, crime & corruption across Europe (legal outsiders' perspective), 126–7
law-abidingness: majority population (legal insiders' perspective), 211, 216–17
law-abidingness: religious and ethnic minorities (legal insiders' perspective), 219–21, 226–7
law-breakers, penalties for (legal outsiders' perspective), 87–8
law-breaking (legal insiders' perspective), 228–9, 233
law-breaking (legal outsiders' perspective), 194–8, 390–2
law-breaking, feelings about (legal outsiders' perspective), 187–8
law-breaking–whose fault? (legal outsiders' perspective), 392–3
law-obedience amongst ethnic and religious groups (legal outsiders' perspective), 195–6
laws and law-enforcement same as rest of Europe (legal insiders' perspective), 355–8, 362–4
laws contrary to one's religion (legal insiders' perspective), 175–6, 179–81
lawyers (legal insiders' perspectives on how public view their profession), 269–73
lawyers (legal outsiders' perspectives on legal insiders), 238–41
lawyers, informedness of, 286, 288
lawyers, trust in, 286, 290
learning from other countries, European and international organisations (legal outsiders' perspective), 319–22
learning from others about law (legal insiders' perspective), 328–9, 336–8
legal fairness and state power (legal outsiders' perspective), 127–8
letter of law (legal outsiders' perspective), 92–3
mediation, informal methods (legal outsiders' perspective), 136–8
'moral values or state power?,' 35, 38
nanny state (legal outsiders' perspective), 89–90
national laws becoming similar across Europe (legal insiders' perspective), 366, 371–3
obeying the law (legal outsiders' perspective), 191–4, 389–90
obeying the law revisited (legal outsiders' perspective), 199–201
obeying v law-breaking (legal insiders' perspective), 202–4, 208–10
Ottoman legal culture, 10, 216, 322, 438
parliamentary supremacy (legal outsiders' perspective), 90–1
personalised trust (legal outsiders' perspective), 185–6
police (legal insiders' perspectives on how public view their profession), 283–5
police (legal outsiders' perspective on legal insiders), 246–51
police, capability and efficiency of, 298–300, 303
police, informedness of, 298–301
police, trust in, 298–300, 305
prosecutors (legal insiders' perspectives on how public view their profession), 279–83
public opinion and law, changing (legal outsiders' perspective), 98
religious law, dealing with (legal outsiders' perspective), 143
terrorism threat (government and security services' response), 101
"truly European," requirements to be, 43

Bulgaria. (cont.)
  Turk Movement for Rights and Freedoms, 50, 220, 255
  Turkish rule, 10

carriers of legal culture. *See* Muslims and Euro-migrants
cartoons, of Mohammad, 409, 414
CBOS, 25
Chairman of the Norwegian Supreme Court, former (Carsten Smith), 64, 109, 270, 274, 290, 330, 357
change and law
  legal insiders' perspectives on 'law,' 64–81
  legal outsiders' perspective, 46–8
Christian tradition (requirement for truly European country), 43–4
Church of Norway, 51–3, 151–2, 213
church *versus* state. *See* religiosity
circumstances v letter of law (legal insiders' perspective), 109
civil disobedience, 119, 139, 142, 166, 170, 174, 177–8, 202, 507
civil law legal family, 9
civil rights and 'war on terror.' *See* war on terror
CJEU (Court of Justice of the European Union), 3, 5, 13, 72, 78, 315, 335, 342–3
clusters of attitudes-approach, 18
common law family, 9
common law tradition, 10
'complex' law, 35, 37–8
concept/meaning of law. *See* law
convergence *versus* divergence, 5–8
corruption
  crime, bribery & corruption (legal outsiders' perspective), 129–31
  government and corruption (legal outsiders' perspective), 199
Court of Justice of the European Union. *See* CJEU
courts
  alternatives (legal insiders' perspective), 148–64
  alternatives (legal outsiders' perspective), 136
  avoiding, 133–5
  law, courts, crime & bribery (legal outsiders' perspective), 199–200
  reasons for turning to, 132–3
crime
  crime, bribery & corruption (legal outsiders' perspective), 129–31
  law, courts, crime & bribery (legal outsiders' perspective), 199–200
Crimean Tatars, 13, 15–16, 49, 63, 142
cultural and legal convergence (legal outsiders' perspective), 322–4
"culturalists," 7
"culture," broadness of term, 18. *See also* legal cultures
'current life-styles' (preferred basis of law), 40–1
'customs and traditions' (preferred basis of law), 39–41

data collection, 23–6
data presentation, 26–7
Data Retention Directive, 84, 345–6
Davud, Mikel, 410
decision-making in court (legal outsiders' perspective), 93–4
democracy, popular, 48–9, 252
Denning, Lord, 112, 346
designer laws, 35–6, 48, 64–71, 79, 311
"designer rulings," 296
"difference-within-sameness," 6
'discipline and order.' *See* 'order and discipline'

Eastern Europe. *See also* European legal culture
  legal nihilism, 11, 36, 46, 83, 86, 124, 190, 201–2, 441
  Western v Eastern Europe, 9–15, 503–5
ECHR (European Convention on Human Rights)
  effectiveness of, 76–7
  Human Rights Act, 67, 75, 342
  interpretations of, 74
  Norwegian law incorporation (1999), 72–3
  Polish legal insiders and, 78

popularity of, 324
Sámi rights, 75
as supra-national organisation, 2, 13
UK and, 346, 508
Eckhoff, Torstein, 108
ECtHR (European Court of Human Rights)
Arold's study, 5
ECtHR or parliament, who should have final say (legal outsiders' perspective), 324–5
EU standards and ECtHR (legal outsiders' perspective), 326–7
perceptions of (legal outsiders' perspective), 324
EEA. *See* European Economic Area
EFTA (European Free Trade Association), 13
EFTA Court, 72, 315
EFTA Surveillance Agency (ESA), 2, 13, 73, 315, 342
E-I standards (European and international standards), 41, 43, 325
E-I-U standards (European, international and universal standards), 342–54
elected representatives (legal insiders' perspectives on how public view their profession), 259–63
England. *See also* religiosity; United Kingdom; war on terror
attitudes, behaviour & law, 43–4
authoritarian republic (legal outsiders' perspective), 88
behaviour and law, changing (legal outsiders' perspective), 98–9
bribes, pressure for (legal outsiders' perspective), 392
Brussels' relations with, 10–11
circumstances v letter of law (legal insiders' perspective), 109
common law tradition, 10
'complex' law, 35, 37–8
court alternatives (legal insiders' perspective), 148–9, 152–7
court alternatives (legal outsiders' perspective), 136
courts, avoidance of, 133–5
courts, reasons for turning to, 132–3
crime, bribery & corruption (legal outsiders' perspective), 129–31
cultural and legal convergence (legal outsiders' perspective), 322–4
'customs and traditions' (preferred basis of law), 39–41
ECtHR, perceptions of (legal outsiders' perspective), 324
ECtHR or parliament, who should have final say (legal outsiders' perspective), 324–5
E-I-U standards (legal insiders' perspective), 342, 346–8
elected representatives (legal insiders' perspectives on how public view their profession), 259–63
EU standards, laws, regulations & minority rights, 49–50
Euro-migrants adapting to law (legal outsiders' perspective), 395–6
Euro-migrants' law-abidance, background influences on (legal outsiders' perspective), 397–9
Euro-migrants obeying the law (legal outsiders' perspective), 394–5
Euro-migrants' reasons for obeying the law, 199–201
'fair' law, 35–7
government and corruption (legal outsiders' perspective), 199
government and parliament (legal outsiders' perspective on legal insiders), 251–5
government and parliament, capability of, 305–8
government and parliament, trust in, 305–7, 310–11
government officials (legal insiders' perspectives on how public view their profession), 263–8
government officials (legal outsiders' perspectives on legal insiders), 238
government officials, fair treatment by (legal outsiders' perspective), 128

England. (cont.)
government regard for law across Europe (legal outsiders' perspective), 385–6
'helpful' law, 34–6
judges, 112–13
judges (legal insiders' perspectives on how public view their profession), 273–9
judges, fairness of, 291, 295
judges, informedness of, 291–3
judges, prosecutors, juries (legal outsiders' perspectives on legal insiders), 241–6
judges, trust in, 291, 297
law, courts, crime & bribery (legal outsiders' perspective), 199–200
law, dealing with (legal outsiders' perspective), 142–3
law, flexibility or rigidity (legal insiders' perspective), 108–17
law, flexibility or rigidity (legal outsiders' perspective), 91–5
law, good v bad, 32–5
law, images of, 32–64
law, influences on (legal outsiders' perspective), 48–9
law, preferred basis of (legal insiders' perspectives), 51, 55–7
law, preferred basis of (legal outsiders' perspectives), 35–41
law, preferred basis of (revisited) (legal outsiders' perspective), 97–8
law, reflect or reform (legal insiders' perspective), 102–8
law, reflect or reform (legal outsiders' perspective), 95–9
law, stepping outside (legal insiders' perspective), 117–23
law, stepping outside (legal outsiders' perspective), 99–101
law, stricter, 44–6
law, stricter enforcement (legal outsiders' perspective), 131–2
law, unreasonable or unjust (legal insiders' perspective), 165–70
law, willingness to break (legal outsiders' perspective), 189–90
law and change (legal insiders' perspectives), 64, 66–7, 75–7
law and change (legal outsiders' perspectives), 46–8
law as freedom or order (legal outsiders' perspective), 86–8
law as justice or oppression (legal outsiders' perspective), 86
law as power of the state v the people (legal outsiders' perspective), 187–9
law enforcement and law (legal outsiders' perspective), 128–9
law in principle v law in practice (legal outsiders' perspective), 386–8
law-abidance amongst public (legal outsiders' perspective), 389
law-abidingness, crime & corruption across Europe (legal outsiders' perspective), 126–7
law-abidingness: majority population (legal insiders' perspective), 211, 213–14
law-abidingness: religious and ethnic minorities (legal insiders' perspective), 219–21, 224–5
law-breakers, penalties for (legal outsiders' perspective), 87–8
law-breaking (legal insiders' perspective), 228–32
law-breaking (legal outsiders' perspective), 194–8, 390–2
law-breaking, feelings about (legal outsiders' perspective), 187–8
law-breaking–whose fault? (legal outsiders' perspective), 392–3
law-obedience amongst ethnic and religious groups (legal outsiders' perspective), 195–6
laws and law-enforcement same as rest of Europe (legal insiders' perspective), 355–8, 360–1
laws contrary to one's religion (legal insiders' perspective), 175–8
lawyers (legal insiders' perspectives on how public view their profession), 269–73

lawyers (legal outsiders' perspectives on legal insiders), 238–41
lawyers, informedness of, 286–7
lawyers, trust in, 286, 289
learning from other countries, European and international organisations (legal outsiders' perspective), 319–22
learning from others about law (legal insiders' perspective), 328–9, 331–4
legal fairness and state power (legal outsiders' perspective), 127–8
letter of law (legal outsiders' perspective), 92–3
mediation, informal methods (legal outsiders' perspective), 136–8
'moral values or state power?,' 35, 38
nanny state (legal outsiders' perspective), 89–90
national laws becoming similar across Europe (legal insiders' perspective), 366–8
obeying the law (legal outsiders' perspective), 191–4, 389–90
obeying the law revisited (legal outsiders' perspective), 199–201
obeying v law-breaking (legal insiders' perspective), 202–6
parliamentary supremacy (legal outsiders' perspective), 90–1
personalised trust (legal outsiders' perspective), 185–6
police (legal insiders' perspectives on how public view their profession), 283–5
police (legal outsiders' perspective on legal insiders), 246–51
police, capability and efficiency of, 298–300, 302
police, informedness of, 298–301
police, trust in, 298–300, 304
prosecutors (legal insiders' perspectives on how public view their profession), 279–83
public opinion and law, changing (legal outsiders' perspective), 98
religion (preferred basis of law), 55–7
religious law, dealing with (legal outsiders' perspective), 143
terrorism threat (government and security services' response), 101
"truly European," requirements to be, 43
ENP. *See* European Neighbourhood Policy
ESA. *See* EFTA Surveillance Agency
ethnic and religious minorities
law-abidingness (legal insiders' perspective), 219–28
law-obedience (legal outsiders' perspective), 195–6
EU. *See* European Union
EU standards, laws, regulations & minority rights (legal outsiders' perspective), 49–50
Eurobarometer Survey, 5, 259, 351
Euro-migrants. *See also* Muslims and Euro-migrants
obeying the law (legal outsiders' perspective), 199–201
overview, 378–9
European, international and universal standards. *See* E-I-U standards
European and international legal integration, 64, 82
European and international standards. *See* E-I standards
European Convention on Human Rights. *See* ECHR
European Court of Human Rights. *See* ECtHR
European Economic Area (EEA), 1, 72, 315, 318
European Free Trade Association. *See* EFTA
European legal culture, 503–11. *See also* legal cultures
conclusions: looking to the future, 509–11
data collection, 23–6
data presentation, 26–7
dimensions of, 21–3
introduction: common Europe, 503
legal insiders v legal outsiders, 506–7

European legal culture, (cont.)
legal transfers and European integration, 507–9
measuring, 17–18
methodological approach, 8–9
one European legal culture or several?, 1–29
thick descriptions, 18–20
Western v Eastern Europe, 9–15, 503–5
European legal integration. *See also* legal transfers
European and international legal integration, 64, 82
globalisation and, 5–6, 13–14, 21
introduction, 1–2
term meaning, 3
European Neighbourhood Policy (ENP), 1
European Union (EU), 1
Data Retention Directive, 84, 345–6
EU standards and ECtHR (legal outsiders' perspective), 326–7
EU standards privileging minorities (legal outsiders' perspective), 327–8
how to handle EU/UN standards (legal outsiders' perspective), 325–6
linguistic plurality of, 70
euthanasia, 39
Evangelical-Lutheran faith, 51–3. *See also* Church of Norway
"Exit." *See also* obeying or breaking the law
introduction, 125, 135
legal insiders' perspective, 145–64
legal outsiders' perspective, 136–8
external influences on the law and legal system
legal insiders' perspective, 340–54
legal outsiders' perspective, 319–28
external learning. *See* legal transfers
external legal culture, 4. *See also* popular legal culture

'fair' law, 35–7
fair treatment by officials, 128
'fairness and legal rights. *See* 'justice, fairness and legal rights'
families, legal, 2, 9, 317
FGs. *See* focus groups
focus groups (FGs), 23–6. *See also* war on terror
forced marriages, 56, 154
Ford, Glyn, 1, 503
foreign governments/ & international organisations (influences on law), 49
former Chairman of the Norwegian Supreme Court (Carsten Smith), 64, 109, 270, 274, 290, 330, 357
Friedman, Lawrence, 1

'general moral values' (preferred basis of law), 41–3
general perceptions of law in action, 126–32. *See also* legal outsiders' perspective on 'law in action'
Glasgow Airport bombing, 409, 413
globalisation, 5–6, 13–14, 21
glocalization, 6
good v bad law (legal outsiders' perspectives), 32–5
government and corruption. *See* corruption
government and parliament (legal outsiders' perspective on legal insiders), 251–5
government and parliament, capability of
Bulgaria, 305–9
England, 305–8
Norway, 305–7
Poland, 305–8
Ukraine, 305–7, 309–10
government and parliament, trust in
Bulgaria, 305–7, 311
England, 305–7, 310–11
Norway, 305–7, 310
Poland, 305–7, 311
Ukraine, 305–7, 311–12
government officials
fair treatment by (legal outsiders' perspective), 128

legal insiders' perspectives on how public view their profession, 263–8
legal outsiders' perspectives on legal insiders, 238
government regard for law across Europe (legal outsiders' perspective), 385–6
Greek Goddess of Law *(Themis)*, 33–4, 386–7
Guantanamo Bay, 410–11, 436, 442–3
Gypsies. *See* Roma community

harmonisation, voluntary, 10–11
'helpful' law, 34–6
homosexual relationships, 39, 43, 57
Human Rights Act, 67, 75, 342
Human-Etisk Forbund, 53
hybridization, 6
hyper-regulation, 30, 66–7

IDIs. *See* in-depth interviews
"illiberal" legal transfers, 6, 22–3, 28–9. *See also* religiosity; war on terror
ILO Convention 169, 75, 344
ILO (International Labour Organisation) Conventions, 13, 335
in-depth interviews (IDIs), 23–6
informal practice, 19, 36, 291, 510
informedness of judges
Bulgaria, 291, 293
England, 291–3
Norway, 291
Poland, 291, 293
Ukraine, 291, 293–4
informedness of lawyers
Bulgaria, 286, 288
England, 286–7
Norway, 286
Poland, 286, 288
Ukraine, 286, 288–9
informedness of police
Bulgaria, 298–301
England, 298–301
Norway, 298–300
Poland, 298–301
Ukraine, 298–302
institutional restrictions, 18
instrumental perspective, 184, 236. *See also* obeying or breaking the law
internal legal culture, 4. *See also* professional legal culture
international and European legal integration, 64, 82
International Labour Organisation. *See* ILO
IRA (Irish Republican Army) terrorism, 14, 406–7, 409, 434–5, 447
Islamic legal culture, 3, 12–13

Jakobsen, David, 410
Judeo-Christian legal culture, 3, 12–13
judges
Bulgaria, 115–16
England, 112–13
judges, prosecutors, juries (legal outsiders' perspectives on legal insiders), 241–6
legal insiders' perspectives legal insiders (like themselves), 291–8
legal insiders' perspectives on how public view their profession, 273–9
Norway, 109–12
Poland, 113–15
Ukraine, 116–17
judges, fairness of
Bulgaria, 291, 295
England, 291, 295
Norway, 291, 294
Poland, 291, 295
Ukraine, 291, 295–6
judges, informedness of
Bulgaria, 291, 293
England, 291–3
Norway, 291
Poland, 291, 293
Ukraine, 291, 293–4
judges, trust in
Bulgaria, 291, 297
England, 291, 297
Norway, 291, 296–7
Poland, 291, 297
Ukraine, 291, 297–8

judicialisation, 30, 64–5, 68, 129, 205, 286
juries (legal outsiders' perspective), 246–7. *See also* judges
'justice, fairness and legal rights,' 32–3, 81, 86, 386
justice or oppression. *See* law as justice or oppression

Kiev Rus' baptism, 61
kneejerk legislation, 37, 49, 66, 310–11
Krekar, Mullah, 14, 409, 414, 433, 442

law. *See also* legal insiders' perspectives on 'law'; legal outsiders' perspectives on 'law'; obeying or breaking the law; role of law
  behaviour and law, changing (legal outsiders' perspective), 98–9
  'complex,' 35, 37–8
  conclusions, 81–2
  dealing with (legal outsiders' perspective), 142–3
  designer laws, 35–6, 48, 64–71, 79, 311
  everyday life and, 30–1
  'fair,' 35–7
  good v bad law (legal outsiders' perspectives), 32–5
  Greek Goddess of Law *(Themis)*, 33–4, 386–7
  'helpful,' 34–6
  images of (legal outsiders' perspectives), 32–64
  influences on (legal outsiders' perspective), 48–9
  'justice, fairness and legal rights,' 32–3, 81, 86, 386
  law, court & parliament (legal outsiders' perspective), 90–1
  law, courts, crime & bribery (legal outsiders' perspective), 199–200
  laws contrary to one's religion (legal insiders' perspective), 175–82
  legal insiders' perspectives on 'law,' 50–81
  legal outsiders' perspectives on 'law,' 31–50
  'moral values or state power?,' 35, 38
  'order and discipline,' 31–3
  overview, 30–1
  'people involved in making or applying the law,' 31–2
  popular culture and, 4
  public opinion and, 98
  'unfair and oppressive laws,' 32–3, 86, 386
  unreasonable or unjust, 165–75
  'written laws, rules and regulations,' 31–2
law and change
  legal insiders' perspectives on 'law,' 64–81
  legal outsiders' perspective, 46–8
law as freedom or order (legal outsiders' perspective), 86–8
law as justice or oppression (legal outsiders' perspective), 86
law as power of the state v the people (legal outsiders' perspective), 187–9
law enforcement (legal outsiders' perspective)
  crime, bribery & corruption, 129–31
  law and, 128–9
law in action. *See also* "Exit"; legal insiders' perspective on 'law in action'; legal outsiders' perspective on 'law in action'; "Loyalty"; "Voice"
  conclusions, 182–3
  general perceptions of, 126–32
  introduction, 125
law in principle. *See also* Muslims and Euro-migrants; role of law
  law in principle v law in practice (legal outsiders' perspective), 386–8
  public ideals and attitudes towards law in principle, 85–95
"Law on Deported People," 63
law-abidance. *See also* Muslims and Euro-migrants
  amongst public (legal outsiders' perspective), 389
  Euro-migrants, background influences on (legal outsiders' perspective), 397–9

law-abidingness (legal insiders' perspective). *See also* obeying or breaking the law
  ethnic and religious minorities, 219–28
  the majority population, 211–19
  past and present, 202–11
law-abidingness, crime & corruption across Europe (legal outsiders' perspective), 126–7
law-breakers, penalties for (legal outsiders' perspective), 87–8
law-breaking. *See also* obeying or breaking the law
  how people should relate to law-breakers (legal outsiders' perspective), 144–5
  law-breaking–whose fault? (legal outsiders' perspective), 392–3
  penalties (legal outsiders' perspective), 87–8
lawyers
  legal insiders' perspectives on how public view their profession, 269–73
  legal insiders' perspectives on legal insiders (like themselves), 286–91
  legal outsiders' perspectives on legal insiders, 238–41
lawyers, informedness of
  Bulgaria, 286, 288
  England, 286–7
  Norway, 286
  Poland, 286, 288
  Ukraine, 286, 288–9
lawyers, trust in
  Bulgaria, 286, 290
  England, 286, 289
  Norway, 286, 289
  Poland, 286, 290
  Ukraine, 286, 290–1
lay judges (legal outsiders' perspective), 246–7. *See also* judges
learning from other countries, European and international organisations (legal outsiders' perspective), 319–22
learning from others about law (legal insiders' perspective)
  Bulgaria, 328–9, 336–8
  England, 328–9, 331–4
  Norway, 328–31
  Poland, 328–9, 335–6
  Ukraine, 328–9, 338–40
legal anthropologists, 17
legal borrowing, 6
legal change and legal transfers. *See* legal transfers
legal consciousness, 2, 17
legal controls (legal outsiders' perspective), 89–90
legal cultures. *See also* European legal culture
  actors in, 3
  'adaptive,' 379–83
  causation and, 18
  clusters of attitudes-approach, 18
  convergence *versus* divergence, 5–8
  criticisms of concept, 66–7
  "culture," broadness of term, 18
  defined, 2
  dimensions of, 21–3
  institutional restrictions and, 18
  legal transfers and, 5–8
  levels of, 2–4
  measuring, 17–18
  religious traditions and, 3
  studies of, 4–5
  systems' approach, 17–18
  thick descriptions of, 18–20
legal dualism, 36
legal fairness and state power (legal outsiders' perspective), 127–8
legal families, 2, 9, 317
legal insiders (perceptions of legal insiders). *See also* legal outsiders
  conclusions, 312–14
  elected representatives (legal insiders' perspectives on how public view their profession), 259–63
  government and parliament (legal outsiders' perspective on legal insiders), 251–5

legal insiders (perceptions of legal insiders). (cont.)
government officials (legal insiders' perspectives on how public view their profession), 263–8
government officials (legal outsiders' perspectives on legal insiders), 238
introduction: people making, implementing and applying the law, 237–8
judges (legal insiders' perspectives legal insiders), 291–8
judges (legal insiders' perspectives on how public view their profession), 273–9
judges, prosecutors, juries (legal outsiders' perspectives on legal insiders), 241–6
lawyers (legal insiders' perspectives on how public view their profession), 269–73
lawyers (legal insiders' perspectives on legal insiders), 286–91
lawyers (legal outsiders' perspectives on legal insiders), 238–41
legal insiders' perspectives on how public view their profession, 258–9
legal insiders' perspectives on legal insiders (like themselves), 285–6
on legal outsiders, 201–2
legal outsiders' perspectives on legal insiders (summary), 255–8
legal outsiders v legal insiders, 506–7
overview, 27–8
police (legal insiders' perspectives on how public view their profession), 283–5
police (legal insiders' perspectives on legal insiders), 298–305
police (legal outsiders' perspective on legal insiders), 246–51
prosecutors (legal insiders' perspectives on how public view their profession), 279–83
legal insiders' perspective on 'law in action'
"Exit," 145–64
laws, unreasonable or unjust, 165–75
laws contrary to one's religion (legal insiders' perspective), 175–82
"Loyalty," 145
"Voice," 164–75
legal insiders' perspective on 'role of law,' 101–23
circumstances v letter of law, 109
law, flexibility or rigidity, 108–17
law, reflect or reform, 102–8
law, stepping outside, 117–23
legal insiders' perspectives on 'law,' 50–81
assessment of change, 64–72
causes of change, 72–81
law, preferred basis of, 51–64
law and change, 64–81
perceptions of change, 64
legal mentalities, 2
legal nihilism
Bulgaria, 92, 209, 216, 236, 314
Eastern Europe, 11, 36, 46, 83, 86, 124, 190, 201–2, 441
Ukraine, 79, 92, 117, 218, 236, 314, 339
legal outsiders (perceptions of legal outsiders). *See also* legal insiders; Muslims and Euro-migrants; obeying or breaking the law
external influences on the law and legal system, 319–28
legal insiders' perspective on, 201–2
legal outsiders' perspectives on legal outsiders (like themselves), 185
legal outsiders v legal insiders, 506–7
legal outsiders' perspective on 'law in action'
courts, avoidance of, 133–5
courts, reasons for turning to, 132–3
"Exit," 136–8
government officials, fair treatment by, 128
law, dealing with, 142–3
law, stricter enforcement, 131–2
law-abidingness, crime & corruption across Europe, 126–7
legal fairness and state power, 127–8
"Loyalty," 143–5

religious law, dealing with, 143
"Voice," 138–43
legal outsiders' perspective on 'role of law,' 84–101
authoritarian republic, 88
behaviour and law, changing, 98–9
decision-making in court, 93–4
government and security services' response to terrorism threat, 101
law, court & parliament, 90–1
law, flexibility or rigidity, 91–5
law, reflect or reform, 95–9
law, stepping outside, 99–101
law as freedom or order, 86–8
law as justice or oppression, 86
law-breakers, penalties for, 87–8
legal controls, 89–90
letter of law, 92–3
minorities, special laws for, 95
minorities and law, 94–5
nanny state, 89–90
parliamentary supremacy, 90–1
public ideals and attitudes towards law in principle, 85–95
public opinion and law, changing, 98
legal outsiders' perspectives on 'law,' 31–50
attitudes, behaviour & law, 43–4
EU standards, laws, regulations & minority rights, 49–50
good v bad law, 32–5
law, images of, 32–64
law, influences on, 48–9
law, preferred basis of, 35–41
law, stricter, 44–6
law and change, 46–8
quality of law, implementation & enforcement of law, 44–6
"truly European," requirements for country to be, 43
legal positivism, 108–9, 349
'legal rights and fairness.' *See* 'justice, fairness and legal rights'
legal transfers (legal change and legal transfers), 507–9
conclusions, 375–7
convergence *versus* divergence, 5–8
cultural and legal convergence (legal outsiders' perspective), 322–4
defined, 2
ECtHR, perceptions of (legal outsiders' perspective), 324
E-I-U standards (legal insiders' perspective), 342
EU standards and ECtHR (legal outsiders' perspective), 326–7
EU standards privileging minorities (legal outsiders' perspective), 327–8
European legal integration (legal insiders' perspective), 355–65
European legal integration, introduction, 315–16
external influences on the law and legal system (legal insiders' perspective), 340–54
external influences on the law and legal system (legal outsiders' perspective), 319–28
failure of, 7
how to handle EU/UN standards (legal outsiders' perspective), 325–6
"illiberal," 6, 22–3, 28–9
laws and law-enforcement same as rest of Europe (legal insiders' perspective), 355–65
learning from other countries, European and international organisations (legal outsiders' perspective), 319–22
legal culture and, 5–8
looking to the future, 365–75
national laws becoming similar across Europe (legal insiders' perspective), 366–75
overview, 316–19
potential for external learning (legal insiders' perspective), 328–40
legislation, kneejerk, 37, 49, 66, 310–11
letter of law
circumstances v letter of law (legal insiders' perspective), 109
legal outsiders' perspective, 92–3
liberal transfers, 6, 28

linguistic plurality, EU, 70
Lipka Tatars. *See* Polish Tatars
Lockerbie Bombing, 413
London bombings, 405–6, 409–10, 413
"Loyalty." *See also* obeying or breaking the law
  introduction, 125, 135
  legal insiders' perspective, 145
  legal outsiders' perspective, 143–5

Madrid train bombing, 410, 415
McDonald, Ken, 406
meaning/concept of law. *See* law
mediation, informal methods (legal outsiders' perspective), 136–8
Meshere, 146, 161
methodological approach, 8–9
minorities (legal outsiders' perspective)
  EU standards privileging minorities, 327–8
  law and minorities, 94–5
  special laws for minorities, 95
minorities & special interests in COUNTRY (influences on law), 49
Mohammad cartoons, 409, 414
'moral values or state power?,' 35, 38
'morality of the lesser evil,' 405
most different systems design, 9
most similar systems design, 9
Movement for Rights and Freedoms, 50, 220, 255
Muslim Arbitration Tribunal, 154
Muslims. *See* war on terror
Muslims and Euro-migrants as carriers of legal culture
  'adaptive' legal cultures, 379–83
  asymmetric adaptation, 396–7
  bribes, pressure for (legal outsiders' perspective), 392
  conclusions: culture, context and behaviour (legal outsiders' perspective), 402–3
  Euro-migrants adapting to law (legal outsiders' perspective), 395–6
  Euro-migrants' law-abidance, background influences on (legal outsiders' perspective), 397–9
  Euro-migrants obeying the law (legal outsiders' perspective), 394–5
  Euro-migrants speak for themselves, 399–402
  government regard for law across Europe (legal outsiders' perspective), 385–6
  introduction: carriers of legal culture, 378–9
  law in principle v law in practice (legal outsiders' perspective), 386–8
  law-abidance amongst public (legal outsiders' perspective), 389
  law-breaking (legal outsiders' perspective), 390–2
  law-breaking–whose fault? (legal outsiders' perspective), 392–3
  long-term adaptation: Muslim minorities, 383–93
  obeying the law (legal outsiders' perspective), 389–90
  short-term adaptation: Euro-migrants, 383–5, 393–402

nanny state (legal outsiders' perspective), 89–90
national legal cultures
  as level of legal culture, 2–3
  research focus, 3
nationally representative surveys, 24
nihilism. *See* legal nihilism
9/11 terrorist attacks, 405
Nordic legal family, 9
normative perspective, 184, 202, 235. *See also* obeying or breaking the law
Northern Ireland, terrorism, 406
Norway. *See also* religiosity; war on terror
  attitudes, behaviour & law, 43–4
  authoritarian republic (legal outsiders' perspective), 88
  behaviour and law, changing (legal outsiders' perspective), 98–9
  bribes, pressure for (legal outsiders' perspective), 392
  Brussels' relations with, 10–11

Chairman of the Norwegian Supreme Court, former (Carsten Smith), 64, 109, 270, 274, 290, 330, 357
Church of Norway, 51–3, 151–2, 213
circumstances v letter of law (legal insiders' perspective), 109
'complex' law, 35, 37–8
court alternatives (legal insiders' perspective), 148–52
court alternatives (legal outsiders' perspective), 136
courts, avoidance of, 133–5
courts, reasons for turning to, 132–3
crime, bribery & corruption (legal outsiders' perspective), 129–31
cultural and legal convergence (legal outsiders' perspective), 322–4
'customs and traditions' (preferred basis of law), 39–41
ECtHR, perceptions of (legal outsiders' perspective), 324
ECtHR or parliament, who should have final say (legal outsiders' perspective), 324–5
EEA, 1, 72, 315, 318
E-I-U standards (legal insiders' perspective), 342–6
elected representatives (legal insiders' perspectives on how public view their profession), 259–63
EU standards, laws, regulations & minority rights, 49–50
Euro-migrants adapting to law (legal outsiders' perspective), 395–6
Euro-migrants' law-abidance, background influences on (legal outsiders' perspective), 397–9
Euro-migrants obeying the law (legal outsiders' perspective), 394–5
Euro-migrants' reasons for obeying the law, 199–201
Evangelical-Lutheran faith, 51–3
'fair' law, 35–7
government and corruption (legal outsiders' perspective), 199
government and parliament (legal outsiders' perspective on legal insiders), 251–5
government and parliament, capability of, 305–7
government and parliament, trust in, 305–7, 310
government officials (legal insiders' perspectives on how public view their profession), 263–8
government officials (legal outsiders' perspectives on legal insiders), 238
government officials, fair treatment by (legal outsiders' perspective), 128
government regard for law across Europe (legal outsiders' perspective), 385–6
'helpful' law, 34–6
judges, 109–12
judges (legal insiders' perspectives on how public view their profession), 273–9
judges, fairness of, 291, 294
judges, informedness of, 291
judges, prosecutors, juries (legal outsiders' perspectives on legal insiders), 241–6
judges, trust in, 291, 296–7
Krekar in, 14, 409, 414, 433, 442
law, courts, crime & bribery (legal outsiders' perspective), 199–200
law, dealing with (legal outsiders' perspective), 142–3
law, flexibility or rigidity (legal insiders' perspective), 108–17
law, flexibility or rigidity (legal outsiders' perspective), 91–5
law, good v bad, 32–5
law, images of, 32–64
law, influences on (legal outsiders' perspective), 48–9
law, preferred basis of (legal insiders' perspectives), 51–5
law, preferred basis of (legal outsiders' perspectives), 35–41
law, preferred basis of (revisited) (legal outsiders' perspective), 97–8

Norway. (cont.)
- law, reflect or reform (legal insiders' perspective), 102–8
- law, reflect or reform (legal outsiders' perspective), 95–9
- law, stepping outside (legal insiders' perspective), 117–23
- law, stepping outside (legal outsiders' perspective), 99–101
- law, stricter, 44–6
- law, stricter enforcement (legal outsiders' perspective), 131–2
- law, unreasonable or unjust (legal insiders' perspective), 165–7
- law, willingness to break (legal outsiders' perspective), 189–90
- law and change (legal insiders' perspectives), 64–6, 72–5
- law and change (legal outsiders' perspectives), 46–8
- law as freedom or order (legal outsiders' perspective), 86–8
- law as justice or oppression (legal outsiders' perspective), 86
- law as power of the state v the people (legal outsiders' perspective), 187–9
- law enforcement and law (legal outsiders' perspective), 128–9
- law in principle v law in practice (legal outsiders' perspective), 386–8
- law-abidance amongst public (legal outsiders' perspective), 389
- law-abidingness, crime & corruption across Europe (legal outsiders' perspective), 126–7
- law-abidingness: majority population (legal insiders' perspective), 211–13
- law-abidingness: religious and ethnic minorities (legal insiders' perspective), 219–24
- law-breakers, penalties for (legal outsiders' perspective), 87–8
- law-breaking (legal insiders' perspective), 228–30
- law-breaking (legal outsiders' perspective), 194–8, 390–2
- law-breaking, feelings about (legal outsiders' perspective), 187–8
- law-breaking–whose fault? (legal outsiders' perspective), 392–3
- law-obedience amongst ethnic and religious groups (legal outsiders' perspective), 195–6
- laws and law-enforcement same as rest of Europe (legal insiders' perspective), 355–60
- laws contrary to one's religion (legal insiders' perspective), 175–7
- lawyers (legal insiders' perspectives on how public view their profession), 269–73
- lawyers (legal outsiders' perspectives on legal insiders), 238–41
- lawyers, informedness of, 286
- lawyers, trust in, 286, 289
- learning from other countries, European and international organisations (legal outsiders' perspective), 319–22
- learning from others about law (legal insiders' perspective), 328–31
- legal fairness and state power (legal outsiders' perspective), 127–8
- legal traditions of, 10
- letter of law (legal outsiders' perspective), 92–3
- mediation, informal methods (legal outsiders' perspective), 136–8
- 'moral values or state power?,' 35, 38
- nanny state (legal outsiders' perspective), 89–90
- national laws becoming similar across Europe (legal insiders' perspective), 366–7
- obeying the law (legal outsiders' perspective), 191–4, 389–90
- obeying the law revisited (legal outsiders' perspective), 199–201
- obeying v law-breaking (legal insiders' perspective), 202–5
- parliamentary supremacy (legal outsiders' perspective), 90–1

personalised trust (legal outsiders' perspective), 185–6
police (legal insiders' perspectives on how public view their profession), 283–5
police (legal outsiders' perspective on legal insiders), 246–51
police, capability and efficiency of, 298–300, 302
police, informedness of, 298–300
police, trust in, 298–300, 304
'popular democracy,' 48–9, 252
prosecutors (legal insiders' perspectives on how public view their profession), 279–83
public opinion and law, changing (legal outsiders' perspective), 98
religion (preferred basis of law), 53–5
religious law, dealing with (legal outsiders' perspective), 143
terrorism threat (government and security services' response), 101
"truly European," requirements to be, 43
Norwegian Criminal Code, "Blasphemy paragraph," 54–5
Norwegian Humanist Society, 53
Norwegian police trade union *(Politiets landsforbund)*, 45
Norwegian Supreme Court Chairman, former (Carsten Smith), 64, 109, 270, 274, 290, 330, 357
Nygaard, William, 409

obeying or breaking the law (legal outsiders' perceptions). *See also* civil disobedience
conclusions, 235–6
ethnic and religious groups, law-obedience, 195–6
Euro-migrants' reasons for obeying the law, 199–201
government and corruption, 199
instrumental perspective, 184
introduction, 184–5
law, courts, crime & bribery, 199–200
law, willingness to break, 189–90
law as power of the state v the people, 187–9
law-abidingness: ethnic and religious minorities (legal insiders' perspective), 219–28
law-abidingness: majority population (legal insiders' perspective), 211–19
law-abidingness: past and present (legal insiders' perspective), 202–11
law-breaking (legal insiders' perspective), 228–35
law-breaking (legal outsiders' perspective), 194–8, 390–2
law-breaking, feelings about, 187–8
legal insiders' perspective on legal outsiders, 201–2
legal outsiders' perspectives on legal outsiders (like themselves), 185
normative perspective, 184, 202, 235
obeying the law, 191–2, 389–90
obeying the law revisited, 199–201
personalised trust, 185–6
oppression or justice. *See* law as justice or oppression
'oppressive laws.' *See* 'unfair and oppressive laws'
Orange Revolution, 64, 173, 210, 262
ORB, 25
'order and discipline,' 31–3
order or freedom. *See* law as freedom or order
ordinary people in COUNTRY (influences on law), 49
Ottoman legal culture, 10, 216, 322, 438

Palin, Sarah, 56–7
parliament
ECtHR or parliament, who should have final say (legal outsiders' perspective), 324–5
government and parliament (legal outsiders' perspective on legal insiders), 251–5
law, court & parliament, 90–1
parliamentary supremacy (legal outsiders' perspective), 90–1

parliament and government, capability of
  Bulgaria, 305–9
  England, 305–8
  Norway, 305–7
  Poland, 305–8
  Ukraine, 305–7, 309–10
parliament and government, trust in
  Bulgaria, 305–7, 311
  England, 305–7, 310–11
  Norway, 305–7, 310
  Poland, 305–7, 311
  Ukraine, 305–7, 311–12
'people involved in making or applying the law,' 31–2
perceptions of legal insiders. *See* legal insiders
perceptions of legal outsiders. *See* legal outsiders
personalised trust (legal outsiders' perspective), 185–6
plan of book, 27–9
Poland. *See also* religiosity; war on terror
  acquis communautaire, 49
  attitudes, behaviour & law, 43–4
  authoritarian republic (legal outsiders' perspective), 88
  behaviour and law, changing (legal outsiders' perspective), 98–9
  bribes, pressure for (legal outsiders' perspective), 392
  Brussels' relations with, 10–11
  circumstances v letter of law (legal insiders' perspective), 109
  'complex' law, 35, 37–8
  court alternatives (legal insiders' perspective), 148–9, 157–60
  court alternatives (legal outsiders' perspective), 136
  courts, avoidance of, 133–5
  courts, reasons for turning to, 132–3
  crime, bribery & corruption (legal outsiders' perspective), 129–31
  cultural and legal convergence (legal outsiders' perspective), 322–4
  'customs and traditions' (preferred basis of law), 39–41
  ECtHR, perceptions of (legal outsiders' perspective), 324
  ECtHR or parliament, who should have final say (legal outsiders' perspective), 324–5
  E-I-U standards (legal insiders' perspective), 342, 349–50
  elected representatives (legal insiders' perspectives on how public view their profession), 259–63
  EU standards, laws, regulations & minority rights, 49–50
  Euro-migrants adapting to law (legal outsiders' perspective), 395–6
  Euro-migrants' law-abidance, background influences on (legal outsiders' perspective), 397–9
  Euro-migrants obeying the law (legal outsiders' perspective), 394–5
  Euro-migrants' reasons for obeying the law, 199–201
  'fair' law, 35–7
  government and corruption (legal outsiders' perspective), 199
  government and parliament (legal outsiders' perspective on legal insiders), 251–5
  government and parliament, capability of, 305–8
  government and parliament, trust in, 305–7, 311
  government officials (legal insiders' perspectives on how public view their profession), 263–8
  government officials (legal outsiders' perspectives on legal insiders), 238
  government officials, fair treatment by (legal outsiders' perspective), 128
  government regard for law across Europe (legal outsiders' perspective), 385–6
  'helpful' law, 34–6
  judges, 113–15
  judges (legal insiders' perspectives on how public view their profession), 273–9

judges, fairness of, 291, 295
judges, informedness of, 291, 293
judges, prosecutors, juries (legal outsiders' perspectives on legal insiders), 241–6
judges, trust in, 291, 297
law, courts, crime & bribery (legal outsiders' perspective), 199–200
law, dealing with (legal outsiders' perspective), 142–3
law, flexibility or rigidity (legal insiders' perspective), 108–17
law, flexibility or rigidity (legal outsiders' perspective), 91–5
law, good v bad, 32–5
law, images of, 32–64
law, influences on (legal outsiders' perspective), 48–9
law, preferred basis of (legal insiders' perspectives), 51, 57–60
law, preferred basis of (legal outsiders' perspectives), 35–41
law, preferred basis of (revisited) (legal outsiders' perspective), 97–8
law, reflect or reform (legal insiders' perspective), 102–8
law, reflect or reform (legal outsiders' perspective), 95–9
law, stepping outside (legal insiders' perspective), 117–23
law, stepping outside (legal outsiders' perspective), 99–101
law, stricter, 44–6
law, stricter enforcement (legal outsiders' perspective), 131–2
law, unreasonable or unjust (legal insiders' perspective), 165–6, 170–1
law, willingness to break (legal outsiders' perspective), 189–90
law and change (legal insiders' perspectives), 64, 67–9, 77–8
law and change (legal outsiders' perspectives), 46–8
law as freedom or order (legal outsiders' perspective), 86–8
law as justice or oppression (legal outsiders' perspective), 86
law as power of the state v the people (legal outsiders' perspective), 187–9
law enforcement and law (legal outsiders' perspective), 128–9
law in principle v law in practice (legal outsiders' perspective), 386–8
law-abidance amongst public (legal outsiders' perspective), 389
law-abidingness, crime & corruption across Europe (legal outsiders' perspective), 126–7
law-abidingness: majority population (legal insiders' perspective), 211, 214–16
law-abidingness: religious and ethnic minorities (legal insiders' perspective), 219–21, 225–6
law-breakers, penalties for (legal outsiders' perspective), 87–8
law-breaking (legal insiders' perspective), 228–9, 232–3
law-breaking (legal outsiders' perspective), 194–8, 390–2
law-breaking, feelings about (legal outsiders' perspective), 187–8
law-breaking–whose fault? (legal outsiders' perspective), 392–3
law-obedience amongst ethnic and religious groups (legal outsiders' perspective), 195–6
laws and law-enforcement same as rest of Europe (legal insiders' perspective), 355–8, 362
laws contrary to one's religion (legal insiders' perspective), 175–6, 178–9
lawyers (legal insiders' perspectives on how public view their profession), 269–73
lawyers (legal outsiders' perspectives on legal insiders), 238–41
lawyers, informedness of, 286, 288
lawyers, trust in, 286, 290
learning from other countries, European and international organisations (legal outsiders' perspective), 319–22

Poland. (cont.)
learning from others about law (legal insiders' perspective), 328–9, 335–6
legal cultures of, 10
legal fairness and state power (legal outsiders' perspective), 127–8
letter of law (legal outsiders' perspective), 92–3
mediation, informal methods (legal outsiders' perspective), 136–8
'moral values or state power?,' 35, 38
nanny state (legal outsiders' perspective), 89–90
national laws becoming similar across Europe (legal insiders' perspective), 366, 368–71
normative perspective, 235
obeying the law (legal outsiders' perspective), 191–4, 389–90
obeying the law revisited (legal outsiders' perspective), 199–201
obeying v law-breaking (legal insiders' perspective), 202–4, 206–8
parliamentary supremacy (legal outsiders' perspective), 90–1
personalised trust (legal outsiders' perspective), 185–6
police (legal insiders' perspectives on how public view their profession), 283–5
police (legal outsiders' perspective on legal insiders), 246–51
police, capability and efficiency of, 298–300, 302–3
police, informedness of, 298–301
police, trust in, 298–300, 304–5
prosecutors (legal insiders' perspectives on how public view their profession), 279–83
public opinion and law, changing (legal outsiders' perspective), 98
religion (preferred basis of law), 57–60
religious law, dealing with (legal outsiders' perspective), 143
terrorism threat (government and security services' response), 101
"truly European," requirements to be, 43
police
legal insiders' perspectives on how public view their profession, 283–5
legal insiders' perspectives on legal insiders (like themselves), 298–305
legal outsiders' perspective on legal insiders, 246–51
police, capability and efficiency of
Bulgaria, 298–300, 303
England, 298–300, 302
Norway, 298–300, 302
Poland, 298–300, 302–3
Ukraine, 298–300, 303–4
police, informedness of
Bulgaria, 298–301
England, 298–301
Norway, 298–300
Poland, 298–301
Ukraine, 298–302
police, trust in
Bulgaria, 298–300, 305
England, 298–300, 304
Norway, 298–300, 304
Poland, 298–300, 304–5
Ukraine, 298–300, 305
Polish Tatars (Lipka Tatars), 15–16, 57–8, 95, 219, 410–11, 436–7
politics, *judicialisation* of, 30, 64–5, 68, 129, 205, 286
Politiets landsforbund. See Norwegian police trade union
polygamy, 63
popular culture, law and, 4
'popular democracy,' 48–9, 252
popular legal culture, 4
positivism, legal, 108–9, 349
potential for external learning. *See* legal transfers
professional legal culture, 4
prosecutors
judges, prosecutors, juries (legal outsiders' perspectives on legal insiders), 241–6

legal insiders' perspectives on how public view their profession, 279–83
prostitution, 39
Prussian Rechtstaat culture, 10
public ideals and attitudes towards law in principle, 85–95

al-Qaeda, 407, 412, 414, 429–30, 433. *See also* war on terror
QSR NUD*IST, 26
qualitative methods, 23–6
quality of law, implementation & enforcement of law (legal outsiders' perspective), 44–6
quantitative surveys, 23–6

reelle hensyn, 108
religion
"illiberal" legal transfers, 28–9
laws contrary to one's religion (legal insiders' perspective), 175–82
legal cultures and religious traditions, 3
religion as preferred basis of law (legal outsiders' perspectives), 40–2
religious law, dealing with (legal outsiders' perspective), 143
religion as preferred basis of law (legal insiders' perspectives)
England, 55–7
Norway, 53–5
Poland, 57–60
Ukraine, 61–3
religiosity (role of religiosity in European popular legal culture)
conclusions, 498–502
conflicting authoritarianisms: church *versus* state, 475–501
impact of religiosity on attitudes towards law (legal outsiders' perspective), 458–61
impact of religiosity on European legal cultures, 454–6
introduction, 454
religiosity (legal outsiders' perspective), 456–8
religious attitudes to law and (stronger first decile), 462
'secular authoritarianism' and (weaker second decile), 460–2
religious and ethnic minorities
law-abidingness (legal insiders' perspective), 219–28
law-obedience (legal outsiders' perspective), 195–6
religious law, dealing with (legal outsiders' perspective), 143
'respect for ethnic and religious minorities,' 43–4
'respect for sexual minorities,' 43–4
risk assessment. *See* war on terror
role of law. *See also* legal insiders' perspective on 'role of law'; legal outsiders' perspective on 'role of law'
conclusions, 123–4
introduction, 83–4
law, flexibility or rigidity (legal insiders' perspective), 108–17
law, flexibility or rigidity (legal outsiders' perspective), 91–5
law, reflect or reform (legal insiders' perspective), 102–8
law, reflect or reform (legal outsiders' perspective), 95–9
law, stepping outside (legal insiders' perspective), 117–23
law, stepping outside (legal outsiders' perspective), 99–101
law in principle, public ideals and attitudes towards, 85–95
legal insiders' perspective, 101–23
legal outsiders' perspective, 84–101
Roma community, 50, 146, 161, 195–7, 220, 225–7, 250
Roman-Germanic law, 10
rule of law, 83. *See also* role of law
Rushdie, Salman, 409
Russian legal culture, 10

Sámi rights, 75
Satanic Verses (Rushdie), 409
Scandinavian legal family, 9
secular authoritarianism. *See* religiosity

secular system (requirement for truly European country), 43–4
September 11th attacks. *See* 9/11 terrorist attacks
Smith, Carsten, 64, 109, 270, 274, 290, 330, 357
socialist legal family, 9
Socis-Gallup, 25
"Soviet Man," 31, 273
SPSS, 26
state power
  law as power of the state v the people (legal outsiders' perspective), 187–9
  legal fairness and state power (legal outsiders' perspective), 127–8
state *versus* church. *See* religiosity
strict v flexible law. *See* authoritarian republic (legal outsiders' perspective)
structured, open-ended IDIs, 25
sub-national legal culture, 2–4
supranational courts, 13, 21–2, 64–5, 73
supranational legal culture, 2–3, 5, 13
systems' approach, 17–18

Tatars
  Crimean Tatars, 13, 15–16, 49, 63, 142
  Polish Tatars (Lipka Tatars), 15–16, 57–8, 95, 219, 410–11, 436–7
Ten Commandments, 42, 54, 58–9, 62–3, 227
Ten Commandments model, 91–2
terrorism. *See also* war on terror
  Bhatti, 410, 414, 433
  Bin Laden, 14, 409–10
  Breivik, 280–1, 408
  Bujak, 410
  Davud, 410
  Glasgow Airport bombing, 409, 413
  government and security services' response (legal outsiders' perspective), 101
  IRA, 14, 406–7, 409, 434–5, 447
  Jakobsen, 410
  Krekar, 14, 409, 414, 433, 442
  Lockerbie Bombing, 413
  London bombings, 405–6, 409–10, 413
  Madrid train bombing, 410, 415
  9/11 terrorist attacks, 405
  Northern Ireland, 406
  al-Qaeda, 407, 412, 414, 429–30, 433
Themis (Greek Goddess of Law), 33–4, 386–7
thick descriptions, of legal culture, 18–20
TNS Gallup, 25–6
"transferists," 7
transplants. *See* legal transfers
triangulation, 23
"truly European," requirements to be, 43
trust, personalised (legal outsiders' perspective), 185–6
trust in government and parliament
  Bulgaria, 305–7, 311
  England, 305–7, 310–11
  Norway, 305–7, 310
  Poland, 305–7, 311
  Ukraine, 305–7, 311–12
trust in judges
  Bulgaria, 291, 297
  England, 291, 297
  Norway, 291, 296–7
  Poland, 291, 297
  Ukraine, 291, 297–8
trust in lawyers
  Bulgaria, 286, 290
  England, 286, 289
  Norway, 286, 289
  Poland, 286, 290
  Ukraine, 286, 290–1
trust in police
  Bulgaria, 298–300, 305
  England, 298–300, 304
  Norway, 298–300, 304
  Poland, 298–300, 304–5
  Ukraine, 298–300, 305
Turk Movement for Rights and Freedoms, 50, 220, 255
Turkish rule, Bulgaria, 10

UAOC. *See* Ukrainian Autocephalous Orthodox Church
UGCC. *See* Ukrainian Greek Catholic Church

UK. *See* United Kingdom
Ukraine. *See also* religiosity; war on terror
attitudes, behaviour & law, 43–4
authoritarian republic (legal outsiders' perspective), 88
behaviour and law, changing (legal outsiders' perspective), 98–9
bribes, pressure for (legal outsiders' perspective), 392
Brussels' relations with, 10–11
circumstances v letter of law (legal insiders' perspective), 109
'complex' law, 35, 37–8
court alternatives (legal insiders' perspective), 148–9, 162–4
court alternatives (legal outsiders' perspective), 136
courts, avoidance of, 133–5
courts, reasons for turning to, 132–3
crime, bribery & corruption (legal outsiders' perspective), 129–31
Crimean Tatars, 13, 15–16, 49, 63, 142
cultural and legal convergence (legal outsiders' perspective), 322–4
'customs and traditions' (preferred basis of law), 39–41
designer laws, 35–6, 48, 64–71, 79, 311
ECtHR, perceptions of (legal outsiders' perspective), 324
ECtHR or parliament, who should have final say (legal outsiders' perspective), 324–5
E-I-U standards (legal insiders' perspective), 342, 352–4
elected representatives (legal insiders' perspectives on how public view their profession), 259–63
EU standards, laws, regulations & minority rights, 49–50
Euro-migrants adapting to law (legal outsiders' perspective), 395–6
Euro-migrants' law-abidance, background influences on (legal outsiders' perspective), 397–9
Euro-migrants obeying the law (legal outsiders' perspective), 394–5
Euro-migrants' reasons for obeying the law, 199–201
'fair' law, 35–7
government and corruption (legal outsiders' perspective), 199
government and parliament (legal outsiders' perspective on legal insiders), 251–5
government and parliament, capability of, 305–7, 309–10
government and parliament, trust in, 305–7, 311–12
government officials (legal insiders' perspectives on how public view their profession), 263–8
government officials (legal outsiders' perspectives on legal insiders), 238
government officials, fair treatment by (legal outsiders' perspective), 128
Greek Goddess of Law *(Themis)*, 33–4, 386–7
'helpful' law, 34–6
instrumental perspective, 236
judges, 116–17
judges (legal insiders' perspectives on how public view their profession), 273–9
judges, fairness of, 291, 295–6
judges, informedness of, 291, 293–4
judges, prosecutors, juries (legal outsiders' perspectives on legal insiders), 241–6
judges, trust in, 291, 297–8
law, courts, crime & bribery (legal outsiders' perspective), 199–200
law, dealing with (legal outsiders' perspective), 142–3
law, flexibility or rigidity (legal insiders' perspective), 108–17
law, flexibility or rigidity (legal outsiders' perspective), 91–5
law, good v bad, 32–5
law, images of, 32–64

Ukraine. (cont.)
law, influences on (legal outsiders' perspective), 48–9
law, preferred basis of (legal insiders' perspectives), 51, 61–3
law, preferred basis of (legal outsiders' perspectives), 35–41
law, preferred basis of (revisited) (legal outsiders' perspective), 97–8
law, reflect or reform (legal insiders' perspective), 102–8
law, reflect or reform (legal outsiders' perspective), 95–9
law, stepping outside (legal insiders' perspective), 117–23
law, stepping outside (legal outsiders' perspective), 99–101
law, stricter, 44–6
law, stricter enforcement (legal outsiders' perspective), 131–2
law, unreasonable or unjust (legal insiders' perspective), 165–6, 173–5
law, willingness to break (legal outsiders' perspective), 189–90
law and change (legal insiders' perspectives), 64, 70–2, 78–81
law and change (legal outsiders' perspectives), 46–8
law as freedom or order (legal outsiders' perspective), 86–8
law as justice or oppression (legal outsiders' perspective), 86
law as power of the state v the people (legal outsiders' perspective), 187–9
law enforcement and law (legal outsiders' perspective), 128–9
law in principle v law in practice (legal outsiders' perspective), 386–8
law-abidance amongst public (legal outsiders' perspective), 389
law-abidingness, crime & corruption across Europe (legal outsiders' perspective), 126–7
law-abidingness: majority population (legal insiders' perspective), 211, 217–19
law-abidingness: religious and ethnic minorities (legal insiders' perspective), 219–21, 227–8
law-breakers, penalties for (legal outsiders' perspective), 87–8
law-breaking (legal insiders' perspective), 228–9, 233–5
law-breaking (legal outsiders' perspective), 194–8, 390–2
law-breaking, feelings about (legal outsiders' perspective), 187–8
law-breaking–whose fault? (legal outsiders' perspective), 392–3
law-obedience amongst ethnic and religious groups (legal outsiders' perspective), 195–6
laws and law-enforcement same as rest of Europe (legal insiders' perspective), 355–8, 364–5
laws contrary to one's religion (legal insiders' perspective), 175–6, 181–2
lawyers (legal insiders' perspectives on how public view their profession), 269–73
lawyers (legal outsiders' perspectives on legal insiders), 238–41
lawyers, informedness of, 286, 288–9
lawyers, trust in, 286, 290–1
learning from other countries, European and international organisations (legal outsiders' perspective), 319–22
learning from others about law (legal insiders' perspective), 328–9, 338–40
legal fairness and state power (legal outsiders' perspective), 127–8
legal traditions of, 10
letter of law (legal outsiders' perspective), 92–3
mediation, informal methods (legal outsiders' perspective), 136–8
'moral values or state power?,' 35, 38
nanny state (legal outsiders' perspective), 89–90

national laws becoming similar across Europe (legal insiders' perspective), 366, 373–5
obeying the law (legal outsiders' perspective), 191–4, 389–90
obeying the law revisited (legal outsiders' perspective), 199–201
obeying v law-breaking (legal insiders' perspective), 202–4, 210–11
Orange Revolution, 64, 173, 210, 262
parliamentary supremacy (legal outsiders' perspective), 90–1
personalised trust (legal outsiders' perspective), 185–6
police (legal insiders' perspectives on how public view their profession), 283–5
police (legal outsiders' perspective on legal insiders), 246–51
police, capability and efficiency of, 298–300, 303–4
police, informedness of, 298–302
police, trust in, 298–300, 305
prosecutors (legal insiders' perspectives on how public view their profession), 279–83
public opinion and law, changing (legal outsiders' perspective), 98
religion as preferred basis of law (legal insiders' perspectives), 61–3
religious law, dealing with (legal outsiders' perspective), 143
terrorism threat (government and security services' response), 101
"truly European," requirements to be, 43
Yanukovych and, 173–4, 342
Ukrainian Autocephalous Orthodox Church (UAOC), 62
Ukrainian Greek Catholic Church (UGCC), 62
Ukrainian Orthodox Church (Kiev Patriarchate), 62
Ukrainian Orthodox Church (Moscow Patriarchate), 62
'unfair and oppressive laws,' 32–3, 86, 386
"United Europe," 1
United Kingdom (UK). *See also* England
ECHR and, 346, 508
government regard for law across Europe (legal outsiders' perspective), 385–6
unreasonable or unjust laws, 165–75

"Voice"
introduction, 125, 135
legal insiders' perspective, 164–75
legal outsiders' perspective, 138–43
voluntary harmonisation, 10–11

war on terror. *See also* terrorism
combating terrorism v rights and freedoms, 417
conclusions, 451–3
external pressure and, 440–4
FG discussions (perceptions of terrorism), 413–16
"illiberal" legal transfers, 6, 22–3, 28–9
impact of risk and religion, 426–32
impact of risk assessment on general public, 423–5
impact of risk assessment on 'paying the price' to combat terrorism, 425–6
impact of risk assessment on respecting, changing, or disregarding the law, 426
introduction, 404–13
law, staying with or stepping outside (perceptions on terrorism), 419–21
legal insiders' perspective, 432–9
'morality of the lesser evil,' 405
perceptions on how to fight terrorism, 447–51
protecting civil rights v combating terrorism, 444–7
quantitative surveys: general public and Muslims (perceptions of terrorism), 416
reacting to international pressure, 421–3

war on terror. (cont.)
respect for law & threat of terrorism by rule of law (legal outsiders' perspective), 407–8
risk assessment, 423
Westergaard, Kurt, 410
Western v Eastern Europe, 9–15, 503–5. *See also* European legal culture
'written laws, rules and regulations,' 31–2

Yanukovych, Viktor, 173–4, 342

Lightning Source UK Ltd.
Milton Keynes UK
UKOW05n0956190916

283314UK00003B/47/P

9 781107 050358